sex

Sex Magazine #1-10
2012-2015

Selections from Sex Magazine Issues #1-10
Edited by Asher Penn

Foreword by Brendan Fowler
Introduction by Asher Penn

Issue #1 Cover: Costello by Rachel Glaser
Art: Danny McDonald by Asher Penn 10
Music: No Neck Blues Band by Asher Penn 20
Fashion: Victoria Bartlett by Hannelore Knuts & Johnny Misheff 26
Film: Bill Strobeck by Maggie Lee 34
Design: Manuel Raeder by Asher Penn 40

Issue #2 Cover: Sick Look Revisited by Natascha Goldenberg
Art: Jordan Wolfson by Asher Penn 48
Fashion: Thuy Pham by Asher Penn 56
Design: Harsh Patel by Asher Penn 62
Film: Grant Falardeau by Asher Penn 70
Technology: Laurie Spiegel by Dena Yago 74
Comics: Deth Kop by Gobby 82

Issue #3 Cover: Eckhaus Latta / Essex Olivares by Asher Penn
Art: Sam Pulitzer by Asher Penn 86
Music: Total Freedom by Asher Penn 94
Music: Solomon Bothwell & KCHUNG Radio by Asher Penn 100
Film: Steve Hanft by Jamie Krasner 106

Issue #4 Cover: Melatonin Fashion Story by Amalia Ulman
Art: Petra Cortright by Asher Penn 116
Music: Venus X by Asher Penn 124
Fashion: Gerlan Jeans by Avena Gallagher 130
Life: Cali Thornhill DeWitt by Asher Penn 138
Comics: The Mayor's Pussy by Brian Blomerth 146

Issue #5 Cover: Martine Sorrondeguy by Mateus Mondini
Music: Ratking by Aaron Bondaroff 152
Music: Young Male by Asher Penn 158
Fashion: L.D. Tuttle by Avena Gallagher 166
Life: John by Coco Young 170
Life: Maggie Lee by Asher Penn 174
Nonfiction: Hammer Blue by Kayla Guthrie 180

Issue #6 Cover: LA Women by Nate Walton
Music: Lansing-Dreiden by Annie Pearlman 186
Music: Brian Gibson by Asher Penn 194
Fashion: Peggy Noland by Cali Thornhill DeWitt 202
Life: Durk Dehner & the Tom of Finland Foundation by Michael Bullock 208

Issue #7 Cover: Suspicious Fashion: C.E by Natascha Goldenberg & Kiki Kudo
Art: Korakrit Arunanondchai by Asher Penn 216
Psychology: Andrew Feldmar by Asher Penn 222
Business: Toby Feltwell by Asher Penn 230
Life: Doc Martens by Al Bedell 238

Issue #8 Cover: Jacksonville by Nathan Antolik
Art: Olia Lialina by Jacky Connolly 246
Art: Jacob Ciocci by Asher Penn 252
Video Games: Nina Freeman by Asher Penn 258
Music: Juiceboxxx by Asher Penn 264
Music: Odwalla88 by Brendan Fowler 270
Fashion: On Bacon Index By Rosemary Kirton 280
Film: Alexa Karolinski by Fiona Duncan 286
Design: Frank Kozik by Asher Penn 292

Issue #9 Cover: Beebe Woods by Gabrielle Tillman
Art: Torbjørn Rødland by Asher Penn 300
Music: Princess Nokia by Milah Libin 304
Fashion: Susan Cianciolo by Asher Penn 308
Film: Making Daisy Park by Air Pop 314

Issue #10 Cover: Caught But Not Yet by Raffaella Hanley
Art: John Michael Boling by Asher Penn 322
Art: Lynn Hershman Leeson by Jacky Connolly 330
Music: B L A C K I E by Juiceboxxx 336
Video Games: Arcane Kids by Asher Penn 342
Comics: Julien Ceccaldi by Fiona Duncan 350
The End: China Chalet by Adam Tetzloff

Book Cover: Photo by Maggie Lee, featuring May Hong, styled by Kiki Kudo

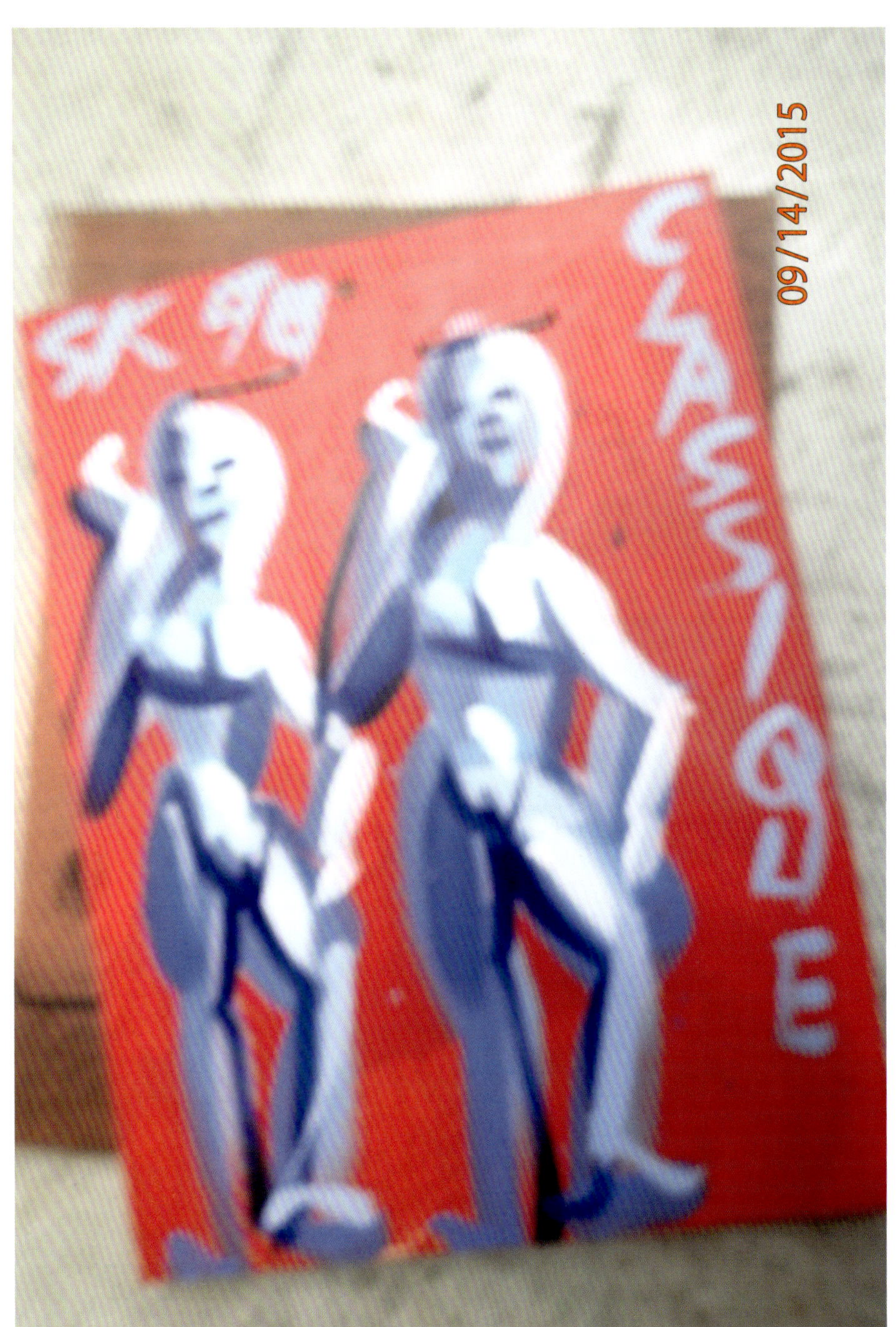

SK 96
CLASSIQUE
09/14/2015

Foreword
by Brendan Fowler

In 1986 I moved from Berkeley to rural Maryland, I was eight years old and I experienced severe culture shock. Music and skateboarding saved my life, giving me a
lifeline to what I thought of as the outside world of culture (and apparently,
somehow, I think, setting me up for life as an artist later). In this time before
the internet was happening, magazines and zines were my main connection to this
"outside" world. I read all of the skateboarding magazines (I still think about
Transworld during GSD's art direction days, and the first few years of SLAP were
so epic) and music magazines; Spin was actually really good at points, in it's own
way; Raygun was great for what it was; Rap Pages early Vibe was rad; Sassy and
it's rare brother magazine, Dirt were even sort of rad for corporate magazines.
Around 1995 I was really into Index Magazine and this zine called Tuba Frenzy.
Both revolved around the interview format, Tuba Frenzy especially. I wanted more
interviews, and so I thought I should make my own thing. I just wanted to conduct
and publish interviews. So I made two issues of this thing called Sex Sells
Magazines. The interviews and most of the editing for a 3rd issue were actually
done, but I tried to co-publish it with Alife in 2002, and bless them but it got
too complicated and never came out. I totally forgot about that. It was going to be
300 pages long, more like a book.

So, the name Sex Sells Magazines sounds so incredibly dated now. It wasn't until I
sat down to write this did I even realize that this is 20 years ago we are talking.
I was in high school, and angry-ish. It was just post-rrriot/3rd wave feminism,
1996, and before high schoolers were talking about trans, marriage equality, sex-
positive or even slut shaming. Any Sex in western mainstream culture was still
kind of taboo. My dad, who lived in the San Francisco Bay area had just came out
and I think he was enjoying this moment in his life for it's political radicalness
as much as anything. He was really into this magazine coming out of the bi-sexual
community called Anything That Moves, so he had a shirt of their logo. "Sex Sells
Magazines" was a way for me to fold a sort of critique of the mainstream magazine
world into this thing that was really a not-so sexy collection of interviews with
artists. Obviously, Sex does not sell magazines like it used to, but apparently
nothing does, as magazines hardly even sell anymore. The name was also a kind of
game, using the word "Magazines" (plural) in the title of a magazine (singular). 🙂

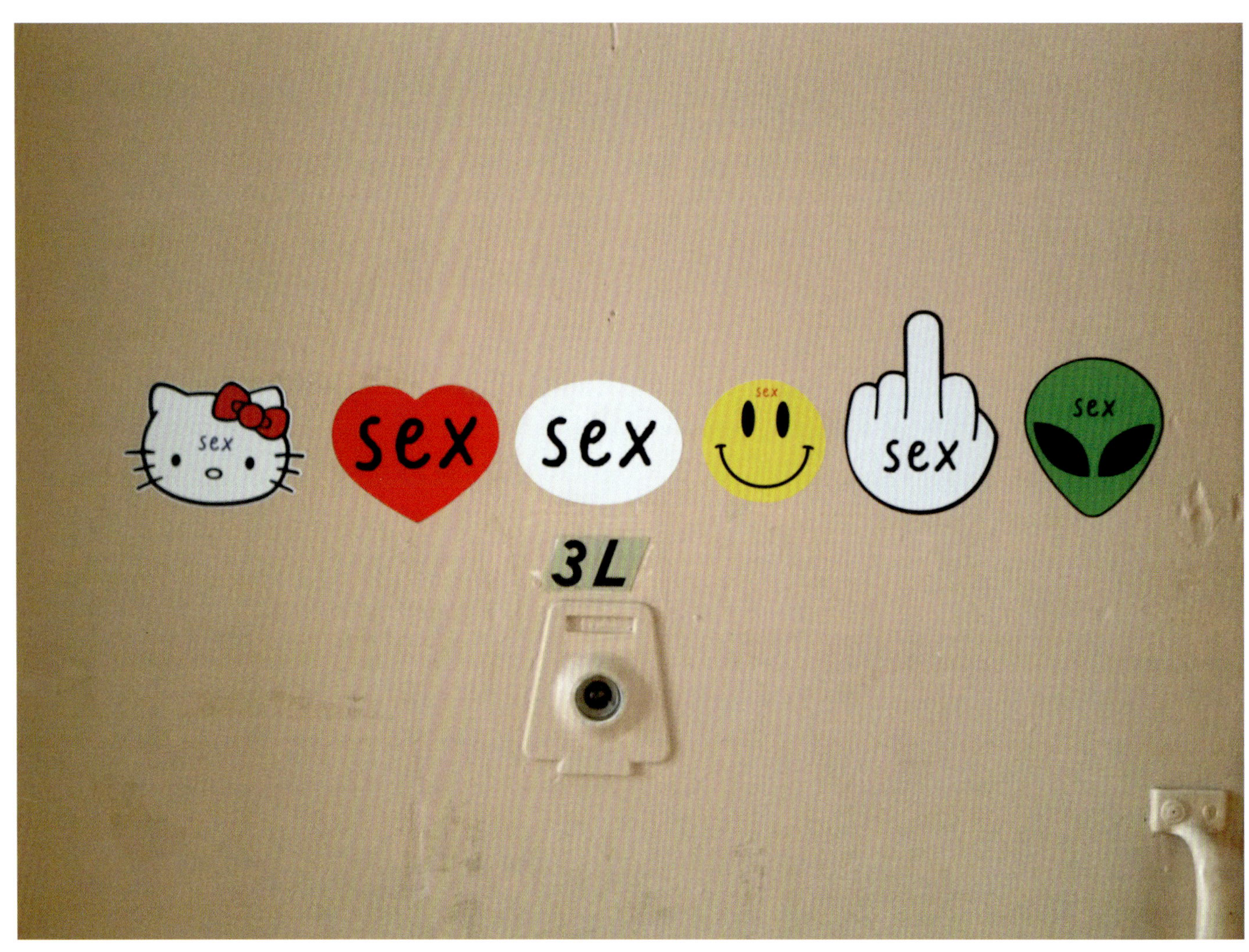

sex
sex
sex
sex
sex
sex
3L

Introduction
by Asher Penn

Sex Magazine started with zero experience or knowledge of how to run a magazine or a website — just a desire to make a publication that championed the ideas and attitudes of a new generation. We wanted to cover the artists we felt were being overlooked or forgotten. We didn't want to work in press cycles — we wanted our articles to be timeless. Sex couldn't be alienating or academic: it had to be on the level. Most importantly, we wanted to showcase the spectrum of different ways creative people can live their lives.

In 2012 mainstream cultural production was at an all time low while the most interesting things were happening in the fringes and online. In the face of a bored, oversaturated art market, the death of independent cinema, music labels incapable of supporting talent, and established magazines losing touch with their audiences it was clear that the only route forward was to start something new. Sex Magazine was not alone in this desire to begin working from the ground up, finding camaraderie with many of the groups and individuals in these pages who had enough faith in themselves and their peers to start something and instill it with value.

At a period when magazines were identifying themselves as artworks, Sex was the opposite. Arguably conservative and neutral by design, our innovation came directly from the inspired, exceptional, creative people who would fill our site and launch parties. The fact that Sex was an internet magazine also helped to bridge a disconnect between print and digital publishing, allowing us to bring legitimacy and quality to online creativity at a time when it's validity was in question.

Since Sex launched a lot has changed. Many of the people we were the first to profile have gone on to greater exposure and awareness, in effect redefining the mainstream. Compiling this book and seeing this collection graduate from web to print has affirmed what I always suspected — we have been living in a truly exciting, transitional period in art and culture. It's been an absolute pleasure to work with the people who made it happen and an honor to commemorate their work in this publication. ☺

Left: My Door, 2014. Photo: Asher Penn

Sex Magazine #1 Fall 2012

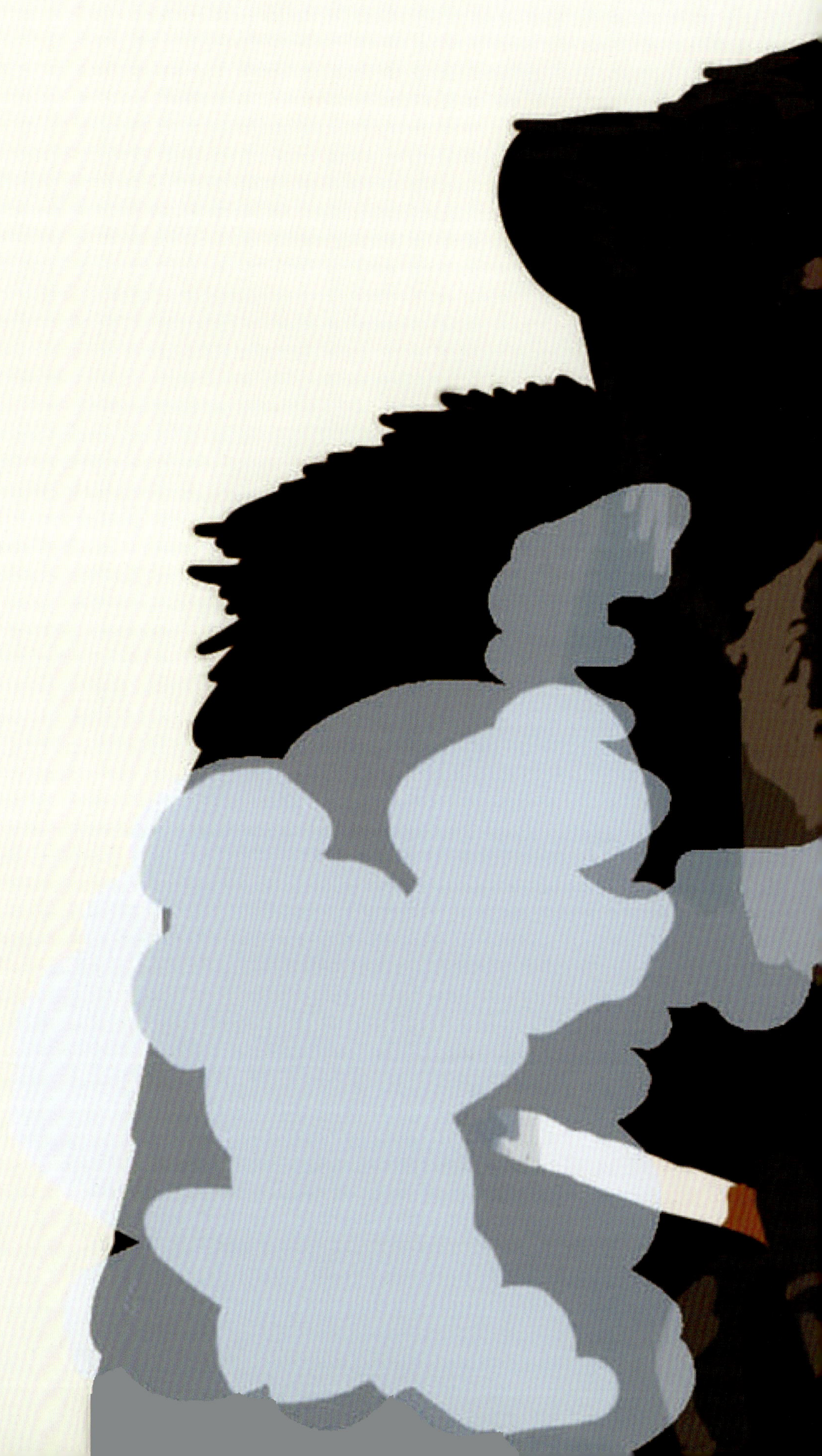

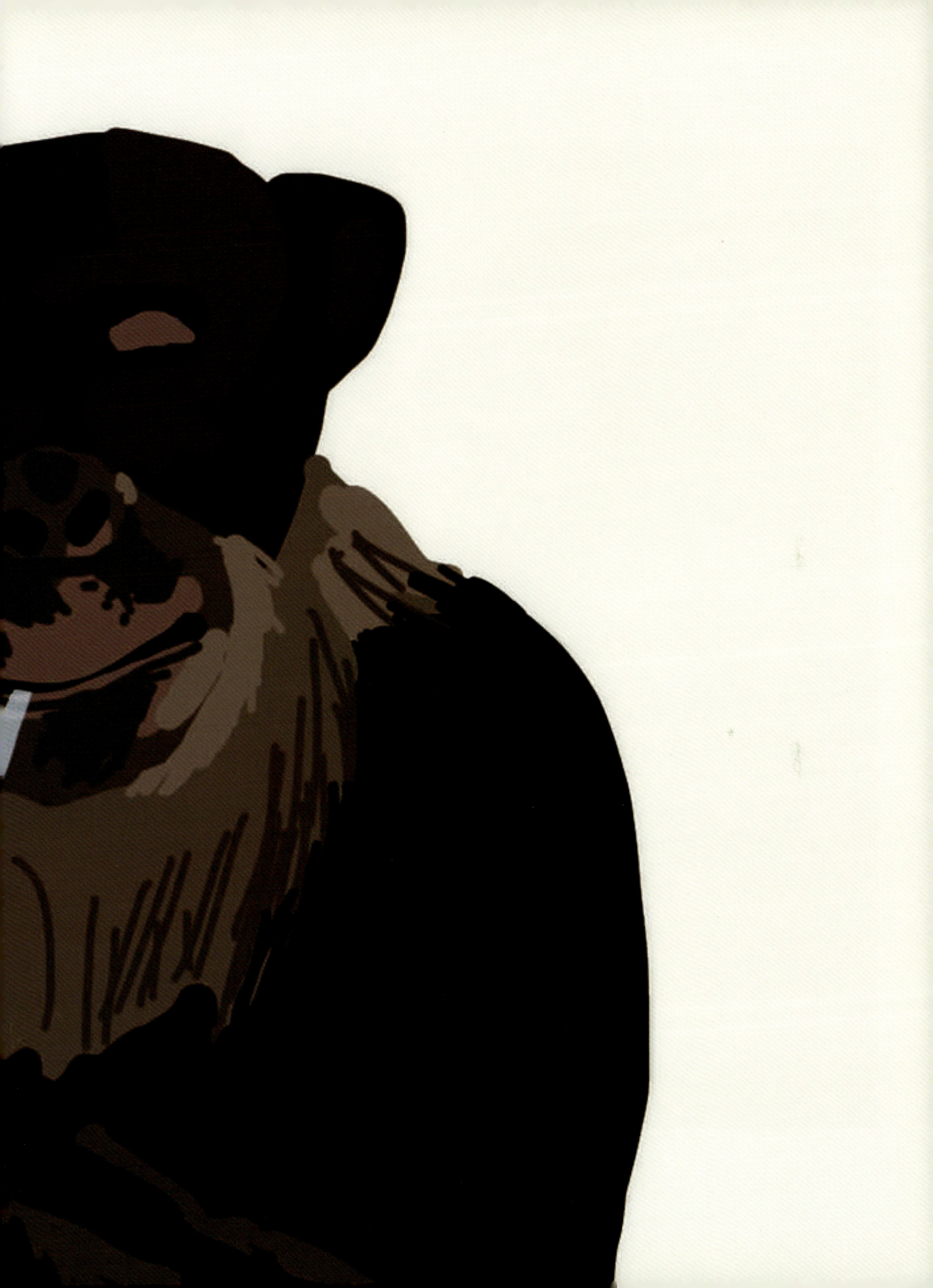

Danny McDonald
"You know that story about the monkey's paw?"

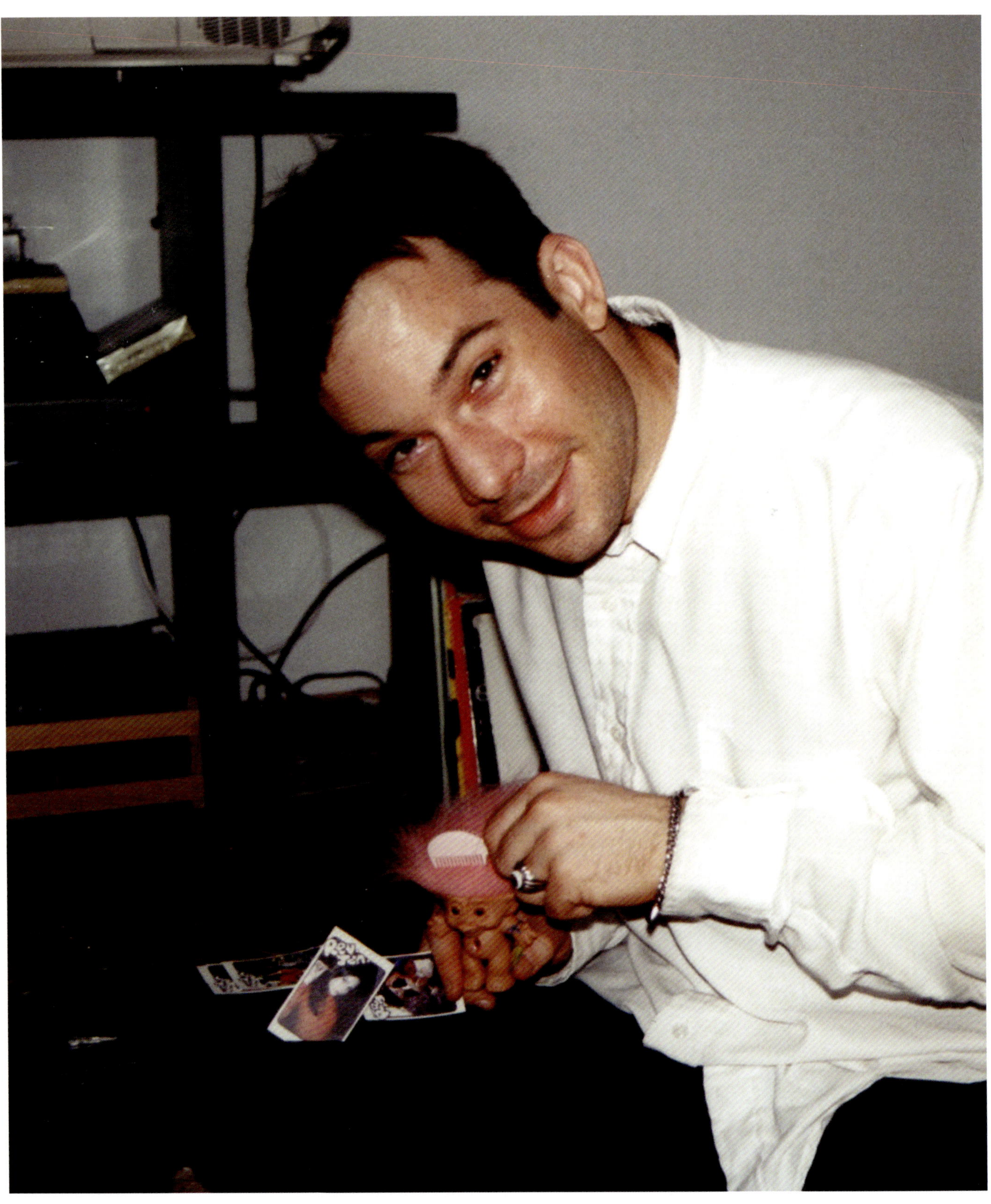

Interview by Asher Penn
Portrait by Rosalie Knox

Since moving to New York in 1989, Danny McDonald has done a lot of different things in the art world: A member of Art Club 2000, manager of the influential gallery American Fine Arts, and founder of the mysterious independent jewelry line Mended Veil. Most recently, his dioramic sculptures were featured in 2010's Whitney Biennial. Throughout these career transitions, McDonald's creative labor has quietly maintained honesty and integrity on a social and economic scale: a true anomaly within the unregulated market of the art world.

Where are you from?
I'm from LA. I moved to New York for Cooper Union after high school.
What was Cooper Union like?
It was really great. The school is based on the Bauhaus model, so the first year you have to do basic things that everybody has to take. There are no majors declared. It's almost like a deprogramming process. It was really good for me because by the time I had graduated from high school, this arts high school, I had developed a particular style of working. I had already done a lot of work and shown my work and won awards and sold a bunch of stuff.
Were you a teen art star?
Not an art star by any means, but I had done a real body of work. At Cooper it was good for me to break that down and get re-educated.
What work were you were doing in LA?
The work was assemblage with the French pronunciation. In a way its very mechanical, like the work I do now.
Remind me what assemblage is?
It's found object art, when all the parts are subsumed into the whole. Like Joseph Cornell or George Herms.
Was that why you got into Cooper?
I don't think that it was a foregone conclusion. I got an early admission but I didn't apply to any other schools. It was incredibly cocky. I don't know what I would have done if I didn't get into Cooper because I had no other plan and no money.

How did you get involved with Art Club 2000?
Art Club 2000 had started before I graduated from college. Two of my friends, Patterson Beckwith and Craig Wadlin, were interning at American Fine Arts. At this point in the history of AFA a lot of artists had left the gallery, the economy had collapsed, galleries were closing...
How many years into AFA was this?
Well Colin [de Land] would say "Whenever you start counting," but some iteration of AFA had been around since 1986. He had a lot of success in '89 and '90 too, but Colin's idea of what should happen and where a lot of artists wanted to go with their art wasn't the same. I think he was looking to do something different.

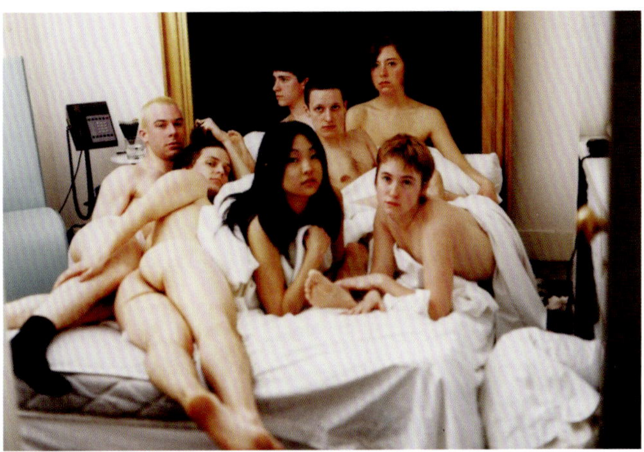

Art Club 2000, Untitled (Paramount Hotel Nude 1), 1992-93. Image courtesy Danny McDonald

Which is what Art Club was?
On some level Art Club 2000 was like a "fuck you" to what Colin saw as art world careerism. He wanted to see what would happen if you just took some young people who didn't have much to lose and put them in the position of putting on a show and talking about it. He got the idea to give Craig and Patterson a show, but then thought it might be more interesting if more people were involved. So he suggested we brought some friends, the limit being seven people. Craig and Patterson chose some friends which included myself and some other people.

Was he looking at your work?
Colin didn't want to see our work. He
wanted to create a discursive project
where we would talk about stuff for
almost a year before we would figure
out what the show would be about. We
had weekly meetings and would talk
about things we'd seen and shows.
There would be speakers that would
come in. Colin was using the Socratic
method: "Why make an exhibition, what
is this place, what is a gallery, how
can this be?"

It sounds kind of exhausting.
It was. I think for Colin it was a
chance to give us some information
that we wouldn't have had or would
have take us longer to get... How
the art world functions and art
doesn't function, how exhibitions are
made, why they're made, and how the
works are made, and how the works are
collected. How the media reception
of an artwork can completely change
its meaning.

They don't teach you that in school.
He wanted to see what would happen
if that information was brought to
the table earlier...and to do it
in a way where in the end it was a
collaborative work. It wasn't like
you had everything to lose if it
completely failed.

So you weren't selling anything?
We certainly toyed with the idea
of, "Lets make a work that will
sell," and how to do that. There
was no expectation of ever selling
anything. Mostly it was about trying
to frustrate whatever normal impulses
there were for making art and figure
out what was maybe latent or hidden
under the surface.

What would be a typical meeting?
There was this one memorable
meeting where Colin was like, "This
is going to be a working meeting,"
and we helped to move the gallery
from 40 Wooster to 22 Wooster. At
night. Rolling copy machines down
the street.

Why at night?
Because he was escaping from the
previous lease.

What was Art Club 2000's first show?
It was about The Gap. At the time
The Gap had an advertising campaign
called The Individuals of Style,
which used a lot of artists and
actors and musicians. Annie Leibowitz
was one of the photographers, and
Cindy Sherman eventually did one.
They were these beautiful black-and-
white photos that were billboard size
and on the bus shelters.

**When Uniqlo got started they did a
similar campaign with Kim Gordon,
Ryan McGinley...**
It was just like that. The clothes
that were so anonymous they would let
your individuality shine through:
you wear your old leather with a gap
T-shirt. At that point we saw The Gap
like Starbucks, it was everywhere,
we wanted to show it as a symbol
of conformity. That was the subject
of our critique... But it was also
this thing beneath the realm of what
most institutional critique would
focus on. We started buying clothes
from The Gap, doing photo projects
with them and then returning them.
The later, The Gap came out with
these ads that were just like that.
Everyone's wearing the same clothes
and everyone is doing synchronized
dance routines. A lot of people seem
to think our photos were parodying
that campaign but that happened after
what we did.

**So you did a show of the photo
prints?**
No, the photos were something that
had emerged from documenting our
meetings and eventually became this
sort of side project the group was
doing. Colin was very reluctant to
show the photos because he understood
or suspected that the photos would
become the focus of any attention
that was paid to the project, and
that is exactly what ended up
happening. He made us print them 8 x
10 and they were in the second room
of the show. Despite that, our first
show became the most recognizable
show that we did and got a lot of
media attention.

     Danny McDonald by Asher Penn

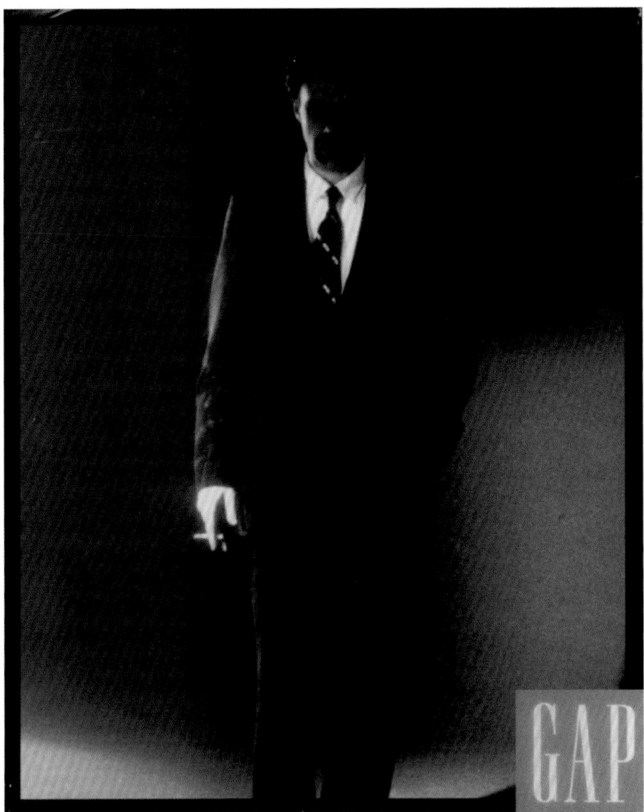

Art Club 2000, Untitled (Individuals of Style Portrait Center/ Artforum CDL Gap Ad), 1993. Image courtesy the Estate of Colin de Land

Why did it cause such a splash?
That had a lot to do with the emergence of "Gen-X" and the media blitz that surrounded it. We became sort of grouped in with Sean Landers and Rita Ackerman: Gen-X artists. Those photos replayed in print more than in the context of the exhibition.

How did you guys respond to that?
We basically didn't do another self portrait ever again.

What were the other elements of The Gap show?
A lot of Art Club was involved in different forms of research. We did ad hoc research projects about whatever we were looking at. With The Gap we went through their garbage, found a lot of information that we eventually generated into content for the show like employee handbooks and their logs. One manager would write a log to the next, what celebrities had been in, notes on how to prevent shoplifters.

That sounds a bit like Mark Dion's work which focused on research.
It bears mentioning that Mark Dion was one teacher that all of us had. We all came to American Fine arts to look at some slides of his work. That was how we were first introduced to the gallery.

The SoHo So Long show was also research based, right?
Yes. Everyone at that time was talking about Chelsea. Colin's girlfriend had moved to Chelsea, and there were basically 3 or 4 galleries there. It was clear a lot of people were moving there and we wanted to find out why. We wanted to find out why the people who weren't moving why were staying. We interviewed critics, gallerists, and collectors.

It was done with a sense of humor though, right?
All of our stuff was done with a degree of lightheartedness and fun. That was something that Colin always insisted on, although a lot of times it wasn't fun. The point was to be self-implicating in the critique and to not take ourselves too seriously and to take everything with a grain of salt.

Was that a theme that ran throughout AFA in general?
That would be hard to say. A lot of serious artists showed at AFA but there was a lot of funny stuff that went down. I mean, when you talk about somebody like Andrea Fraser, there is great humor in that work, but it's pretty serious stuff. With Art Club there was a degree of amateurishness that was part of the fun. Alongside us people were doing their own work in a totally different tone. There was always some element of parody and parodying the act of making an exhibition, which at that point we saw as a project; the idea of doing an exhibition and trying to change the world with it was a somewhat dubious and hilarious prospect, but we were actually trying to do that.

What were some other shows you did?
We did a show called 1970 which was also a series of interviews with nine artists. With SoHo So Long we interviewed collectors, gallerists and critics because we felt like this decision to move to Chelsea had nothing to do with artists. For 1970 we asked simple questions to nine older artists: things like, "What is the difference between 1970 and now in the art world and living in NY?" That show was great. Interviews with great people.

What was your first impression of American Fine Arts?
The first show I saw was a group show Colin had curated. There was a giant Jeff Koons sculpture of a police officer and a bear, a Vito Acconci convertible clam shelter which was this clam that was covered in clamshells, and some classic Joel Shapiro figure. I think the second show I saw was Andrea Fraser's May I Help You? It was incredible.

What was that show like?
She had hired three actors to play three gallerists. The show was hung with surrogate paintings all the way around the gallery in a broken line. The paintings literally functioned as surrogates for an art exhibition. A gallerist would approach you, welcome you to the gallery, and speak to you as if you were a collector, while showing you works of art. The script that they used was taken from various sources and pieced together with text from works that you were obviously not looking at. It was psychologically really complex.

How did you end up working at American Fine Arts?
Art Club 2000 did our first show in the summer of '93 and I ended up working there the end of that fall.

You worked there until it ended, right?
Yeah, '93 to 2004.

What was your first position?
At the beginning I think Colin had reduced his staff to one person. My friend Patterson and I had basically

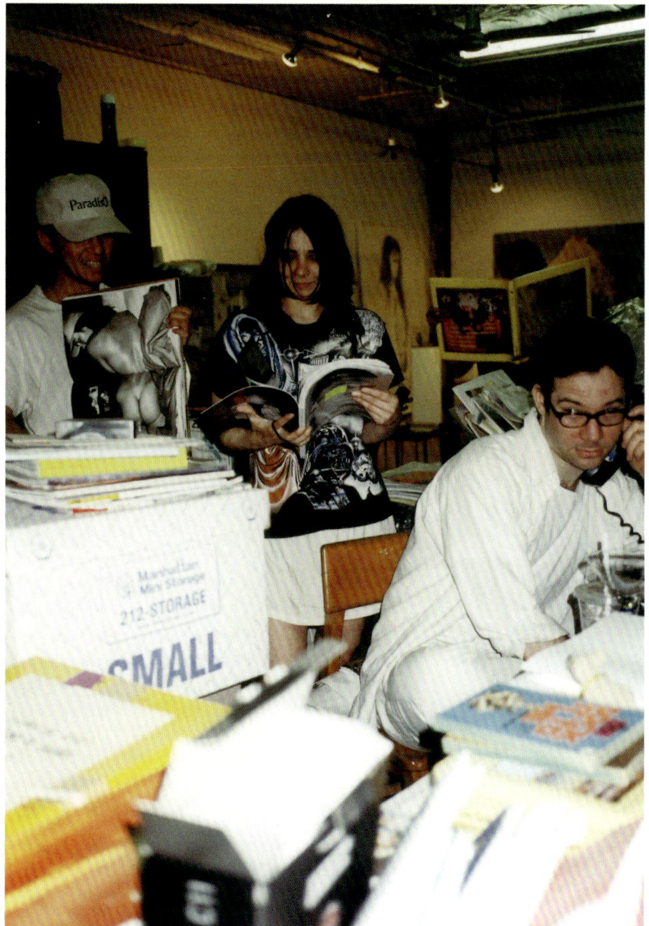

Taka, Lizzie, Margaret & Danny, American Fine Arts, 2002. Photo: Rosalie Knox

no idea what we were going to do after school. We saw it as an opportunity to work with someone we'd already had experience working with. My first job there was managing the archive and handling slide requests but it quickly evolved into being everything. Colin wanted everyone to be able to deal with whatever situation was arising. There wasn't a strict structure to who did what in the gallery with the exception of Christine who was in charge of all the accounting. The gallery office was open, so it wasn't this kind of thing with a front desk with some anonymous person sitting there. It was a different dynamic.

Did you help put together shows and work with artists?
Yeah, sometimes. Every show was a different situation. There was a lot of crazy stuff.

How did the gallery change?
I would say I started working there at a point of transition. When we moved to the second space on Wooster, Colin cut the gallery in half so that the gallery would never do single solo shows: every show would be in one of two different rooms. This was part of his program against the career-driven, overblown-ego, genius-artist thing. The second room was called the Reuben room, named after the Reuben Gallery. I'm spotty on the history of this, but I think it was a gallery in the 60s where the artists would help each other install exhibitions. It was a modern model.

What was the end goal of this model?
Colin was trying to put a stop to whatever he saw as detrimental to the process of art; The machine that artists get plugged into where the gallery benefits and the artist benefits but the art becomes a sort of stagnant and self-replicating rehash of whatever it is that sold.

Have those ideas stuck with you?
Yeah. It's something that in a lot of ways makes it difficult to make work, especially in a context where a lot of things railed against and hated by Colin are now the dominant way things operate. The corporatization of gallery practices and the way that galleries have multiple locations and huge galleries, generally just less experimental in their approach...the museumification of galleries, that kind of thing. What Chelsea became. Definitely it made it hard to want to participate. When I was at AFA, the fact that I was in a gallery all the time made it hard for me to make art. That's part of the reason I began the jewelry line. It was an opportunity for me to do something creative that was outside of the art context.

You also saw the gallery switch from SoHo to Chelsea too. Was that for economic reasons?
Economic reasons were the deciding factor. It became clear that if the gallery were to survive it would have to move to Chelsea.

How did the gallery deal with those kinds of pressures?
It was a constant struggle. Colin was interested in sales and wanted the artists that he showed to sell, but that didn't make him choose works that were going to sell. In the end, Colin would end up floating the gallery through money he made during the Armory Show. The whole period I worked at AFA it wasn't a money making enterprise. It barely survived even with great personal sacrifice both on his part as well as from the people that worked there. When Pat Hearn died in 2000 we were running two spaces. Pat Hearn Gallery was officially closed but there were two memorial shows spanning two periods of Pat's gallery. Pat had wanted her gallery closed and wanted Colin to move his gallery into her old space. It was really hard. Colin was reluctant to move. I remember at one point he wanted to turn Pat Hearn Gallery into a nightclub. He didn't like being in Chelsea. He didn't like what happened.

He was responding to it.
Well, yeah, Colin was always making a stab at whatever was the status quo.

What was it like being an employee at American Fine Arts?
When I watch the show The Office, it reminds me a lot of our situation. There was an aspect of torture through comedy with Colin. It was like a clubhouse, but it was also high-stress, low-money all the time, and that created even more stress. At the same time there was a lot of fun involved in it. I think Colin thought that if it wasn't going to be fun, he wasn't interested in doing it. It's kind of ironic because I know that it wasn't fun most of the time for him. Especially after Pat got sick and died and he got sick, it was a nightmare. He got screwed over a lot, but he was kind of a clown. The play aspect was an important part of it for him on a philosophical level and that made it livable.

What was it like working for him as a young person?
It was like young artist kids trying to help somebody, who's not a normal businessperson, run a business. His management skills were not good. He'd sit down to show you how to do something on the computer and then he would end up reconstructing the program.

Were people nice to each other at the gallery? Was it a competitive environment?
I think the aspect of financial gain and seniority in any office makes that game sort of more tough. At AFA, more than anything we were competing for Colin's attention.

So here still wasn't that psychological warfare that is associated with some galleries.
Oh, no way. While there were constant discussions, meetings, reforms, and strategy sessions about selling, there was never any pressure to sell. It wasn't something you had a quota for or you were going to get in trouble for. There was some ridiculous commission structure that he set up at one point, which was like a fraction of a percentage. I never bothered to try to collect any of that.

When Colin died, you ended up managing the gallery, right?
Well, basically Christine, who was the co-director with me, and I inherited the gallery with the idea that we would continue it by virtue of the space and being in Chelsea in this great location. Obviously a lot of artists would leave but a lot would stay. Colin had the idea that the gallery could continue. He had signed a 10-year lease to continue renting the space and the landlord, through controversial and possibly nefarious means, ended the lease. At that point we had to decide whether we were going to go for a real estate hunt, raise funds to do that, which was just impossible after everything we'd been through, or close the gallery.

How did you start making jewelry?
I started making jewelry in the mid 90s...like, '95, '96. It was something that I did for my friends and for fun. Then I started collaborating with Susan Cianciolo.

This was a period of time when a lot of artists were turning to fashion.
Yeah, Bernadette Corporation was making clothes. A lot of my friends were stylists and photographers. There has always been a lot of crossover between art and fashion but this was in part driven by economics. This wasn't the bubble economy era of the art world, and that must have had something to do with it. It was easier to get together a group of T-shirts or something and get people to buy them than it would be to sell an artwork. There was no real insecurity as to whether fashion was lower than art. I think it was seen as another possible venue for getting ideas out there. It was exciting.

Your first collection was for Susan Cianciolo, right?
Yeah. I worked with Susan on her tenth runway show. The jewelry was offered with the collection. I basically started doing it because I needed the money. The idea of doing the collection and making orders and sending them to stores was something I knew nothing about. I had my doubts that I would be able to do it, but thought it would be fun to try. I was getting a lot of encouragement.

What did the first jewelry pieces look like?
Kind of like absurd jewelry that might look normal from far away. Then up close it tells a story or performs some kind of narrative that's diabolical or sort of gothic. Each collection looked really different from the next. One of the first pieces was the 1984 quarter. It was a quarter from the year 1984 made to look really old. My friend Jess Holzworth, who worked at AFA at the time made this pamphlet to sell my jewelry and helped me write some descriptions. For the 1984 coin we

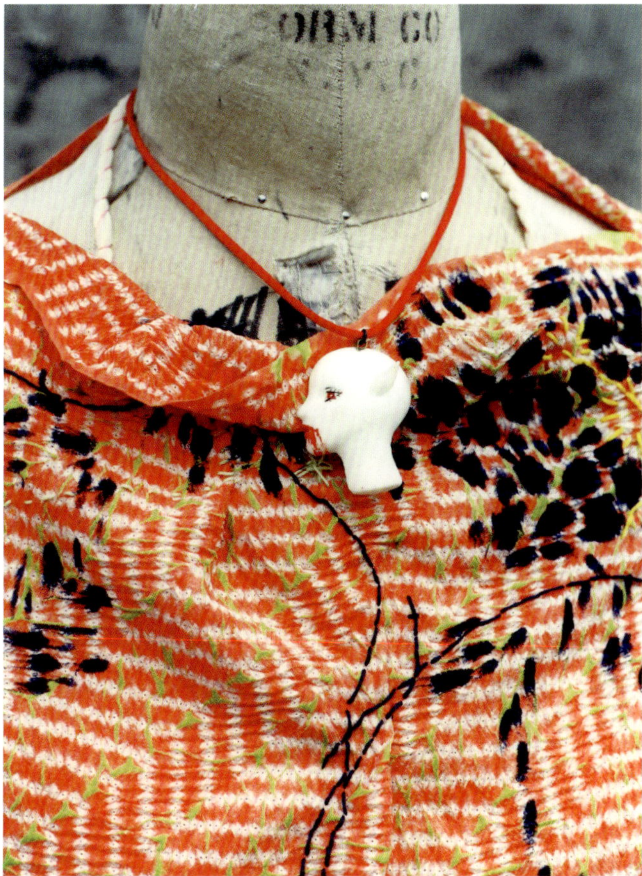

Mended Veil, Vampire Profile Pendant, Susan Cianciolo Run 3 Collection, 1996. Photo: Rosalie Knox

wrote "Ignorance is strength and
this is one strong piece of jewelry.
Supplies are limited due to scarcity."
**I love how Mended Veil pieces are made
out of figurative elements, while
jewelry is traditionally abstract.**
That's the strange combination of
influences for how I make things.
Sometimes the history of jewelry
would be part of the piece or maybe
it would just look like a classical
necklace with a twist. Some of them
are more language based, like the
bad luck bracelet. A lot of them
have literary influences, from sci-
fi and fantasy stuff. Basically every
collection was a story in my head,
with different characters and jewelry
to go with it. Every season was
thematic: The notion of how themes
are stereotypically represented with
all these symbols. Jewelry is always
symbolic, which is why I think it's
so interesting.

How is jewelry always symbolic?
Even the most pedestrian sort of
jewelry is tied to long-standing
histories of jewelry making, which
are based on symbols that keep
coming back. The eye, the cross,
stuff like that. It has always been
this thing that is personal but
also culturally reflective of its
origins. It has an aura of magic or
wealth.
**Were you collecting jewelry before
you made it?**
Not really. My grandmother was a
big jewelry person. She had a big
collection of turquoise and antique
jewelry that I spent a lot of time
going through as a kid. The first
pieces of Mended Veil were made from
whatever broken pieces of jewelry she
left after she passed away.
Do you wear your jewelry?
No, its bad luck.
**It's bad luck to wear the jewelry
you make?**
No, my jewelry is bad luck. The
idea that "this is my lucky thing"
— that's the thing about jewelry
I find so fascinating. People
immediately want to ascribe some
sort of belief system to this
inanimate object that they are
wearing. I often try to do things
that were doing the opposite of
that. Bad luck bracelet. You know
that story about the monkey's paw?
No.
The monkey's paw is a hand of a
monkey that gives a guy three
wishes. And each wish is worse
than the next. He asks for money,
his son is killed in an industrial
accident...
He gets the insurance money.
Yeah, so the guy wishes for his son
to be alive again and the corpse
arrives revived at the door and the
guy has to use the last wish to
erase the first two. So a lot of the
jewelry I make is for people that
are willing to confront superstition
as a questionable belief. I'm trying
to make stuff to make people think
about those things.

Do you still make jewelry?
I stopped in 2009. I don't think I exhausted all possibilities but I definitely took it to the point where as a business I was either going to have to up my game and expand it or stop doing it. I ended up being on this constant scavenger hunt for things, not just a certain color of bead but a certain size and shape of bead that relates to the next bead, like a spectrum idea. This stuff became almost impossible to get and then production had to happen. I spent a lot of time in the bead district looking for things that didn't exist anymore...5 months after I made the sample.

How many pieces would you make for a collection?
It would depend. I would make 30 odd pieces per collection and then I wouldn't know which one the buyer wanted or which one the customer would respond to. I would have to be ready to make 100 of something and for that reason I had to buy a lot of stuff that didn't get used. Then for things that were ordered heavily I would have to buy stuff that didn't exist in the quantities I needed. Because they were artworks in a way, it was very specific and it became very time consuming.

Did you do lookbooks?
Yeah. This one was called The Dungeons of Mended Veil and it was a vampire slayer's charm bracelet, with all the stuff you would use to kill a vampire if you were a vampire slayer. Dungeons and Dragons: dice...

What do you think when you see other people wearing your jewelry?
It usually makes me happy. People have a tendency to say, "Look I'm wearing one of your necklaces!" before I really have a chance to notice it. But I'm usually more concerned about the condition of the jewelry. Trying to see if it's held together OK. A lot of the methods I used to put these pieces together were not traditional and as a result they sometimes fell apart.

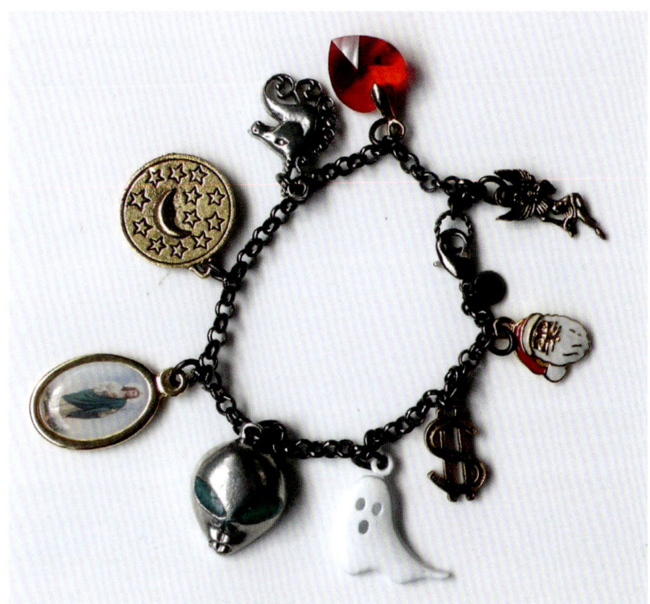

Mended Veil, Questionable Beliefs (Charm Bracelet), 2006. Image courtesy Ooga Booga

You've recently started making artworks again, right?
My show opened the day the stock market crashed. I somehow managed to get out of the art world before the last bubble and then got back in...

What motivated you to make these pieces?
I'd had this stuff going around my head for a long time and I guess it was always my secret plan to make work again. Enough time had passed since the gallery closed that my exhaustion with the art business was waning. I was also getting tired of the fashion cycle, having to do two big collections every year and doing production the rest of the time. I was invited to be in a show, and that's when I first started making these pieces. I had been collecting action figures and playing with them, on top of my TV or whatever. For me that work went back to my initial influences in LA and the kind of art I was making at that time — people from the beat generation, doing awesome assemblage and found object art — combining that with my influences having worked at American Fine Arts. I wanted to make stuff about my life and the people around me. I started

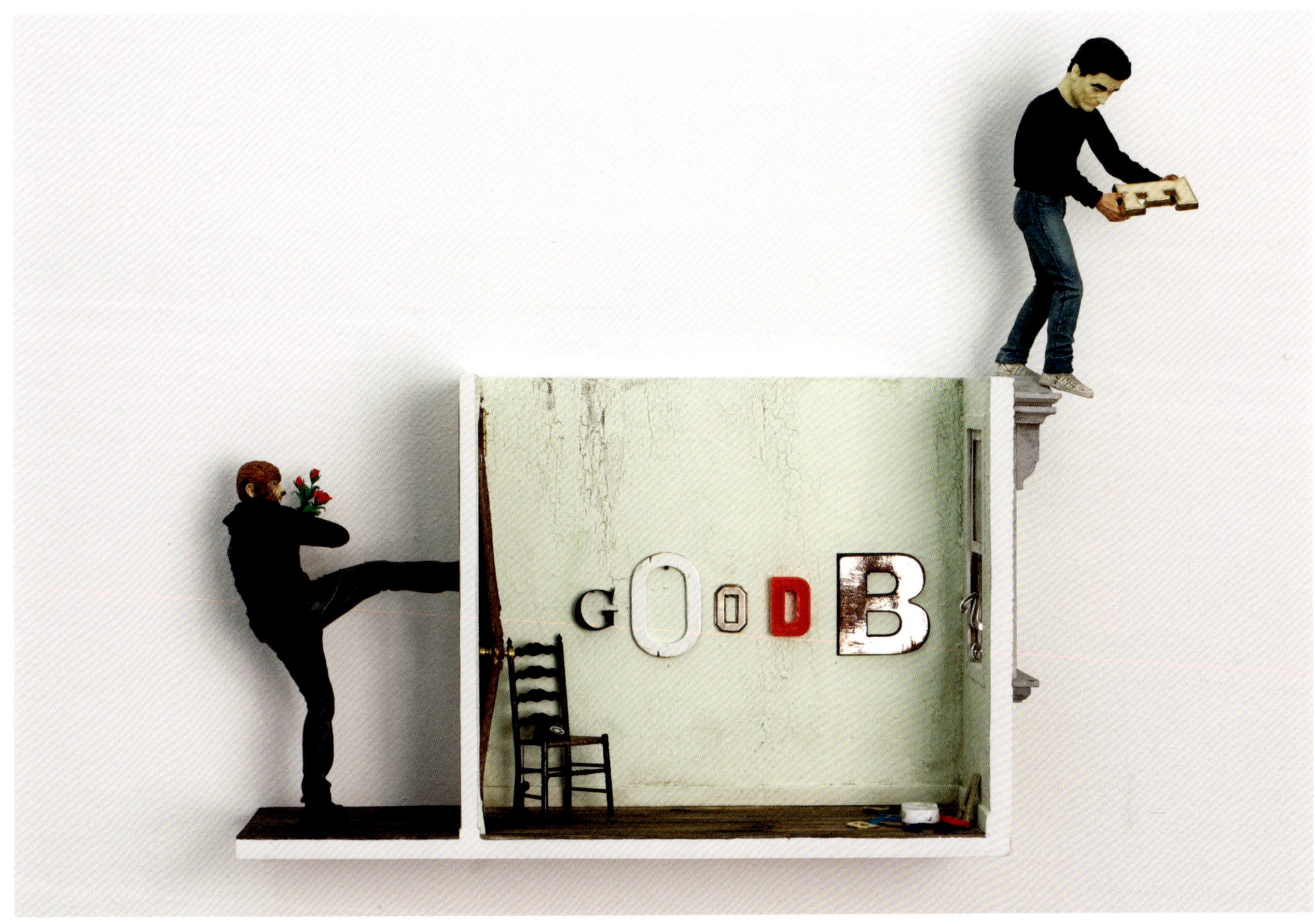

Danny McDonald, Goodbye (The Wolfman and Frankenstein), 2008. Photo: Thomas Mueller

thinking about getting older and being an artist, but living an outmoded lifestyle that doesn't really have much play anymore.

Your new works feel kind of gossipy. I keep trying to figure the parallels out, who is who.

They're a bit like scenes from soap operas. Somebody described them as being a "dilemma driven practice." These are situations that are faced by people all the time. I was making it in the context of this big boom of buildings going up in Manhattan, and everyone having great art careers and museums expanding...
I sort of made this work about people who got left behind. Bohemian Monsters, the title of the show, was about becoming a monster — where you're a spectral reflection of a time that existed before, looking at another context which you don't really fit into.

What are you working on now?

I basically took a year off, which was supposed to be relaxing but has sort of driven me crazy. Now I am trying to decide what my next move will be. I'm working on something now I can show you. This one is sort of about the credit crisis.

Is that Beetlejuice?

It's Uncle Sam. The chest-burster from Alien is coming out of his ass. The alien's mouth is a credit card offer, one of those "your name here" kind of things, and then there's a vulture perched on Uncle Sam's shoulder...

Wow.

It's like a political cartoon that keeps fucking with your head over and over again.

How do you think you accomplish that?

I like to think that they're good sculptures. ☺

No Neck Blues Band

"The poetry that is involved in NNCK is not a poetry that I would expect anyone else to understand or read as poetry, but it is poetry to me. Therefore I will address it as such."

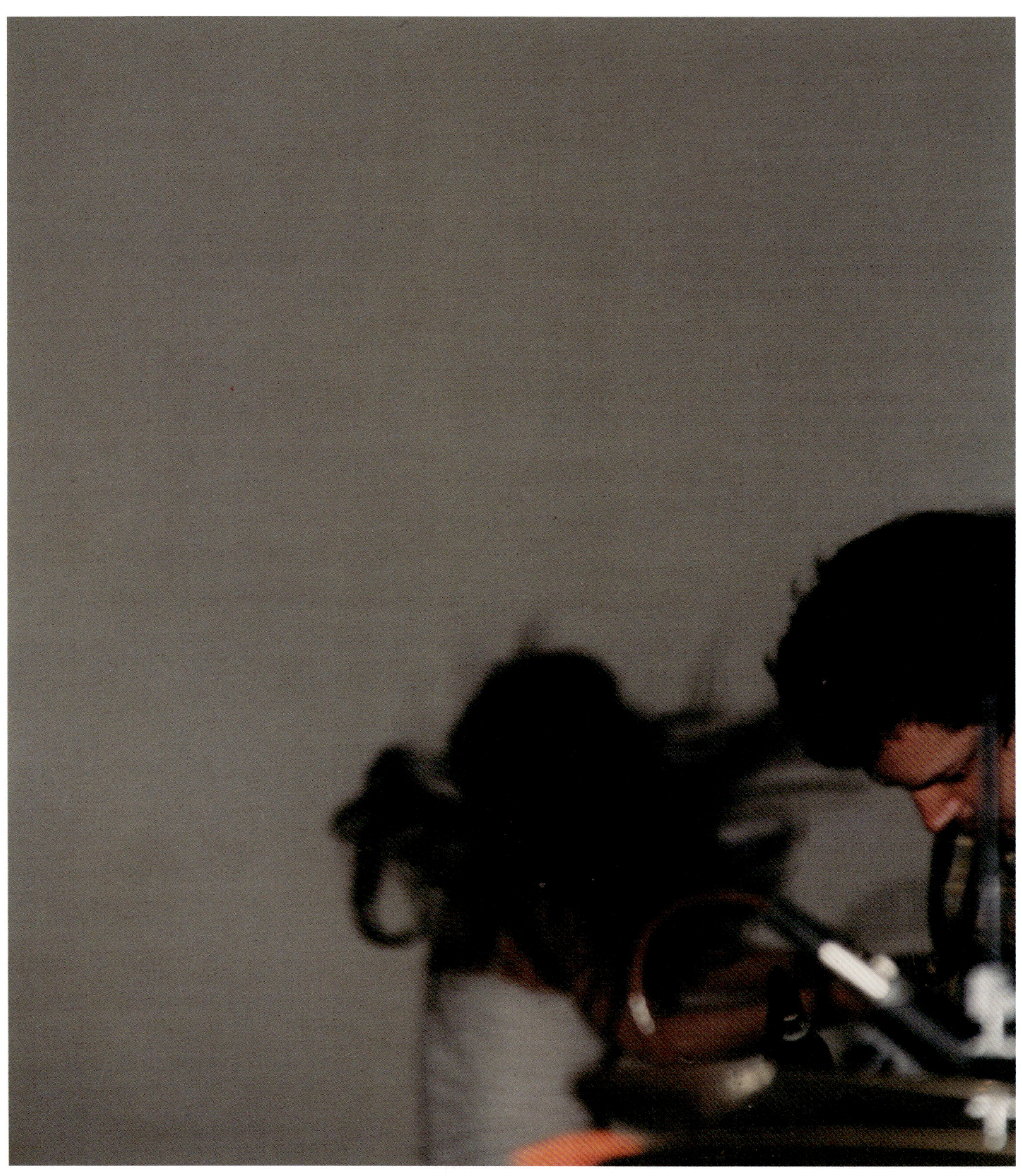

Interview by Asher Penn
Images courtesy NNCK

For almost twenty years now, No Neck Blues Band have remained a truly singular entity within experimental music. Once dubbed "the greatest band in the universe" by Thurston Moore, NNCK's countless records and live performances have consistently eschewed classification as a reminder of what makes music (or sound) so sacred: something that cannot and maybe should not be explained.

How did NNCK start?
It started in '93 with myself and Jason Meaher after we dropped out of the University of Buffalo, where we hated it. We came back to New York, and started playing together and going to a lot of shows.

What were you going for at the beginning?
We were making the effort to become the band that we wanted to see. This was drawn from bands that we were seeing, research, and life experiences happening at the time. We were going out all the time to see what was out there and this was influencing us. I don't feel like that story is all that different from a lot of other people's experiences at that age. We were in our early twenties. We existed behind closed doors for about a year.

When was this?
This is the early 90s. We spent about a year figuring out how to get on a schedule where we were meeting up regularly.

Initially it was just the two of you?
Also Pat Murano. That was the core. We fooled around with having a drummer. Being green about what free music would yield, I think we thought we needed a drummer, a proper drummer...

What do you mean free music?
I would describe it as a sort of explorational form that was met with impulse. Without knowing what was to come or what would reveal itself to us. The kind of sound exploration we ended up doing helped us to eschew the form of a traditional band.

If I heard a recording would I kind of recognize it as NNCK?
That's hard for me to say. I don't think that there was much going on with these early sound fragments that we were creating. There were some points of reference to get us through. It was like we made an outline and then we would try to follow the outline.

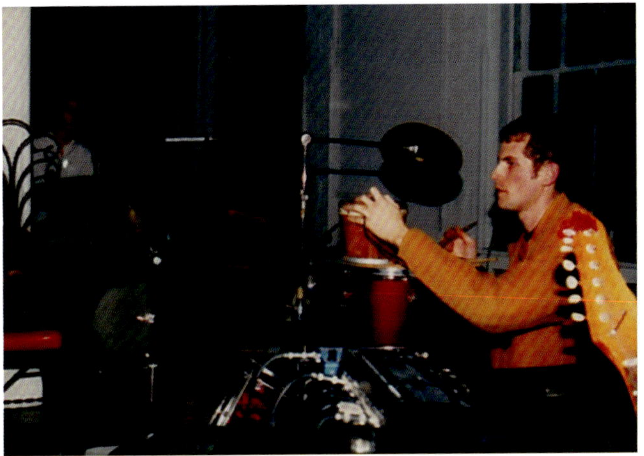

No Neck Blues Band, Susan Cianciolo Show, 1996.
Photo: Cris Moor

The early 90s were a big time for indie rock, alternative rock...
We were taking that stuff in, and probably anything else that you could mention that was in the air at that time. We were going out four to five nights a week to see concerts, shows.

Who were you seeing?
Bands like Unsane, Cop Shoot Cop, the earliest incarnation of Jon Spencer Blues Explosion. We were friends with these people. The band that was very important and took us under their wing was Circle X from Louisville, Kentucky. They were older guys who played this no-wave kind of art-rock. They were these guys who had read continental European philosophy and were staging these odd performance art gestures, with sculptural objects on stage. They were a conceptual band that would do things that were not rock and roll in a way that was much more compelling to us than what was common at the time.

So you eventually abandoned the structural outlines?
Once we didn't need the outline of a set or a structure for what we perceived to be our songs it became intuitive. We started to learn how to find it almost as much as make it and started to recognize the thing that NNCK would be. That is when more people started coming in. It was always people who were exposed to the music who came to us and said, "I want to do this also." We knew that they heard the same thing we were hearing or they were experiencing the same impulse to do this thing.

Were you surprised?
It was always, and remains, surprising to me that anyone cares. It was really surprising at the time. We were cutting more and more of our ties with what a normal present-ation would be. The shows were getting longer, involving treatments of the space in order to disorientate the audience.

Were you finding inspiration outside your peers?
AMM really had an impact on us. They were a famous free music group, one of the forefather's of this kind of thing. We saw them at Contact Studios in '94. We also saw video footage of a band from Japan called Hijokaidan, which means Emergency Stairs, one of the famous noise groups, if not the most famous noise group in the world. Becoming aware of this band and seeing glimpses of some footage from Japan in the 80s was really radical exposure and we felt privileged and informed by seeing just glimpses. This liberated us. We didn't need to be apologetic for these ideas that we had about our performances.

What is NNCK's relationship to Japanese music?
There was always something that resonated with us about extreme Jap-anese noise music and film. We would eventually become involved with this woman at Beecher Cove called Mico, the last person to join our group, who had a background in Butoh dance.

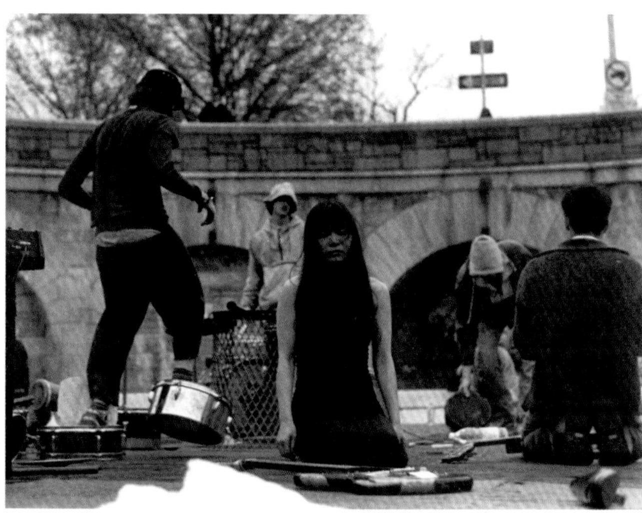
No Neck Blues Band, Riverside Park, Orthodox Easter, 1998. Photo: Sara Press

She brought a whole dimension of this dance of darkness that is connected to Japanese post-World War II psychology. I don't know if it was the emergence, or the struggle that happened based on the Americanization of Japan, but there is a kind of fearless philosophical certainty to a lot of Japanese music and art that resonates with us.

I read in an interview that you don't like the terms mystical or spiritual to describe what you do.
Well, we certainly are not a commercial enterprise. When the red phone rings in our house you know it is not because we are getting paid. It is coming from a different authority. It is something else, something that I am not going to define. We are not thinking along the terms of the characterization of what it is. We are too busy finding it.

It sounds like scientific exploration.
The people who make up NNCK are all dyed in the wool bookworms and aesthetes. These are people who spent all of their time absorbing information, looking for understanding, the essence of things. People who have dedicated their lives in their entirety to this acquisition of understanding, and knowledge.

What is your relationship to New York?
Being in New York, we are hiding
in plain sight. We're not in some
compound working on our secret
project, our secret truth, our secret
precious thing. This has gone on in
plain sight the entire time. We prefer
to not even go inside a venue in order
to do it. We would prefer to do it in
public, always. We want to make our
music in an integrated way with what
happens in the city, and what happens
in the city is not a removed thing —
it is a frenetic, connected thing.
**NNCK has always struck me as being
particularly urban.**
I have had no other experience than
an urban experience. I don't know
what to compare it to. We decided
early on without even discussing, that
everything and anything would be fair
game to introduce to the equation.
It would serve the whole and be
integrated. There was never a line that
was drawn that said, "No, we can't."
**I read that you toured with Trad Gras
och Stenar, which surprised me, but
also made a lot of sense.**
We could really relate to what those
guys had done with their band. They
became a straightforward, rock-
orientated group as far as their
methods, but those guys started out
very much along the lines of what it
is that we do.
How was it touring with them?
It was great. As soon as we started
to play shows with them their music
started to emerge inside of our
music and vice versa. You would hear
traces of us in them. In the bigger
picture I would say it was neither of
our music.
What was the space you had in Harlem?
The Hint House. We had it for about
twelve years. It was a joint venture
of I think seventeen people. We were
renting it from a private landlord,
who eventually sold it to Columbia
University who then decided to build
their art campus there. You don't
beat Columbia, or the Catholic
Church. They tore down the building,
which I was happy about.

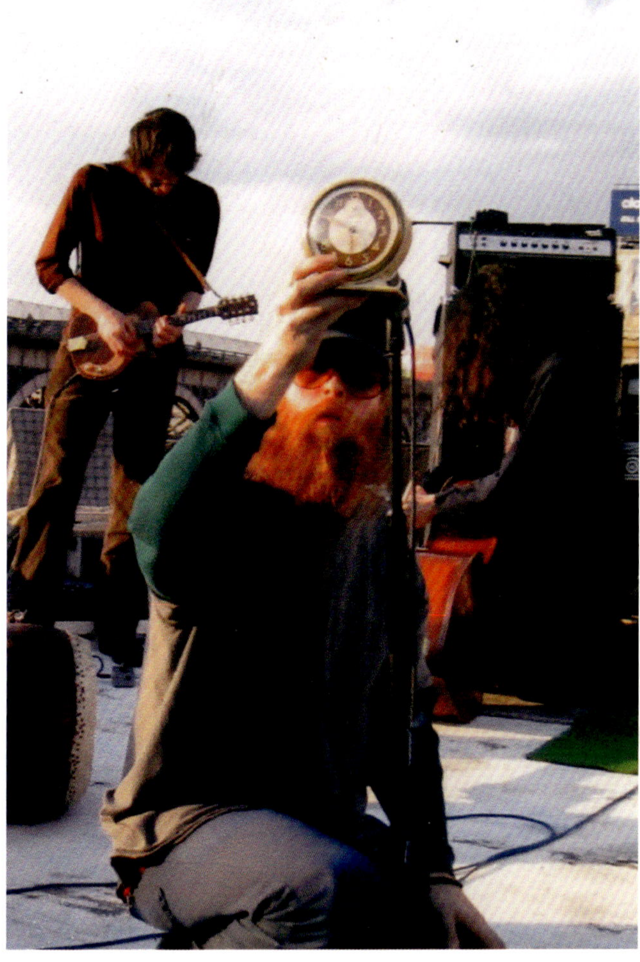

No Neck Blues Band, Hint House Roof, 2006.
Photo: Brian Leitgeb

Was it actually a house?
It was a three-story loft space.
**Did all the members of the band live
there while you had it?**
Various people lived there from the
group at different times and also
other people who were marginally
associated with the group — friends.
It was really important to our
development to have a place to go.
It was 2,500 square feet. It was not
divided with walls but demarcated
into two artist studios. At least
1,000 square feet of that space was
our permanent playing field. No one
lived in that room. The living space
was above. It was three stories. We
did shows. We recorded the album
Qvaris in that space. We had a lot of
great people play up there including
John Fahey.

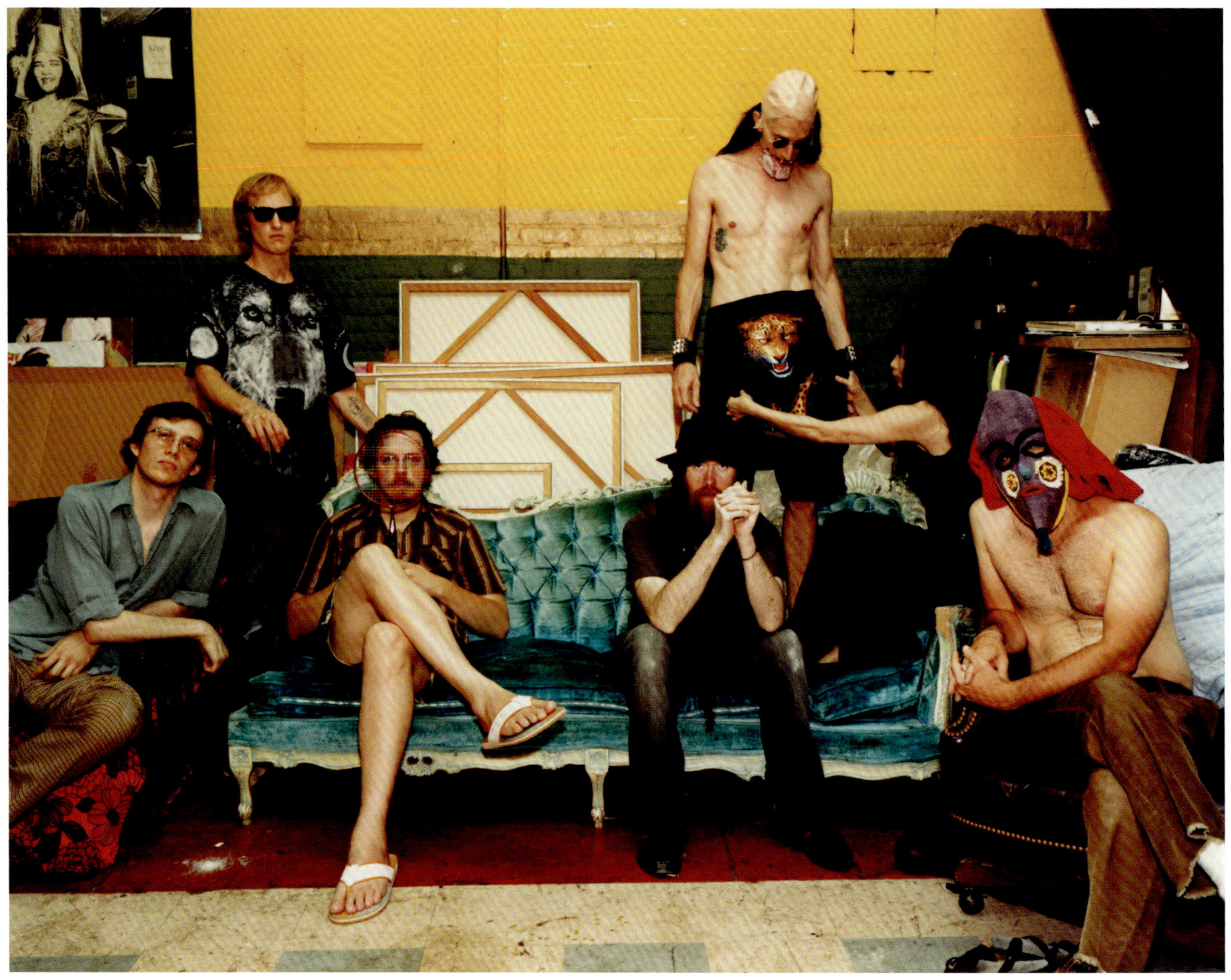

No Neck Blues Band, Hint House, 2006. Photo: Brian Leitgeb

How did the space change your work?
We had been nomadic prior to that
for about a year. Our first studio
was on 195 Christie Street, but we
were thrown out for insubordination.
Then we played Columbus Park weekly,
right below Canal Street. That was
interesting, and necessary in our
learning experience. When we got the
building in Harlem we had the entire
building. There were no neighbors. We
weren't beholden to anything but our
own intentions. That transformed the
band into something that was fully
functioning as opposed to something
that we were making an effort to
create. Those sessions in the Hint
House felt like much more. We would
come to the sessions because NNCK
would be happening.

Did you always meet once a week?
That was the standard. There were
points where we met everyday.
**I read a quote where somebody in the
band said, "I wish I was a poet.
When I read poetry I understand what
it means."**
The poetry that is involved in NNCK
is not a poetry that I would expect
anyone else to understand or read as
poetry, but it is poetry to me.
Therefore I will address it as such-
I will give it that respect. A lot of
imagery, ideas, and strategies of the
band are poetic gestures that are
done deliberately and consciously.
It becomes a poetic gesture to make
records, to do performances, to
exist, to vouch for the name, to know
that we are that thing.

    No Neck Blues Band by Asher Penn

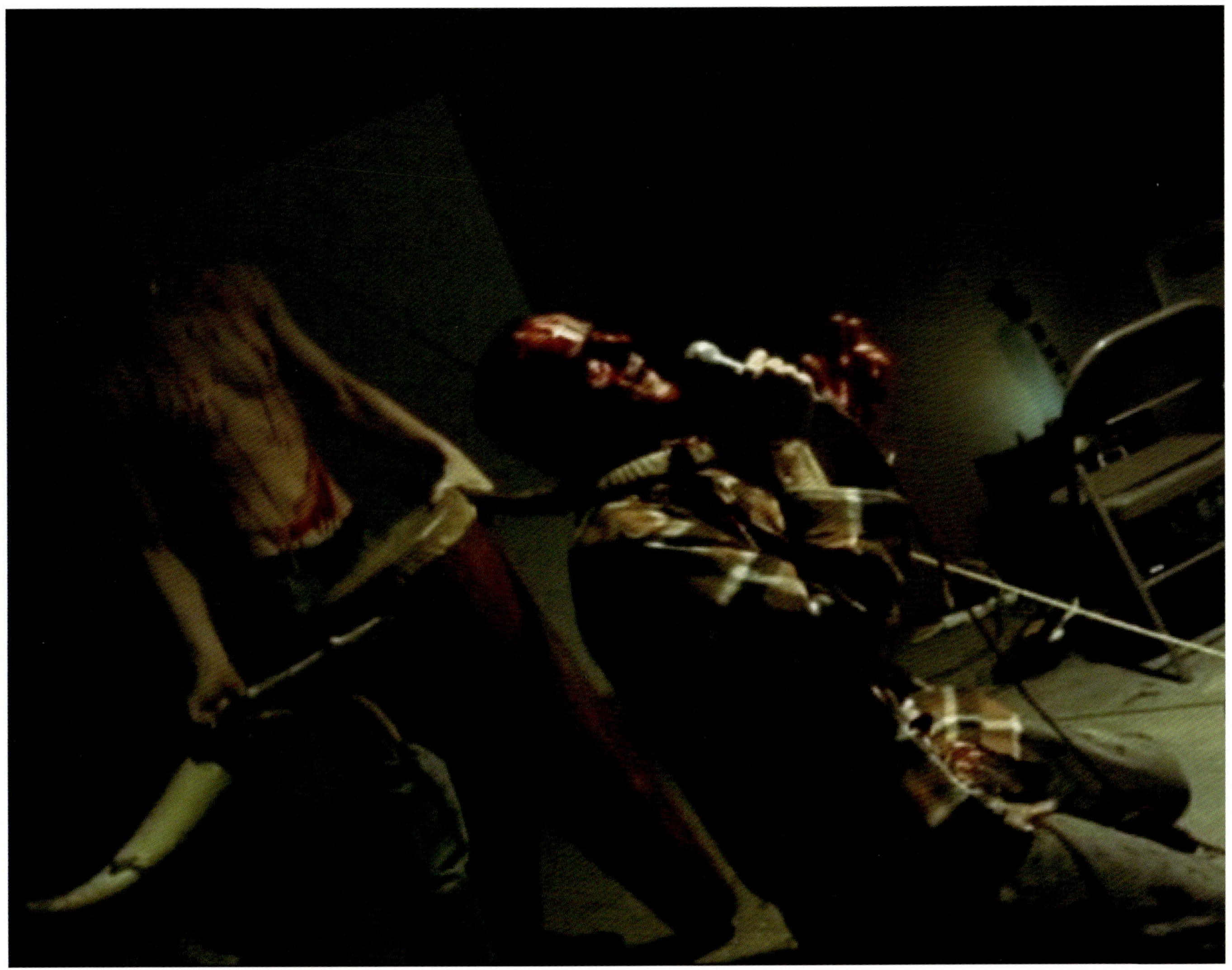

No Neck Blues Band, AT 6AM WE BECOME THE POLICE, Directed by Adam Egypt Mortimer, 2009.

You guys have been together for almost 20 years. That is a long time for any project.
It has been really interesting to watch what has happened in 20 years. For us there is something that runs through that 20 years that is NNCK and we think that it is worth something. I don't think it would really ever stop.

Do you guys think of NNCK in terms of music or sound?
In making it I think we have come upon some music. There has been music that has occurred based on our efforts to open up the possibilities of sound. Music came pretty slowly. There was an understanding of how we heard what was happening. I could hear a show start before anything happened.

It's like the quiet before the storm.
I could hear it begin in what the noises in the room were and it would take no effort on the part of the group to fall into that sound. The evolution of it musically took fine tuning, being able to hear what it was that was happening. Then all of a sudden music is available, totally possible. You can just fall in and we have fallen in before. We don't stay there. It is not important for us to continue to make what other people would recognize as music, but it does happen.

What is improvisation to you?
Improvisation comes with connotations that sounds like an exercise. With NNCK, we base our music on what I would call an impulse. ☺

Victoria Bartlett
"Styling should be about self-expression and independence."

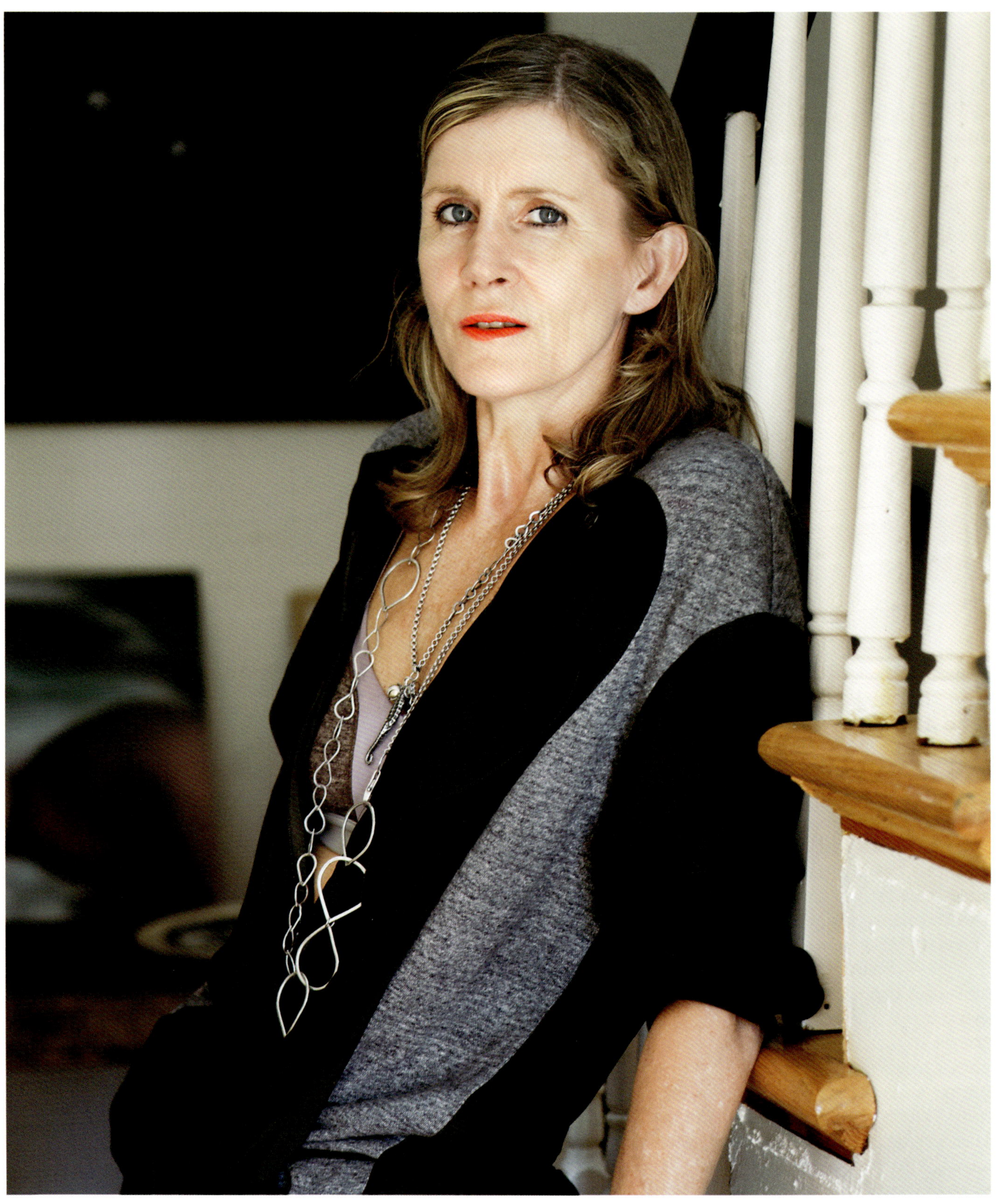

Interview Part I by Hannelore Knuts
Interview Part II by Johnny Misheff

British expat Victoria Bartlett is a
pioneer in the field of styling and an
auteur within the fashion industry.
Building her reputation on her
collaborative work with Steven Klein
and styling music celebrities like
Björk and Madonna, Bartlett eventually
returned to design, launching VPL
(Visible Panty Line) — a lingerie
apparel line that popularized the
underwear-as-outerwear aesthetic.
Bartlett's work in fashion routinely
sets her apart: a "personal style"
that is entirely visionary.

Part I: Hannelore Knuts
This is gonna record, no?
They're gonna think you're in a Latin
restaurant.
But we are.
What do you want to start with? When
I came to New York?
Yeah, and why.
I came in the 80s. A certain wave
of people were coming over. It was
a whole insurgence of the Brit
movement, the New Romantics. I
remember my first night out, there
was broken glass on the streets and
it was as if they were diamond laced
— the streets were sparkling. It was
straight out of a movie — my dream
New York — and I just fell straight
into doing projects.
What kind of projects?
I came here wanting to do something.
I wanted to design. I paired off
with this guy Jeffrey Costello.
We did one collection, BC, for two
seasons and then we were bankrupt. We
sold in stores in the East Village.
I also did a whole printed thing
where I did T-shirts with this woman
Pinky Black. We did multicolor Haile
Selassie Chanel T-shirts, which we
were selling at Michael and Gerlinde
Kostiff's store, The World. They were
the guys who did Kinky Gerlinky. But
then I got into just doing parties.
With all of your friends?
That's what New York was about. I've
always liked the collaborative thing
and New York was that from the
beginning. People grouped together

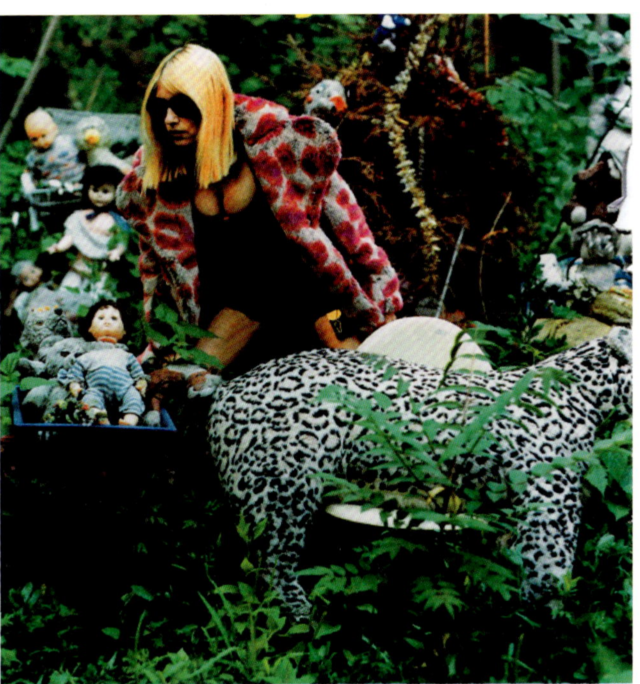

Kim Gordon styled by Victoria Bartlett,
Interview Magazine, August 1992. Photo:
Steven Klein, courtesy BMP Media Holdings, LLC

and would just think up ideas. We
would be sitting at David LaCha-
pelle's studio, chatting, bored, and
then, "All right, everyone get naked, you're gonna be blue, you're
gonna be purple..." So we'd all get
body-painted and then do the photos.
A lot of stuff was spontaneous.
Could you make money with that?
No, I didn't make money really
until I met up with Steven Klein.
We ended up together and started
collaborating. He brought me into
the commercial world and I brought
him into the underworld. We merged
our interests. We'd set up shoots
from Wigstock, but we'd move it onto
Steven's roof and he'd have a set
designer build a set. We'd all go up
there and have a banquet and then
he'd shoot. We'd go to like
Palladium on Halloween and have
someone on an elephant. He'd have
an elephant go into a club and we'd
shoot. It was about integrating
everyone you knew and what happened
at night. For me, it was more the
liberation of being able to create
these scenarios, characters, like
making editorial film art.

That's the secret of a good picture.
It was also the times. New York was a
different place. Now it's very groomed
for tourism. The areas you can go into
now weren't safe. Parts of the Village
were really dangerous. Chelsea was
just Mega Sex City, with fur and drag
queens and hardcore gays. I think for
that reason people were afraid of New
York and so it was less crowded. It
gave people room. It's never going to
come back because the city is groomed
for businesses. I think it was just
very pure.

How did VPL start?
When VPL started, I didn't wanna do
it as a collection. The first concept
was with Mary Frey. We talked about
doing a label called Difficult Brown.
We wanted to do underwear, but like
fast food. She was doing this Slush
Puppy stand at the time. We wanted to
have a stand and revolving menu, but
with underwear and everything packaged
like fast food. Very Japanese, kind of
gimmicky, but that's where VPL started
from. At the same time, I went to
Japan and they wanted me to open the
first stylist store there. It would
have been great. I told them I would
only do it if I could do underwear,
and I designed the store. It was all
plexi with all the underwear in poster
books or in huge photo cubes.

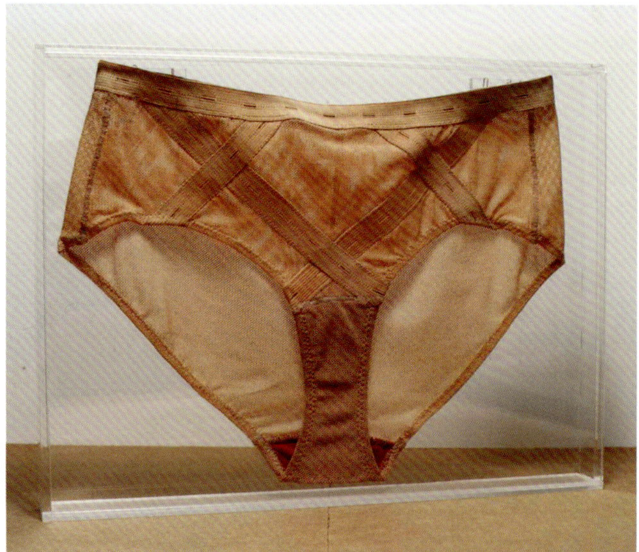

VPL, Sheer Underwear in Plexi, FW03.
Photo: Maciek Kobielski

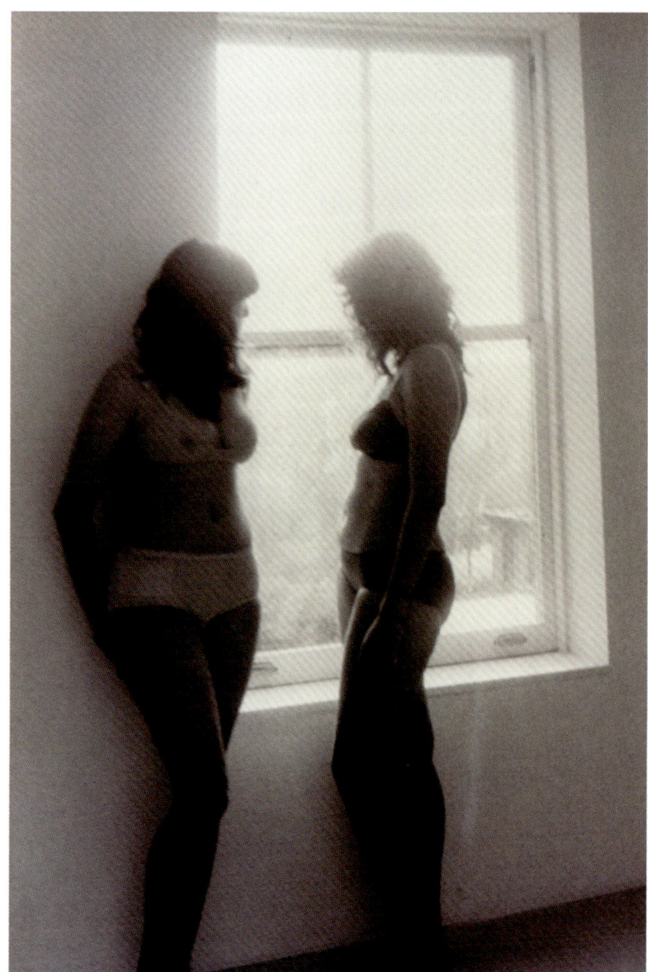

VPL, FW03. Photo: Mark Borthwick

It sounds amazing.
It would have been amazing, but
they had a crash. That's where it
started though. I was thinking about
underwear that was visible outside.
I called Jeffrey Costello, and asked
him to do this capsule collection
with me. It was all medical and
surgical — we wanted it to be dual
functional.

How was it functional?
All the underwear had loops for your
key rings and anything else you
could attach. All the underwear had
pockets. You could put your tampons
in them. We called them travel
panties. It was actually a really
cool concept. You were in the first
show.

With the doctors.
Mark did all the photos and Marcelo
did a film. We literally only had
sixteen looks; that was all we had.

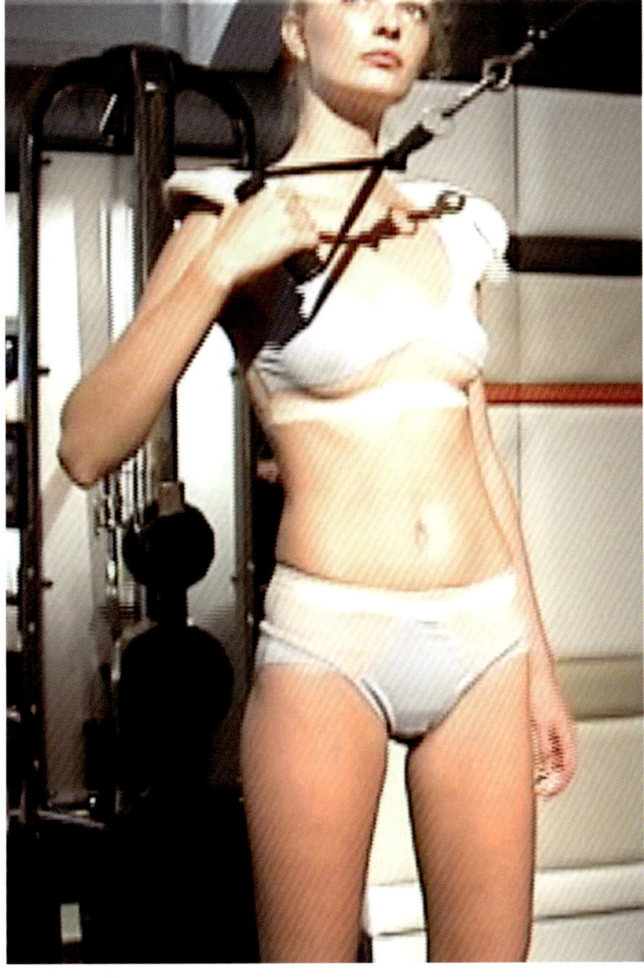

VPL, SS05.

But, you know, it's underwear...
It was cool because no one was doing it
at the time.
Did you do a second season right after?
The second season we did a skateboard
bowl. Andy Kessler, who passed away
a year and a half ago, was the most
infamous old-school skateboarder on
the East Coast. He built every ramp
and skateboard bowl you'd see. I had
this raw space, a 16,000-square-foot
space that Darryl K and I divided.
Andy built this 200-foot-long ramp
that was nude and red in the space. I
asked my friend Jill Nichols to paint
it, not knowing how long it was.
She was like, "To this day I could
have fucking killed you." She was
painting night and day. Then we had
these female pro-skateboard champions
skateboard back and forth. It was so
great because we could get people
involved. Everyone was excited.

And they all did it...wow.
Were you in that one?
**No, I remember the doctor and then
the gym.**
I remember you asked me, "Do you have
a cocktail? What do you do? You do
the weights and a cocktail?"
**That was the only time I've ever had
fun in a gym.**
That was pretty funny. I guess, I've
always been into concepts and the
theatre of stuff. Did you do the
one in the industrial building? We
built the frame of a house, like in
Dogville. You had to walk through it.
We had VPL doormats on either side so
you could wipe your feet.
**And that evolved into your way of
working.**
I always swore that that's not what
I wanted to do, but I actually love
doing it. I think in life things
have a progression and things change
because of circumstance. When Kiki
came on she formulated a business out
of it.
**And now you've returned back to
styling.**
Yeah. I love styling.
**Some designers are more stylists than
they really are designers.**
I think it helps having done styling.
A lot of designers don't have a
styling background and can't think
up concepts. They only think of
clothing. I start with what I want
to do, which is more like putting
together a photo shoot. It's almost
like working backwards. I start at
the finale — that's where my concept
spawns from. The theater of it has
to excite me. You get into the
peripheral things and then you do
the main clothes and then you have
to do the more fundamental things.
I can't do it the other way. When
VPL started, it was more like an
interactive space for me where you do
the designing, but you also bring in
an exterior world.
**You have to bring in your community,
your family.**
For me, it's always the family. I
outsource the family unit.

I feel that you enjoy the fact that you can give a platform to people who need it.
It's the give and take that's so important. I also know the people, so there's a personal dialogue. That's why I never understood the idea of hiring people you don't know. Groups like the Bauhaus or the Beat Generation fascinated me because it was groups of people who grew together. It's a family unit and from within it you grow and get better ideas.

It's not about you, its about making something for everyone.
The idea of "me," which happens a lot in design, I find boring. I think there's a bigger thing in sharing ideas with people and sharing experience and experimentation that's more exciting. I hate the concept of people trying to own their things because it's so self-indulgent. The most creative times in history are really about people getting together and sharing.

You keep finding young kids. You always have a young family.
I don't believe in generational things. That's the beauty of staying slightly young mentally — you stay open.

You're not afraid of a young name. You have a good eye and you trust your eye.
And I'm a Peter Pan.

And you're a Peter Pan.
I'm eternally young.

I hope this thing is taping all this. Any last words for me?
What's always fascinated me about you is that we're so similar. You're someone who's very independent — however you're not a loner, you're not reliant, you're very strong, and you're someone who likes to collaborate. You have a genuine sensibility. You imbue a mix of all these elements, you're not a one trick pony. You do many things because creatively you think in that way. I think it's a really modern way to be and it's inspiring to be around.

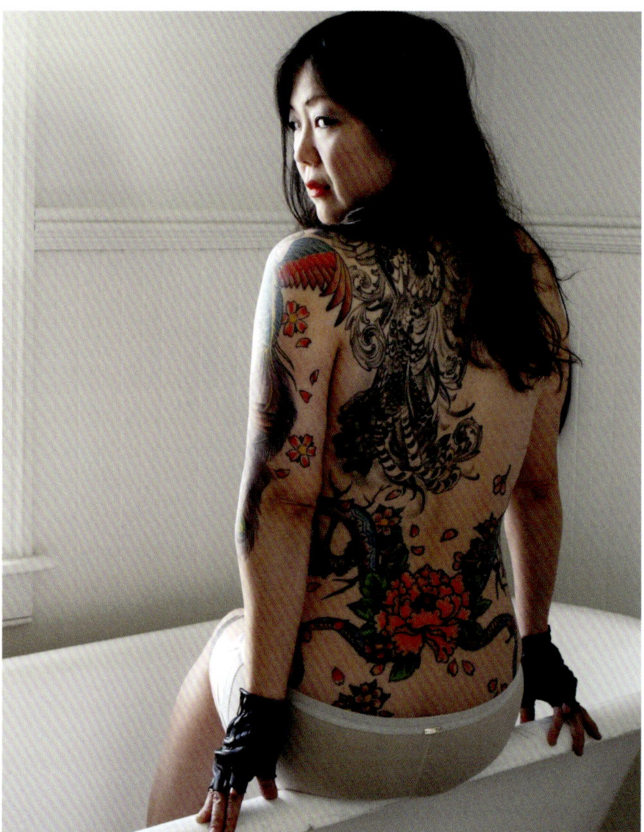

Margaret at John's House, Underwear by VPL, 2009.
Photo: Jack Pierson

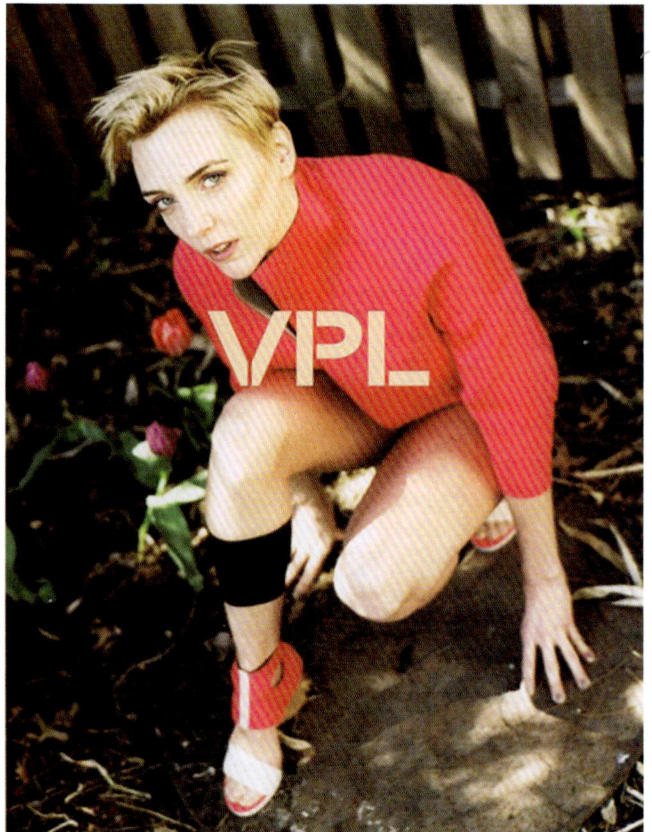

Hannelore Knuts, VPL, 2014.

Part II: Johnny Misheff

I'd like to talk about this period in the 90s when stylists were really coming into their own, the beginning of the era of the celebrity stylist.
There were probably only a handful of stylists at the time. Ray Petrie started it in London. There was Joe McKenna and Laurie Goldstein. We were a new brigade. There were all these articles about Camilla Nickerson and Andrew Dosmuk. Our group was more wacky and avant-garde. It was more about independent style and just styling to make a point.

Is that what the magazines wanted?
Advertisers didn't have the rights to tell you what you needed to do. You would dictate to them. You could do whatever you wanted with the clothes to create a look.

What magazines were the most fun to work with?
They all were back then. Even doing Elle in England at the time was so different from what it is now. We would do spreads of all the trannies for a lot of magazines that don't exist anymore. It was an almost trannified world in a funny way. Things were extreme. Lady Gaga could've been created then, but she isn't a natural transformation of how it was. People lived that and did it. They weren't produced into it.

This must have given you all an immense feeling of power.
There were no rules or restrictions. It was an open field to do what you wanted. Music was also big, so I was working with all the singers and musicians in the beginning.

Like who?
Deee-Lite. I styled their video "Groove Is in the Heart."

You did that one?
I did it for $800. The whole thing — twenty people. We were all in it. I'm in it. I've got a wig on. We're all dolled up.

How did that come about?
I used to do parties with Kierin and Dmitri, who were both in Deee-Lite. Dmitri was my DJ and Lady Miss K

was my go-go dancer. Miss K needed to do this video, so it was all our friends getting together, doing it on a minimum budget, and asking every favor in the book to get clothes from people. Deee-Lite was known in an underground way, but then it exploded. I remember Pat Fields was huge then. Everyone wanted her clothes. Her store was incredible. Half the stuff in the video came from there.

I forget the name of your band. Cheap something...
I was in a band that never played called Cheap Date. We rehearsed and did recordings, but never performed live because there was only one real musician in the group. But we did a lot of press.

Without ever playing out?
Yes, because we dressed extravagantly. We would wear these ridiculous outfits, like German fräuleins.

Where are those recordings now and why have you never played them for me?
I probably have one of my tapes somewhere, but I don't have a tape player. Go figure.

I get the sense that everyone was helping everyone back then. Who did you work with most, if anyone in particular?
I did a lot with Jeffrey Costello before we became partners for VPL. Before that we did a Madonna video together.

Which one?
Fever. We intended to use all Gaultier clothes — that was the whole concept. Then I got a phone call from Madonna saying, "I opened the box of clothes and I don't like them." It was 7 PM the night before. I called everyone I knew. I was begging people, "You gotta let me come by!!!" I called my friend at Vivienne Westwood and he flew in to do it, but then we ended up using one of my own Westwood pieces, the gold one with the wings and miniskirt that looked like a gladiator outfit.

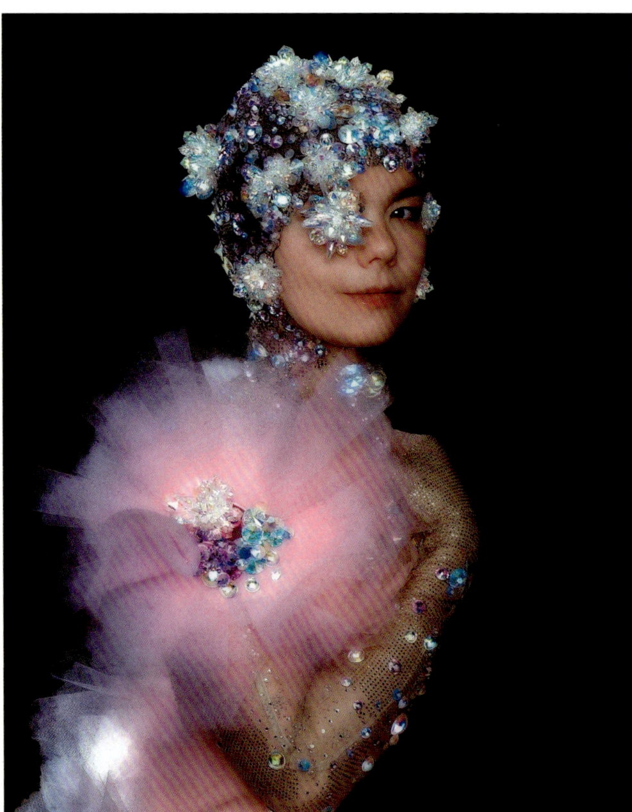

Björk, Vespertine Promo Shoot, Styled by Victoria Bartlett, 2001. Photo: Warren du Preez & Nick Thornton-Jones

You styled Trent Reznor too, right?
Trent Reznor was actually a client of mine for a year. He asked me to do all the clothing for Nine Inch Nails. He wanted deconstructed and distressed clothes. Jeffrey would make them and I would be on my roof oiling them, fucking them up, wearing them down, aging them.
What year was that?
It would be in the mid 90s.
Downward Spiral era.
None of them drank. It was this hardcore band and they'd have fruit shakes. I really liked Trent. He was great. I don't know who was responsible, probably his record company, but I got ripped off and never got paid for a lot of stuff.
That's on the record! What about Björk?
She was incredible, such a character. She knows what she wants, but is very open to you being creative. The thing that's great about her is that she's excited about you performing as an artist as well.

What happened to the styling world? It doesn't feel as fun as what you're describing.
The industry changed. Now you've got a list of advertisers and that's what you use. It's made stylists lazy. It's all about picking a product. Styling should be about self-expression and independence. People loved Gaultier and Montana, but it would be mixed in. It was about integrating personal style, mixing, and matching.
Is that why you wanted to branch off and do your own line?
Yeah. It was like my hands were tied, it was quite crippling. There was also no real gratification. You become the schlepper, the one who's responsible for anything that goes wrong. I found it unsatisfying because you never really owned what you did. I trained in design, so I wanted to go back into it, but in a different way.
It's ten years later and people are loving it.
They better. In the future I hope that VPL becomes the biggest phenomenon.
It's become an institution. I love the shows in particular.
Tenfold from what it started as. There are always the best looking crowds at the shows.
Best looking crowds. Everyone knows each other. Everyone loves each other. You create an environment within this business structure that you have.
You can't sell out to the industry. You have to love it for the reasons you love it. The reason I love fashion is the theatrics of it. Obviously, I have to do the commercial side, which is challenging, but it's interesting to break those boundaries.
I hope people start getting inspired again, thinking out of the box.
It takes individuals. I think we have a couple of those running around.
There definitely are.
They just need to be given the platform. We need to raise them up. 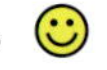

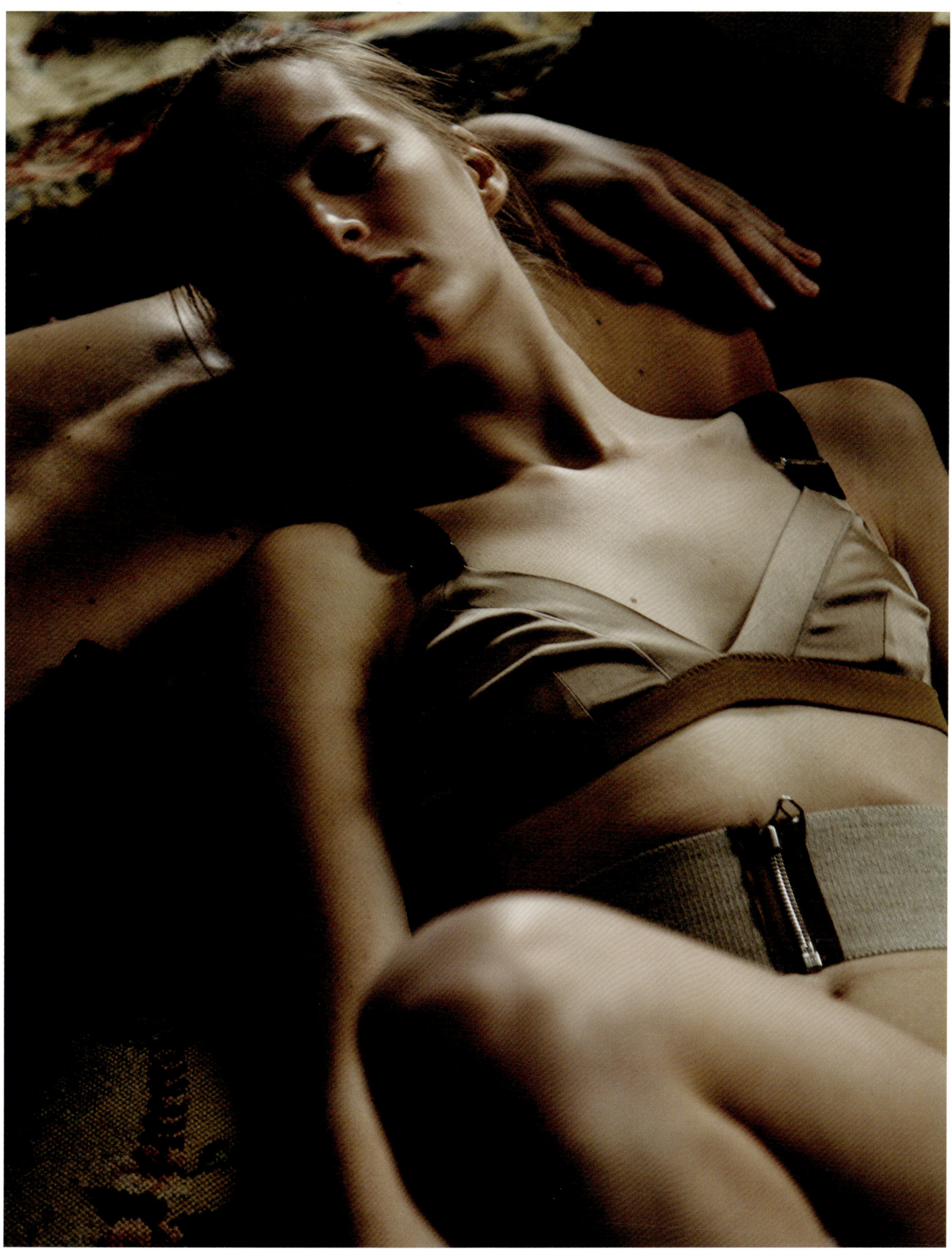

VPL, FW09. Photo: David Armstrong

Bill Strobeck

"In Philly I saw like two homeless guys blowing each other
and eating McDonald's afterwards."

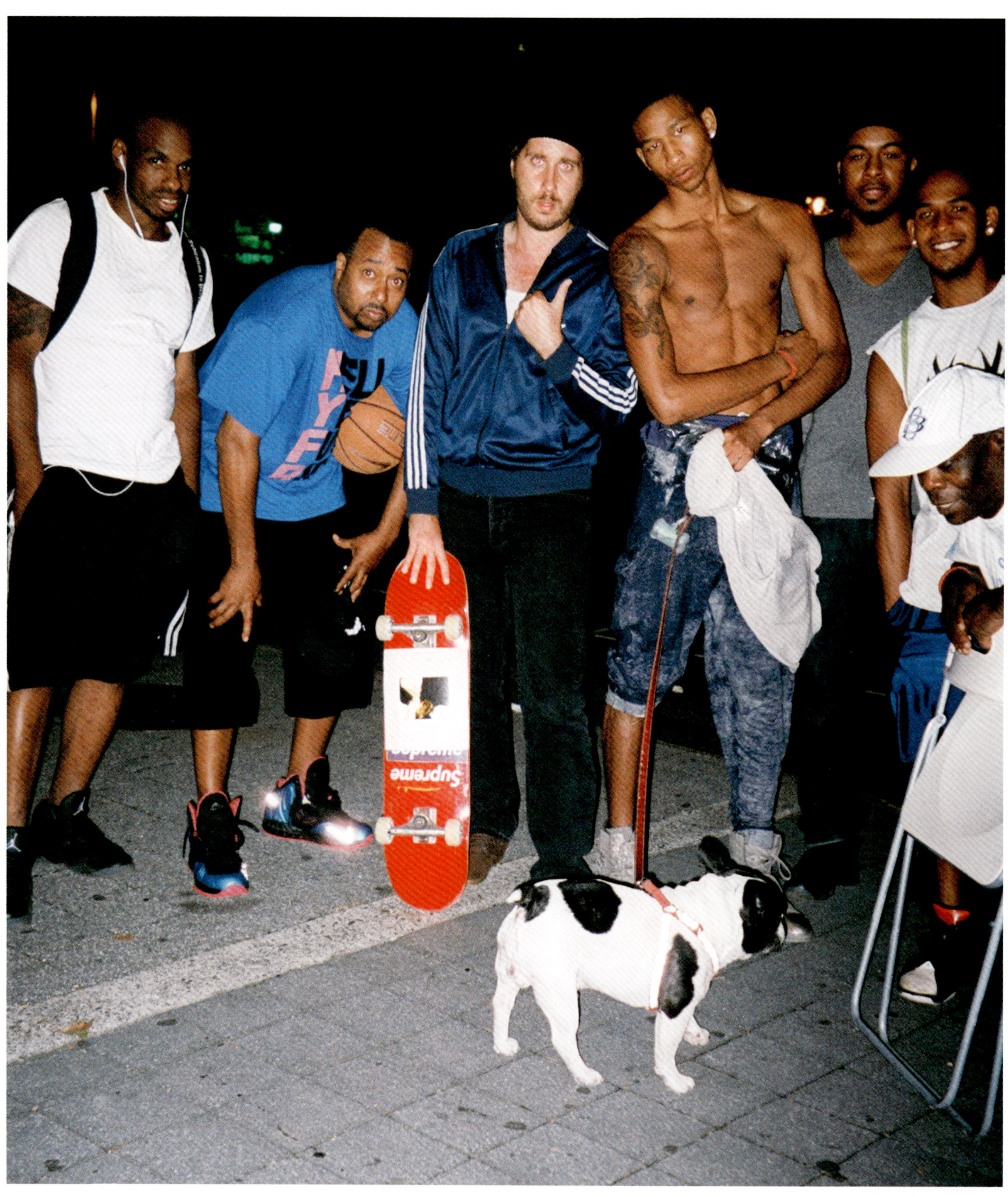

Interview & portrait by Maggie Lee
Images courtesy Bill Strobeck

The first time I met Bill Strobeck I was filming something and he took a cashew from a snack bowl and put it between his fingers, moving them like there was a person dancing with a cashew hard on. He was wearing a leather daddy hat with a chain on it and a denim jacket. We didn't really talk. A decade earlier, I was in my bedroom watching his video for Alien Workshop's Photosynthesis. What was the deal with Jason Dill's bedroom in that video? I remember wishing my room was allowed to be that messy. He had one mattress on the floor and one mattress up on the wall without sheets, and there were one million receipts on the floor. None of the clothes were on his clothes hanger. That film was an East Coast thing. I loved the style and wanted to recreate and surround myself in how it made me feel. Ever since, I have been following Bill's work. Whether it's photographs or films, they are so iconic and timeless. Damn, Bill is so sick!

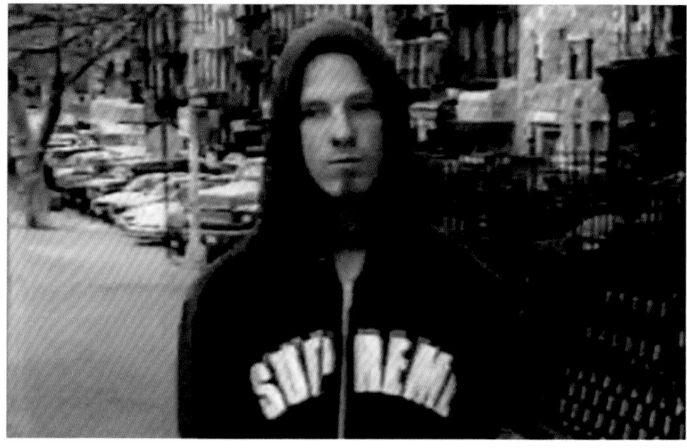

Photosynthesis, Alien Workshop, 2000.

How did you dress when you were a kid?
When I was really young my mother would take me to thrift stores to get all my clothes. She didn't have that much money really, and probably would go there just to buy shit for herself. I went through a lot of different phases in my teen years. No joke, I would show up to school wearing slippers and random shit like that. I would also shop at Big and Tall stores because as skaters we wore oversized clothes back then.

Were you a weirdo?
I wasn't weird, I was real normal... at least I thought I was normal.
You were a skateboarder. Did you dress like a skater?
I started skateboarding because of the style of it. Skateboarders looked cooler back then. They for sure looked different than everybody that I went to school with, and that was very attractive to me. The skateboard culture wasn't really around me. I wanted to look like the kids I saw in the magazines. I would go to school with bleached hair and stuff like that, like I was part of some cult that was just so much bigger than this small thing that was happening at my school.
Were you going to shows?
I started going to hardcore shows around '92. At the time all these rad cultures would go to these shows: skaters, people that wrote graffiti and liked hip-hop. Kids that didn't even like the music would go — they would all show up to this one thing and hang. I think everyone kind of felt normal. No one was judging each other. It didn't feel like there were any walls up.
Why did you want to move from Philadelphia to New York?
I lived in Philadelphia for seven years. Time had taken its course and it became really boring to me. A few of my friends had moved to the city, so I moved here as well.
What year was that?
I moved here in 2002, but I was coming up here since '98, filming skating and stuff.
How did you first start working for Alien Workshop?
I had been given a camera as a gift and started filming a lot. One of the guys that was on the team lived in Philadelphia had asked me to film him. He ended up being a pretty dominant guy in skateboarding, especially in Philadelphia. The people at Alien Workshop were getting all the footage. Eventually they just asked me to work for them.

Were you nervous? You were pretty young, right?
I was a little nervous at first, being so young and filming people that I looked up to. I was like 19 or 20.

Was that when you met Jason Dill?
When I met Dill he had just moved to New York. He was so wrapped up in the style of the city. He was taking all this shit in that was happening here, like a sponge, and putting it into his skating. It was very artistic and inspiring to be around. I felt like I was making a project with him. He had a vision, and he wanted to do it, and it felt like I was helping him create his vision.

What's your favorite Dill tattoo?
I don't know, but he has a Winnie the Pooh on his arm. It's kinda funny because this other Irish kid that I grew up with named Kevin Griffen, who I was best friends with, was obsessed with Winnie the Pooh as well. Then I moved to New York and met Dill and we became really good friends. He would get his girlfriend all these Winnie the Pooh things he'd find. It's so weird, cause him and Kevin are born in the same month.

Can we talk about filming Mark Gonzales on roller skates?
Yeah. I had seen a photo of Mark on roller skates that someone posted online and noticed he was in New York, so I hit him up. He said that the next day he had some free time to meet up. The day came and it happened to be 99 degrees outside. He told me he wanted to roller skate from the Lower East Side below Delancey Street all the way up to 63rd and Lexington, which is pretty far, especially on a day where it's supposed to be over 100 by noon. I ended up following him with the camera and kind of just let him do what he wanted. It's how it always is with him. He does what he does and you document it in the way you want. The crazy thing is I ended up almost getting killed.

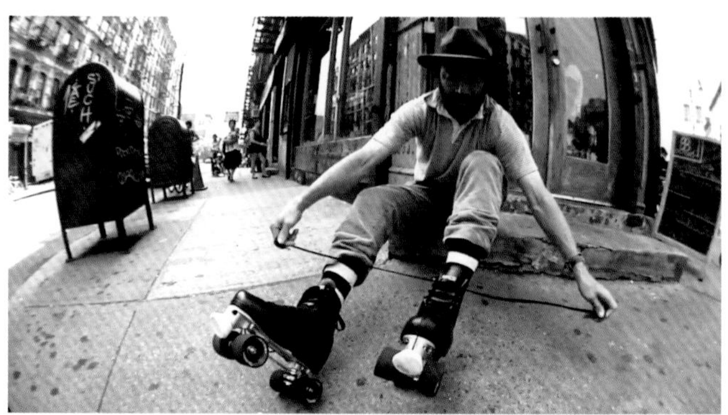

$TUD, 2012.

What happened?
He went under this tractor-trailer that was waiting to turn, I went behind him filming, and my backpack had hooked on a screw that was underneath. My arms were still in my backpack, I couldn't move, but I shook it off, it unhooked, and I ran out from under the trailer. All the guy driving had to do was press the gas and the truck would've ran me over. I was by the back wheels, It was scary. I think Mark was even scared.

What is one of the gnarliest things that you've seen?
In Philly I saw like two homeless guys blowing each other and eating McDonald's afterwards.

What are your dreams like?
My dreams are really all over the place. I'm a really imaginative person in general. I've never had dreams where I'm dying or falling. They're just really loopy and weird. If you could record them I wouldn't even have to make a film, I would just put those out every month.

Why do you think that teenage girls love skateboarders so much?
Girls just love skateboarders. Skateboarding is a weird, rebellious thing, or at least it was at one time. The sound of skateboards going down the street will make you turn your head for sure. Girls do it too. Girls love skateboarders — they're dirtbags, but fun dirtbags.

Who was your first crush?
When I was younger my mother was really sick with schizophrenia, so

I lived with my aunt and my uncle. My aunt's friend lived five houses down from us and she had a daughter that was probably six or seven years younger than me. Since my aunt hung out with this lady, and they were best friends, I was forced to hang out with this younger girl. I remember trying to kiss her once. My aunt and uncle ended up moving away, so I had to move away too, and I wasn't around that girl anymore. Sometimes I feel that I hang out with all these young girls because of that girl.

Is that why you always have like a handful of friends that are girls?
I dunno, they're all super free and fun. I also grew up with three ladies. I grew up with my mother, my grandmother, and my grandmother's friend.

Grandmother's friend?
Yeah, she lived with us, so I grew up around all women. I'm really comfortable around women. I have female tendencies maybe. Pisces is the feminine sign. You're probably looking at me thinking that's kind of funny, but I really believe in astrology.

I believe in it too. What are some films that have inspired you?
I love old Depeche Mode videos by Anton Corbijn, some stuff that Dennis Hopper has done. The Paradise Lost documentary was really fucking strong when I first saw it. It is a fucked up story, but those kids were interesting to watch. I could watch something like that, and make something based off the feeling I get from that. Anyway, a couple of those movies were made by Dennis Hopper, like the Last Movie. When I watched it, I was, like, "This is what I think a movie should be like." He was super fucking out of his mind at the time he made that. I like that there's scenes missing and shit.

What else is it that you like about Dennis Hopper?
Well, the fact that he's a total original. He was very rebellious in

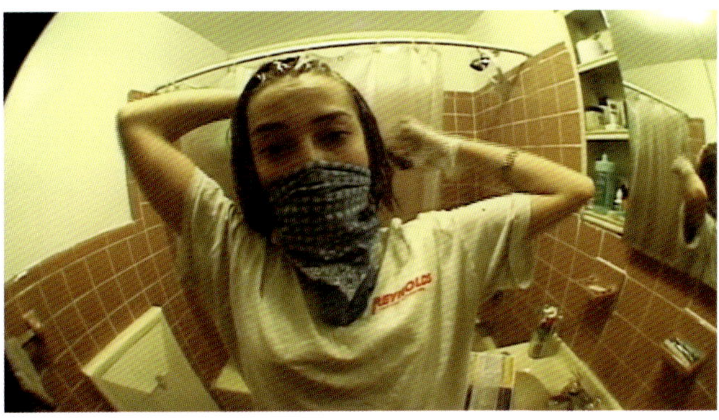

Sister, 2010.

such a smooth way. I don't watch that many movies. I have, like, thirty movies I watch over and over. It's hard for me to watch newer movies. There's titles wherever he wanted them. And he made that after Easy Rider, which was such a big success. He was, like, "Well, fuck. Now they're gonna give me money to make the movie I really want to make." I just feel like that's such a solid movie. He was going against the grain. He did it. It's awesome. He's got a super solid career to look at.

What about Paradise Lost?
The filmmakers just caught something that I was instantly attracted to. I think my work was influenced by that. The people that I choose to document have very strong personalities. They kind of make my work. It's a little bit of me and a little bit of them, and it kinda makes one big thing. Without the people that I've documented, my work wouldn't be as strong. It wouldn't be as good. I get glued to certain people because I'm attracted to their personalities, the way they act, the way they are as people, because they just don't act at all. They just do their thing. They all are very different too, and there's something about them that I want to capture and show everyone else in the world. If you take away those people from everything I've done, the special things wouldn't even be there anymore. The special things wouldn't be there at all.

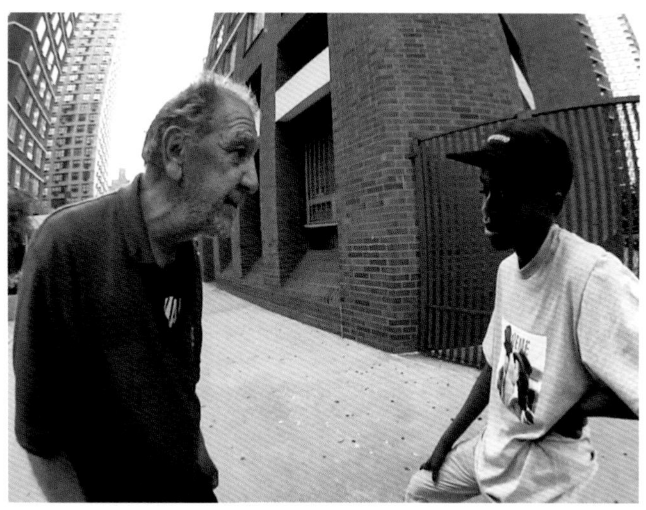

Buddy, Supreme, 2012.

What else inspires you?
I can hear a song and the feeling
I get will help create an image.
The feeling of all these things
together creates a new thing. That's
what art is: the projection of the
things that have happened to you and
your hang-ups. How you feel that
day, what you ate an hour ago, it's
just all one thing. When I made My
Lovely Mess that was just what was
happening at that time in my life.
I could take that same footage, the
same exact footage, and edit it next
month, and it would be a totally
different film.

**What was the process for editing the
movie My Lovely Mess?**
Well, you had asked me to do
something for that film night that
you put it together. That movie
literally only took four days to
edit. I had footage laying around
that I had filmed: I had gone on a
trip to Jamaica, I had footage of
my mother from the year before, and
the girl that lives in my family's
house. All that was within a year's
time. I just had it laying around.
When you asked me to do it, I had
to put something together because I
only had a few days. I took all
this footage I had and tried to make
it into a film. That's how that
worked out, I just made something
that flowed out of a bunch of scraps
that I had.

Yeah, and it worked out so well.
It worked. I'm really happy with
that. It was a small thing, and no
skateboarding. I thrive on trying to
do stuff outside of skating. I've
done skateboarding for so long. This
one is more personal to me than
anything I've done.

How much stuff do you shoot?
When I'm out filming skateboard
stuff — and that's been fifteen
years now — I film other stuff too.
If there's something else going on,
I'll film it. I have hundreds of
hours of footage, which goes back to
what I was saying about documentary
stuff. That's what it is. I'm just
filming the day that I'm living in.
I'm filming the people I'm with. I'm
filming things that are around me.
That's my day. Then I'll go back and
use eight seconds of it. My job is
filming what goes on in my life.

**Do you ever feel weird behind the
camera? Or awkward?**
I don't feel weird behind the camera.
I actually feel really comfortable.
I'll just walk up to a stranger, and
start talking to them. When you have
a camera, and it has a lens that's
really big, and you're up close to
someone, and you don't know them, it
freaks them out. I feel like I'm
super good at jiving with people.
Just the other day, I got like
some lady on the street with her
boyfriend. They were maxed out or
something. They were fighting, and
I was up the street from Supreme, out
here in L.A., and I walked by them,
they were fighting. I'm, like, "Hey,
can you talk about what's going on
up the street?" Next thing you know,
the girl had her tits out, and the
guy was slapping them around and
talking about how he had so much
money...and they were homeless.
That's what I'm saying. Stuff just
happens like that to me. Any of the
skate videos, they're packed with
all that. For skateboarding, you
could do a hard trick and it doesn't
matter to me. I'm over that.
Personality is the trick.

Are you attracted to that, or does it come to you?
I want that. I go home, I watch that, and it speaks in volumes. My mother was schizophrenic, and I was around that. I feel pretty comfortable walking up to somebody that I feel is homeless or schizophrenic on the street. I don't scare them. I don't feel freaked out, and maybe they don't feel threatened by that. I try to go with the flow with what that person's about.

That's a good motto. You also seem to be unafraid to mix digital cameras and, like, high 8. How do you decide what camera to use?
I just did that thing with Chloe Sevigny for Opening Ceremony. I had the cameras lying around my apartment, and I hadn't used them yet, so I used them. It's short, and it only took a couple hours. It's a little bit of today and a little bit of the past. The cameras are old and we're in the present. If you look at somebody from the 60s, you know they're from that time.

And you put them on the internet.
I like doing projects where I can show them in a free, free, way. A free-ish style. Like with making videos and films, when you put them online, you don't need to go through anyone to do that. When it goes online, it's your thing, it's exactly the way you wanted it. I like that style. You do that, and then somebody might see that and say, "I want something like this. I'm gonna give them the creative, and the cash to make it," which I think is the raddest thing ever.

So true. And you're creating things that teenagers are looking at, and people in small towns.
Totally. When I was younger I would order videos from a skate shop in Florida, and it would take two weeks to get to me. I would get this tape, and would watch it over and over, and that would inspire me.

I see you as an artist that can make commercial work that's your work — no one can replicate it, it's something that only you can do.
That's the best thing about doing everything yourself and doing it your own way. Having your own vibe to it without trying. This is what I feel — that this clip should be cut here, then this clip should be back two clips, it should be before this clip. Any of the things that I've made have been a process to me. I have to turn up the volume here on this clip. You have to do this here. You have to put this person here. Its things you probably don't even notice but making a film for me is like putting a puzzle together.

What's one thing you don't want anyone to know? [laughter]
Something that I don't want anyone to know?

That's a weird question. I just wanted to see what you would say.
I'm pretty open. I'm a pretty open person, I don't think I leave too much hidden. My way of feeling comfortable is just spitting it out and getting it over with...

What's something you want to tell everyone?
How about, "Fuck you"...and, "Stop on over and hang out at my apartment...it's a fun place to kick it." ☺

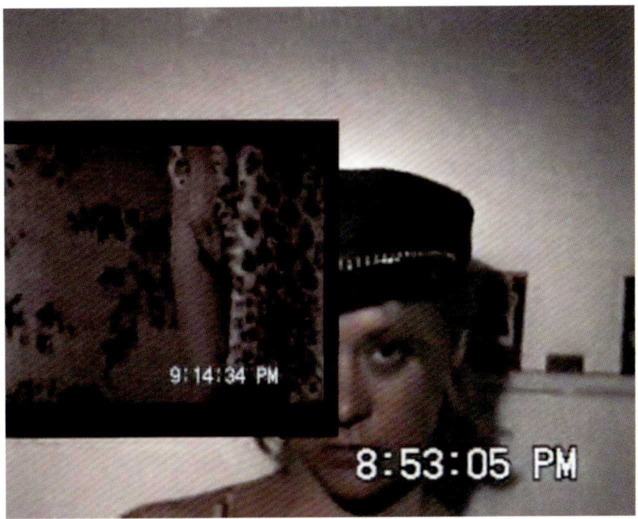

Where's Bambi?, Opening Ceremony, 2012.

Manuel Raeder

"I think it's very crucial to produce in order
to figure out an alternative way of working."

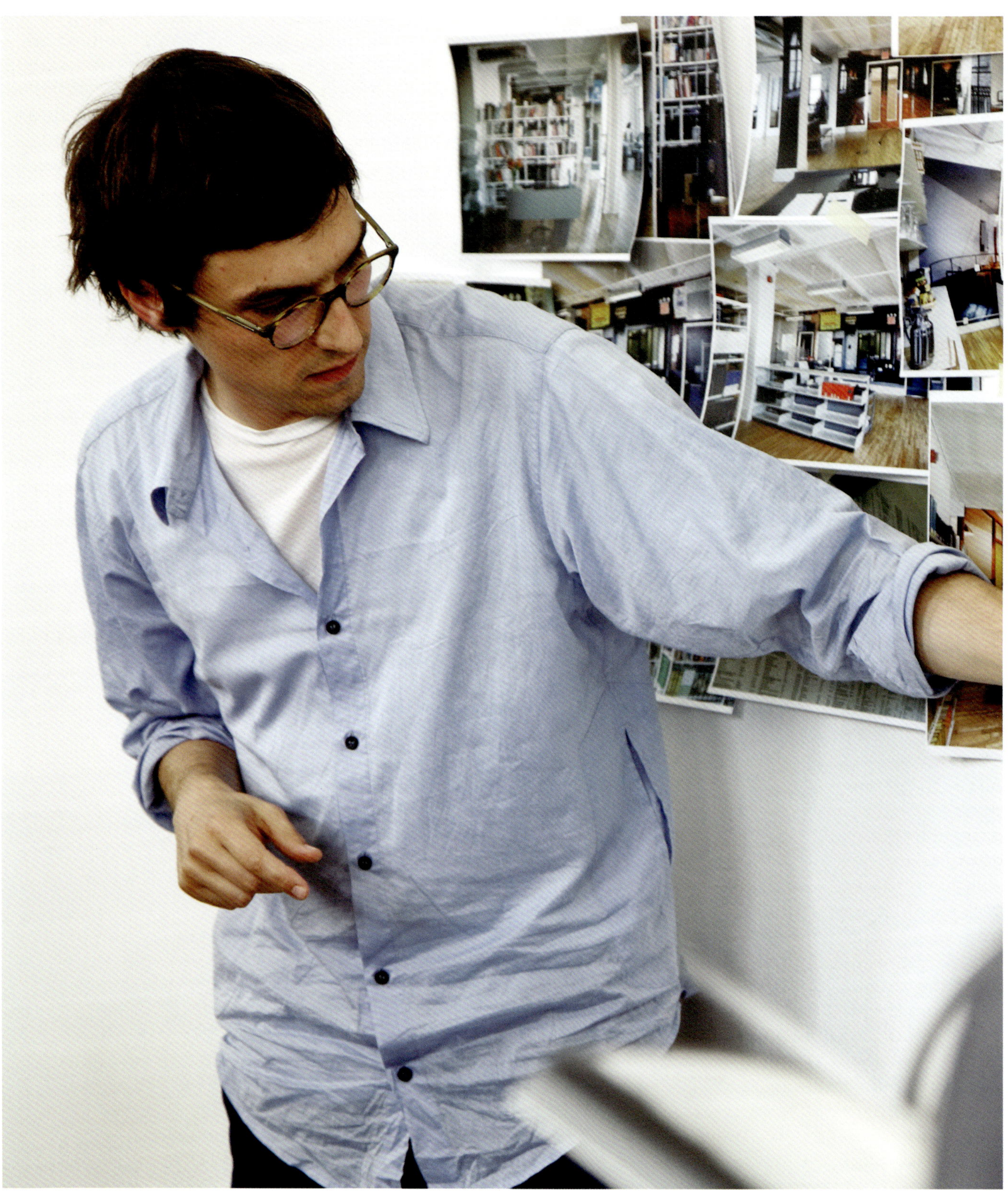

Interview by Asher Penn
Portrait by Ulrich Gebert

Manuel Raeder is best recognized as the longstanding graphic designer for German fashion label BLESS, a brand whose public identity is as unusual and open-ended as the clothing they make. His formal and conceptual fingerprints appear clearly only if the receiver holistically investigates the full spectrum of his projects, collaborators, and clients. This includes publishing houses such as Walther König and Sternberg, artists like Michael Krebber and Sergej Jenson, and the imprints he runs with fellow designer Manuel Goller, such as My Bauhaus is better than yours and Bom Dia Boa Tarde Boa Noite. Through these projects Raeder's constant is consciousness: a willingness to engage with material he is working on and respond to it in the moment, with no allegiance to what he did yesterday or what he will do tomorrow.

What was your experience like going to school?
When I started to study in London I was a little bit naive. I didn't really know what graphic design was. It seemed more free than a course like sculpture or painting. I didn't know what I was gonna do, or what was gonna happen. That didn't really matter so much because afterwards at the Jan van Eyck Academy it was much more about me defining my own profession, or defining my own practice in a way. There I started getting into theory, experimenting with printing and different things, book making, figuring out how to bring those together.
Was the plan always to work as a graphic designer?
No, it happened organically. When I was living in London I started working with friends, people who were surrounding me. Most of them were either involved with music or with the fine arts. Friends asked me to start doing fliers for gigs, artists started making me do invitations for exhibitions, things like that.

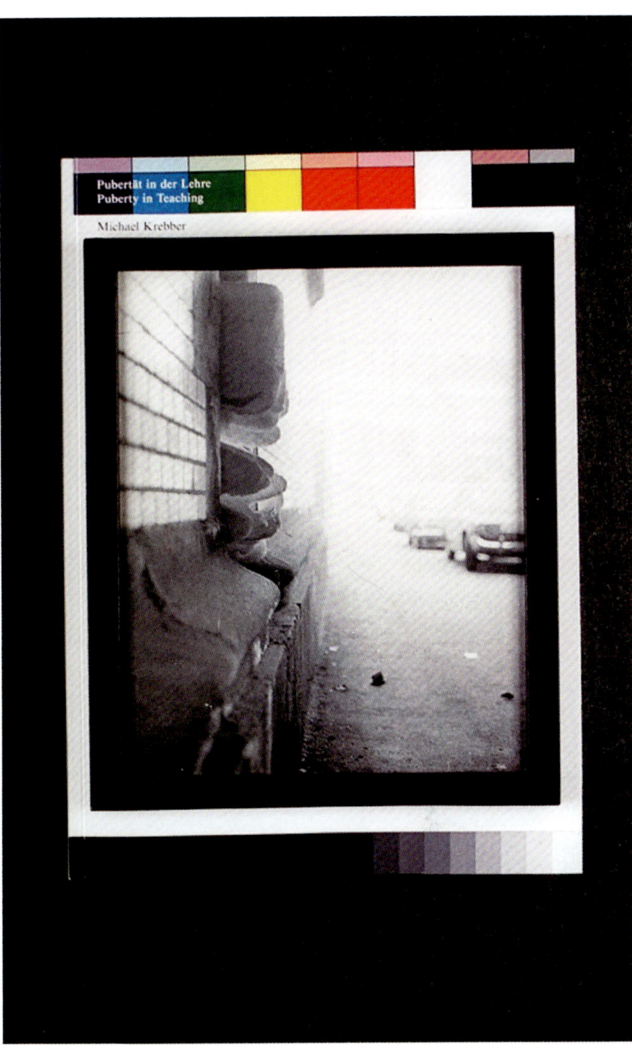

Michael Krebber, Puberty in Teaching, Walther Koenig, 2008.

And it led to more projects?
I started working with some magazines, doing interviews with artists, musicians, eventually doing the layout...
What's your relationship with the artists you collaborate with?
Every time it's different. There are no set rules for it. It really varies. There are some artists that I've now made the fifth or sixth book with. After such a long time you have a totally different level of communication. It's usually about trust. Sometimes it might take time, sometimes it can be very fast, sometimes it could happen within one or two weeks. Sometimes it can take years to create a space of mutual understanding.

Images courtesy Manuel Raeder

Is there something in this creative dynamic you consciously pursued?
It became very clear when I was at the Jan van Eyck Academy, because I had already worked for a while in design. I was still very young, and hadn't had much experience, but I wasn't convinced about a profession that tries to persuade itself through pushing through an aesthetic, making it's aesthetic look nice and labeling it as a way to survive. I thought, "Oh my god, if I work in this profession I'm gonna be bored. I'm gonna be so bored doing the same thing over and over, so how can I create a praxis for me that I find challenging?" This question has always been present in my head since I started working as a designer: How can I detach this praxis and make it suit me and not me suit the praxis? I started looking at different things, like how books were made in the 60s and 70s, Fluxus, conceptual art books, and so on. I found it interesting that even when a designer works outside of the parameters they are usually trained in, a book can still work as a carrier of condensed information. It's not the typeface, or the color, or the grid, but the structure that surrounds it — such as editorial questions, or how it comes together more generally. This is what I still enjoy now, and what I have been busy with the last ten years.

What is My Bauhaus is Better Than Yours?
It's basically a collective. It started as a thesis project for some students at the Bauhaus University in Weimar. I was advisor for their BA, so I was an advisor for this project. The idea developed into a company that could go beyond this final exam and have it's own life. There are two founders, Manuel Goller and Daniel Burchard, and then there are other associated people who work on it. The idea is that it enables production of furniture and distribution in a more independent way. So they have some of my furniture in the program, but it's not my company in that sense.

What is your relationship to Bauhaus?
Well, the title My Bauhaus is better than yours is of course an ironic joke. It relates to what is accepted as a classic design standard. Especially in Germany, where Bauhaus is considered a classic, people are not so open to new, young design or things that might be out of the ordinary. The title is saying that something new, a new way of thinking, might actually be a new classic. In German design there is very little risk, especially in graphic design and furniture. Design is historically linked to a commercial aspect that has more to do with promotion. But design is not about that, it's also about human beings, and relationships. It's about how someone relates to an object, and what this object means or what it says. There are a lot of young contemporary designers that are still thinking about these things, expanding on these ideas, and suiting them to a more contemporary context.

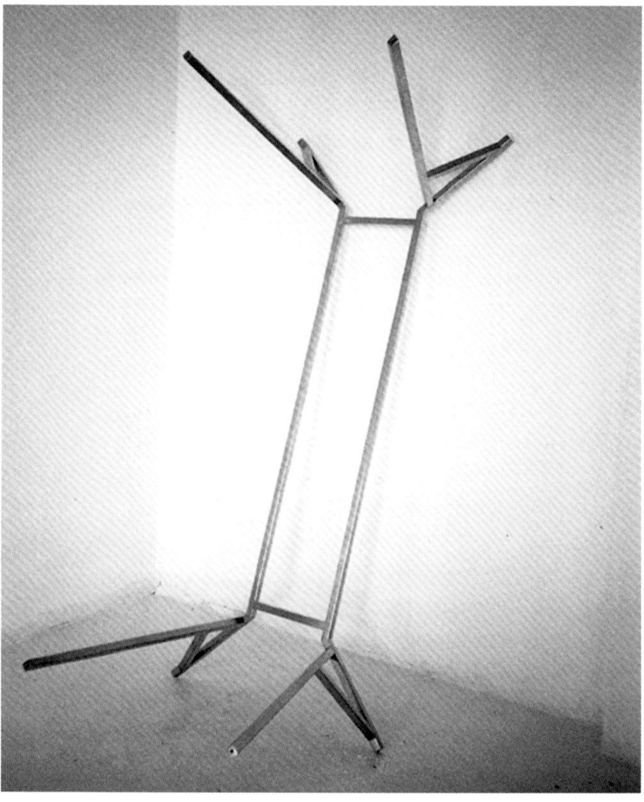

My Bauhaus is Better Than Yours, Architect's Table, 2011. Photo: Manuel Goller

How did you get involved with BLESS?
It was quite a coincidence. A mutual
friend always said that we should
get to know each other because the
way I was thinking about graphic
design was very much related to how
they were thinking in fashion. I had
never heard about them, I didn't
know who they were, and I had never
worked in fashion before. My friend
told me to call them when I was in
Berlin or Paris. At one point I was
in Berlin for a visit and ended up
meeting Ines Kaag at her studio. It
turned out that we're from the same
village in the south of Germany. We
never knew each other, but there was
an immediate, strong connection. Our
perception about the world and design
were connected. We became very close
friends. One week later, they asked
me if I wanted to do the book about
ten years of BLESS. I said, "Yeah, of
course, I would love to," but I had
never really heard about BLESS. They
started showing me their stuff and I
began working on the book. Two weeks
later they called me again and said,
"Hey do you want to do all our graphic
design?" That's how the collaboration
started growing over the years.
**That's when BLESS really established
itself. How did you incorporate
yourself into what they were doing?
Were you riffing on what they had
already?**
The first collection we started
working on together was number twenty-
three. They already had twenty-two
collections where they had worked
with other graphic designers, and a
lot of it was actually them doing
things themselves. Eventually they
found that they had no time to do it,
so they really needed someone that
they could maintain a dialogue with.
The company was growing at that point
and they began doing projects every
six months in Paris. They have always
had a very strong opinion about what
design is. The first thing we worked
on together was the look book, which
came out every six months. BLESS
doesn't have classic fashion shows

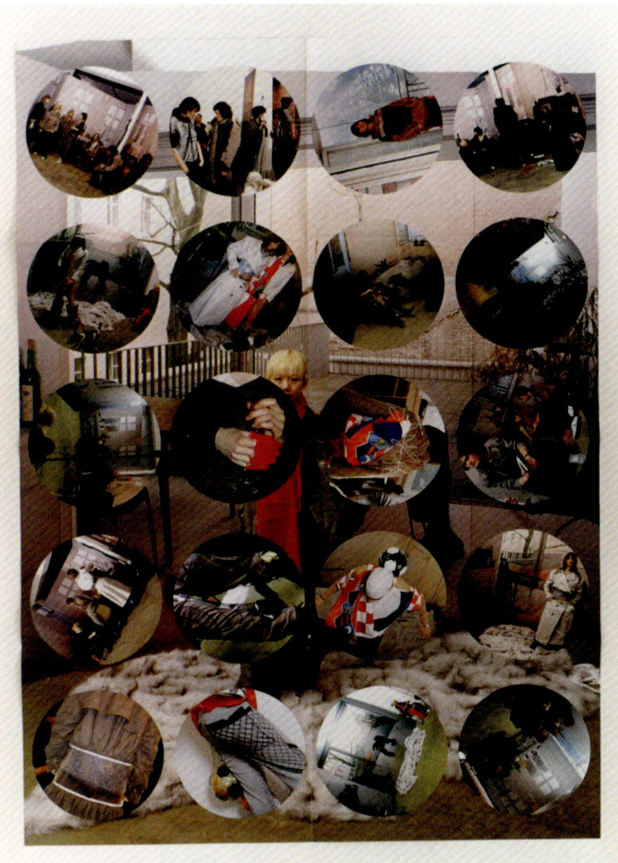

BLESS Poster, 2008.

where models walk on the catwalk,
where the clothes are presented by
tall, slim models. Instead they
invite all their friends to come to
the show and wear the clothes. So
almost every show has the same faces.
Whether it's a dinner or a football
match, the people wear the clothes and
the press is invited. So I thought we
should consider the look book in the
same way. It's a way to escape the
industry so that it's not about the
reaffirmation of clichés. How could
the photographic language of the look
book function in the same way as their
collections and shows do. We came up
with the idea of collaborating with
magazines. We could insert the look
book into existing magazines. This
way we could publish it in a magazine
about cars, or a magazine about food,
animals, photography, art, or fashion.
It could escape from standardized
forms of distribution and reach
another audience.

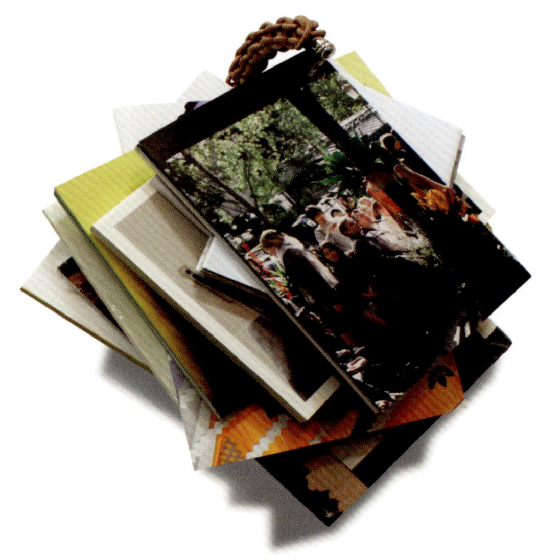

BLESS Collected Lookbook Collaborations, 2011.

**These things are all a big part
of what make BLESS.**
Since they very beginning of BLESS,
there was always a great deal of
concern as to how to represent an
image. BLESS never wanted to have
staged photography and high-end
fashion shoots where everything
was staged and fake just for that
specific moment. It's important
to consider how the woman wearing
clothes in the fashion show is
represented. These are questions that
have always been present for BLESS.
So after the shows they started
asking for pictures from all the
people that attended who had their
own cameras. With those pictures we
began constructing the look book, so
it was an image that was much more
related to the people who attended,
rather than the image constructed by
a photographer hired to produce a
fancy, nice picture. The nice thing
was also that you could see over the
years the same people in each show.
Then we started saying, "Why don't we
start thinking about making a pattern
from it?" The images and language
created by the shows would enter the
collection again. I started getting
involved in textile designs, and we
started making textiles from each
look book that would then come out in
the next collection.

**So your design work actually became
the fashion content.**
There's a cycle. Like a lot of my
work, it's about continuity, not
just the five minutes in Paris when
the collection is presented. It's
also about your life and how you
continue it, and how you can have
certain continuity through that.
**It seems like there are a lot of
norms that you're challenging on a
regular basis. Despite this, you
also manage to be productive.**
Thanks, that's a very nice comment.
I think it's very important to
say no. At the same time I think
it's also important to create
things, to have an alternative.
If you start thinking about the
economy, capitalism, and even the
art world, it's important to have
a standpoint, and yet to still
try and propose alternatives.
This became more evident with the
economic crisis and people being
unhappy about many things such
as the distribution of labor and
wealth. I think it's very crucial
to produce in order to figure out
an alternative way of working. What
could be an alternative set up for
producing, of designing in relation
to that? Also the effect it has on
the environment, the labor force,
distribution...
Where do these philosophies com from?
Well, it's a combination of course.
There is not one specific writer,
or movie, or dialogue. We're all
human beings on the planet and there
are many things that influence us.
A lot of it relates to personal
experiences I have with friends,
people, family. If you are a
designer suddenly under the pressure
to produce very heavily and every
six months, and this is not good
for you anymore, you don't feel
it's right, and it makes you tired
or exhausted, then you need to find
a way to change this. Could you do
it in a different way, or should
you just say no, or quit? These
questions are very present for me.

This reminds me of that early piece you made: "I could have taken an image, blown it up big, and put bold type on it. But I chose not to." It sounds like you were frustrated.
Yes, this text totally originates from that. It's a common and cliché perception that things that are said bold, or in big letters, or with very big bright colors are more important than things that might be small. It's visible on any level, such as architecture. A big building that has cost millions of euros, you know will receive a lot more attention than an organic self-built structure. It's about validation. So you have a huge building, very fancy and glossy, and people love it, but they would never pay attention to a beautifully constructed fence made of cacti that's been there already for many years, growing slowly. Something constructed organically, like people.

How is your studio structured?
Typically there are two people that work here, but it varies. There are no set rules. For example if Manuel is in the studio, he knows what to do, or to generate his own project. I try to make it so everyone always has their own projects. We've had interns here that have basically done a whole biennial. Through curiosity he or she started taking over the whole project and doing almost all the design. The editions for the Biennial came out of this dialogue. It's a three-way relationship. It's not just about me, it's about the artists we collaborate with, the curator, and what position the design takes in relation. And this can all be accomplished through dialogue and discussion, and these decisions can then evolve. And if someone has a very strong personality behind that, even someone that joins the studio and says, "Look, we should do this in this typeface." I think that's really good. I will not go against it. This is what I mean when I say that you can still then make decisions collaboratively and negotiate things through a dialogue.

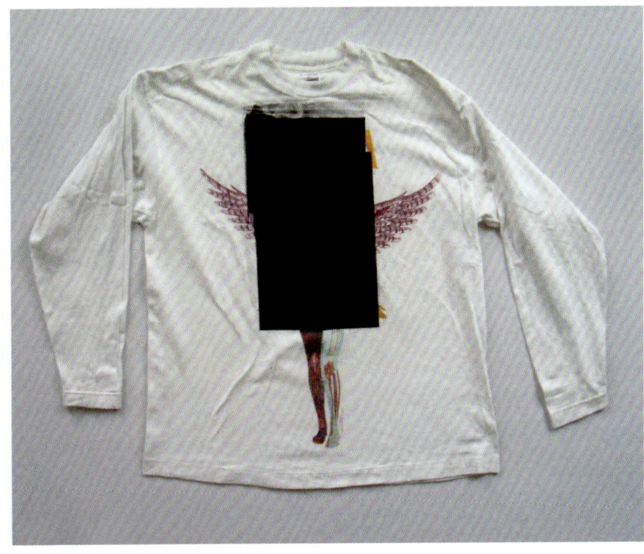

Charity Shirt, 2007.

What's your home environment like? Do you live with the objects you make?
You would be disappointed. It's very simple. I'm not so obsessed with design in that sense. I don't have any known designer furniture in my home if that's what you mean. I have one of the Group Affinity Benches in my kitchen even though it gets a bit annoying after I sit on it for a while.

Are you a spiritual person?
Not really. I try to practice aikido on a regular basis.

How long have you done that for?
Seven years now.

You did an interview with the aikido teacher from Paris in the BLESS book.
Both the founders of BLESS have practiced aikido for many years. The interview was to thank them for introducing me to aikido.

What is aikido?
It's a Japanese marital art that is quite young. It was founded during the war. The idea is that you basically don't answer any violence with more violence. It's about someone wanting to hurt you, but you're basically already air, they cannot even attack you. I don't know if this explains it. It has a lot to do with very round movements. It looks a bit like dancing with two people that do it very well. ☺

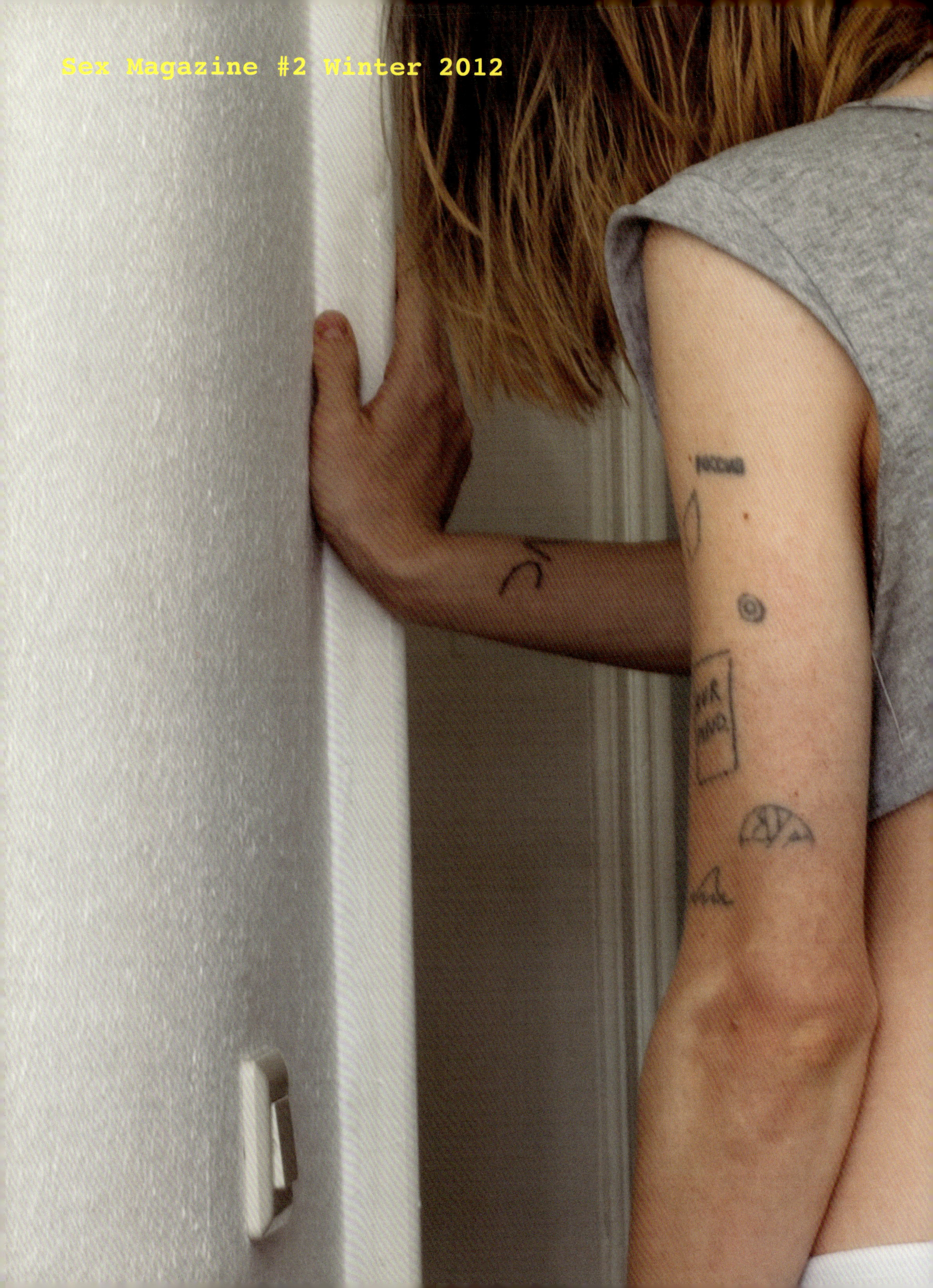

Sex Magazine #2 Winter 2012

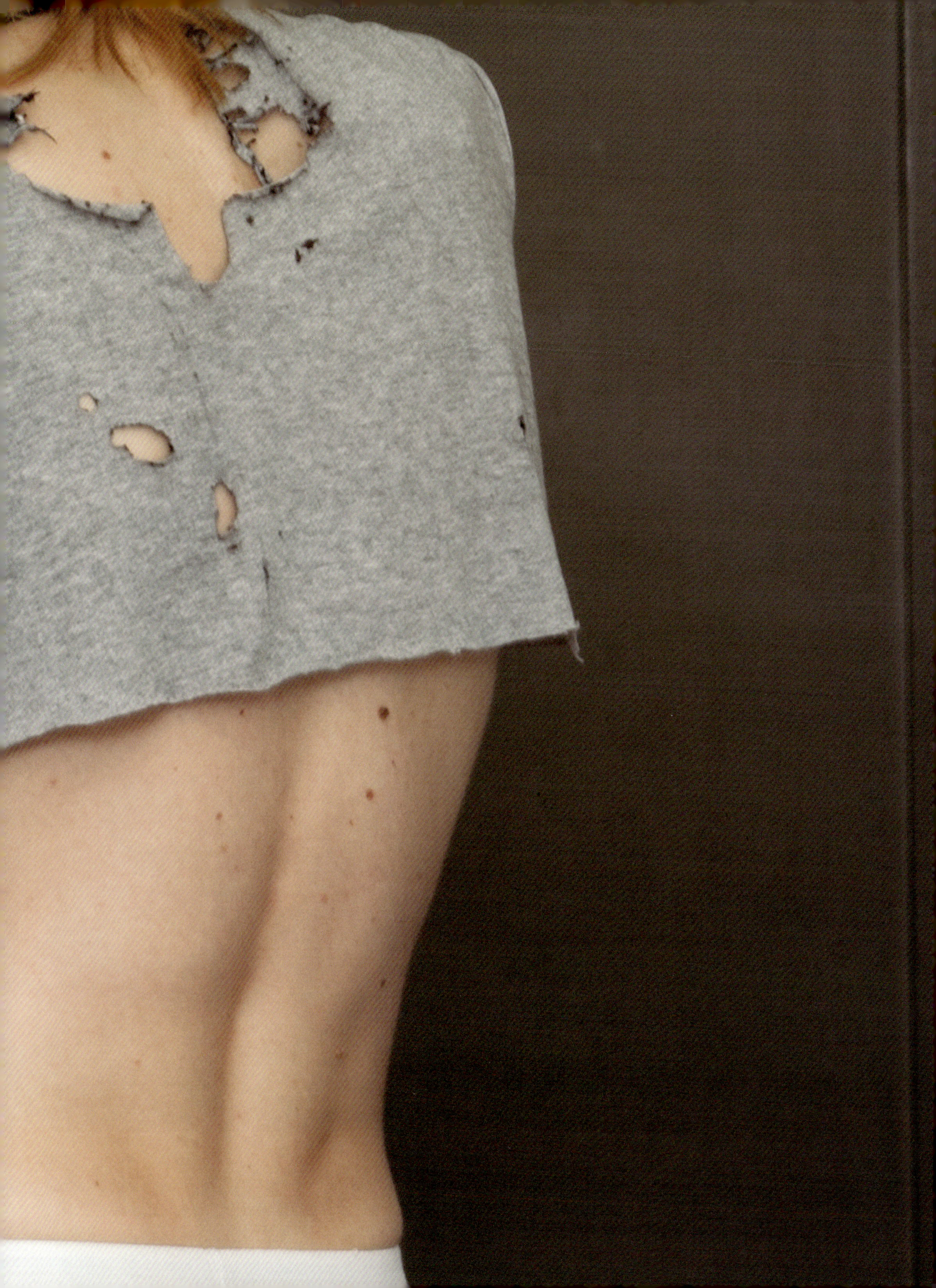

Jordan Wolfson
"Do I think that I'm like Woody Allen?"

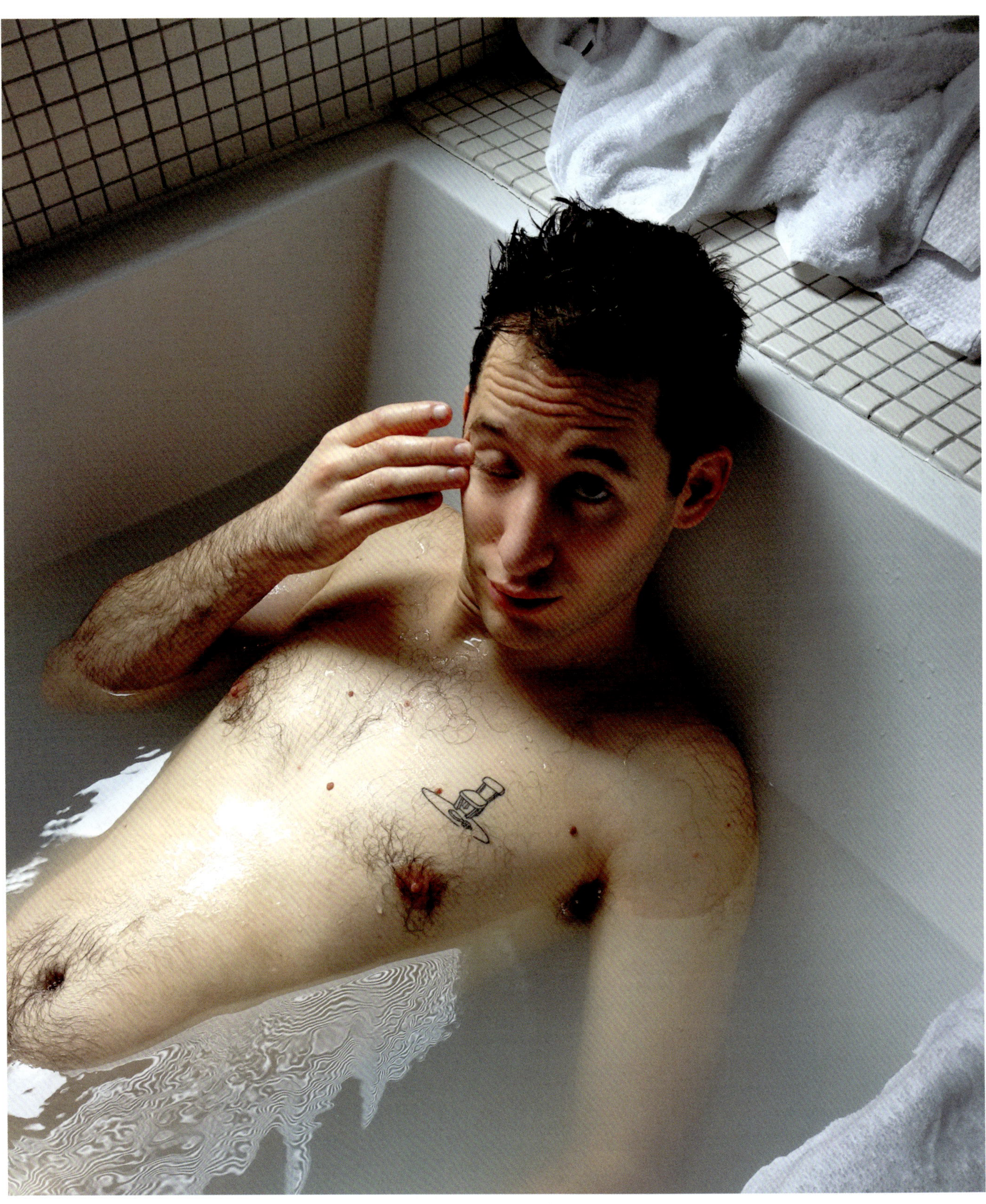

Interview by Asher Penn
Portrait by Clare Ros

Since making his debut at the 2006 Whitney Biennial at the age of 25, artist Jordan Wolfson has shown himself to be one of the most provocative artists of his generation. Eschewing an object-based practice in favor of video installations, Wolfson's works bring an unfamiliar poetics to the genre of pop art, navigating cultural touchstones such as Christopher Reeves, 9/11, Diet Coke, Kate Moss, Hitler, AIDS, Charlie Chaplin, Bob Dylan, and Richard Brautigan. Using the uncanny vernacular of cinema, animation, music, and voice, Wolfson's films are polarizing in their seductive nature, manipulating expectations to a place that is sometimes uncomfortable, sometimes revelatory.

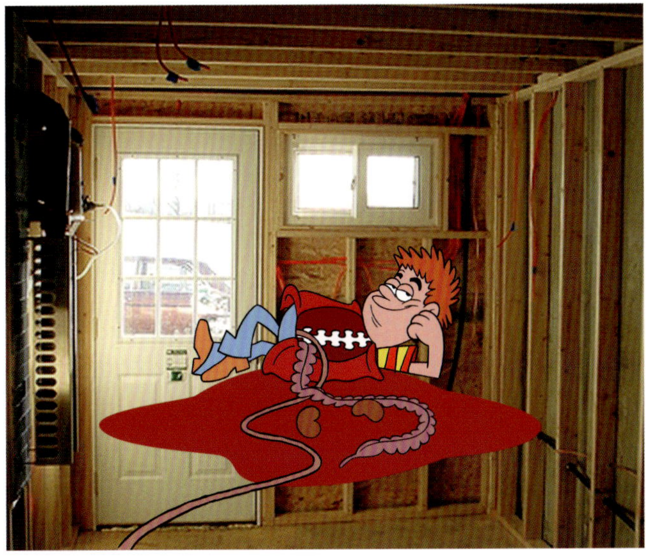
Raspberry Poser, 2012.

What was your childhood like?
I lived on the Upper West Side in New York City until I was ten years old — across the street from the Museum of Natural History. My mom was a psychoanalyst and my father did different types of business things. He still does. I have three older sisters, but I only grew up with one of them. When I was about ten years old, we moved from New York City to our country house, which was in Connecticut. That was in 1990.

Were you sad to leave the city?
I thought it was going to be fun because I used to love being up at the country house, but everything changed. When I lived here in New York City, I wasn't as exposed to these systems of social hierarchy that exist between kids at schools in more suburban settings — I never understood the concept of popularity until I moved to Connecticut.

Why wasn't that a thing in New York?
I don't know. It wasn't fostered. I went to Columbia Grammar on the Upper West Side and there were like ten or fifteen students in the class. There was never an overall structure of cool or not. But once I went to this other school in Connecticut, which was a regular public school in an affluent town, I was always in learning disability programs. In New York they told me I was special and creative and intelligent, but in Connecticut they said, "You have disabilities. We'll help you do your homework." They weren't attuned to what my actual needs were. It was completely unstructured. There were students with developmental issues in the classroom with me. Then there was this whole structure of popularity. It was like this vast network of students and dynamics that I had never been exposed to before. It was very horrible and very frightening to me. I think it really fucked me up and kind of made me who I am today. It gave me a certain distrust of people.

Were you medicated at the time?
Yes, I'd been medicated since I was seven years old with Adderall-type medications for ADHD. We were only an hour outside of New York, but it was a very dramatic difference. I was Jewish and had learning disabilities. I felt like I had been played a really bad hand. But, when I was in New York City, I was still Jewish and had learning disabilities, but it seemed like I was on top of the world. It was traumatic and then I learned about conformity. And I exercised conformity.

What do you mean?
They'd all wear Umbros or Samba
Classics and I had to fit in with
them. Then I got a pair of Umbros
and Samba Classics and felt whole.
I looked down at my body and what I
was wearing, and suddenly I looked
like the other students. I felt
somehow accomplished or settled,
which is a type of conformity. It's
a negative thing.

You were skateboarding back then, right?
Yeah. I think the skateboarding
thing was a reaction. I would skate
up and down on my block in the
city but never knew any tricks. I
always wanted to be a skater, but I
didn't really become one until I was
thirteen or fourteen years old. And
then I went crazy for skateboarding.
I think it was what I needed to
express my individuality and become
autonomous from these other students.

Were you making art in high school?
Not at first, but when I was 16
years old I became extremely into
art making. Before that I was a
hardcore skater. I wanted to become
a professional skateboarder and I was
good, but I didn't have what it took
to become a pro. I saw people who
did and there was a huge difference
between them and me. There were guys
who were able to do these things
that were totally fearless feats. I
just could never imagine putting my
body through that. I couldn't even
comprehend it. Once I started doing
art, everything in my life changed. I
stopped caring about skateboarding,
and I began to lose touch with my
skater friends and skate culture at
large. Art-making was just something
that was bigger than all of that for
me. I looked around and thought that
all these people who were so serious
about skating were misled, or just
wasting time exercising another type
of conformity. I had been part of this
skate culture and I was a conformist.
To a degree I was trading one badge
for another, but making art was
something I felt so connected to that
my reality simply changed.

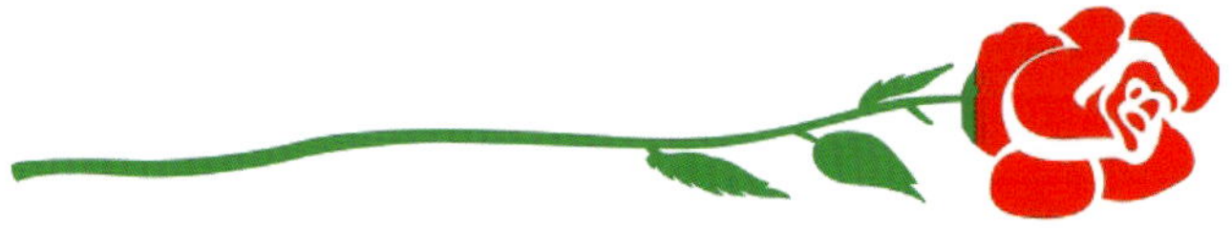

Untitled (Bumper Sticker), 2010.

**I've always thought that there is
a side to skater culture that's
actually super conformist.**
Right, people don't want to talk
about that. They think what they're
doing is about individualism. And
in some ways it is, but it's also
about a type of conformity. I
used to feel like every day I
had to wear a shirt that had
some skate logo on it or I was
betraying something which is kind
of ridiculous to think. But there
are also hugely positive aspects of
skateboarding that have translated
into my art practice. For example:
in skateboarding, you can decide
to learn a trick or do a feat of
some kind. And if you set your
mind to it, you will do it in some
capacity. I remember spending days
upon days learning or perfecting
a trick. Now it's the same in
my art making. I will dedicate
myself completely to figuring out
or finding a solution to finish
an artwork, and it takes time and
sustained effort, but eventually I
reach a solution.

**What kind of art were you exposed
to as a kid?**
My grandparents were collectors,
so they always had art around and
they gave some to my parents. They
were into Larry Rivers, Red Grooms,
and Alex Katz. It was all very
commercial. I think Red Grooms was
probably pretty easy to own. There
was never any Andy Warhol, but
there was Frank Stella. There was
also Milton Avery. I was informed
by that, as a kind of a precursor
to pop art. But there was never any
Rauschenberg or Jasper Johns or
anything like that.

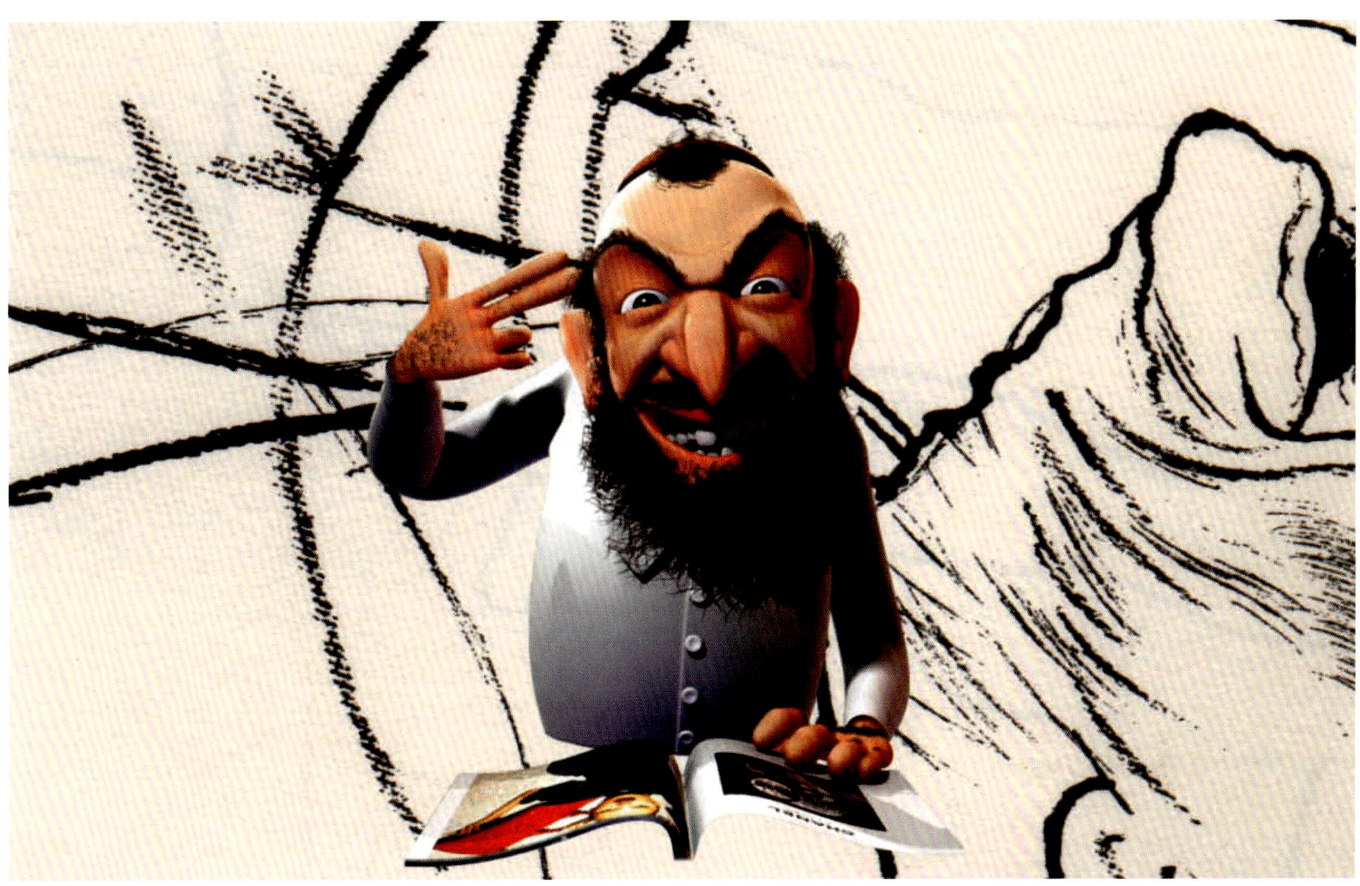

Animation, Masks, 2012.

What about Chagall?
There was Chagall. My mom always had
a Chagall poster up. It was of the
two lovers flying over the village.
**Was Jewish folk art a part of your
upbringing?**
Not really, but there was a lot of
Ben Shahn around. It wasn't so much
George Grosz at that point. There's a
story about how my grandparents had
this copy of Ecce Homo, this George
Grosz book they were really proud
of owning. Then suddenly, they got
embarrassed because their friends
were coming over and they had the
same book. So my grandparents hid it.
I think that's a very negative way to
relate to things, but that's how my
family was about it.
They were self-conscious about it?
It's a vanity thing. They collect
work and think it will somehow
reflect on their character. I talked
to a dealer who was talking to
someone about Animation, Masks, and
he told me that this collector kept

asking, "Don't you think it's anti-
Semitic?" And the dealer said, "No,
I don't think it's anti-Semitic."
The collector was afraid to buy it
because he didn't want to be labeled
as an anti-Semite.
**It's a touchy work. I loved it but
can't really say whether I would ever
want to own it. I like the poster.**
You can watch a film and love it,
just like you can read a book and
love it, but the general attitude
around owning a piece of art is that
it says something about you.
**What do your parents think of
Animation, Masks?**
I think they like it. They think
it's interesting, but it also
confuses them. I think they like
what I'm doing because I've received
acceptance for it. They were very
worried about Animation, Masks. When
I was making it, they were very
concerned for me professionally.
After it was done and they saw it,
they cooled down.

Let's talk about college. We both went to RISD. How was it for you?
For me RISD was a mixed experience. I felt frustrated with the teachers who seemed really behind on art for the most part. But on the other hand the students were amazing, and there was a kind of culture within the students that was positive. You were definitely part of that culture.

I liked it at the time. You didn't?
I felt restless at RISD, mostly because of the way the school was broken up into departments. On the positive side though I felt that I was always able to make my best work in Providence. I didn't realize this until I left for an exchange in Stockholm.

Why did you go to Stockholm?
Because I applied to Cooper Union so many times and was rejected every time. So I thought Europe would be a more interesting place to go. I went to the foreign exchange office at RISD and looked around through different school brochures. I found this place called Konstfack in Stockholm and it just looked incredible. The student work was like nothing I had ever seen before.

What was the work like?
It was much more sophisticated than RISD work, probably because most of the students were older. They came to school when they were between 25 to 30 years old. First-year students at Konstfack were like first-year graduate students at Yale or something.

Can you tell me more about why you weren't happy at RISD?
I felt that the school was sort of on the wrong side of art. I didn't like how teachers saw the world, with a few exceptions. They would teach us what they thought was good, rather than what was relevant in contemporary art. Looking back, I guess they taught us what they thought was relevant, but it still troubled me. I was in the sculpture department, and they weren't like, "This is Charles Ray." They were

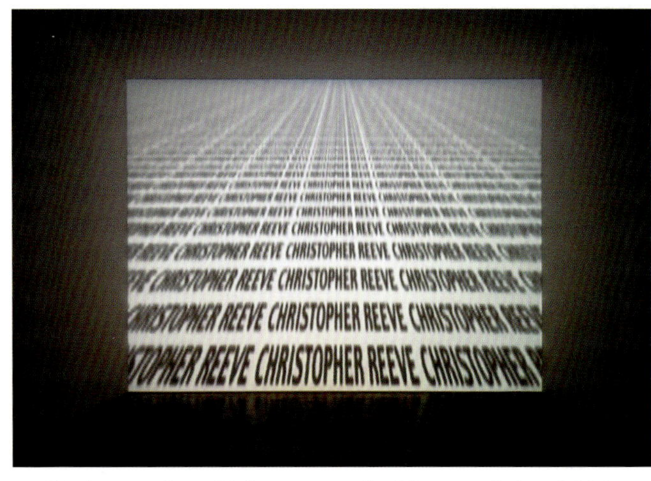

Infinite Melancholy, Kunsthalle Zurich, 2004.

like, "This is Martin Puryear." They were interested in a certain type of craft, but they weren't interested in the objectivity of what contemporary sculpture had become. They never talked about Duchamp. I'm positive, when you were in the photo department, they taught you about Cindy Sherman.

Yeah, because I took photo. They never taught Charles Ray, though.
I don't know much about him at all. He's just incredible. It's not just about the work, but the pacing of the works from one to the next. Then there is also the attention to detail, the kind of attention for him that is evident in each work. For most artists today it seems so much about the shows and the overall practice. So much can get filled in. It's kind of like a plastic pumpkin full of candy: there are lots of different things inside, but you know it's all candy, and it's all in one thing. I don't feel like that's the kind of artist I am.

So what kind of artist are you?
What I feel I'm doing is a sequential line of works. I see it as a path. I want the works to become autonomous, independent. They should exist independently of any exhibition. It might be more similar to how an author works. Or a musician doing records, one after the other. Or a filmmaker. Like Woody Allen, who does one film a year.

What's your take on Woody Allen?
I think he's great. I think that
he's really funny and really, really
smart. I love his movies. I think
it's incredible what he did. It's
amazing to me that he made Sleeper.
And it's amazing to me that he
made Annie Hall. There's a whole
transition between Sleeper and Annie
Hall when he got Bergman and Sven
Nykvist — Bergman's cinematographer
that started working with him later
on in the 80s. The look of his films
changed dramatically. Do I think that
I'm like Woody Allen? No. I don't.
Do you consider yourself a filmmaker?
I don't really think of myself as a
filmmaker. Even at RISD, I was in
the sculpture department because I
wanted to have the choice to make
anything I wanted to. They asked me
to leave at one point. They said,
"Why don't you go to the film and
video department?" But I never felt
like I was a film and video person.
I don't imagine my work being in
film festivals, or in the realm of
commercial cinema or advertising.
I've always thought of myself as a
visual artist. My influences aren't
so much film and video.
**You always struck me as somebody
that had a real appreciation of
filmmakers. When I was working for
you, we were always talking about
them. Bergman...**
I love Bergman. That's different
though, at least to me. Bergman
is hardcore art. Bergman is so
different from all other cinema.
He's so removed. He was a commercial
filmmaker, but he surpasses the
standards for what we consider
commercial filmmaking today — or
even back then. I don't have any
ambition of being a commercial
filmmaker and leaving the art world
to make movies. My brain doesn't
turn that way. I don't think about
interesting stories that could be
made into movies. That's the farthest
thing from my brain. I think of
images in flashes. That's what I'm
inspired by.

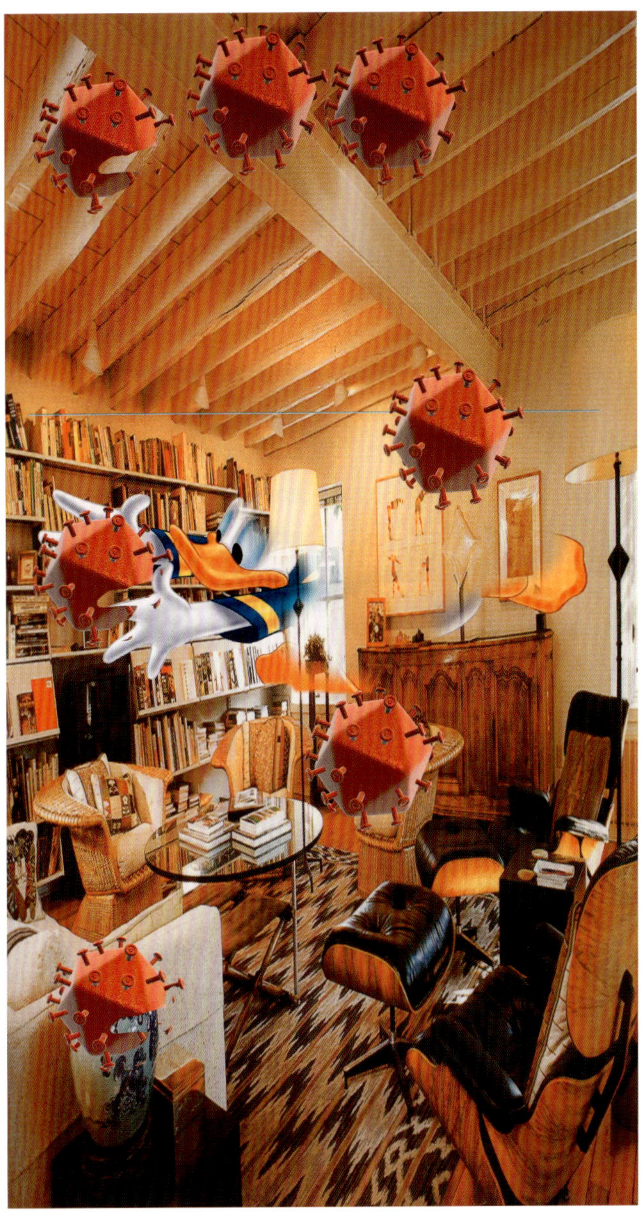

Untitled, Archival Inkjet on Canvas, 2012.

**You've made work about commercial
films. I remember hearing about this
one piece. You recited every word
from the script of Home Alone.**
Oh, yeah, I did that in my senior
year of RISD. I also did Infinite
Melancholy, the Christopher Reeve
video. I did them both at the same
time. I kind of never finished the
Home Alone thing. There were some
technical problems and I had no time.
I had to choose one or the other to
show. I watched some of it recently
with a friend and it seemed really
amateurish. But when I made it, it
was a really massive project to me.

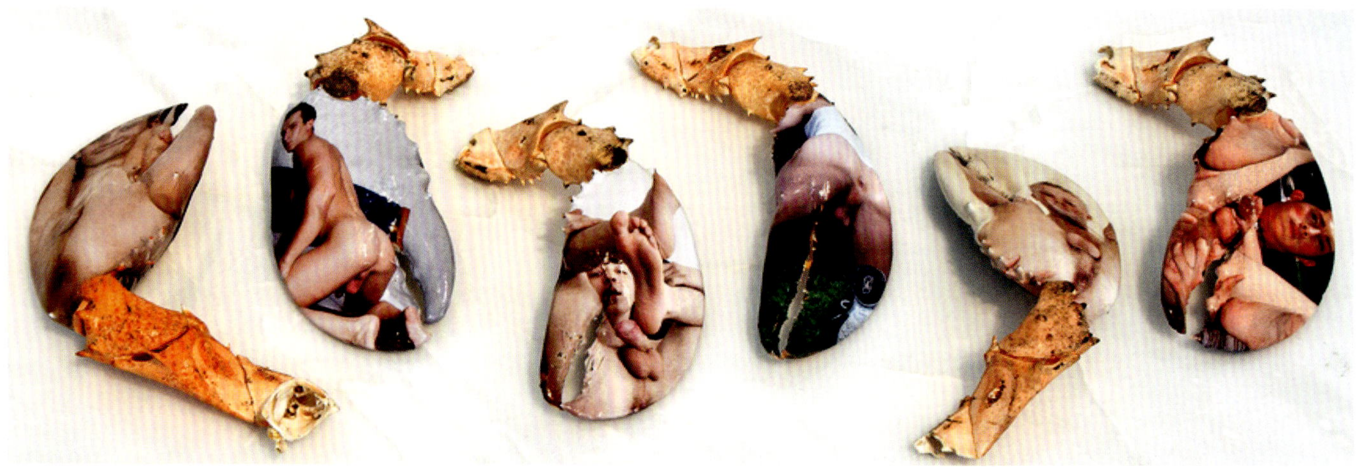

Untitled, Adhesive Digital Print on Lobster Claws, 2011.

Your work doesn't look like a lot of art that I've ever seen. It kind of pushes my expectations of what art can actually be.
Sometimes you spend your time making something that looks like art. It looks good to you because of other art you've seen or know about, and what you know about art history. Eventually, after time and practice, you get over it and break off on your own: you make your own work. It seems really scary at first because there's no one to tell you what's right except for yourself. You can show it to your friends, and they can say, "That's great," but it's not like you can open up some art history book and prove that what you've done is great: "Oh, look, so-and-so did it like that, and I do it like that, so therefore it's a success." That doesn't work. It has to be a leap of faith.

Did you ever feel nervous making it and putting it in front of people?
I get totally freaked out. When I was working on Infinite Melancholy I had to render it at the computer lab at school. It took eleven days to render on this one G4 computer. Originally, it was this flat-planed landscape with a blue sky but eventually I distorted it — I pulled up at the horizon lines. The result was that when you viewed the piece it pulled you in, almost physically. There was no horizon. There was a visceral feeling to it.

It's uncanny.
Yeah, it's strange. The uncanny effect seemed to start happening when I gave up control in the works.

What kinds of people like your work?
I'm always surprised by it because I feel that the things I want to do no one is going to like. Maybe that's just an insecurity of mine — I get worried that people aren't going to get it or that it will be too much. And when I end up doing them because I know I need to do them — because I need to follow through — those are always the best works. I really didn't think Animation, Masks was going to be as critically successful as it was. I didn't think Con Leche was going be as successful as it was either, both critically and commercially. When Animation, Masks was finished I knew that this was how the piece had to be. I didn't care if anyone was going to like it or not. That was a really important place for me to get to, and also a scary place to be. It hasn't been easy. I had a really positive, strong response from friends on the piece, but the first night I showed it in Düsseldorf there wasn't as strong of a response, or at least I wasn't so sure. Later I showed it at Frieze and it was received very well. After that the show with Alex Zachary and Peter Currie was overwhelmingly well received too. I didn't expect it to go like that. I was really nervous.

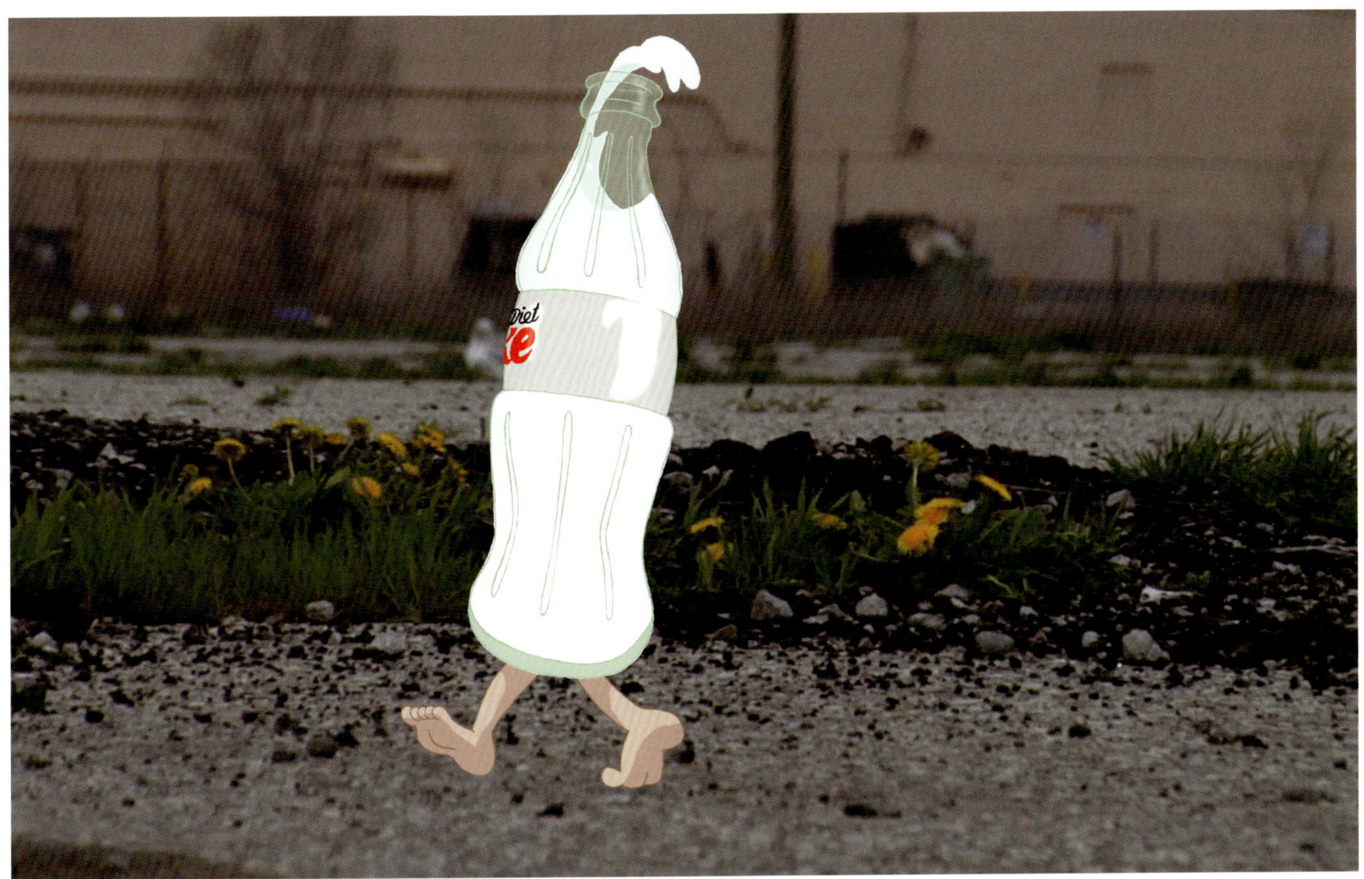

Con Leche, 2009.

When you finish a piece, is there some kind of self-acceptance that happens? Or acceptance of the work?
It's not so much about acceptance; it's more that I have this thing that I've been working on for a certain amount of time. I reached the final deadline, which could hypothetically be an exhibition. Or I just came to the conclusion that I knew it was finished: it's as good as it's going to be and I did my best possible job at it. Then it's finished, it's in the world. I can still change it here and there, fix it up a bit, that's my privilege, but that's the piece — it's done. It's very assuring and comforting to be finished and able to go on. I'm super critical of myself and the work, so I go crazy and don't want to see anybody while I'm working. I have to get to a point where I accept the work as an artwork. Then I can finally accept it as finished.

Last question. Is it true you lived with a Hasidic family?
No, I visited an Orthodox household. Again, I got no answers. I was lost and didn't realize that the answers I wanted for the work had nothing to do with actual Judaism. For the most part I was confused about what I was doing. In the end, I realized that the answers were inside myself. There weren't going to be any specific notes of knowledge that were going to enlighten me as to how to complete the artwork. It was simply a matter of what my own personal directives were, how I saw the world. That was it. Everything else was wasted time.
You tend to waste time when you work. When I worked for you, we made a lot of stuff that didn't get used, like that footage of you on the bike.
A lot of extra stuff gets cut out like crazy. I waste a lot of money and time. I think it's all in the hope that I get to some unique place in the end. ☺

Thuy Pham

"It was a basic business idea, but to me it was a foreign concept."

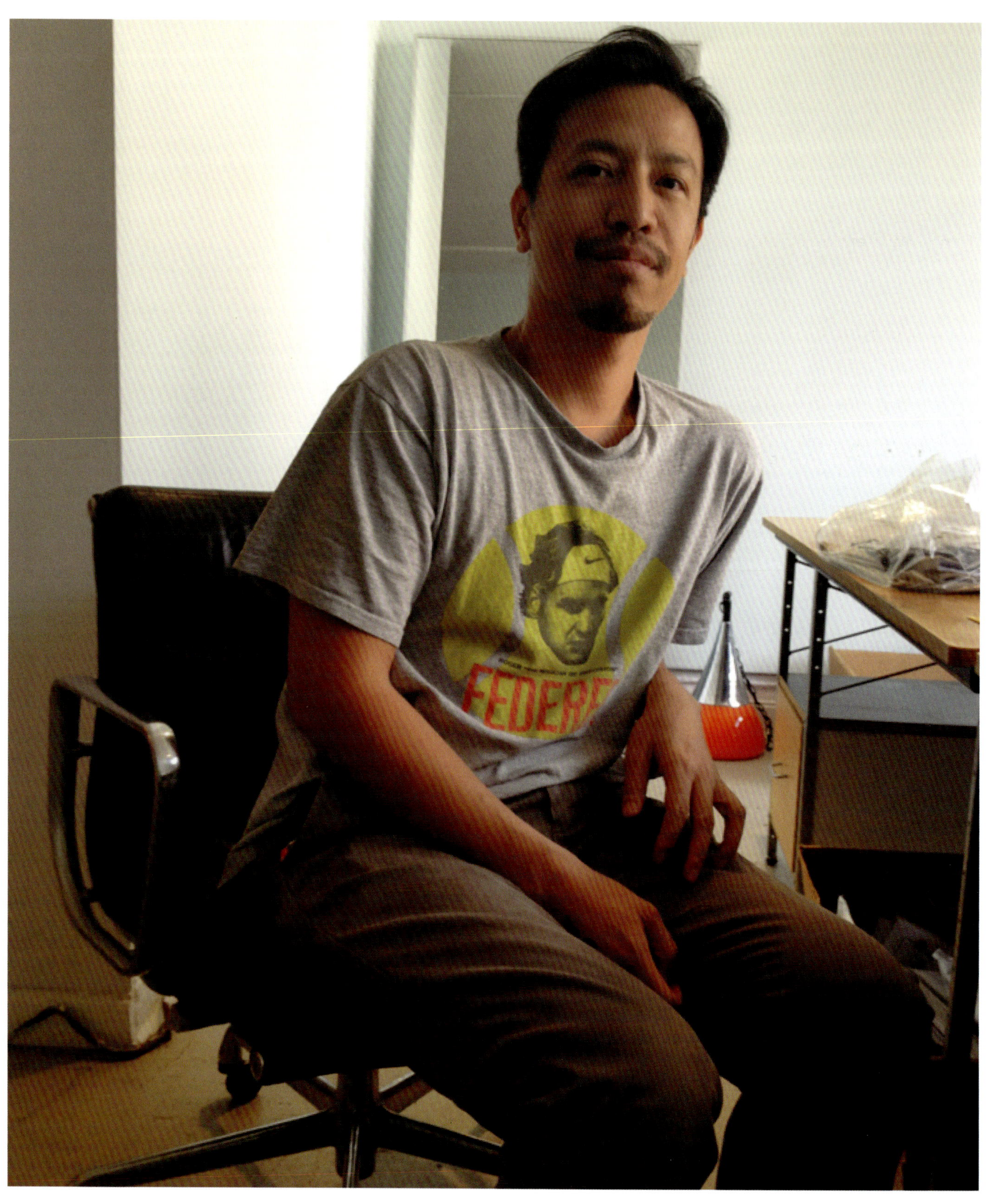

Interview & portrait by Asher Penn
Images courtesy Thuy Pham

Thuy Pham made his debut in fashion as the head designer of 90s art-project-cum-fashion-label Bernadette Corporation, who, along with brands like Imitation of Christ and BLESS, created an independent culture outside of the fashion system. Leaving the group in '98, Pham started United Bamboo, the Downtown clothing line whose deconstruction of classic American styles pioneered an approach towards design and style that would characterize production for the new millennium. Despite these trailblazing gestures, Thuy Pham's approach is surprisingly reserved and simple — steadily working towards improving his product and brand with every season.

You came to New York to go to Cooper Union, right?
Well, before that I went to Virginia Tech for engineering, but realized I wasn't smart enough, and it was really competitive. I switched to architecture almost randomly, which was lucky, because that is how I learned about Cooper Union. Since there was no tuition at Cooper, I thought I should try to get in. We had to submit a home test and I made my portfolio out of sheets of aluminum. It was all etchings. It looked really cool, but the shipping was $600 at the post office because it weighed 30 pounds. I didn't have the money to mail it. On my way home I ran into a friend who was actually driving to New York that night. I gave him $50 to drop it off for me.
And then you got in. That is lucky.
Yeah. My life has always been coincidental — I've had very lucky moments.
So you went from engineering to architecture. That sounds more creative.
My father had steered me away from any kind of profession that had to do with design or art, so architecture was good for me. It's art and design, but in some ways engineering too, so my father approved.

There are a few instances of people who come from architecture and then end up in fashion.
Architecture is a great design foundation. When you start in architecture you can spring into designing other stuff. It's probably the most all-encompassing design discipline. You understand materials, construction, structure. Maybe that's why I think it would be harder for a fashion person to jump into architecture.

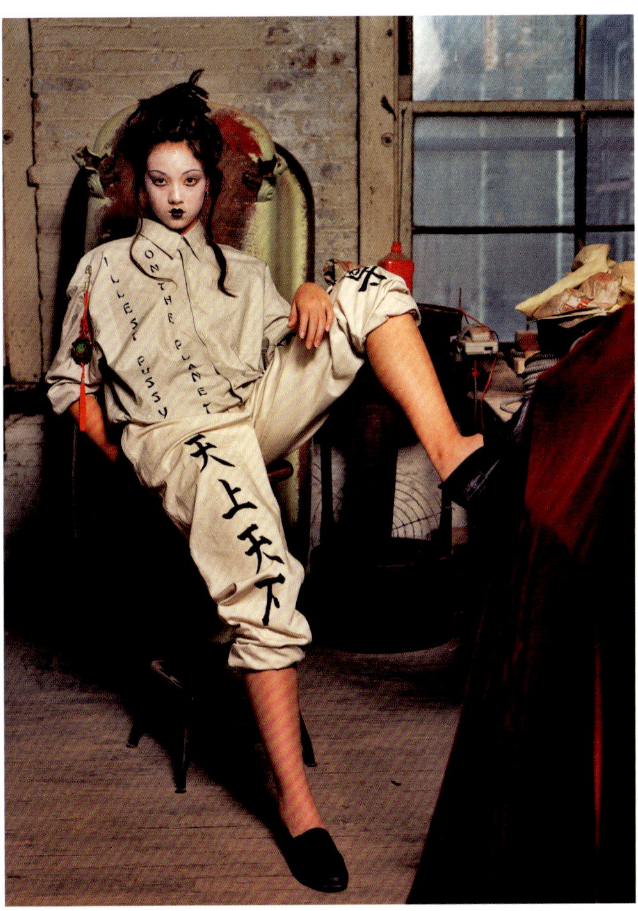

Unpublished Shoot, Bernadette Corporation, 2012. Photo: Cris Moor

Did you graduate as an architect?
No. After I came to New York a high school friend came here to go to FIT for fashion design. I got distracted by NYC life. My friend was going to all the fun clubs with these fun people, while I was building models at Cooper Union all night. Eventually, I started hanging in clubs more than doing homework.

Is this Seth Shapiro?
Yeah. He was doing his clothes and he had a write up in Interview magazine. I thought it was awesome that you could get noticed for making clothes.
It didn't seem that hard to you?
Not at the time. I helped him out and another friend making menswear. By helping these guys, I learned about making clothes.
There isn't much information out there about Seth Shapiro.
Seth Shapiro went to my high school. Then he sort of disappeared. I ran into him in DC right as I left home for NYC and we agreed to become roommates. He had fallen in love with some Christian girl who rejected him because he wasn't Christian. Then he became very Christian himself for a brief moment. Very Christian people came up to my apartment and read the bible. Then for some reason unknown to me, he joined a Moonie cult, which took him to London. They took his passport and belongings. He sold flowers on the street and gave the money to the cult. No one could get in touch with him. After this episode, he showed up again about a year later. He told me about begging on the street. It was when he came back to New York that he started his fashion line. He's the one that made the fashion line first, but more like an artist than a designer.
He was selling fashion to the art world?
Yeah, I guess. And then Bernadette is his cousin.
And you guys really connected too?
At Cooper Union, I was really into postmodernism and so was Bernadette. It was almost required reading for the late-90s generation of architects. Bernadette was interesting because she tried to bring this postmodernism to the fashion world, approaching it like an art project. Bernadette had a strong desire to deconstruct things in a semiotic sense. With postmodernism, you deconstruct something, take it out of context. Bernadette liked to recontextualize pop culture. Like,

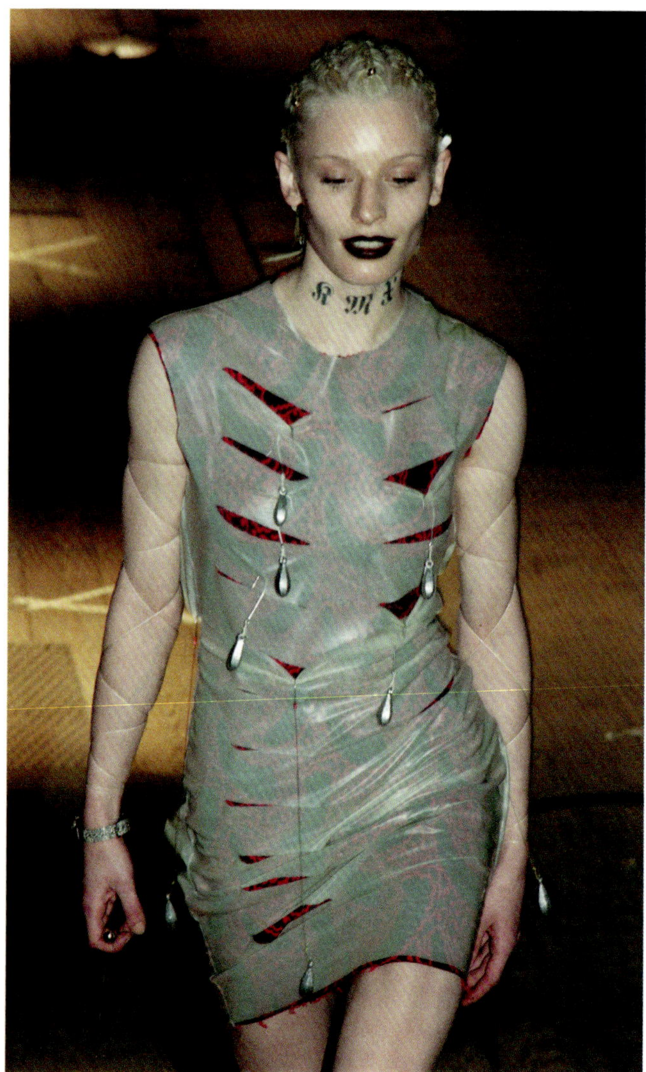

Bernadette Corporation, FW97. Photo: Cris Moor

how hip hop kids use brands as signifiers, changing the intended meaning. The Ralph Lauren Polo brand acts a signifier of the WASPy image, but is popular in the inner-city precisely because of that image. The deconstruction aspect isn't intentional but shows how meaning can easily slip and disintegrate in different contexts.
What was the dynamic of the group?
Bernadette was the stylist. As the designer, I tried to help her make some clothes. Antek was a filmmaker. I've always been a really hands on person — I know many computer programs, I know how to sew, etc. I'm like a craftsman. I like to make stuff. Bernadette likes to produce images. Antek likes to write or talk concepts.

How many collections did Bernadette Corporation end up doing?
Just four collections. I would say that two of them weren't even really collections.

How did it end?
I had a falling out with Bernadette Corp. I wanted them to be more serious about business since I had so much responsibility on the clothing side. They disagreed.

How did you meet Miho?
We got two interns when we started producing the clothes for Bernadette Corp., Siri and Miho. Later, Siri and Miho sublet my space for their own clothing brand. Their approach was so different from mine. They would put, say, $5,000 in a pot and then try to make $10,000 from it. It was a basic business idea, but to me it was a foreign concept. I began to help out with the clothes and eventually gave them a brand name.

You named them United Bamboo?
Yeah. After a while Siri wanted to do his own line but Miho and I kept doing United Bamboo.

What year was this?
This was 1997.

I looked up United Bamboo on style.com. The earliest show they had was in 2004. What did you do for seven years?
We focused on expanding our company. Eventually we decided to do fashion shows because we wanted more press. Before that we had tried to stay low-key.

What was the concept behind United Bamboo?
With Bernadette Corporation, the clothes were more like Alexander McQueen's fantastical pieces and punkish anti-authority attitude, but I've always liked Comme des Garçons' architecturalish approach to design. I have the same problem with CdG as I have with experimental architecture: it's great in a vacuum, but sometimes it's too weird in the context of real life. I also liked Ralph Lauren at that time as a business. He was basically the biggest American brand name ever.

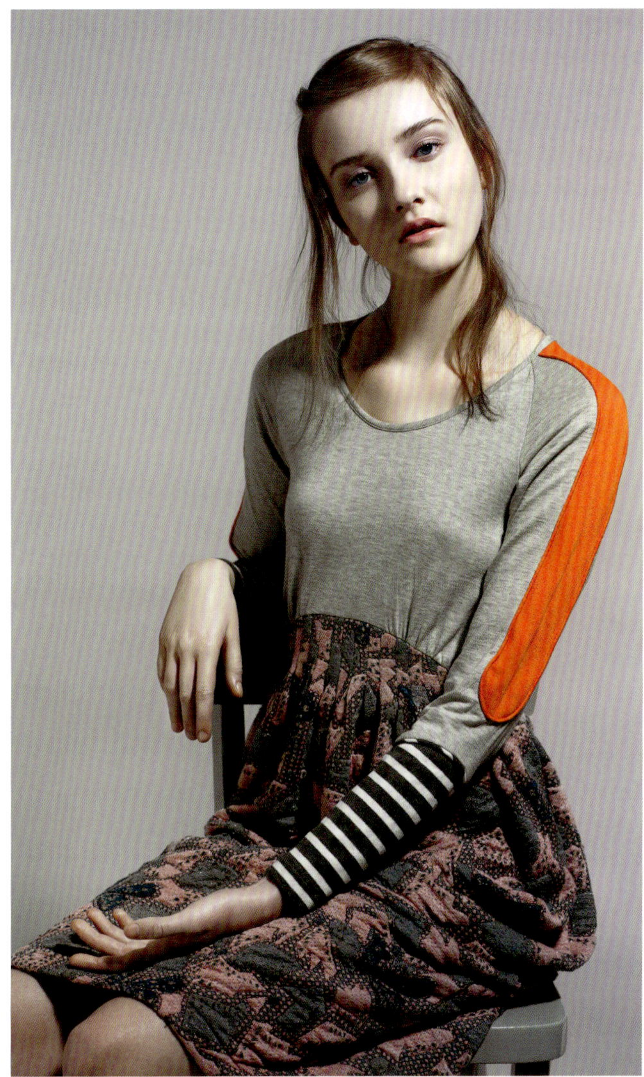

United Bamboo FW05. Photo: Cris Moor

What's his deal?
I read that he was born Ralph Lifshitz, a Jewish guy who became successful marketing this image of the Northeastern, upper-class lifestyle. It's equally absurd for a Jewish or Vietnamese guy to make a preppy brand. I thought it'd be easier to take something that already exists and recombine it rather than try to be original, kind of like music sampling or remixing. This is the lesson I took from postmodernism. Ralph Lauren has spent millions to cultivate a certain preppy idea. People already recognize it as a kind of "archetype" so I can just take it and use it as a "sample." People understood that right away, in the same manner as recognizing a P. Diddy tune.

Were you guys making womenswear or menswear?
Just womenswear. All very preppy looking. Except something about it wasn't right.
Where did you sell it?
Steven Alan was one of the first people that really supported Bernadette Corporation. He carried United Bamboo and also sold our line in his showroom. We also sold to all the smaller shops in New York. It was really beneficial for us to sell in Japan. It helped that Miho is Japanese. Japan is an island nation and in their culture individualism is really discouraged. If a Japanese person breaks out of that, they consider that to be quite an achievement, especially if he or she gets noticed in another country. We did well in the Japanese market, more so than in the U.S.
United Bamboo seems like a company that Americans might think comes from Japan. When I first saw your ads it was kind of unclear.
Yeah, sometimes it works to your advantage, but sometimes it doesn't.
What do you mean?
Fashion is full of contradiction. People want you to change all the time, but, at the same time, they don't want you to change at all. They want consistency, but if you do the same thing all the time they call it boring. So the brand identity or the underlying theme must remain the same, but every season I need to do something different. I don't have a different idea each season. Instead, I have an overall brand story where I try to show the progression from season to season by how we get better as designers. The things that we design become either more intricate or more subtle.
So there is a goal of improvement instead of just making something new for the sake of it.
Exactly. Each collection is neither an endpoint nor a destination. It's like a cut off point of where you really are at that moment.

That's a nice way of looking at it. Imagine the pressure if the brand was your name.
Because the brand is not in my name I don't have a personal attachment to it. I try to look at the brand as something that we gave birth to but took on a life of its own.
The brand dictates the next logical step to you.
Yeah, exactly. A lot of people don't actually understand design. They think it's like sketching, but the sketching part is just the beginning. Making clothes involves a lot of organization, especially making an entire collection. The parts have to fit together. You choose a fabric and consider at least a certain amount of styles. They require a certain minimum and if I can't sell that amount of stuff, then I can't use the fabric. For me, I judge a designer not on how good the product looks, but on how they make everything work together.
You mean how they can run an effective business?
Yeah. Design students often send me portfolios, but I can't tell who will be a good designer just from sketches. When you work with people you can tell if they are going to be good or not because the good ones make things easy.
What does Miho bring to your collaboration?
We mainly design women's clothes and somehow I never really trust my instincts. Before we design something I talk to her a lot. I usually do more of the actual design part. I'm more technical in our team.
How did the Cat Calendar come about?
Ten years ago we made little clothes for our cat and a friend photographed it. We put the picture on our wall. People who came over really liked it. We did nothing else with it until our press office said, "Why don't you make a gift, a swag or whatever, to send out to people, like how Pirelli sends out calendars?" We decided to make a calendar. ☺

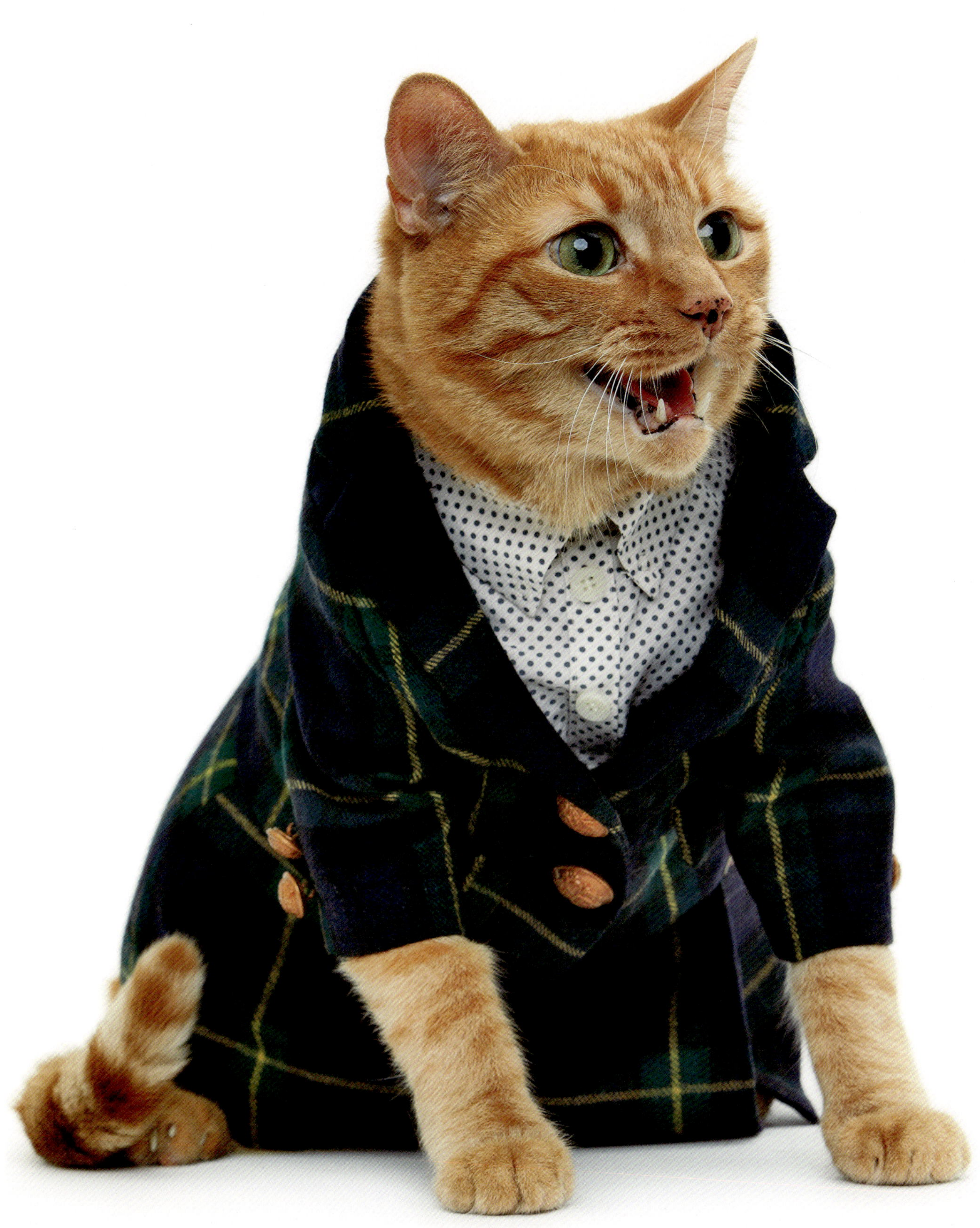

Hobbes, United Bamboo Cat Calendar, 2013. Photo: Noah Sheldon

Harsh Patel
"I have a real talent for picking friends who are more patient and forgiving than I am."

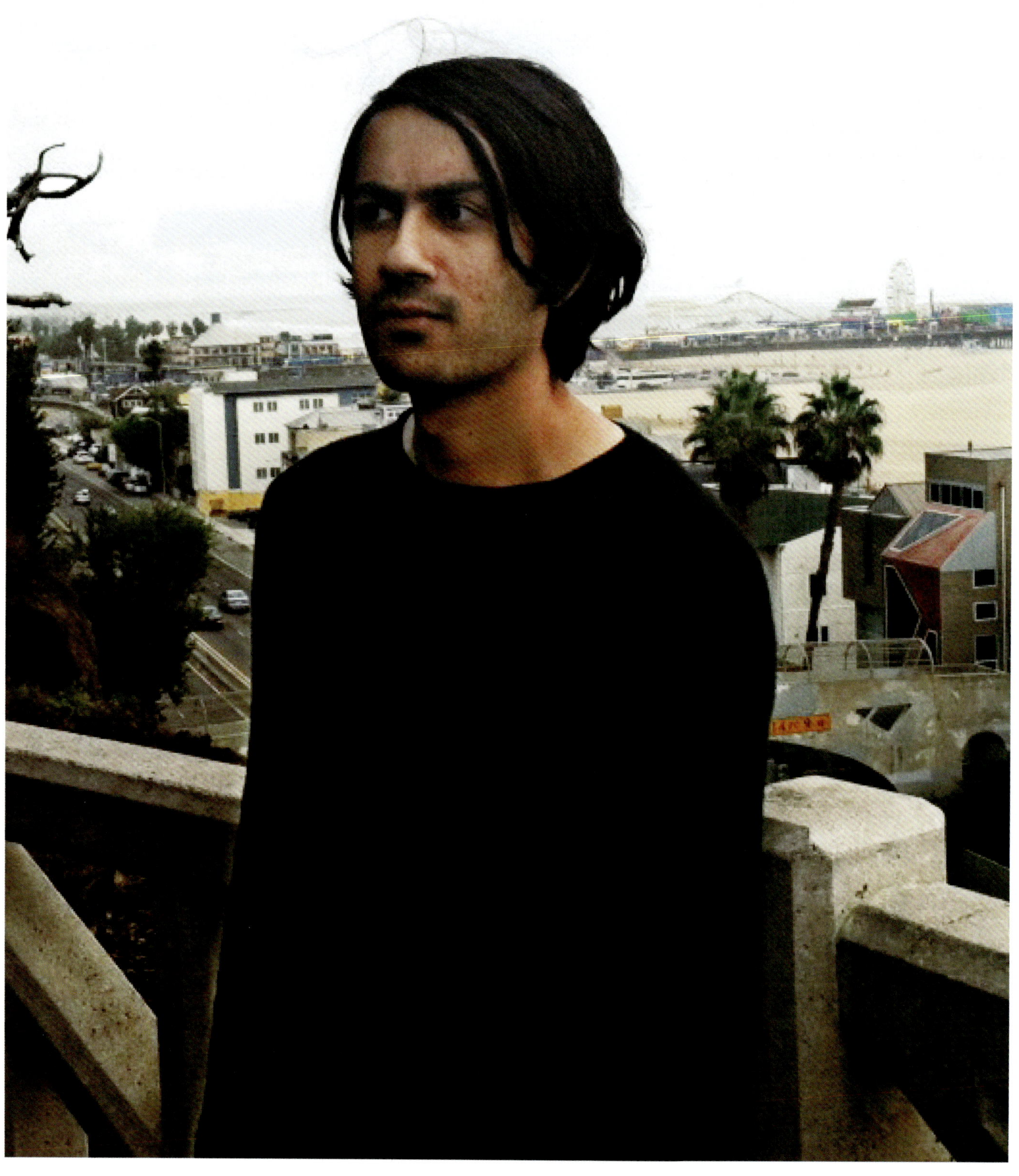

Interview by Asher Penn
Portrait by Jessica Williams

Since making his introduction as the designer of The Blow Up magazine, and publishing house Free Association, Harsh Patel has brought his highly personal graphic sensibilities to collaborations with a shopping list of independent creative entities: fashion designer Rachel Comey, KCHUNG Radio, and stores like X Marks the Bökship and Stand Up Comedy. Through all this he has created several limited-run mail order labels, including Sister, Clenched Fist, Zulu Demon City, and most recently 3DX, whose esoteric distribution system of goods (and information) has quietly refused any norms of independent publishing. Once described as a "pathological outsider" Harsh Patel's work defies the casual colonialism inherent to our culture industry, seeking instead a working model that avoids both exploiting others and being exploited.

You're from Nairobi, and moved to the states when you were nine. How much do you remember about Nairobi?
Everything, pretty much.
How was that part of your childhood?
Africa has a heaviness and a certain type of kindness that nothing's come close to since.
When did you leave?
When I was nine. We moved from Africa to Texas. The very southern part, the Rio Grande Valley. The Southest South in America. It used to be mainly farmland, but it's all getting developed fast.
And you don't think people get Texas?
They get a distant, faraway sort of look when Texas comes up, yeah.
What are some of your first memories of culture?
I spent some summers in India when I was an kid, and we traveled around Kenya on holidays. My family had friends from all over, in a really natural way. My parents can reduce any interaction with any sort of person to timeless sort of concerns, in this style that's really Indian, African, and British at once.

What about mass culture? How were you engaging with it when you were young?
TV, probably. Going up to Austin with friends in high school later on, to record stores we thought were cool. I was also in the habit early on of writing letters, which means that some of those experiences with mass culture were sort of half-imagined.
Who were some of the people you wrote letters to?
Up until high school, I was gonna be a cartoonist so I wrote to animators that I knew of. My best friend was really into golden-era Disney, and knew it up and down. I knew the old cartoon divisions of other places like MGM and Warner Brothers really well. I could call out the production credits of a cartoon before they faded in, just to surprise my parents. The first books I asked them to buy me were about the animation studio systems, and biographies of people like Tex Avery. Then I just started writing letters to people who were in the animation industry proper. I would ask them questions and they were all cool about it. Peter Chung, the guy who made the Aeon Flux show — I remember he was really cool to me.
Were you the same about music?
If we made trips to go buy records in Austin I would go prepared, knowing what I wanted to get or writing or calling ahead of time to make sure that they set it aside for me. Then triple-checking the names and then figuring out how to write to those labels. Before I even moved there, I wrote to the record label Trance Syndicate which King Coffey of the Butthole Surfers ran. I just said, "I live in this pretty small town, I think I'm gonna go to college in Austin. When I'm there, can I do some kind of work for you?" They wrote back and said, "Sure, just wait until you graduate 'cause you're writing to us a couple years ahead of time. But when you're up here, look us up. It's nice that you're so into us."

Images courtesy Harsh Patel

Sister 67, Postcard by Stefan Marx, 2009.

How did you first go online?
They used to send floppy disks like junk mail, and you'd use them to get on the internet for free for a little while in the early 90s. I instantly started checking for stuff, usually music, to see what had made its way on there. Comparing it to its physical counterpart, feeling like it gave me something extra in my understanding or appreciation of it. Trading tapes by mail by searching people's profiles for bands I was into, but couldn't just pick up — that's how I got into a lot of different music. It was pretty much the best avenue as it meant I was generally dealing with a very invested, true type of fan. The best tape I got back then was from a girl in Kentucky I found that way, and it ends up we have friends in common now. Making a few websites that were squarely graphic design experiments and finding other people who did. There were some really great websites back then, like Superbad, Red Smoke, Hell, Turux, and Jodi. All very hard to figure out, and with a real lawless, frontier kind of spirit. Bradford from the band Deerhunter, he made some just "wow" stuff too, some of the best, I think. We did a couple of things together back then. The internet feels a lot more dishonest nowadays than it did early on, but I still think that it's easier for people to be open by writing to each other and imagining each other a bit.

Why did you study graphic design?
I knew I didn't have the discipline to be an animator. I also knew that animation schools cost a lot of money, required time, and meant a very tough time finding work. Something about design, through seeing it applied to music, interested me. I applied to the University of Texas in Austin. I had heard it was really good, and pretty selective, and could overlook your bad grades if your portfolio was strong enough. The program wasn't called "graphic design," it was just "design." The bigger idea of design, like furniture and buildings, too. They even had us make a teacup, and explain how you held it and what that meant. At the time, I was frustrated because I only wanted to make printed things. Today, I am very grateful for it. Graphic design as a field has some of the most fucked up identity politics out there. People who seem to have no idea who they are. Starting out that way kept up the idea in my head that it's a social activity first. Anyone who's any good at it is a people person, loves people, understands psychology, understands society.

How did you end up in New York?
I graduated in 2004 and was living in a cheap apartment in Austin, doing freelance a few days a month, paying the rent, just hanging out. After two months, I had a moment of panic. You know, "Do I just keep living here? It feels like this could go on forever, I don't know if it's meant to be this easy." I was wired a certain way about work and a future, and my imagination as to how to get those things was so limited I thought that the only places I could possibly go without a load of hassle were New York and LA. Then through a friend of a friend, my name was put in a hat with some other names for some MTV work. It came along almost instantly, and they offered more money than I'd ever heard of before: actually a very typical amount for broadcast, but,

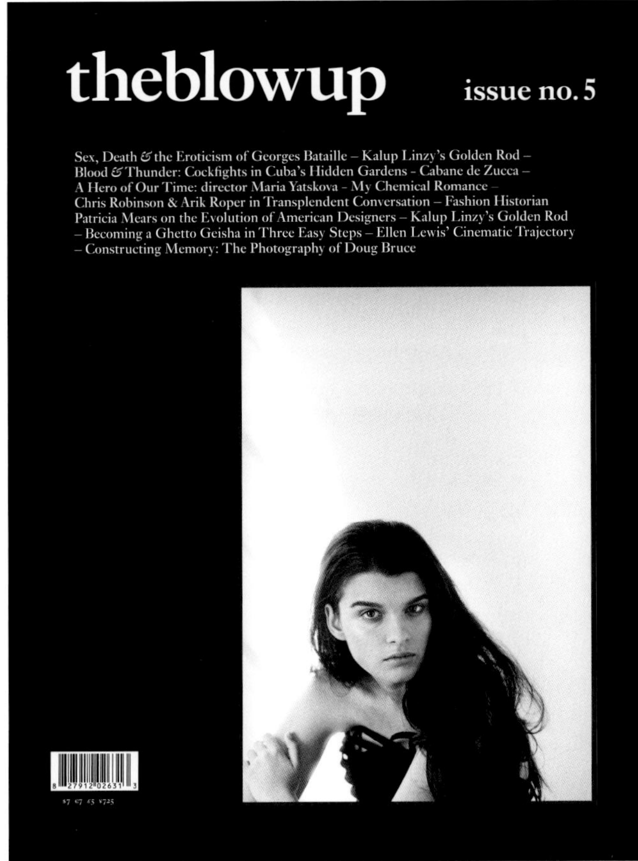

The Blow Up, Issue No. 5, 2005.

beyond any conception I held, so, it gave me some fire. I did the work, hired some friends to help me, got paid, paid my friends, and used the rest of money to move to New York and continue working for MTV.

What was it like working at MTV?
MTV was a hallowed institution then, and one I always thought highly of. Considering how different it was when I was growing up, that sounds a bit strange now. I worked in-house there for a while, and there were some great people there, people I still talk to. Eventually though, that department changed. Some people left their jobs to start their own things, and, in the process, I kind of left. I had friends working in advertising, so I asked them about it. I was in this mode where I had to make money and I didn't understand the city yet. It made sense to support myself that way as it felt like the most textbook type of graphic design, the easiest kind, design as service.

How did you end up working on that magazine The Blow Up?
When I moved to New York, I'd written to this guy Seth Hodes, who at the time was part of this group called Soft Gold. I liked their work quite a bit and showed him some of mine. Figuring he'd recognize my name, as I knew he'd also done work for MTV under the same people who had hired me. Within a month of being up there, we met and he offered me the job of designing this magazine he ran with Matt Eberhart. People downtown liked and respected it. They entrusted me with a tremendous amount of responsibility right away.

What would you say the magazines bigger goals were?
I don't know what Seth's goals were, exactly. I know he put everything into it for sure. For me personally, it was the most simple way to engage with fashion and art at that time. That's all. I think the reason it was liked as a whole, and not corrupt in my mind at all, is because Seth and Matt really enjoyed championing the people and ideas they respected. They knew they weren't giving anybody a meal ticket by publishing them. It wasn't some way for them to get power over people. They were just glad to engage with this small community of people and have some kind of an artifact of that. It was a pretty hands-off process. They genuinely trusted everybody to do their own thing, and trusted it all to work together.

How did The Blow Up differentiate itself from the other magazines that were being made at the time?
I think it had a profound understanding of young people. It existed in a certain place where it put that kind of naiveté next to much headier art and philosophy topics without being the least bit cynical. Considering how young we all were — I guess I was 23 or 24 around that time — it was probably natural that it stood on its own in that way.

**Was this the same time period that
you began doing agency work? How did
that happen?**
Seth and Matt were doing part-time
work a couple days for an agency,
writing copy and doing research.
Stuff that was far beneath their real
capabilities. Not that any of those
clients, some of whom who were really
big, got what the hell they were on
about, anyway. I was just under the
impression that the place we worked
at was The Blow Up's own office until
I figured out it was the agency's,
which made sense, 'cause the magazine
never had any money for anything.
Those agency guys got used to me being
there and threw me some little jobs.
I helped them design pitches to get
money from big clients. A lot of these
pitches were successful, and became
real things, which was surreal. For a
little while, we were not only doing
The Blow Up, but also daylighting or
moonlighting or whatever doing work of
this completely different stature and
of this completely different nature.
Seth didn't like it and got out.
Matt moved on to a better agency.
I ended up staying in advertising for
two years after that, just designing
these sort of informational websites
for Boeing's 787 plane. I'm just glad
that it was two and not four, not five
or six or seven...

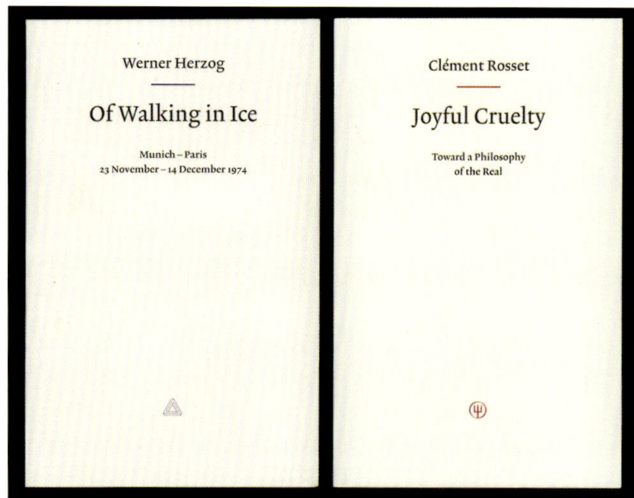

Werner Herzog: Of Walking On Ice, 2008.
Clément Rosset: Joyful Cruelty, 2009.
Free Association.

That was why you moved to LA?
Yeah. LA was really different as far
as making money went, probably the
opposite, but my girlfriend was here
and I knew I'd benefit from the sudden
isolation in West LA. I was torn up
from working so hard and so fast. I
could feel it physically, too.
**Can you talk a little bit about Free
Association?**
After The Blow Up ended, Matt
called asking me to work on a small
imprint he wanted to start: books
in a serial format, the titles
influenced heavily by his schooling
in philosophy, usually long out of
print. He correctly counted on them
to be successful, and on being able
to pay me for my work. We put out
three titles really quickly under his
direction. He also completely trusted
my decision-making in terms of design
with these things that were pretty
new to me.
**That Werner Herzog book Of Walking
in Ice was a big success. It was also
really beautiful.**
I'm happy with it still, proud of what
we did.
**For the record, could you talk a
little bit about how Rat Press ended
up happening?**
Brett Ratner saw one of the Free
Association books and called Matt to
say, "I want to do the same thing."
At first I thought Matt was screwing
around with me, since he knows Rush
Hour 1 & 2 are some of my favorite
movies of all time, and that he
directed those. But he wasn't doing
that. Within a week of that call,
Matt came to LA and we met Brett at
his house. He wanted out to put out
texts about movies, and already had
the selections and rights secured
when he met us. We set this thing up
for him really quickly. It was a very
different kind of engagement because
it wasn't our baby. To this day, I
have not seen a physical copy of those
books. I remember reading them as I
typeset them and thinking a couple
were pretty interesting. One was a
long interview with Marlon Brando.

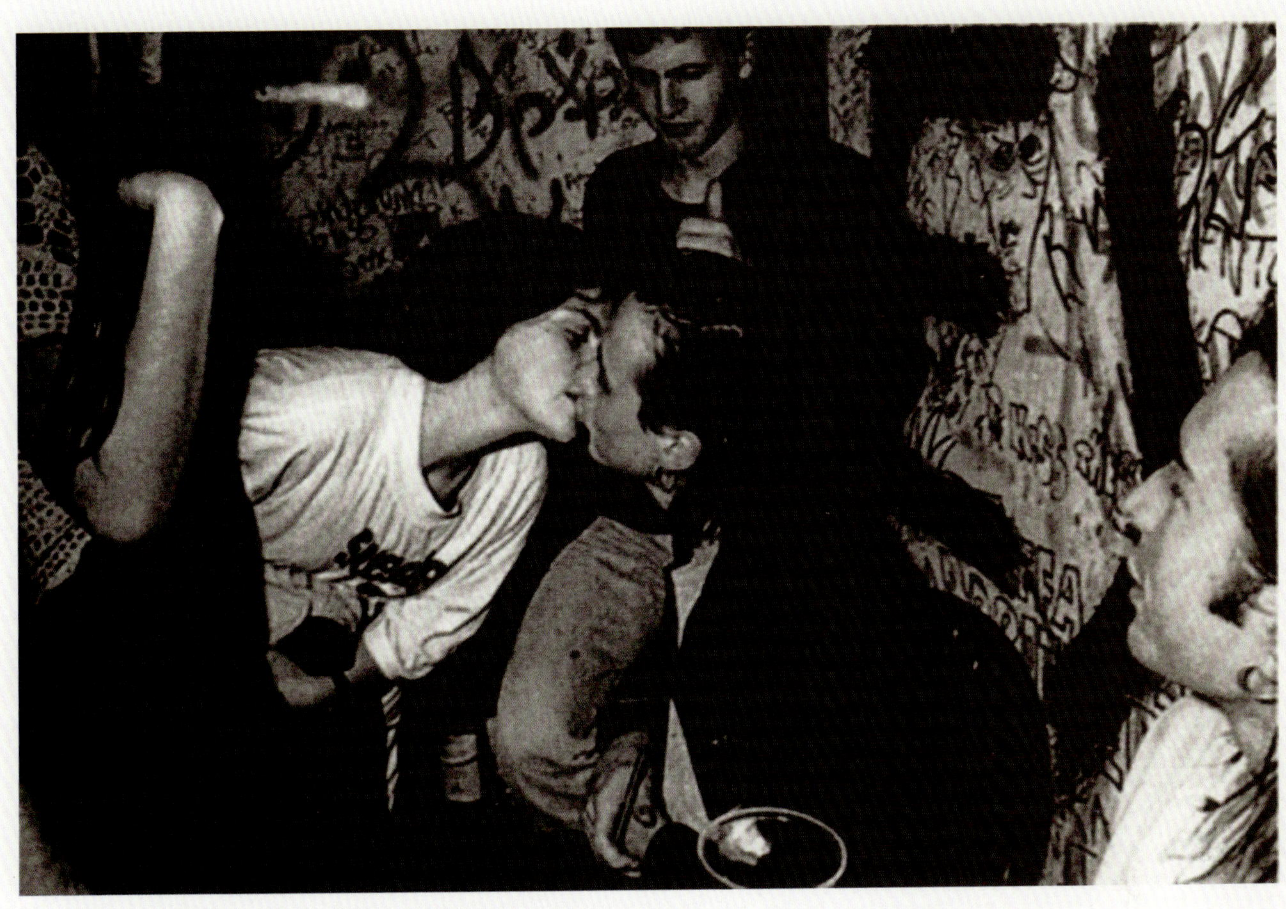

Lesson One, Alternative Invite, Young Art Gallery, 2011.

Didn't you end up spending some time with Robert Evans for one of the books?
Yeah. He's a really nice guy.
Did Free Association inspire Sister?
Sister came a few years after Free Association. Sister came out of an understanding of the realities of large-scale publishing. I knew that if I designed these things a certain way, made them a certain way, and made sure that only certain people got them, you could get the same feeling without all the hassle of that system. At the time I understood it well enough to know I couldn't contend with it.
For the record, what was Sister?
It was a mail order label.
Why mail order?
Mail order was important to me because it meant that anybody could get it, they just had to be paying attention.

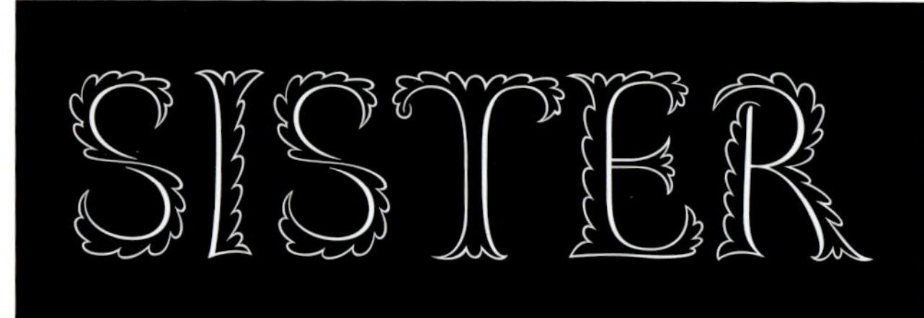

Sister Logo, 2009.

Why was it such small editions?
If you make just twenty copies of
something, at home, and don't even
count on selling them, you get to
just keep working with your friends.
You don't have to set aside three
months to work then sit around biting
your nails about money. You can
make forty books in one year if you
want, and I did. You can keep that
model indefinitely. And, if you're
disciplined about it, which I wasn't,
you could probably make a little bit
of money, or break even with what you
put in at least.

**Did you plan out the whole framework
beforehand?**
Yeah. I think I always do that. Setting
up a plan that's based on ideas and
what type of resources I have. I'm
very used to thinking like that, and
looking for it in other work.

What were the other rules?
Over a year, I would just make one
hundred things, only with friends,
and sell some of it to the people
who knew about it. Then it'd be
gone and there'd be no real trace
left. You couldn't just walk into a
store somewhere and buy the things
in the catalog either. Not that I
wanted my stuff next to something
I may have thought was garbage,
anyway. It was hard to keep track of,
but anybody could have affordably
bought about two thirds of the Sister
catalog that was buyable. Some
people bought a lot, people I've
never met. While it was going on, I
was constantly erasing releases and
replacing them, too. So there was
actually a total of about one hundred
thirty things, but I redacted enough
to where it was just one hundred
like I'd planned.

**Not everything on the list was for
sale. The site kept on changing.**
Sometimes, you could buy them, and
sometimes you couldn't. Depends on
what my mood was. It was personal.
**What were the things that you were
looking for in the people you were
publishing?**
You were the first one.
**Yeah, I was really surprised and
flattered that you asked me. I also
didn't totally get it. I remember a
long conversation on the phone where
you explained how you were thinking
about the project.**
I believe in getting a good start on
something. Your book set up a lot for
what was gonna happen after. I didn't
know you as well as I do now, but I
knew enough to bet so much on that
one. I had to trust your work, and
where it was headed, and I expected
the same in return.
**Was Sister your first project
without a client?**
No, I've been doing work like this
for a long time. I used to make
fonts, and would sell them online.
I've also done other things that had
time limits, things that come and go
and are then buried. I would rather
they stay buried, so I don't ever
want to talk about them, but they're
still important to me. The label I
have going now, 3DX, is the first
one that has no end planned. I have
done enough of these now and put
them to bed that I'd like one to
just go on forever.

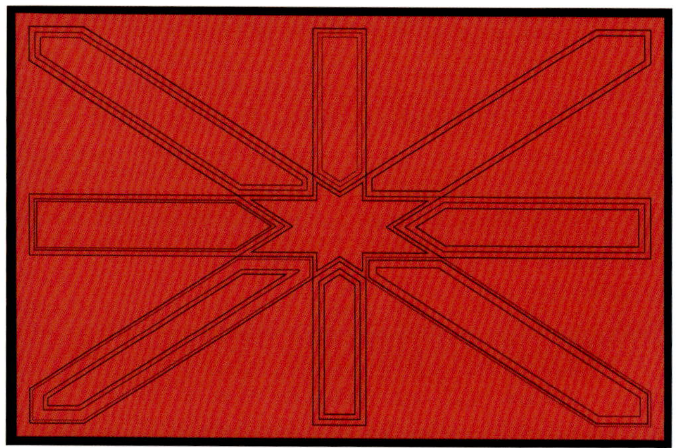

3DX, Exploder, 2012.

There were also discographies for other labels, like Sarah Records.
Yeah. I looked around, and couldn't find that information when I really wanted it. So I had to make it myself, put all that information together from these places that usually have incomplete information about these things I admire from a distance. Afterwards, I have some kind of instinctual thing to want to put them in a form that I think is deserving of their beauty. I'm careful when I make those things that it's understood that I am not asserting any kind of alignment with it, or that I own any of it. Nor that I have any kind of a "real" understanding of it just by making that. I hate when people do that, it's a punishable offense. Those things were always sold for zero profit, too. I stuck by that, and a couple of people responded favorably. I was always scared that someone from XPRESSWAY Records would be upset that I did this, but, I found out they weren't at all, which was great. I mailed them a few copies last year.

You also collect a certain type of music and share it on the internet.
Yeah. The work I put into that helps me think bigger things through. What I like about this music is it's based on a way of making things and sharing things that is special, but tried and true through other music, like dancehall. If I dedicate a few hours a day looking for it — and it's pretty hard to get through any traditional channel — talking to other collectors and serious listeners, while making sure I'm not piggybacking on someone else's culture, then it sort of keeps me in check about everything else. I don't use my real name, there's no branding, no ad dollars, no book or documentary in the works. In order to keep my privileges as a trader and collector, I have to make sure I'm square with the producers, MCs, DJs, and listeners in equal. That's some of the enjoyment for me anyway, making sure I don't screw that balance up.

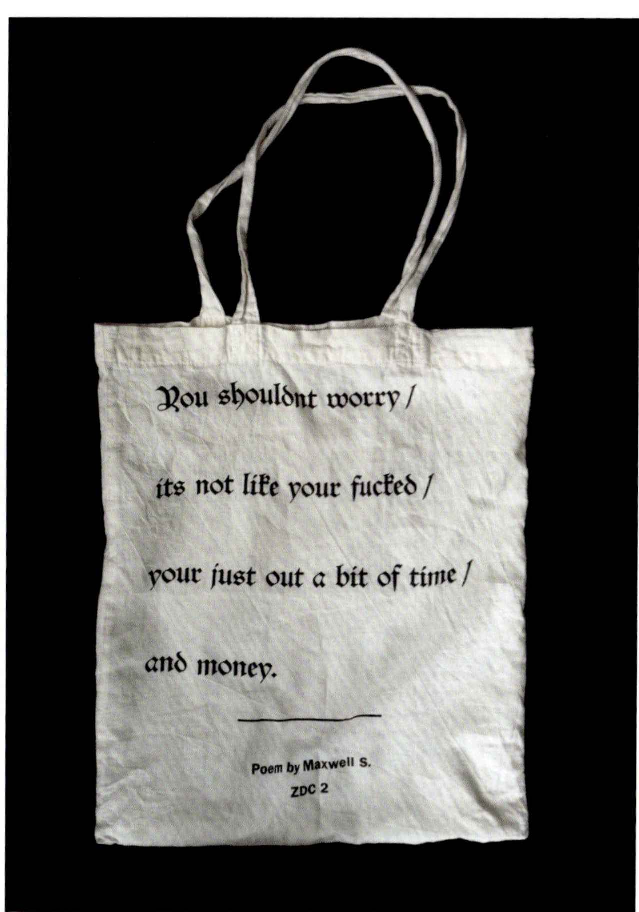

ZDC2A, Poem by Maxwell Simmer, 2010.

Sister set up a specific style of collaboration. You also do design work for a spectrum of independent companies. Is it the same?
I've worked with a lot of people in the same way before. They know that I'm paying super close attention, closer than most anybody else. So they already know that I'm going to do something that is about them first and me second. They know that they're handing it off to me, and they're gonna see it when it's done.

That way of working seems to really cut out micromanaging.
There's no micromanaging because it's usually a handoff. My close friends know I never talk about my work process or ask about theirs, or solicit feedback on work from them, or give them feedback on anything they're working on. So, it's in line with that. I have a real talent for picking friends who are more patient and forgiving than I am, too. ☺

Grant Falardeau
"Anyone who says they have a favorite flower is fucking crazy."

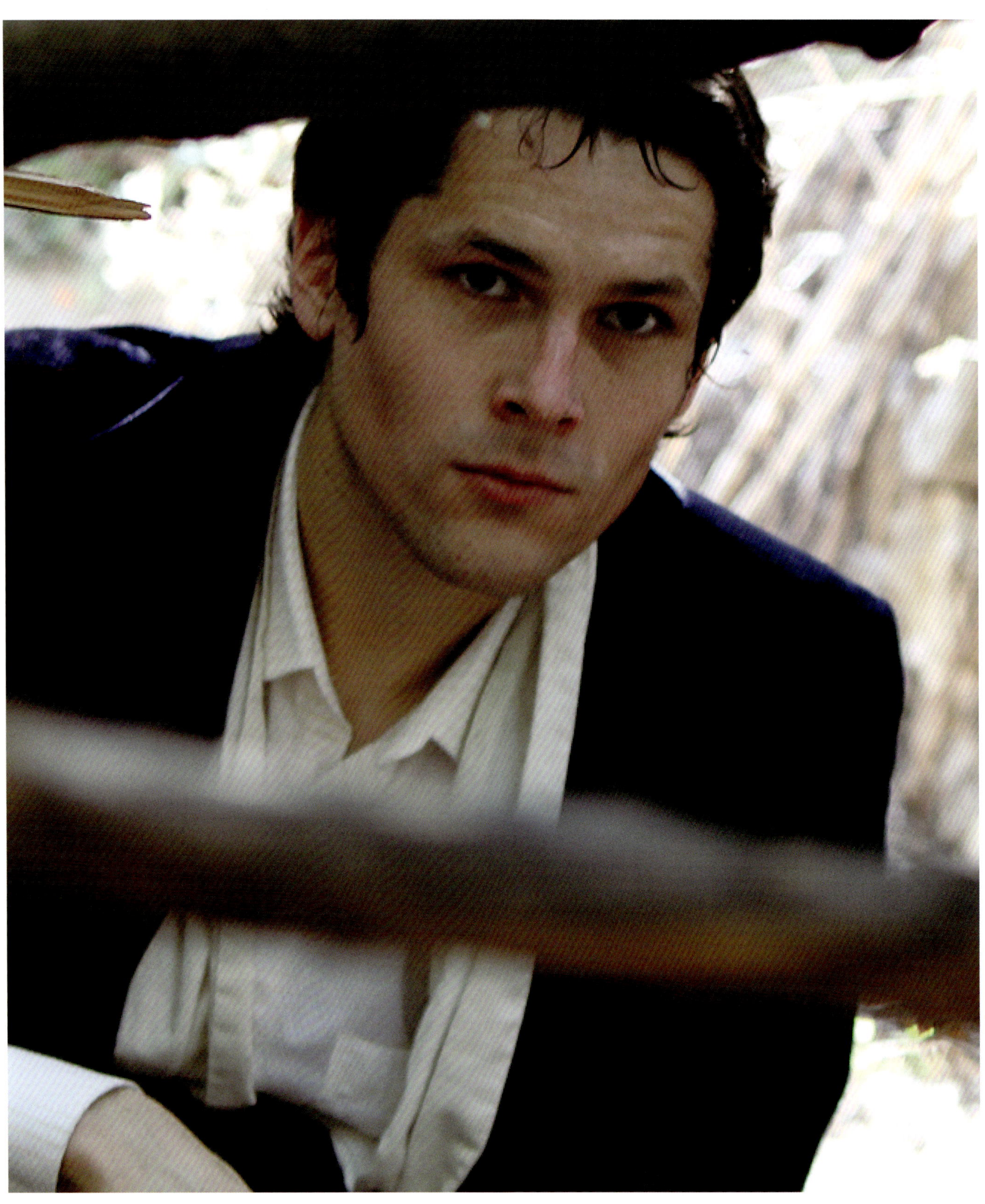

Interview by Asher Penn
Portrait by Elena Aragón

Over the past decade Los Angeles based filmmaker Grant Falardeau's mercurial output has included short films, music videos, television series, novels, poetry, and drawings. Working consistently in collaboration with a tight-knit community of friends, with little regard for the Hollywood or "Independent" system, Falardeau's films show a rare combination of sincerity and play — a joyful reflection of a beautiful mind.

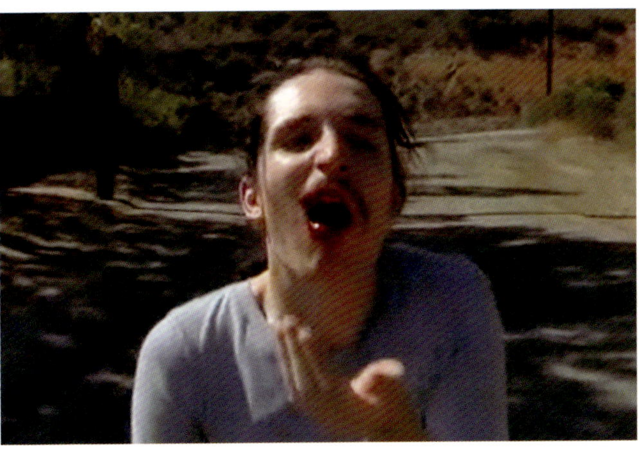

Frito Lo, 2009.

How do you flirt with people?
You just focus on the butterflies... I'm flirting with you right now. You gotta duck and groove around them. Focus on that sweet spot. Keep your eye on the prize. Remember, we're all just livin' it for the good juice.

Have you ever done drugs?
I dabbled...but a lil' dab'll do ya. I only occasionally drink alcohol now. But I always say I wish I was high on every drug — feeling exercise endorphins, swallowing food, having an orgasm — all at the same time. Wouldn't that be the best moment?

How old were you when you first fell in love?
Supposedly I kissed the doctor on the cheek as he held me upside down to spank me when I was born. Momma tells this story every once in a while. I believe it's the truth.

Do you have enemies?
Everything. A bad sandwich. Getting the flu. Flubbing up a sentence. A button popping off my pants. I'm battling my enemies all day long, man. I'm learning to be zen about it, though. Sometimes a bowl of cereal will fall on my lap and I just look up happy.

Are there any people you hate?
People, no. I have nothing but love and compassion for people. Even the jerks out there. Even the rotten, self-centered assholes rubbing coffee grinds and putrid tapioca on themselves at a dump.

Are you religious?
Everything is a miracle.

What kind of car do you drive?
A big blue one. She's falling apart. She's filled with props and wigs and costumes, just in case. Half her doors won't open and her speedometer is on the fritz. But let's keep on going.

Do you ever talk to kids?
I live for children. Around Halloween, I saw a little boy dressed as a cop in a book store. He was a couple feet away from his mother, looking at some magnets, out of her line of vision. I was waiting for a friend, just browsing too. I thought up several cop questions to ask him. But the more I refined my quips in my head, the more I felt my questions go down the wrong path. What started off as, "So, officer, catch any bad guys today?" became, "So, you're a policeman? Find any criminals?" I could just imagine his mother stealthily whipping around to clobber me with her purse, so I abandoned the effort altogether and just waited for my friend. I should have gone with my gut, then that kid and I could've shared a chuckle.

What's the most disgusting thing you have ever eaten?
Fiberglass.

What is your favorite flower?
Anyone who says they have a favorite flower is fucking crazy.

How do you like to spend your money?
Making movies.

Have you ever committed a crime?
Yes. Who hasn't? Even nuns jaywalk.

Images courtesy Grant Falardeau

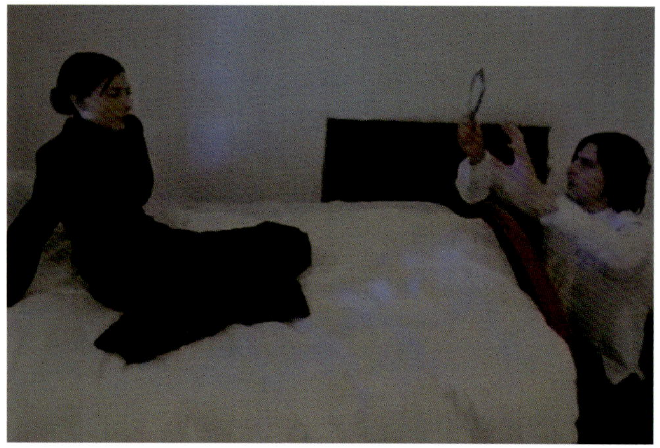

White Dove, Sister, 2013.

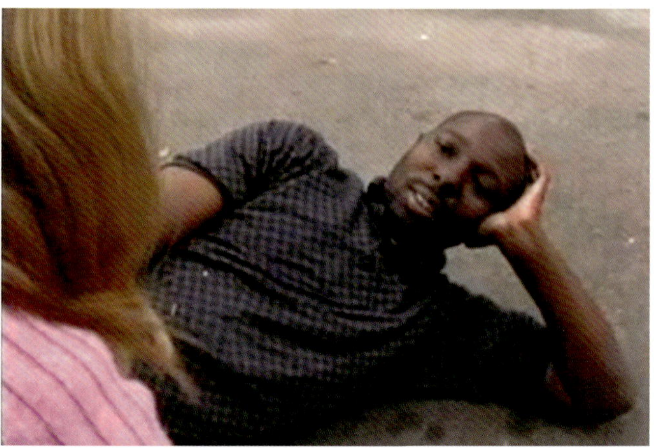

Rob Nakeem Bombastic, 2007.

How much time do you spend alone?
I spend a lot of time alone. I'm
alone and then I'm surrounded by
people and we are all laughing. Then
I'm alone again.

**Have you ever written something and
said, "This is too much?"**
Yes. As a matter of fact, a few
questions ago you asked who my first
love was and I immediately thought of
the joke, "Does jacking off to Mary
Poppins count?" But I didn't say it
because it was too much.

Have you ever approached a celebrity?
No. Celebrities deserve extra privacy.
Unless I'm introduced, I try to keep
my distance. I think the general
public should make a conscious effort
to ignore celebrities. We need to
level the playing field and ignore
them for their own sake. Trust me,
it's good for them, it's the next
best thing to anonymity.

**Do you collect anything? Do you have
any prized possessions?**
I collect hats by accident. I don't
wear hats, they're for my movies! I
prize the art I have acquired over
the years... I wish I could afford to
frame it.

Have you ever broken someone's heart?
Absolutely. On a daily basis. It's a
tragedy. And no one is the same after.

Have you ever seen a ghost?
I saw a ghost. I was walking through
a nice neighborhood one night and I
looked in a window and I saw a ghost
sitting at a table feverishly reading
a dictionary.

Do you believe in "research"?
Appropriate planning and research
is key in any process, but as far
as art is concerned, in it's truest
sense, no. It's dangerous to the
artist because research helps form
techniques and style. Art has
nothing to do with research, it
has to do with experience... The
wayward search. Creation has nothing
to do with the past, so research
ultimately means nothing. It's like
conceptual art. I don't believe
in conceptual art. It relies on a
concept from the past, usually by
way of research, that doesn't exist
in the experience. It's bullshit.
People get research tangled up in
the act of making art constantly.
This produces failed art. Or no
art at all.

What's your motto?
Love a color rainbow.

**What do you think you'd be like if
you were a woman?**
Tall and sexy. I'd make love at least
twice a day. I'd eat apple wedges and
nifty little tea sandwiches.

Have you ever been in a fight?
Nothing major. Just pushing and
punching and shoving and yelling and
screaming. Nothing cool, like a brawl
that happens on the tops of classic
cars at drive-in movie theaters where
the rules are nobody can touch the
ground. No, nothing like that.

Have you ever met an Indian?
I am an Indian. Apache. I'm from
Geronimo's family.

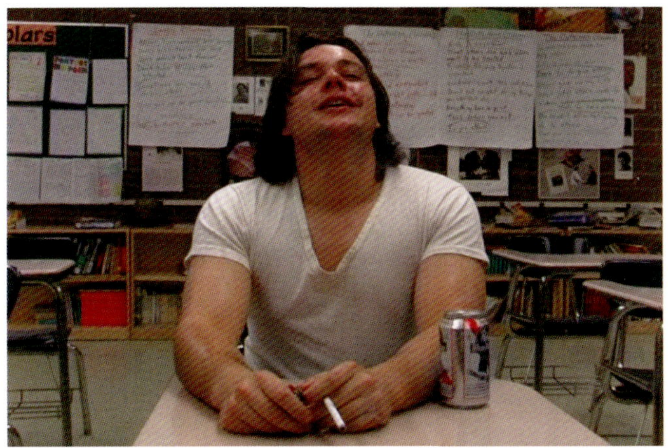

Desafianado, 2009.

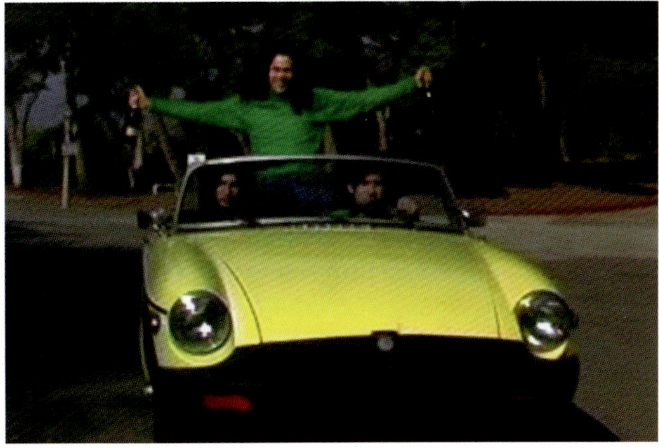

The Parrot Gang, 2009.

What makes you cry?
Thinking about my mother dying.

What is the funniest thing Miles Jopling has ever said to you?
That's a tough one. Just the other night, we drove by a strip club. I said, "It would be funny if I rolled down the window and screamed, 'Baby, you're a star! Fuck you!'" Miles immediately impersonated the voice of a stripper with a string of hilarious comebacks. In his impersonation, she referred to us as "kids" in a sort of crumbly, world-weary Latina accent. It was funny.

What kind of music do you like to dance to?
I like to dance to a new type of music. I have the names of all the musicians written down on a slip of paper somewhere. I could draw the instruments on a napkin for you. Really...I like this kind of music... it's real world class...spot on, kind of stuff.

Do you think smoking is cool?
I think smoking is spiritual. I'm Geronimo's boy — what do you expect?

Do you see a tailor?
I don't have the money for that now. Although my cousin just recently embroidered a flower onto his shirt at a shop in Atwater for a couple of bucks. Supposedly they have a big binder of designs to choose from. It's like a "Grandma approved" way to get a tattoo. I like that.

How do you feel when you're writing?
In the moment.

Is it true you were a fat kid?
Yes I was. I would just hunker down in front of the TV and eat food all day. One of the saddest moments at that time was when my very skinny best friend was teased by one of his older brother's friends for having a tiny gut. I stood there waiting for him to tear my ass to shreds. But he didn't even acknowledge my presence. I was so fat, so utterly large, I wasn't on his insult radar. When you are fat you know what it feels like to be invisible.

Do you ever read movie reviews?
Yes, though I find that very few critics share my views. If somebody writes a review of my work I vow not to read it. It's not conducive to the artist. People say you need to grow a thicker skin or learn from the mistakes critics write about. It doesn't work that way. The only way to get better is to make mistakes. A critic once told me that a specific movie I made failed because it lacked "establishing shots" and had "bad sound." He was right about these problems, but now, in hindsight, I know the piece did not fail. But he said it so knowingly, he seemed so sure about it, that I took his suggestions on the spot. I remade the movie with the added shots and better sound. That was a failed piece. I learned two things by doing that: never listen to critics, and never do the same thing twice and expect the same results. ☺

Laurie Spiegel

"When you're writing the software for yourself,
you get something that really thinks like you."

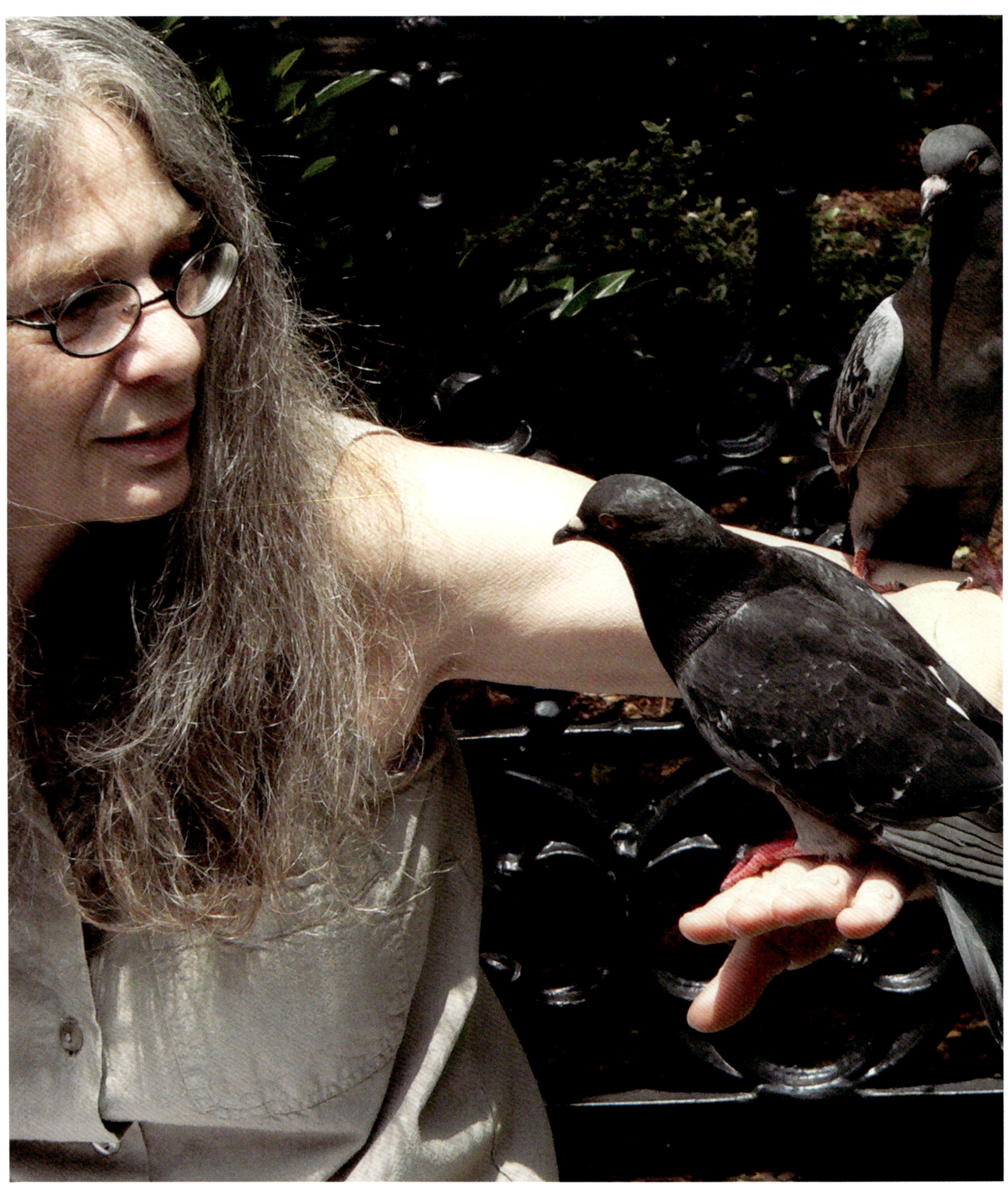

Interview by Dena Yago
Portrait by Peter Schmideg

Laurie Spiegel is a composer and a humanist software developer. Composing musical works, as well as the programs used to create them, Spiegel is celebrated for her seminal albums "Unseen Worlds" and "The Expanding Universe," and included in such varied arenas from the Voyager Spacecraft of 1977 to the recent Hunger Games soundtrack. Her work on the GROOVE system at Bell Labs and the countless sounds she developed at the Experimental Television Center has made her elemental in both the history of computer programming as well as New York's experimental music scene. She is a feminist, animal rehabilitator, programmer, and writer whose presence and work over the past forty years has charted a seismic shift in technology, in our relationships to the tools we use, and how these tools have reshaped the lines of creative production.

How did you first start working at Bell Labs?

I had been working with analog synthesizers — with the Buchla system in particular, an instrument by Don Buchla — and I was frustrated with it for a number of reasons. Analog synthesizers had no memory, so you couldn't save your work. You'd use these machines oftentimes in a shared studio. You'd be working for four hours and then you'd have to leave as the next person came in. You'd never get your setup or music back exactly the way you had it, because nothing could ever be reconstructed quite the same way again. Anyway, in the early 70's, Rhys Chatham invited Emmanuel Ghent and Max Mathews to do a concert at The Kitchen, here in New York. Instead of playing analog synths directly, Ghent and Mathews were using computers to control analog equipment. I remember seeing this and thinking that this was exactly what I needed.

So did you reach out to those guys? Did you know them?

It took me a while to work up the guts, but I called up Emmanuel Ghent and asked if I could be his apprentice. He was working at Bell Labs. I asked, "Can I study with you?" but he said he didn't teach, so I asked if I could volunteer to be his assistant. Max Mathews would look over my shoulder every now and then while I was working there. After about three months he decided I knew what I was doing technically, and he gave me clearance and a badge so I could start working at Bell Labs on my own.

What were you doing there?

I wanted access to GROOVE, which was a new hybrid computer-controlled analog system. The few people who were doing computer music back then were doing non-real-time synthesis. You would put a bunch of instructions into the computer, how you wanted the sounds to be synthesized, and then the computer processed them over a weekend. After that you'd have 30 seconds worth of digital signal computed, waiting for you to play it out of the buffer and record it to tape. It was really slow and completely non-interactive. It was like a computer playing an instrument rather than a computer being the instrument. To create CD-quality audio, you would have two channels of over 44 thousand numbers to calculate every second if the computer is synthesizing the sounds real-time. But when a computer was controlling an analog system, all it has to process is a hundred little control points that might move a sound parameter up a hair, move to some note, or fade a sound down. The demands on the computer were small enough to allow for real-time interaction with the sound at that rate, the way you had with a conventional acoustic instrument.

Were any other big companies bringing in artists to do this kind of work?
Bell Labs was really special. For one, it was a regulated monopoly. Before the government broke up the Bell system in 1984, there was only one phone company in the United States: Bell Telephone. Everybody still thought you could only have one company to connect everybody. It works well if it's just one company, and it was complicated and took years to figure out how to break it into smaller parts to conform with the antitrust laws. So "Ma Bell" was given an exemption to those laws. But in exchange for that, the government mandated that they act sort of like a nonprofit company.

So what was the company culture like?
The atmosphere at the lab was very noncommercial. There was a lot of pure research. The dozen departments that Max Mathews ran researched things like speech synthesis and speech recognition, the structure of human memory, and how our minds do depth perception. There were studies on nonverbal interaction. They were interested in the picture phone, and wanted to see if people talked differently on the phone if they could or couldn't see each other. They were doing a lot of experimental research. It wasn't at all related to making new products. It was for understanding how communication works and how to make it better. It wasn't product-oriented or commercial,they weren't selling telephones. The philosophy of product-making meanwhile was different back then, too. Stuff was built to last longer.

It sounds almost like a university.
It was an atmosphere of people who were really serious about the research they were doing, and they weren't concerned with commercial stuff. They wanted to understand things, create things, and create knowledge. They also recognized that if you're designing something like switching circuits, nobody is going to test them better than a real-time musician. The number of operations and kinds of information that a musician puts out during a live performance is way more than any other kind of interactive user. I had a chance to do those kinds of tests when I was working on another synthesizer project at Bell, built by someone named Hal Alles.

Tell me about that project.
I wrote for Hal's synth in one of the early versions of the C programming language while they were still developing it. I had to program the instrument from another computer in another part of the building. If the program didn't run, I'd have to walk all the way down to this other lab and might discover that it wasn't running because Hal had actually taken the whole machine apart, and he was changing some components. I was also getting memos at the lab saying, "We have just changed the equals-plus sign in C, to plus-equals and installed a new compiler. Please revise all your software." The whole operating system, language, and hardware were under development as I was working. When something didn't run, you couldn't tell whether you had a bug in your program, or there was a bug in the compiler, or they had changed the compiler or syntax but not put out a notice yet, or the hardware or operating system had been modified. All of it was new and still in flux.

That sounds crazy.
The Lab was asked to do a performance for the Motion Picture Association in Hollywood to celebrate "50 Years of Talking Pictures," so we had this deadline for getting Hal's machine up and running and out to Hollywood for a performance. When we finally got it out to LA, it was full of condensation from being cold in the cargo hold of an airplane. We had to take it apart and dry off the circuit cards with hair dryers. During the performance, the Motion Picture people put the synthesizer on this rotating platform that no

      Laurie Spiegel by Dena Yago

one had bothered to tell us about,
so the cables were gradually getting
entangled — pulled tighter and
tighter as the thing rotated on stage!
They stopped the rotation just in the
nick of time and nothing blew up.

So when did you leave Bell Labs?
I left in 1979, mostly because they
got rid of these wonderful old
computers I had been working on.
I was working on these bulky DDP-
224 systems. These were dedicated
systems, which meant only one user
at a time. At the end of January
1979, they replaced these dedicated
systems with more modern machines, or
modern for the time anyway, called
timesharing systems. Timesharing
was a whole new model for using
computers. These new systems were
running Unix, which was also brand-
new. With Unix you could have
multiple terminals and users on one
computer, all sharing processing
power and memory at the same time,
dividing computing power into tiny
slices of time. Because of the
extremely limited processing power
of computers if you were doing music
in real-time or interactively, that
kind of architecture was not going
to work for you. There wasn't enough
processing power to share! You really
needed all the power you could get,
the whole computer to yourself, with
complete control of its timing to do
music in real-time. So if you were
sharing resources on a multiuser,
multiprocess system, real-time music
became impossible. Computers were a
lot slower then.

**So what happened when they junked
these old systems?**
We lost everything. All of a sudden
we had no computers to run all of the
software we were using and developing
for the DDP-224 throughout the
70s. The DDP-224 was old, obsolete
technology to the Labs at that point,
but to me it was my instrument, my
musical voice. I tried to make do by
writing music on paper for instruments
for a while. Then I was given a
prototype Apple II, which was great.

But there was still a real limit to
what you could do on an Apple II. So
when this thing called the McLeyvier
came along, a much more powerful
instrument, I wanted to be involved
with it, and I went to work for the
company that was developing it so
that I could use it.

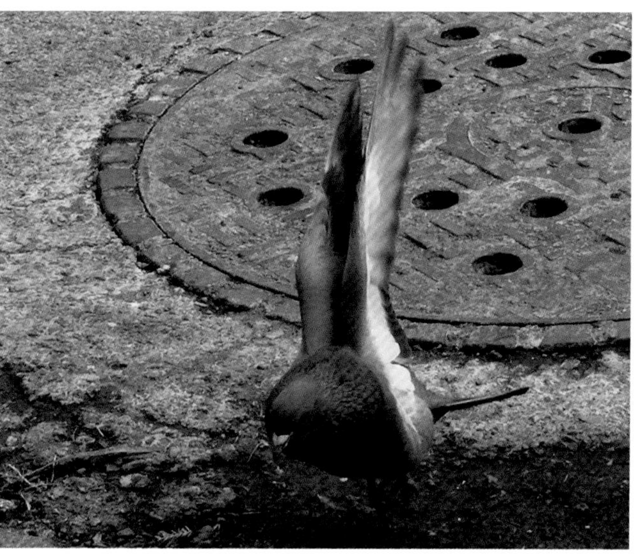

In Canada?
Yes, Toronto. It was the early 80s,
and I was working on the McLeyvier,
developed by David McLey. The
McLeyvier was a music processor that
included an LSI 11/23 computer, an
analog synthesizer and various input
and output devices as subsystems. It
also had faders and lots of audio
and other IO connectors. When I was
doing software for that, I worked
from '82 to '85, up in Toronto.

**So you took this programming job to
continue doing computer music?**
It wasn't so much programming as
being put in charge of software
design — the McLeyvier project had a
staff of programmers.

**What was your relationship with the
Mac people?**
Jef Raskin was my main contact
and friend at Apple. He was the
originator of the Macintosh until
Steve Jobs took it over from him. I
had met Jef back in the 70s, and we
had become friends. He was a really
good musician.

Oh, who knew!
Yeah, two of the best musicians I've ever known aren't even thought of as musicians. Jef Raskin and Marvin Minsky are the two people that I know who can, at the drop of a hat, sit down and improvise a fugue on piano in a million different classical styles.

So Jef was the one who gave you the Apple II?
Yes. One day Jef shows up at my loft and says, "Laurie, I think you're really going to like this. You don't have a computer. You're miserable. I'm going to plug this computer into your TV then I'm going to take a nap in your back room. And while I'm taking a nap, you're going to write your first program on this computer." And I was doubtful, since I had never seen this computer before. And I certainly had never seen this programming language. "You'll figure it out," Jef reassured me, "It's BASIC. It's like a subset of FORTRAN. It won't be a problem for you."

Was he right?
He went and took a nap and by the time he woke up, I had written a little visual mandala generator. I was hooked. It was a prototype 48K Apple II. Jef saw what I made and said, "The computer is yours, you know, keep it."

Were you writing the same kind of algorithms to make visual work that you were writing to compose music?
That's what I wanted to do. I wanted to try to make a visual version of music: a non-referential visual art made of structures of change over time, the way music is made of structures of changing sound over time. I wanted an art that was self-referential, using shapes and colors and textures similar to the way that music uses pitch and loudness and timbre — art that doesn't refer to anything outside of itself, that creates emotion by manipulating our expectations, using structures of repetition and change.

That reminds me, you were involved in that Ursula Le Guin movie, The Lathe of Heaven. How did that happen?
It was a project of at the Experimental TV Lab at WNET, the PBS TV station in New York City. I'd been a video artist in residence there around that time, trying to make visual music, though I ended up mostly doing music for everybody else's videos because they all really needed music. I was interested in the co-generation of image and sound, composing them together at the same time.

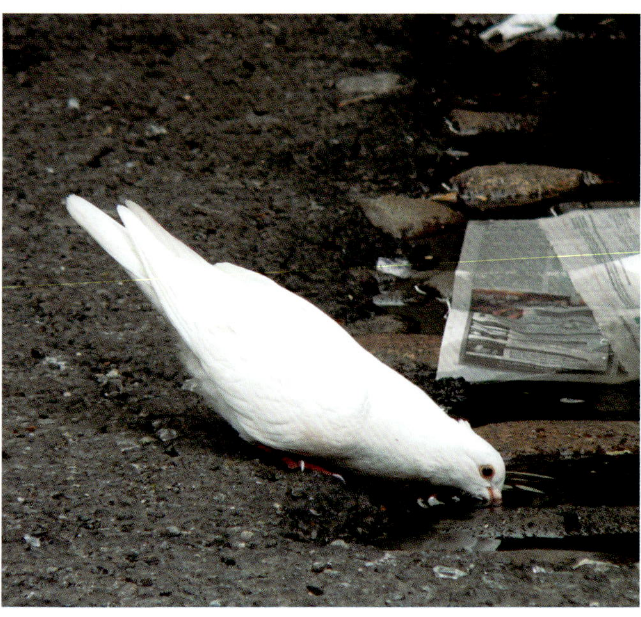

How did that space work?
Each little shared studio was a community of people interacting with each other and collaborating in ways that I think were a big factor in making the '70s in New York the art scene that it was. You had people running into each other and synergistically collaborating and influencing each other's work in ways that you probably don't get now that everybody has a powerful computer studio right at home, and they work alone in their bedrooms. It's not the same as being in a shared space, and in the middle of working on something somebody comes in to your studio and says, "Oh, but what if you did this!"

Was that outlook present with programming and shared computers?

Music was the big thing. The software was only a tool. We were in it as artists, and the goal of the software was to make music and art. People helped each other. Don't forget software wasn't patentable yet. What we really were trying to do was to get some sound that we hear inside our heads out into the air where other people could hear it. We wanted to make it possible to communicate stuff that we saw only in our inner imaginations.

That's interesting.

Imagination is something else I worry about a lot these days. I think it might be getting lost. Everybody is so bombarded and overloaded with media coming at us that we don't have the same access to our imaginations as we used to. Back when I made The Expanding Universe, I would go through my record collection and flip back and forth through my LPs. There was something I wanted to listen to that I couldn't quite put my finger on. I could picture the sound in my mind, but I couldn't find it on a record. So I was led by my internal auditory imagination. If I'd had a record with something like it, I would have just played the record, but instead, I had to make it.

Sounds pretty D-I-Y.

Right, there was a lot more of that mentality toward making artistic and musical stuff, experiences that didn't exist yet. It was like there were new empty worlds that had yet to be populated. A lot of these newer musical forms that are popular now are more like editing- and processing-based stuff like remixes, mash-ups, collages, and montages — new works made out of pre-existing works. I'm not against any of these new forms, but a lot of pretty wonderful music and art came out of staring at the blank canvas. Sometimes it's pure silence that lets you listen to what happens inside your own head. I'm not advocating meditation or anything drastic, but I think an occasional media fast is probably a really good idea for people in the arts.

How'd you end up with an email address @xanadu.net? That's Ted Nelson's project, the original blueprints for hypertext and the web.

Having been somewhat involved in computer graphics but not officially doing computer graphics, I decided to go to SIGGRAPH, which is the Special Interest Group on Computer Graphics and Interactive Techniques for computer professionals. I don't remember who gave me Marvin Minsky's number, probably Maryanne Amacher, but they said "Call him. He loves music." So I did, and said I was a composer, and Marvin said to come over right away. I went to Marvin Minsky's house, and found him out on his unmowed front lawn in a T-shirt, throwing something like hubcaps to see if he could decapitate dandelions. We went inside and messed around on the piano and we hit it off well. Then he took me over to the Artificial Intelligence Lab where I first met Ted Nelson.

This was at MIT?

Yes, Ted and I became good friends. I wasn't part of the team that worked on Xanadu when they actually had a team working on the software. At one point Ted told me that he didn't ever want to lose my email address, so he would give me one on his server and, that way, he would always be able to reach me.

Were you, or was anyone, ever really using Xanadu? Was there a point where it was functioning?

"Functioning" is kind of a relative term. It was more a proof-of-concept level of function for a model and a set of standards and rules. Ted published a paper called The Hypertext in 1965, and it was so far ahead of its time. It was based on an evolution of Vannevar Bush's Memex concept, which goes back to 1945 when computers were still just analytical engines. The thinking was: the human mind doesn't just go in one line sequentially in the way text is written. You have all these streams and parallels and branches when you think.

Ted always wanted to write the way his mind worked, to be able to really express how he thought. Vannevar Bush's Memex model is really an associative linkage of ideas, and bits of information that are connected by association. With Ted's model, everything was bi-directionally linked. The web, as it has evolved, is much closer to a paper with footnotes, where you click on the footnote and you get the reference. Xanadu was a much more complex and fluid model of how different documents could be organized in relation to each other. Ted really feels like we've all been duped by something inferior with the way that the web has turned out. When I think about what my expectations were for computer music — compared to what happened after all these companies moved in and started trying to create products for the music software market — I realize that those two divisions of labor, technology creators and users, hadn't been separated from each other yet back then.

So how do you feel about that separation, since you've created so many of your own tools?
I have really weird mixed feelings For a long time, I felt it was really illegitimate even to use pre-fabricated sounds, and now there are all these people out there just selling pre-fab sounds. I mean, everybody should create their own sounds. That's part of why we're in the medium, so we can create our own sounds, and the nature of the sound is part of the vision of the music that you're trying to realize. Sure I use other people's software, but I've gotten a lot further musically with my own stuff. My CD Unseen Worlds was done mostly with the software Music Mouse, which I wrote for my own use, and that a lot of other people used later on too. When you're writing the software for yourself, you get something that really thinks like you. I don't think I've

either produced the same quality of results or had the same level of excitement and involvement in the creative process using software by other people. But making software has gotten a lot more complicated. The systems have gotten a lot more complicated.

Do you write much software now?
I would love to get back to writing software again. I miss that level of total immersion, getting down inside the sounds, as opposed to just looking at them from outside, through an editor. There's a level of detachment that's built into that whole model of music software. The concept of an editor is completely different from the concept of a musical instrument. A lot of it has to do with the nature of time and how time is experienced. And, in music, it's really easy to fall into representing time as a bunch of equal points across a line, the way you see notes on a score or points on a timeline. But that's not how you experience it if you pick up a guitar, or you sit down at a keyboard or you're making up music from your head. You're inside of it, and the perspective is that you are riding the timeline, rather than looking at the timeline. It's the difference between looking at a road from up in an airplane, versus being in a car racing down the highway. There's a deeper level of involvement when you're in the car, when you don't know what's coming up next or how the flow of traffic is going to change the way you're moving. That's the feeling I like to have.

Like you're deep in traffic?
Yes, like I'm down there on the highway, moving along, rather than just looking at it from above. That's really stretching the metaphor, but that's about as close as I can probably get right now to what I miss in most software I've used that I didn't write myself. As for visual art, I don't know. I'm trying to think of what might be analogous.

You're always outside the canvas, or the image, or the frame — looking into it — but you can also be completely inside the frame when you're working, you can let it become your world.

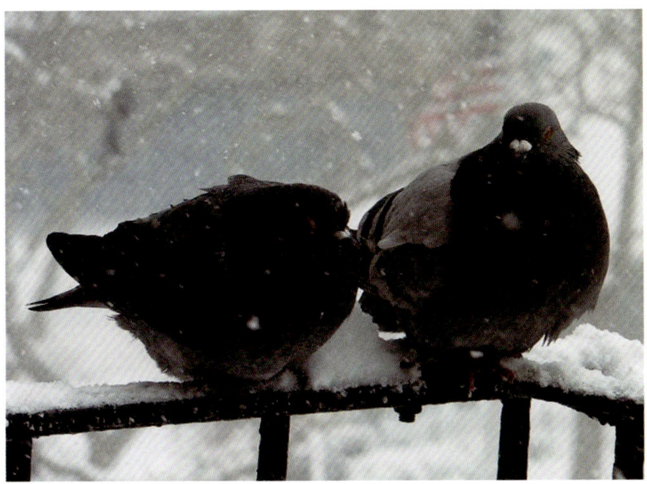

That's sort of sentimental...
A lot of software introduces a certain distance between you and the material. I would love to do more software, if I could catch up with the technology in terms of my own programming skills, which are from the dark ages. I mean, I started as an old-fashioned procedural language programmer. And object-oriented languages? I just don't think that way. It's a different paradigm for how things connect. It's like a foreign language that I have to translate, whereas old-fashioned procedural code comes natural for me. A procedural language is more like, "I do this, and then I do this, and then depending on this thing, I might do this or I might do that." It's like one decision at a time, moving through a creative process. It feels more similar to being a person. If I'm sitting here with a pencil, writing down a piece of music on paper, that's how I think. Improvising and composing music is just plain procedural to me. There are no objects or abstractions about communicating entities in my experience. Does that make sense?
Yeah, it does.

In a way, I'm hanging on to things that have worked for me in the past. I still have a Mac Plus in my studio and I still use it at times. I just don't want to get rid of some of my old software for earlier Macs that has to run in the Rosetta emulator. And I also keep a G4 that runs Classic or OS 9 for even earlier software. There's a lot of really good old stuff out there that's worth keeping.
It's important to keep the good old stuff.
There should be the ability to emulate earlier computers in every new computer. Musical instruments have always been cumulative. The piano coming along didn't wipe out the harpsichord. Acoustic instruments didn't die out when we got electronic instruments. We have both, and we're really glad to have both. Every new generation of computers should make more things possible but not wipe out the older stuff we could do. But sometimes newer systems can't run the older software. Older hardware, meanwhile, breaks down. Connectors get corroded, and you can't get replacement parts for old technology. There also may be no way to connect old gear to modern networks. The rate of turnover just gets faster and faster, too. I'm not saying this from nostalgia because the old times were better, because there is a lot that is so much easier to do now. God it's wonderful what technology can do today! But we didn't lose the paintbrush when we developed computer graphics. The paintbrush is really important, and it still can do incredible things that probably only a paintbrush can do, no matter how good a graphics tablet gets. You know, there's nothing like a pencil. I love pencils. What would it be like if, because we have keyboards to type on now, we could no longer have pencils or pens? ☺

Deth Kop

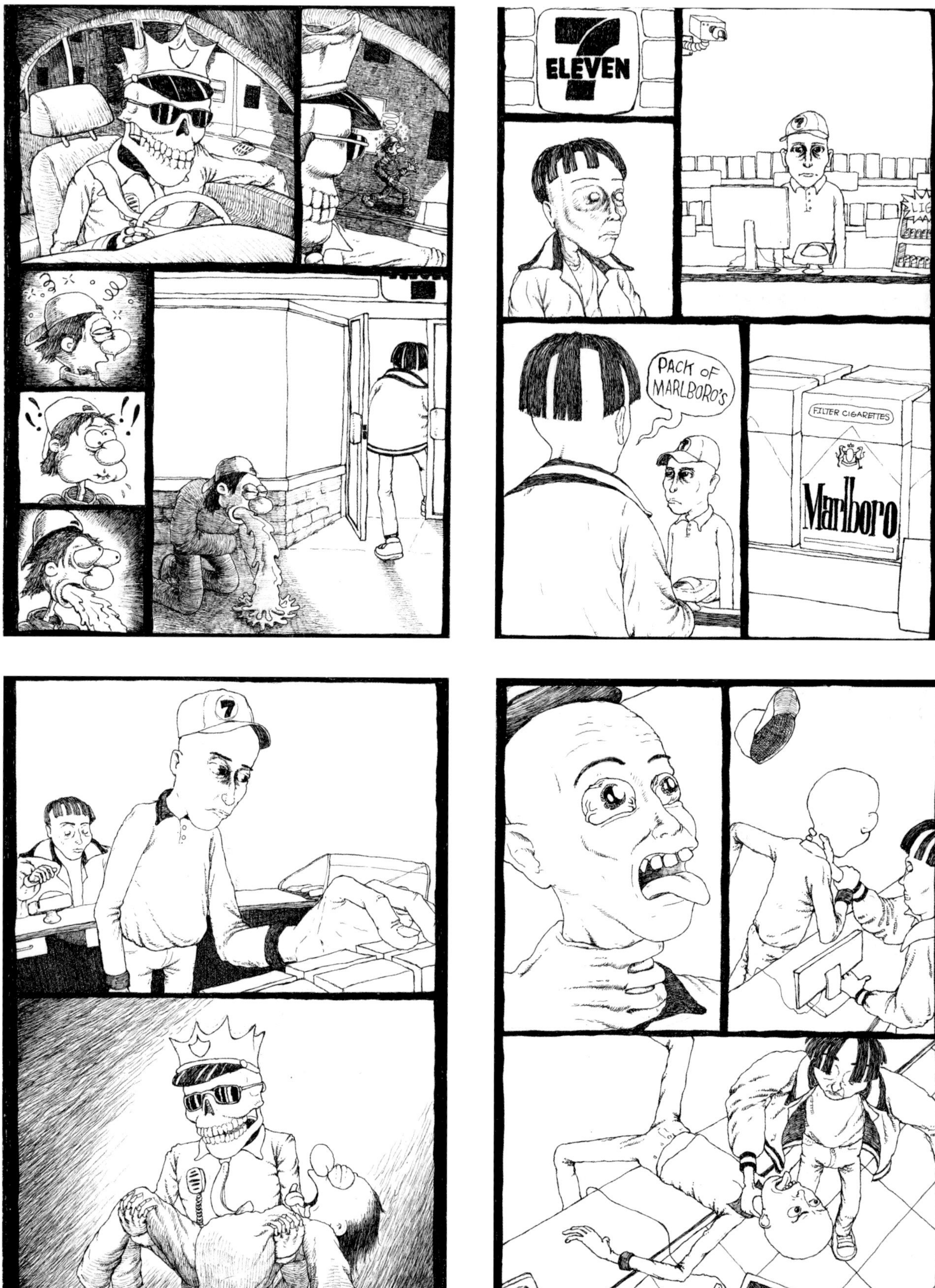

By Gobby

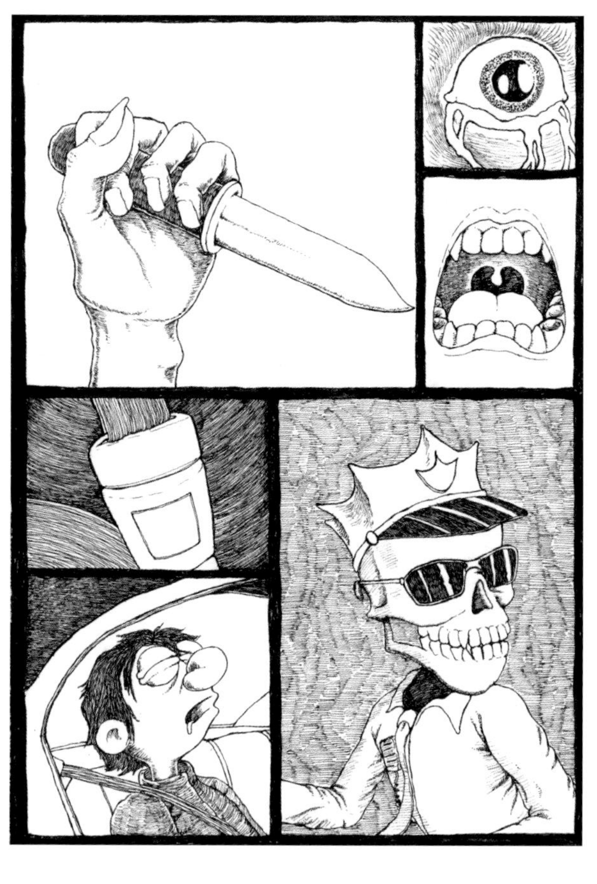

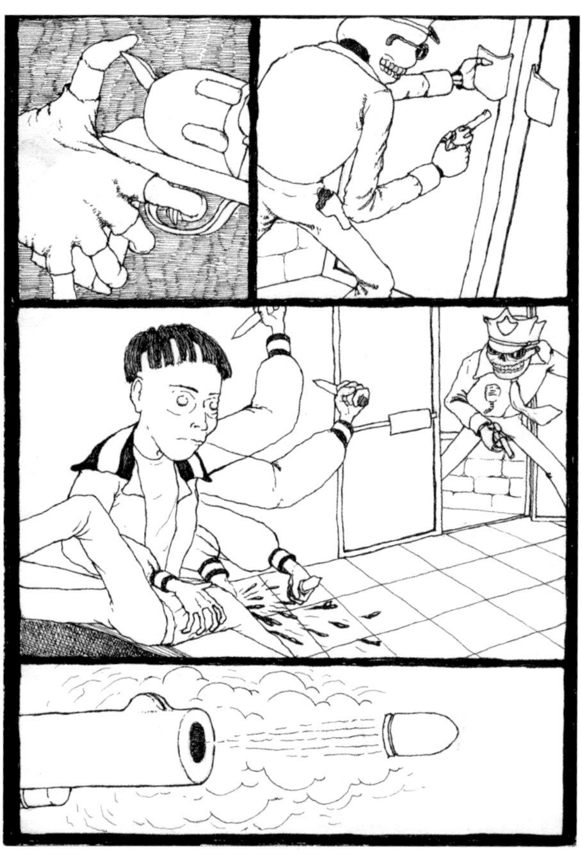

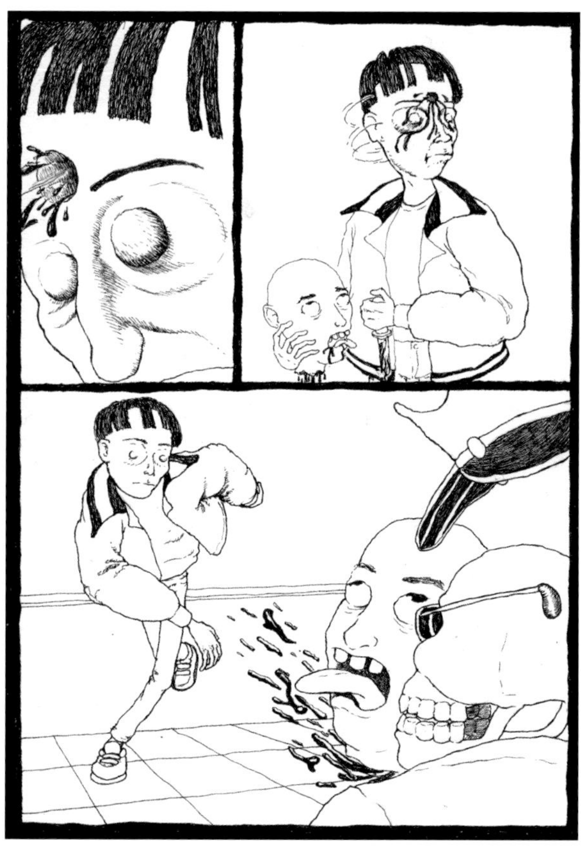

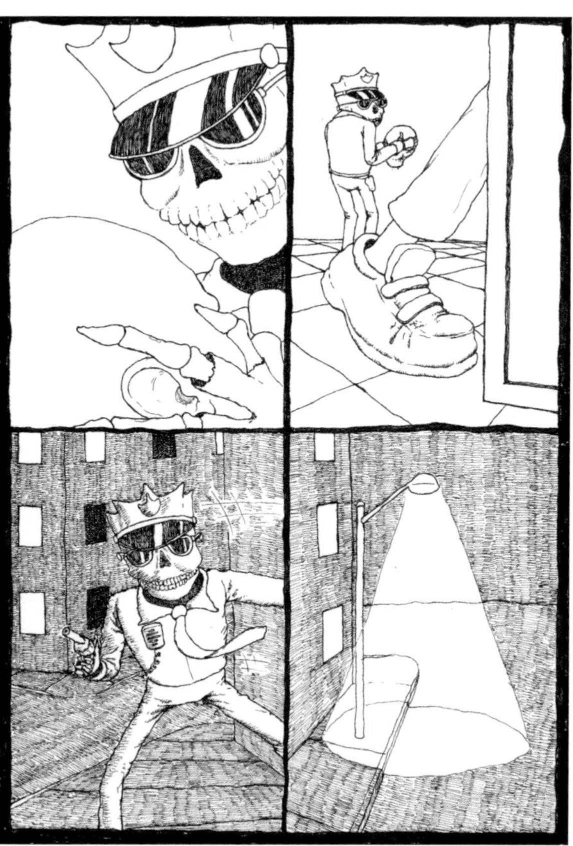

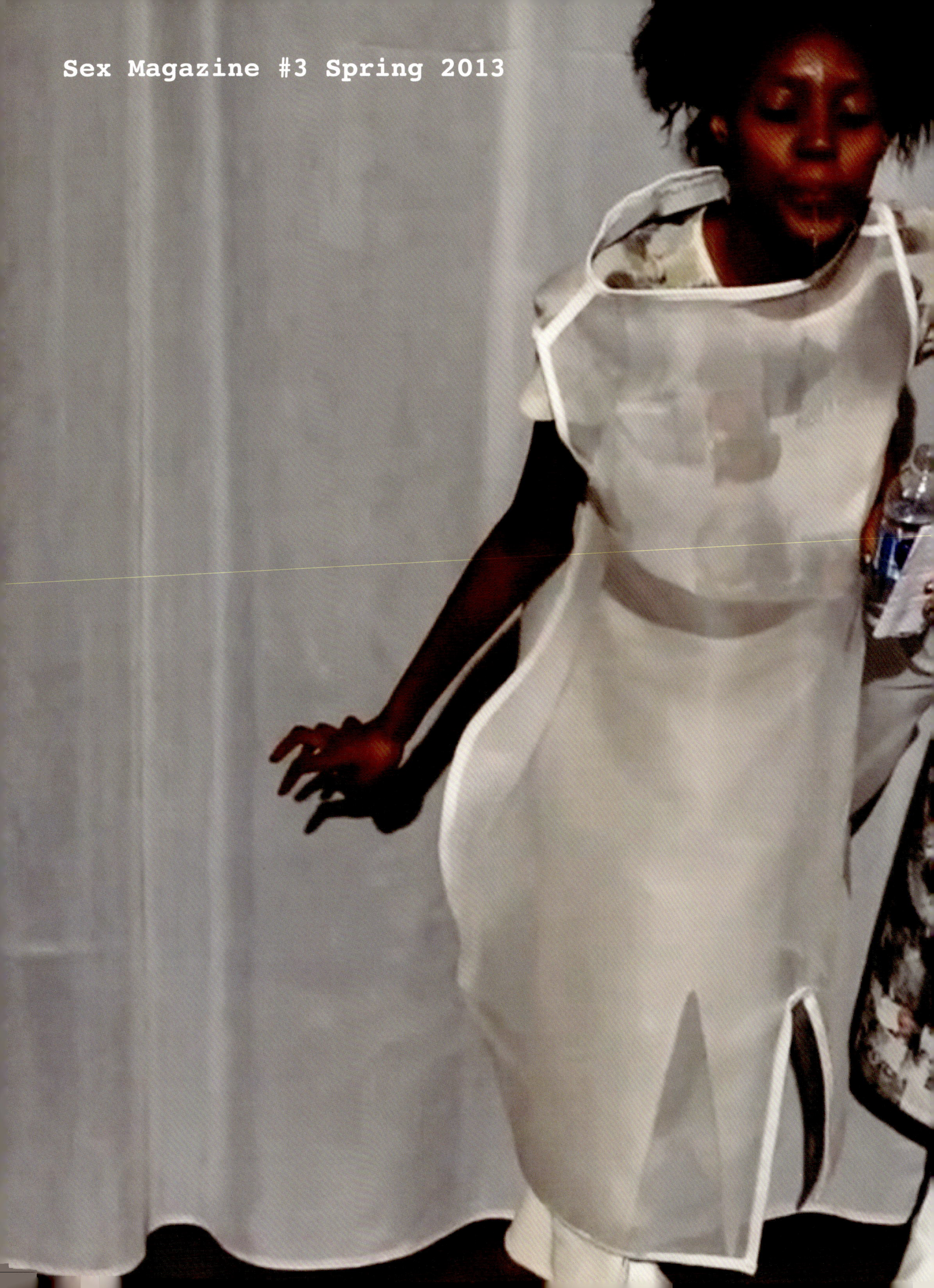

Sex Magazine #3 Spring 2013

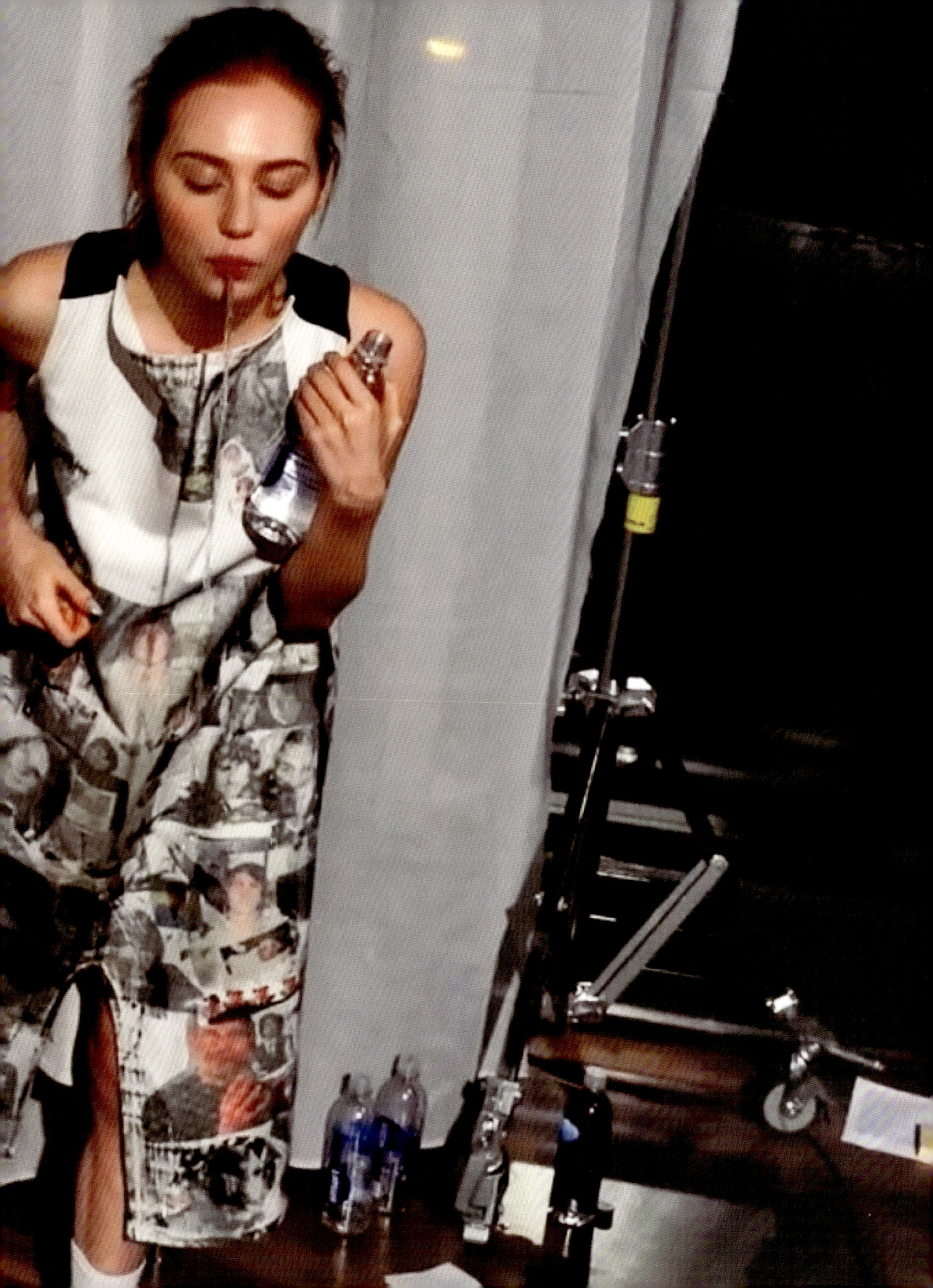

Sam Pulitzer

"Imagine you're in class trying to understand why painting is coming back on the market in 2005. Then you go to this performance and you get really high and think: why do I care about all that other shit?"

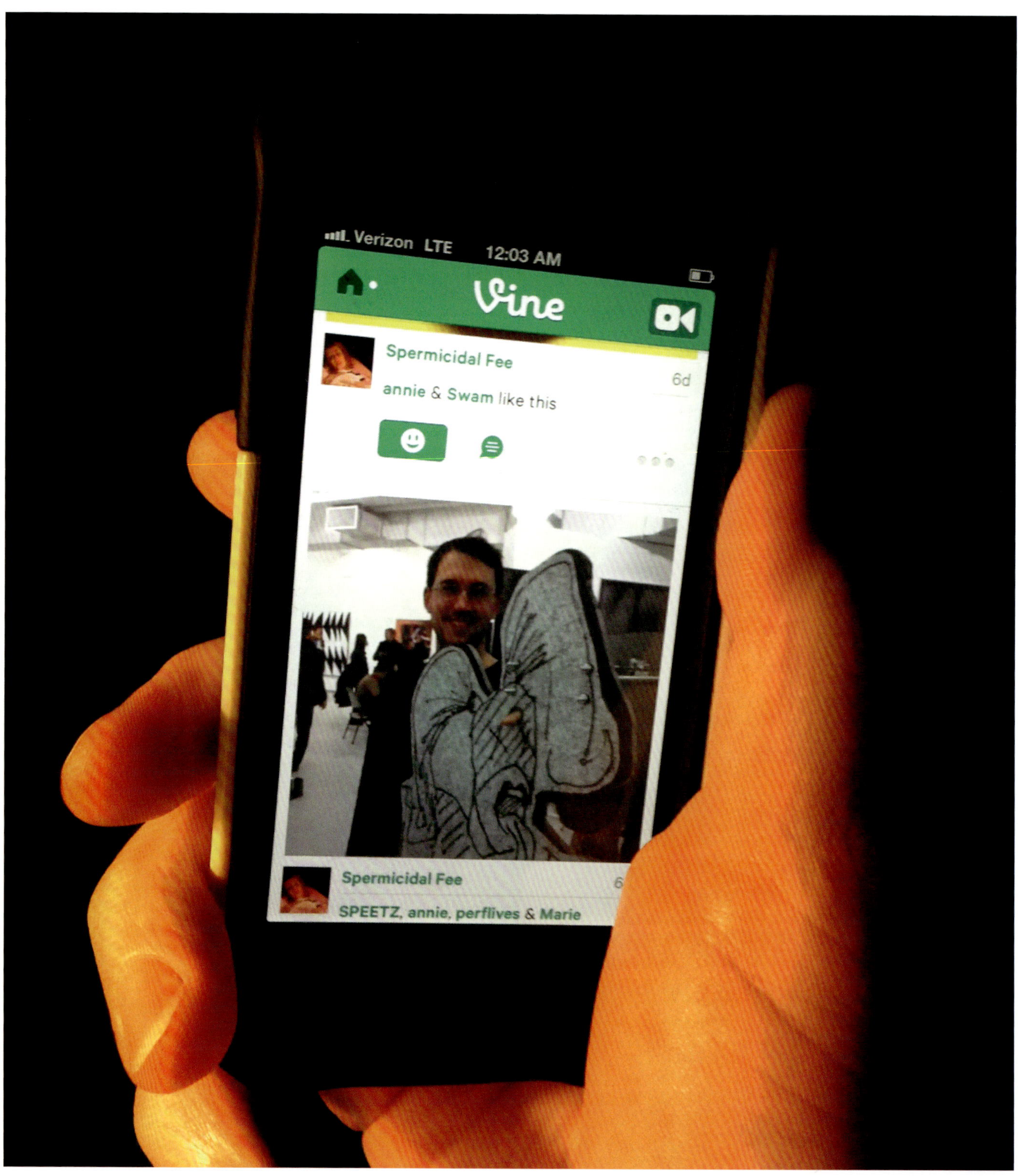

Interview by Asher Penn
Images courtesy Sam Pulitzer

I first came into contact with Sam
Pulitzer when he was a photography
student at Rhode Island School of
Design. Two years younger than me,
Sam immediately stood out from his
peers with an encyclopedic cultural
knowledge and work that was radically
different from what his colleagues
were producing. Since graduating
in 2006, Pulitzer has gone on to
make a singular impression on the
New York art world, gaining infamy
for his semi-anonymous hate-core
blog Jerry Magoo, critical writings
in magazines like Artforum, and
memorable exhibitions at artist-run
galleries including Real Fine Arts.
Pulitzer's output has consistently
manifested as a response both to his
personal life and what he sees going
on around him, using art and writing
as a tool to trespass and profane the
institutional structures that define
its distribution and reception.

**We met at RISD. Why did you decide
to go there?**
I don't know. I didn't want to go to
Bard. I wanted to be in a city, but
I didn't get into any colleges in
New York.
You wanted to study art?
No. It was between art and writing.
And then I thought maybe I should
just study art. I'm glad I did. I
think everyone I meet from liberal
arts school is okay, but they're just
not the same.
Art is more fun?
It's definitely more fun. It's got
a more exuberant sense of pleasure.
On the other hand RISD was really
conservative. At least while I was
there. RISD is a design school, so
it's got a lot of kids that are
really looking to have a career right
out of college.
Right.
School was school. I met you. I
liked Providence. It's a beautiful
place. Freshman year was delightful.
But then sophomore year when you're
in the major and you think: ugh,
this sucks.

You weren't into it.
I hated the darkroom. It made my
skin break out. But I decided I
didn't want to switch majors. I
didn't want to switch schools and
spend more time in college. I just
wanted to get out of there as soon
as I could in a way. Not that I tried
to graduate early because I didn't
like being a good student. I didn't
have a great attitude.

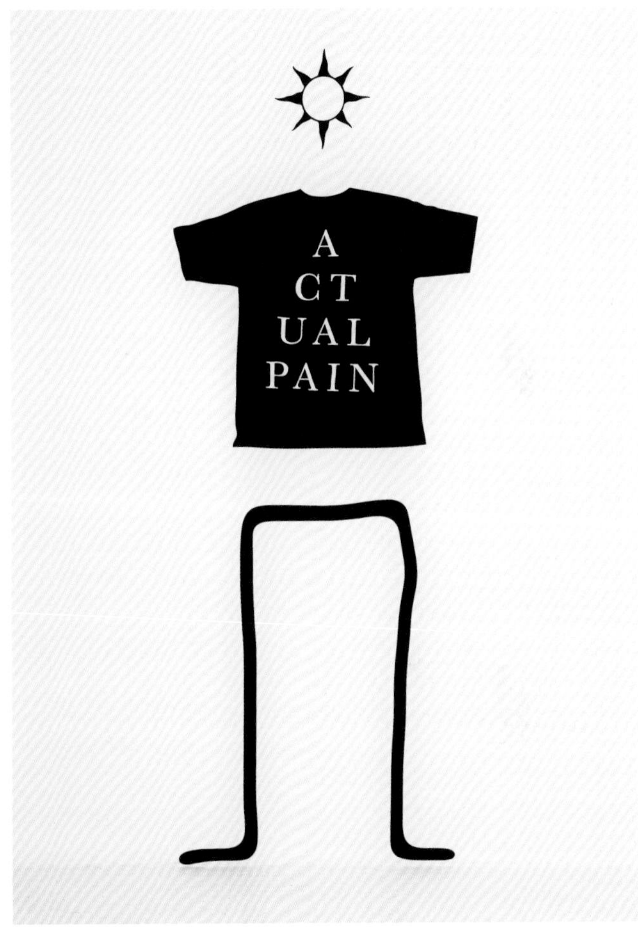

A Soundless Head, 2012.

Were you even into photography?
I don't know. I liked art. I was
very pretentious. I was very into
what you see at museums. RISD is
good in the sense that it has an okay
library. It also has a great video
library. I spent so much time there.
I also took courses at Brown. That
school sucks, too. But honestly just
being in Providence was great. Going
to see shitty screamo or noise rock
shows, that was great.

What was the story with your senior show, Community Power Walls?
I was thinking a lot about being in Providence, my experience of being in school. I was starting to be more serious about reading and understanding theory and things like that. I was starting to understand myself as an institutional subject. At the same time Providence offered all these wonderful alternatives to how creativity can be produced, outside of official institutions.

Like Fort Thunder.
Yeah. Or the Sickle, wink wink. Imagine you're in class trying to understand why painting is coming back on the market in 2005. Then you go to this performance and you get really high and think: why do I care about all that other shit? But maybe that's more of an attitude I have now than I did at that point. We were in college in the boom years. A lot of what was being praised by teachers and discussed back then was really about what was selling.

So, what was in the show?
I just bought three generic sheets of dry wall — like four by eight feet or whatever — and then I painted a really hideous mural on each one, like in a funky-café kind of manner. One was good, two were horrible. And so the two bad ones I just turned into a merch table with the mural facing down so you didn't see it. It sat on two saw horses, which I "commandeered" from the sculpture department. And then I put all of these posters on top of that, maybe also a print or two.

You put photo prints in frames right?
I was thinking about this tension between rough, austere work and the framing that happens in institutions. I had this meeting with the dean at one point, I think just to get the alcohol for the opening. Anyway, in his office I saw all of these framed artworks. It was work by the good students. I wasn't a good student. I thought: fuck these good students. I'm going to frame my work the same way. I wanted to pickle my work in these same frames.

What were the images you framed?
They were like half analog, half digital photo collages. Some of them were hideous as fuck, and others had a more artisanal, sophisticated touch. I framed and hung all of them on the drywall and throughout the space.

There was so much pressure on those senior thesis shows I remember.
I was just having fun. I think I just had a chip on my shoulder that didn't want to conform. For me it went from: why the fuck am I in school? To: why do I want to be an artist? To: why am I in school to be an artist? And finally: how do I find an effective compromise? And then there's the show. How do you find pleasure in being subjected? I'm very romantic at heart, actually. I felt pinioned by this gargantuan school that just wanted my money.

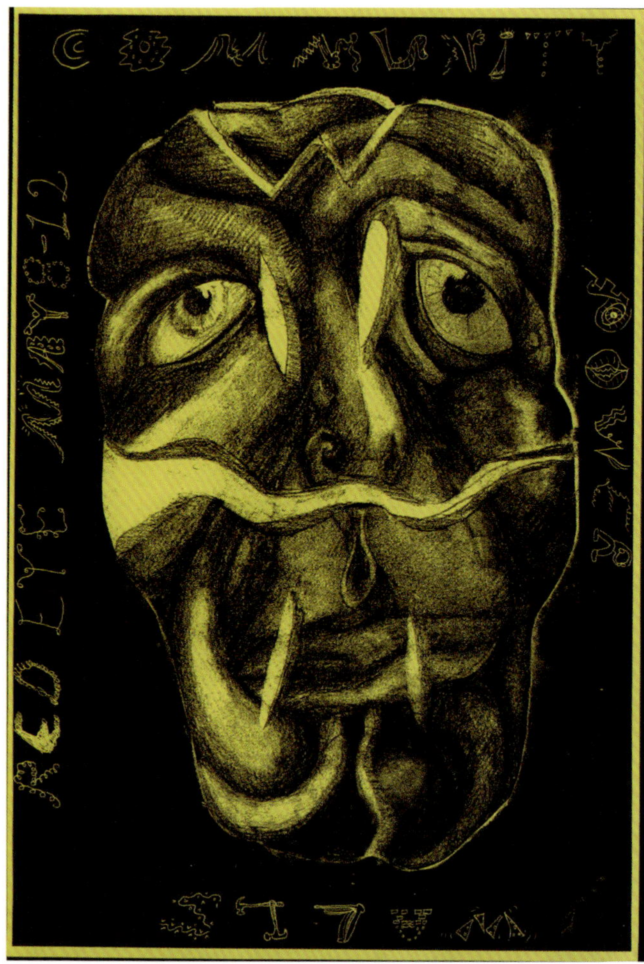

Community Power Walls (Poster No. 10), 2006.

      Sam Pulitzer by Asher Penn

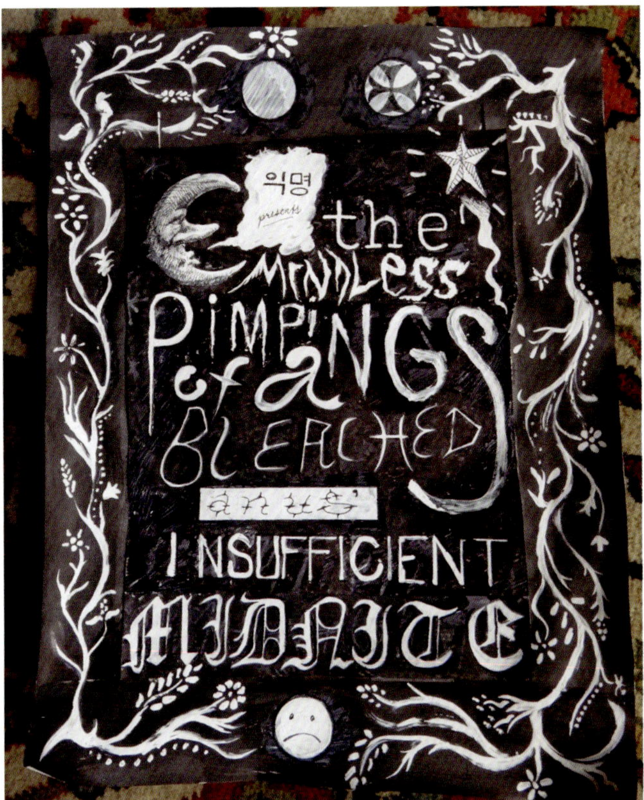
The Mindless Pimpings of a Bleached Anus'
Insufficient Midnite (in progress), 2013.

Kinda like Stockholm Syndrome.
It's more like: how can you break out
of a prison if you don't know you're
in it? Everything is about learning.
You got to school, you learn. Does
that make us get more jaded about the
universe? Or do we get more absorbed
in the Veils of Maya, to speak like
a hippie? I wanted to make work like
that. That was what I liked. I like
work that's about being a little
fucked up, but still having the
appearance of intelligence. I mean,
I do have four eyes.

Like a fucked up dork?
That's my psychic dilemma right there.
It's just my careerism. I want to be
fucked up, but I'm trying to find a
efficient compromise.

**Then you moved to New York and worked
at Greene Naftali. How was that?**
It wasn't an easy job. It felt like
getting paid to go to grad school.
I learned a lot. You don't learn
anything in college. You learn when
you're actually doing the thing you
want to be doing.

**What were you learning at the
gallery?**
I learned how the fiction of
contemporary art is created. I
learned how to write a press release
in an hour.

You wrote them in an hour?
It's easy to write a press release.
You're wearing a mask when you write
it. It's anonymous. I mean, not
really anonymous, but anonymous
enough. I think my best writing has
been press releases.

How come?
I like when writing is instrumental-
ized. I like when it's put to use.
That's what the blog was.

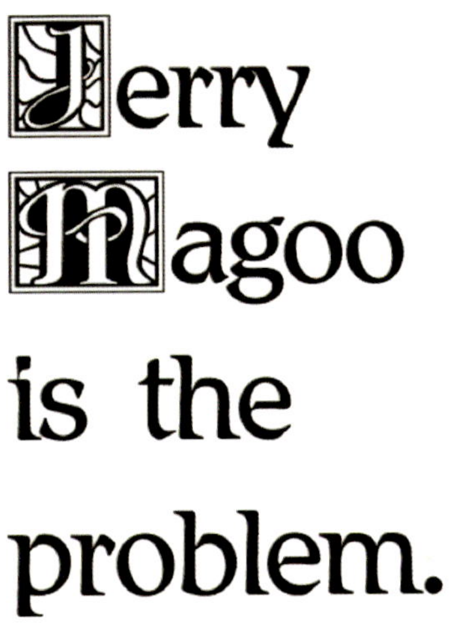

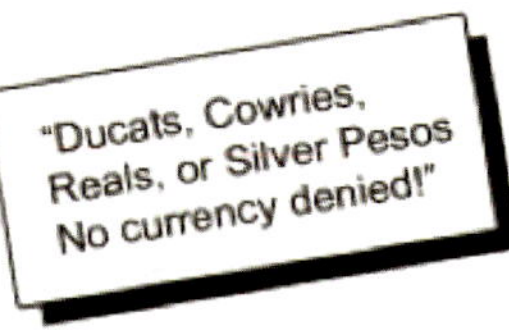

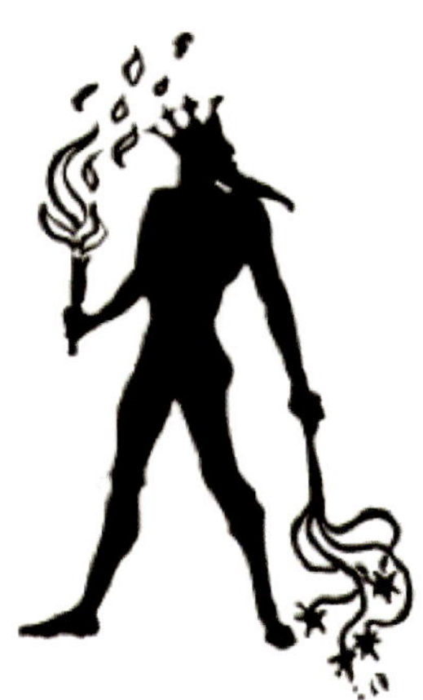

Jerry Magoo, 2011.

**You were trying to instrumentalize
your writing?**
I was trying to become a better
writer. I felt that I better start
thinking about what I want to be
doing as an artist or something like
that. It was totally self-serving.
The whole blog form is made to
market. Every brand that exists has a
blog to promote themselves. For me,
honestly, it's been a promotional
tool. Granted, now I'm disclosing
the fact that I've done it. Everyone
knows it. They've known about it for
a long time.

There weren't that many art blogs around at the time, right? Like, there was Art Fag City, Contemporary Art Daily...

Jerry Magoo started out around the same time as Contemporary Art Daily, and the difference was simple: one blog wore white clothes, one blog wore black clothes. One was a prep, and one was a despondent goth, or something like that. If you want to be a "good artist" you want the positive feedback of seeing yourself on Contemporary Art Daily. But if you're on Magoo, it's negative feedback. In a way, it all came out of listening to noise music. I like listening to negative feedback as a thing that comes out of my speakers. I love the positive feedback too, sometimes — nice harmonic scales. But in the end, it's all low level cybernetics, volunteer police work, to point fingers toward the writing of "better" behavioral procedures.

You fielded a lot of negative feedback. People would always ask me if I knew who it was and their next question would be, "Why are they doing that?"

The criticism was always this: you should be more discursive. You should be more self-reflexive. This was coming from people that studied at the Whitney ISP program. But look: I'm a fucking blogger, I'm trash, I'm sub-human. I adapted my writing to the form. I didn't want to transcend the blog form at all. I wanted to make writing that was halfway between a shitty emo reaction to the world around me, and all the back talk that clogged up my brain after working at a gallery for a few years, mixed with the now commonplace habit of looking at too much art online.

In some ways it was like irresponsible criticism.

One person compared me to a terrorist, which maybe I am. I just like using words for their power, as opposed to their capacity to drum up pleasant visions of what's going on. I don't like pleasant visions.

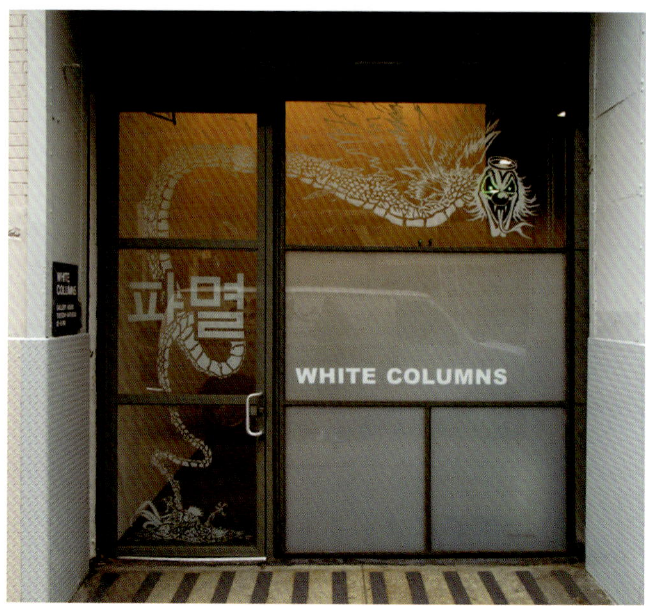

Ruin (with Bill Hayden), 7th White Columns Annual, 2013.

You once told me that band Brokencyde was an inspiration.

I remember first seeing that band online and thinking: is this what these fucking kids are doing these days? It was just disgusting, horrible. It wasn't even well crafted. It seemed imbecilic. It had this rough quality that was completely unpolished, completely unsophisticated. It lacked everything that you'd expect from someone that had, say, gone to college. Its affinity with Magoo should be obvious.

Your first show at Real Fine Arts was called Hogg. The show was centered around these digital photo collages.

I based that show on what I was seeing people we went to school with doing online at the time — people had these blogs and they would just spend hours posting images on MySpace and Facebook. It was utterly pathetic.

Now that I think about it, the show was kind of laid out like a blog scroll.

Yeah. The narrative of the show was Hogg — the story of this little child who just gets fucked by this group of people. The first image in the show is an angelic boy, and the last image is a sculpture of an angelic boy in a cemetery.

I read Hogg after you did that show. It's a really intense book.
At the end of the book it's just this boy and Hogg at the end of their adventure. Hogg is going to take this boy to the middle of nowhere and just turn him into a dog, a sex slave — so the boy walks away. Aside from maybe this anti-coupling message, There's no real moral. It's just porn.
After reading the book I liked that I could think of them as illustrations.
I wanted to use art as a way to think about narrative and subjectivity without such a formal bearing on the custodial traditions of painting or sculpture. I was seeing all these fucking goody-two-shoes artists around me. Like preppy, post-Krebber,what-the-fuck painters with some sort of intellectual vibe. I had no patience for that. I wanted to be a different type of artist. Since my teen years, I've spent a lot of my time looking at conceptual art and thinking "blah blah blah, the remaining possibilities." I wanted to make a show that had something more rooted in what I always understood about that work, about conceptual art. But really what they got was something like if Mike Kelley had died a sad blogger.

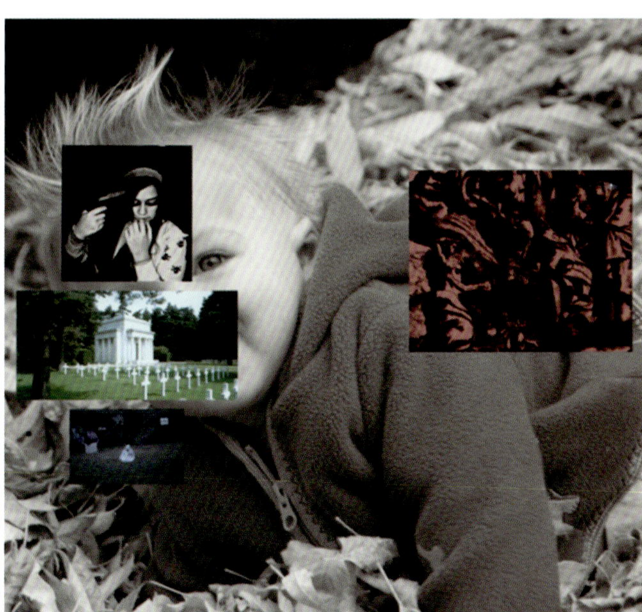

Untitled (Hogg), 2009.

What about your second show at Real Fine Arts, Hogg 2? That was kind of a sequel, right?
For that I was trying to install a very problematized discotheque, or something like that. A broken discotheque.
Is that why you used lasers?
Yeah. These were lasers that don't move, that die all the time, that just point to these ear gauges on the floor.
Wait, why ear gauges? Was this a Brokencyde thing?
I position these gauges to prevent one from looking into a space outside from its gallery setting. And the disco experience is about producing an inside. You go out to discotheques and you get caressed in a bathtub of lasers — it's great. It's a communal situation. The art world has these similar environments that produce an inside — a very exempt, specialized inside, where a particular social economy of touch is brokered. The one thing about the laser works which I'm most proud of is the way they touch the viewer. How many artworks out there actually touch people that come to see them?
I always catch you touching art. You're not supposed to touch it, let alone have it touch you.
The lasers do, you can put your hand in the way and they're touching you. It's also about looking: how do you look at a laser? You can see a shine emitted from the laser device, and the laser point where the beam meets some solid surface. You don't really see a laser beam until it's interrupted. So a laser can define an inside space. How do you look from a particular inside to an outside? Maybe these terms are confused nowadays.
You've been doing a lot of work with decals lately. Those touch the gallery walls. Is there a connection?
No doubt. But I landed on that material largely thanks to its convenience.

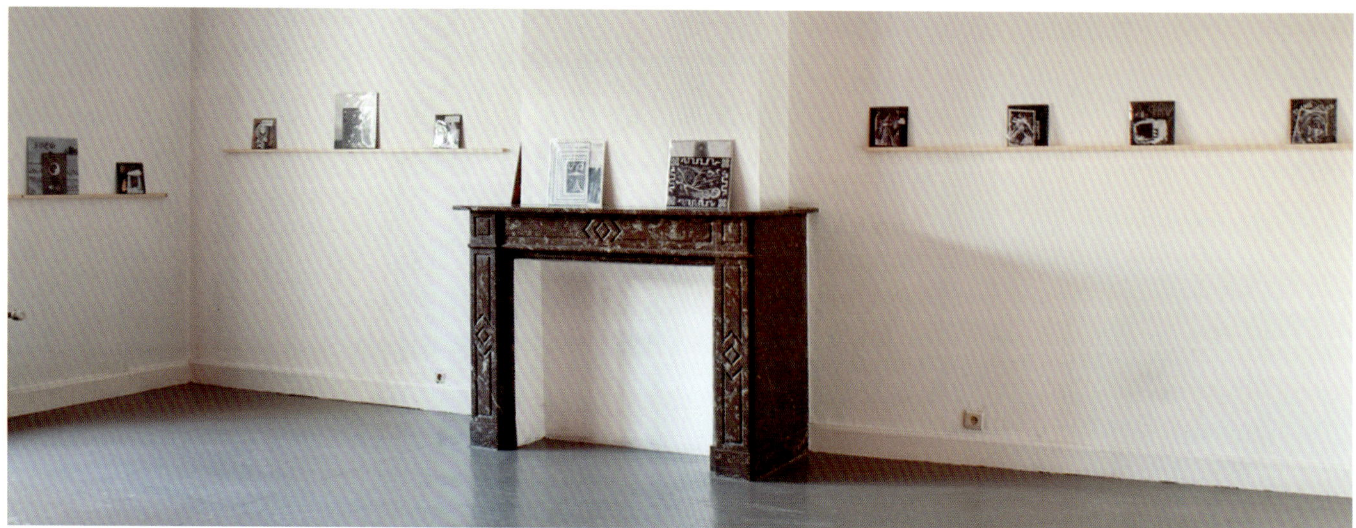

Sotoso Installation, Brussels, 2012.

Your most recent show in Brussels looked a lot like a boutique record store. You buy a lot of vinyl right?
Yeah, I do. It's an Achilles' heel. I can love a record as much as I love art, which is cheesy. I hate a lot of shit. I'm pretty despondent about some things. For example I hate shopping. When I do it, I like to buy things that are like a uniform I can put on. But when it comes to buying records, that's different. I get immense pleasure listening to particular moods that some people are capable of producing.

Were the records in the show ones you'd already bought?
I owned most of them, I was looking to sell them. Then I thought I could sell these for ten dollars apiece online, or I could make them into a show. I wanted to make an installation that was a record store, but barely a record store at that — a broken one like the discothèque. I took all the seriousness of these musicians who made these records that I really cared about, and the art and packaging of it all — and I used it to problematize my work, specifically these drawings where my actual hand is present. I was inflating their value, in a way, but it was intended as a comment on the way "less serious" cultural interests aid the marketability of contemporary art like a happy parasite.

And your drawings were inserted in the record sleeves?
Yeah, they're just slipped in the plastic sleeves. When I graduated college I was working on drawings. You've seen them. And the drawings in Brussels are basically made the same way, with the same material.

I wanted to ask you about something recent. You did a text piece at this rave, Lixxxtapussy, using that Dickface font Bill Hayden and Nicolas Guagnini made.
A thousand dicks in that pussy.

Ha ha, yeah. It reminded me how there has been this thread of poetry in your work for a while.
I love poetry, yeah. It's beautiful. I'm a bit of a philistine with poetry now. I read it when I was a teenager. I wanted to study writing, so I've always given a little bit of interest to it. I never studied it in an academic sense, and feel sorry for those that have.

I feel like in the last decade a lot of artists explored poetry. It felt like an open field.
So is art. So is everything.

Yeah, you're right.
You have to economize what you're doing to make it work. You have to bring it to life, bring it in to being. You have to offer it presence, you know what I mean? Plumb it from absence to presence. ☺

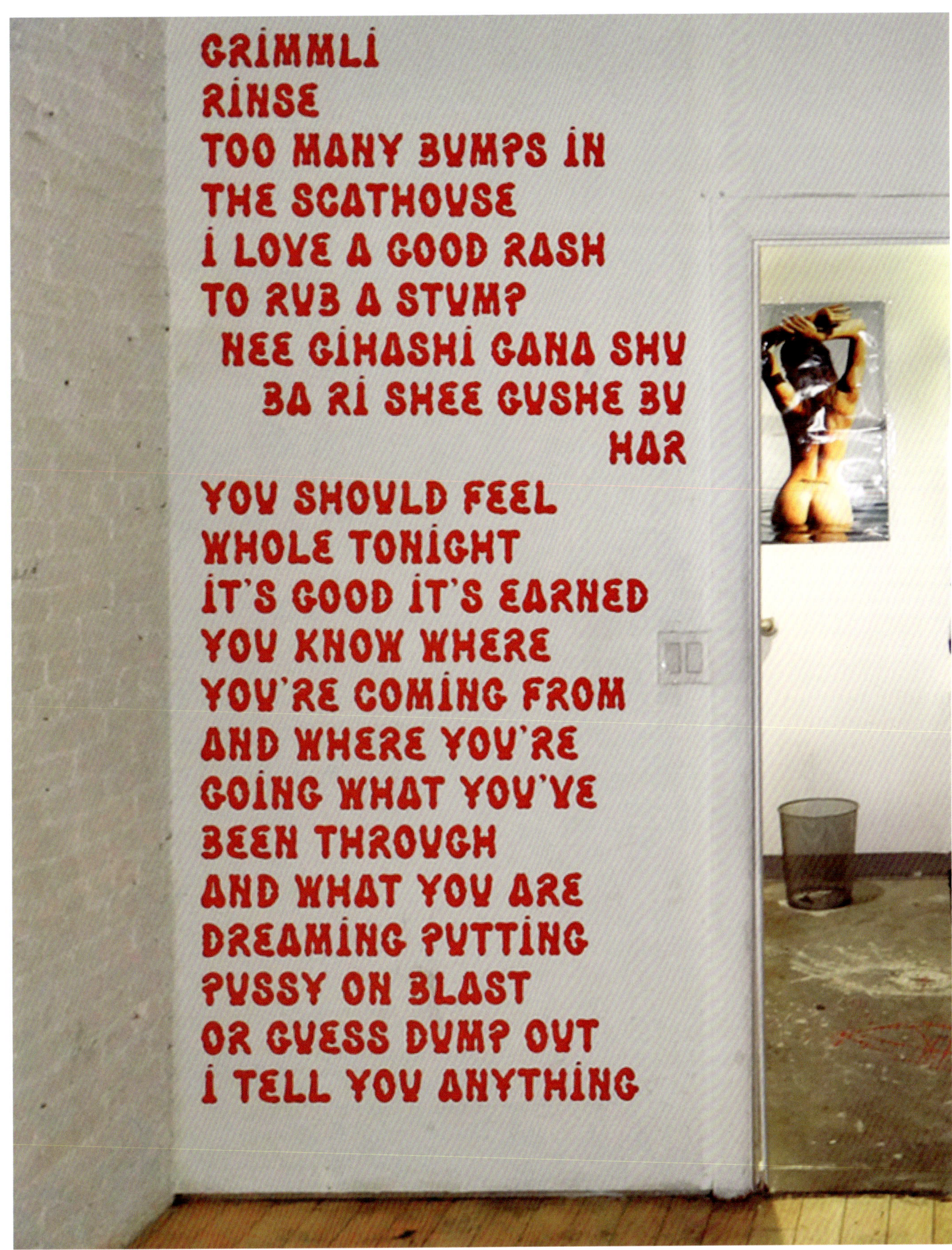

Ha (with Bill Hayden), Lixxxtapussy, 2013.

Total Freedom

"No one really wants to be comfortable. I take that back.
People are excited by being made uncomfortable."

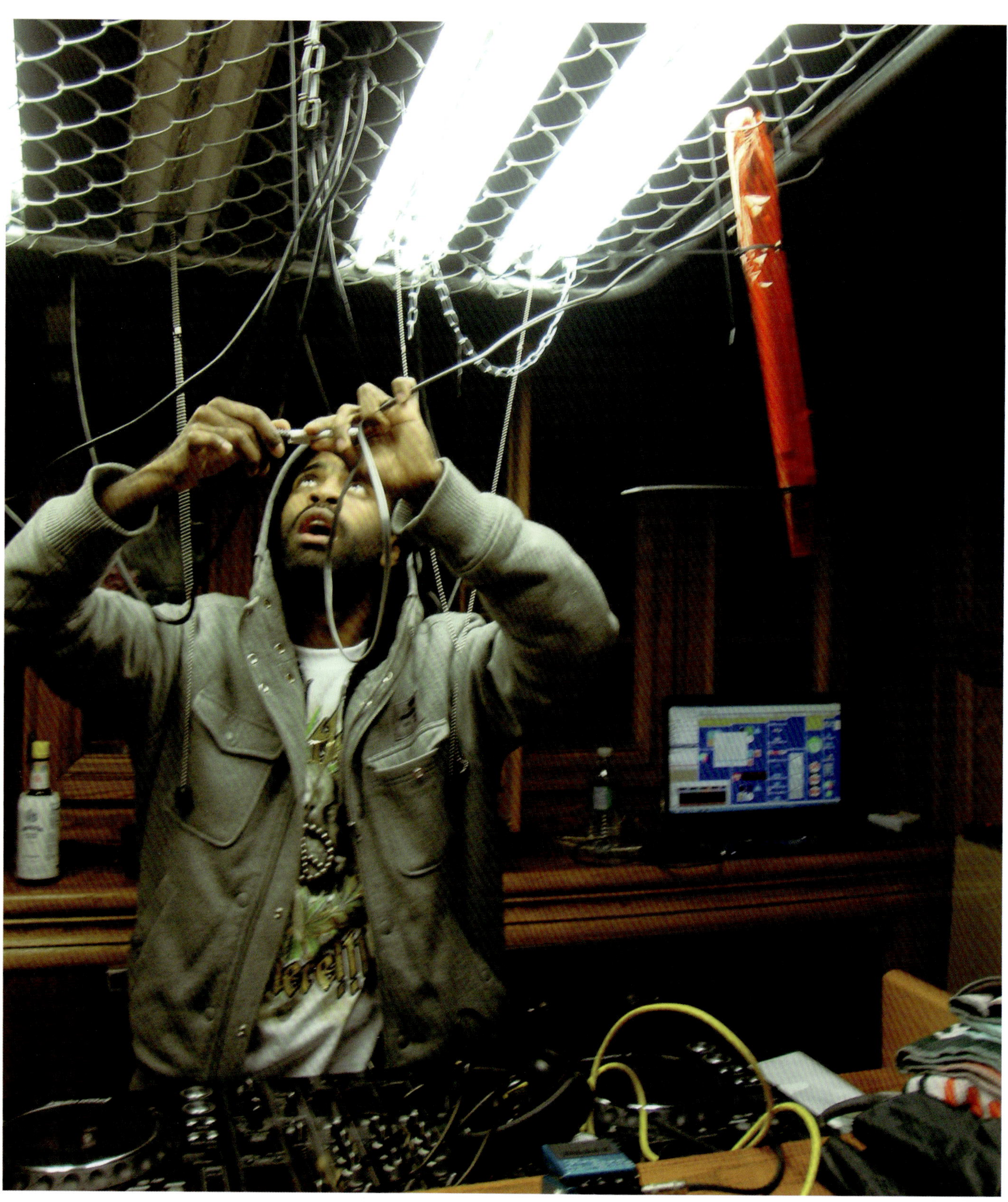

Interview by Asher Penn
Portrait by Liz Rywelski

In the midst of a boom in dance
music culture, Ashland Mines, a.k.a.
Total Freedom, stands out.
While fulfilling the civic duties of
any active DJ today — parties, mix
tapes and remixes — Mines' output has
eschewed convention and genre in
favor of new sounds and experiences.
Coming to electronic music via
experimental noise, Mines' approach
is dictated by his moniker —
exploration, discovery, and freedom.

How did you first get into music?
I grew up playing music. I grew up
with instruments.
**What kind of instruments did you
play?**
All the kids in my family learned
stringed instruments — the Suzuki
method. I played cello. Everybody in
my family played something like that.
Did you guys ever play together?
Yeah.
That's cool.
It is.
Where are you from?
I grew up in New Jersey. I moved to
the Seattle area with my family when
I was like 16.
Did you go to Olympia and Yoyoagogo?
Yeah I would take the bus.
**That was a really good time for
that stuff.**
Yeah, it was. I was happy when I
moved out there. In Jersey, I lived
in the country — it was suburban,
borderline rural. I had to pull a
whole lot of shenanigans to go to any
show. To see a band or go buy records
was just difficult. Then I moved to
this college town in Washington,
there were a few record stores, a few
all-ages venues. I was so happy to
be around that. I had also grown up
thinking K records was really cool,
so I was really happy to be able to
access that easily.
**I had a lot of fun when I went there
too. It would be a house party with a
live band in a living room. Everybody
would dance. The scene was really
good on a social level.**
I would agree, for sure.

How did you end up in Chicago?
I went to Chicago on vacation just
to visit and never went back. Chicago
was way more fun than Seattle.
Were you going to college there?
No, never.
Did you start DJing in Chicago?
I had been playing a bit already.
What were you playing?
I was just playing whatever was cool
at the time. I played a lot of weird
American folk stuff and noise. That
was my general area. I worked forever
to get DJ gigs. It was like at a show
between bands or at a restaurant
during brunch. I played at precisely
one nightclub in Chicago the whole
time I was there. I would put on
shows on a small scale whenever I had
friends in town that needed a place
to play.

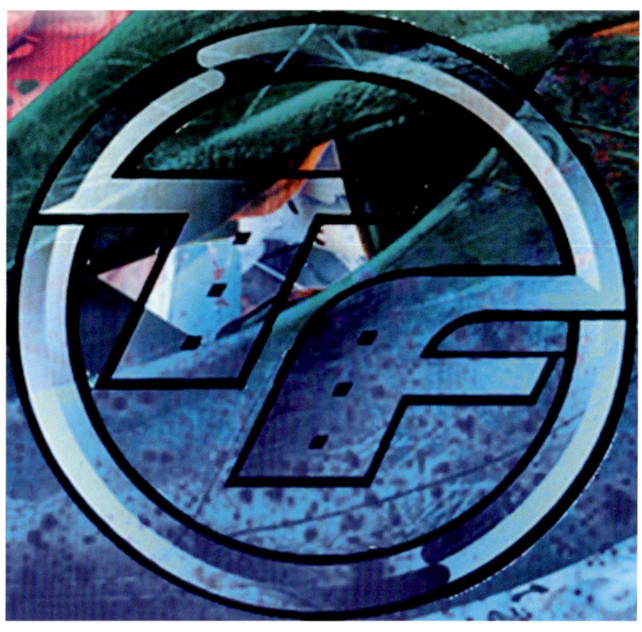

Total Freedom Artwork, 2010.

**There is still an element of noise
music when you DJ.**
When I started DJing I played
noise stuff all the time. Later on
it wasn't a decision to keep it
around...it just happened naturally.
The world developed, there were new
things I had never heard before that
were exciting to me, and I started
playing them in addition to other
sounds that were interesting to me.

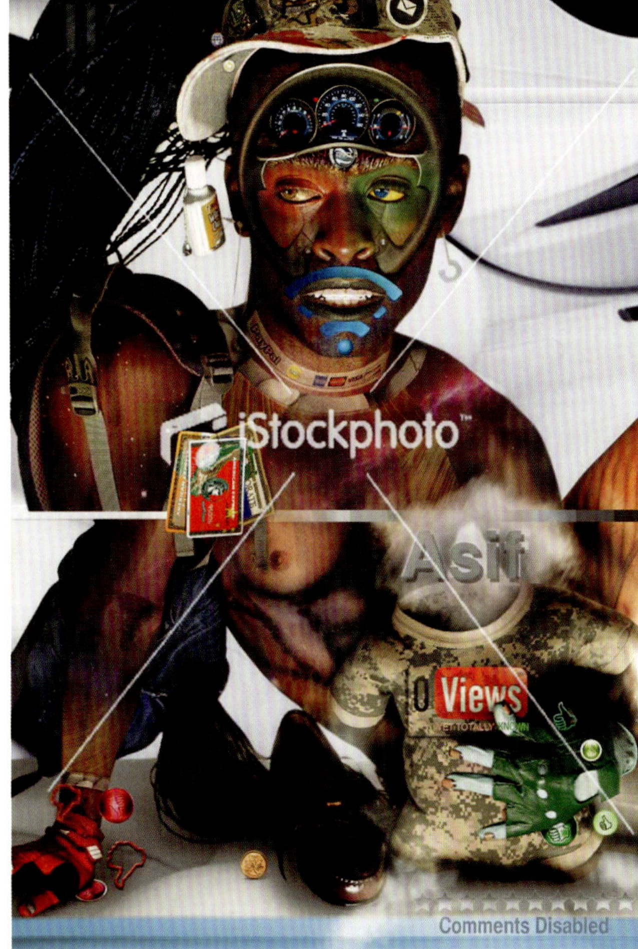
Total Freedom, Ryan's Web, W Magazine, 2010.
Photo: Ryan Trecartin

What were the sounds that you were finding interesting?
Just stuff I found on the internet. For a while I didn't know what the internet really was, as far as music was concerned. I didn't know how to use Soul Seek and Napster really at all. I wasn't really diving in terms of mining data off the internet. When I finally figured out what the internet was, what I saw were all these different access points to music that I had previously never heard of, never seen. That was really exciting to me in 2005, 2006.

Were you sharing your sounds on MySpace and stuff, too?
I was participating, but only because I felt like it was good karma to do that. I still don't think anyone has really downloaded anything from those places that I used to publish.

I remember seeing you in one of Ryan Trecartin's films. How did you meet?
I met Ryan, Rhett, and Lizzie by accident at a leather bar. We got along really great, and then they moved to Philly. We kept in touch in terms of being friends and also collaborating a little bit. Eventually they moved back to LA.

I've always felt there were parallels between your music and Ryan's.
I am definitely a fan of the music that Ryan makes and the music that Lizzie Fitch makes. I wish there were correlations between our aesthetics that way. I just don't think I am on the same plane at all. Ryan's a jazz musician and I am a trash picker.

Was Wildness your first night in LA?
It wasn't Wildness, but Wildness was the first one I cared about at all. I just made a lot of choices along the way. Generally before that it was roll down a hill and see what it ends up like. I made choices about who I was doing it with and where and what the goals were for the experience that people would have in there. And it worked.

What were the goals?
We just wanted to give something that made sense in the space, worked with what the space was already giving off. Something that anyone would want to come to, but no one would feel completely comfortable at. No one really wants to be comfortable. I take that back. People are excited by being made uncomfortable.

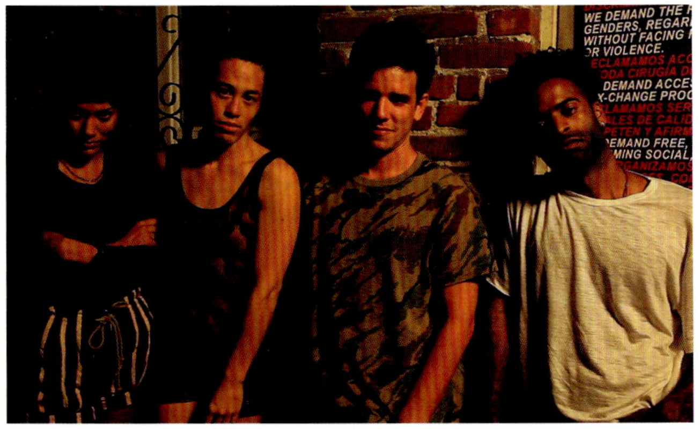
Still from WILDNESS, 2012: Wu Tsang, NGUZUNGUZU (Asma Maroof and Daniel Pieda), and Total Freedom.

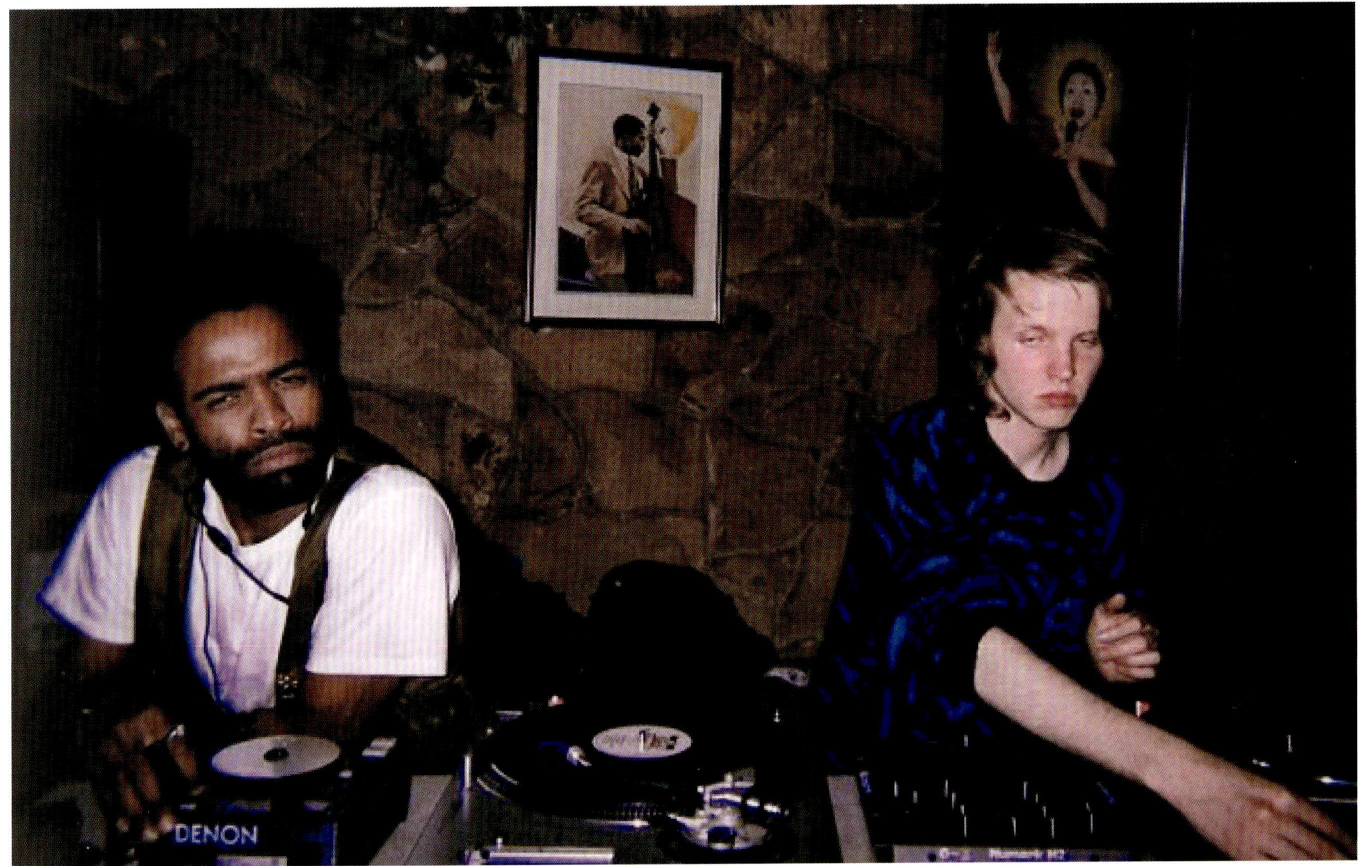

Total Freedom & SFV Acid, Grown, 2012. Photo: Ashley Huizenga

What was the music like?
We were all playing a lot of stuff and playing at the same time. Me and the other regular DJs, Asma and Daniel. I would always bring lots of electronics and stuff to play over the set as much as possible.
It was a weekly party right? I've always heard that is really hard to pull off.
It was a struggle every week. We would walk out of there with $20, and half the time some of us were like, "What the fuck are we doing?" But it was free and the drinks were cheap. We wanted it to be free. For everyone.
How did it change over time?
Well, it became popular. Eventually, here were too many people there, which was really good for the bar and really fun for us, but really different than how it had started out...which was a lot of fog and 5 people in the room and me and the other DJs being really weird.

What was Grown?
Grown was like the opposite of Wildness. Wildness stopped really abruptly in a way we didn't plan — it landed on us. I had already planned on doing this new weekly thing. Grown was just a different environment, different clientele and different management style. It was a jazz club that was really comfortable and cozy. It was sedated and comfortable and chatty — like a party that was based around having conversations and cute girls. That was the idea. Come and talk to cute girls or feel like a cute girl.
That sounds fun. What kind of music would you play?
Classic house. It was all inspired by Zane Reyolds a.k.a. SFV Acid. He would bring his equipment and play live occasionally if I could force him into it. Then I would DJ and he would DJ. He had these 2 friends that would come and DJ every week — really intense vinyl-head teenagers. That was that vibe.

Mustache Flyer, Brian Skiff, 2013.

What year was this?
2010 I think. I would say things
really intensely changed for a large
group of people, not just my friends
and people directly involved, when
the bar where Grown was closed.
Basically, everything in LA closes
at 1:45 AM and that's kind of the
time everyone wants to go to bed here
anyway — it's special to stay up
till 6 AM on a weeknight. You could
smoke there...it was kind of lawless,
but also really clean. Miki's place
was insane, it felt like another
planet. I am sure there is nothing
like that going on at all. Once that
place closed droves of people had to
replace that with something. I have
no idea what it is, but cokeheads
have to go somewhere.

**How did you start playing at Mustache
Mondays?**
I heard from a friend that there
was this new party downtown that we
should check out. I ended up going by
myself. I saw this stripper I thought
was really cute and I thought "Shit,
I need to work here." I found out
who was managing the party and asked
him if I could DJ. I started DJing
there every week. That slowly turned
into me sideways booking people even
though it wasn't my party.

So it kind of became a hub.
It is the hub for sure. I have to go
there tonight. It has been five and
a half years that I have been going
there every week that I'm in town.
It's also the club where I learned to
DJ the way I DJ today.

What did you learn?
I learned to beat match and play
dance music for people who want to
dance. That was not something I
understood or even thought about
before really. I definitely got that
idea from Telfar. He got me booked
for some show with him, the first
night at Santos I think. Before that
point I would play electronic stuff
but never in a way you would assume
a DJ does. I didn't know anything at
all about mixing and putting beats
together at all.

**Whenever I see you play it always
feels like a really different set
each time.**
Oh my god, please print that. My
biggest fear ever is that people will
see me playing and say he's playing
the same set he played last week. I
have never prepared a set ever, but
sometimes something cool will happen
by accident, and I will end up doing
it every time I play for months. I
am always terrified that someone is
going to clock me on that.

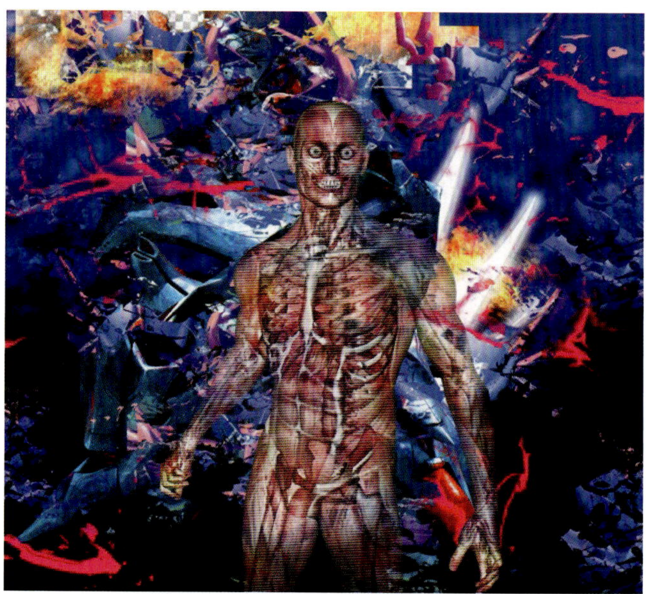

Blasting Voice, Teenage Teardrops, 2012.

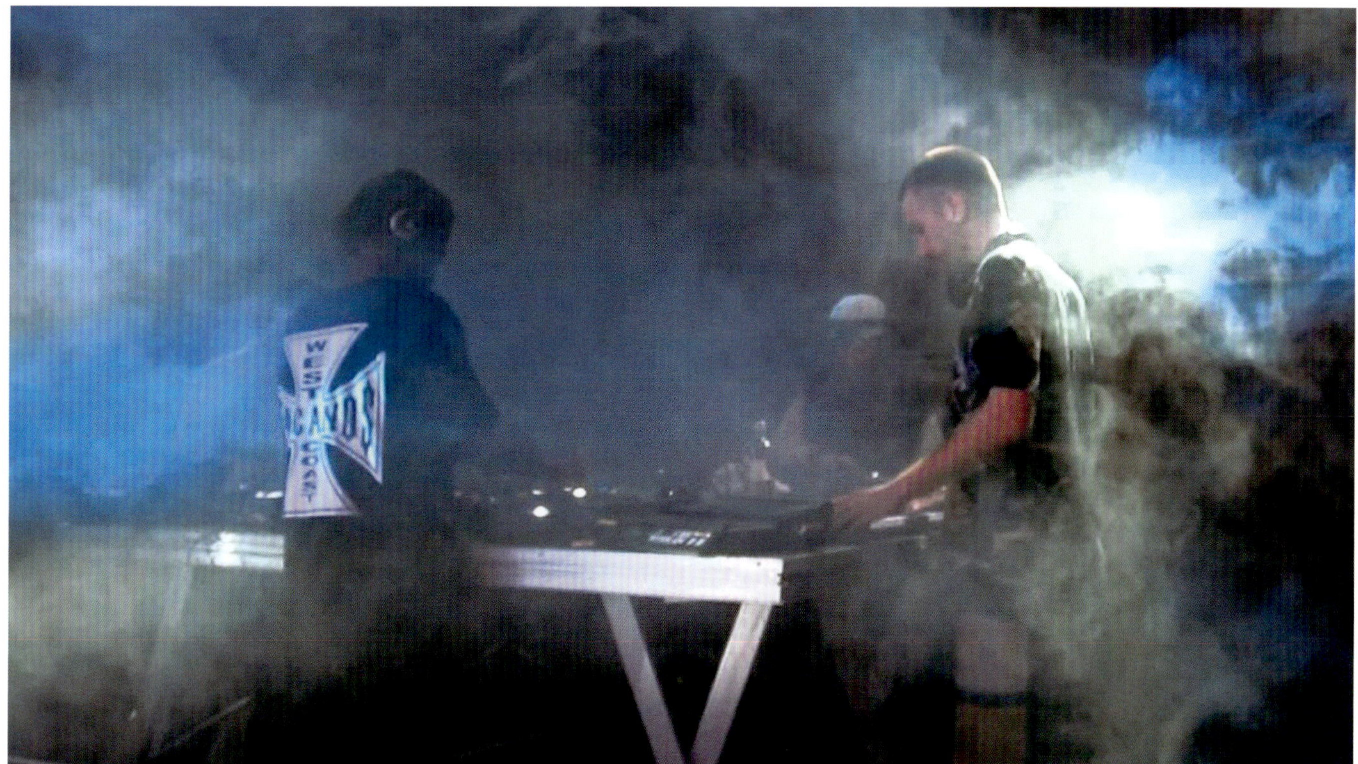

Nguzunguzu, Total Freedom, and Kingdom, Bologna, 2012.

You don't prepare for your sets at all?
I try to always have new music to play, but I don't put together a set list or anything.

How much time do you spend looking for music?
At the moment, none. I'm so old and bored by the idea of looking through files on the internet that some teenagers threw up there. I have been doing that for so long. Everything I play now is something my friend made or something my friend found and gave me...or something that came from the time I spent on the internet in 2006. I can't tell, maybe I am in a phase. I think sometimes it is not the right way to act, given my job.

You think that a DJ should be constantly looking for new music?
I am a DJ that doesn't really make music, so, yeah, I am supposed to be digging. In 2013 I haven't like, for instance, looked for any new hip hop. It is just not there, I can't do it.

No new obscurities.
Nothing, not even anything obscure. I don't even know. Maybe the springtime will bring it out.

I remember your Opening Ceremony mix. You had this YouTube video of this girl singing a cappella and you filled it out with beats. I thought it was a really cool way to mix fidelities.
That particular song was this B celebrity, Teyana Taylor. I am a huge fan of hers. That was something she recorded one morning when she woke up or something. It's cool that we all have access to those ridiculously private experiences and productions. Dealing with that kind of material is kind of a new thing. I mean, it's not that new anymore, but it's still kind of new.

Last question. Have you always loved nightclubs?
I don't know about always, but I definitely do. I see no end in that. It's like this big mix of different emotions my brain is driven to by being in just the simplest most basic club. Like, just a fog machine and some rotating light, some darkness and a speaker. There is a lot to think about, a lot for my brain to play with. ☺

Solomon Bothwell & KCHUNG Radio
"We've lowered the bar."

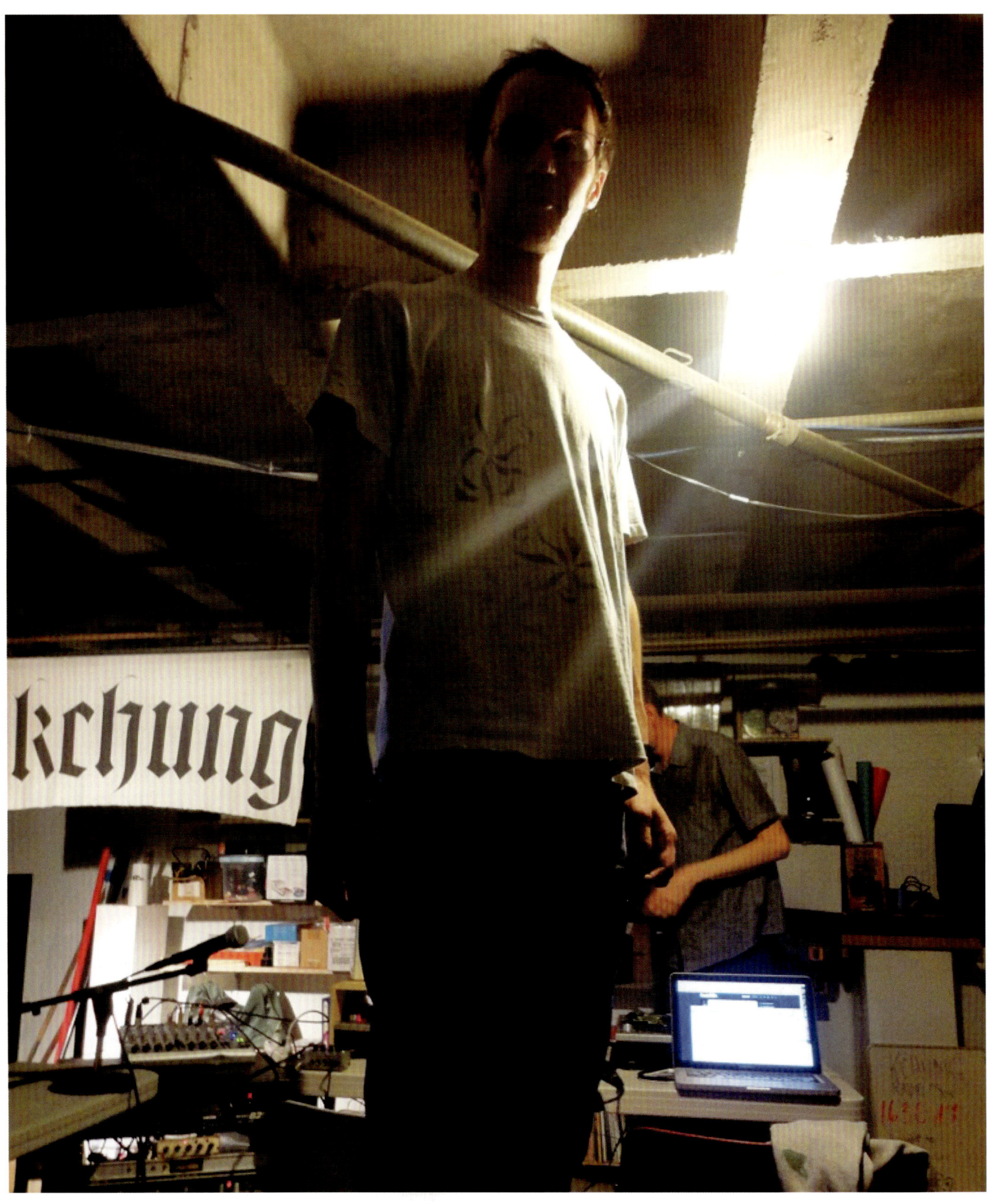

Interview by Asher Penn
Portrait by Cali Thornhill DeWitt

KCHUNG Radio is an independent radio station based in Los Angeles. Founded in the summer of 2011 by Solomon Bothwell, KCHUNG Radio has gone from broadcasting on the streets, to hosting over 63 shows and 140 hours of original programming a month, which can be streamed live online, or heard IRL on the radio waves of Chinatown. With an organizational structure that defies the conventions of artist-run spaces or non-profits KCHUNG Radio has in less than two years shown the potential of radio in the new millennium and established itself as an essential hub within Los Angeles' creative community.

Hey Solomon?
Hey man.
How is it going?
Good. I just got a new apartment, so I'm pretty excited about being out there.
Where is it?
It's in Chinatown.
Is it walking distance from the radio station?
Yeah, two blocks.
Where did you live before?
I lived in my studio for a while, which is next door to the radio station. I've kind of distanced myself a little bit now that I've got an apartment. Before that I lived in Hollywood.
What do you do in your studio?
I do fabrication for artists, musicians, and galleries. The studio is sort of a workshop for that. I have a wood shop and an electronics workbench. Lately I've been working for a lot of musicians, modifying gear and stuff like that.
What kind of modifications to the gear are you doing?
I'm working for this guy who has these samplers from the 80s that used floppy disks. I'm just replacing the floppy drives with floppy drive emulators that use an SD card. You can have 100 floppy disks on one SD card that you load in instead of needing a grocery bag full of disks.

How did you get into electronics?
I guess when I was in college, but not through class or anything. I met a couple of guys who were older — one of them was this homeless guy named Steve who was this total fucking genius. You could just pick some arbitrary integrated circuit, tell him the name of it, and he could recite the data sheet to you. I had this other friend who was into radio stuff who would travel all over the world fixing stuff for people. After school I kind of stopped doing the electronics stuff for a while.

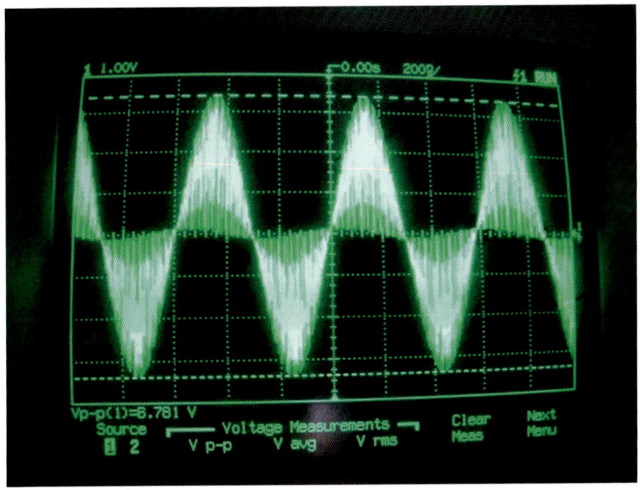

KCHUNG Radio's Modulated Carrier Wave, 2012.

What did you study in college?
I kind of dropped in and out of school so I studied a lot of different stuff. I'm really close to finishing a bunch of degrees. I was in a music program for a while, then I switched into technocultural studies. And then I decided to take art history on top of that; I tried to add philosophy, too. They are all pretty much finished, but I've been in and out of school for forever.
All at the same school?
I've been to a million different schools. I went through this phase where I figured out all the loopholes to take classes on different campuses in different departments. Now I've maxed out my units and I still don't have any degrees. It's really fucking stupid.

Did you do any college radio stuff?
A little bit. At UC Davis I had a
radio show for a while. I helped
out with the studio engineering when
bands would come in to play live
shows or record.
What was your show?
It was a late-night thing where
I played free jazz and modern comp.
I enjoyed that quite a bit actually.
At UC Davis they have a really good
music archive, going back about 40
years. Original releases of some
pretty cool stuff.
How did KCHUNG start?
When I first moved back down to Los
Angeles, I didn't really know what
I was doing so I thought I might
volunteer at a radio station. I went
to KXLU and a few others, but it
seemed kind of complicated and not
really doable for someone who wasn't
working within their system.
Did you end up interning there?
No, I ended up dropping it. Then a
couple years later I was at the
Mountain School and there was a guest
lecturer from KCRW. He kind of rubbed
me the wrong way. I wasn't into his
whole thing, and got the impression
that other people felt the same way.
After the class ended, a bunch of
students were all hanging out in
Chinatown, and I was like, "I could
start my own radio station and it would
be way cooler than KCRW." I wasn't
really serious, I was just blowing off
steam. Harsh Patel, who was at the
Mountain school with me, looked at me
and said, yeah you should do that.
Ha ha, wow.
The next day Harsh emailed me all
these graphic design examples for
this station that didn't exist. He
was already willing to put in work.
I thought, maybe this is a cool idea.
So, I started telling people that I
was starting a radio station and
everyone seemed pretty into it. It
just became more and more real as if
people were expecting it to really
happen. Before we knew it there were
a ton of people submitting show
proposals and asking to get involved.

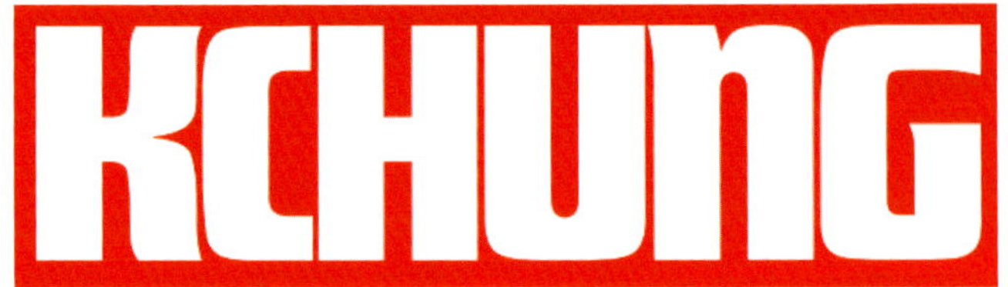

KCHUNG Logo, Designed by Harsh Patel, 2011.

What was the first broadcast?
My friend Luke Fischbeck said we
should do an event. I got a little kit
transmitter and Luke emailed a bunch
of people. We did this afternoon event
on Chung King Road. It was super fun.
You didn't have a space or anything?
No. Harsh kept telling me that we
needed to have weekly live shows. I
wasn't opposed to it, I just had no
idea how that could actually happen.
We didn't have a space, and we didn't
have any equipment — we just borrowed
everything for each event. Eventually
Luke offered us his Chinatown studio
for a month, just to see how it went.
People donated equipment, as long-term
loans or gifts. Things just started
to build up.
And you already had a schedule?
The schedule happened really quickly.
Almost immediately we had more people
wanting shows than time available. We
scrambled to find a new space when
Luke came back to town. Our second
studio was in a basement on Chung
King Road. It was slightly larger and
allowed us to have a somewhat expanded
schedule, but it was a temporary move
and came with weird restrictions on
what we could and couldn't do. We
have since moved into another new
space that is much larger and allows
us to do pretty much whatever we want.
How often were you broadcasting?
At first it was just one night a week.
Then we added a second night. I was
there every week for both of those
nights. Then we added a third night, and
at three nights I was like, "Oh man,
this is a lot of work. I don't know if I
can do this many," so I stopped adding
shows. Then a couple people offered to
help with station managing. We split it
between more people, and we were able to
add a fourth night.

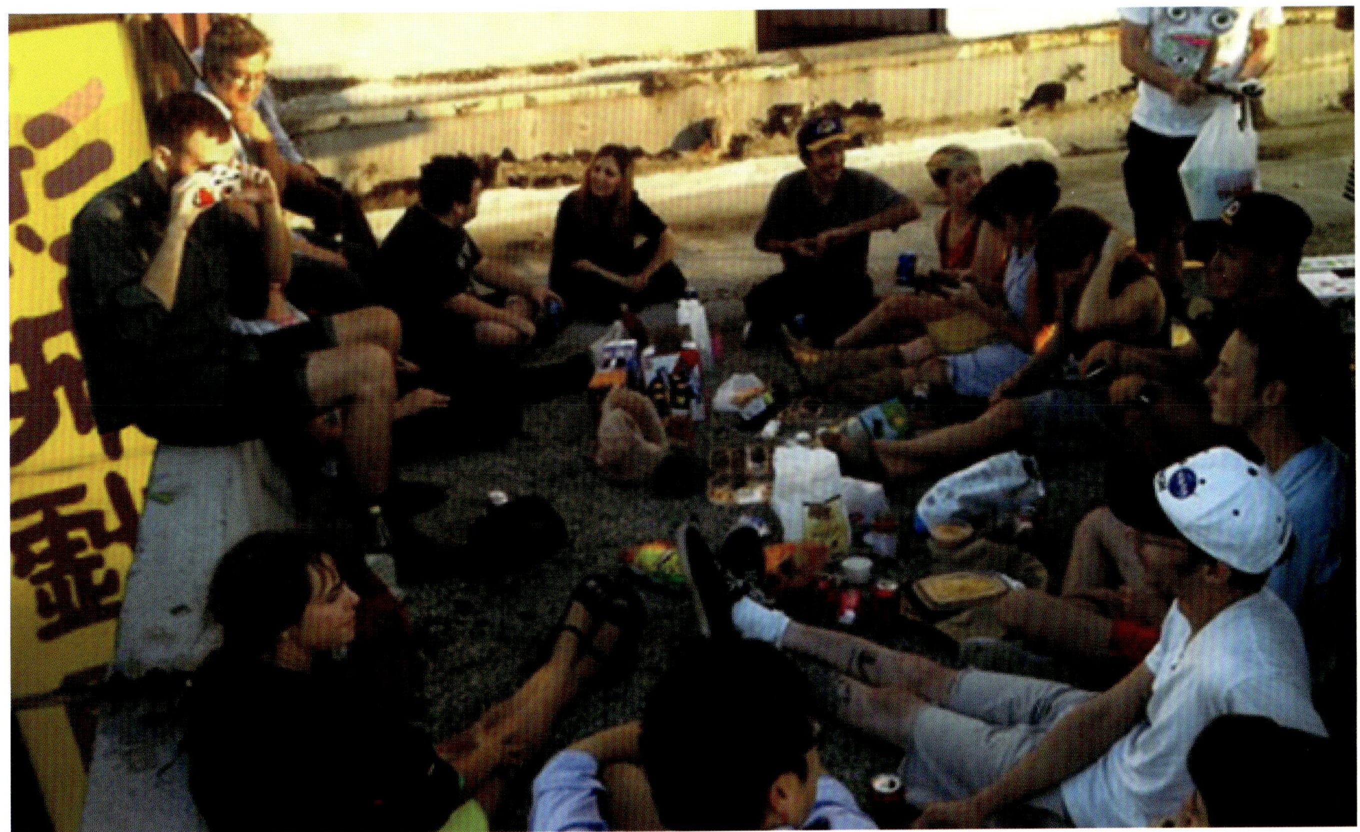

KCHUNG Roof, 2012.

But you were still kind of the manager of the whole thing?
Yeah. At one point last summer I was actually really overwhelmed with it. There were about 25 shows at that point. There were a ton of people and there were all these expectations. We were doing events all the time. I was doing a lot of the work and was really stressed out. So I sent out an email — I basically said that if KCHUNG doesn't get more organized with more of an infrastructure then I'm gonna shut everything down.
You were done with it.
I couldn't deal with it anymore. But that kind of got things going. Since then, we've escalated the infrastructure. Every couple of months things change. At this point it's really started to emulate the structure of a community radio station. We have a general manager, a music director, a PR person, an engineer, a finance manager, a mixtape production team, etc.

How are people getting these jobs?
Since no one really gets paid you can't really expect anyone to do anything, so people kind of pick a job title that appeals to them. Then they just do the things that make sense for them to do under that job title. There were attempts in the past to create these kind of positions and it never really worked out.
Is it expected that if somebody has a show they are going to make some kind of contribution in terms of helping run the radio station?
Well, practically speaking the biggest concern is rent. So people are asked to pay a certain amount per month — a pretty reasonable amount of money. As far as non-monetary contribution, I mean it's always great when people want to do something, but there is no expectation. I've tried expecting things from people in the past and I end up disappointed. You can't expect someone to do something they don't want to do.

How do you get a show on KCHUNG?
It's pretty simple. You just have to
have a little bit of patience, and be
willing to send an email.

**What happens when someone sends
you an email?**
You get a form — the form is a
new thing. In the past there was
no form. The form just covers
your availability and what you're
interested in outside of doing a
show. I guess there is a thing where
it asks you to describe the show
you want, but as far as I know that
doesn't matter.

**So you really don't try to curate the
shows or anything.**
No, not at all. I am really insecure
and don't want to make important
decisions like that. In the past when
people emailed me show proposals I
would not read the description. I
just put their name on the list. We
have a waitlist for when spots become
available — like if we add new time
slots, or somebody stops doing
a show.

**So the variety of shows happened
organically?**
Yeah. The only reason why it might
seem curated is people tend to find
out about the station through their
friends. Someone has a show, and then
they bring a bunch of their friends
over. Then they all want to get
shows, so they get on the list and
then they get shows, and they bring
their friends. Everybody is pulling
their social circles into it, and
then they start to overlap.

**It seems like a lot of people have
discovered a whole new approach to
radio at KCHUNG. There are things
that are happening that are really
experimental. There's a lot of
uncharted territory.**
I think that is because no one really
has any idea what they're doing. When
the station first started it was
really kind of unclear what could
or couldn't happen, what was fun,
what wasn't fun. I was just talking
to John Burtle yesterday about this
topic. You know him right?

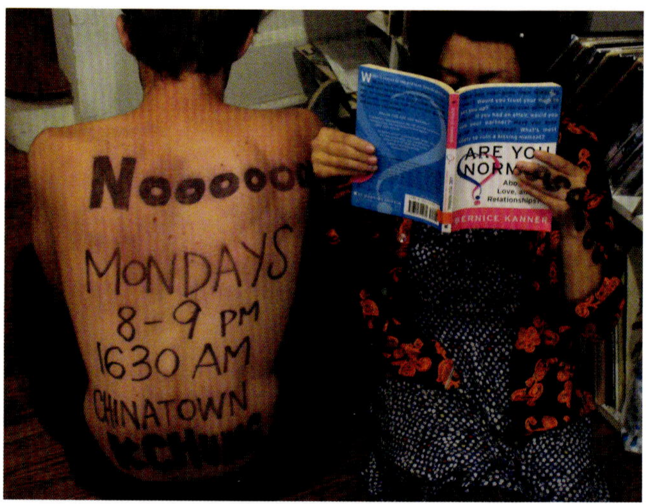

John Burtle & Guan Romg, Nooooooooo Flyer, 2012.

**He does that show Nooooooooooooooooo,
with Guan right?**
Yeah. Their show is a pretty good example of the kind of experimentation
you're talking about. He was saying
the first time he and Guan did their
show — afterwards he asked me, "So was
that okay?"

What did you say?
He has this really funny way of
impersonating the expression I made. I
mean, I had no idea. I had no context,
they had no context.

Then it kind of became their style.
They just kept doing it the way they
were doing it. Now, it's been two
years so people can listen to a bunch
of things, and see how different
people approach it.

The archive is great for that.
If you are willing to put in a little
work to figure out how to navigate
it you can see the changes in a
particular show. You can see how
shows spawned other shows.

There are also these weird one-offs.
That's happens when so and so had to
stay an extra hour because some
other person missed their show, and
then this other person showed up and
they did this impromptu thing. Those
two people never would have done a
show together but there it is for one
episode. And it's got a weird name.
It's always pretty cool when that
happens. There are these moments where
everything kind of mixes together.

KCHUNG is streamed online as well as archived online. How important is it that it gets broadcast on analog airwaves as well?
Well, terrestrial broadcasting is important to me but I'm not sure how important it really is for KCHUNG Radio. I think it is part hobby and part obsession. It's not very practical because your range is limited to Chinatown. You can't even drive down the freeway and listen. You have to park your car in Chinatown to listen to it.

But you get a kick out of it.
I just like the idea of doing something that's really happening. It's really in the air.

Is the organization of KCHUNG informed by anything? Things you've read or experienced?
I would say that the organizational structure of the station is definitely informed by the experiences I've had with political organizations and with collective housing. I've had some experiences with both of those and had things that I liked and things that I really hated about both.

So where did that leave you?
I just didn't want to create an organization based on a consensus model or anything like that. Honestly, I don't think that style really works. Maybe if someone were to hear me say that they'd say that's fucked up, but I don't care. It's just a radio station. It's not dealing with people's lives in any serious way. People need to be able to make decisions on their own. It shouldn't be this big vote from everyone involved for anything to happen.

What is the official status of KCHUNG right now? You're not a non-profit, right?
That's a hot topic right now. Currently we are operating in this weird gray area. We're not incorporated. We're not a non-profit, or an LLC. I don't even know what those things mean, but it's not any of those things.

The lack of status is just because there is really no need?
Well, our overhead in the past has been really low. There was no rent in our first space. The second space was only $200 a month, so it was really easy to raise the money between everyone who was involved. Now we have a new space and more overhead, and more people involved. The ongoing question is how are we gonna raise money? Do we need to step out of the gray area and become something else? I'd rather not be a non-profit, or a for profit, or whatever it is, just because it seems like a lot of work. Then again I don't know. We could get in trouble. I don't really know how this works. This is all pretty new to me.

How do you guys deal with the money you have?
We have a PayPal account. Someone volunteered to have it attached to their bank account. We're working on the honor system — we won't cause problems for that person's bank account and that person won't steal the money. Everything else we try to deal with in cash. The whole setup kind of prevents us from raising money, so it's kind of problematic.

How has KCHUNG impacted your personal life?
Well, I've met people through KCHUNG who have become some of my closest friends who I cannot imagine living without. That's the most important thing for me.

That rules.
Everyone involved in KCHUNG is doing it because they enjoy it and want to participate. They are genuinely interested because they think it's fun — not because they can get something out of it. You're not gonna get a job at a commercial radio station because you're at KCHUNG. It's not gonna make your art career. It's low expectations. It doesn't really matter if it works or doesn't work. I don't know. We've lowered the bar. ☺

Steve Hanft

"I got to rework his script and put some weird ideas in there...
like Kate Moss making the guy eat Fruit Loops."

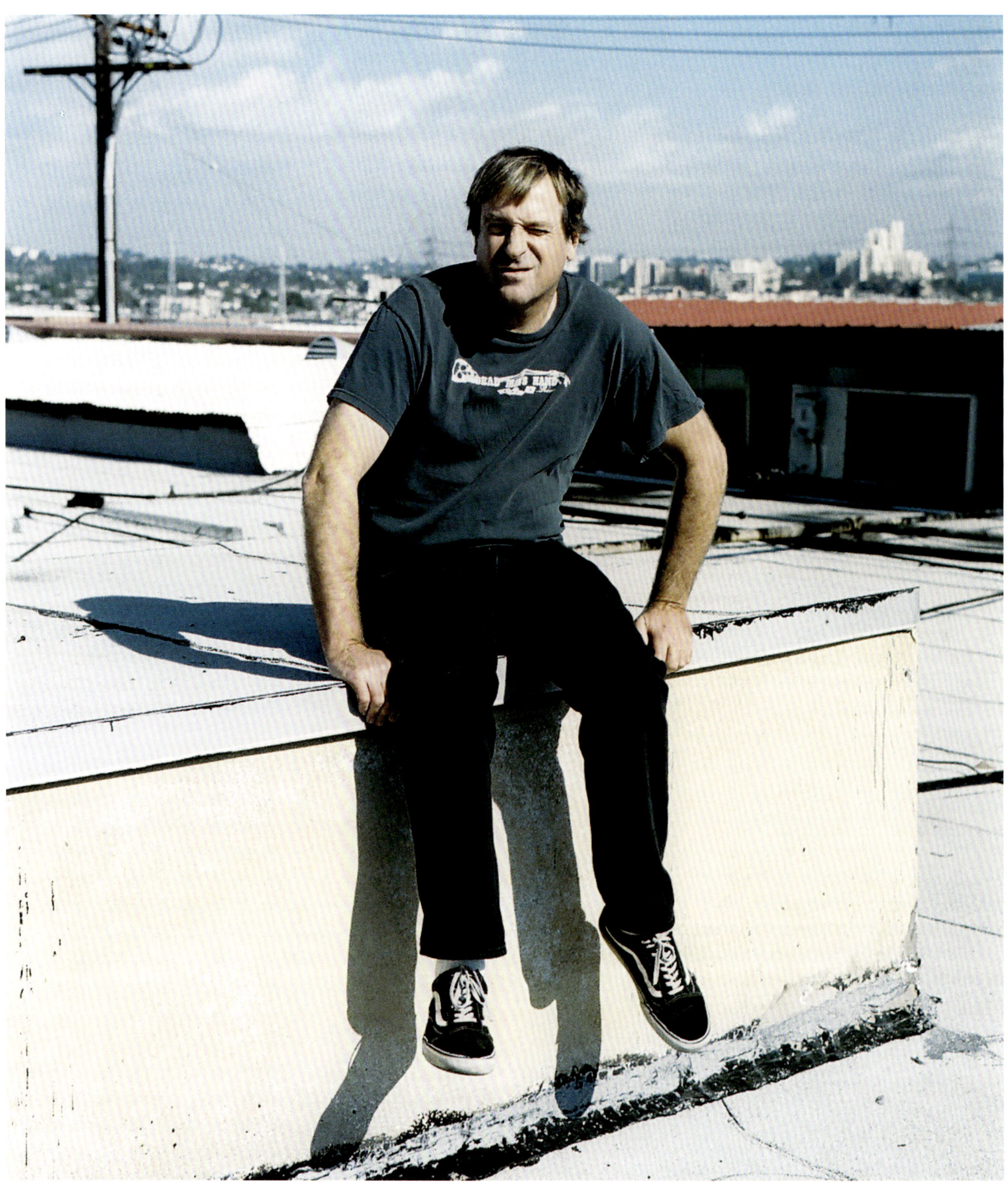

Interview by Jamie Krasner
Portrait by Cali Thornhill DeWitt

I was introduced to Steve Hanft's work when I was about 15. I remember watching a compilation show on MTV, something like "120 Minutes Flashback" on music videos of the 90s. Beck's video for his song "Loser" stood out — flaming squeegees, aerobics in a graveyard. It was all good. I ended up finding a bunch of other videos he directed for Beck, L7, ICP. Eventually I was lead to his feature film, Southlander: Diary of a Desperate Musician, the story of a guy who loses his white Monotron synthesizer and journeys through LA to find it, coming in contact with a bunch of weirdos throughout (Beth Orton, Beck, Hank Williams III, Ross Harris, Mark Gonzales), most giving great and strange performances. It seemed like it had been shot freely and retained that raw sensibility and humor I loved from his music videos. The drunk dream sequence of Ross Harris playing guitar and lip syncing his song in a diner is still one of my favorites.

Did you study filmmaking?
Well, I started out with photography, black-and-white, printing and everything. At some point I wanted to break away from just doing stills and get into moving imagery — some dream stuff. I went to California Institute of the Arts. I studied experimental live action film. I received a BFA and a MFA because I went for five years.

You're originally from L.A.?
I was born in Ventura, and I also lived in Fillmore and Simi Valley. Little, tiny towns in Ventura County.

I read that before you started making music videos you made a full-length movie.
Yeah, my MFA thesis feature was called Kill the Moonlight.

What was the film about?
The main character was named Chance. He was a stock car racer who was not a winner. He was a loser. There was this area called the Saugus Speedway, his environment, and I wanted to see what it was all about.

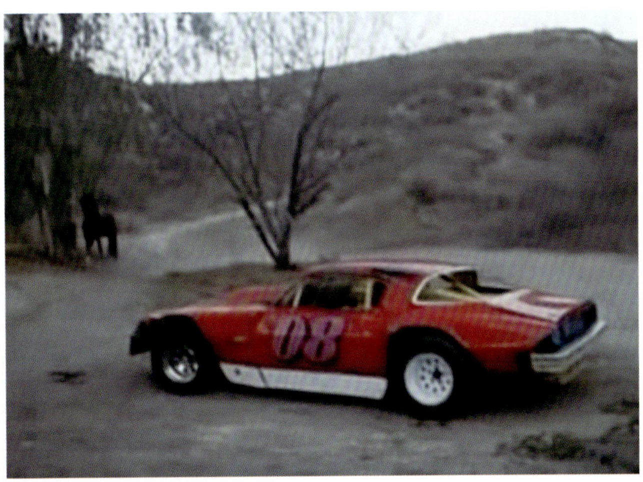

Kill the Moonlight, 1991.

What was the vibe of the movie?
There was just no romanticism involved in that film. That was the experiment, to make a feature narrative film with a story that doesn't have a moral. I just wanted to make something that was anti-romantic. Something that just is what it is.

Beck is on the soundtrack. How did you guys meet?
I was working on Kill the Moonlight in about 1990, and going out to a lot of shows — Nirvana, The Melvins, the whole grunge rock scene. I'd see Beck, and he would jump up on stage. He wasn't on the bill, but he would just play a song. I liked his songs, and so I asked him to do some music for Kill the Moonlight. He liked the film a lot and we started to collaborate. I think the song Loser is based on the film Kill the Moonlight.

Asher told me that you were in a band called Loser.
I had a band called Loser before I met Beck. It was with Steve Hillenburg, who's the creator of SpongeBob. He was the guitar player with our friends Clare and Carlos. We would all jam at CalArts. After I graduated from CalArts, my band broke up, and I just started jamming with Beck and some of his friends. And we just kept the name Loser. Beck got a little record deal with Bong Load, around the same time that he was jamming in our band.

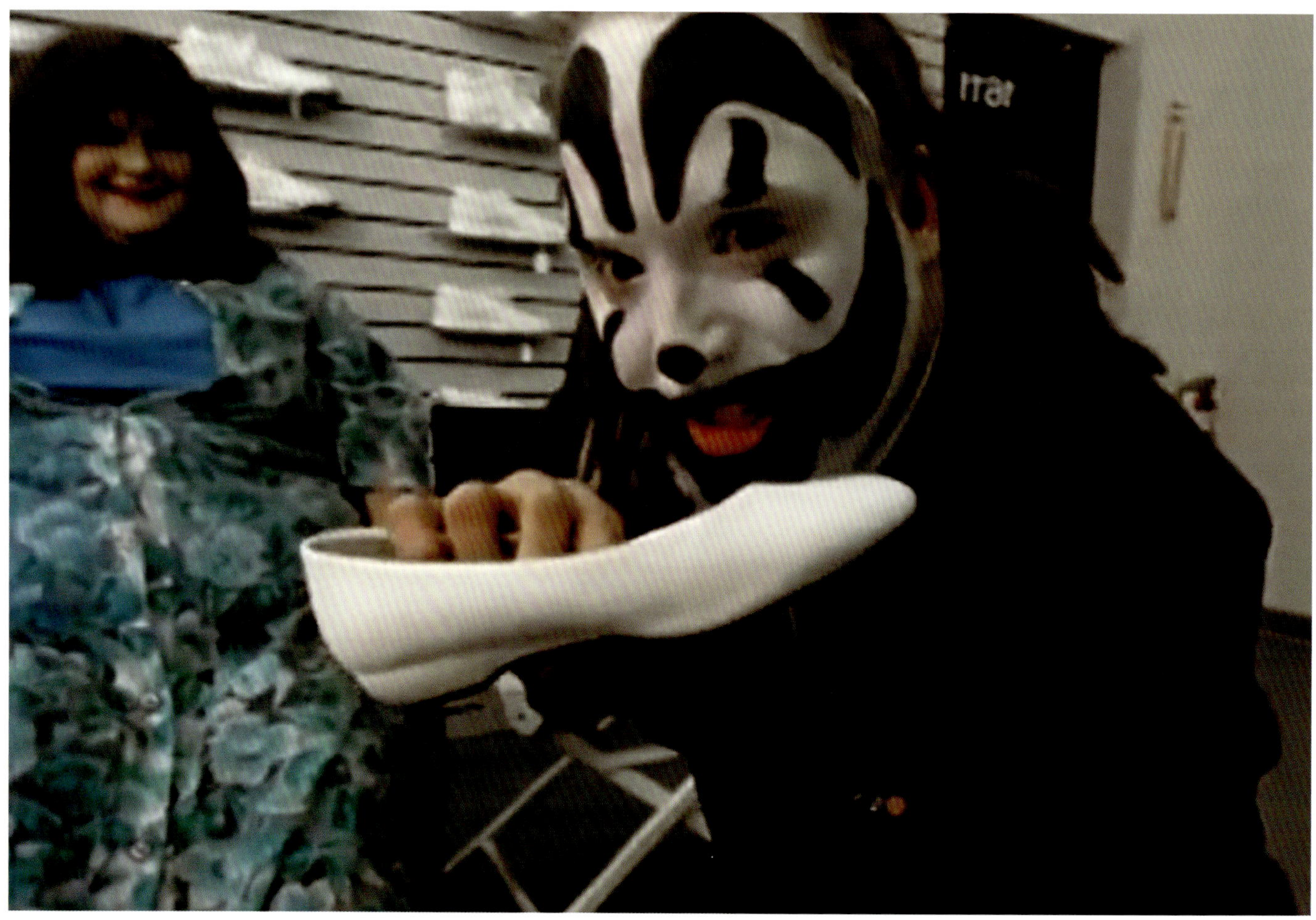

Insane Clown Posse, Hokus Pokus, The Island Def Jam Music Group, 1997.

What other bands were you in?
Liquor Cabinet. Arrowhead Man. Sexy
Death Soda. Tommy & The Demons.
Several others, Mime Crime. That was
all silent.
Like miming?
Yeah. Like air guitar.
OK.
We recently played at the Troubadour.
We opened up for That Dog.
**You guys just get on stage and like
mimic a band? With your hands?**
We take it pretty seriously. The
audience laughs a lot, but we try and
get real serious about our timing.
We have songs with different mimes
in them. At the end of the show, we
always chainsaw something with a
real chainsaw.
Like what?
Like a cake. One time we chainsawed
the coffin that we used in the Loser
video. I think Mime Crime was in the
Loser video. Some of the guys.

How did the Loser video come about?
Well like I said, Beck had got a deal
from Bong Load records, and they gave
us $300 to make a video. I had some
film in my fridge with a bunch of
different stocks — black-and-white,
color, fast, slow, different speeds. I
thought it would look cool to have a
music video with 16 different stocks
of film. I made a storyboard that had
a coffin moving through town.
**There's this one film by Luis Buñuel
where there's this moving coffin...
Simon of the Desert?**
Yeah, I was referencing that film,
which was actually referencing
some other film from 1914 by this
surrealist...I forget her name. I
would see so many experimental films
at CalArts that I don't remember. My
mother was a film librarian there,
and so we were always projecting
experimental films in the living room
instead of watching regular TV.

That sounds cool.
Yeah, it was. That coffin in the video was originally made for the band Loser. Beck would play most of the first song inside the coffin and then would kick it open, come out and play the solo.

After Loser came out you started directing a ton of music videos, right? Were those only for the bands you were into?
The first two years, I only did music videos where I liked the band. Then, around '96, I had this huge stack of CDs of people that wanted me to do videos. I figured I would write treatments for all of them.

So you stopped being discerning by your personal taste.
I mean, I did the L7 video, the Blues Explosion, and the Beck videos. They're my friends, I loved doing it, but it wasn't a way to get big budgets and start shooting on 35-millimeter, which is something I wanted to try. They might be the worst band in the world, but they were popular. I decided that was a good reason to make a video. It really changed my entire way of thinking.

I really like the Insane Clown Posse video you did.
I really liked working with them. They were very creative in a really original way.

So those ICP videos were both your concept?
Hokus Pokus was my concept. The other one, How Many Times was theirs.

Were you into both?
I like directing somebody else's concept. I didn't get to do that too often. I normally write my script. The Primal Scream Video I did was written by Irvine Welsh, who wrote Trainspotting. He wrote the treatment for the video, and then he started to direct it, but didn't wanna finish for some reason. I jumped at the chance. They were like, "Kate Moss is gonna be in it. And Devon Aoki." I got to rework his script and put some weird ideas in there...like Kate Moss making the guy eat Fruit Loops.

This reminds me of that documentary you did for Elliott Smith, Strange Parallel. It starts out as this typical portrait and then gets super bizarre.
That was so weird. I was hired to make a documentary on him. I went over there to Portland and met with him before, without any cameras. We just talked for like two days. What I got out of it was like he wanted it to be fucked up. Those were his words. I was like, "Well, what if you wrote down some of your dreams?" He said he didn't remember any, but the next day when he was driving me to the airport he told me he had had a bunch of dreams. We sat there at the Starbucks and wrote them all down on the napkin. That was the script.

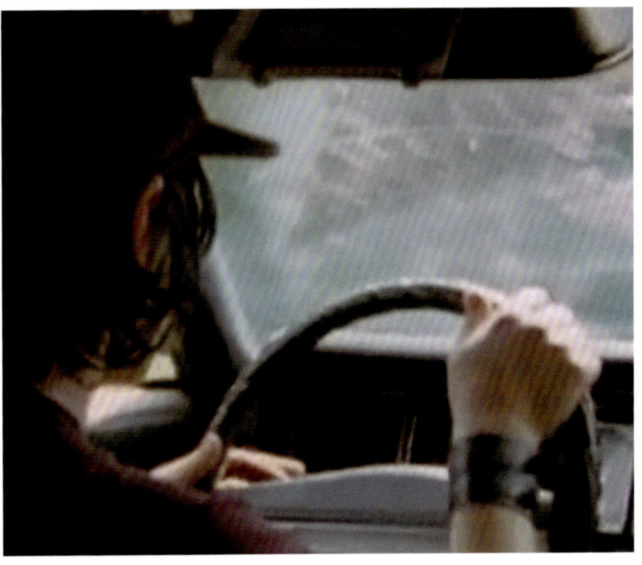

Elliot Smith, Strange Parallel, 1998.

That sounds totally different from making something for Hootie and the Blowfish.
Strange Parallel was like a return to my roots with experimental filmmaking. My documentaries are like my features: they are all a diary in the form of film, not some straight voice-of-god type film. With Elliott's film the script was a dream come true. He was a huge Beatles fan and wanted films like the Beatles — rock and roll films that are weird and funny.

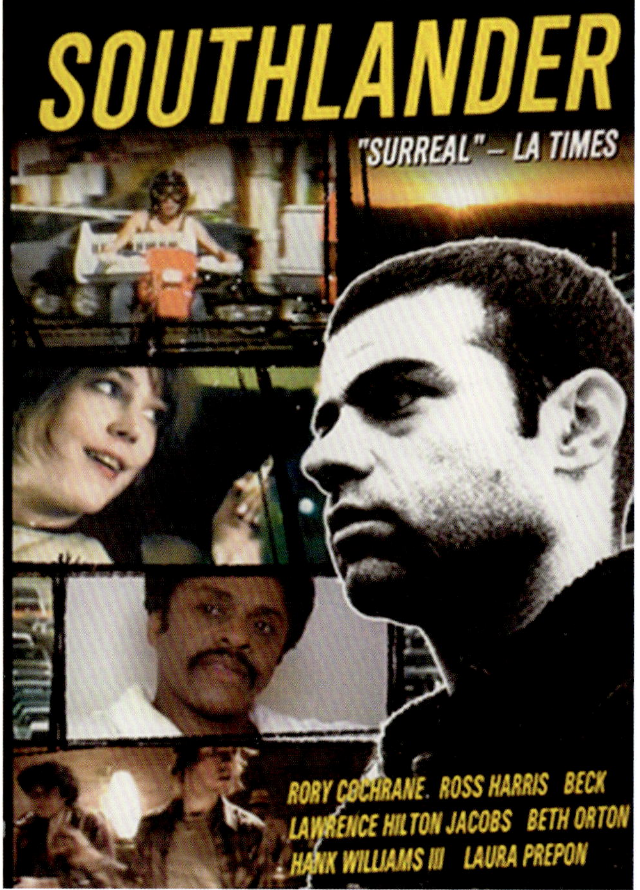

Southlander, DVD Cover, 2003.

How did Southlander start?

Propaganda Films was a production company that was begging me to sign to do music videos. This was at a point where I was trying to break into Hollywood to make features. I noticed that they had produced a couple of really great features: Barfly and Wild at Heart. I told them that I would sign with them if they put it in the contract that they would produce a film down the line.

And that was Southlander?

Yeah. I was working a lot at the time so it took a couple years to edit. That's why it didn't come out until 2003. It was written and shot in just a couple weeks. There's no real script, it was just a six-page treatment.

I was wondering about that.

We wrote a lot of the dialogue, but there would just be pages that we'd bring. It wasn't a complete script or anything.

Southlander costars Ross Harris, who's acted in a lot of your videos.

I work with him all the time. He directs, too. He just directed a Vans skateboard commercial.

He kind of steals some scenes he's in.

You know he was also the little kid star in Airplane.

Ha, so he's been acting awhile. How did you meet him?

I met him at Greenpeace. We were both going door to door asking for money to, you know, help ecology. He had this house in the valley where he'd have these crazy parties. Beck and I would jam out there.

I saw those Ray Ban commercials you made recently. They're awesome.

My friend Benzo directed those and I produced them. When he told me about the first one I was like, "I could produce the shit out of this video." I ended up starring in it, too. We just focused in on his concept which was a magic trick, and somehow hammered it together with camera tricks and tests and things.

Are you guys using reversal?

I'm not allowed to reveal it. There's one guy named Captain Disillusionist on YouTube and he's got this video where he explains every shot, how it was done. He's got most of them right, but he's got a couple wrong, and we're not gonna let him know. If you make the trick so hard to figure out people with silver spray paint all over their face will analyze it for like, 30 hours. Then it just gets more hits.

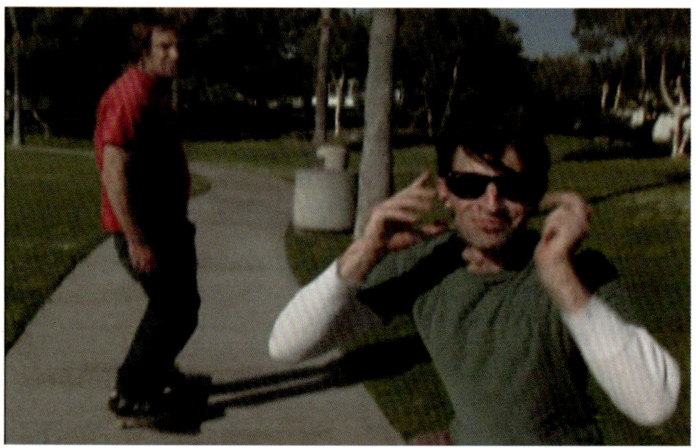

Sunglass Catch, Ray-Ban Films, 2007.

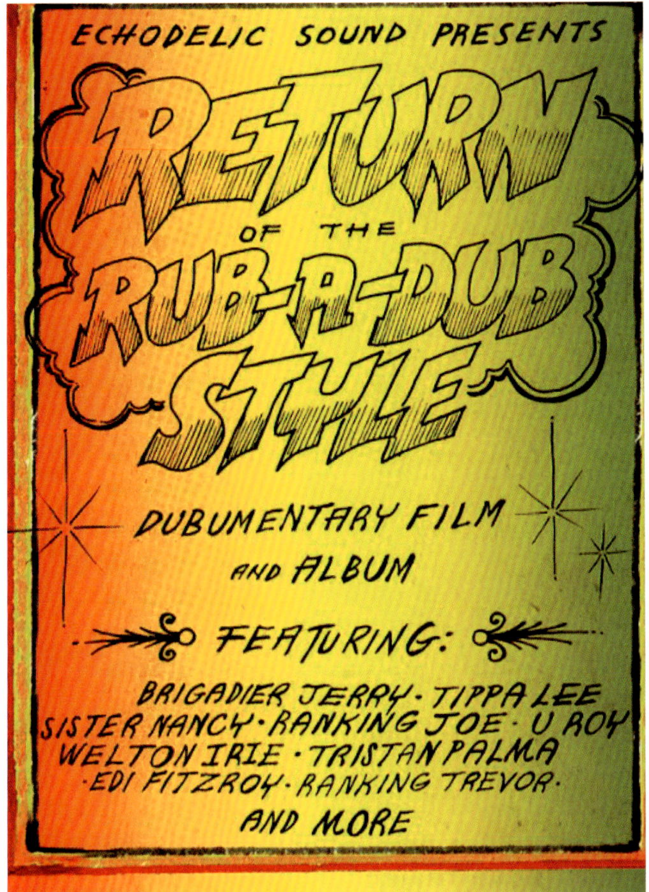

Return of the Rub-a-Dub Style, Poster, 2008.

I like them for that reason too.
It's funny because I was trying to get into Cannes Film Festival my whole life. With my features and short films... And when I finally get in, it's for the sunglasses ads.

What other projects have you been working on lately?
Mostly squeegeeing out improvised zero budget films. Making videos, shorts, producing and acting in friend's films. For a year or two I slowed down on directing music videos to take care of my Ma. During that time I finished two feature scripts. I kind of went back to the drawing board on how to write a movie. Now I'm back to shooting and editing music videos every day, which is wicked. Seeing how people respond on the regular kind of proves my theory that a film made less commercial is actually more popular than something made by the squares in the commercial world.

You've made a lot of videos recently?
I've made six music videos since the start of 2013. The momentum of traveling, shooting, and editing is sending me to a whole new level. I'm stoked. It's a great way to live, you know?

What about your recent documentary?
A friend of mine runs this club in LA called the Dub Club. All my friends were spinning records there and reggae bands would play. One of 'em started flying in his Jamaican DJs — they call the DJ the guy who raps on the mic — flying these legends in from Jamaica. I started getting really interested in sound system culture. I got to meet all the main artists because they're not so popular in Jamaica anymore, but they're popular here. All the underground rockers and DJs, who understand that the root of hip hop is reggae. They want to hear the original style of toasting on the mic. So I was documenting the performances as well as interviewing the people who came out to see these guys on those nights. We were basically just filming over four years with like really cheap cameras — camcorders that could film in like no light — just trying to capture something that's happening.

It sounds good though.
It's got good sound because it's just 3 tracks...a 45 vinyl that's a great Dub band recording in Jamaica from 1970. Then another wire is coming right off the microphone of the guy doing the live lyrics.

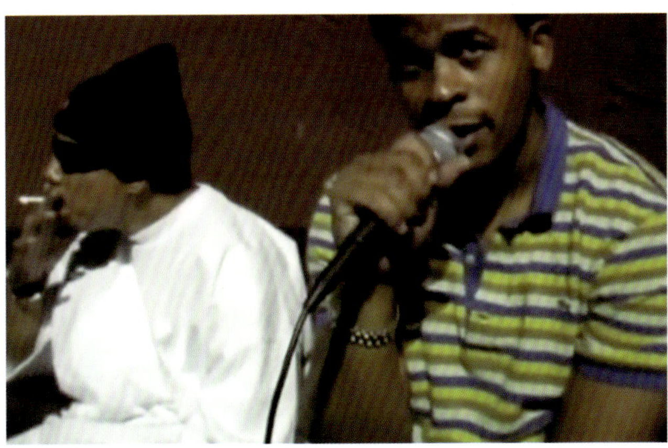

Return of the Rub-a-Dub Style, 2008.

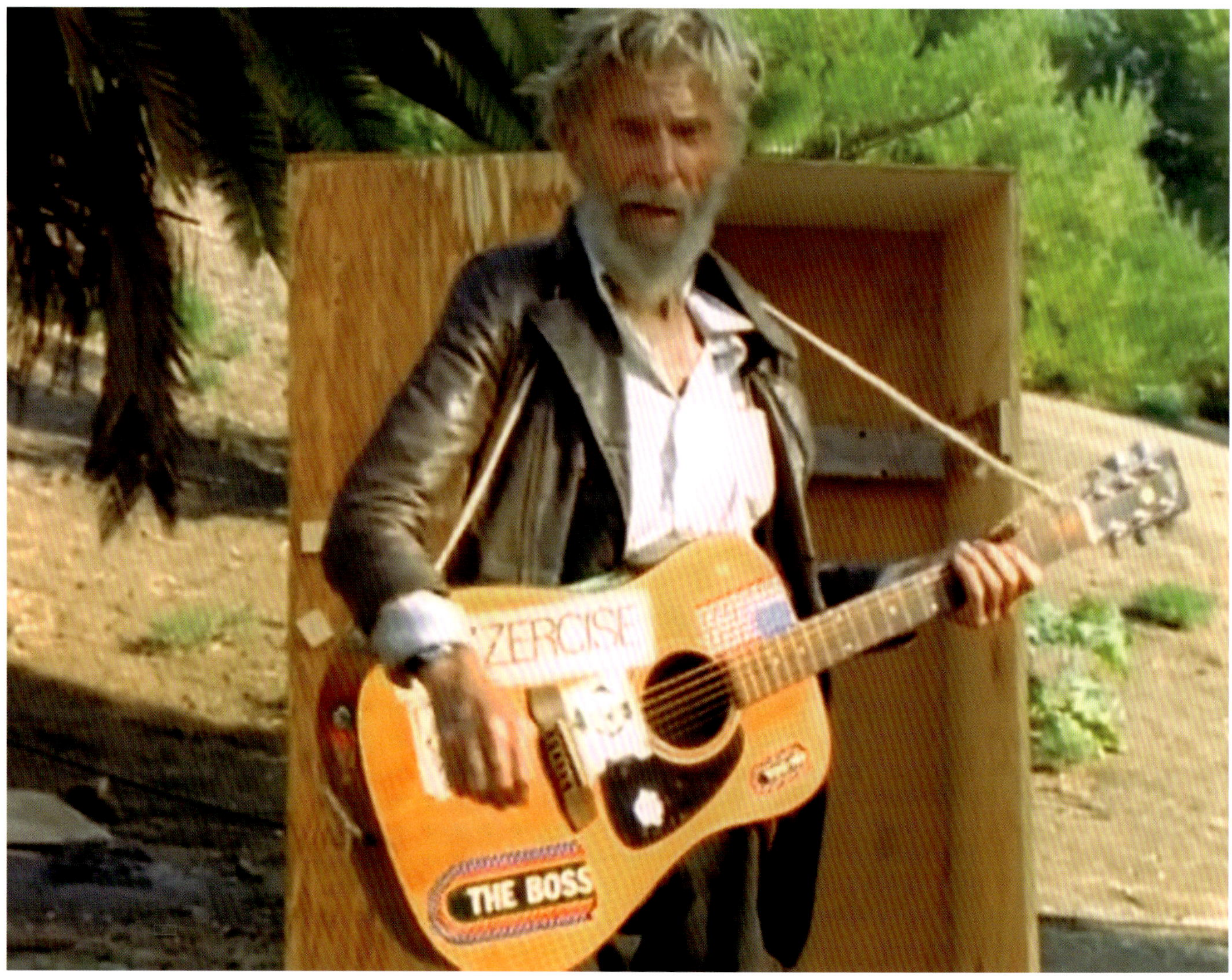

Beck, Loser, 1993.

It sounds super live.
The lyrics are so live, they make up
the lyrics on the spot, and so it's
going right into that sound. Into the
mic line on the camera. It's just
immediate.

**I really like the female DJ in the
documentary, Sister Nancy.**
I mean, she is the greatest female DJ
on the mic, ever. Her song Bam Bam is
a huge hit, and mashes up any dance
floor. I am ultra inspired by her.
When you're around her, it's intense.
She keeps it very, very real.

**Does that club still have those
nights going on?**
It's like a thousand people every
Wednesday night. Nonstop. It's been
really blowing up.

What are some things that inspire you?
Growing up surfing and just being out
in nature has always been the biggest
influence on my filmmaking. Watching
the light is really important in film
and just experiencing the elements.
It's totally different from the
digital world — the outdoors are where
a lot of creative things happen.

What else?
Watching Mexican TV and not being able
to understand it. In Mexico, people
are working with what they have and
that's what I do. Mexican film and
television producers are an influence
because their humor is a different
style than like, Two and a Half Men.

This is cool. One more.
Mark Gonzales is definitely one of my
biggest influences.

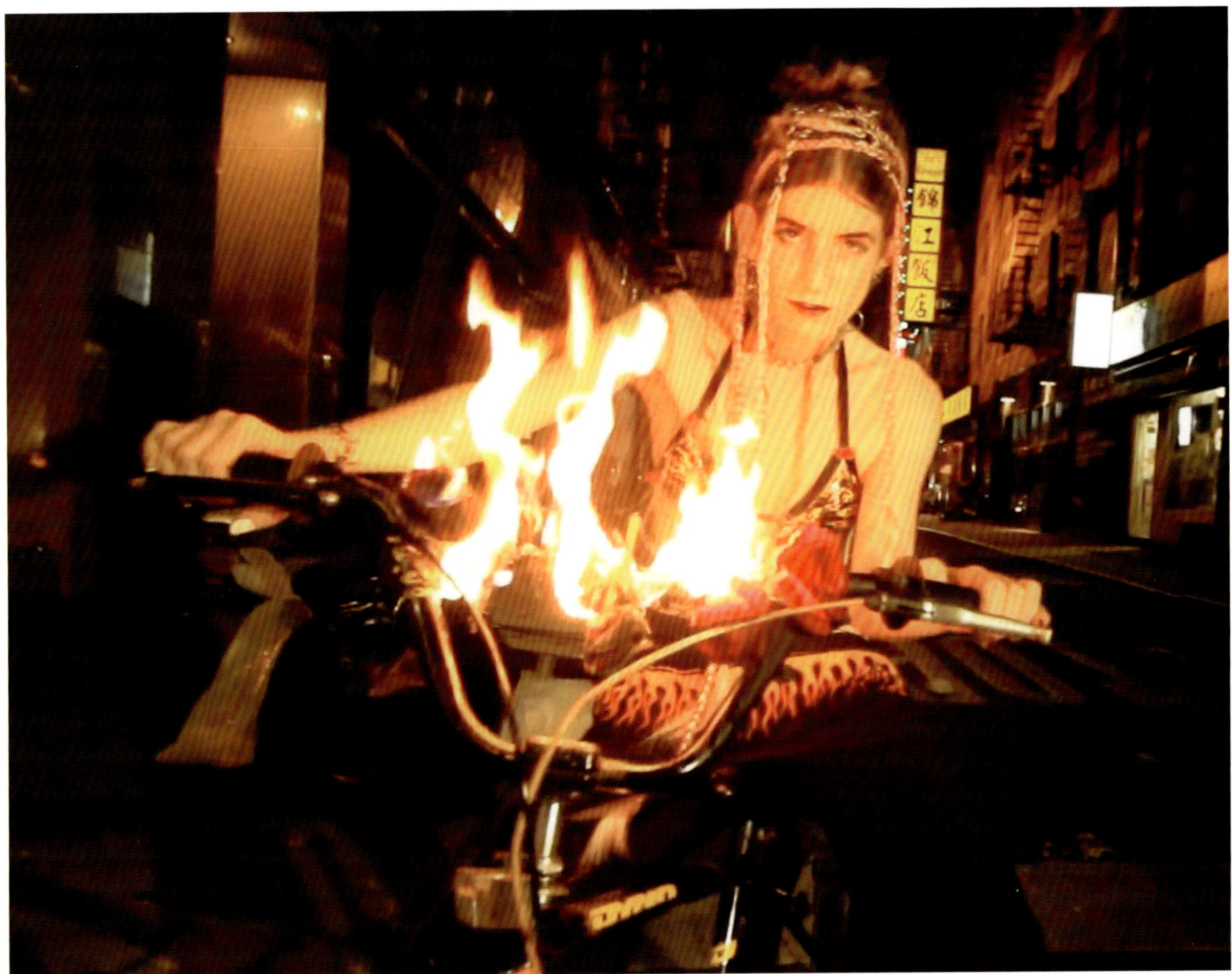

Seth, Fish Oil, 2013.

He's been in some of your films, right?
Yeah, he was in Southlander. He was
in the Beck Pay No Mind video.
With that one Mark Gonzales, and Beck
together, the three of us collaborating
on that video...it was perfect.
Mark Gonzales skateboarding at midnight
all around LA. And then at the bar.
Some of our moms having some drinks.
That part was creepy.
It was meant to be a little creepy.
We were trying to get at Beck's poetry.
I think it's one of his best songs.
Beercan is great too.
Yeah, those guys in the video raiding
the house are real homeless guys. We
just went to the mission, and were
like, "We're filming a video, and we're
gonna pay you guys to come crashing
into this house and eat all the food."

Oh my god.
It was a friend's house. That was
a real learning curve, working with
that many homeless guys.
**Wait, do you work with homeless dudes
a lot?**
I put a lot of homeless people in my
music videos. I also always pay a
lot of money. A lot of them will
want to get dropped off at the liquor
store after.
**OK. My last question is... I am in,
like, two bands right now. Would you
consider making a video for me?**
Will you send me the track?
**I just finished two different albums,
I'll send you both of them.**
Yeah, that'd be cool. I can't wait
to hear it.
Yeah, I'll send it to you. Cool! 🙂

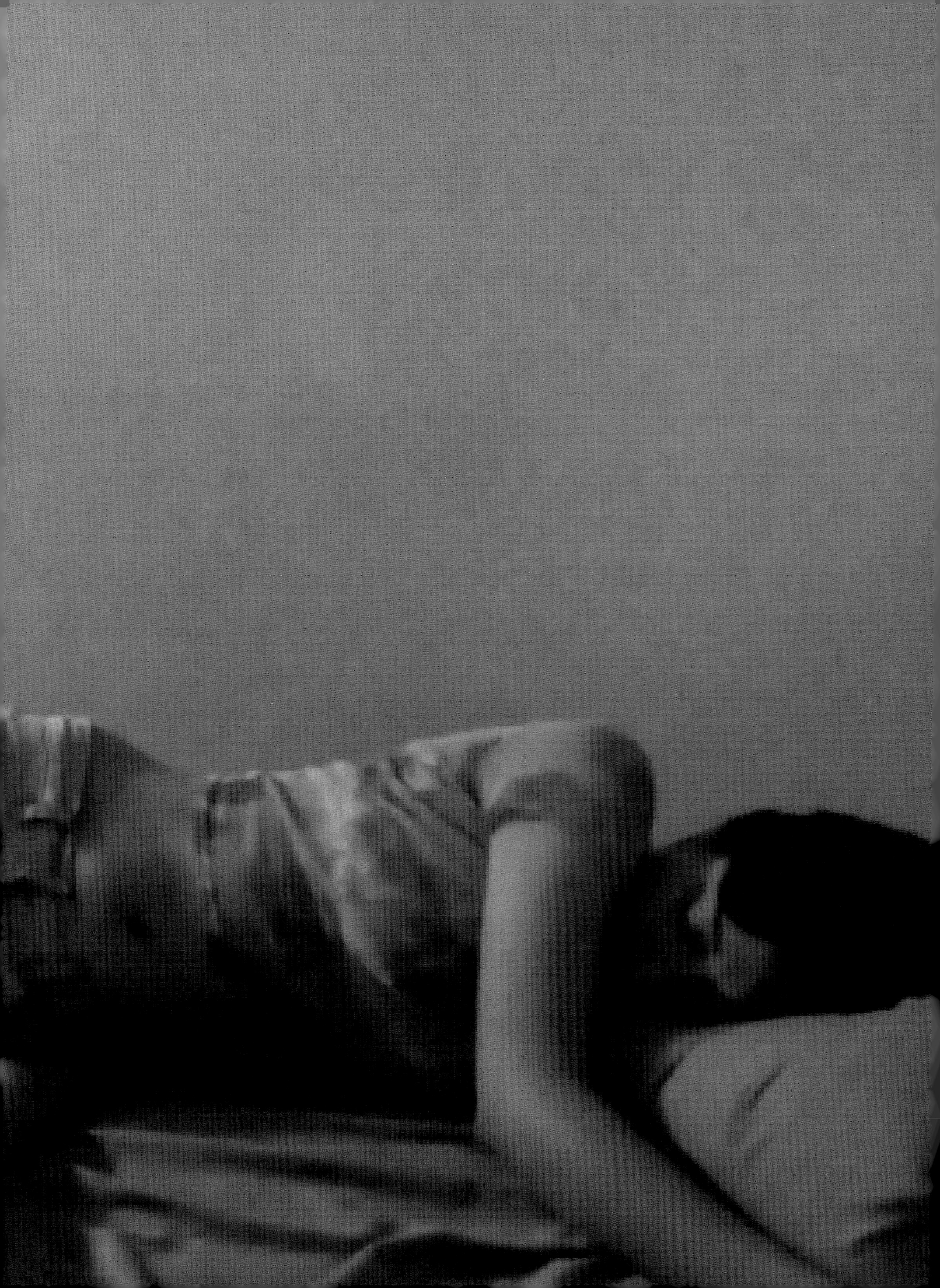

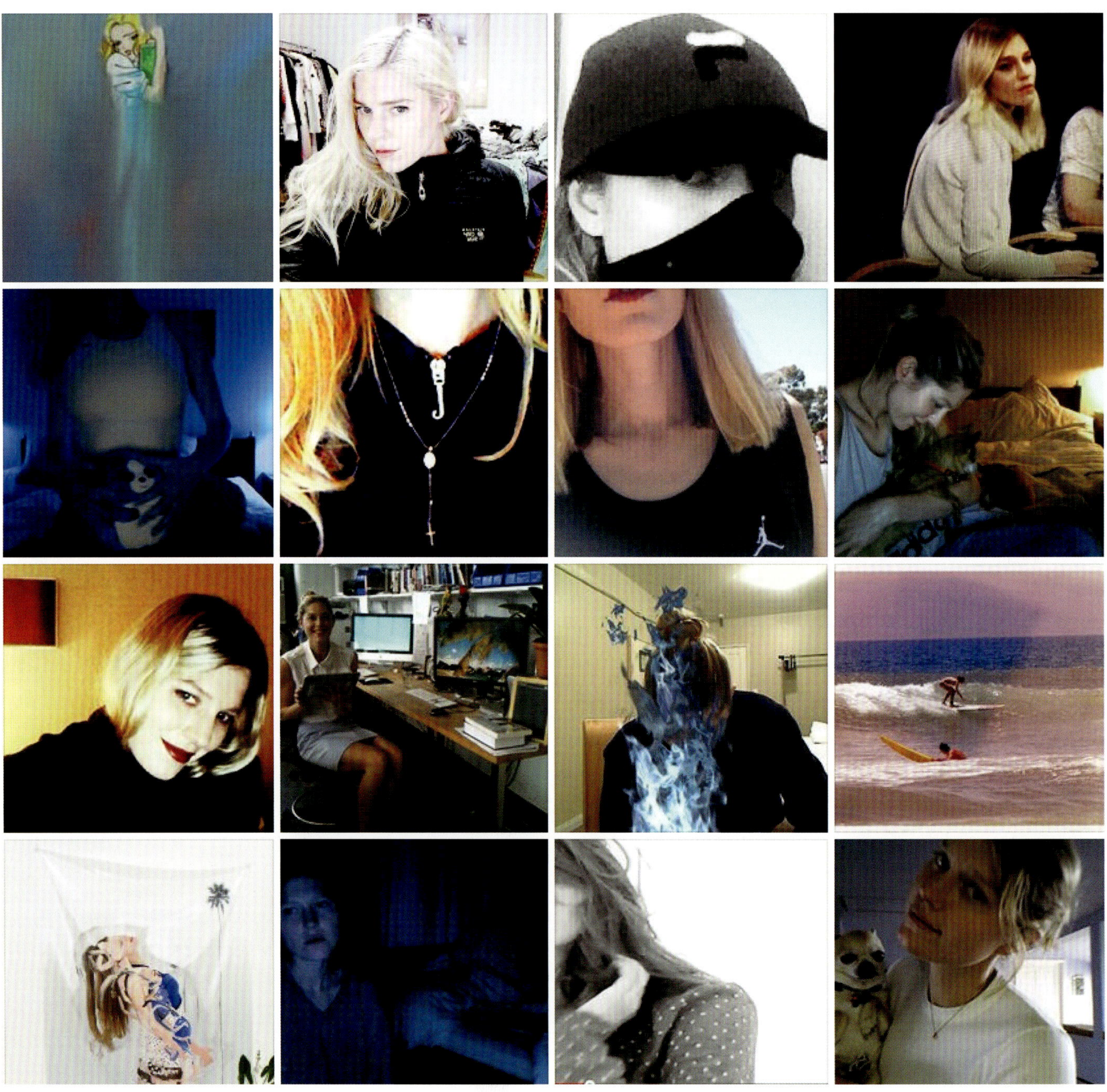

Interview by Asher Penn
Images courtesy Petra Cortright

Last year, the celebrated cyberpunk novelist Bruce Sterling described the work of Petra Cortright as, "Weird in a way that net art never has been before." This was one of the first public acknowledgments of a broader cultural phenomenon: the emergence of a new generation of digital-native artists who never knew art before computers and the internet. Since 2007 Petra Cortright has used her website and social networking platforms to share her videos, gif animations, and Photoshop works, building a massive following both in and out of the art world: Her video "vvebcam" got over 60,000 views before it was taken offline by YouTube for mis-tagging, and she was one of the youngest artists to be featured in the 2009 Venice Biennale. Through all this, Petra has managed to avoid online art's worst clichés of self-referentiality, instead showing a return to the traditional interests that have historically preoccupied artists — formal discovery and personal expression.

Were computers around in your house from when you were born?
Yeah, I had a computer since I was one. My dad had one of the first Macs.

Why did your family have Macs?
My dad was the head of the Art Department at USCB. I think early on a lot of artists used Macs. When I was in school most people had PCs until I guess the late 90s, when they started making the candy-colored iMacs. Then those got super popular.

What kind of stuff did you do on the computer?
I was really into SimCity 2000. I never really played video games like Nintendo — they were too violent and scary. Even Donkey Kong was stressful. I liked computer games. With SimCity, you could edit the landscape. I would just do that, for the longest time.

What would you put on the landscapes?
Like thousands of trees, waterfalls and stuff. I didn't really care about the game. I also remember really early drawing programs. One was kind of like Kid Pix but it was black and white. That was when I was really little.

Most kids like to draw. Did you prefer to draw on computers?
It was more fun. With computers you can do stuff that's way more complex than what you can do with your hands.

It's complex but it's also super easy.
I've always had a friendly, playful relationship with computers. It always felt really natural, like an extension of drawing. It was just a way to be creative.

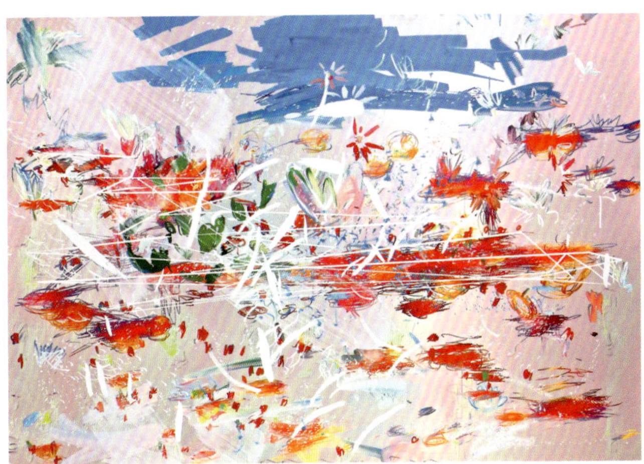

A.D.I.D.A.S., 2013.

So your parents were in the arts?
Yeah. My dad died when I was four-and-a-half. He was a master printmaker and sculptor. My mom has a master's in Painting from Berkeley. Also, one of my parents' close friends was Marcia Tucker who founded the New Museum. I grew up with a lot of art and artists around.

What was your first experience of going online?
I guess it was AOL. My mom got AOL pretty early. She was a member of all these chat rooms for widows. I remember she had this printed out list of emoticons. There were smiley faces, all these words next to them, like happy, sad, hugs...

Hugs?
It was just two brackets, and that
meant hugs. I wish I still had that
list. It would be so good to look
at now, this printed-out list of
emoticons.

Were you going to chat rooms, too?
Not really. It's hard to remember the
internet before Google. The first
time I used Google I was in the fifth
grade. The librarian was telling
everyone to use Google instead
of Yahoo because it was better. I
thought it was a weird word.

What about Google image search?
I specifically remember my first
image search. I searched for trees.
Like, "green trees." And it was really
overwhelming because there were so
many pictures of trees, all at once.
Before, you could only look at books.

So you were into it.
I was totally obsessed with image
search after that. It's still that way
when I work. I feel no need to take a
photo of anything. If you can't find
exactly what you want to find, you can
usually find something better than
what you were looking for.

**When did you start putting stuff
online?**
It was in high school, so around
2001. I had LiveJournal and wanted to
put images up.

**Had you been saving your computer
drawings before that point?**
Not until I was posting them online.
Then it became important. Before
that I didn't even think in those
terms, because no one else was going
to see it. I think there's a really
strong link with people sharing stuff
and saving stuff — posting something
online, and the validation that comes
with that. It is kind of hard to
separate at this point.

**Were your friends at school on
LiveJournal?**
My friend Jaime, who now makes music
under the name M.E.S.H. got me into
LiveJournal. He went to my high
school and I had a crush on him, so I
was always trying to impress him. He
introduced me to other people online.

Like who?
There was this thing called
NowGoCreate, a website created by
Damon Zucconi, Mike Tucker, and Milan
Zrnic. I ended up meeting so many
people from NowGoCreate in person.

What was NowGoCreate?
It was kind of like Deviant Art for
people in 2002 learning Photoshop. It
had a snarky, fine art approach. There
weren't that many people on the site,
maybe 30 — it wasn't a big thing at
all. Jaime Whipple was on it, Jessica
Williams, Will Simpson, Ilia Ovech-
kin...a lot of people that were in the
surfing club Loshadka. Many ended up
going to Cooper Union and MICA.

What would people post?
People would post typography, projects
that they were working on, photos.
It was in that era of graphic tees,
when Adobe Illustrator was really
cool. Stuff like a bunch of triangles
with crows flying.

**Were they trying to get dialog or
critiques for it?**
Yeah. You would post something, and
then people would try to flex their
pre-college, art-school talk about
it. Things would sometimes get pretty
heated. It was not good.

What were you posting?
I was posting really shitty Photoshop
work. I wish I had posted more
drawings that I had done, but I was
trying to post cooler stuff which
in retrospect was not cool. It was
just trendy.

**You were on that site Nasty Nets too.
Was that like NowGoCreate?**
No. You had to be invited to Nasty
Nets. I think it started maybe a year
before I was invited to it. It felt
like a big deal. I was scared to post
at first.

Who was on it?
Pretty much everyone that was a
member of it was an artist. But you
wouldn't post your work. You would
post things that you found on the
internet, things that you thought
other people would be interested in.
One time I posted my own work, but for
the most part it was found images.

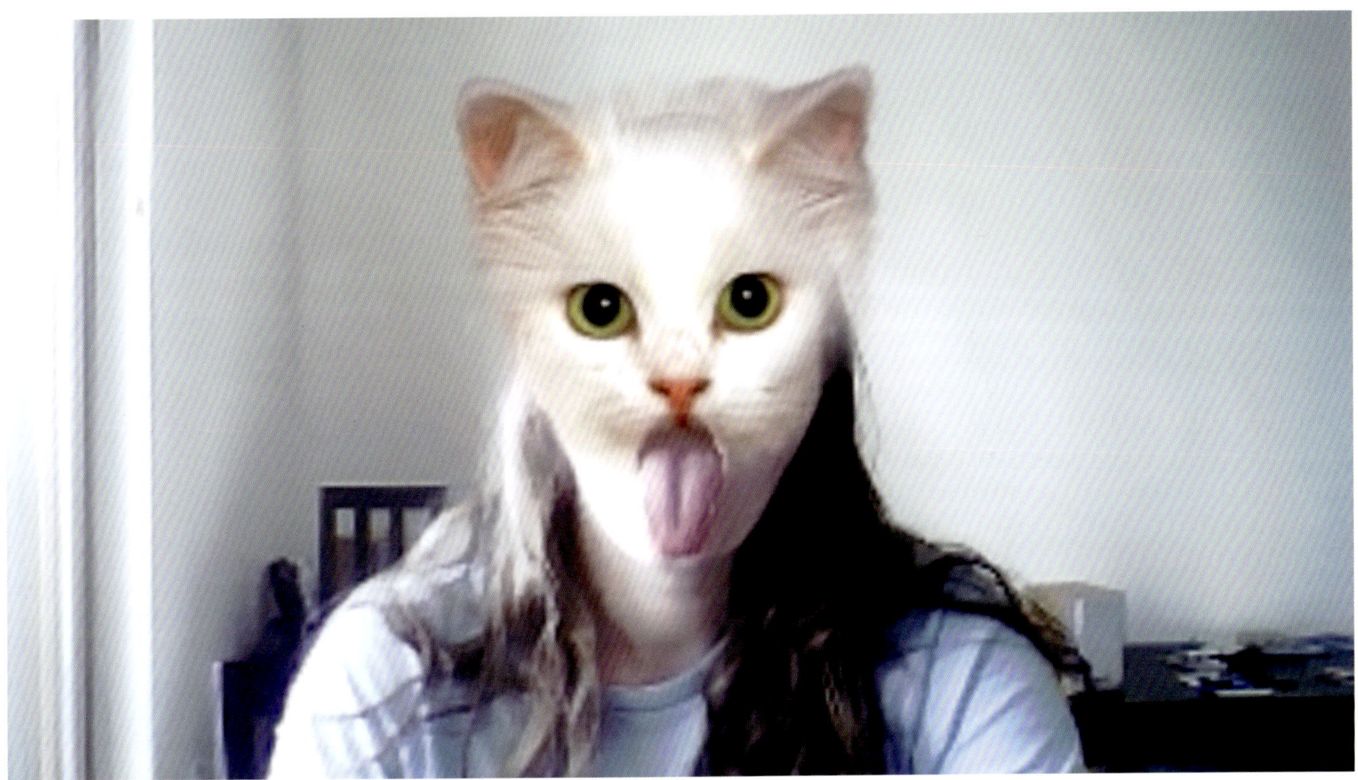

cats spirit spsit spit, 2008.

So it was a community for sharing things you found?
Yeah. Recently there was this panel discussion and one of the founding members described it in this really good way. He said, "Art sometimes happens here." Sometimes posts that people did would be considered work.
I was looking at the comments on some posts. People seemed really sincere.
Everyone was super nice. There were some Nasty Nets trolls on there too, for sure.
There also seemed to be a major reverence for jpegs and gifs.
Well, this was before animated gifs got played out — before Google+ came out and there was suddenly such a clusterfuck of animated gifs.
Suddenly they were totally available.
Yeah, which changed the appeal for sure. I hate talking about technology this way because things change, it's not necessarily a good thing or a bad thing, it's just what happens. Things just got more popular and less rare and exciting. You get desensitized to it. The patience of digital culture is so limited now. If you can get someone to look at something that you posted for two seconds, you've already conquered the day. People are getting shorter and shorter attention spans, which is okay. It's just how it works.
You went to art school right? What did you study?
Well, I wanted to do graphic design. I really liked computers and so I thought that was my only option. But graphic design sucks, having to work for other people sucks. I'm a terrible employee.
Where did you go to school?
CCA, then Parsons, but I dropped out.
Why did you drop out?
I had a really hard time with the living situations. I lived in five different apartments and they all ended in horrible disasters. The first one, there was carbon monoxide leaking. The second one, there was toxic mold. The third one, there were bed bugs. The fourth one, there was a flood. And the fifth one was a fire. The last one was kind of my bad. I had too many candles. There was no structural damage, though.

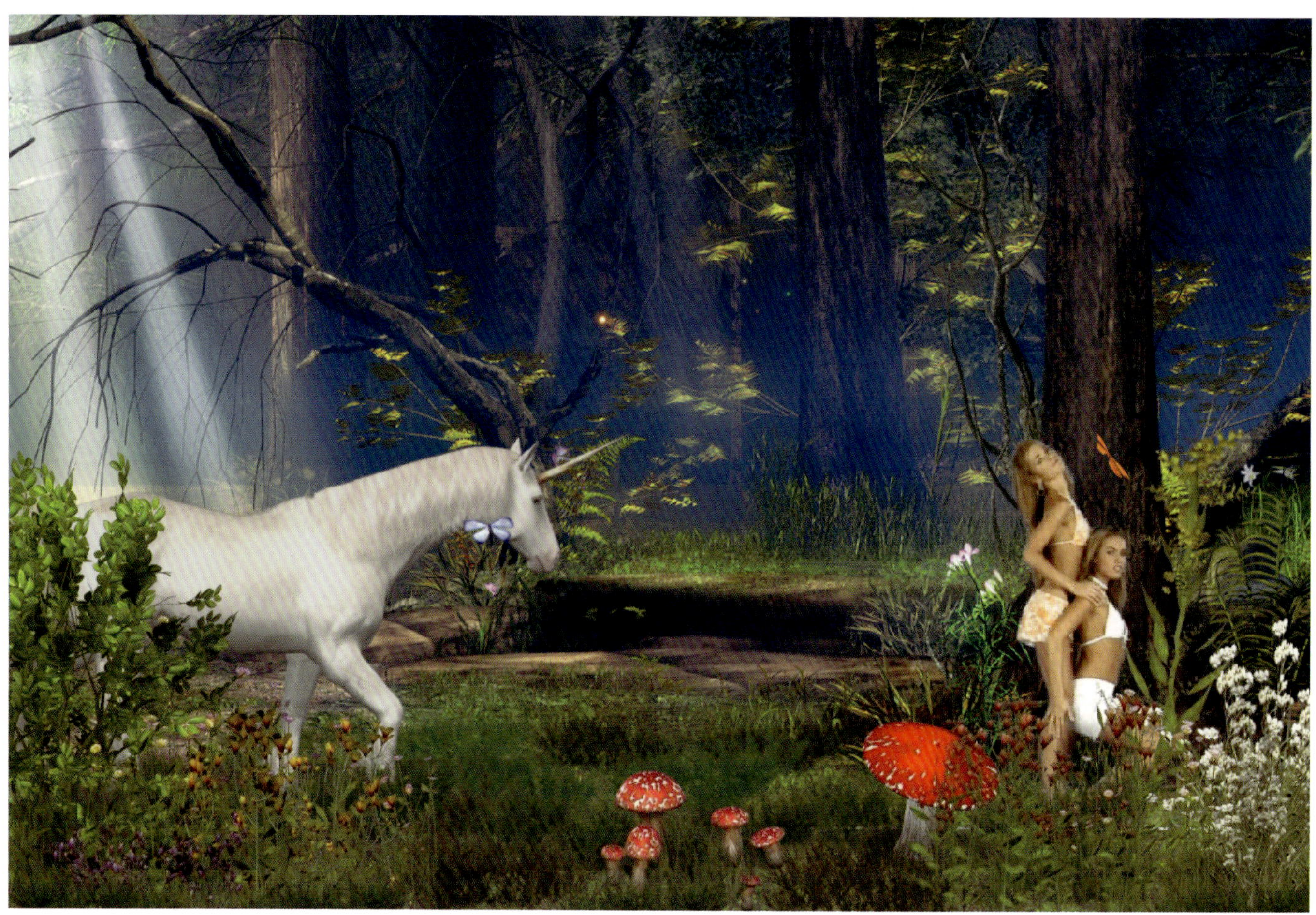

Enchanted Foreststrippersnopeleeasy2girls[1], 2012.

It sounds like the ten plagues.
It was a little cartoony. I remember
so many subway rides, being exhausted
for every reason, but none having to
do with school. Things like finals
didn't even register on my distress
level of what was happening. School
seemed like the easy part of it,
honestly.

What was your first website?
It was my homepage, which I started
in 2007. I haven't updated the look
of it since 2008, so all the animated
gifs and stuff have been there for
five years. It's kind of a problem
— I know this sounds like such a
white net girl problem (lol) — but
I'm tired of people asking me about
animated gifs in interviews.

Ha.
In a weird way it gives an impression
that I'm a crusader for nostalgia or
for older internet, but I also make
work with new technology. I like both.

**I was looking at your site today. I
like the wallpapers for the videos.**
I like being able to customize. Even
just doing a wallpaper behind a
YouTube video makes a big difference.
It changes the context a lot.

**Are you supposed to watch the videos
with the backgrounds?**
I try to make it nice and at least
more special, but it's not a
requirement to see it that way. I'm
very relaxed about how people view my
work. I'm really grateful if people
look at it at all so it doesn't
really matter if it's on YouTube or
on my website.

**At what point in all this did you
start to regard yourself as an artist?**
I feel like I still have trouble with
that sometimes. Making the website,
it seemed like such a big deal,
putting stuff on there and listing it
as a piece. That was before I had
sold anything.

What was the first work you sold?
I had a show in 2008 at a gallery in Dallas, Texas, called And/Or.
You were making physical art objects?
They were only made for the show. The gallerist wanted to make prints of the pixel paintings, and some drawings. That was really straightforward but then he wanted to also show a webcam video I made.
How was that weird?
I just had never priced work before so I had no guidelines. The prints seemed kind of straightforward, you just sell them for whatever you normally sell a print for. With the webcam video, I had no idea. I wanted some automatic way to figure it out because it was really stressful.
What did you end up doing?
As a joke I said, "I wish that I could price the video by YouTube views or something." The gallerist thought it was a good idea. From the start, that's how I've always priced the videos.
So you only make objects when someone gives you a show?
Yeah, because I've never had a studio. I've never really had a reason to make physical stuff unless there was a show, with resources and money. I never pay to have the things produced.
That's a pretty unusual way in general for an artist to work.
It makes sense if you're lazy and poor. I'm also just so flexible with everything. Anything that I make can have so many final forms. It seems like a lot of pressure to decide the best way to show something.
Was SimCity 2000 kind of inspirational for your landscape videos?
Yeah, definitely. I've always also really liked nature. The house that I grew up in Santa Barbara was on this hill and one side of it had this huge view of the mountains and the other side was the ocean. It was like a 360-degree view. I grew up looking at this scenery. I guess the landscape stuff that I do on computers is like a logical extension of that.

Landscapes are also a pretty classic subject matter for art.
Yeah, I don't question it too much or anything.
Whenever I look at your videos I wonder how you made them. It looks like a customized hack of automatic filters.
I always like that. To me it seems so obvious. For 95% of them, there is no post-production whatsoever, they're all live. I use webcam software that has live effects. So when they're being made, it's like directing and editing and post-production all at once. Most of my work takes 20 minutes to make. They're almost half performance and then half documentation. It's all these things at the right time. They're really playful and sincere, and I don't really know what I'm doing until after it's done.
What inspires you to make a new video piece?
When I first do it, its something that I just really want to do. I make more videos when I'm restless. I make the still images when I'm more relaxed. I don't think I can really do good work in Photoshop unless the house is clean.
I read an interview where you said that you felt your daily practice was similar to a painter.
There are some days when I wake up, and I'll be really in the mood to listen to loud music and fuck around with the webcam. Then there are days when I wake up, and I just want to upload brushes to Photoshop and not talk to anyone and just paint. When I use Photoshop, I'll usually start with a blank document, which is kind of like a blank canvas. I would never say that I'm a painter because that's so technical. I don't consider myself a precise person. I guess that's why I like computers, because I can be really precise. Except somehow I've found a way to mess that up. My desktop is a nightmare — I need to organize it.

In terms of being technically skilled with the computer where do you fit in the spectrum?
I think I'm above average. I definitely know more than the average woman. If I really want to know something, then I usually figure it out on my own by researching. I really have to want to know how to do it, like teaching myself Flash for these pieces that I've been working on.
The wallpapers.
Yeah, with the strippers. I hate Flash so much, it's the worst, dumbest technology.
How long have you been working in Flash?
Since the end of 2011. And it's only because I really wanted to work with the stuff.
What about your placement of yourself in your own videos? How did that start?
When I made the first one I really didn't have so much intent for it as a piece. When I posted it on YouTube, Paddy Johnson wrote about it on her website Art Fag City, which was really weird. I didn't think about it as an art piece at all, really. It was just this weird video of myself, like an extension of taking a picture of myself.
You were also doing lots of crazy hashtags right?
That got me in trouble on YouTube. It was this huge list of default internet spam keywords that you would put in the index of your website to get more hits. It's this super, super long, really, really nasty, awesome list — I mean, it's kind of outdated, because the first celebrities are Britney Spears and Paris Hilton. Now I guess it would be Kim Kardashian.
So people would come to your page and see the wrong thing.
Yeah, and they would write super negative comments on the videos, which I was really into. Having anyone take the time on YouTube to say anything at all seemed like a big deal to me. I'm always interested in having people respond to anything that I do.

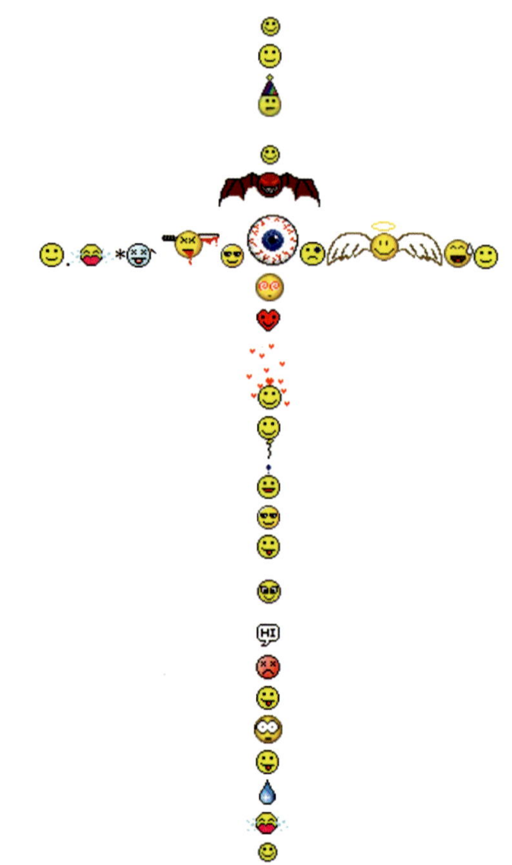

Homepage Artwork, 2004–present.

Even in a negative way.
I'm into the negative stuff. I started getting really into replying to people. Whatever they said to me, I would reply back, but a hundred times nastier. Honestly, the comments that I would write, I can't even say them out loud. They're really gnarly language. Whatever tone someone was using in their comment, I'd answer them the same way. It would either be super positive or super negative. If anyone said anything mean to me I would just be the worst. Like really bad things. I feel like the minimum I would say back to people was, "Thanks for the view, peasant." I was really into calling people peasants. I guess the "thanks for the view" thing was because of the pricing.
You were also racking up the value of the video.
Yeah. I didn't even have the video catalog at that point but I had that in my mind anyways. The value came through viewership.

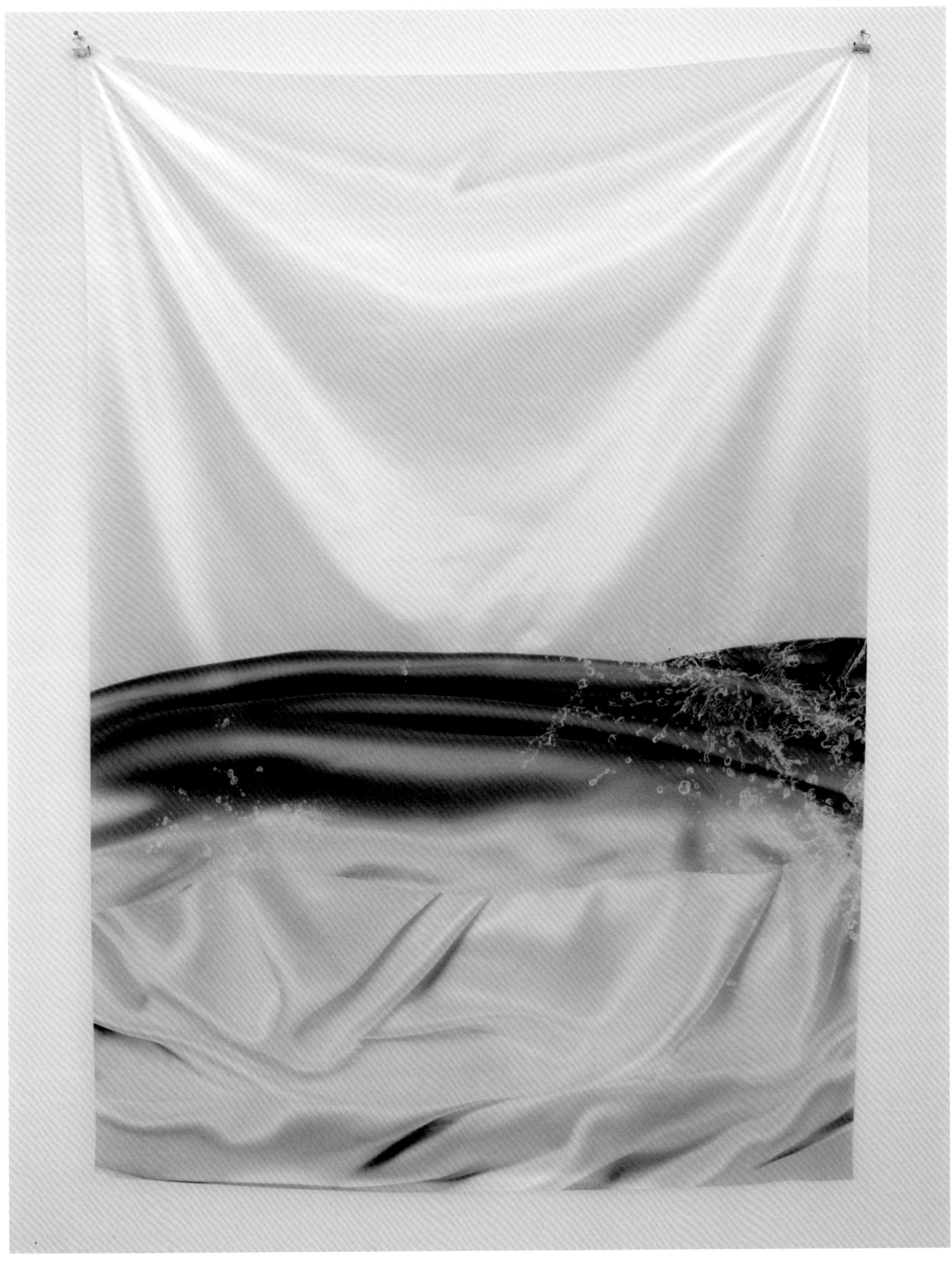

SO WET, Preteen Gallery, 2011.

Venus X

"I didn't look for hip hop because I grew up around it.
I was looking for something else."

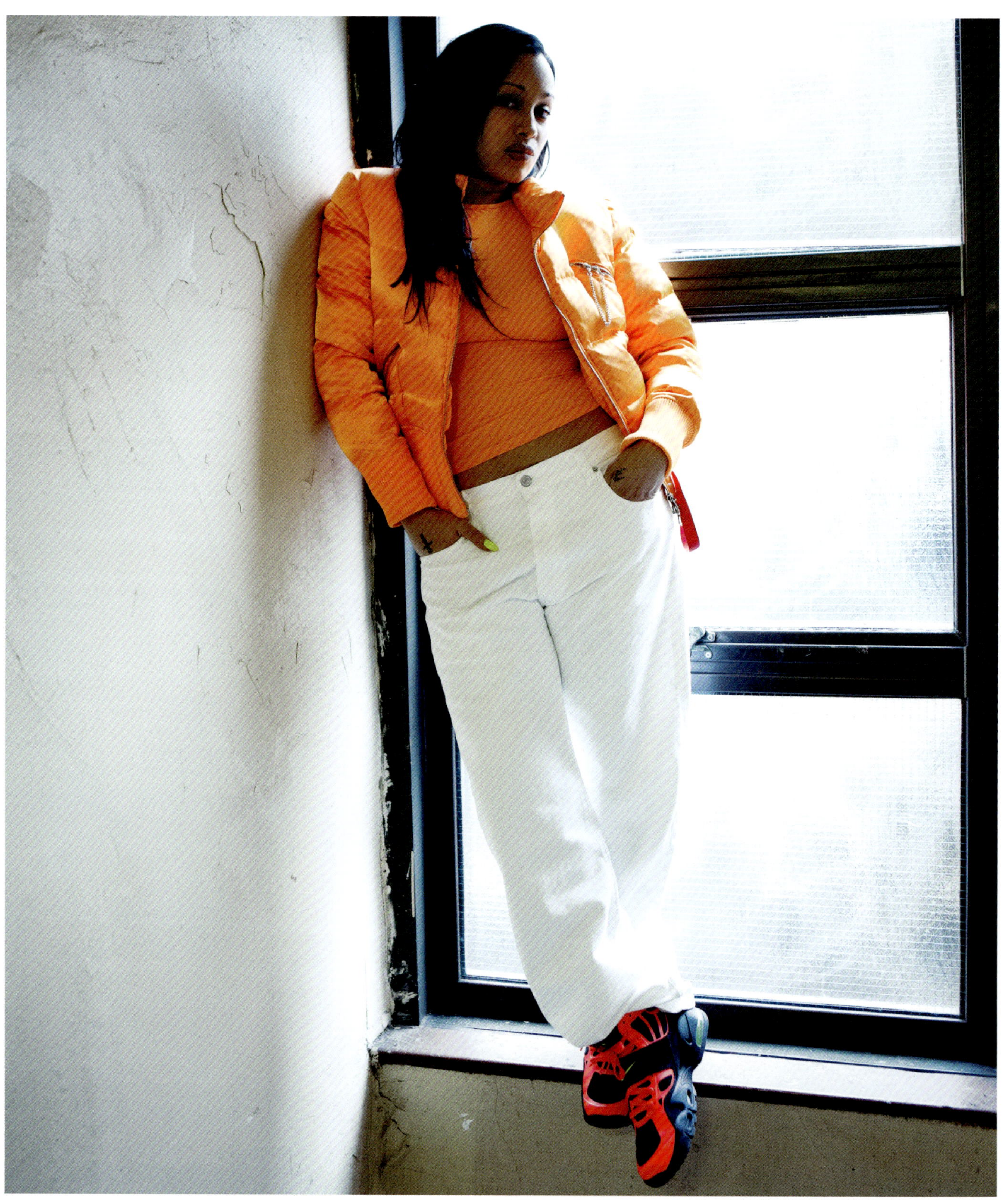

Interview by Asher Penn
Portrait by Brayden Olsen

When Venus X began her GHE20G0TH1K party in New York in 2009, there was no way she could have imagined what it would become: an international cultural phenomenon encompassing music, fashion, nightlife, art, and politics. The vanguard public that Venus X first attracted cut across seemingly divisive boundaries in NYC nightlife — GHE20G0TH1K was black, white, gay, straight, trans, slutty, high fashion, low-brow, and thoroughly lawless. It was also the defining context to debut the talents of now-celebrated acts like Total Freedom, Nguzunguzu, and Physical Therapy. While today Venus X is an internationally touring DJ and there are literally dozens of warehouse raves happening in New York City each month, GHE20G0TH1K still stands apart — largely due to Venus X's unrelenting commitment to the scenes she catalyzes and nurtures, as well as the talented and wild people that come to inhabit them.

This place is great for interviews.
I came here for the first time with one of my mentors. I heard this used to be the Hip Hop Hotel, where everybody used to stay back in the day. I do all my interviews here. It has good juju.

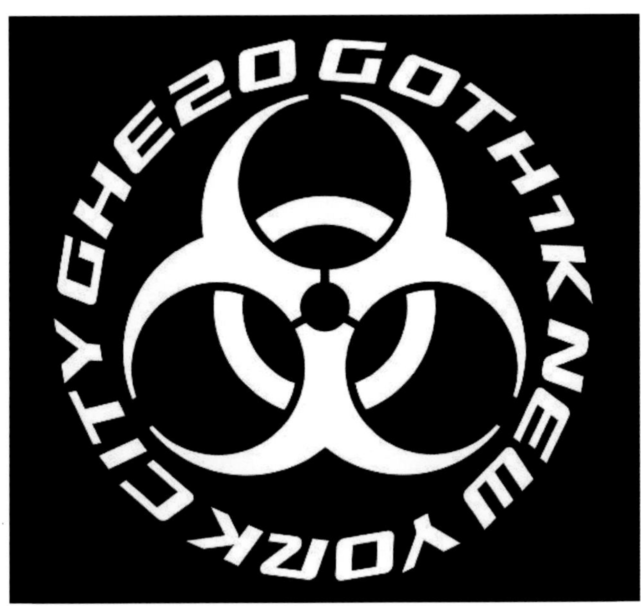

GHE20G0TH1K Logo, 2012.

You have a mentor?
Well I have a lot of different mentors. Lizzie from Gang Gang, Santigold, Mos Def...
How did you connect with them?
It happened really naturally. Lizzie used to come to my party and then she took me and Shayne on tour with her for a couple weeks to open up for Gang Gang. These days Lizzie will take me to the spa and be like, "Girl, it's going to be okay, you don't have to quit." She reminds me that it takes time to level out.
Having older people to talk to helps.
Yeah. Because if your family life is off, if your spiritual shit is all fucked up and you're an artist, you can't really function. Most artists don't know that because they think it's all about music and it's not. You have to be superhuman when you're touring. You're playing all these shows, and you're not really making that much money, and people don't respect you yet, you don't have hotels necessarily, you're sleeping on floors — you've got to be really balanced to put up with all that shit. It was really hard before I had mentors. It's been really amazing to have a couple people who will just tell you you're on the right path, even if you don't take the super-pop road. Before I never had that much guidance.
We met when you were at The New School.
Yeah, but I never finished. I was too busy doing events, like talks and shows and GHE20G0TH1K. I didn't care about school. School was stressful.
What were you doing before you started GHE20G0TH1K?
I was taking photos of punk bands mostly. I was obsessed with drummers. I wanted to be a drummer but no one would teach me. It was a boys club. So I just took pictures. I would take pictures of all these crust punk bands from St. Marks who used to hang out there, like Big Gunz and Cerebral Ballzy when they first started — I have polaroids of one of their first practice sessions. I followed some bands out to South by Southwest.

Images courtesy Venus X

Were you hanging out at places like Todd P venues? ABC No Rio?

A little bit. A lot of Rock Star Bar.

What was that place?

It doesn't exist anymore. It was a hardcore punk venue on South 5th and Kent. That was the hot spot. I would go to lots of house parties with bands and different kids. The typical shit where you're at a house party and it's kids puking, fucking, a band playing in the basement It's a hot mess. There's a radical bookstore upstairs and they're selling anarchist leaflets and shit. It was really special, even if the music wasn't that good. The kids who went there were awesome.

How did you start DJing?

I would watch all these people DJ drunk and think, "I can do that." I asked my friend to teach me, which he did — not very well — but I managed. I actually got my first real lesson DJing live at Top Shop in front of hundreds of people.

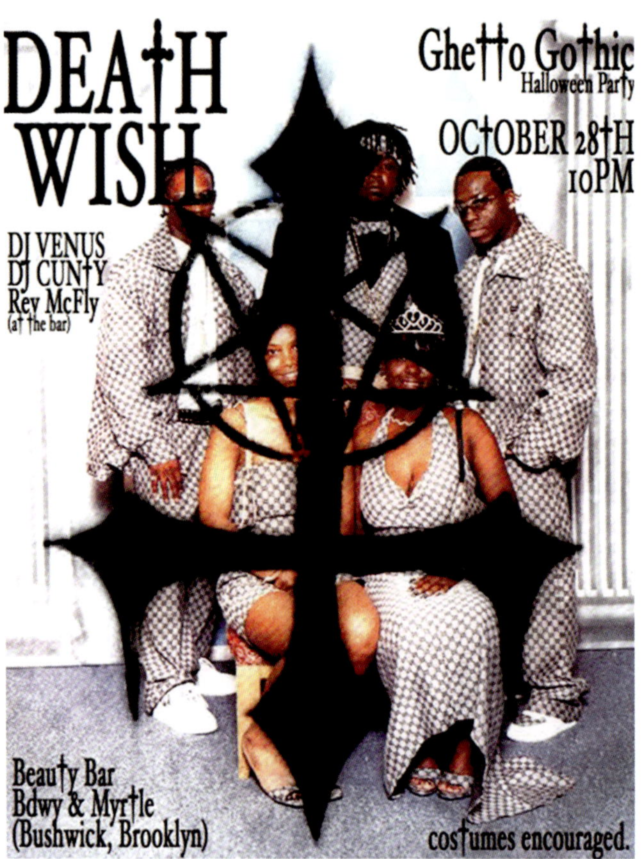

GHE20G0TH1K Flyer, 2009.

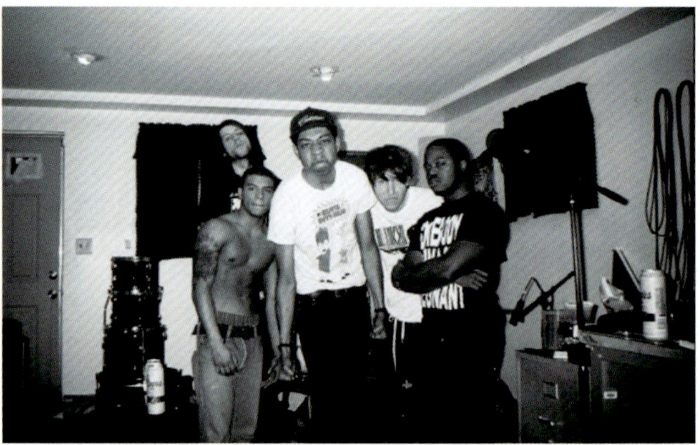

Cerebral Ballzy, 2007. Photo: Venus X

I remember when that happened.

Yeah there were lots of local DJs getting booked. I got around $75 to play for two hours during my friend's set. He was like, "Fuck it, I'll show you how to mix two songs and you can do it for the rest of the time." So I did it.

What inspired you to actually start GHE20G0TH1K?

I was going to Weird at Home Sweet Home, which at the time was super coldwave, like, white goth. Then I was going to hip hop parties that I felt were more like black goth — you have people talking about murder and shit, that's gothic. It's not American gothic or Irish-Celtic gothic. It's a different kind of gothic. I decided I wanted to start a party where I could play both and mix them up. I liked what some Witch House people were making like Salem.

What was your exposure to hip hop?

Well, I was a waitress at the 40/40, Jay Z's club. At the height of the 40/40, the VIP room was packed with Jermaine Dupri, Rihanna, Ne-Yo, Beyoncé. I was 19 years old waiting tables, serving $10,000 alcohol tabs to these people. I didn't look for hip hop, I grew up around it, so in my free time I was trying to rebel, not just from that job but also from my family and my upbringing, which was very urban, very hood. My dad was a drug dealer, money launderer. He did a lot of crazy shit, which I didn't mind, but I had never been exposed to anything punk, anything independent.

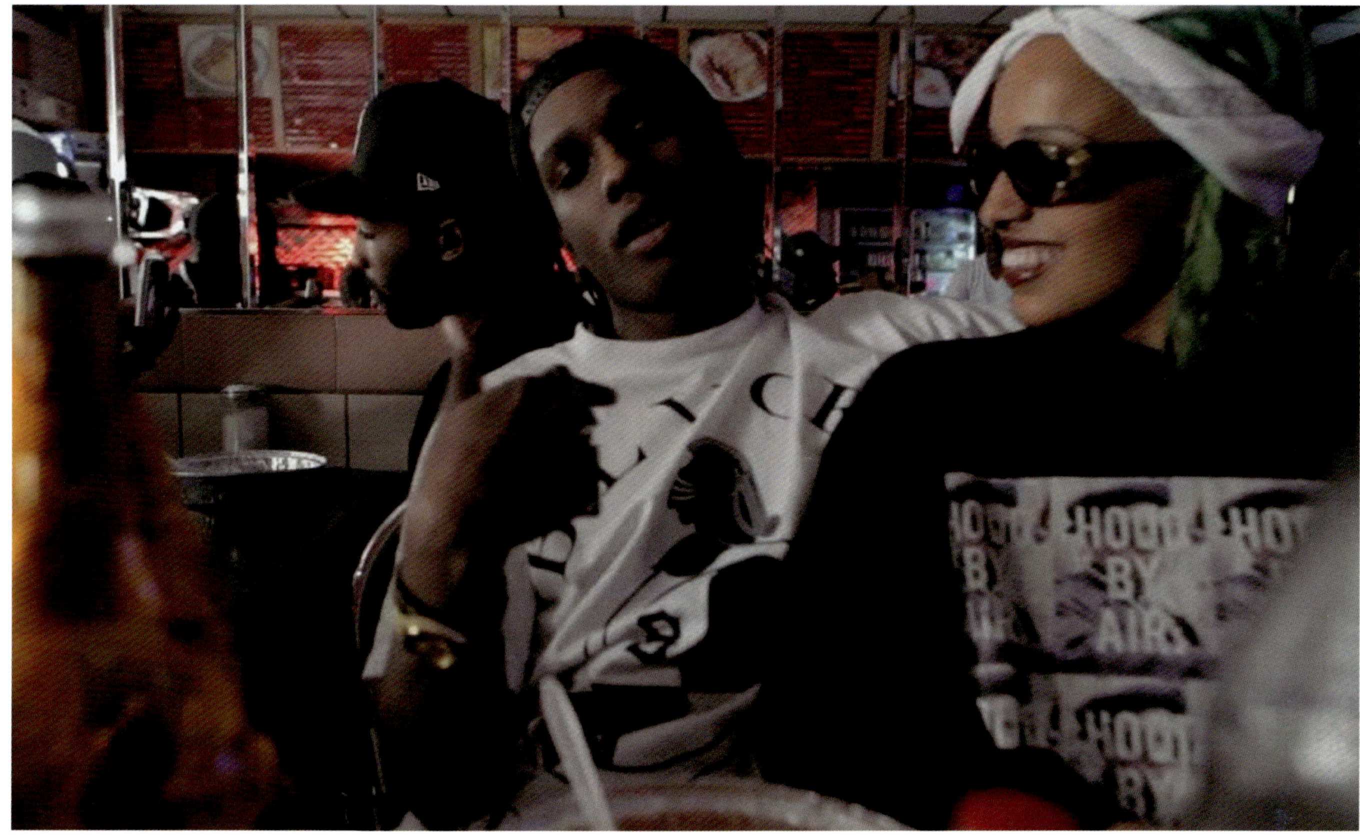

ASAP Rocky, Peso, 2011. Directed by Abteen Bagheri & ASAP Rocky

So you were kind of rebelling against hip hop culture?
It didn't even coincide with what I was learning. I was learning about militancy, gender, feminism. I was learning about all these things that were basically saying hip hop is whack. So I was a little punk girl. I wore Doc Martens and baby doll dresses. I wore a big jean jacket that my grandma had from the 80s. I wouldn't have fit in at any hip hop venues.

Where was the first GHE20G0TH1K?
It was at Beauty Bar. I DJed by myself the whole night on my iPod and my laptop — two channels. We did it monthly and I packed the place out both times. Then we did it at Legion Bar on Metropolitan and packed that out as well. The manager at Metropolitan offered me the space on Orchard Street, Gallery Bar. We started doing GHE20G0TH1K in the basement there. He was a great bartender, a great manager. He knew exactly who to give free drinks to and how to take care of everybody.

So from the start it was really a reflection of your social life.
My personal social life, yeah.

What music were you playing?
Nine Inch Nails, Christian Death, Cocteau Twins, Sisters of Mercy... A lot of 70s punk from the early years. Adolescents, Wire, or Public Image Limited. Really hardcore, angry, political shit. Then we also played nasty Dipset, Juke from Chicago, which at that time was still really dark — it was at the beginning of the whole genre. Witch House stuff, Salem...whatever we wanted.

How did the music evolve?
I was listening to lots of different kinds of stuff everywhere, learning about music from different perspectives, so it kept growing every single time I DJed. By the time I got to Orchard Street I had been going to Kingdom parties. I wanted to get him involved because I knew that I had a different audience that wanted to hear his music.

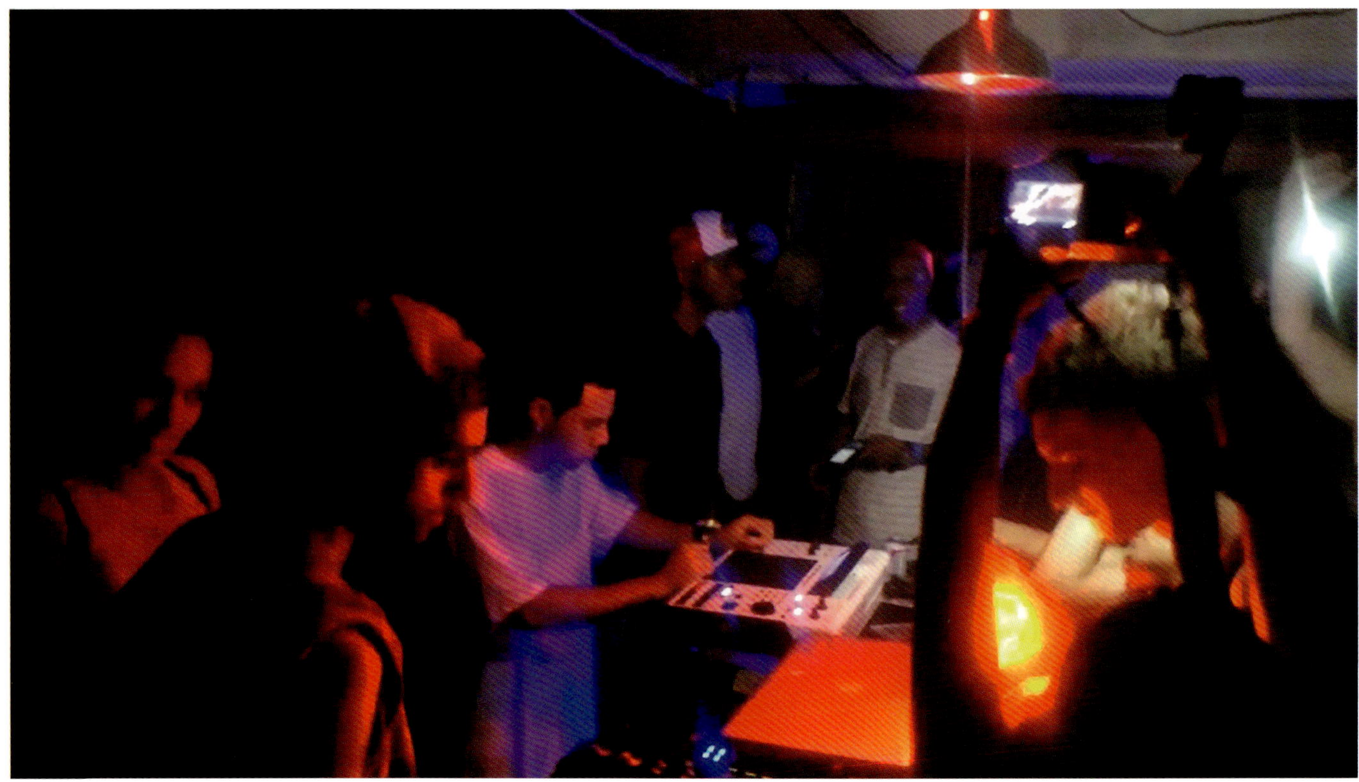

AraabMuzik, GHE20G0TH1K, 2011.

There are a lot of DJs that got their first real visibility at GHE20G0TH1K: How did you guys find each other?
Every relationship was different. I knew Shayne from when I was 19. He was DJing with Physical Therapy who went to New School; we saw each other at the bagel shop, getting coffee. I took classes with House of Ladosha who introduced me to Kingdom. He had all these other connections like Ashland and Nguzunguzu. With all these people GHE20G0TH1K transformed from being a punk and hip hop party to being a ghetto goth party. It took on its own identity, and it became something by everybody bringing their own one-hour labor.

How long were you at Orchard Street?
We were monthly, then biweekly, then every other week. We were on Orchard for about a year and a half, and then we went to Grand Street.

Was this with the same manager?
He's my boy. He ran Orchard Street and he was the one who ran the warehouse. We were a team. GHE20G0TH1K changed when he moved to Florida and the Warehouse got shut down. I've been bringing it back slowly, with people from that team.

The parties on Grand Street were awesome. You never really knew what you were going to hear.
Yeah, you might hear acid house, you might hear hip hop, you might hear a gay guy rapping, you might hear a punk band. You never knew because I was programming from my personal relationships.

You would hear or see something you liked and would want to bring it in.
Yeah. So when my friends were playing industrial goth, I said, "Yo we got to get them to DJ or to perform." That's my mentality. It wasn't, "People are going to think it's weird, that's not a DJ." Fuck that. If people don't like it they don't have to come back. I don't care.

I remember one night seeing AraabMuzik there. It was like a mosh pit.
We couldn't announce it because we didn't pay him the right fee. We couldn't book him solid so it was a secret thing. That party was out of control.

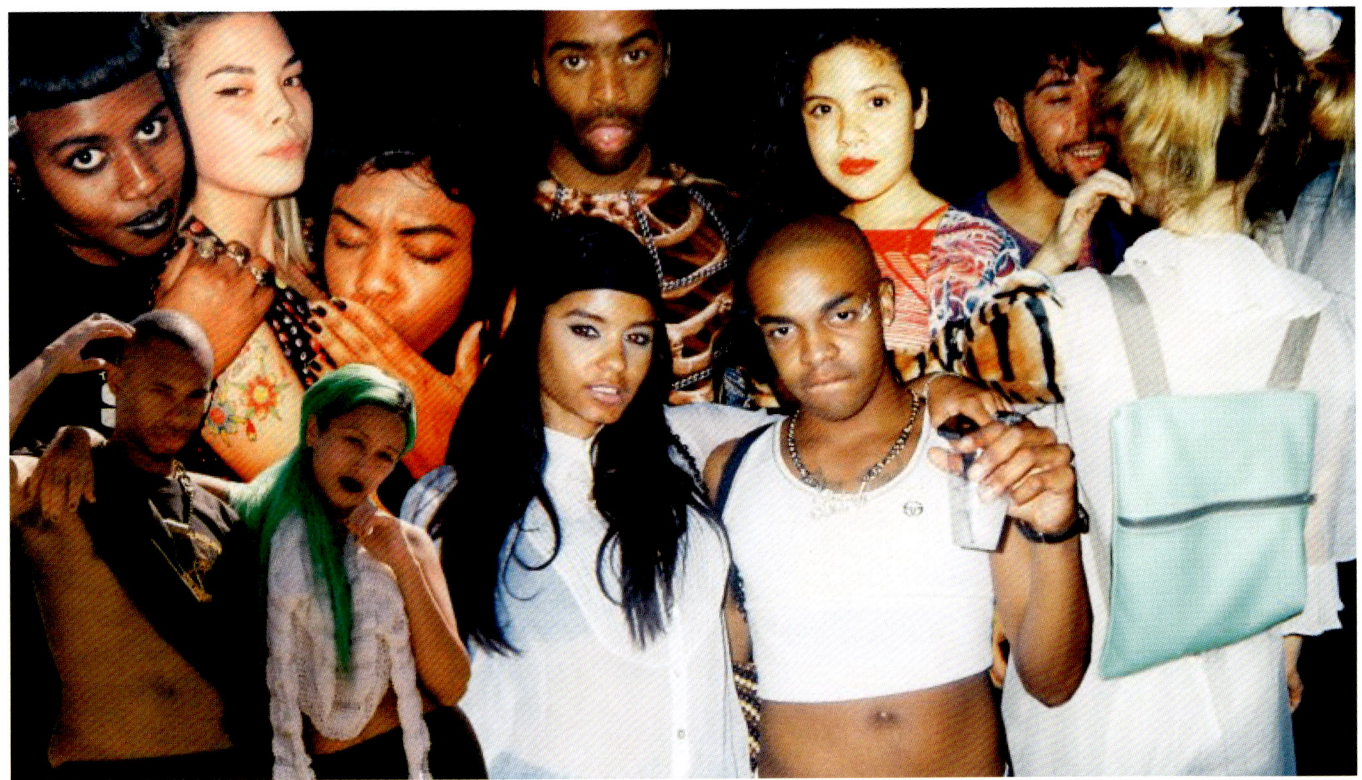

GHE20G0TH1K Collage, 2011.

Now it seems like there are 20 raves going on every weekend in Bushwick.
They say imitation is the best flattery, but it does create some competition. I just care that our parties are good when we do them. I don't want to be monopolizing the experience. If I inspire people to do something, that's awesome. Hopefully they won't be too in my shit, doing exactly what I do, but it happens a lot. A lot of promoters are sneaky. Why wouldn't you hire the same kind of lineup if you see that it's working for somebody else?
So since Grand Street shut down it's just been you? You don't have a partner?
Yeah, I've been doing everything by myself. That's why I use different venues — like SOB's, Santos, Westway, these spaces in Bushwick — they've got their own system in place. I don't have to run the bar. I can't really do the consistent warehouse party like I used to. My homie was really responsible for holding down that illegal venue so I could make sure that everybody feels good and that all the right people are in place, working and playing.

How has the internet played a role in all this happening?
Oh my God, the internet was my MetroCard. I could go anywhere and I could talk to anybody. I could book people. I could listen to music on YouTube from all over the world. I could download things from anywhere.
It was also how people learned about GHE20G0TH1K.
Kids were watching us build the party, the invites, taking inspiration from the lineups and stuff like that. It created a very loose but clear network of people around the world that felt the same thing. They were all about the same age, they all had the same kind of influences from just being young at the same time. It was cool. GHE20G0TH1K was really one of the pioneers of bridging this internet generation with a real experience, which is something that kids are struggling with. How do you materialize all that shit you do online? And how do you meet up with those people that you talk to all fucking day? Come to GHE20G0TH1K. Go be there. ☺

Gerlan Jeans
"It's about bringing design back to the people."

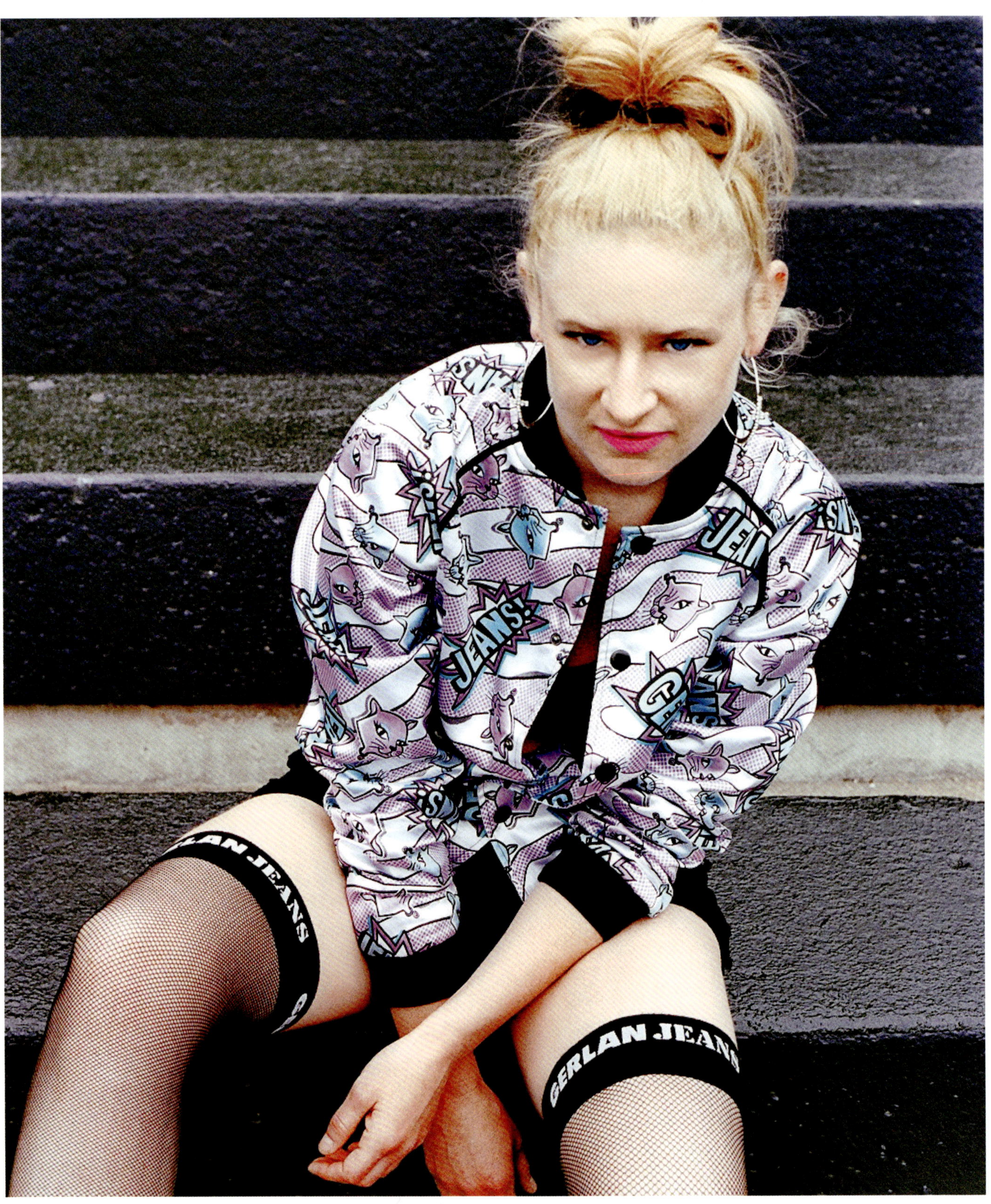

Interview by Avena Gallagher
Portrait by Maggie Lee

Since 2009, the collections of Gerlan Jeans have brought a much needed return to teen irreverence and self-expression into the arena of street fashion. Independently owned and operated by designer Gerlan Marcel, previously known for her print designs for Jeremy Scott, Gerlan Jeans uses printed graphics to combine the best looks of American alt culture — goth, hippie, skateboarding, punk, raver — into inventive garments that celebrate the attitudes and values of youth culture. Whether it's Mall Witch, Minnie Mouse, or Gerl Power, the message with Gerlan Jeans is always the same: positivity, inclusivity, and fun.

Now, these are your drawings from what age?
I think I was probably eight or nine. It's summer wear. The shorts are brightly colored palm trees with a yellow sunset behind them. She's wearing a bathing suit, which has pineapples on it. "They have become in popular demand from the Gerlain buyers."
So exact in your pricing at such a young age.
"She was rewarded in 1986 for being the best and prettiest girl in America" as you can tell from her amazing look. She has no arms or legs — "...she's been with us for about a year. She's very popular and has been in great demand to be put in this magazine. She is wearing a cool summer skirt with a pastel colored shirt. The shirt is $16.27."
You still haven't been told how to spell fashion yet.
I was the worst speller.
It's still "fasoin."
"This is Yvonne Mendemon who was fired because she started to flert..." E-R-T. "...she started to flert with our cameraman but is back with us now."
Was this how you thought fashion was?
I must have been looking at some sort of catalog.

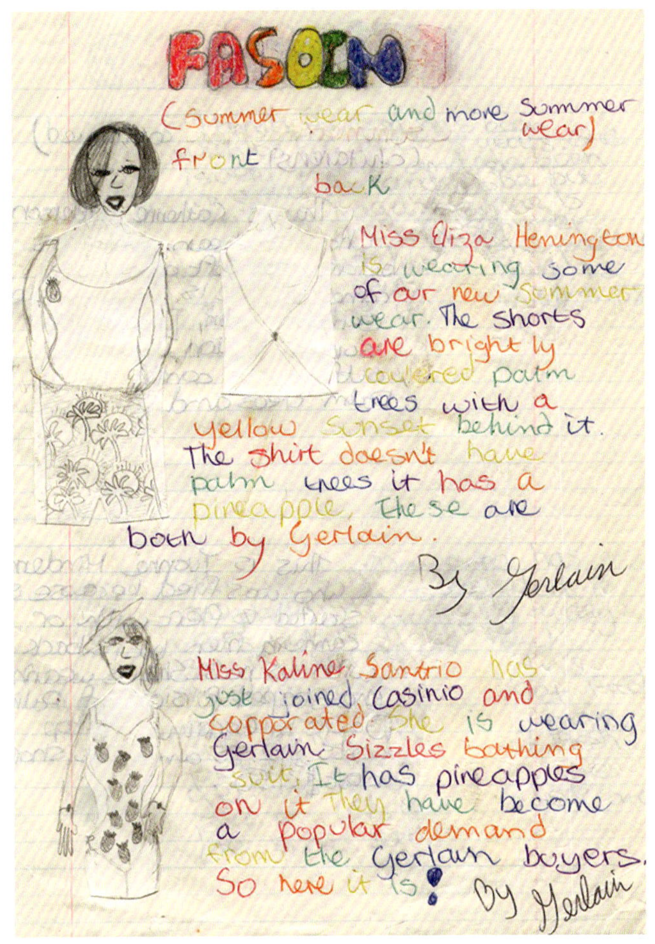

Gerlan Drawings, 1986.

So you weren't looking at magazines?
I don't really remember reading fashion magazines or anything. I do remember getting a subscription to Rolling Stone and thinking it was the coolest thing ever.
Look at your little prints. They're already very Gerlan.
It's very Guerlain by Gerlan. My dad took us to Paris when I was 15, and there are all these pictures of me in front of the Guerlain store. With maroon 90s hair. I had a leather jacket with a Black Flag sticker on the back that I just thought was the coolest.
How Chic.
I was actually really concerned with not being chic enough in Paris. I remember I would wake up really early, spend two hours getting ready to go out on the streets. Obviously, in my brain, somehow, this leather jacket with the Black Flag sticker helped the situation.

Images courtesy Gerlan Marcel

What was your favorite mall to go to growing up?
The Galleria. Every town in America had an "upscale" mall called the Galleria. They had a glass ceiling and huge tropical plants with mini waterfalls everywhere. It was the chicest! Plus they had a flagship Esprit store!
That Esprit store had a smell that was the exact same all over the world, at all of their locations.
Everything in the store transported you into this idea. The brands were so hyper realized.
Then there was UNITS, which was a completely different animal.
Units had an amazing concept. It was like a modular system for dressing. The woman who started it, Sandra Garratt, was American. It was basically a mass-market sensibility of what Yohji Yamamoto had been doing.
Like a tube that was a skirt but could also be a dress.
A lot of what American Apparel was originally, is based on this UNITS structure. The whole store was modular designed to match the clothes. It was a revelation in a mall in Ohio!
In the same role, then, we have the old Banana Republic.
And their sub-label "Outback Red." The store was full-concept safari. They really went there with the interiors. The stores were designed with all of this kind of salvaged wood, foliage, vintage safari helmets. The ads in the magazines were that too.
At our Banana Republic, there was a broken-down jeep in the middle of the store.
They had one at the Galleria. It was so "Out of Africa." You had a full concept for a store and a full concept for the clothing...they were 4,000% dedicated to their vision!
In those days did you know you wanted to get into fashion?
No, not at all — I wasn't sure what I wanted to do but I knew I didn't want to be told what to do...

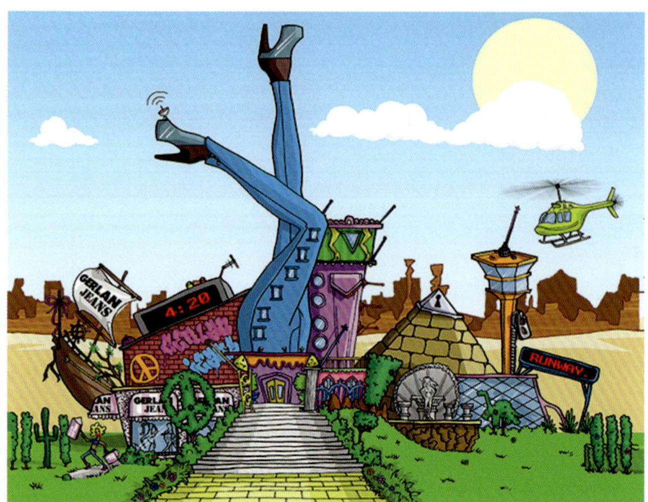

Gerlan Jeans Corp. Headquarters - Jeans, Nevada.

Did you go to college?
When I graduated high school I decided to go to Hampshire College because it was this totally alternative place where there were no grades, no exams, and farm animals roaming the grounds. But I deferred my enrollment for a year, so I could have some time to just do whatever the fuck I wanted to do. I just wanted to experience as many things as possible, without limitation.
How were you able to do that?
I had this book of intentional communities — politically correct word for communes — all over the United States. Me and my best friend planned this trip for basically two years, when we were still in high school. I was obsessed with On the Road, The Electric Kool-Aid Acid Test, and Wilderness, a book of poems by Jim Morrison. We built our own food dehydrator and spent like eight months living on all these various communes. We eventually settled on the West Coast for a period of three months or so in Deadwood, Oregon. I lived in this old-school bus.
And what kind of community was it?
It was based on Quaker principles of living, that had started in the 70s. Me and my friend were the youngest members by like 20 years. After living there and being on that trip, I realized I wanted to be on the move; I didn't want to be in one place. That was when I decided to go on permanent tour with the Grateful Dead.

Why the Grateful Dead?
It was about the music and choosing
your own adventure. I feel very
lucky to have had this outlet. When
you're young you just want to go off
and experience things on your own,
it's pretty scary. How are you going
to support yourself? How are you
going to feed yourself? What do you
do? But here was this self-existing
environment in Grateful Dead land.
It was like this traveling economy
— a little world and village. There
was buying, selling, bartering, and
trading — a full support system in
place with total acceptance and no
boundaries. The Grateful Dead allowed
me total freedom at a very young age.

What happened when school started?
I was still on Grateful Dead tour,
driving to shows on the West Coast
in my friend's grandmother's Cadillac
and occasionally driving back to
Hampshire College for class on
Mondays. I wanted to travel more than
I wanted to be in any type of school
environment... I had always wanted
to live in Greece because I had seen
these photos of my dad when he lived
there in the 60s, all sun-kissed,
weaving on a loom in that Grecian
light. So, I found some weird, little
art school with like three people
in it and moved to Paros, a little
island in the middle of the Cyclades.

What kind of art were you making?
I was painting. It was very Grateful
Dead inspired. Everything was very
goddess-y, swirly. I was imitating
a lot of styles, but I didn't have
one of my own. I met this teacher
who suggested I stop limiting myself
to one medium.

Were you thinking about fashion?
I made clothes on the Grateful Dead
tour. I was totally self-taught.
I mostly made "boob-curtains" It
was literally a strip of fabric
around your boobs with a gathered
"curtain" covering your stomach and
an embroidered Star of David or a
mushroom on the front. That's how I
started really sewing and putting
stuff together.

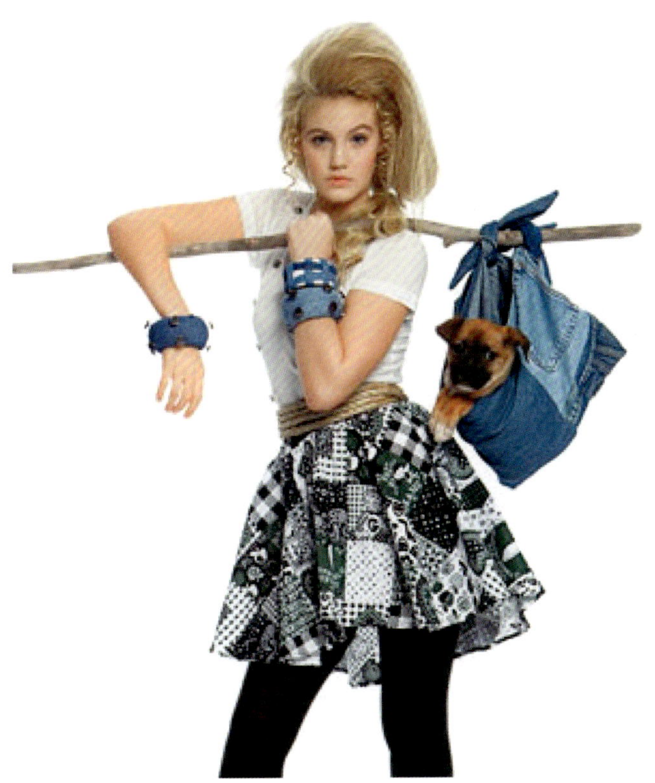

God Bless These Jeans, F/W 2011.

But you weren't anti-fashion?
Obviously, Grateful Dead kids were
kind of anti-fashion, but there was
a look, a full-on uniform, which
I was super into. Patchwork boob
curtains, pipe pouches, embroidered
dreadlocks, peyote stitches, Jnco
Jeans and the heyday of Alien
Workshop and Poot...

What did you do after Greece?
I went to Oregon College of Arts and
Crafts in Portland, and began doing
a "surface design" course. It was
weaving and dying with natural fibers
and beads and things. It was not
fashion related, most of my fellow
classmates were moms going back to
school, making potato-stamp-print
casserole covers.

But you were making printed fabric.
Yeah and I was making stuff out of
it. But I barely knew how to even sew
or do any of that stuff. I realized
that OCAC wasn't the right place for
me either. I basically quit and just
started working as a buyer at Buffalo
Exchange and other odd jobs while I
was taking night classes in pattern
making and sewn construction.

How did you end up at Saint Martins?
I had this friend, Jen, who I had met while traveling around with this sound system called S.P.A.Z. (Space Pirate Audio Zone) — post Grateful Dead — and she had gone to London for some sort of summer class in fashion. She made all these outrageous clothes, like turquoise fake fur coats with big eyeballs as pockets. She would sell them at this store in Portland that carried all this weird Cyberdog-inspired rave gear made by West Coast designers. I basically wanted to be her. She had crazy dreads that she dyed all different colors of blue and purple and I did the same. She had these Swear platform sandals with daisies on them, which I bought in the same color. People would sometimes mistake us for each other and I always loved it.

And she encouraged you?
She was like, "Well, if you really want to do this, why don't you do it in London?" That was how the whole thing got started. I had no idea that there was this school called Saint Martins that all these famous people went to. I just felt like that was the place. I actually didn't get into Saint Martins when I first applied...

But you went to London anyway?
I went to London anyway and ended up at the London College of Fashion. I was very lucky to have this amazing teacher, David Kappo, who taught at Saint Martins and said to me: "You should be doing Print at Saint Martins. What are you doing here?"

He was able to make that happen?
He arranged an interview that changed my life! I'd been to all these different schools, traveled all these different places but when I got to Saint Martins, I felt home. It's like this incubator to just figure out what your creative process is, and what your creative voice is, with no boundaries. There were also a lot of critical judgments, which is good. If you haven't cried by your second year at Saint Martins, there's probably something wrong with you.

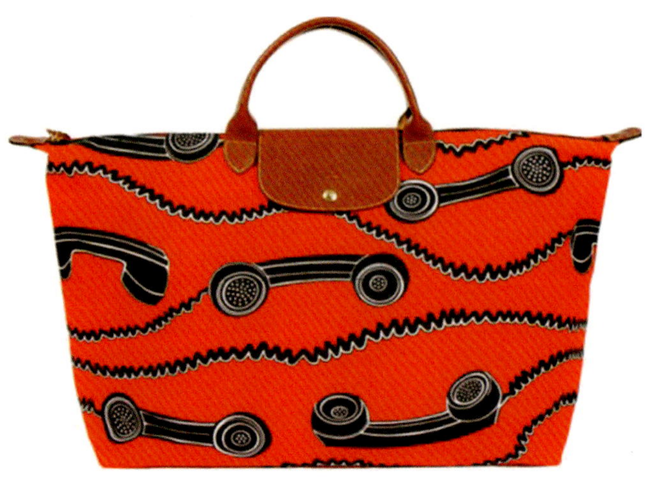

Jeremy Scott X Longchamp, 2010.

How did you start working with Jeremy Scott?
Weirdly, my dad had sent me an article from The New York Times years before. He was like, "This guy's from the Midwest and he sounds interesting."

I remember that article. There were pictures of him hanging out with his mom.
Yeah, his dad made barbecue ribs backstage at the show. At Saint Martins, you took a year off before your graduate collection to intern for designers. I spent six of those months working for Jeremy Scott.

How did you contact him?
I remember calling a store that stocked Jeremy Scott and asking if they knew who did his press. I finally got the phone number of People Revolution and called. They told me to send my resume to their office, but I insisted on getting his studio address. This went on numerous times until I obviously annoyed the pants off them, and they gave me the address. A week after sending in my resume, I got an email back and it was literally from Jeremy! A few weeks later I was staying at his guesthouse in the Hollywood Hills!

Did you like it?
I was in hog heaven as soon as I got there. The guesthouse was next to the studio which was in the garage. I was there for six months doing

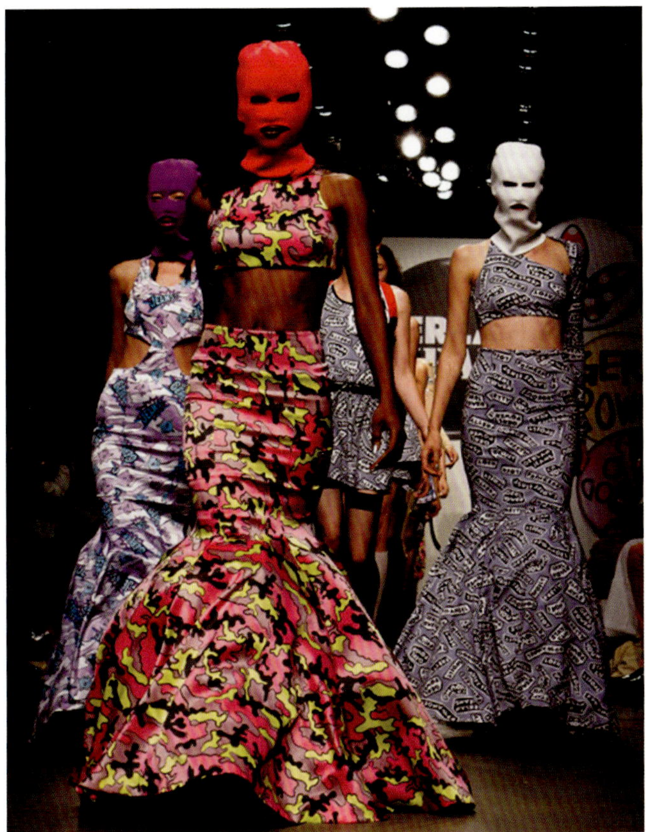

Gerl Power, SS13.

everything from drawings prints and graphics to managing the studio and making costumes for Björk and Fischerspooner. He asked me to come back and work for him. So I was designing prints for Jeremy while I was doing my graduate collection in London. The day after I showed my graduate collection at Saint Martins, I flew back to LA to work full-time for Jeremy.

What was your working process like together?
Aesthetically we were both totally in tune so I wasn't sacrificing my creativity to give him what he wanted. Sometimes it would be something really abstract like a dream he had where there were hot dogs fighting and they had boxing gloves. I would then develop the graphics by hand. The mummy print and the phone with the never-ending line...they were literally sketched in pencil or ink and then scanned and put to fabric.

Was LA the first time you ever went into a Hot Topic?
Oh my God.

Was that a major moment?
It's almost like I can't even remember, because it feels like such a visceral part of who I am. It was at the Highland Mall in Hollywood. The Hot Topic there was so outrageous. I used to just go there for a Sunday stroll and then stop by the oxygen bar kiosk.

How long did you stay in LA?
Two years. I came to New York in late 2006. The vibrancy and fantasy of LA was so invigorating after five years in London but I missed having that close-up interaction with humanity that is so hard to find in LA where everyone is trapped in their cars.

What was your first fashion job in New York?
Designing women's outerwear for Coach.

Was Coach a culture shock?
Totally, but I was super into it. It was an exciting contrast to my past experiences, seeing how that corporate structure worked and how the design process in that environment functions

It must have been quite a gearshift for you aesthetically.
It was definitely a challenge... it's less about big ideas and more about really refined details, like having a three hour meeting about the dimensions of a coin pocket. It was a lot about designing a new liner for the same jacket shape made from different materials season after season. I have great respect for the details but it can get a bit monotonous after awhile — there was so much more I wanted to express!

Is that why you decided to start your own label, Gerlan?
I felt I had a very specific story I wanted to tell, opinions I wanted to express, and a vision I wanted to share. I wanted to contribute to the zeitgeist and have a conversation culturally. The medium that I just felt most drawn to was printed graphics. It's literally about wearing your opinions on your clothes. I needed to create a platform to be able to do that and the only way was to really start something on my own.

THE ORIGINAL
GERLAN JEANS

Gerlan Jeans Logo, 2013.

Not only a clothing company but a brand identity as well.
It's all about creating a fully realized, immersive brand story that allows your customer to interact and participate in the story being created. Even if it's just a subliminal thing, your customer is contributing to the language being constructed. It's idea-driven, not trend-based work.

Amen. Why specifically denim?
I was really, really obsessed with printed denim growing up. "Jeans" was also a nod to the concept of a diffusion line, without the diffusion. It was about bringing design back to the people. Ultimately the goal is to be mass market, as opposed to a niche thing. A huge part of it is inclusivity, and it comes from a genuine place. For me, it's not about being an artist. It's about being able to produce these ideas in multiples because that's what makes them powerful.

This gets back to the idea of mass market too.
If these designs could go to a factory somewhere, there would be boxes and boxes and boxes of this stuff being shipped out globally, galaxy-wide, and then people could participate in this message and add life to it. Because I'm not producing thousands and thousands of garments, the price point is too high. A lot of the people who love Gerlan Jeans can't afford Gerlan Jeans.

But you know there is a buying public for it out there.
There are all these Gerlan Jeans knockoffs being made in Asia and they're selling it in huge numbers. You see them on their websites for 25 bucks. I can't compete with that price. So, yes, there is a mass audience that's ready for it.

Your second collection was funded with Kickstarter. How did that work?
A friend introduced me to the founder of Kickstarter. It was a relatively new thing at that point, mostly being used to self-finance independent film and music. He gave me all these sweet insider tips and tricks on how to make the most of it.

Did you feel Kickstarter was in sync with the brand identity for Gerlan?
It felt really congruent with the motivations for doing the line to begin with. This was literally putting it into the hands of the people. There was this overwhelming outpouring of love and support from these people who believed in this vision and wanted to contribute to making it happen and being a part of its story. You don't have to rely on the fashion establishment to make it happen.

What's your process when you put together a collection?
Idea-wise I'm on overload all the time. Conceptually, collection development evolves in a very organic way. With the SS12 "Mall Witch" collection, the jump-off point was about investigating that moment when you realized you wanted to be alternative. Its such a contradictory time...that moment when you're trying to embrace what makes you different but at the same time you're still self-conscious about the things that make you different.

Do you often have teenagers in mind when you're making your collections?
I always have teens on the brain. That's such an exciting time, when you're really discovering your style, and you have this combination of fearlessness and naiveté. Being young to me is a state of mind, it's not an age thing. People are constantly saying to me they think I am really young just because I'm so enthusiastic. That blows my mind because enthusiasm should be part of life no matter what your age! That kind of energy and attitude is important to me. Spreading peace and love through print and color. ☺

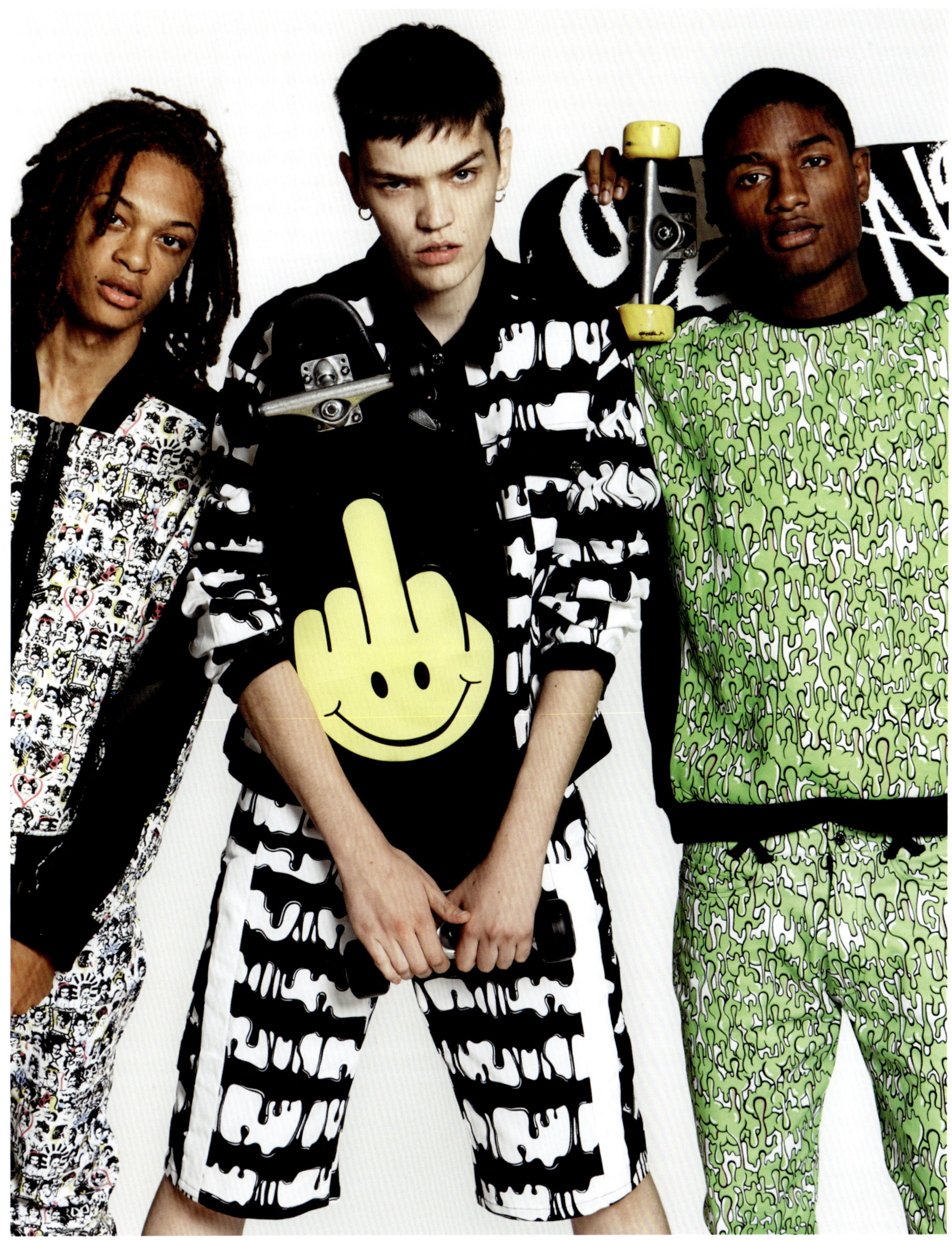

Mall Witch, SS12. Photo: Danielle Levitt

Cali Thornhill DeWitt
"Some people shouldn't get it."

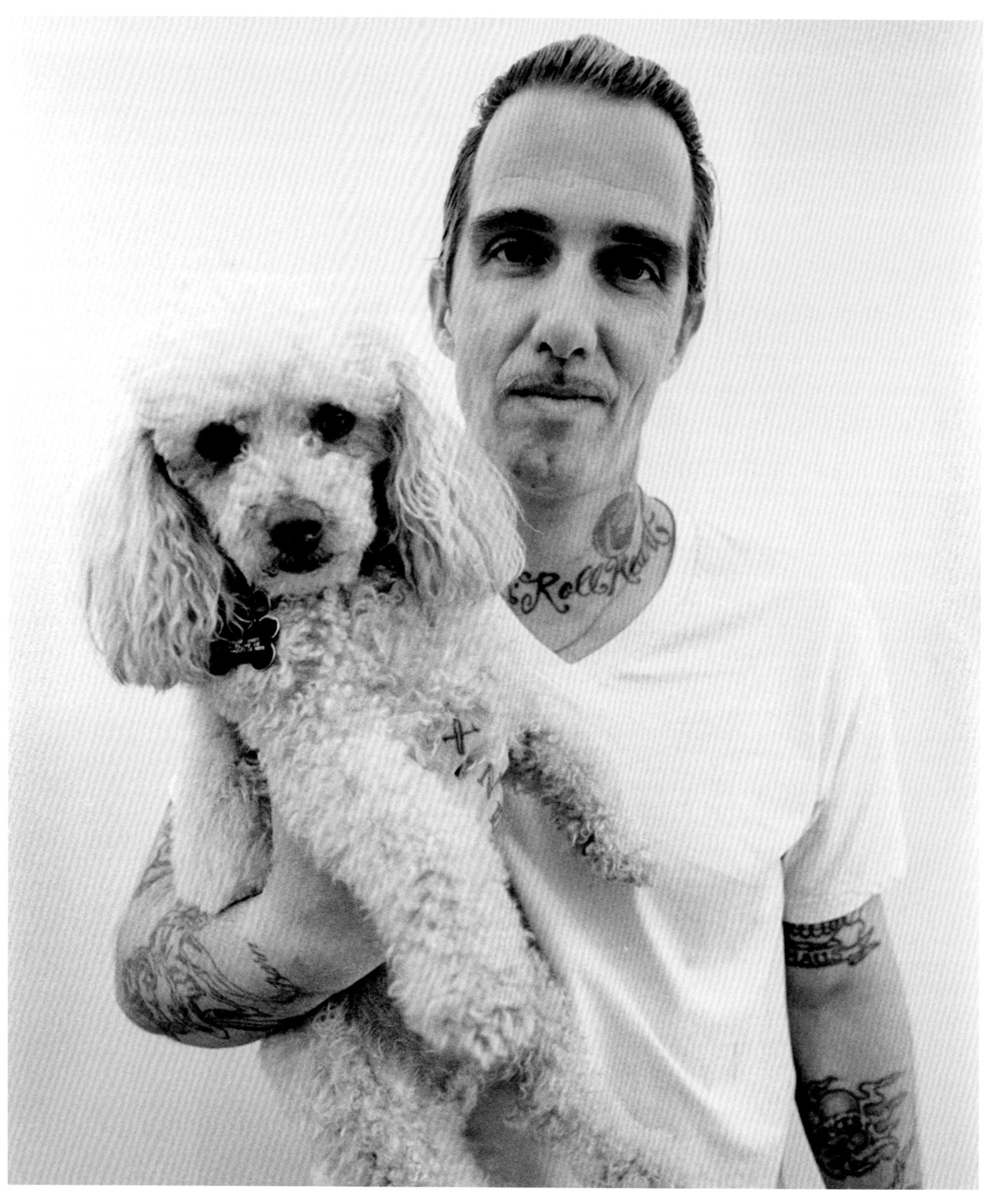

Interview by Asher Penn
Portrait by Susan DeWitt

In Los Angeles, Cali Thornhill DeWitt is considered by many to be one of the most selfless participants and aggregators of the city's DIY culture. DeWitt runs an independent record label called Teenage Teardrops, maintains a 500-page-deep photo blog called Witch Hat, and hosts a weekly radio show on KCHUNG Radio called Zen Mafia — a moniker for a veritable gang to which he belongs, although actually who or what the Zen Mafia is remains decidedly unclear. DeWitt also organizes art shows, concerts, makes fliers, posters, T-shirts, zines... it's honestly hard to keep up. While creative work for many people seems ultimately oriented towards some kind of career, Cali has refused any system oriented towards turning creativity into capital, instead making his "work" about supporting and empowering the people around him: his friends and family.

Where were you born?
I was born in Sidney, British Columbia, on Vancouver Island. In my first three years we lived in Port Renfrew, Prince George, and Salt Spring Island. My dad was a logger. We moved to California when I was three years old.

Why did you move to California?
Because my dad went to college here. He loves California. He ate his first taco in 1963 at the age of 20, on Sunset and Alvarado. He had lived here and loved it until he got a draft notice, so he boned out back to Canada.

Where did you live when you moved?
The San Fernando Valley. The gigantic suburb, the endless suburb. Late-70s/early-80s SFV was very Fast Times at Ridgemont High.

What got you into music?
I think it started from my dad. He loved jazz, and was really well versed in it. I didn't like it when I was a little kid, but there was always music in our house. My mom listened to country, my dad listened to jazz, and somehow that meant they had a Rolling Stones record.

So you were got into rock and roll?
Yeah, my first favorite song was "Paint It Black." My dad also nurtured the things that I liked. He took me to see Rock 'n' Roll High School in the theater. He took me to see The Decline of Western Civilization in the theater when I was like seven. He took me to see the Who movie, The Kids Are Alright, when it came out.

That's cool.
I think those things affected me more than I think he thought they would. He just thought they were funny, the rips in the Ramones' jeans, Darby Crash's attitude, but I was really into it.

What kind of work did he do?
He does home renovations and finish carpentry and stuff. He turned 70 this year and he still does it.

So did you play music at all?
No, never. I have tried to learn the piano a few times but I don't have the discipline for it. What I would want — my fantasy — would be to play piano like Chico Marx, but I don't have the determination for that I don't think.

So with music you've always been OK in the audience?
I'm a fan first, and music was my first favorite thing.

Were you going to shows when you were a teen?
All the time. My first show was a D.O.A. show in 1982 when I was nine. I had a twelve-year-old friend who took me.

What kind of shows were you going to? Who were you seeing?
I would go and see stuff like the Butthole Surfers where some goth band would open and some shitty hardcore band would be on the bill. That was cool. It was the late 80s, so there was great hardcore: D.R.I., C.O.C., Cro-Mags, Born Against. All the straight edge, youth crew stuff: Pushed Aside, Inside Out, Chain of Strength, etc. There were also bands like Infest and Man Is the Bastard starting to play and get on my radar.

Were you intimidated by the hardcore punk scene?
I mean, punk shows were super violent in LA. It was scary. I remember walking into a fucking Descendants show when I was 13, and within five minutes I had gotten head butted by a grown man, in the face. There was a lot of violence, a lot of fighting, a lot of stabbings. We had a lot of gangs in LA at that time, and I was not about that.

But you still went.
I still went because to me it was like the best thing that you could do. There was freedom in that music. That's why the fighting tripped me out, because it didn't seem to have a place in it. It seemed like it should be like a safe place instead of an unsafe space.

Were you into art in your teens?
Yeah. My dad always took us to the museum and there was always a lot of books in our house. I liked art and always drew, but I never even knew that there was such a thing as art school until I was like 30. Which is weird because I think that's something I would have probably done if someone had told me about it. Actually I probably wouldn't have done it, but I would have considered it.

What were you doing between 18 and 30?
I was having a mostly harsh time. I was doing a lot of drugs; I did drugs until I was 28, and that commanded most of my creative time.

When did you start doing drugs?
I started doing drugs young. I dropped out of school when I was 16. I had lots of friends, was very social, but really didn't do anything. I really think I didn't do anything except party. I had all kinds of like fun. I mean, it was fun until I was 20.

You spent eight years not having fun?
For me it's not fun to have to be a drug addict. I don't regret it, and I had a lot of important experiences during those years, but at a certain point it became clear that I was living an incredibly selfish and wasteful life.

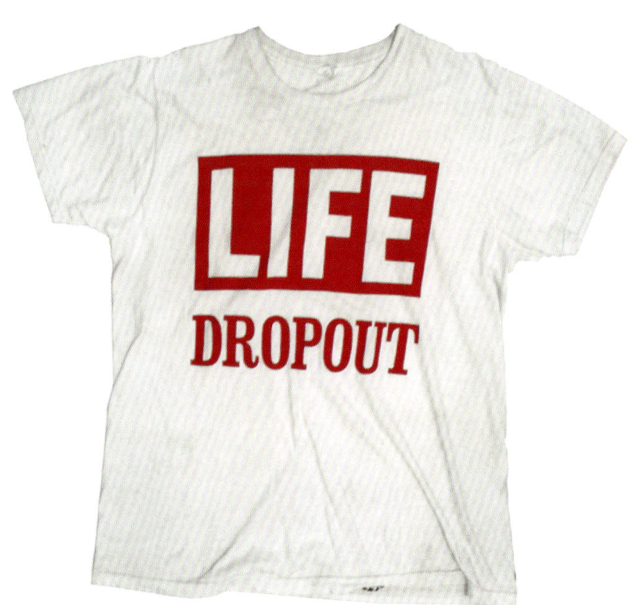

Life Dropout T-shirt, 2011.

At the same time, you spent a lot of time with some really creative people during that era, right?
I was witnessing great stuff ever since I was young. I was always in the middle of something important. If I liked something I was pretty passionate about it. I always liked to find the thing that feels the most honest for that moment. So I would put myself in the middle of it.

But you didn't really participate?
At times I was part of a community, and when you are active within a group of people you are participating in a way, but I definitely could have done a lot more. I had a lot of opportunities to be a part of different things. When I was young I felt like I was growing up faster than my peers, like I was ahead of my time, but now looking back I was an incredibly slow starter. I couldn't get to the next step of producing things. I was on drugs and I was afraid.

Did you have any opportunities to work in the music industry at large in the 90s?
I used to think when I was a kid that a good job for me would be an A&R guy. That was something that people wanted to be then, and I got that job when I was 21.

What label were you doing it for?
Geffen. I didn't make a lot of money
at all, but I had an office that I was
supposed to go to. I would go there
and sit there and not know what I was
supposed to do. I was so confused and
bummed out the whole time. Seeing
how major record labels work and
how people treated music just really
solidified what I learned when I was
like 13 from Crass records.

Which is?
Just be fucking independent and create
your own world, your own reality and
don't try to play with those people.
Just don't do it. If you can say no to
them directly, do it, because it feels
good. They are used to people lining
up to kiss their asses.

What brought you to sobriety at 28?
I mean I had been brought to sobriety
many times in my twenties. I had been
in lots of rehabs and I had had much
uglier moments in my life. I knew
what to do. I had been going to AA
for like six years on and off. When I
finally got sober I was a bartender.
I did that for three more years.

So you don't mind being around drugs?
I should say that I'm pro-drugs.
I think drugs should be legal. I
think a lot of people benefit from
them. I think I benefited from them
at first. And if someone I know is
really fucking up, I might not even
say anything to them. If they want to
talk about it I'm down to talk about
it any time, but preaching doesn't
work in any area.

**Once you got sober you started being
more active creatively?**
I had been involved in things as
much as I could be already. I always
booked shows and made flyers, but my
lifestyle at the time made me not
totally reliable. I mean I wasn't a
thief, I wasn't ripping anyone off, I
just couldn't always be counted on to
show up. When I was sober I started
being more active. I was just trying
to nurture my community, whatever
that was. I realized that good
intentions were one thing, but not
enough at all.

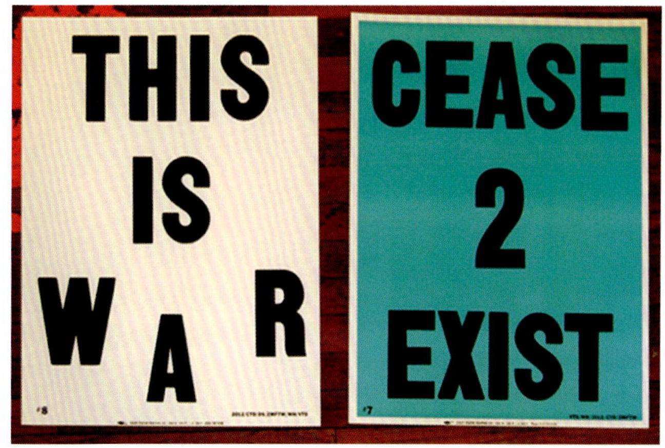

Modern American Opinion, #7 & 8, 2012.

**So you've been involved in music.
Have you ever produced it?**
Like sitting in a studio? No. I don't
like that part of it; I don't like
editing. Anything that feels like
school doesn't appeal to me you.

**So it's more like just making the
record happen?**
Yeah. At first I was working with
other labels but there was always
compromise when you worked with other
people. I don't want to compromise.
I would rather work to make the
money and spend it myself on making
something.

**So that is why you started Teenage
Teardrops?**
Yeah. Since 2006 we've put out almost
50 releases.

Has it always been vinyl?
It's vinyl, tapes...there have been
some books. A "release" on Teenage
Teardrops can be anything I want it
to be.

What were the books?
I put out my brother Pat's first
book, which I should really reprint.
I put out a book of Mark McCoy, who
is a Brooklyn artist that I love,
and a dear friend. There's been a
bunch of zines in there. I released
a zine of my mother Susan DeWitt's
photography.

How do you choose who you work with?
Everyone I've worked with on Teenage
Teardrops is a friend. When I decide
to work with someone, I already love
and respect them as people and as
artists.

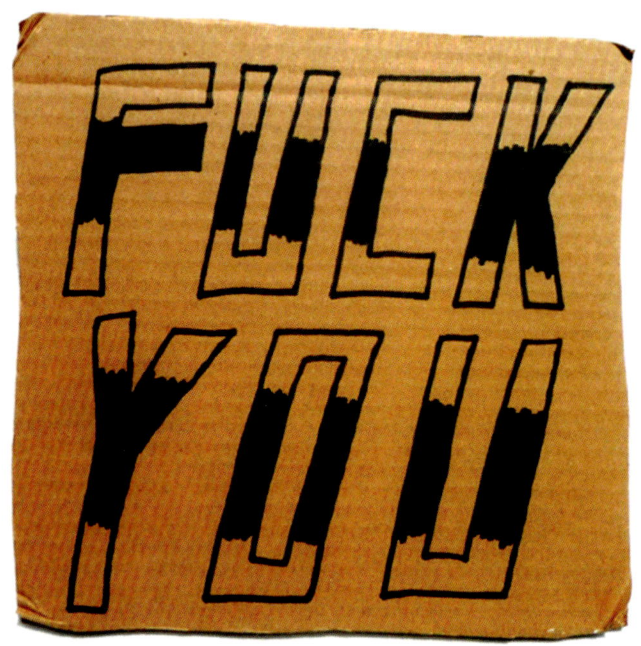

Crazy Band Album Art, Jesse Spears, Teenage Teardrops, 2012.

Were you thinking of TT as a business?
It wasn't a business idea because
I didn't know how it would work.
It became clear over the years that
it was not a business for me. I
understand how you can make it a
business, but for a truly independent
label to make a little bit of profit
you have to work very hard in a
certain way. Some people are down to
do that, but I'm not down to do that.
I'm not down to like hire a publicist,
I'm not down to take out ads. Anyone
who I make a record with or whatever,
I say, "We're going to make it as
beautiful as you want it and as we
can, and it's going to be so nice,
but I'm not a real record label."
Just so they understand and they
don't have expectations in that realm.

How involved are you in the production?
I get as involved as they want me
to be. I really like designing the
covers, and usually they let me
do that, but they don't have to.
The best case is if we collaborate
somehow because that's really fun.

And you distribute them afterwards?
With declining sales in the record
world in general, I just wind up
mostly selling them online one at a
time through the mail.

How did you meet the Zen Mafia?
I met Jesse and Jenna at the same
time about seven years ago. Soon
after that I met Deanna and the
twins. Nate and I were already
friends. We'd already been hanging
out, all of us, all the time. They
all kind of changed my life. Like,
Jenna and Jesse, they were only
21 but their level of honesty was
shocking to me. I was really into
it. I didn't really realize it at
the time, but they did teach me a
lot in that realm.

How did the name Zen Mafia come about?
The first time I heard the phrase
was at a party in the Hollywood
Hills. Deanna started screaming it.

Why did she start screaming?
It wasn't unusual for her to start
screaming at a party or anything.
It was just a funny thing at the
time. But then a couple of days
later Anthony started the Tumblr.

Who was on the Tumblr?
We all had access to it. Everyone
posted whatever they wanted, but it
worked within the group well — we
were communicating with each other.
We would also gas on kooks and lame
local trends, whatever. It's a
place to dump the Internet garbage
can. A place to collectively say
"fuck you." Everyone has their own
style on there. We did that for a
while and the name stuck. We all made
hats and shirts and shit over time.
Crew gear.

**I feel like you're downplaying it a
little bit.**
Maybe? I think it's the just the name
of our family. The idea that you make
your own world with your friends is
really important. I love the world I
live in, but it is a creation of me
and my friends...

Which is like a family.
We treat each other like family. We
tell each other the truth. Sometimes
it's mean, but we take care of each
other. I want this house to be
somewhere where anyone could come
over and there is food and a place to
hang out and be safe.

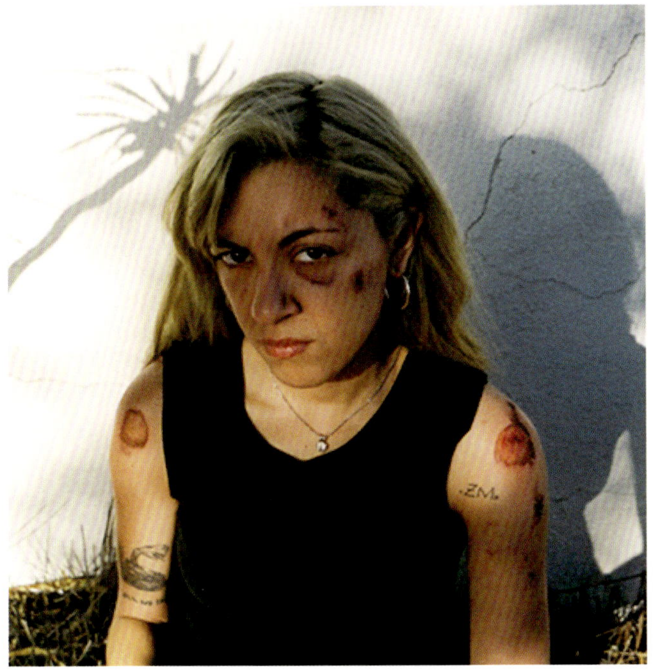

Jasmin Romero after Bike Accident, 2013.

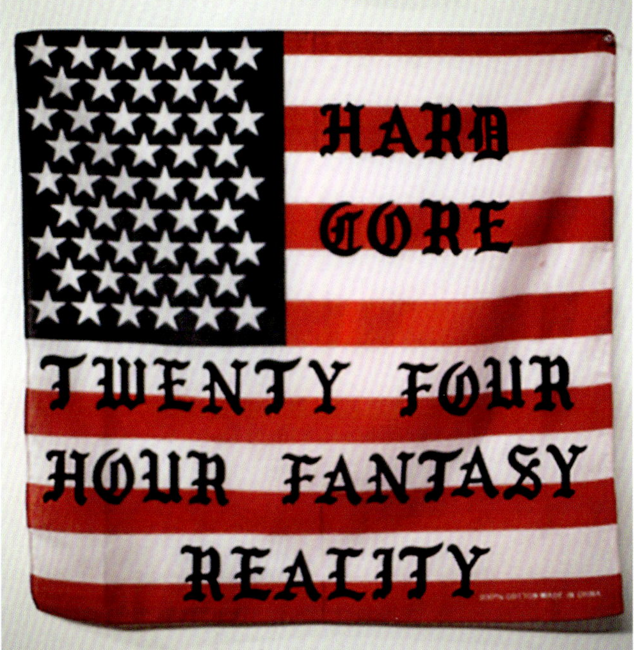

The Zen Mafia Show Flyer, KCHUNG Radio, 2014.

And people do.

Yeah. Like yesterday Jasmine just had that crazy accident on her bike, and today she called me and asked me to take pictures of the wounds. Then it turned out she hadn't been able to wash her hair because her arms were fucked up, so then Jenna fills up a bucket with warm water and washes her hair while we're taking pictures. I just think that's so special. I also think that anyone could do that. Anyone could love their friends and make it an important thing.

What do you think Zen Mafia has allowed creatively?

I think it gives everyone permission to go all the way. When you have a group of people you respect, you can tell them your ideas and they can tell you what they think, and then you can build from there. You can go as far as you're comfortable going. People will tell you the truth but they'll also up you. It's really good to have people upping you all the time. And I will do whatever I can to help anyone in this game to do their thing. The main goal is to feel good about what you do and to make your friends laugh or feel something — to make your friends feel good about what you do. It can be confusing when you go out into the rest of the world, but that's okay.

Because some people don't get it.

Some people shouldn't get it. I don't want to appeal to everyone. I don't like everyone. There's a lot of fucked up people out there, a lot of vampires and scumbags, which makes it even more important to strengthen and embolden yourself with your group of friends. It's more important than ever to reject things, and to only allow what matters to you into your life.

To be able stand up and collectively say "fuck you."

I think of Zen Mafia crew as the ideal modern American family. Because we're telling the truth, and we love each other, and we're not going to do any of the fucked up shit that we're supposed to do, and we won't lie to you or fuck you over. People should know up front how you feel and what you will and won't take part in. If someone expects something out of me that they shouldn't, I think of it as my fault, like I am not communicating my ideas/ideals clearly enough.

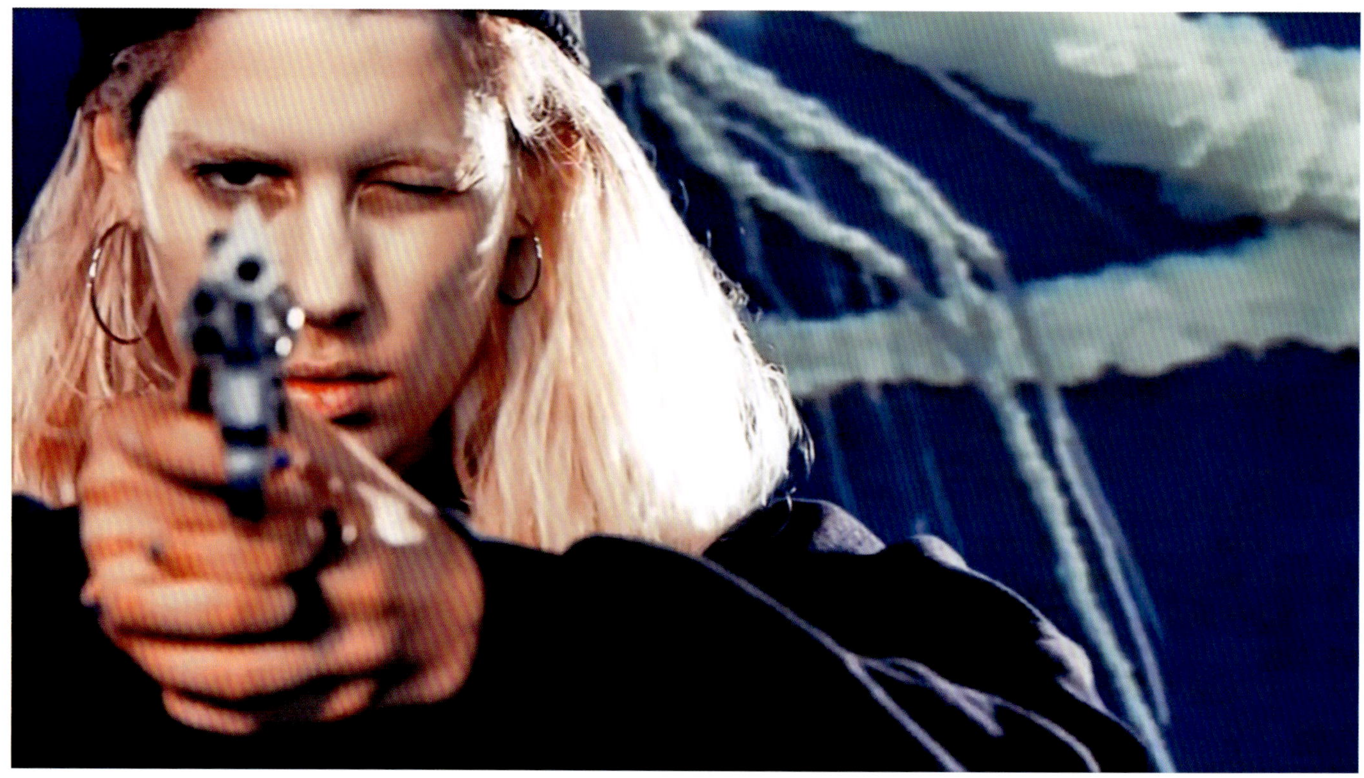

Antwon, Dyin' In The Pussy, 2013.

Was the Zen Mafia your first radio show?
Yeah pretty much.
How did you find out about KCHUNG?
I think because of Fishbeck. I had already known him from putting out a Lucky Dragons album. He sent out an email invitation. Initially the Zen Mafia show was supposed to be all of us, but over time it became mostly me and Jenna. A lot of people got their own shows. Any one of our friends can show up any week. At this point there's at least 50 hours of the shows archived and downloadable, which is pretty rad.
The aesthetic of the show was always very raw. I felt like I had never heard radio like that before.
Right off it was like a party show where everyone wanted to talk on the microphone. I feel like that's so unprofessional that it's good. We always have the mics turned all the way up. Musically it was so many different kinds of music. I have so many records, that for the first year the idea was to never play the same song twice. We would just bring 20 or 30 records from home that I hadn't listened to in a while.
You've been making music videos recently, right?
That's a new thing. I hadn't been pursuing it but I like doing it.
What was your first video?
Dunes, who are an LA band.
That video's great.
Thanks man. I put out a single from them. They were doing a project where they wanted to make ten videos, so they asked me to make one. My friend, Dan O'Sullivan, who is this awesome cinematographer and editor, had always said I should direct a video and he'd shoot it. So we made it and it was a good experience. We wound up making five or six more in the last year.
Where do you get your inspiration when you make your videos?
It's always different. For Hoax's video my inspiration was The Long Goodbye. See how far off track I got? I need a starting point and then I see what happens.

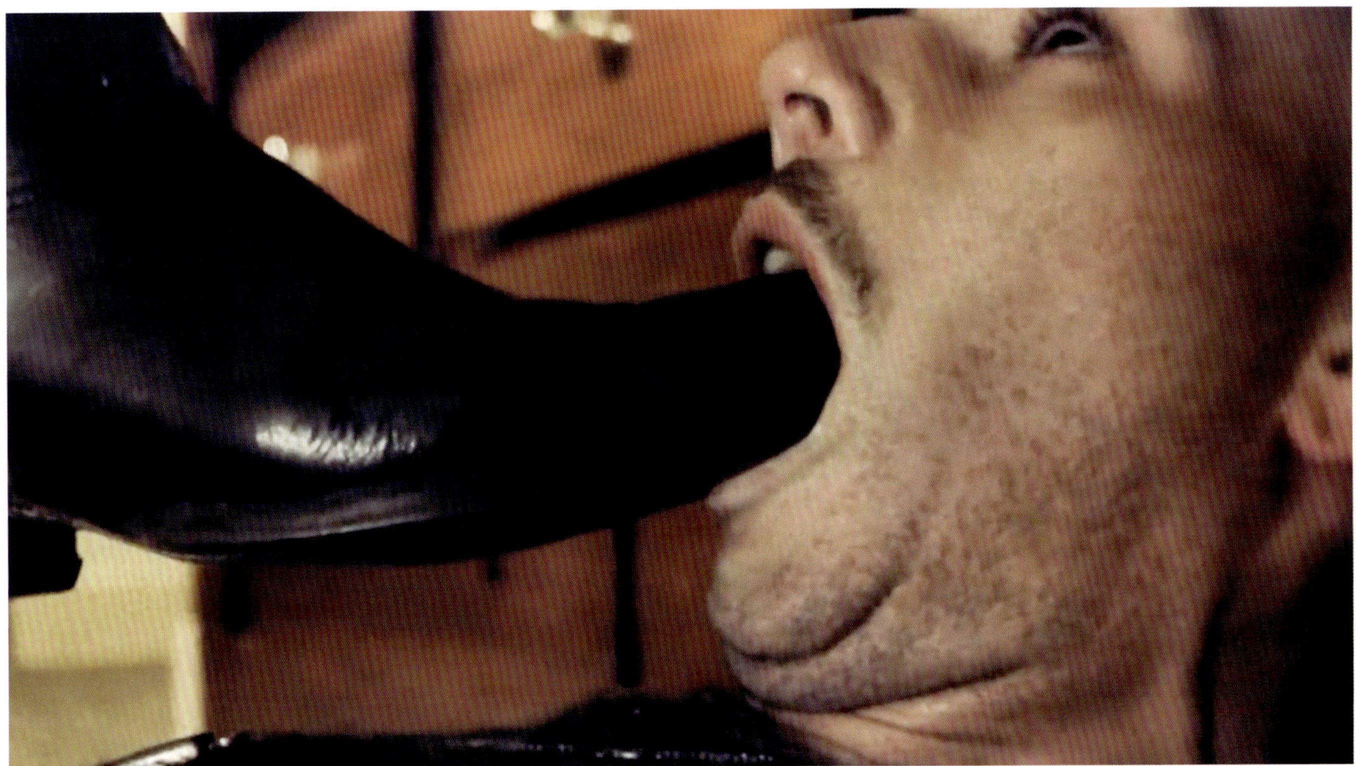

Hoax, Fantasy, 2012.

You were always taking photos before you were making videos.
I love doing that. I think that really started for me with Nan Goldin. When I was 19, with a skate board and a backpack just staying on people's couches and stuff, I always had a black book for drawing and The Ballad of Sexual Dependency in my backpack. It's weird, her friends are really important to me, because I looked at the photos of her friends so often. I feel that way about my friends.

Nan Goldin's photos really glamorized drugs and violence. I feel like your photos are different from that.
Well, the fucked up glamorization of sex, drugs, and rock and roll style is so boring to me, and so prevalent. It sells so much. It's such a dead end, because if you die young, you lose. So I do believe in playing a more positive part, but positive on your own terms. Like maybe a lot of people wouldn't recognize my life as positive but I see it that way.

How long have you been showing your photos?
The first time I had a show by myself was on my 30th birthday. I took Polaroids every day for a year, and then I put them up on a wall in order. There were like four thousand Polaroids or something and I whittled it down to like fifteen hundred. It was totally insane.

You've also been having art shows lately.
For sure. For years I've been putting things on the internet and some people have kept up with it. I've gotten opportunities from that and it seems to be more lately. I just try to do it in a way that I'm happy with it, and have no expectations. I'm less fearful every year, and as that's happened I'm more free with my thinking and my creativity. I am a very late bloomer you know, and so there's a little bit of an under-lying franticness because I feel like I'm just getting started. Luckily people in my family seem to live to like 95 on a diet of hamburgers and gin, so I think I still have a lot of time. ☺

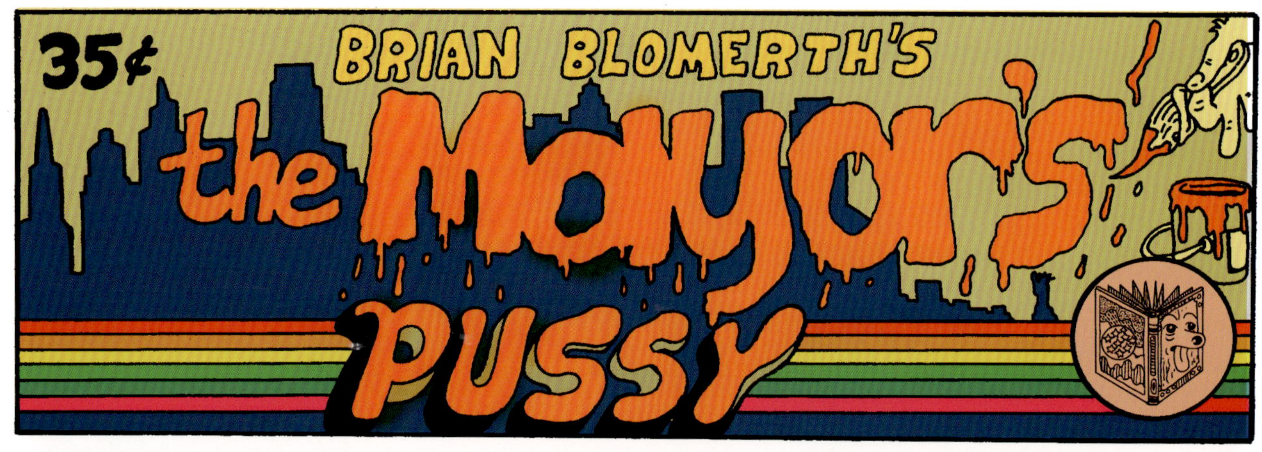

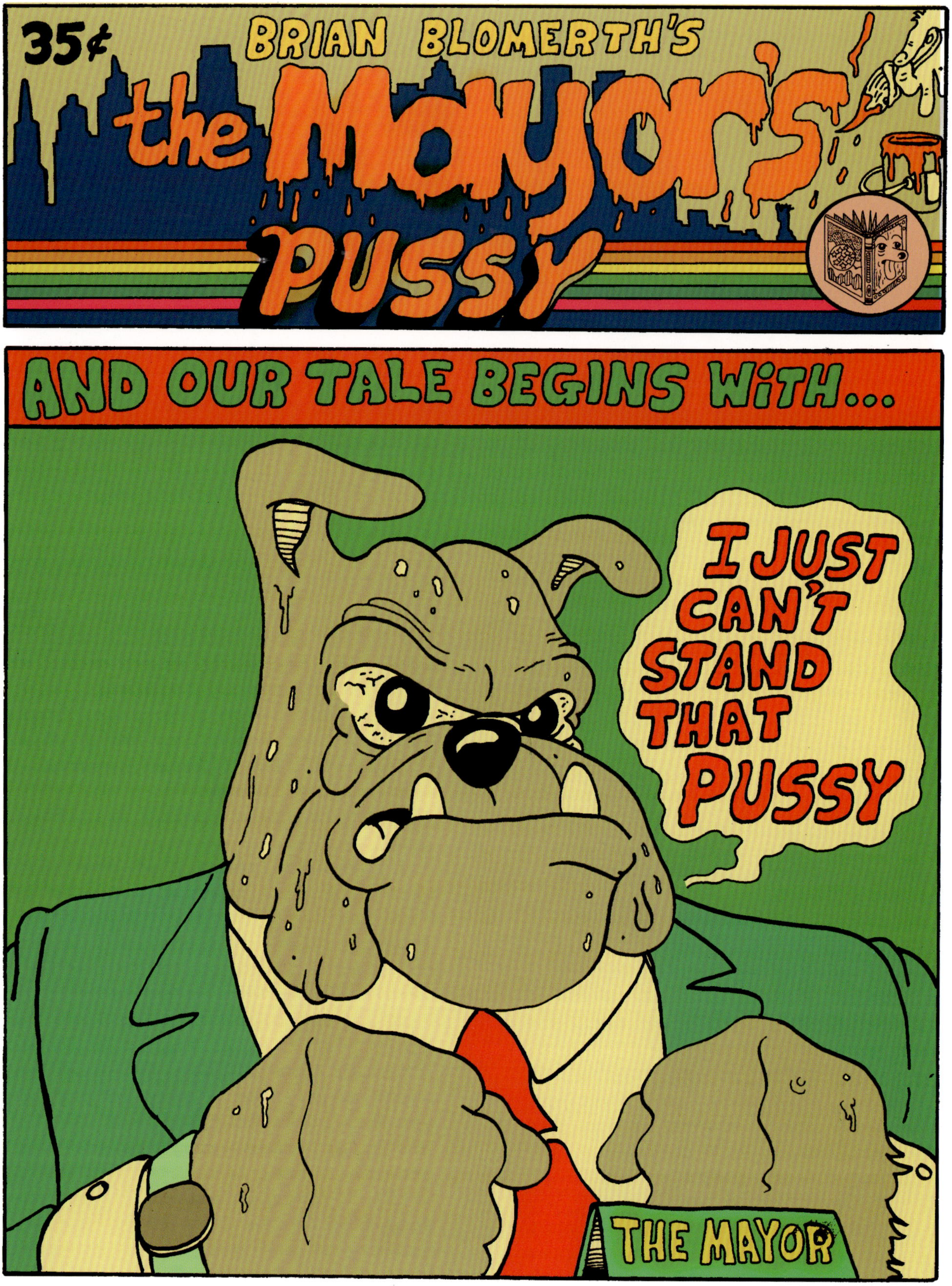

By Brian Blomerth

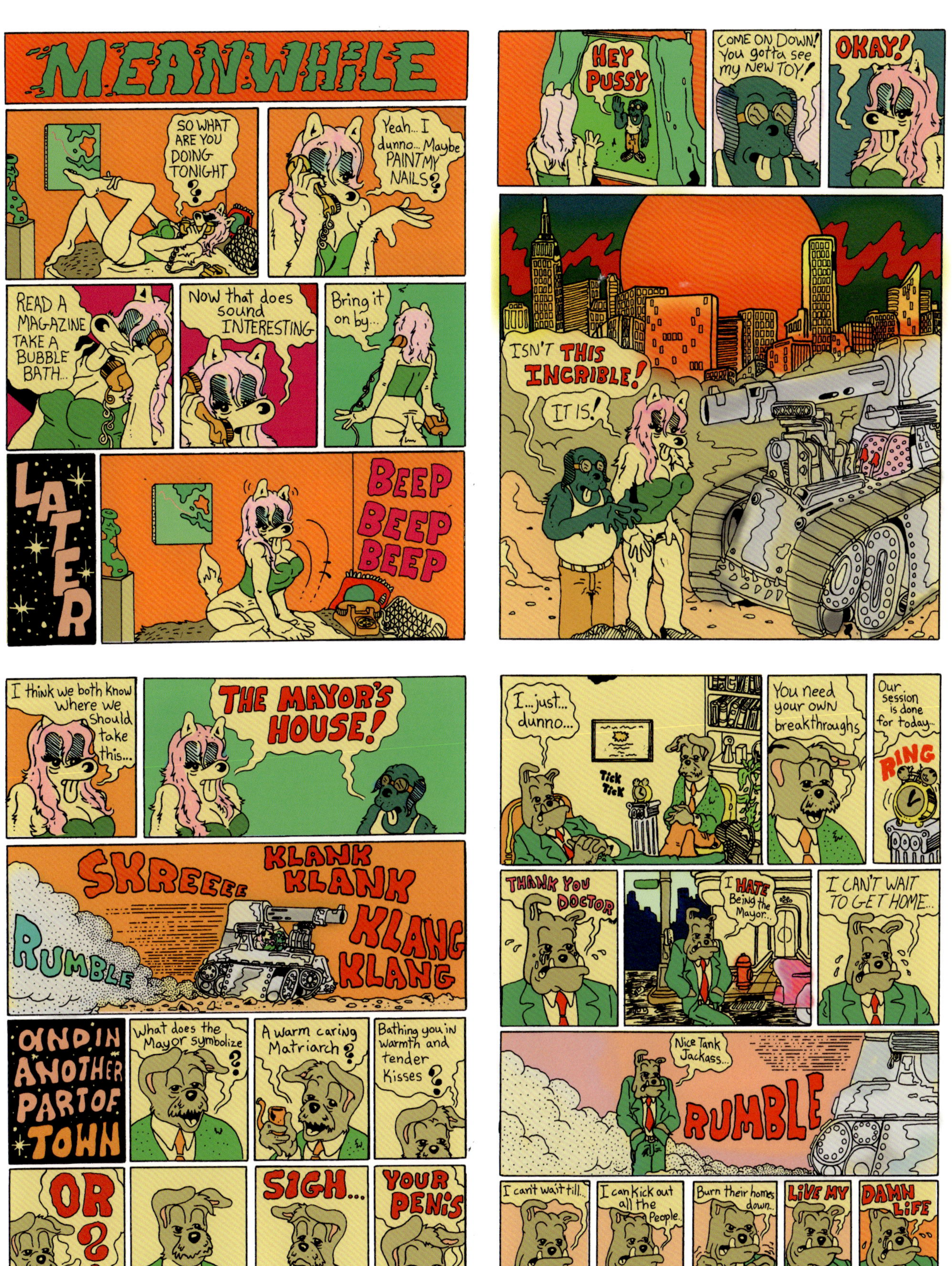

MEANWHILE

SO WHAT ARE YOU DOING TONIGHT?

Yeah... I dunno... Maybe PAINT MY NAILS?

READ A MAGAZINE TAKE A BUBBLE BATH...

Now that does sound INTERESTING

Bring it on by...

LATER

BEEP BEEP BEEP

HEY PUSSY

COME ON DOWN! You gotta see my NEW TOY!

OKAY!

ISN'T THIS INCRIBLE!

IT IS!

I think we both know where we should take this...

THE MAYOR'S HOUSE!

SKREEEE

KLANK KLANK

KLANG KLANG

RUMBLE

AND IN ANOTHER PART OF TOWN

What does the Mayor symbolize?

A warm caring Matriarch?

Bathing you in warmth and tender Kisses?

OR?

SIGH...

YOUR PENIS

I...just... dunno...

Tick Tick

You need your own breakthroughs

Our session is done for today...

RING

THANK YOU DOCTOR

I HATE being the Mayor...

I CAN'T WAIT TO GET HOME...

Nice Tank Jackass...

RUMBLE

I can't wait till...

I can kick out all the people.

Burn their homes down...

LIVE MY

DAMN LIFE

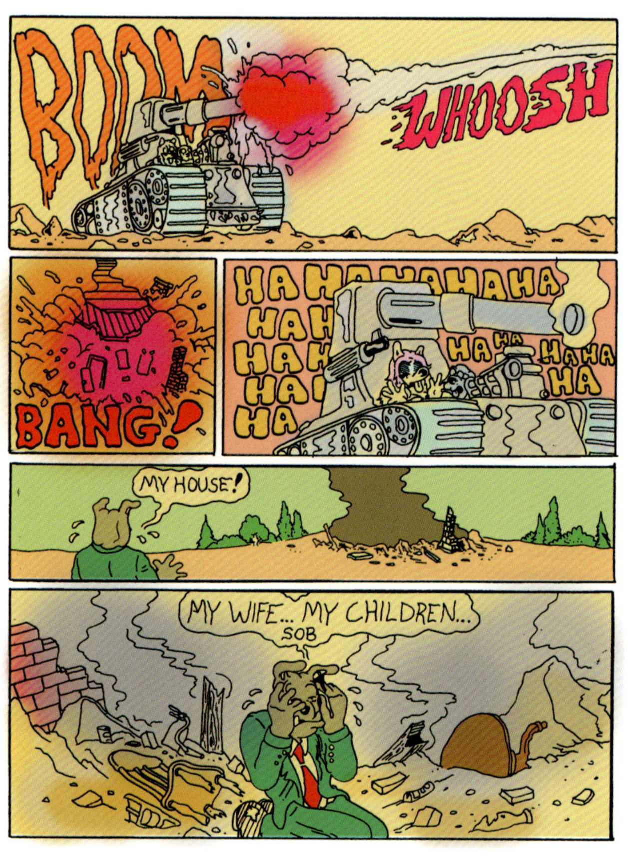

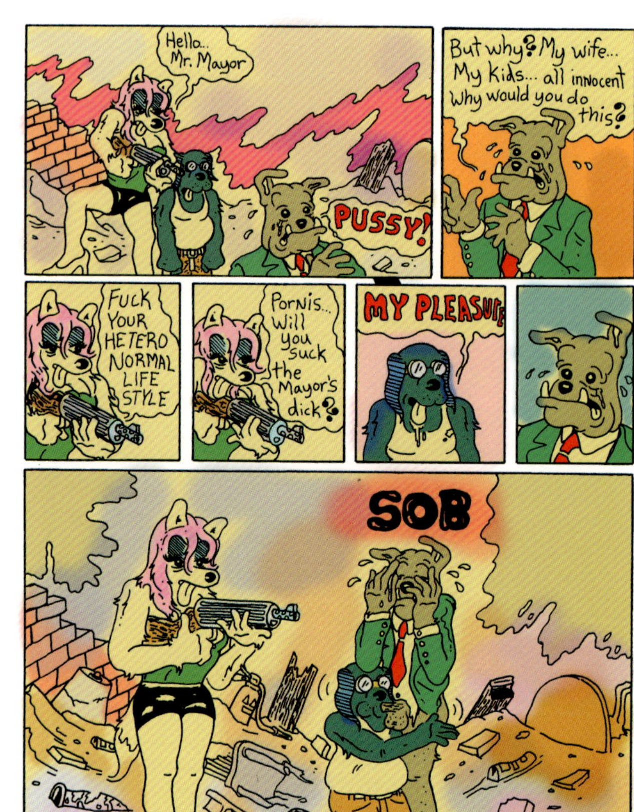

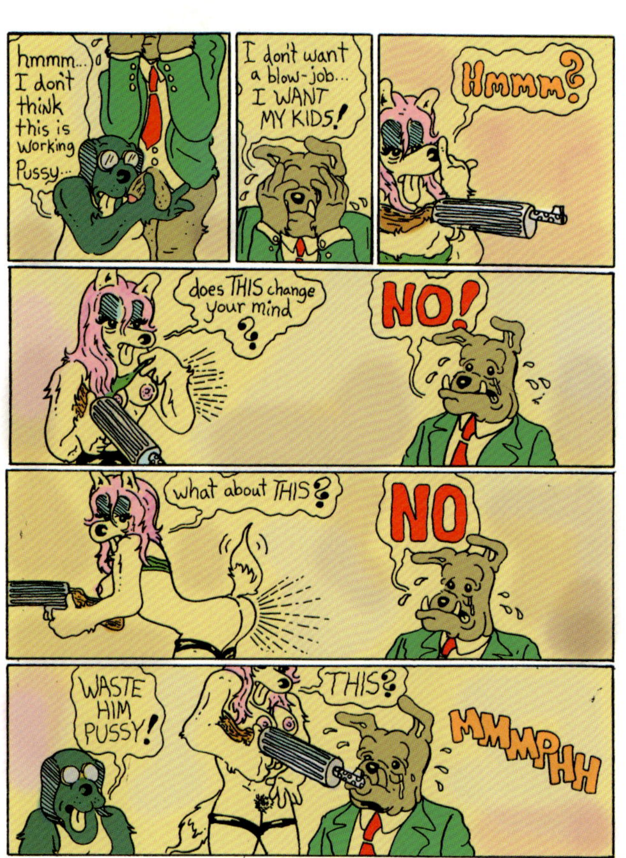

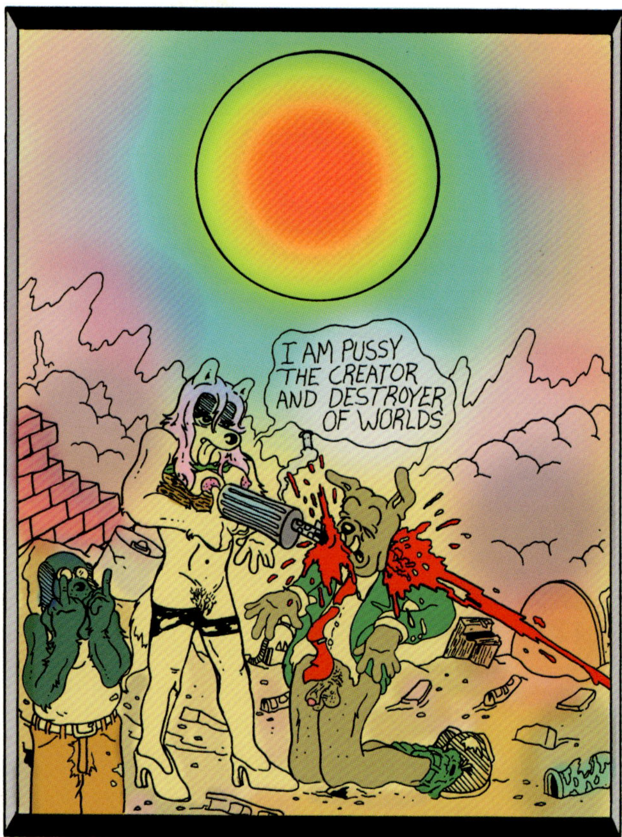

     The Mayor's Pussy by Brian Blomerth

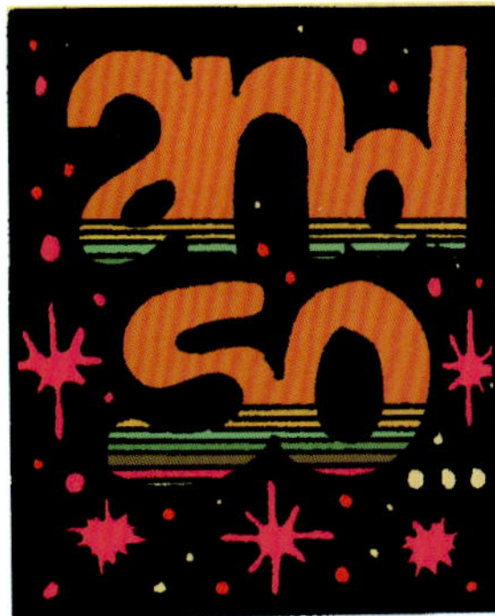

2nd so...

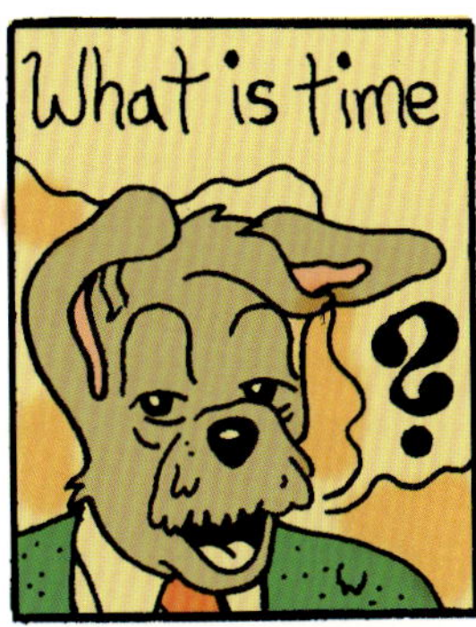

What is time

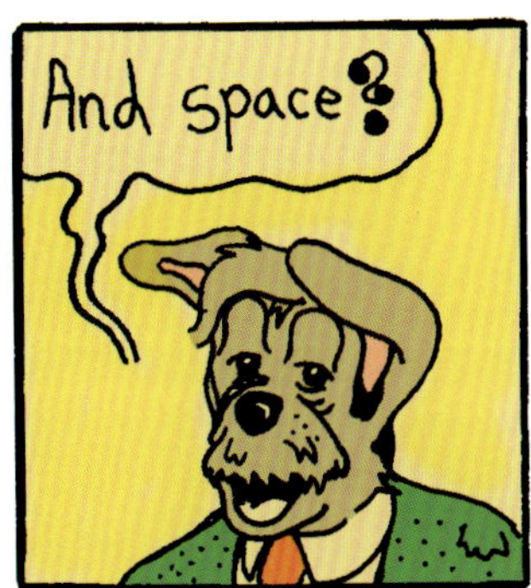

And space?

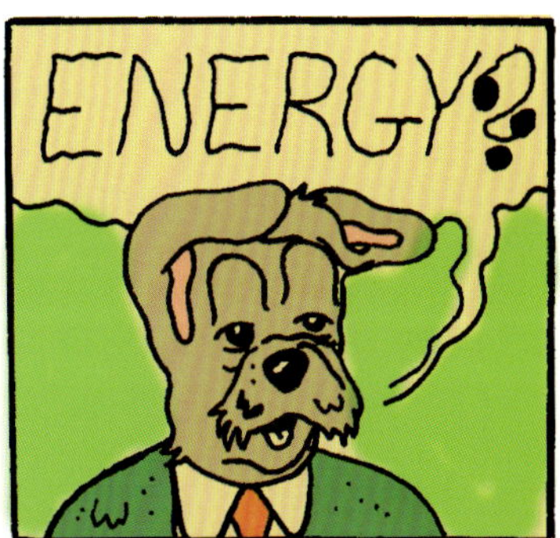

ENERGY?

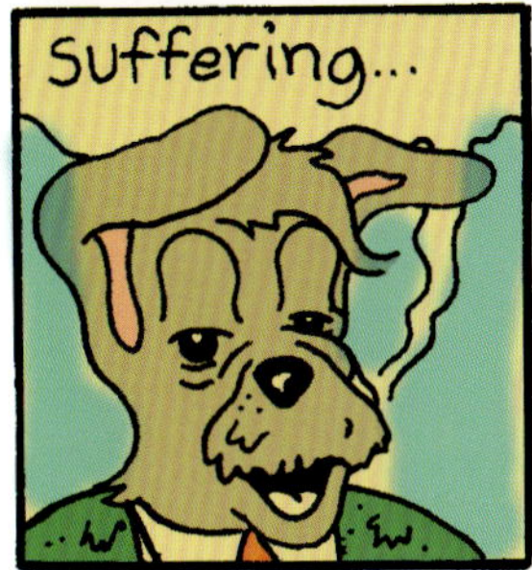

Suffering...

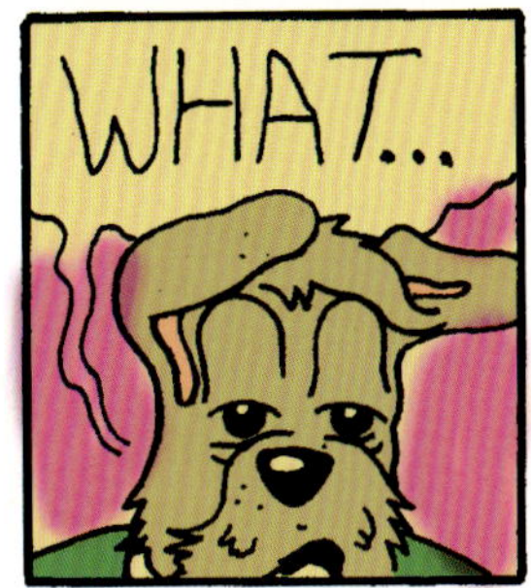

WHAT...

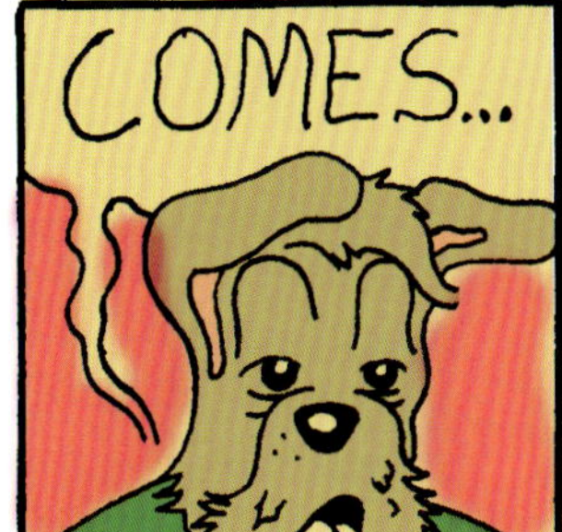

COMES...

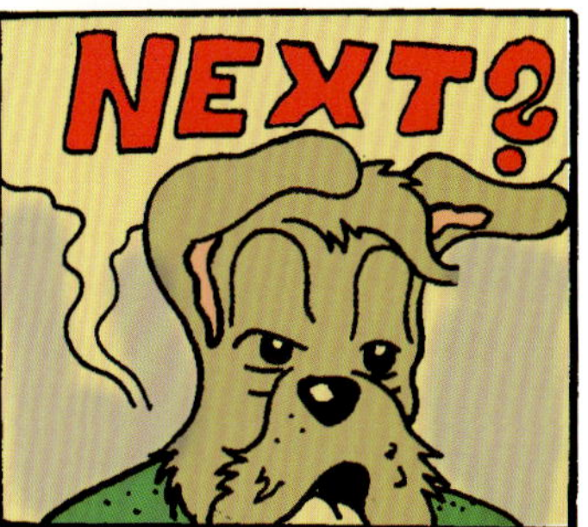

NEXT?

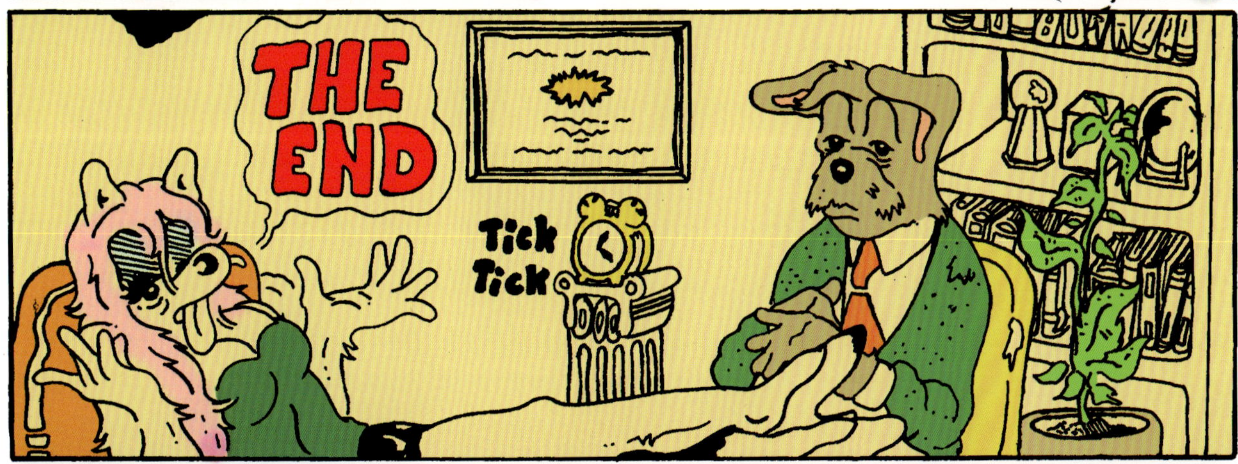

THE END
Tick Tick

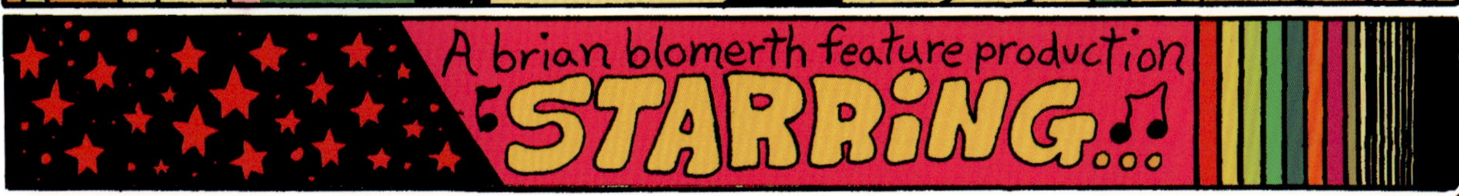

A brian blomerth feature production
STARRING...

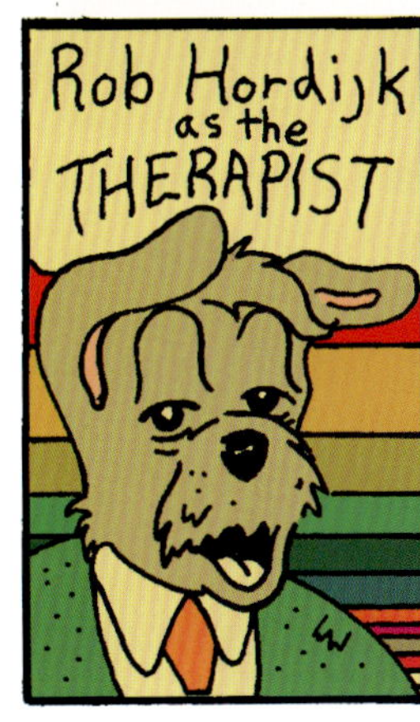

Rob Hordijk as the THERAPIST

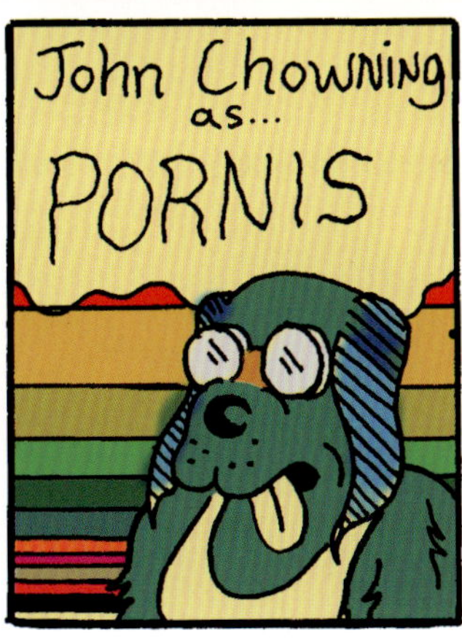

John Chowning as... PORNIS

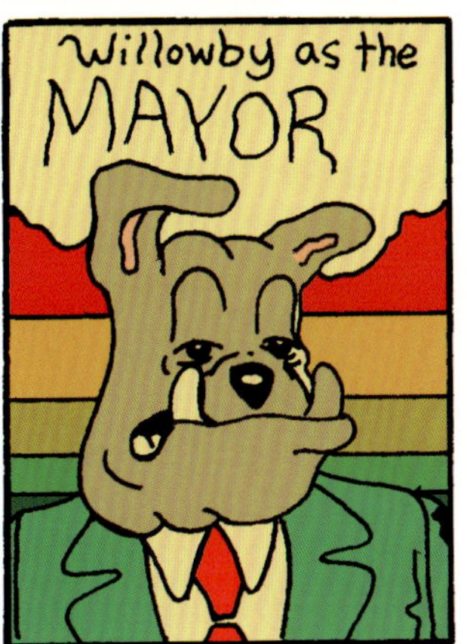

Willowby as the MAYOR

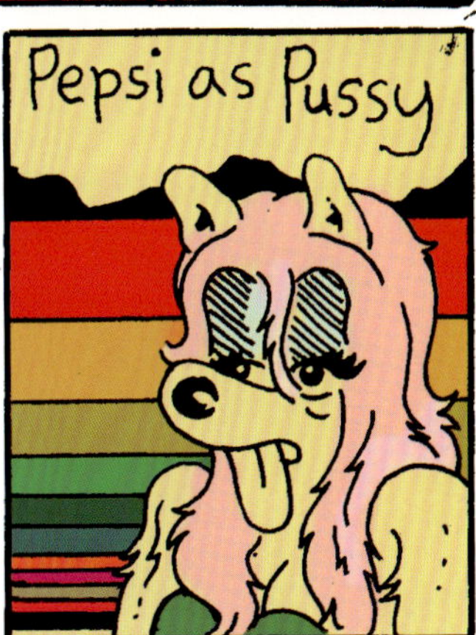

Pepsi as Pussy

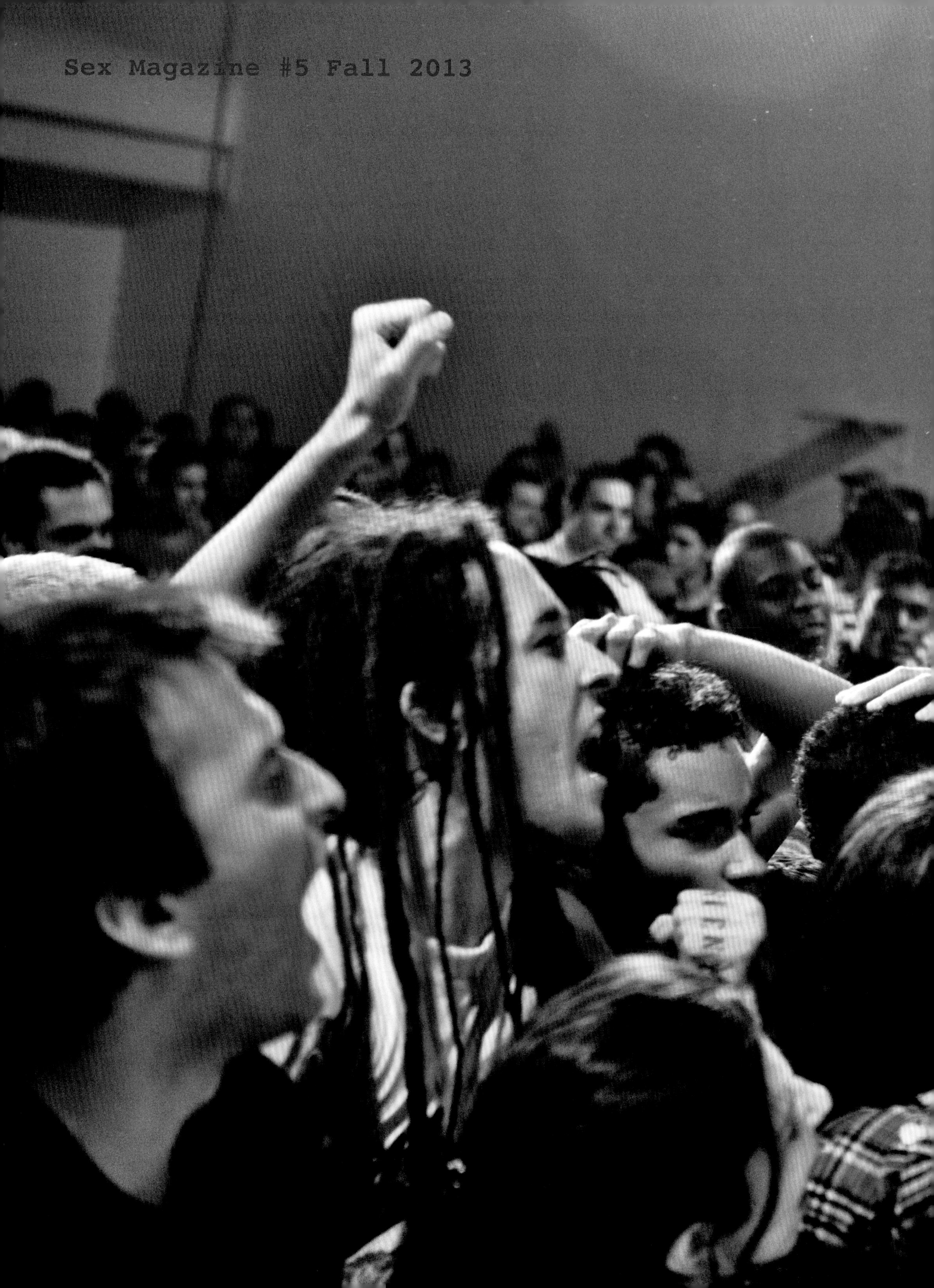
Sex Magazine #5 Fall 2013

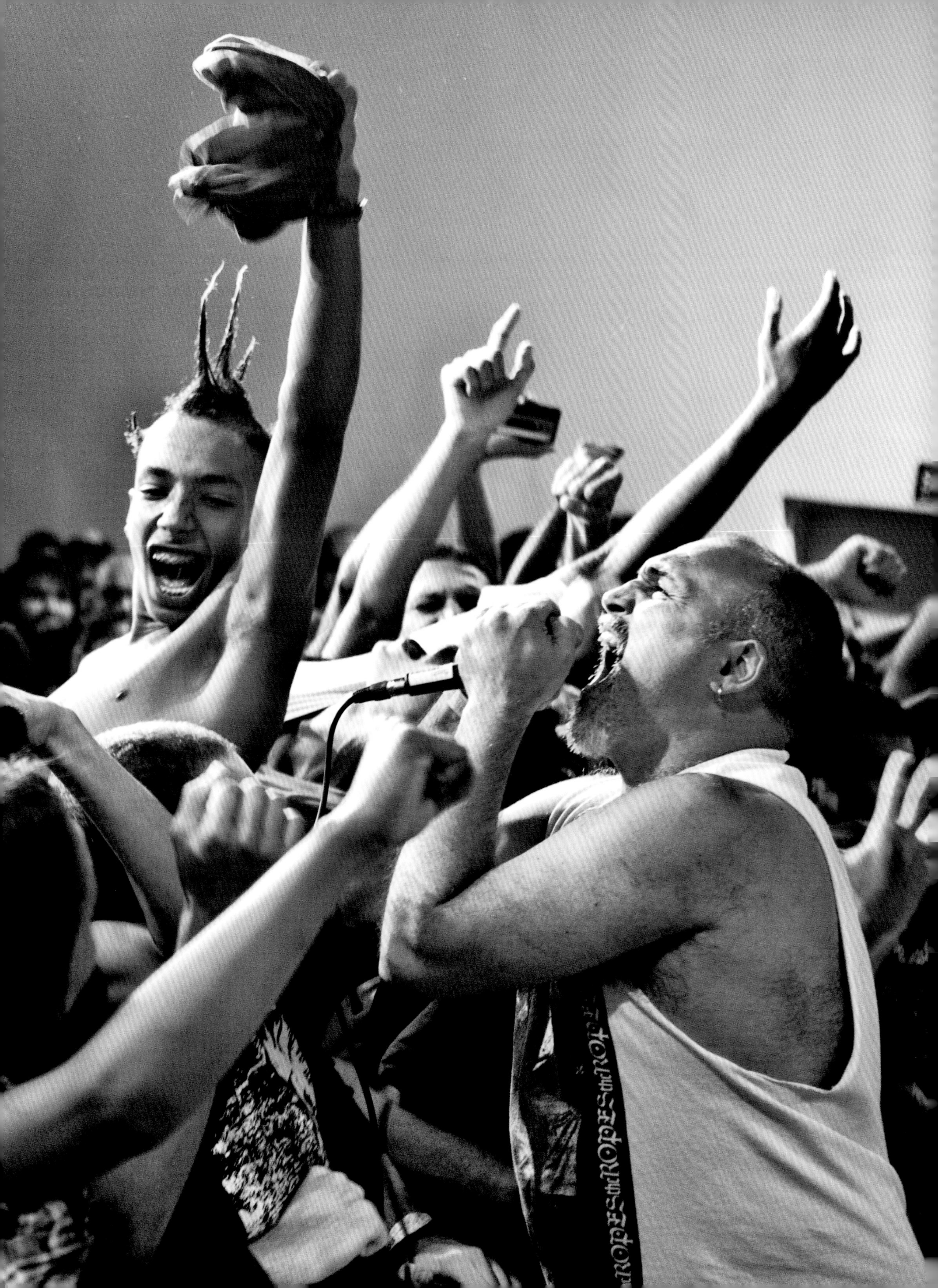

Ratking
"Never name it."

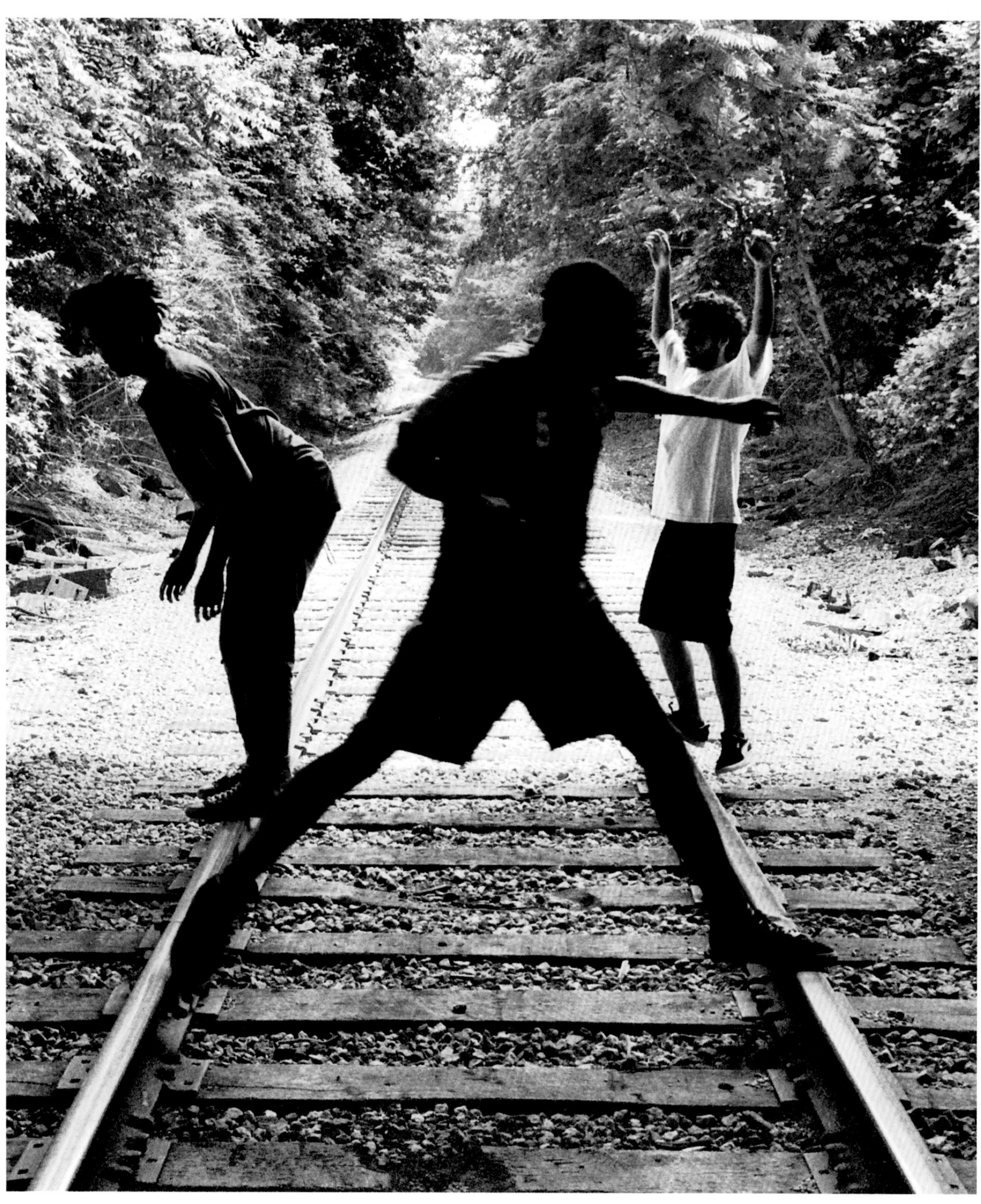

Interview by Aaron Bondaroff
Portrait by Jon Puglia

It's possible that NYC-based rap trio Ratking laid down their 45 minute live set at least once a week this summer — whether touring with groups like Death Grips and Trash Talk or playing their hometown, everywhere from Webster Hall to Fitness Center for Arts and Tactics. This emphasis on live performance isn't the only thing that separates Ratking from the majority of hip hop released today, whether mainstream or independent. The combination of Sporting Life's live beats, Wiki's flow as an MC, and Hak's vocal stylings made their debut EP Wiki93 on XL records an instant anomaly both as a studied 90s throwback and a direct vision of the future. With their first full-length LP due out this October, Sex decided to reunite Ratking with Aaron Bondaroff, one of the groups earliest supporters.

Yo, yo, yo, yo, yo. What's good, what's up, what's the deal, Know Wave Radio, hanging out. It's a hot Thursday. I like to say Nervous Thursday just for the good old days of Video Music Box — shout out to Crazy Sam, that was a big part of my upbringing. I got a lot of noise in the background today, it's a proper New York City interview, hanging out sesh at the Know Wave. You'll be hearing drilling in the streets because the city's on the ever-changing. Special show today, got my homies, got the team — Know Wave Radio, Ratking 001 — the first interview I get to do with these guy, who I've know for a pretty long time. What up Wiki?
Wiki: It's good, how you doing?
You looking good. You feeling good?
Wiki: Yeah, feeling good. A little sick.
Wait, Sporting Life can you put a little background music on for me so we could, like, kind of get the vibe going? Who's in the Know Wave studio?
Wiki: Got Sporting Life, Hak, Johnny Problems. Johnny is our body guard/merch man/whatever-dirty-work-we-need-to-get-done man.

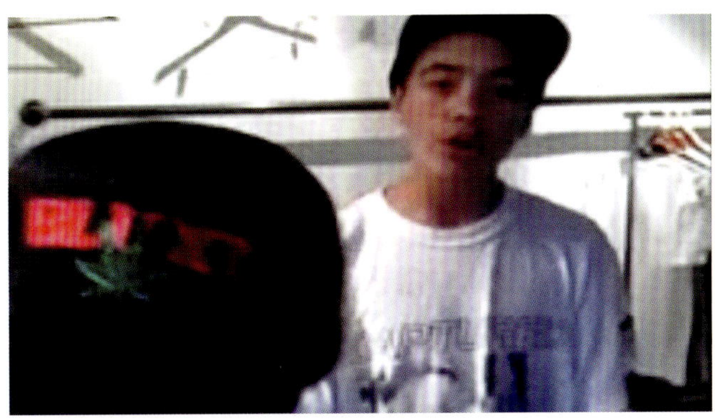
Lil' Wiki & Googs, Off Bowery Productions, 2008.

Making it happen. Making it happen in Manhattan.
Wiki: Downtown, Browntown, Dirty Don — remember that shit?
Wait a minute. Downtown, Browntown, Dirty Don...fuck I don't remember how it goes. I just remember from cook ups to hook ups, to make ups to break ups, I'm napping, I'm nodding, I'm never not...I can't remember. It's my old rap. I could probably come out of retirement and do a quick hook for Ratking.
Wiki: Of course, of course.
I know there's a lot of paperwork these days to work with you guys... So let's just get right into it. Wiki, what's up, where you from originally?
Wiki: I'm from the Upper West Side.
And what's your background?
Wiki: My dad's Puerto Rican, my mom's Irish-American.
I'm right with you man. Puerto Rican, Jew, you know.
Wiki: Of course.
I knew when I first met you, you were still in high school.
Wiki: I think I was in the eighth grade.
That's not high school buddy. That's junior high school. I remember when you and Rob rolled through and dropped some freestyles on me. Rob was your A&R back then cause he kind of kicked down the door first. He was like, "Yo, my man, he got rhymes." Did you finish high school?
Wiki: Yeah, I graduated. I got good grades too.

Left: Hak, Sporting Life & Wiki

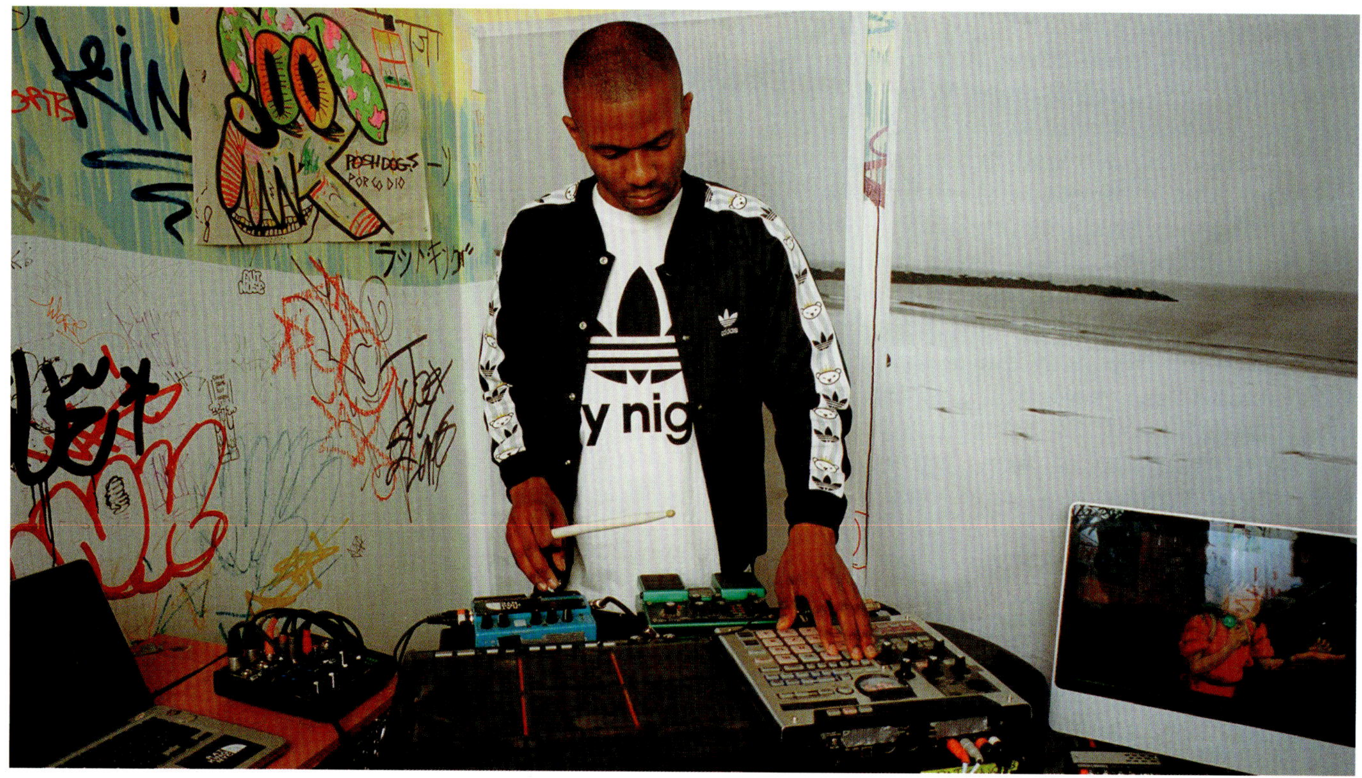

Sporting Life, 2014. Photo: Ari Marcopoulos

When you were in high school people knew that you were rapping right?
Wiki: Yea, people knew by my senior year. People started realizing that Ratking was popping up.
Hak, grab the mic, are you younger? How old are you?
Hak: We were in the same grade. I'm '94, but Wiki's a year older than me.
Is that what the 1993 EP refers to?
Hak: Yeah.
Damn, 90s babies. That's cool, that's a good year. What about you, Sporting Life, where were you from?
Sporting Life: I'm from Birmingham, Alabama.
How did you get into making music?
Sporting Life: I started making beats right before I moved to New York. That was 2006. My older brother moved here first. At the time he wrote and spit and I was gonna make beats for him.
What were some of the musicians or sounds that were inspiring you at that time?
Sporting Life: I was inspired by Beastie Boys and shit like that. Pharrell. Early Kanye, DJ Toomp. But, you know, you can't emulate forever.

I was the one who introduced Hak and Wiki to Eric, right?
Wiki: Yeah, I was just kind of rapping over like instrumentals, putting videos up on YouTube. You sent me some of Eric's beats and shit and we ended up meeting at that park jam. Hak was there too.
So Hak was a part of Ratking from the beginning?
Wiki: Hak always did a lot of visual art, that was kind of more his thing. After a while, he just kind of eased his way into the group. It was just like, "Oh, of course." It just made sense.
I know it's bullshit with titles and all that nonsense, but what do you guys consider yourselves? You guys pull inspiration from a lot of different places.
Wiki: I think in the end it is what it is. It's forming as it goes. We try to pull in a lot, we reference and recycle. The three of us all have a different angle on everything. I try to be the most pure in the spirit of hip hop, to really keep that authenticity. Hak's not a rapper and

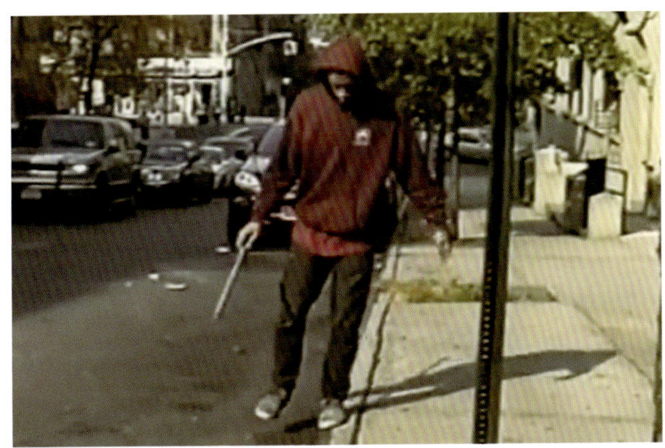

Hak, Car Hater, 2011.

he's not a singer: he's an artist that just uses those mediums. And then Eric's really influenced by a lot of noise music, like Black Dice and Animal Collective, as well as the hip hop he grew up on. I think we take those inspirations and try to tighten them up as much as possible, play it as live as possible.

You're coming from so many different places. You don't want to get caught up in categories.

Sporting Life: Yeah, never name it.

Hak, you're more like a performance artist. I've seen you perform a few times, but it was a while ago.

Hak: At first, honestly, I was really uncomfortable in my own skin being on stage. Now I enjoy it. I always try to find something new and take risks during live performances.

When you guys play shows, do people know the songs? How do they react?

Wiki: In the city we have a bit of a fan base, whether it's our friends or our friends' friends. This one show, when we played Piece of Shit everyone was spitting during the whole thing. That was pretty dope. When we're out on the road, on the other hand, we have to win over the crowd. In the beginning they're not really with it. During our first tour no one was really clapping at the end of our shows. For the last one with Death Grips, there was applause, everyone was feeling it. Everyone was going to the merch table, checking it out. It's working. The project's working.

When I met you, you were MC Patrick, and I told you that you should be Lil' Wiki, cause you were like an encyclopedia. You were educating me.

Wiki: I liked being named. To me that was some old school shit — to be named by an older cat. I thought that was kind of dope and the name stuck.

Do you go by Patrick or by Wiki? Does your family call you Wiki?

Wiki: My dad actually calls me Wiki which is a little weird. I don't know, my boys call me Wiki and they call me Pat.

How did the name Ratking come around? Does it have some kind of meaning?

Wiki: It just kind of encompassed a bunch of ideas we were thinking about at the time we started. It's kind of a tough name. You can't really fuck with it. It looks dope when you write it too.

Sporting Life: A Ratking is just like a bunch of rats when they get into a certain situation. They become tangled and have to kind of live as one organism. I don't know, a lot of people are creeped out by it.

You guys got some good rat stories? I want to hear some rat stories.

Wiki: I'm honestly pretty scared of rats.

I'm fucking freaked out by rats.

Hak: What's your rat story?

I remember like in Williamsburg I had an apartment on Manhattan Avenue in the late 90s. There was just rats galore, rats everywhere. I would come home at night and they would be on my stoop in b-boy positions smoking blunts. These rats were holding shit down. They were like blocking me from getting into my place. I would open my front door and all the rats would run up the stairs before me and find spots to hide. I'll be like watching my TV and all of a sudden a rat would walk in front of the TV — like, "Look at me!" — and keep going to my kitchen. Then it would drag the whole garbage bag into the other room. They were like baby pit bulls.

Hak: I think you might be the Ratking.

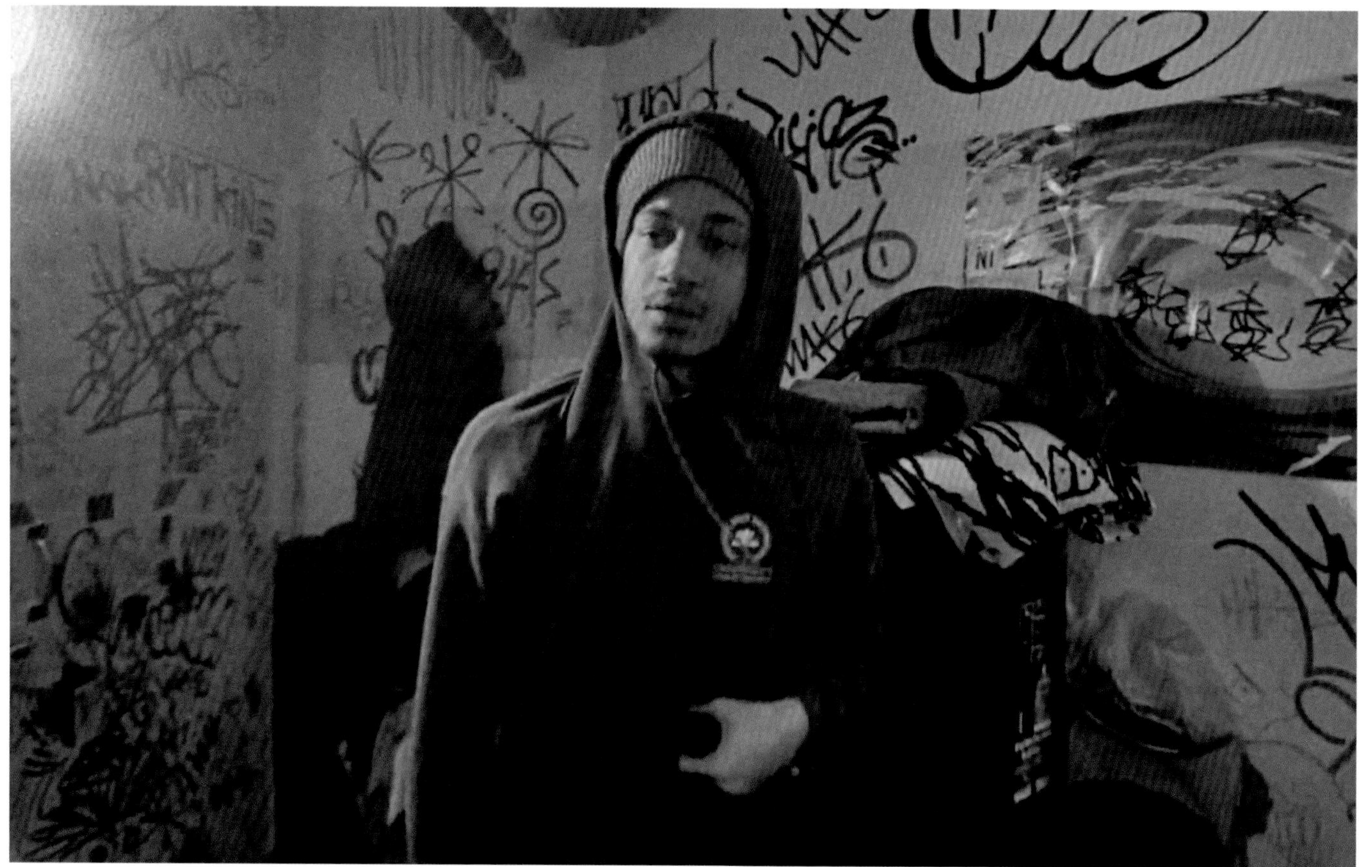

Piece of Shit, Directed by Ari Marcopoulos, 2013.

How long have you guys officially been Ratking now?
Hak: Two and a half years.
Pretty new. What are some of the other young bands that you guys play shows with?
Hak: The Illuzion with Salomon Faye and Rebel. DJ Dog Dick from Far Rockaway. He's actually helping us out with the record and he's featured on some tracks. Wavy Spice is on the album too. Kaila Paulino from the Bronx. Show Me the Body.
But you also work with your peers, your community. Like Letter Racer.
Wiki: Letter Racer are kind of all our artist friends. We're all trying to help each other out, whatever it is, art or music.
You also work with some older cats. I know Ari Marcopoulos did a video with you guys.
Wiki: Yeah. He had this art show and asked us to play that. Then he filmed the video for Piece of Shit. It was a live version of the song.

What are you going for with your videos?
Sporting Life: I don't know if there is an overarching message. We were talking yesterday about a new video we're trying to do called CANAL. With anything you create I think the content has to be dope, but so do the means by which you create it. That's the ill combination. That's the only rule we use to make things.
It's really important for you guys to perform live, right? That's kinda rare now in hip hop.
Wiki: Yeah. Our songs are changing as we play. It's part of the writing process. Sometimes playing live might make it that we're off for a sec, but that might make something new happen that's even doper than the recorded version.
Sporting Life: It also takes hip hop away from what I feel big business and success brought it to — that stage versus crowd kind of mentality. "We've got chains, we've got shoes, we fuck all your girls, it's us versus you."

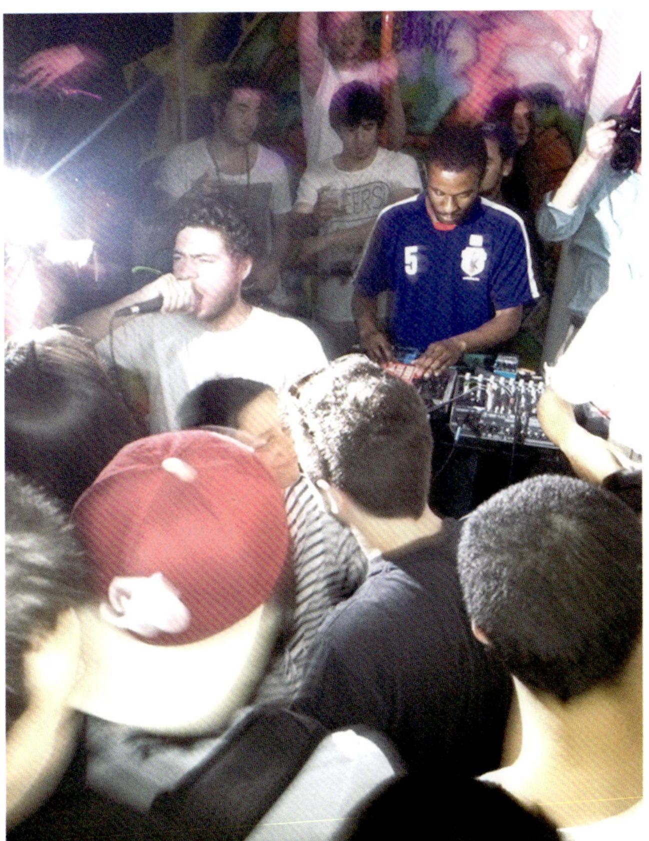

Ratking, Gallery 69, New York, 2013.
Photo: Asher Penn

Playing it live I feel bridges the gap between the people on stage and the people in the crowd, because they see you moving to the music and they're feeling it. It's all of us dancing to the same thing, not me stunting on you from an elevated position on stage.

You bring a lot of punk energy to rap.

Wiki: You don't have to scream, rip your shirt off, or crowd surf to be punk, but if you set up a certain situation, then you're going to want to scream naturally. You might smack yourself in the face with the mic if you're feeling a song a certain way. If somebody on the outside considers that punk — then whatever, that's the word, but it's just the outcome of what you're feeling at the time.

Hak: You've got to handle yourself in real time. It kind of humbles you because you have to realize it takes practice. It also sets you apart, raises the bar to a degree of difficulty for what you're trying to do.

Wiki, who are some of your MC influences?

Wiki: I mean, I'm influenced by everything. But specifically? Definitely Jay Z's Blueprint Volume I, II, III. A lot of Cam'ron. Freeway. I'll be like telling Eric, "This is like some Freeway shit but on a jungle beat from my voice." You would never connect it back. ODB is a big influence too. On the new album I definitely go mad drunken style on my ad-libs. There's definitely some Minor Threat, Bad Brains, Germs-type shit on the album too.

You guys are doing pretty well. You're with XL, you're playing pretty major venues. Why do you still play small gigs?

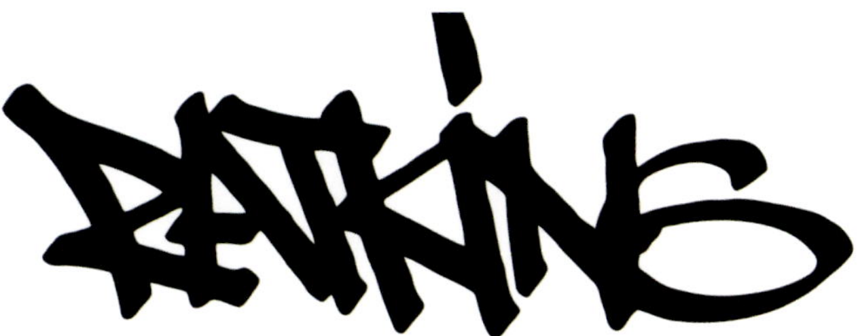

Ratking Logo, Designed by Arvid Logan, 2013.

Hak: We try to play shows anywhere we can play shows. Our friends have this venue called Apostrophe, which is kind of a gutted Bodega turned art gallery and performance space. We played a bunch of shows there and it was always a good mixture of kids from the neighborhood, adults from the neighborhood, and other people from everywhere. At a lot of those shows we're on the same level as the crowd. I love switching it up from being on stage to being on level with the people we're speaking to.

Wiki: A lot of the shows that we play in Bushwick will draw kind of a hipster crowd...but Apostrophe really does bridge the gap between hip hop and new shit. Once I had the flu and missed a show we played there but saw the footage later — I remember seeing all these Spanish kids from the neighborhood bouncing out! They get to see and hear something new. It's just dope, it's good for everyone. 😊

Young Male

"I love to see someone who's halfway crazy doing their thing, whether it's making dance music using a metal box with some knobs on it, or a guy smashing somebody's hand with a hammer."

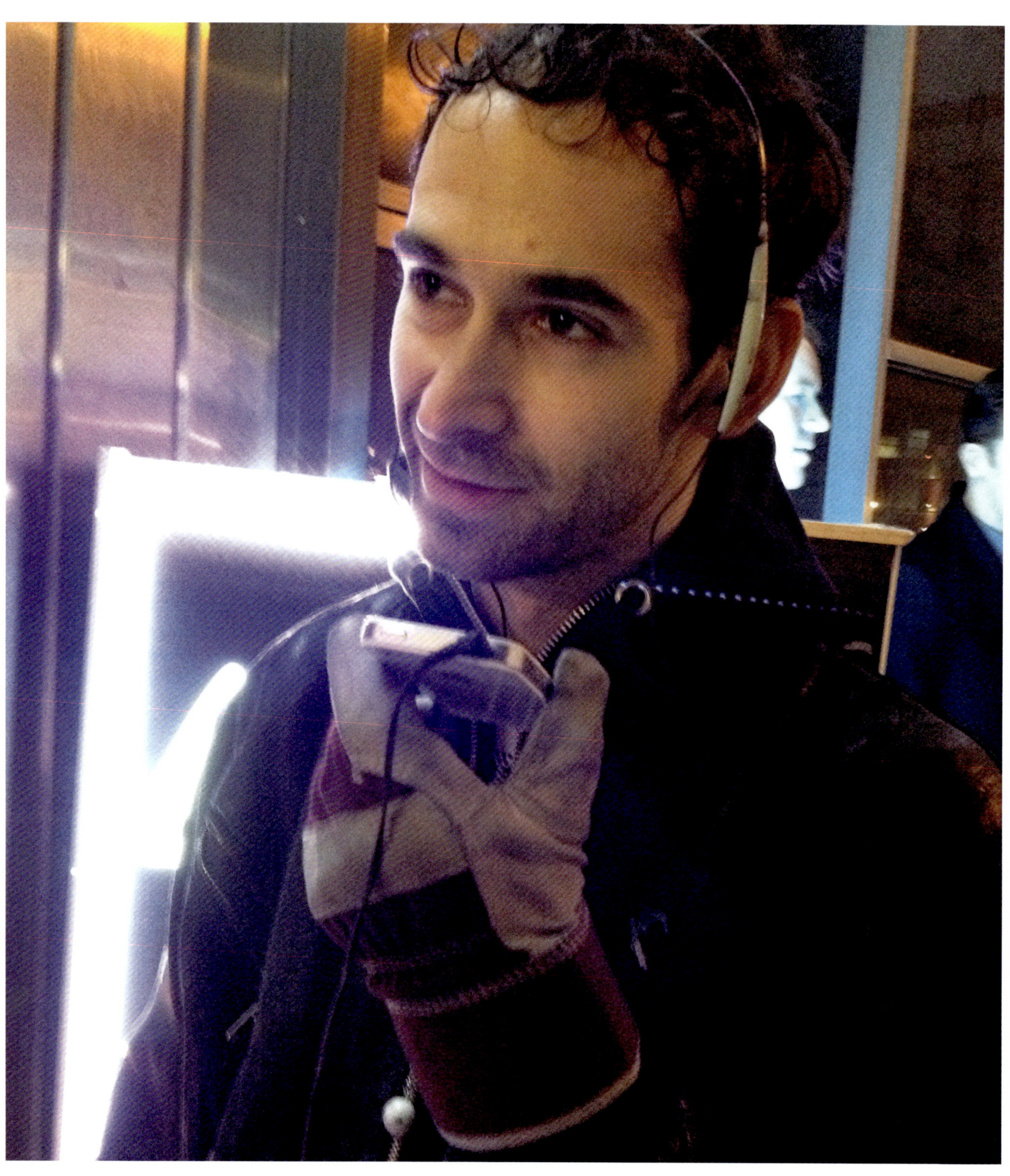

Interview & portrait by Asher Penn
Images courtesy Quinn Taylor

A year since releasing his first EP on artist-owned label White Material Records, New York-based Young Male (Quinn Taylor) has gone from virtual unknown to "local techno god." With a musical background steeped in underground noise, Young Male's recordings and live performances have brought a remarkably unique voice to today's often homogeneous landscape of electronic music. Now an internationally touring DJ and producer despite minimal hype from the standard industry legitimizers, Young Male is a rare example of an artist reaching a continuously growing audience with only hard work and killer music.

I didn't know you were from New York.
Yeah, I was born in Midtown I think. My mom owned a loft in Union Square on 16th Street, but it was a different fucking place then. Really different. People wouldn't walk across the park at that time. It was full of drugs and pretty violent. She moved because she got robbed at knifepoint in her own house while I was in the crib next to her. We ended up on the other end of Long Island in a small farming and fishing town called Greenport.

But you grew up in Virginia. How did you guys end up moving there?
I went to a really good wrestling camp in Virginia the summer between 8th grade and 9th grade and while I was there wrestling, my mom drove around Virginia looking for spots to move to.

How did you get into wrestling?
Going to middle school in Long Island was fucking hell man. I got bullied so much. It was brutal. I just wanted to be stronger and understand my body a little better. I was tired of feeling small and weak.

How long did you wrestle for?
Two years. I was a decent wrestler. I would've continued in high school if I hadn't started skateboarding. Skateboarding was so much more fun, and the other people that skated were way fucking cooler than the kids who wrestled.

Were you good at skateboarding?
I was never that good. I think you have to be this certain type of person to get really good. The best skaters that I knew weren't that athletic, they were just willing to jump down 12 stairs. You have to have some weird blind faith. It's not easy to pinpoint. Kids like that don't necessarily think they're good enough to do those crazy tricks, they're just not worried about hurting themselves. It's pretty amazing.

Did you play any other sports?
I played football in middle school. I loved it. I was a cornerback, the guy who covers receivers. I was pretty good. I got an interception in almost every game.

Were you bigger when you were younger?
No, I was smaller. I've always been kind of cursed by being a small athlete. I think I weighed like 112 pounds in high school. But all my life I've loved watching and playing sports. I'm a huge MMA fan.

You go to the gym a lot now, right?
That's a big part of my life. I really consider it an important thing to do. Exercising is essential to keeping your brain healthy. I haven't been going lately. I have no money and my gym membership is on hold.

It's an expensive gym?
Right now I have a fancy gym. It's expensive but it's kind of worth it. I mean, there are hot girls to look at, you're never waiting too long to use a treadmill or to use equipment. The towels are nice. It's way easier to actually get yourself to go the gym when it's not a shithole.

Let's get back to Virginia. Were you going to shows in high school?
Yeah, at least once a month there'd be some cool show at the local college. We were close to D.C. so all these bands from there would play. I saw the Makeup play one of their first shows. Blonde Redhead came to play before they'd ever released an album. I saw Fugazi when I was like 13.

Were you playing music?
I hung out with these kids that were kind of music prodigies. They weren't classically trained but they'd been making music since they were really young. We all played music together in a ton of bands. When I think about it, there's nothing then or now that sounded like what we were doing. It was pretty weird. It's so rare that anyone ever makes anything that doesn't sound like a million things before it. This shit really didn't sound like anything.

How often would you guys play?
We would play music every day. My friend had a shed that was sound insulated and we had all our music equipment in there. It was a pretty amazing life at that time. You go to fucking high school, you leave at like three in the afternoon, you barely spend any time of your day there, and then you go and you hang out with your friends and play music. It was awesome.

Were you a good student?
No, I was a bad student. I got like Ds and Cs, and the occasional B. I just wasn't a fucking goody two-shoes kid. I didn't want to do that shit. I wanted to go skateboard and play music and play video games. So I just didn't do my homework.

What about art?
I didn't give a shit about art until I went to pre-college at RISD. I wasn't even planning on going to college. I thought it was just this crazy waste of money, and I never liked kids that were obsessed with school. Then my mom convinced me to go to pre-college, which was fun, not to mention there were weird, pretty girls walking around everywhere. It seemed like the coolest thing to do at the time. After pre-college, when I went back to my high school art class, I thought I was a serious artist. [Laughs] I was drawing fruit in a fucking bowl and cow skulls and shit. God...

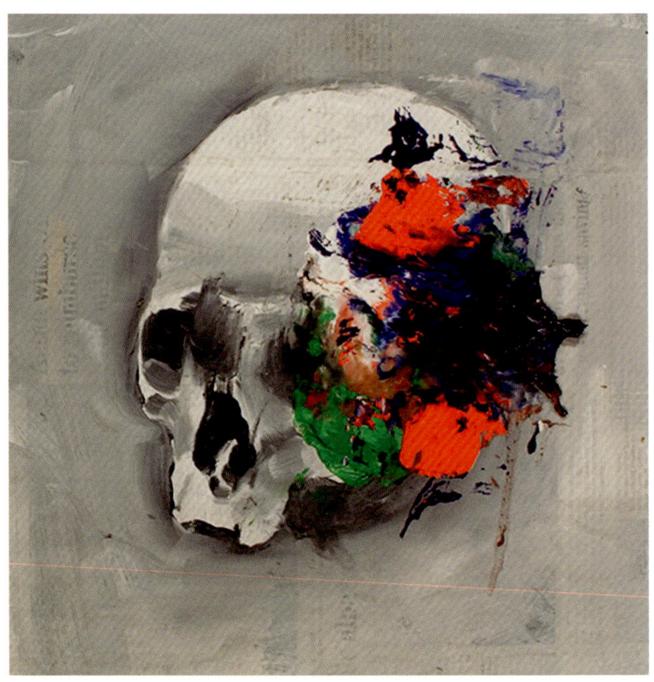

Greatest Hits! volume3, 2008.

So you went to RISD.
Yeah. I studied painting and then transferred to sculpture. I don't think I learned that much. I'm glad I went. I had an OK time. I learned how to draw and got a little better at not procrastinating, but most importantly I got to meet all these fucking strange, cool people that I still know today. People who have truly influenced me in deep ways. I definitely believe that the people you meet in school are what make going to school valuable. I mean those relationships can last the rest of your life.

It's also really hard to separate RISD from Fort Thunder at that time. When did you first go there?
I went when I was a freshman. One of the first weeks of freshman year actually, I went to a big wrestling event there. They had this big DIY wrestling ring with ropes. Everyone would wear insane costumes. There was a lot of fake blood. There was also some guy doing play-by-play on a megaphone and some crazy music pumped through some totally blown out system. It was honestly chaos. It blew my mind, it was a formative experience.

So you'd go a lot?

Everyone went to Fort Thunder events. When you heard that there was something there, you knew you had to go check that shit out. I really consider myself lucky to have gone and seen a place like that.

What was your first impression of Lightning Bolt?

The first time I saw them play was in a parking lot in the middle of a cold-ass Rhode Island winter, surrounded by parked cars with their lights on. It was post-apocalyptic as fuck. It was incredible seeing two dudes do so much with just a bass and drums — they were doing so much sonically with just two instruments. The idea of doing a lot with limited means still influences the shit that I do now. I think that's part of the reason that I use such a simple live setup with just a drum machine and FX pedals. That was also the first time I'd seen a band bring their own P.A. to a show. They were people who were obsessed with music and wanted to play it, and they would do whatever it took to make it happen.

Providence has pretty high standards for music in general.

That's the hardest place to play. They're the harshest critics without a doubt. If you play there, you'd better play your best fucking shit because you're playing for a group of some of the sickest musicians living in this country. They've seen a LOT of music and they know some real shit when they see it.

There's an ethos to it.

Yeah, and there's also a really high value placed on performers being real human beings there. Expressing yourself in your own fucked up way, however insignificant it might feel. Learning about what the fuck it is that YOU like, not what your best friend likes, not what is popular at that moment, y'know? It takes a lot of courage to do that. It's not easy, it's often humiliating, but I think it's worth the struggle.

What was your first solo music project?

I had a noise project that I never performed where I just used a homemade oscillator and distorted vocals. I would run the microphone through this fucking gnarly distortion pedal so the vocals were unintelligible. That was the first time I did any real experimental shit. I still do some stuff like that in private. I have private music projects that exist only in my bedroom.

How did you learn about electronics?

My friend Christopher who does Brown Recluse Alpha and Daily Life taught me all that stuff. He spent a lot of time explaining schematics and giving me lessons on how to build simple circuits. He taught me how to build all the basic components of a synthesizer. He was kind of my mentor.

I didn't know that.

He was the first person I saw playing noise music. It totally turned my life upside down. The first time I saw him play was a really important moment in my life musically. I've never seen him play another show like it since.

What did he do?

He played this cassette tape that he made. It was drum machine loops that were distorted and blown out, which he sang and spoke over. It was so simple but so powerful. He had a shitload of little toys, plants, and some spinning lights sitting on his amp, too. I remember that he was wearing mismatched shoes and was smiling like a maniac while he was playing. I knew I was watching an unusual person doing an unusual performance. Halfway through his set, the amp died. He kind of threw a fit, and started just smashing the amp on the floor in front of the audience while it was buzzing and feeding back. I actually remember thinking to myself, "Goddamn...THAT was fucking cool."

How did you transition from making noise to getting into techno?
Well, it's kind of funny. Remember in 2006 when iTunes had streaming radio? There were tons of stations, all sorts of genres. Black metal stations, 80s stations, 90s, anything you wanted pretty much. I'd just gotten my first computer and I would always stay up late as fuck listening to the cheesy trance stations. "Trance Around the World" I think was my favorite show. Deep into the night I would be drawing, working on art, and listening to that stuff. Finally I had this thought that it would be cool to make this music that at the time I secretly loved. This slowly led to me doing Young Male.

Where did the name come from?
The name comes from this cardboard sign written in Sharpie that I found in Providence outside of a huge old mill building. It said: "YOUNG MALE WILL PAY YOU $200 TO KICK ME IN NUTS 200 TIMES AND BEAT ME WITH BASEBALL BAT 200 TIMES Come to the yellow door and Holler. ask for GERM".

Wow.
I know... So I took that sign. I had it on the wall in my room for a while. Then a friend was putting on a show and asked me to play solo and asked what my name should be on the flyer for the show. I was like, "Uh, I'll be called Young Male." I liked that the name hinted at personal ads for sex that you'd find in local newspapers or something you'd see on craigslist. There was a weird feel to it in that sense, and it was also a simple and basic description of me. I am young, I am male, I am a little desperate. [Laughs] Young Male felt like the perfect name.

What was the first Young Male show?
It was at RISD. All I had at that time was a synthesizer and cassette tapes. The cassette tapes had drum loops on them and I would play synth over top of them. Nothing was sequenced, I played everything by hand. It was corny, but it was also pretty cool. It was primitive, but people were psyched.

How did you end up losing the synthesizer and just using your drum machine?
When I moved to NY, no one was interested in what I was doing. The only gigs anyone was asking me to play were back in Providence. So I was going to Providence playing these shows, and I couldn't bring all my equipment. Eventually I made this decision to just bring my drum machine because that was all I could carry on the bus. That was the beginning of playing live sets like that.

Playing live with limited equipment.
It was cool when I finally just played with the 909. I don't think that it was that common for people to see some guy with just a drum machine.

But nobody in NY would book you?
The only person who would let me play shows was Alex Field — DJ Richard — at his house on 10 Stueben Street. That was the sickest venue in New York by far in my opinion. I miss it badly.

How long had you been playing?
I'd been doing that stripped down version of Young Male for about a year at that point. I've been working on this project for about seven years now.

Did the music you were making change when you moved to NY?
Definitely. That first year in New York, that shit was hard. You can't get a job. You have no money. Girls fucking don't give a shit about you because you're nobody. People do not want to book you to play shows. I just felt alienated. I was making techno in my bedroom, alone, and walking around my neighborhood at night, alone. That's what I would do Friday and Saturday nights while everyone else was at whatever cool party was happening. I was not at those parties, I was at home, chilling with my cat, listening to alienating music and making alienated music. Somehow that was therapeutic and it did change the sound of what I was doing. It made it way darker, way more dystopian. I was channeling what I was feeling and I liked how dark it was becoming.

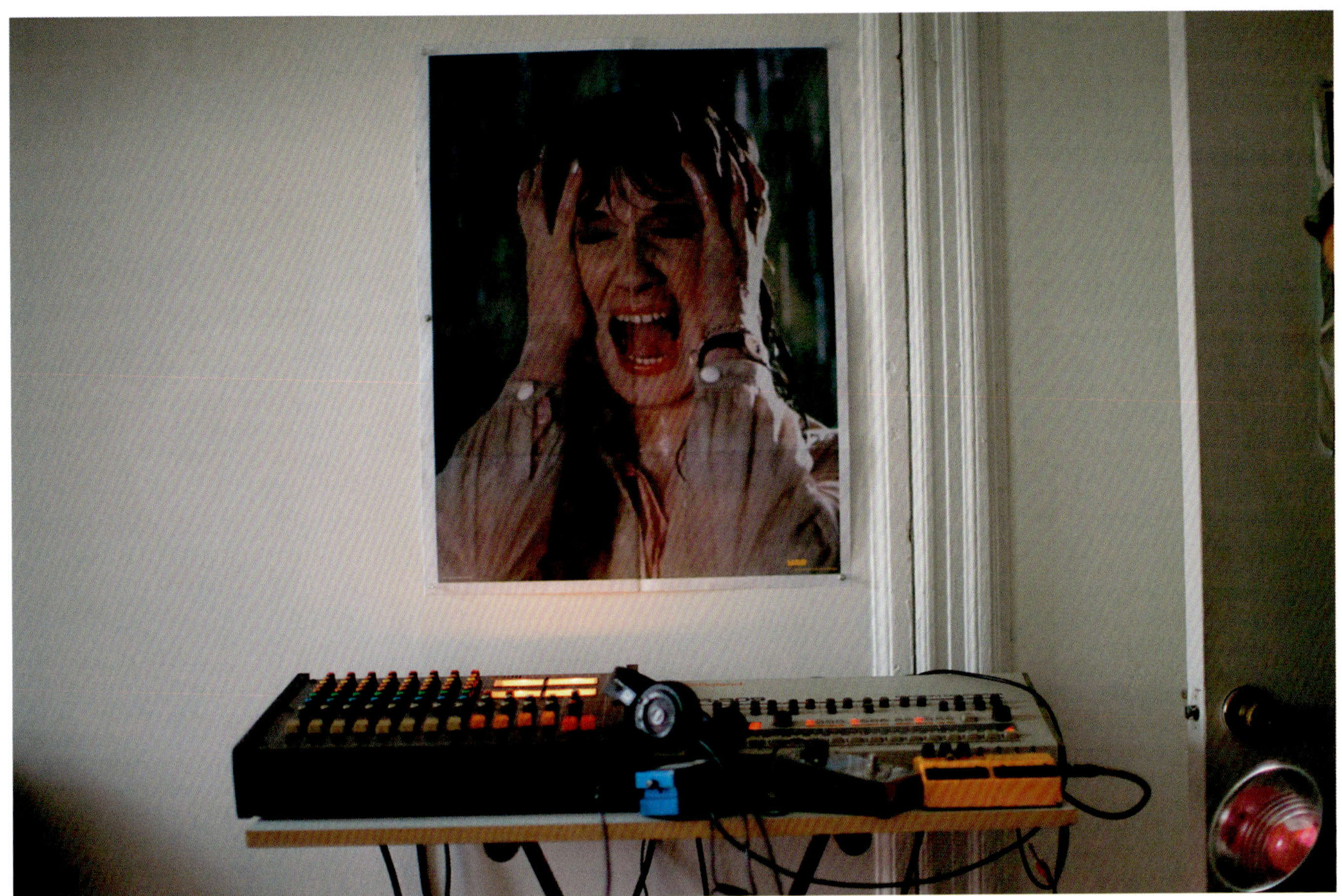

Setup, 2013.

I have always felt Young Male was a form of self-expression.
It's the first musical expression I've made where I feel like there's a good chunk of me in there. Obviously, it's inspired by a bunch of different things and anyone who listens to techno can hear them instantly. I would never deny it. But there's a good 70% of me in there, which is a lot. I think most people are lucky to even get 50% of themselves in whatever they're making.
For some reason I feel like your Twitter helped with that too.
I mean, yeah. My Twitter isn't about my music, but you're right. I learned about being myself via Twitter. I use it as a diary for my thoughts, laid out for anyone who feels like reading it. The thing is, because there's an audience you have to keep it pretty honest. If you're writing in a way that's not a true reflection of yourself, it shows pretty quickly.

I was expressing this part of my personality that usually only my closer friends get to see. It's a little depraved, but it's made me more brave in terms of being honest about who I am.
So it does relate to your music.
It all wraps into one ball. The internet has helped me learn to express myself, not only as a person, but sexually and musically too.
Some people have told me that there are parallels between Young Male and some Detroit techno from the 80s.
Yeah, I remember when you mentioned that a while ago. That's a great compliment. I hope it's true. Techno was created by black dudes in Detroit that were simplifying house music and warping it into something that expressed the alienation they were feeling. It was being made in this collapsing industrial city that had been forgotten about and left to dissolve.

So Detroit is at the root of it.
Yes. Techno was being made using instruments that no one wanted. I think that Detroit is similar to Providence in a lot of ways and that probably creates some parallels with what I'm doing. It's an old manufacturing town where all the manufacturing has left. The people are still there, no one has any money, but they're still making their music in isolation. So I guess I feel like I come from a similar situation in that sense — a bleak landscape of forgotten middle-class and industrial ruins.

And Young Male sounds like that?
I try to work that sound into the tracks I produce. I honestly haven't listened to enough Detroit techno to be an expert. There are certain producers I love and my music probably sounds reminiscent of that stuff.

I've always thought it sounded like John Carpenter soundtracks.
The soundtrack to The Thing inspires almost every musical thing I ever do. I mean it's so perfect. That entire score is just that one synthesized note with delay on it, echoing sporadically through the movie. So fucking haunting.

The soundtrack for Drive is also good. You wouldn't shut up about that movie.
[Laughs] I love to see someone who's halfway crazy doing their thing. Whether it's making dance music using a metal box with some knobs on it, or a guy smashing somebody's hand with a hammer. Getting to see someone take it a little bit over the edge is always sick.

I wanted to ask you about White Material records. I love every release so far, but don't really understand how it has set itself apart from any other label out there.
I don't totally know either. This is a complex question and I don't want to overstep my bounds, but I'll try to answer it. I honestly haven't thought about this subject too much because the label is still in its infancy and I don't want to get too caught up in figuring out what it is and what it isn't. There's an undeniable magic though. I think with White Material you're seeing a group of artists and friends who developed together in one place and have worked together over a long period of time. It's pretty common for record labels to cherry-pick talent from all over the world without having a direct connection to the artist. I also think it's exciting for people who are into techno to see a record label be created and run by young people. I think there's a relationship to punk and noise culture as well that's a little different from other labels, both aesthetically and in attitude. This probably comes from us all being surrounded by so much DIY and noise culture in Providence. I think that when your audience understands that an actual person is making this stuff they're psyched. They feel like, "Hey, I can do this too!! I can start something!" There's nothing I get more excited about than a new track by my friends. I'd always wanted to start something fresh and have the opportunity to say, "This is what WE love, and this is MY vision, here it is if you want it." I don't want to just join something that already exists.

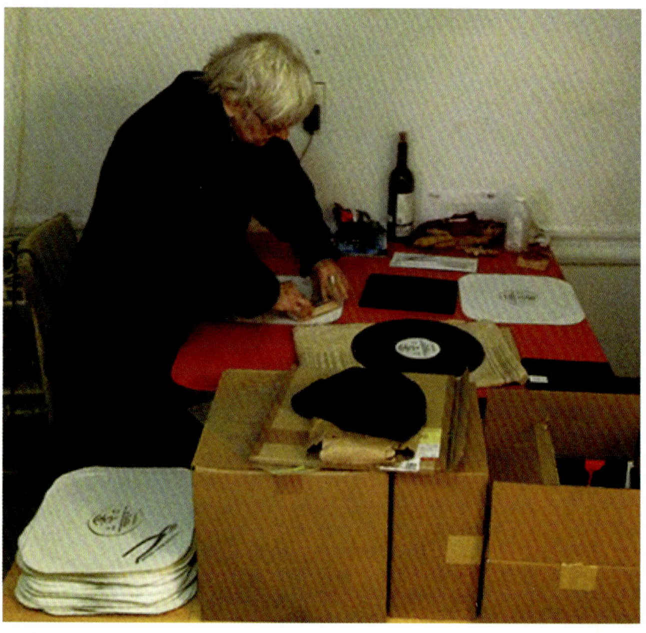

Quinn's Mom Stamping White Material Sleeves, 2012.

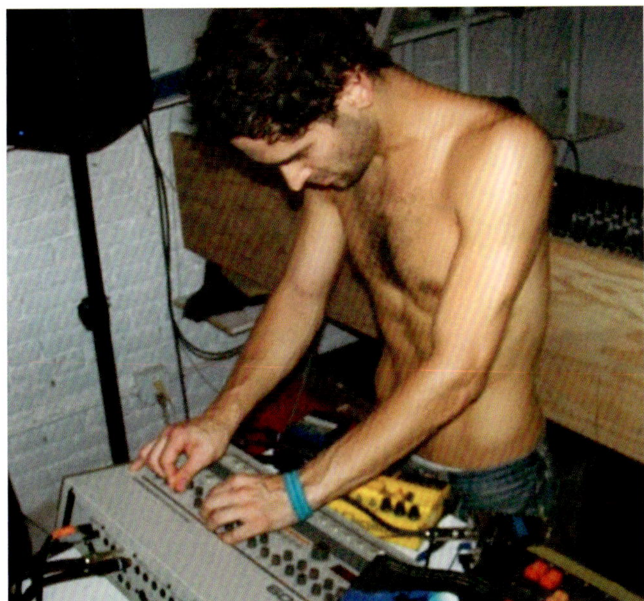

Young Male, Steuben St. Loft, 2012.

So most electronic musicians want to join other labels?
I don't know what anyone else wants. I've just spent too much time in my life making someone else money and giving my creative gifts and time to other companies to use. I don't care about joining something that already exists. I want to do something that's close to my heart. I think that every-thing White Material does has a strong feeling of care because it's ours. We started this thing from scratch.
That reminds me of you playing Boiler Room last week. That was weird.
I wish I'd known that the fucking Boiler Room was sponsored by Red Bull. It felt odd man. If I'd known, I might not have played. I know Red Bull does a lot of good things for a lot of artists and they aren't an evil company. I respect that they want to sponsor good things, but why not just donate a bunch of money anonymously. They don't do that because these shows act as advertisements for them basically. They are aligning themselves socially with "cool," "creative" scenes. I don't mean to be negative, and I know a lot of people disagree, but I don't want a fucking soda company to co-opt the creative things I do. I've worked so hard for so long. That's not my dream.

You liked it when they did that space thing.
Yeah I loved it. That was a beautiful gesture, especially since our government plans on giving up on space exploration. I told everyone I knew to watch that. But, it's one thing to sponsor a guy jumping out of a plane in space, where the stunt doesn't exist without the funding. It's another thing for Red Bull to slap their name on these events that are organized by, and performed by, self-sufficient, interesting people who have been given this miraculous musical gift. These shows happen without big companies' sponsorship. Music in general doesn't need big companies to make people pay attention to it. These institutions blow up artists for a month and then afterwards you're tossed and no one gives a shit. I make this music for people who love music. That's it. I want to give this gift to people who want to go to a club and feel free. We don't need to make some giant company more money by allowing them to pretend that they're showing us what's cool. They don't know what's good. Their taste is not cool, their taste is not interesting. You're letting this amazing thing that you've worked on for years and years and years be co-opted in two seconds by a soda company. It feels wrong. I want to be a person and not another advertisement. I'm just trying to stand up for what I feel is right.
I think that's why I freaked out at the boiler room thing. They didn't seem to be taking it seriously.
I mean, I don't care if people take what I do seriously or not. I do hope they get something from it or can relate in some way. I enjoy it. It's one of the few moments in my life that I feel completely alive and free. When I perform you're getting to see a little bit of my fucking soul. I know I'm being dramatic here, but you get to see what I do while I'm alone in my room, day in, day out. It's very personal. So yeah, that's serious. ☺

LD Tuttle

"I'm not into decoration — for me that's not what
designing shoes is about."

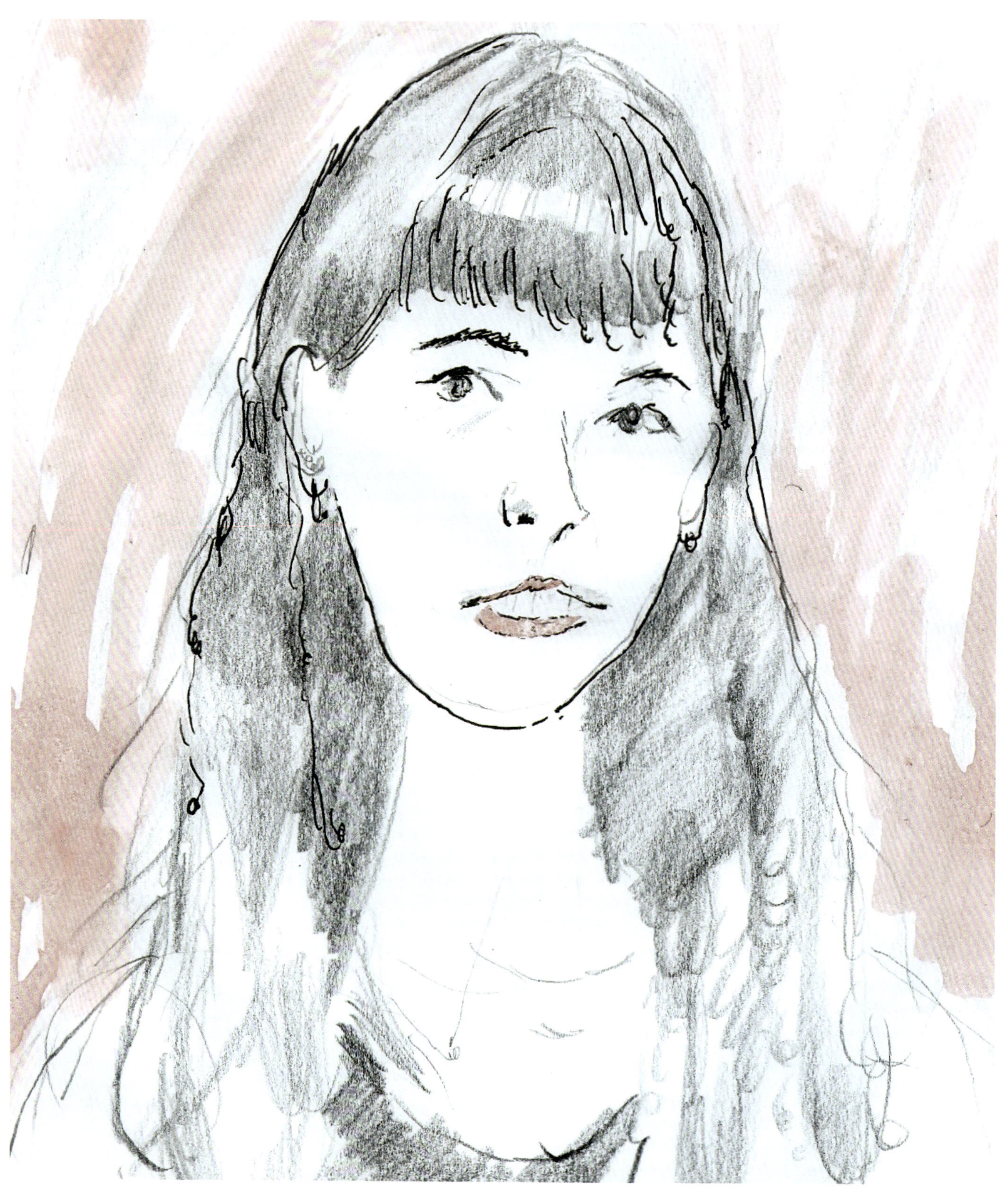

Interview by Avena Gallagher
Portrait by Alissa McKendrick

LD Tuttle shoes are difficult to describe: Often comprised of unconventional shapes, materials, and cuts, the shoes are anomalous as they seem to defy any literal trend and genre. Designed entirely by Tiffany Tuttle, the shoe's straps, zippers, and heels operate in ways that seem impossible, all the while maintaining a functionality rooted in the craft of shoemaking. Having collaborated with brands like VPL and Helmut Lang, Tiffany Tuttle's designs insist on trailblazing new territory in form, leaving exciting new aesthetics in their wake.

Were you interested in fashion growing up?

I loved making things. I learned how to sew when I was really young, five or six. I made my sister a doll, I knitted weird scarves, I made rugs. I always liked doing stuff with my hands. I kind of stopped doing that when I started dancing.

How did you get into dancing?

Well, lot of young girls dance. I loved dancing, I begged my mom to let me take ballet classes when I was seven. I kept dancing all through school. I was going to be a ballet dancer.

I can see that in your legs. I was like, "She has got some pins on her, this girl."

After high school I went and joined this professional company in Las Vegas, but when I got there I realized I didn't want this as a profession. Like anything, you have to be really committed, but it's 20 times more commitment with dance. You only hang out with dancers, it's the only thing you talk about. I missed having other things in my life, so I went to college and studied history.

Where did you go to school?

Princeton. While I was there I started to get into fashion. I applied to FIT and went that route.

Did you study shoemaking at FIT?

Not at all. But I was at Rebecca Taylor, assisting. She didn't do shoes at the time but we would do

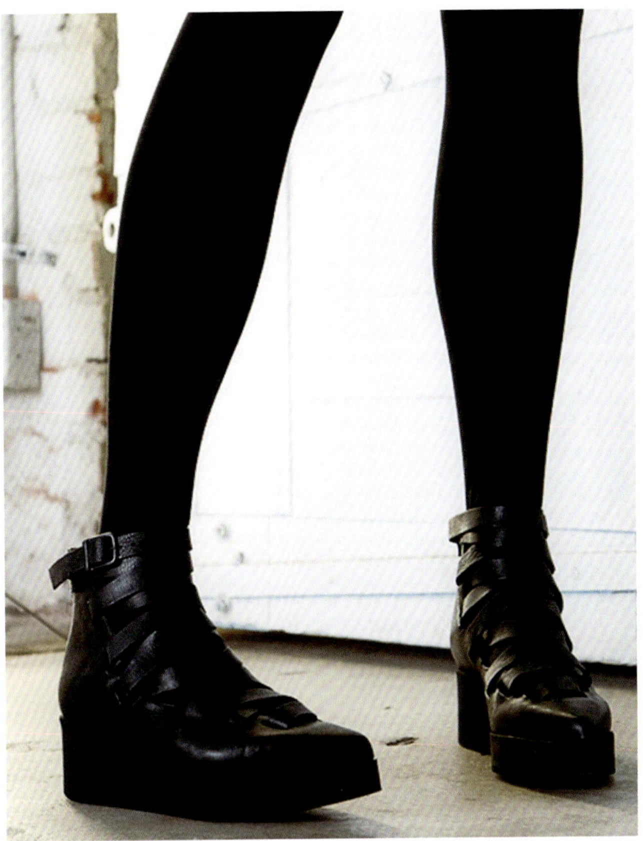

The Blind, AW13.

shoes for the runway, so I got to work on that a little bit. Shoes had always been something I was into, so I decided it was a good idea to just make the switch. I went to this shoe school in Milan.

How fabulous.

It was very technical. Most of the people studying there were sent by their employers — like a shoe factory that might be paying for employees to learn the trade. I came from a design background and knew nothing about the practical side of making shoes. My background was almost the complete opposite of almost everyone else there.

It sounds like an old art there.

I am so glad I did it. Clothes are complicated but shoes are 20,000 times more complicated. It really helps to understand how the entire shoe is put together. I find when working with clothing designers, I am often trying to explain five times why something will work or won't work. It's really hard to understand until you have seen it made.

Images courtesy Tiffany Tuttle

I'm sure. I can think of my own experience wearing shoes that are properly made, not wearing shoes, and wearing shoes that are not properly made. There is a huge difference and there is so much to balance visually and physically. Everything you are working with is also on a smaller scale than clothing. With clothing if you are in production and a pair of pants isn't fitting you can take it in and just modify it. You can't do that with shoes. It changes everything. To say you want to change the heel height by 7mm is to start from the beginning.

One thing that tripped me out recently was seeing really difficult high heel shoes become so trendy that they are being sold at this mass market level. You wonder about people's safety. People are clomping around in these giant fashion platform shoes that cost...
Yeah, $40. That whole extreme platform heel, it's crazy.

Your shoes always look very complicated to design.
My shoes are not insanely complicated in terms having 50 million little straps — it's the original concept that can be quite difficult. Some pattern makers I worked with told me that I was totally crazy. In Italy they love to be super dramatic: "This isn't a shoe, Tiffany!" They love to complain, but they also really like the challenge of creating it.

Why do your shoes have to be manufactured in Italy?
Well they don't. Most shoes are made in China nowadays. I started out making them in Italy because it interested me and now I love everything about it. I have done a few different freelance projects in China and there is a big difference. It makes me feel really lucky to be able to work in Italy.

I have one pair of your VPL boots. You feel like you are stepping on a lot of layers. They are quite built.

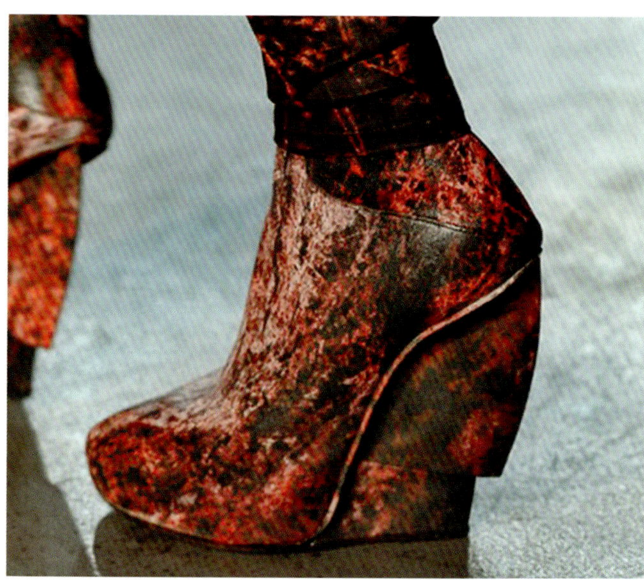

Helmut Lang, AW12.

Italy is a place where you can still do that.

I forgot to ask, do you think there is some connection between the shoes you design and ballet shoes?
Definitely. I spent the first 18—19 years of my life staring at my feet and other people's feet and legs, worrying about how good my arch was. It becomes such an obsession for a dancer. I still really relate to shoes in that way. Shoes are about movement — it's not just this pretty high heel, it should be a three-dimensional object that can move and be looked at from all different angles.

You can do anything in your shoes, even the high ones. Thank god.
It's so crazy — some women can wear extremely high heels, look amazing, and walk really well.

And be comfortable.
But a lot of women can't. It's easy to look ridiculous when you can't walk.

Have you ever considered also making clothes?
No. I love clothes, I love fashion, I love looking at shows and reading about it, but I do not want to do it. Another thing that drew me to shoes was how focused it was. It is just this one little thing that you wear. I really like the specificity of it.

**Do you remember the first shoes that
you designed?**
I remember the first shoes I actually
had made. They were very different.
Just more simple, more traditional.
The thing about shoes is it takes a
lot more knowledge to do the more
interesting things. It has been a
progression. You deal with the heels
that you have at first because that's
what you can work with. Then you grow
and find a factory that is willing to
develop things with you.

**How would you describe your design
aesthetic?**
I get asked this question all the
time. For me, I try to create
something that is both utilitarian
and romantic. It has some sort of
mystery to it, a hidden beauty. At
the same time it's super clean: with
the silhouette, the lines of the
shoe. I am not into decoration — for
me that's not what designing shoes is
about. It's about creating beautiful
lines and also letting the shoe and
the material it's made from do its
own thing.

**There can be so many different
shapes in a shoe. They really inform
everything you are doing.**
Your whole silhouette.

It is that subtle.
The other day when I flew here, I was
wearing these shoes, and I hated the
way they felt with my pants. It was
driving me crazy all day. I don't
really obsess, and I looked like a
bum, I was in a sweatshirt...but it
was about the way the silhouette was
working and the way it felt that was
bothering me. I think shoes are
really important that way.

**Do you approach a collection with a
central idea or are you picking up
where you left off the last season?**
Both. Ideas from last season are what
immediately come to the front as I
start the new season, it's what happens switching from one season to the
next. It's nice because maybe you have
some concept you are working with in
spring but it will really change and
develop into something new in fall.

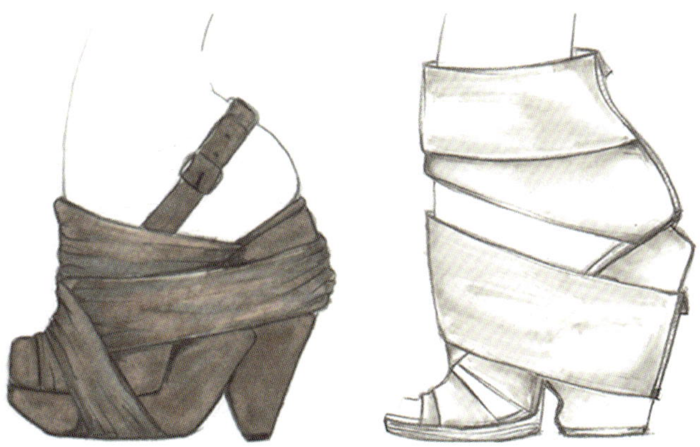
The Lean AW10, The Moon SS10.

**I think it is defiant to create
something that isn't changing at the
same rhythm as the fashion industry.**
I guess that's true. I think it's
important to work with your ideas and
see them grow and change organically.
That was the great thing about
working with Victoria Bartlett — she
works the same way. She does her own
thing her own way.

**You have so many different textures.
Sometimes in one shoe you will have
a bunch of them, and also your
construction often becomes quite
textural. The materials themselves
are also tactile and very earthy.**
To me that's when things have
character, for lack of a better word.
You can look at a leather and see so
much in it. I tend to be drawn to
that stuff where you can really see
the highs and lows in the leather and
different colors in one.

**What do you feel LD Tuttle shoes do
to a person's outfit?**
Make it worse? I hope that they work
with different styles but have a life
of their own at the same time.

I think that's true.
As a designer you obviously have
this ego — otherwise you wouldn't be
designing at all. You are trying
to create something unique, your
own special thing. At the same time
I think another reason you are a
designer is you see amazing people
around you. Like "look at that girl,
her style is incredible." You would
never want to change that, you just
want to be a part of that. ☺

John
"Who the fuck is this guy?"

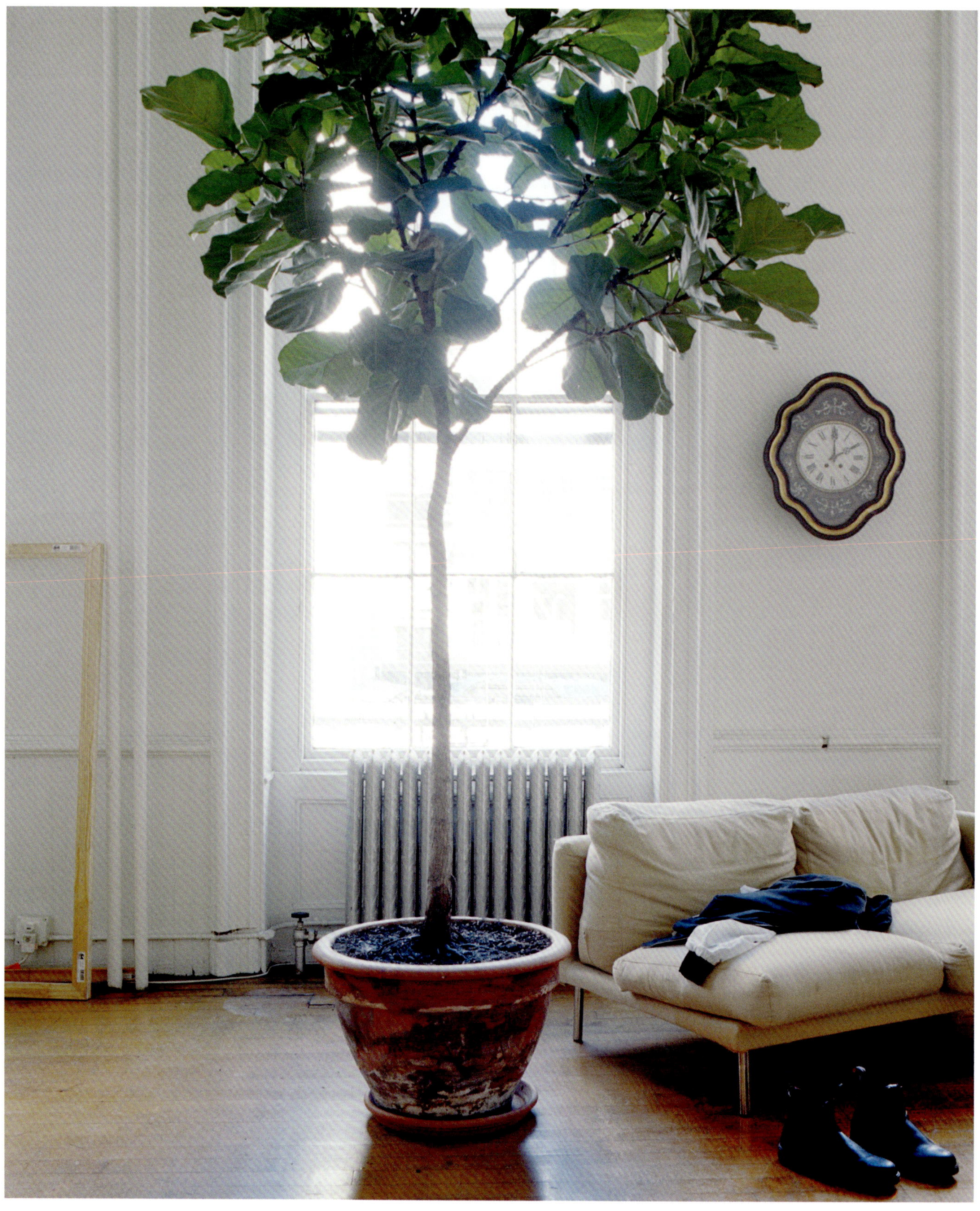

By Coco Young
Photo by Oto Gillen

Who the fuck is this guy? The sneakers he always wears. His hot 21-year-old girlfriend...where did he find her? His apt in Tribeca. In his apt: Throwing magnets on his fridge while his girlfriend's Swedish friends were sleeping on his couch. He showed me the throwing magnets game, then he's like, "Do you do drugs?" Who the fuck is this guy? I hear he works on Wall Street? Is he a weird stalker/creep? Or is he a genius? Is he perverted?

* * *

The dinner party had technically ended but no one was getting ready to leave any time soon. Familiar faces were loitering around the huge smoky loft. Some bodies were crouched on the floor holding cigarettes, others on the couch taking iPhone selfies and tagging John's Instagram name.

I knew John through social media more than I knew him in real life. The first encounter I had with him with him was a Facebook message I received on July 22, 2012 saying, "You seem very interesting, Coco." I didn't respond. Shortly after, I began to notice the mention of his name around town. This was the first time I ever went to his apartment. I had been drinking at my friend Shulan's on West 12th Street when we heard that John was "having people over." I forget if we walked or took a cab but I do remember walking into the Tribeca loft and wondering, "Who is this guy?"

The tree planted in the center of his living room was so tall that its leaves brush against the 18-foot ceiling. People wondered aloud how it got there in the first place. A stack of dirty porcelain plates on a wooden table matched John's casual all-white outfit. Worn-in Reebok sneakers peeped out under his wide legged Levi's. A baseball cap was negligently placed on top of his heavy head of hair, making him look like one of those purposely sloppy "celebrities are just like us!"

That night I did ecstasy thinking it was ketamine because they both look the same. My friend Alex, meanwhile, was on John's MacBook Pro, playing Aqua. John's girlfriend Cece was dancing next to him. She was wearing a pair of baggy jeans and one of John's white dress shirts. Standing there, moving in place, she looked like a young mermaid, an explosion of blonde, Swedish hair flipping in the air as she danced. Her flawless skin picked up the expensive looking studio lights above. Her full lips parted to sing the lyrics:

"I'm a Barbie girl, in a Barbie world."

Her voice revealed perfect teeth covered in shiny metal. She was as beautiful as Mariel Hemingway in Woody Allen's Manhattan, but with braces. I wanted to understand this dynamic because, despite the age difference, John and Cece appear to have something real. As she was dancing to the sound coming from his speakers, effortlessly dressed in his clothing, she looked at him tenderly.

* * *

What is so amazing about John is that everyone either knows him or knows of him. He is connected to every social circle in New York but no one seems to know how or why. Whenever someone asks him a question about his life, he answers by talking about a book or movie. He is liked, even loved, by many, but after asking around a bit, I came to realize that I wasn't the only one perplexed by this character. Even a few weeks after this dinner party, I couldn't shake the curiosity I had about John. Usually when a person captivates me, I want to photograph them. This was different. I wanted more from John than to capture the way he looks. I started thinking about the artist Sophie Calle, and how she follows people.

Although Calle will often choose a person randomly, she is able to make a portrait of them by decreasing the distance between herself and her subject, by following them until they become a real part of her life.

On March 25 at 7:21 PM I was editing photos when I received my first text message from John. I had no idea how this person got my phone number and I was a bit perplexed at first. All it said was "Hi Coco. U miss me?" and immediately after: "LOL lets hang out soon". I started piecing the identity of my anonymous texter together after a run-in with John at an art opening, when he asked me why I never responded. I nonetheless maintained his number unsaved, as I wanted to keep the novelty of an unregistered set of digits popping up on the screen of my iPhone.

The distance between John and I was already getting smaller: one day he sent me that Facebook message, and now we are acquaintances. Distance is a measure, a malleable quantity and maybe the distance between John and I, engaged with social media, could be reduced even more if we tried. Instead of asking to take his picture (which I don't think would have captured his intricacies), I decided to focus my attention on him as a whole. I got to know him in order to compose this portrait of him.

I started by looking on the internet: besides his heavily muted Facebook and Instagram accounts, nothing, absolutely nothing exists about him. Very odd for someone who goes to most parties and knows everybody. I asked around about him, and there's no shortage of rumors: he has a secret high-powered job, was a piano prodigy by the time he was 13, and, more recently, was spotted by a friend of mine crawling out of the trunk of a Jeep with four other people on a sunny afternoon — apparently returned from some rave in Brooklyn.

John was known for curating his parties with specific and eclectic groups of people like someone might curate an art show with coveted, in-demand works. Originally I thought that John was hitting on me, but then I realized that he was just interested in pulling me into his circle. Decreasing the distance between him and I would be easy.

On Sunday, May 26, I woke up at noon to a text from John inviting me to a dinner party at his place that very night. The dinner was in honor of Cece, who was returning to Sweden for a while. I was really excited and asked my friend Daria to come along. We were supposed to bring wine but we got a six pack of Stella from an overpriced deli on Broadway near John's apartment. The narrow staircase of his Franklin street building felt like a hallway leading to a club. As we got closer to the door, step by step, the volume of the music and the cigarette smoke increased. We didn't really know anyone there but John greeted us with a sparkling white smile.

A group of young Swedish girls were scattered around the living room table. They were chain-smoking Marlboro Lights with the mannerism of Hollywood actresses. These young girls seemed to be playing dress-up in their mothers clothing and had certainly mastered the affects of maturity. They gave themselves away washing down pieces of homemade sushi with clumsy gulps of champagne. John was the master of the ceremony, a moving center of gravity around which everyone seemed to be in orbit. As a director, he was in his element.

That night I wore my most opaque red Chanel lipstick. I think John liked it because he asked if he could wear it after he shaved. He ran into the bathroom and came out without his typical five o'clock shadow.

I handed him my tube of lipstick which he deftly applied without once glancing into a mirror. That night, I tried to talk to him a few times, asking him casual questions without seeming too eager. John gave short answers and would change the subject by making a joke or introducing me to another one of his guests.

Around midnight, he made an announcement: the party was moving to some Korean nightclub in Chinatown, an obscure place he was at that time frequenting as a DJ. Our small group followed his orders and vacated the apartment. We all walked together from his apartment to Mott street. As we entered the club, I realized the manager was waiting for him. Many guests were there already, sipping on vodka sodas and Tsingtaos, waiting. The black lights inside made everything fluorescent and blue. John's teeth glowed and seemed whiter because his lips were still dark from the red lipstick. John disappeared into his crowd and I didn't see him again that night.

*   *   *

This is what happens when John picks you up on the 4th of July. You're waiting on East 13th Street and Avenue A. The wheel of a rented white Audi pulls up on the curb right next to you. The driver's side window rolls down. John doesn't say anything. He's wearing a baseball cap and wraparound sunglasses. They're the kind you wear when you go skiing. Three other girls are crowded in the back of the car. You don't know them. They are going to annoy you. You start talking because you don't want to hear anyone else's voice today. You're stuck in traffic going into the Holland tunnel. The girls are laughing, you feel like puking. A dog barks. There's nowhere to go. Black Skinhead plays on the radio. This is Independence Day. John is doing 80 on the highway headed for the hamlets of eastern Pennsylvania.

Gun laws here are practically non existent. You hear the pops in the air. You know you're getting close. The gravel cracks under your feet as you jump out of the car. You're at the Sunset Hill Shooting Range. Everyone who works here is strapped. You take the earmuffs off for a second because it's hot.

A guard barks at you immediately. John is laughing. John is always laughing. He takes a picture with his iPhone. He tries to crowd you and the other girls for a picture. You don't want to be in it. John is jumping up and down and yelling something at you. He is pointing at an assault riffle.

"I want you to shoot it."

The gravel cracks under your feet. The gravel is littered with empty shells. It's family day at the range. A 14-year-old boy raises an M4. His father stands behind him. Proud American. Your hands are shaking. You're gripping a matte black AK-47. The gun is too heavy for your boney shoulder. The instructor shouts in your ear. None of his words make sense. John stands behind you. A butterfly of fear grows inside your stomach. You clinch your hand with anxiety and start picking at the cuticles of your index finger with your thumb. It bleeds a little. You pull the trigger.

*   *   *

I could text John right now and say, "what's up." Maybe we would meet at La Colombe for an iced coffee and talk about people we know or laugh about the 4th of July. But if I were to ask him a question, something simple about his life — because the distance between John and anyone else in the world can never be completely eradicated — he would probably change the subject and start talking about some film he likes, maybe The Good, the Bad and the Ugly. ☺

Maggie Lee
"SmaSh the staTe and then take a nap"

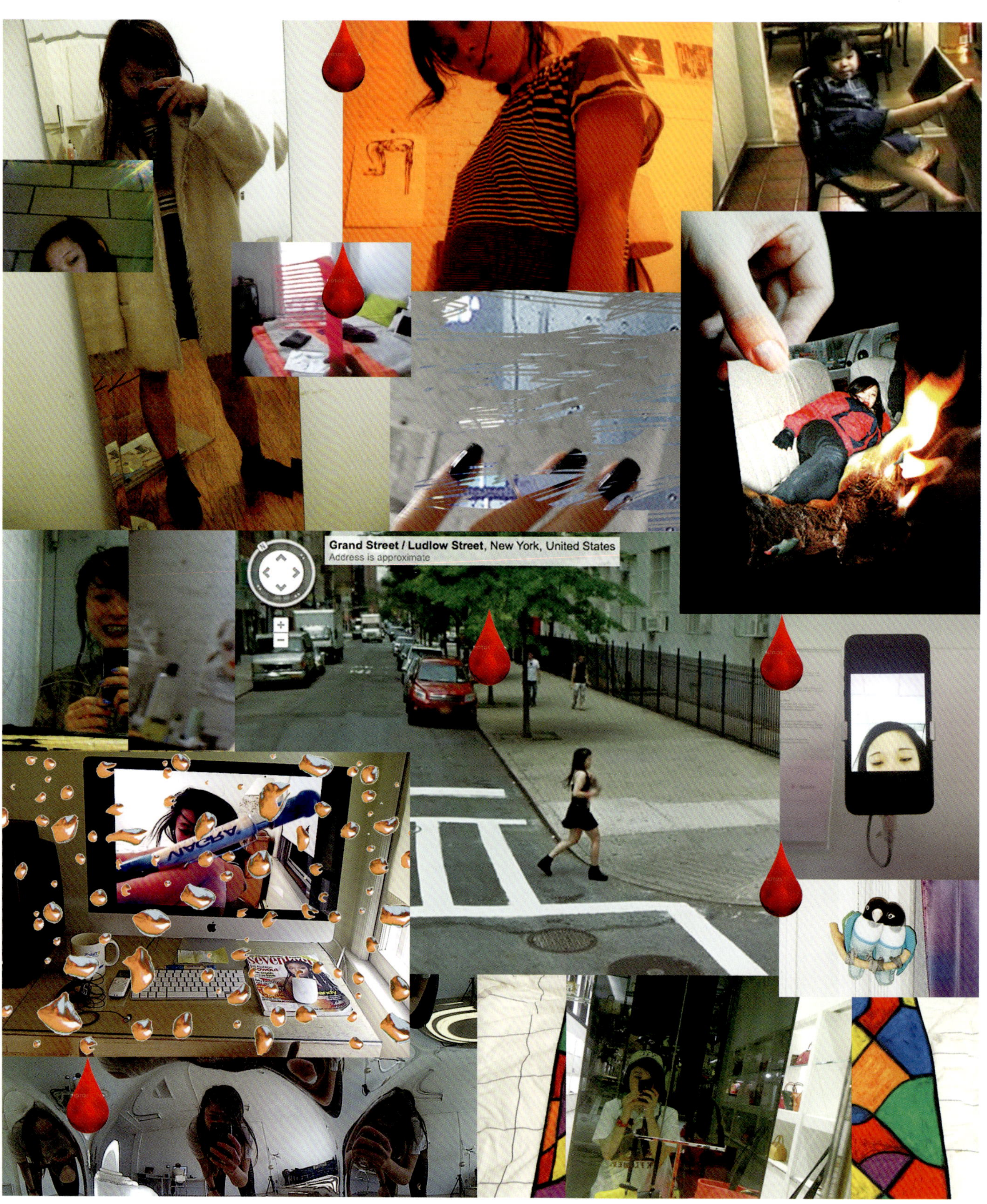

Interview by Asher Penn
Images courtesy Maggie Lee

If you're a reader of Sex and don't know who Maggie Lee is, we're a little bit confused. Maggie has been down with Sex since day one, contributing fashion stories, interviews, portraits, as well as constantly sending in videos, photos, poems, and descriptions of her dreams for our blog. She's easily one of the most prolific, hard working, and cool creative people living in New York today, so we decided to interview her in her favorite format: The questionnaire.

What's your middle name?
...my birth certificate, SS, and state ID all have different middle names. my dad's eyes are closed on his state i-D.

How old are you?
26

How tall are you?
5 ft.

What sign are you?
Leo, moon in Pieces

Where do you live?
123 Lil' Puddin' Road, NYC, USA, come over!

Where were your parents' jobs?
Howard Johnsons, Lord and Taylor, Pings Restaurant, Mings Restaurant, Far East Magic & Acrobatics.

What was your favorite TV show growing up?
Eerie Indiana, Round the Twist, Are You Afraid of the Dark?, Aeon Flux, MTV Subterranean, Liquid Television

What was your favorite toy?
I have this peach toy that looks like a peach but its cement, you can put it in a fruit basket with real fruit. It becomes a game when people want to eat it, because it's not real, its a toy... peach game.

What was the first record you bought?
presidentsoftheunitedstatesofamerica

Did you ever go to camp?
I went to camp at Pratt Institute when I was 15 and went to a bar and someone bought my friend a beer and i had some of it. It was at this place called The Gardens. That building collapsed though. I still don't know how I got in...

Were you a rebellious teen?
SmaSh the staTe and then take a nap

Did you get good grades?
They were OK - I would usually stay up until 4am and then would be so sleepy at school. i think punks somehow found their own hidden cirriculum, IDK, i didn't like high school.

Were you popular in high school?
I think I was popular until one time I got my face painted at a town fair and no one talked to me after that. And then my face was tan except the part with the face paint so at school I had a decorative tan on my face. IDK. I looked 10 when everyone was 14. A blessing in disguise.

What was your favorite class?
Free period, because I would sleep on a cot in the nurses office. One time there was someone else sleeping on a cot and he got up and laid on top of me and pretended he was cumming. it was demented.

What class did you hate?
Math.

Who did you hang out with?
People from a message board

Who was your first crush?
Sho, he had a mushroom haircut

Who was your first kiss?
Jonathan, XOXO. He was my insane crush from 1st grade to 8th grade. He was a bad boy. On April 23rd, 1999, we kissed on a dare like it was nothing. His mother was in the room, we did it when she wasn't looking.

Who was your first Boyfriend?
Sean, a real hottie at the time. It was 7th-8th grade. It took a year of dating to actually make out, and it tasted like swedish fish. We kissed on the balcony of a hotel on a band/orchestra field trip to virginia.

Were you on Makeoutclub?
uh x huh

Did you have subscriptions to any magazines?
Elementary school, it was Readers Digest, not my choice. In 5th grade to middle school it was Seventeen + YM!! In high school I worked at a mailbox copy center and there was this guy that would give me all his Vice Magazines for years.

What was your first website?
M14Sm4sH on Geocities
**Can you name some other websites
you've made?**
M14Sm4sH was MS Paint art and
reviews, I had another one on gURL.
com and it was DIY stuff.
Did your website get hacked once?
Crash and Burn
What's your favorite movie?
Babe
Do you have a style icon?
Lung Leg, Rose McGowan, the cast
and crew of Charmed, when Beck is
interviewed by Thurston Moore, Alicia
Bay Laurel...
**What's the most expensive thing you
spend money on?**
Feelings, art and technology
**What's the cheapest thing you spend
money on?**
Give a penny get a penny

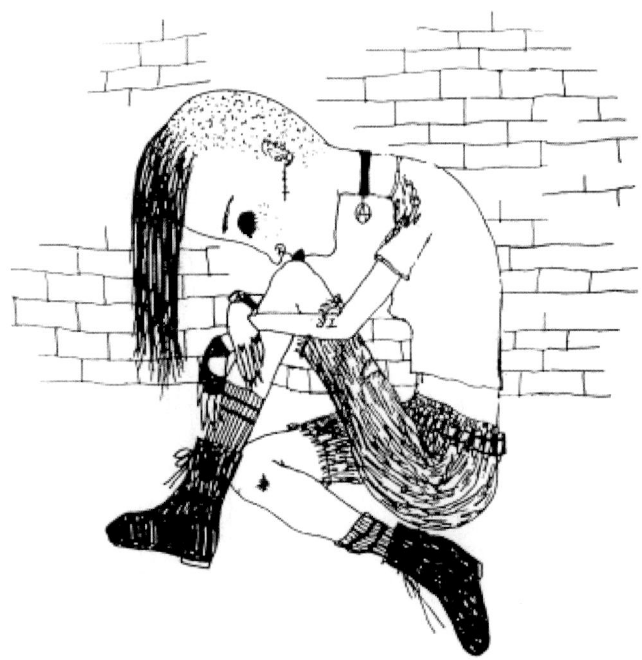

Punk Girl, 2010.

What's your favorite candy?
Peachass marzipan fruit
Have you ever shoplifted?
If I have to, F*k th3 5ySt3M
As a Leo do you identify with lions?
Not really
What's your spirit animal?
Bunny

What's your dream date?
Something...on a hill rolling in
the grass making out in a garden.
an apocalyptic scene where leaves,
flowers, and rain are falling on us and
maybe if there was a DJ and the bass
was really loud and you could feel the
ground shaking that would be sick...
wearing eckhaus latta, COMME des
GARÇONS something
Who is your #1 crush?
I can't say or it won't happen ;-D
**What's your favorite band T-shirt
that you own?**
Silk Flowers
What was your first zine?
No Parents Allowed
Can you name all your other zines?
too embarrassing
Where do you get your groceries?
Mr. KiWi + Mr. CoCo
Where do you shop for clothes?
My sister's closet
Do you see a hairstylist?
Yoko at Salon Shizen
**How much time do you spend a day in
front of a computer?**
carpal tunnel
**What's your favorite way to
procastinate?**
Listen to some music, dance in front
of mirror, and clean room
Do you exercise?
I have two groupons, one for gyrotonics
and the other for pole dancing
**Who's your favorite celebrity you
have met?**
Jeanette Hayes, OMG.
How many cameras do you own?
Blackberry tootsie pop, photobooth,
rangefinder, point and shoot, SLR
Who is your favorite skateboarder?
Jerry Hsu
Name a guilty pleasure?
hehehe
**Who's the coolest band you ever saw
live?**
Rorschach, GBX
Do you write down your dreams?
only when i wear a nicotine patch
before bed
Do you keep a diary?
http://teenopendiary.com/
formyeyesonly ;-D

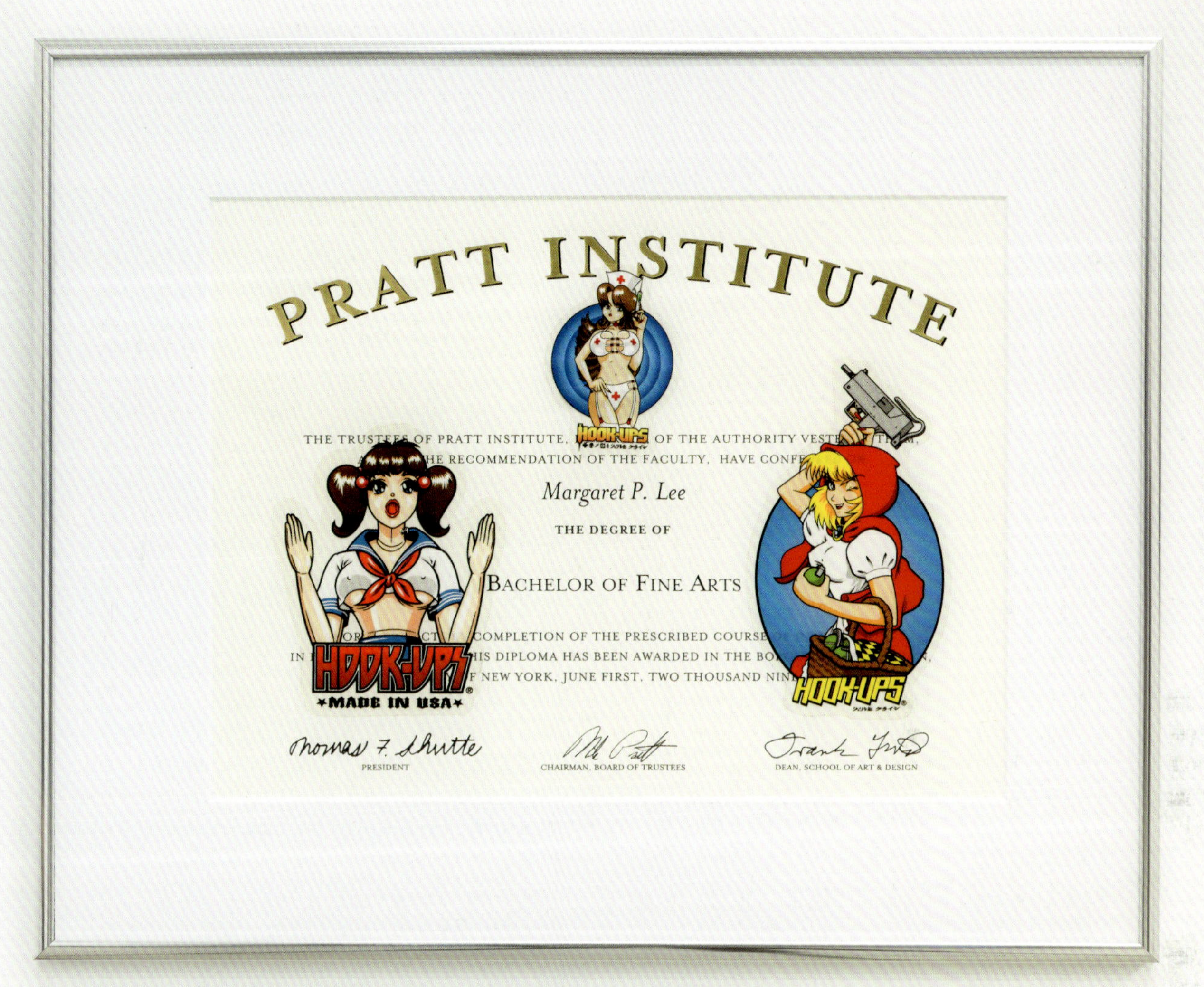

Hookups Endorsement Diploma, Lonely Girl, Maccarone Gallery, 2013.

Who is your hero?
fire erowid, earth erowid

Do you ever meditate?
☮ to you and ☮ for me, ☮☮☮. made from the best stuff on earth for your mind body and soul

What's your favorite food?
Cafe gratitude

What's your favorite color?
Warm orange / salmon/ rust color

Do you like New Jersey?
I like it more now that I don't live there, it's nice to go back. yesterday, i hung out with my uncles. my one uncle made me a spicy tuna hand roll and a green tea on the side and then i went back into the kitchen and my other uncle healed me with gua sha.

How old were you when you saw Kids?
13, on my DELL computer with a sweaty hand on the "minimize" button incase my mom saw.

If you had a boy what would you name it?
Tripp, Crispin, Valentino, Balthazar... ugh I can't think about this right now, stressing me out LOL

If you had a girl what would you name it?
Felicia, Naomi, Mercedes, Prue, Ivy, Seven...

Have you ever had any nicknames?
Magic! That was supposed to be my real name but

Do you have a motto?
go with the flow

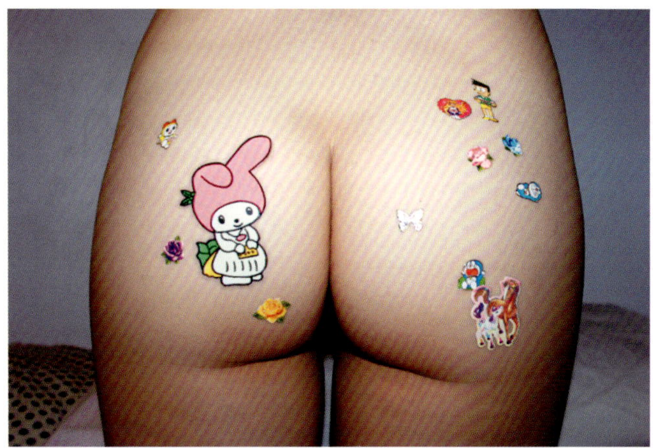

Sexy Cute Ass, 2011.

Do you like dogs or cats?
yes and yes, omg, Hachiko, i want to cry.
What's a good pet name?
Seggaaaa, but when they're bad, it's ......SEGA!
Can you ollie?
Yah, it's like, 1st you just pretend there's a bug on the tail and then you squish it and then with your other foot you flick it off and try to get all the goo off your board, while jumping.
Do you believe in Girl Power?
XGIRL, BOMB ASS PUSSY, KATHLEEN HANNA, TAVI
Do you believe in God?
"In God we bust" — Lizzi Bougatsos
Do you believe in magic?
Magic is like meditation
Do you believe in ghosts?
I'm scared.
Do you like kids?
Yeah! I like when kids make up games that are like inside jokes, so funny.
Have you ever played sports?
field hockey, rugby
Are you good at any video games?
twisted metal black
What swear word do you use the most often?
!@#$%^&*
What's your favorite swear word?
bootyhole, lol, why are u asking me this?? ;-p
What's a turn on?
Bad boys
What's a turn off?
Bad attitude

Do you read comics?
Dame Darcy + Julian Ceccaldi, I'm gonna cry!
Have you ever been arrested?
I had to go to jail one time when I was a baby. I ate mellon candy and watched Beavis and Butthead next to a security screen of the woman who was "babysitting me," sitting in a jail cell, wearing tevas. She left me alone on the beach, and then left me alone at night near the boardwalk and the special effects lights really freaked me out. She bought $100 dollars worth of tie dye clothes for me and her house was wood paneled with cloth hanging on top of a lamp. The cops found us because she was driving drunk with a stolen car and money and my mom had to come 3 hours away to pick me up at jail.
Have you ever crowd surfed?
warped tour @ randalls island, 2001
What kind of art do you like?
i like STOMP, the musical, you know, stuff like that
What's the cutest thing on YouTube?
"Dad makes fun of his son for looking like Marilyn Manson", just watch it cause the son is a cutie and then he gets so much fan mail that Ricki invites him back to the show so he can go out to dinner with 2 admirers in NYC or super milk intro theme song

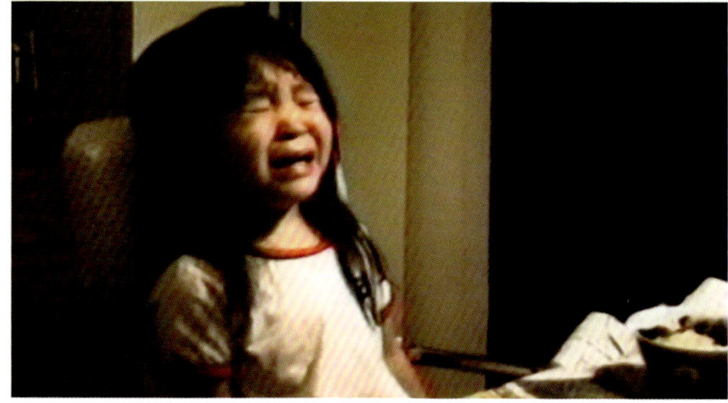

Mommy, Beta Pictures, 2015.

What makes you mad?
injustice, war, hardship, pushy people, fox news
What's the hardest thing about living in NY?
sometimes its hard to be free and have time to yourself to enjoy life.

What's the best thing about living in NY?
The fall is the best. Everything is so crispy. I love the cold air and the leaves and autumn colors. Listen to Aphex Twin and go for a walk. Everything smells better too. I love friends. i love to party with a good sound system. i love checking things out, working, working in the studio, independence, everything!!!

What's your favorite drug?
XOXO

Do you like scary movies?
Only if someone will watch them with me, I like Argento

Do you ever feel emo?
I have this babydoll toy, I've had her forever. Shes black and has freckles and has a pouting face. When I look at her I get emo. She makes me think of culture, history, being a baby, the person who made it, the doll factory, other people who have the same doll toy, everything.

Do strangers ever message you? Are they ever cool?
It use to be teenage zine ppl, then art students, blog readers, psychonauts, then when i worked in a t-shirt store, it was like sneakerheads, and now its just random. the other day a student from my high school emailed me about making a poem for his zine, so sweet.

Why do you keep deleting your facebook?
i wouldn't reply to people's messages but then i would post a good utube and then some ppl got mad at me for not replying or thought i had free time but was ignoring them and then i hated the idea of Facebook but now i'm back on it.

What's your favorite flower?
Icelandic poppy

What's craziest thing you've ever filmed?
girls gone wild. maybe a man on the bridge trying to jump? it freaked me out. he didn't jump.

Did you ever do graffiti? Did you have a tag? Acts of vandalism?
Sometimes i'll collect all my negative thoughts and put it in a crystal and then throw it at someone's window. someone who is a bad person obviously. i think thats feng shui..

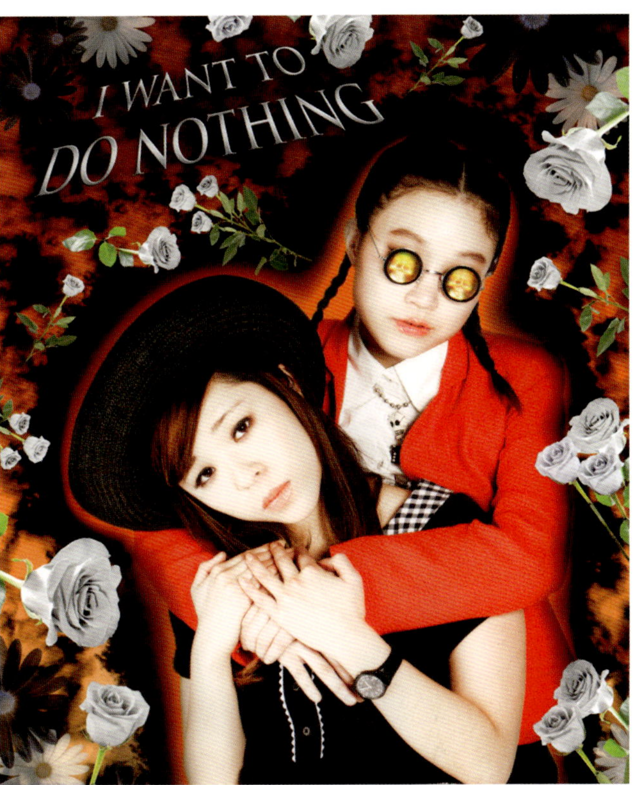

Maggie Lee & Sandy Kim, Pretty Kool-A, Vice Magazine, 2012.

Lucky Number?
1,234,567,890

Have you ever played music or been in a band?
in high school, a hardcore/ thrash band

What's your favorite Nirvana song?
Lithium because my other babysitter use to sing it to me, so soothing.

Are you a packrat?
Trying to be minimal

Are you a neat freak?
On a leash

Did you name your computer?
SEXYCUTEASS OSX 10.8.4

What do you look for in a boyfriend?
They have to be cute, a freak, good style, and good at something cool and make me feel crazy. Ideal bf would make me want to cry and make out and want to do everything, xoxo til infinity.

What's a good karaoke Song?
NIN Closer

Can you write a Haiku?
Thank you Asher Penn
For asking me question
I have to go, BYE! ☺

Hammer Blue

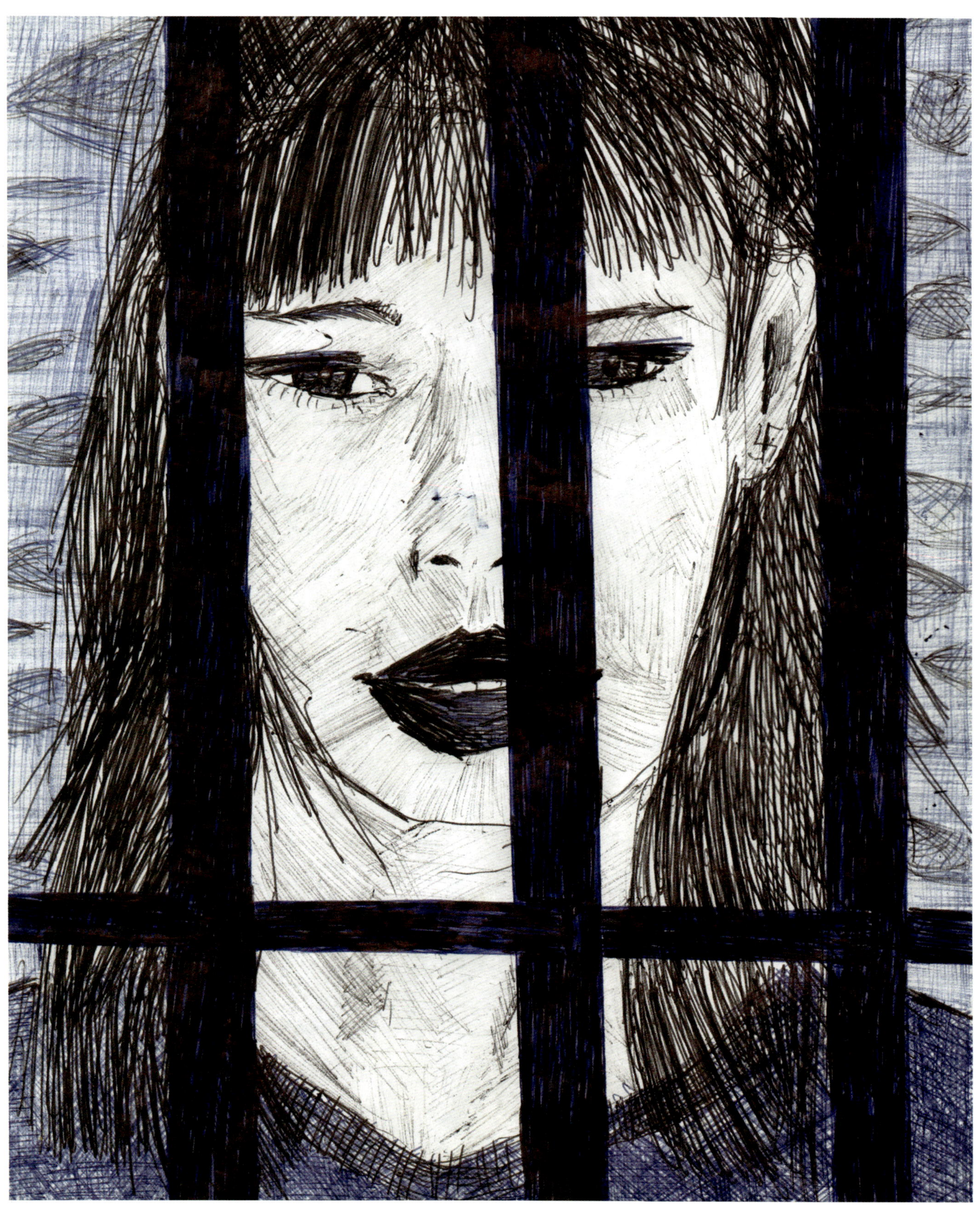

By Kayla Guthrie
Drawings by Asher Penn

"You must've packed in a hurry,"
said the uniformed man as he
sifted through my suitcase, which
lay unzipped on the conveyor belt
at a security checkpoint in the
Philadelphia airport. His hands
passed over dirty underwear,
drawings, a sewing machine, books
loaded into the mesh zipper pocket...

"Yeah, I did."

I remember him assessing me grimly,
and me feeling embarrassed he'd had
to go through my stuff. Then the
clothes were rearranged back over
the sewing machine, the suitcase was
closed and zipped up, and there must
have been some words or gesture made
to indicate that I was free to go,
although that moment escapes me.

Is it wrong to quarantine certain
times in your life — perfectly
innocent weeks or months presumably
no less alive in memory than any
others — to stop and suffocate these
recollections before they become too
insightful? And is it worse to try to
narrate those weeks and months, tell
their stories from this cool remove,
while the memories are still locked
away in dimness, breathing shallow,
confined breaths?

Shortly before I moved away, I
noticed a friend using a neologism
— "hammerhead" — both a noun and an
adjective: hammerhead won't take no
for an answer, will not consider
other points of view. Or, you're
turning hammerhead when you're
obsessed with shortcuts, never mind
that you keep hitting your head
against the wall — again and again.

I didn't really want to know what
I was doing. I thought I would
attend grad school, and move to
New York that way. Work on being an
artist. I guess I was going to get
an internship. Two separate ideas,
but see how I forced past that in my
mind?

Philadelphia was not New York but
it was New York, basically, for our
purposes.

Hammerhead.

We went there as much as we could,
enduring the Chinatown bus ride. It
was only supposed to be a couple of
hours, but usually ended up taking
around four. There was a bathroom in
the back where piss sloshed around
on the floor. We tried not to drink
too much water.

On one excursion I bought a special
pair of shoes from Opening Ceremony.

"I'm on a trip, so I have an
excuse," I said to the salesgirl.
I had saved up some money from my
job at a shoe store in Vancouver.
I'd almost spent it on something
expensive from my work before I left
town, but changed my mind after
discussing it with a male coworker
who said, "You're going to New York.
Buy shoes in New York."

"I wish I had an excuse to buy those
shoes," the Opening Ceremony girl
replied gaily.

"You're my hero, by the way," my
coworker had told me.

Asher put down security deposits and
paid bus fare and did fix-it things
around the house. We bought jugs
of Poland Spring water rather than
drink from the taps. Was there a
problem with the water? I went for
long walks and wrote incessantly:

October 26, 2007

"Feeling ancient." It's like an
overwhelming nostalgia that comes
some days when the seasons are
changing. It makes my skull fill
with color — I'm not kidding — glow
shifting from tiffany to lavender to
royal blue. A synaesthetic buzzing,
punctuated by pink and gold.

Left: Untitled (Philadelphia Drawing), Asher Penn, 2007.

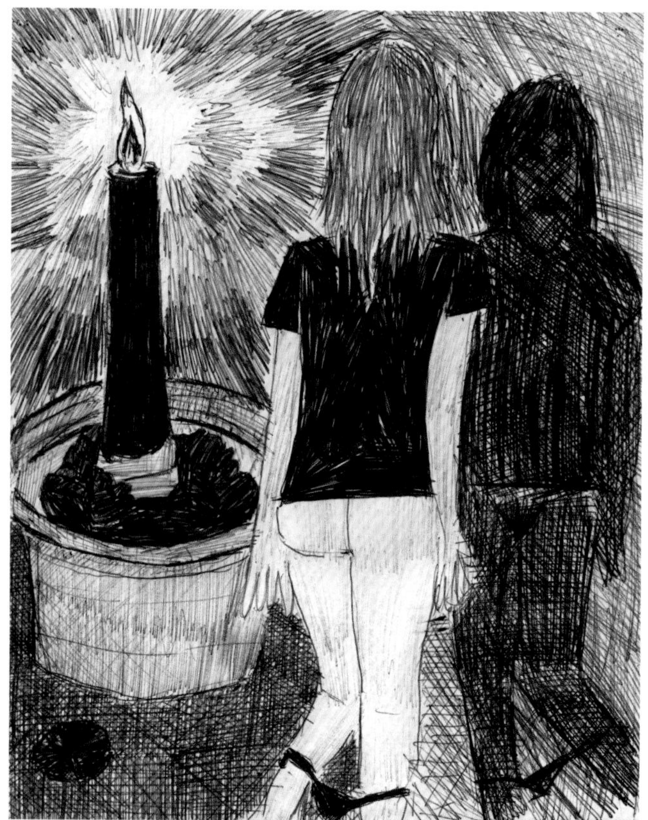
Untitled (Philadelphia Drawing),
Asher Penn, 2007.

I was watching the Indian summer sun
illuminate some leaves swirling on
the sidewalk and something triggered
a warm adoration in me. I let my
head buzz and go for a walk, letting
this feeling take my feet somewhere.
In shadows and corners of streets
I seemed to be looking for a place
inside me that was at least as old as
my first memory.

My room had three windows that faced
the street. Below was an African money
order and phone card place that played
thumping, up-tempo music all day at
an intrusive volume. Our apartment
had two floors and three bedrooms and
we had a roommate, who lived in the
room below mine. He had recently moved
from New York; a Cooper Union alumnus,
boyfriend of our friend, and sculptor
of oversized granny craft objects made
from wicker and fabric. He sang along
to Sinead O'Connor in the mornings,
hitting all the high notes: "Since
you've been gone I can do what-ever I
wa-a-ant..."

His room opened into the common
area with French doors, which he
dressed with curtains. Wall-to-wall
mirrors covered the space, creating
a heightened, drab feel. Mirrored
shelves were mounted in the corners.
Asher photographed my new shoes
and one of my books there, posing
them as he set up the shots with a
tripod.

On Thanksgiving, we went over to
the house of some friends. Before
eating, we all held hands around
the table while the hostess gave a
rambling speech, which ended: "Fuck
you, Mom and Dad."

Then we stuffed our faces, got drunk,
and walked down to the Delaware
river, where it was completely dark
except for a few halogen lights from
some commercial docks blinking in the
near distance.

You couldn't tell what was water
and what was night sky. There was a
full moon but it only seemed to make
everything else blacker, all light
restricted to its white orb. I was
too freezing to think much about how
eerie it was.

Someone cried out about Thanksgiving, or the Delaware, and then
we turned to make our way home. The
walk seemed to take forever, as if
our thoughts and voices slowed down
in the cold.

At the end of November a bunch of us
did acid. I didn't see or realize
anything. I felt alien, alone and
paranoid — and stony, like listening
to the dark moments of a song on the
radio that I was indifferent to. We
were at a park: a ravine, covered in
leaves, variously loud and crunchy
and moist and spongy, down a trail
and up a hill. The trail seemed to
have been a service vehicle road,
the route to a drainage pipe, which
lay further in and was a swimming
spot in the summer.

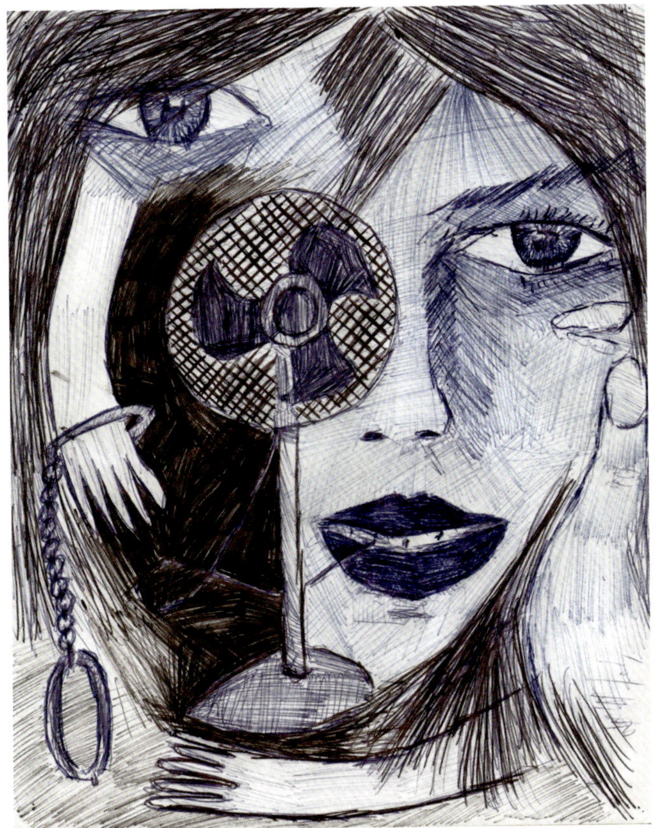

Untitled (Philadelphia Drawing),
Asher Penn, 2007.

At the mouth of the pipe, there was a rope swing and some rocks above still, shallow water. The leaves were supposed to have been turning around this time but the colors were mostly faded and fallen, the trees dull and naked. Thinking back to the mossy forests I was used to, I felt a helpless gloom as one of our group members explained, "It's kind of gone now. It would have been a lot more colorful a few weeks ago, I guess."

I kept asking questions and tried to have fun, exclaiming at the view, but the people in our group seemed immersed in their thoughts, quiet and contained, unintelligible and stupid when they did talk. The day had been overcast and as the light faded it began to get darker.

I felt suddenly achingly hungry, after a long day of wandering in the forest, and blandly expressed that we should get going and eat.

We hiked uphill out of the ravine and left in the autumn night, driving back to our neighborhood while someone chattered about new designer drugs.

We stopped for Mexican food, which I had never much eaten before but always seemed to be eating then, and didn't particularly enjoy or understand at the time - tortillas and rice and cheese and various things, not fresh.

"You can tell she's crazy by her hair — she just picks at it." Asher had said about a member of our group that day.

I thought of this while the girl ordered chicken tacos, and stared at her; I wonder now if she just seemed weird at the time because I was making her uncomfortable.

I chose a vegetarian burrito. When it arrived, I looked at it and sliced it down the middle. Gazing at the slit in the center, I kept preparing to begin. It just sat there and looked at me.

I must have tried putting some of it in my mouth, but couldn't do anything with the lettuce and cooked vegetables and cheese and rice and sauce, so I waited for everyone to finish so I could go home, still hungry and anxious.

November 17, 2007

Closing your eyes you feel the wrapper of your skin resting a quarter inch over the denser mass of your muscles and organs, and the stillness of the bones beneath.

Your eyes are blacked out in your skull, silent mush levitating in dark water. Sometimes you manage to stay so still that a royal blue penetrates the blackness; a deep ballpoint blue that's almost violet. ☺

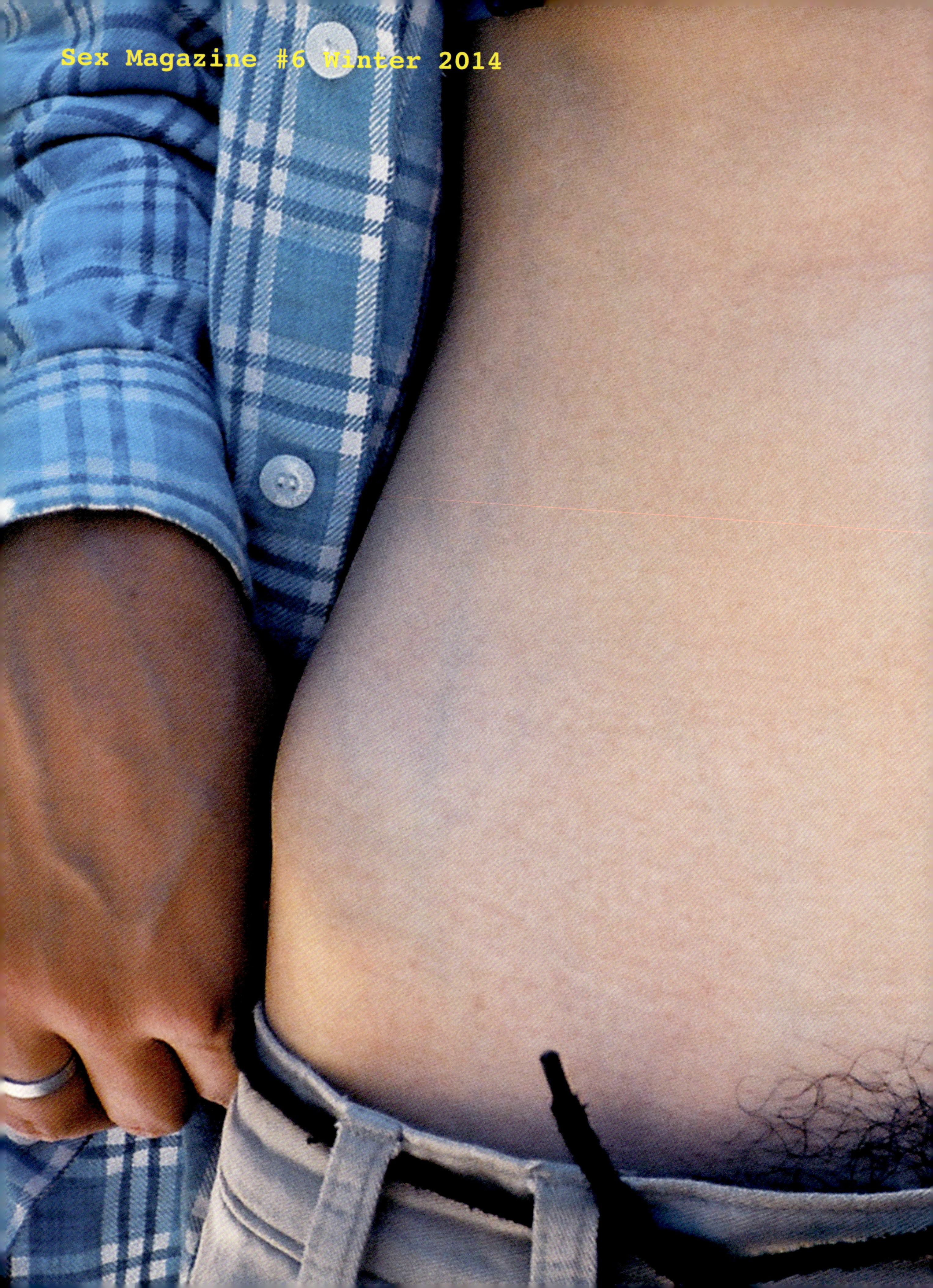
Sex Magazine #6 Winter 2014

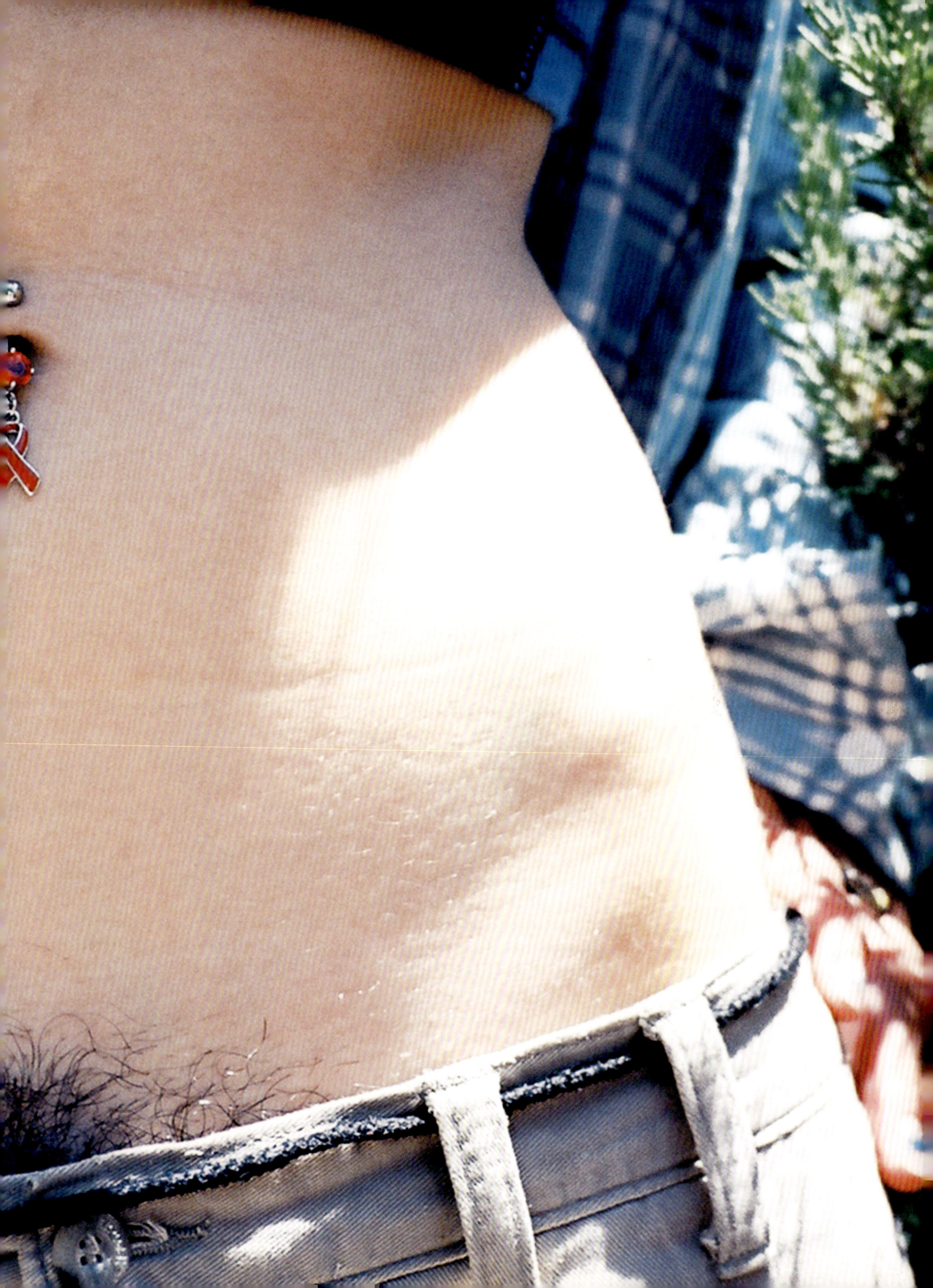

Lansing-Dreiden
"Not everything has to be popular."

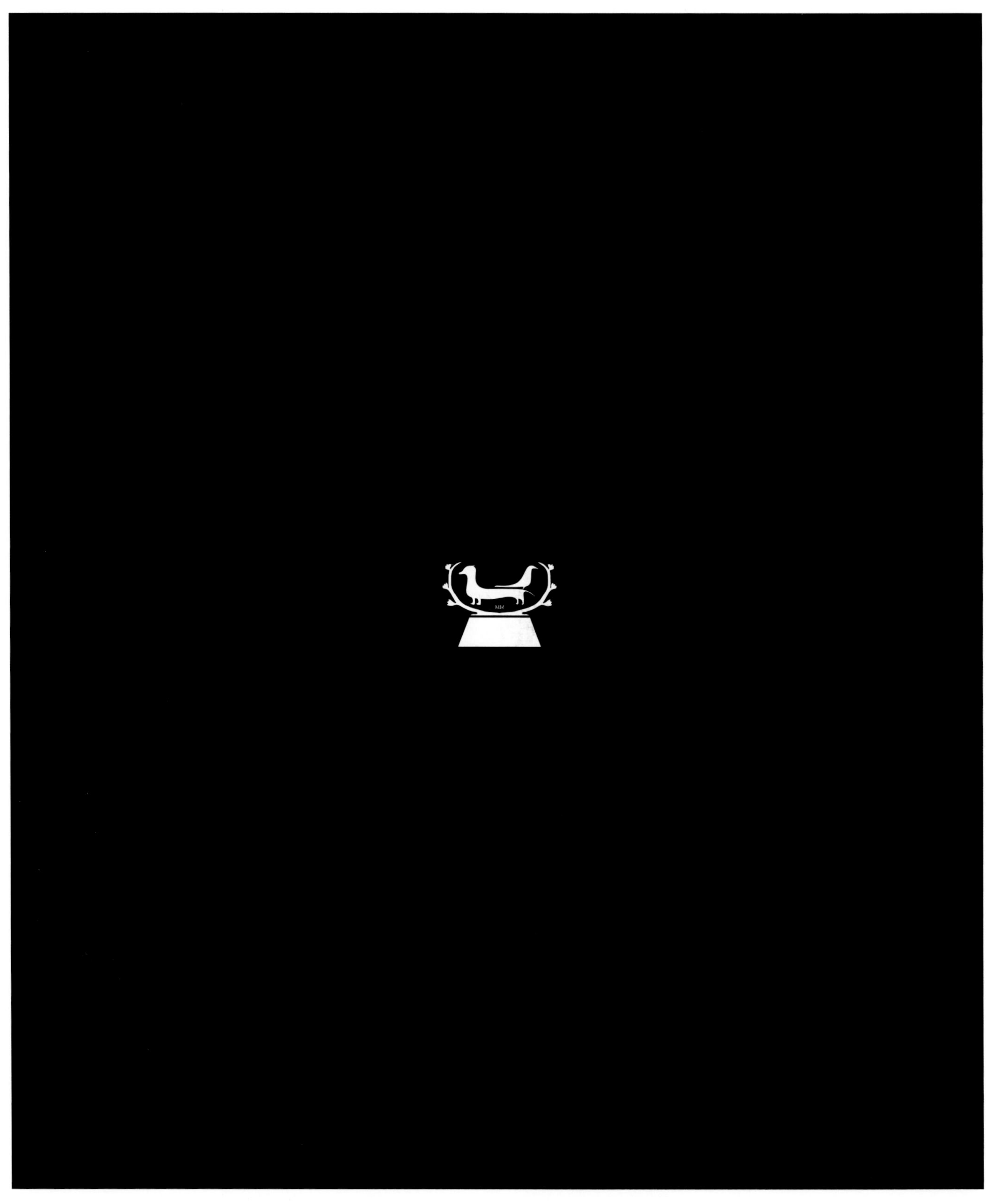

Interview by Annie Pearlman
Images courtesy Lansing-Dreiden

My favorite record in 2003 was self-
released by a group that called
itself a company and hired musicians
to perform their rare live shows.
With only a strange hyphenated name
and logo on minimal black-and-white
packaging, and little else revealed
in the very scant press they received,
you didn't have much to go on except
to check out Lansing-Dreiden's work
for yourself, and you were lucky
if you got that far. Their website
did a pretty good job of sharing
all the "company's" creations,
arranged by year, but no names or
human authorship. Their high-concept
artistic touch could be applied to
anything, from interior design to
literary journals. Lansing-Dreiden's
work was economic, fully realized, and
easy to enjoy, which made it stand out
from the often indulgent, half-baked,
half-hustled New York art scene, but
their unpopular methodologies and
lack of personhood seemed to confuse
or upset others outside of the fine
arts arena. Now, they are re-releasing
their albums again through Mexican
Summer and talking to an old fan.

Okay, so I've been a big fan since
2003, FYI. Huge, huge fan. As soon as
I heard Incomplete Triangle I wrote
to the anonymous email address asking
if you needed an intern.
We wrote back to you?
**You wrote back that maybe it wasn't
right at this time.**
I remember that.
**Yeah, but guess who is in your face
ten years later?**
Hell yeah.
I made it happen.
You're more of a member than any of
us are.
**Okay, so let's talk about the
beginning. You guys are all from
Miami?**
Yeah. It wouldn't have happened
otherwise.
When did you guys first meet?
In early grade school around the
second grade. Our parents were
friends.

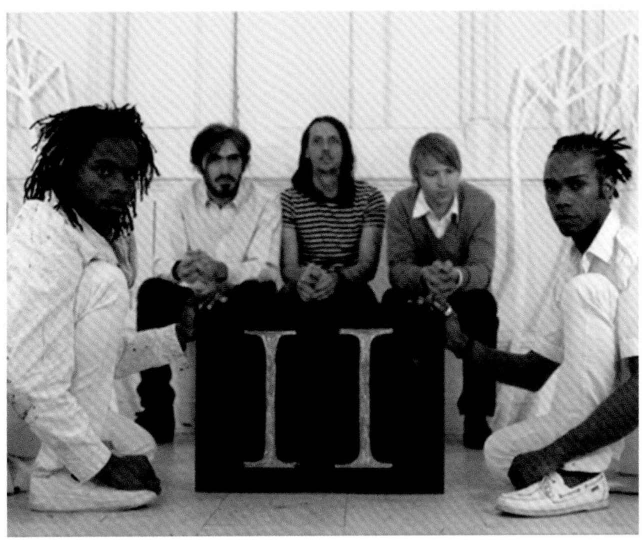

L D Section 2, 2006.

**And that brought you all to NY.
Did you all go to Cooper Union?**
Three of us went to Cooper.
How did Lansing-Dreiden start?
It just came out of a conversation.
Something I think originally from
the frustrations of having a band.
What kind of frustrations?
It just seemed like if you have
a band and you make a video then
the video is less important than
the band. The idea was to create a
company where everything had the
same importance placed on it.
You started it right out of college?
It was that moment when you have to
either get a job or you struggle,
or you try to do both. We all got
jobs but we wanted to make a project
happen that kept us interested in
waking up in the morning.
**Where did the name Lansing-Dreiden
come from?**
Do we have to answer that?
You don't have to answer anything.
We never liked how the band seemed
to always be more of a focus than
their work or music. People always
want to see what the band looks
like, or what the artist looks like
as opposed to what the artist thinks
as exemplified by the work itself.
It's super cliché now, but to us it
seemed more important just to show
the work and not have it attached to
a face.

Lansing-Dreiden sounded established.
We wanted it to feel old, like it already existed. We didn't want to feel like we were making this new cool thing. It was more like the baton got passed from some old dudes.

What freedoms did anonymity afford you?
Well, you could be as perverse or misanthropic as you wanted to be and you'd never catch any direct flack from it.

A lot of people loved your music and were frustrated by all the other stuff. Or intrigued. It was mysterious.
The idea of "being mysterious" was maybe like five or ten percent of our interest in it. We just really didn't want to be associated with it personally. Some of us were actually really shy. When we said that in interviews no one seemed to believe it.

So whatever you released would stand in for that?
Those choices were supposed to stand in for what a personality would be. If you think about the history of people dressing up and performing through masks it's pretty vast. It goes back to Ancient Greece. People like David Bowie, Kiss, or Klaus Nomi dressing up and performing through these alternate characters.

But it was never even a band, right? Lansing-Dreiden was a company.
People thought we were a collective, but we weren't. A collective is a bunch of individuals working together on something. With a company it usually doesn't matter who the CEO is and who the employees are to the rest of the world. The company has a mission and an aesthetic, the cult of personality gets absorbed into the brand image. It has a direction and a goal, and that made more sense to us as a group of artists making work at that time.

And that combined your graphic works, your video, your animation and music.
The point was that you could apply the rules to whatever medium. If you made a video the video would follow the same rules.

What were the rules?
If we try to describe it we're just gonna forget a bunch of stuff that's pretty essential... We had known each other for so long so we all kind of knew what would fit and what wouldn't, what felt right and what didn't.

OK. But there are still some basic rules right?
No proper nouns, no colors... No direct references to the real world. Everything Lansing-Dreiden existed in a fictional world.

Were there references?
You could maybe reference current events, but through fictional storytelling only. We invented names of towns, and of brands and things like that. It was like a parallel universe.

The bizarro Lansing-Dreiden world.
The central objective was to speak through fiction — all of the work stemmed from that. Whether it was a song, drawings, or an installation, it all came from the story.

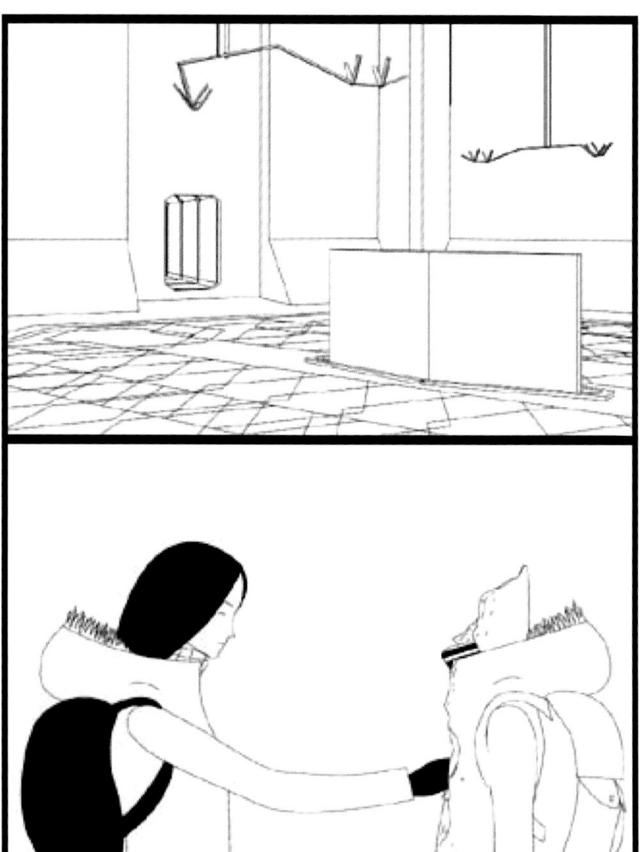

Quiet Earth Stills, 2001.

What was your working process like?
At the studio there were always
sketches and ideas lying around.
Certain ones appealed to everyone more
than others. Those were usually shaped
and refined to convey the next step of
the company's evolution — like
building the story of the company
itself as we went along. Someone would
go and work on stuff and then present
it. Then everyone would be like, "That
sucks, go back and redo it." Or, "That's
awesome, let's use that, but this
sucks." That's how a lot of it worked.
**That sounds like a different practice
for an art studio.**
We were producing each other as a
producer would in the studio. That's
where the sort of cooperation lies.
There really wasn't anything that was
completed by someone without it being
talked about ahead of time, or being
tweaked somewhere during the process.
**It would have gone through the checks
and balances.**
We had access to a group of like-
minded artists with different skill
sets. It's rare when everyone can
kind of get on the same page and make
something that's greater than the sum
of its parts. None of us wanted to be
an artist in the singular sense. Nobody wanted to be a "frontman." None
of that appealed to any of us. We all
wanted to make compelling works of
art, films, music, and were trying to
find the way to do that which gave us
the greatest amount of flexibility.

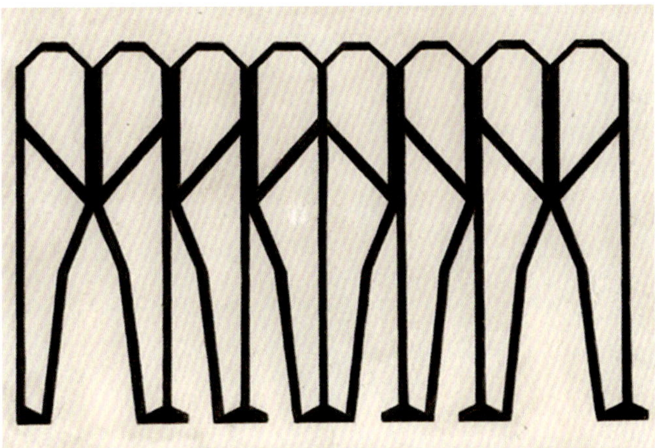

A.E.O.T.N., 2004.

You could actually do what you wanted.
Where it wouldn't limit us the way
"personalities" would, or having to
answer for whatever choices we made.
Really it was more about freedom
and keeping ourselves interested in
ourselves. Trying to figure out a
context where we could put a metal
song on the same album as a drowsy
shoegaze song and a freestyle song.
If you just start with that kind of
goal and you're open to finding the
right way to do that, it's possible.
This also ensured quality control.
The strength of some of the work
comes from the idea of strength in
numbers. Everything had to be ratified
by three other people. By the time
something was completed we all felt
really strongly about it. That kind of
confidence imbued the work.
**How did Incomplete Triangle album
come about?**
The Incomplete Triangle was just
a mix of ideas, but that was the
point — we had lots of different
interests. We were listening to demos
we made and finding the recurring
themes, and then categorizing them.
The categories were based on Ancient
Greek court music. They wouldn't
really play songs — they would play
modes: War, Rest, and Celebration.
That's is the structure of the album.
**It was a surprisingly listenable
album.**
We wanted to make work that was
superficially seductive — pretty on
the surface but still allowing the
listener to delve as deep as they
wanted to. Hopefully the deeper they
delved the more rewarding their
experience would be. I remember that
was an overarching thing that we'd
come back to.
**It was pretty different from the
music being made at the time.**
You have to remember at the time
Peaches was the most popular thing.
You'd go out and people would be
playing Peaches or Outkast. We wanted
to do something that was a little
more serious feeling. We wanted it to
be old, quiet, and dark.

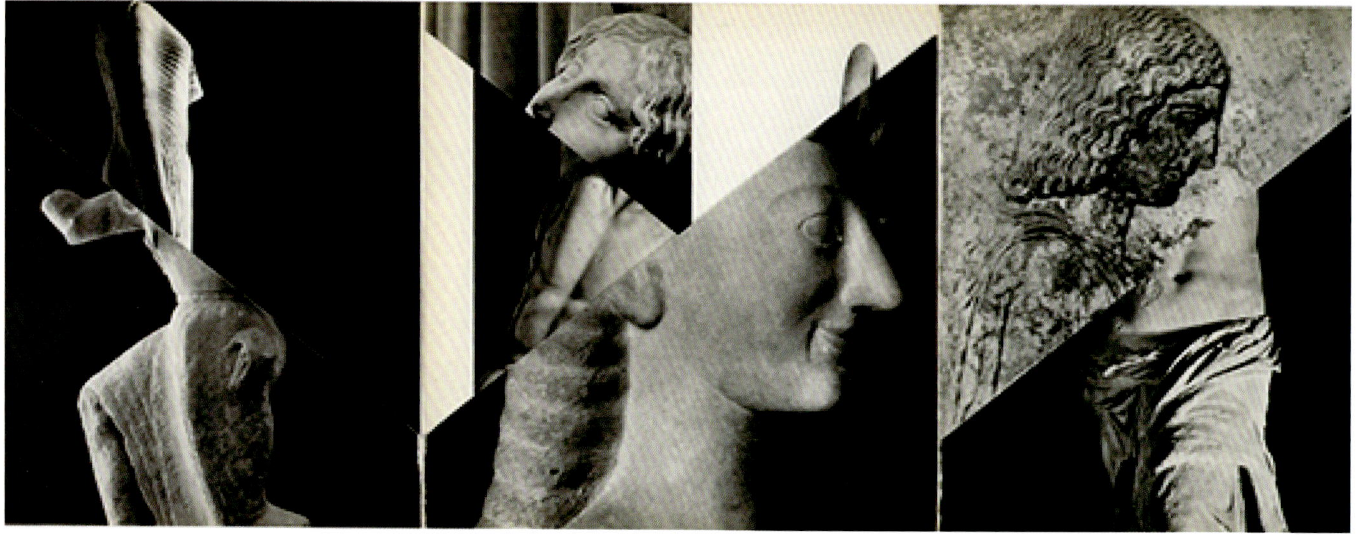

What Was Once One, Rivington Arms, 2006.

My favorite tracks have totally changed over time. Now I'm like all about the techno parts.
That's cool. We can only hope for something like that. The first record was surprising to people that so many genres were touched upon. By the second record people were more ready for that. Then we did a record of hip hop remixes.

What was the reaction to the music?
We always had a great reaction. Everyone pretty much liked and respected what we were doing, to the point it had the ability to be ripped off, which was really the greatest honor. There was a certain point where someone made a fake website of ours trying to bash us. It felt really amazing that someone would spend the time to do that.

Did you get more attention for your music than your art?
Music is easier for people to digest in general... But all the press for the music was really bad. It was always less about the music and more about the company. Like the Pitchfork review.

I totally wrote to the Pitchfork reviewer and defended you at the time. They barely even mentioned the music.
Someone told us from within the walls of Pitchfork that it got a lot of mail. It's just so funny how insecure people are about how they feel about art. Sometimes it seems people just want everything to be the same shit. In general the art was more positively received than the music was, but to a smaller audience.

But the music is what's really lived on you know.
Because music is just a file you download and you can listen to it whenever you want. It's more of an effort to look and think about art.

There wasn't much crossover in the audiences.
There was a block specifically because Jay-Z wasn't talking about Picasso and dancing with Marina Abramovic at the time. There was so little overlap. At the time it was a big thing that Fischerspooner was working with Deitch Projects.

Can you remember how many shows there were, or live performances?
Fifteen at the most. They varied. One time we had two drummers. One time we painted a guy white and had him do some performances for us in Miami.

Was that an actor or someone you knew?
That was an artist we knew that could draw well. There was a lot of overlap with his work and we felt he was perfect for the role — which reprised his role in a music video. It's good to mention that piece just to show that we have had a sense of humor at different points in the project.

L-D Ambassador (Clip 2), 2002.

We got called pretentious a lot. I remember that word being thrown at us. Pretentious, pretentious, pretentious... But Magical realism, parallel universe — it's almost some sci-fi nerd shit. It's like we had a sense of humor the whole time and no one really knew.

So the piece in Miami was meant to express that?
Yeah. And again everyone got mad. No one laughed. They tried to sabotage the performance.

So despite the appeal of the music you kept an equal balance with other practices.
It was really important that we kept the company interdisciplinary — kept all those little trees alive, all those little plants happy and not focus too much on one thing. Even though there was maybe a broader response and also more money being thrown at us for the musical endeavor it was always really important to us to make sure we had new cycles of artwork and visuals too.

Just to keep it interesting.
When you have so many different people you end up wanting to explore different genres.

Can we talk about your influences?
Can we talk about that? I don't think we can talk about that. We were supposed to meet ahead of time and make sure...

There is that group the KLF.
We didn't realize what they were about even when we were doing the Lansing-Dreiden stuff. We knew the music and that they were cool. Looking back there are definitely parallels between what we did and what they did.

They got like a million dollars at some point and burned it, right?
They had a manual for how to be successful: The first thing you have to do is fire your band and sell all your instruments because you're gonna need money to pay for a studio and hire an engineer to make your music for you. Then you have to go and get a book of records for hit songs and just lift an old one, change the lyrics a little bit, buy an accompaniment...

What about brand identity? That seemed like an ongoing element of Lansing-Dreiden.
We were into taking things that shouldn't be branded and turning them into something more commercial. I think it's a preoccupation that a lot of artists have had in the past. The idea that a brand could tell a story is not new — look at a culture like ancient Egypt where the aesthetics, religion, belief system, government, and architecture all kind of said one thing. Now there are companies like Nike. They can make a commercial that's just fast cuts of athletes about to start running with the sound of an orchestra tuning and then you just throw a Nike logo on it and it's completely understandable.

The context of a brand changes everything.
Because we're trained to accept a brand as something that can come at you from all these different directions — you identify all those things as the same thing. We found that idea really interesting. It's not so much that we were interested in creating a brand — it was more that the language of doing so was really interesting.

****

Lansing-Dreiden is a company that
sees no distinction between art and commerce
—or anything else. Hence, the output of the organization may
manifest itself in various forms, from video to music to product design
to the construction of narratives. All Lansing-Dreiden projects are fragmentary,
mere stones in a path whose end lies in a space where the very definition of "path" paths.

****

Profile from www.lansing-dreiden.com, 2000.

Was your website a part of that?
Today it's totally normal for an artist or a band to have a website, videos...a kind of unified aesthetic. We were operating at this moment where the internet was pretty new. It felt like more of a statement back then. Nowadays, forget about it.

How important was it for you guys to consider your audience?
We never understood who our fans were. To this day we don't know what people think. You put out a song, you make a drawing, you make a video... Each person is gonna have their own relationship to it.

Anonymity plays into that too.
Because we were anonymous we didn't have that interaction. New York is a very social city and in order to do really well you have to be a social meme. That's one of the reasons why this project came to a slow halt. Our gallery ended, and we weren't out there talking to other galleries. We never had been.

Did you guys work on other stuff outside of Lansing-Dreiden?
Not really. We all had jobs but none of them were really satisfying our creative impulses.

Does Lansing-Dreiden still exist?
Totally. There is always the option for someone to lay a cool mil on us.

Were there projects that didn't get to do because of lack of financing?
Tons. There was a whole building we wanted to construct to build a performance stage and a viewing room, and a fucking gallery space. We only got around to like one half percent of the stuff we wanted to make. We wanted to make feature films, video games...

Did you turn down any opportunities?
There were offers to unmask us or something in the past for prominent press, and we couldn't do it. We loosely got offered like licensing opportunities for our music on commercials or something that we also turned down. Looking back it still looks like the right thing to do.

Do you consider Lansing-Dreiden to be a success?
No real entity like us has succeeded because it's difficult to pull off. If things are going really well you're doing something wrong. You gotta question it. It was always just about making Lansing-Dreiden work. None of us had those other goals.

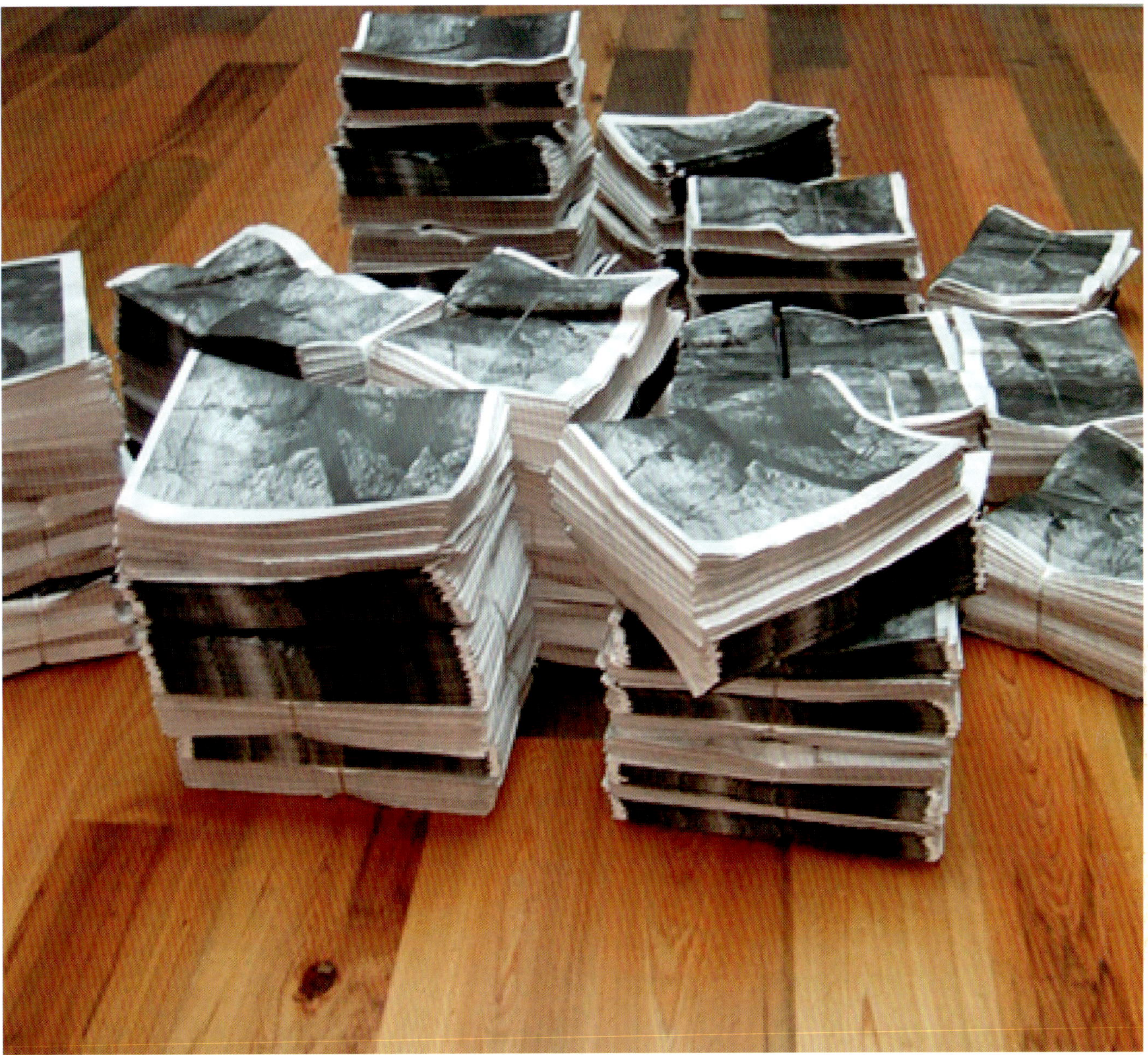

Death Notice, 2006.

It seemed unrealistic to have a smash hit, tour the world, be in the best museums.

You didn't expect it to do that.
None of us wanted to be famous. We were turned off by that idea. The KLF talk about how the repercussions of having a number-one hit in the UK could be life-changing in a super negative way. You can either run the route of like being this frozen version of yourself for the rest of your life in order to maintain the success that you had with that one hit, or you can do what a lot of people do which is try to prove to your audience that you can do all these different things. It just seems like a brutal disfigurement.

You don't need that.
Some movies are gonna be seen by millions of people. Some movies are really small movies that have a limited audience that really appreciates it. Not everything has to be popular. There is a lot to be proud of in just those six years or whatever where it was actually working. There is plenty to explore if anybody gives a shit. ☺

Brian Gibson

"It's nice to work on something where you're
not competing with anybody that you know."

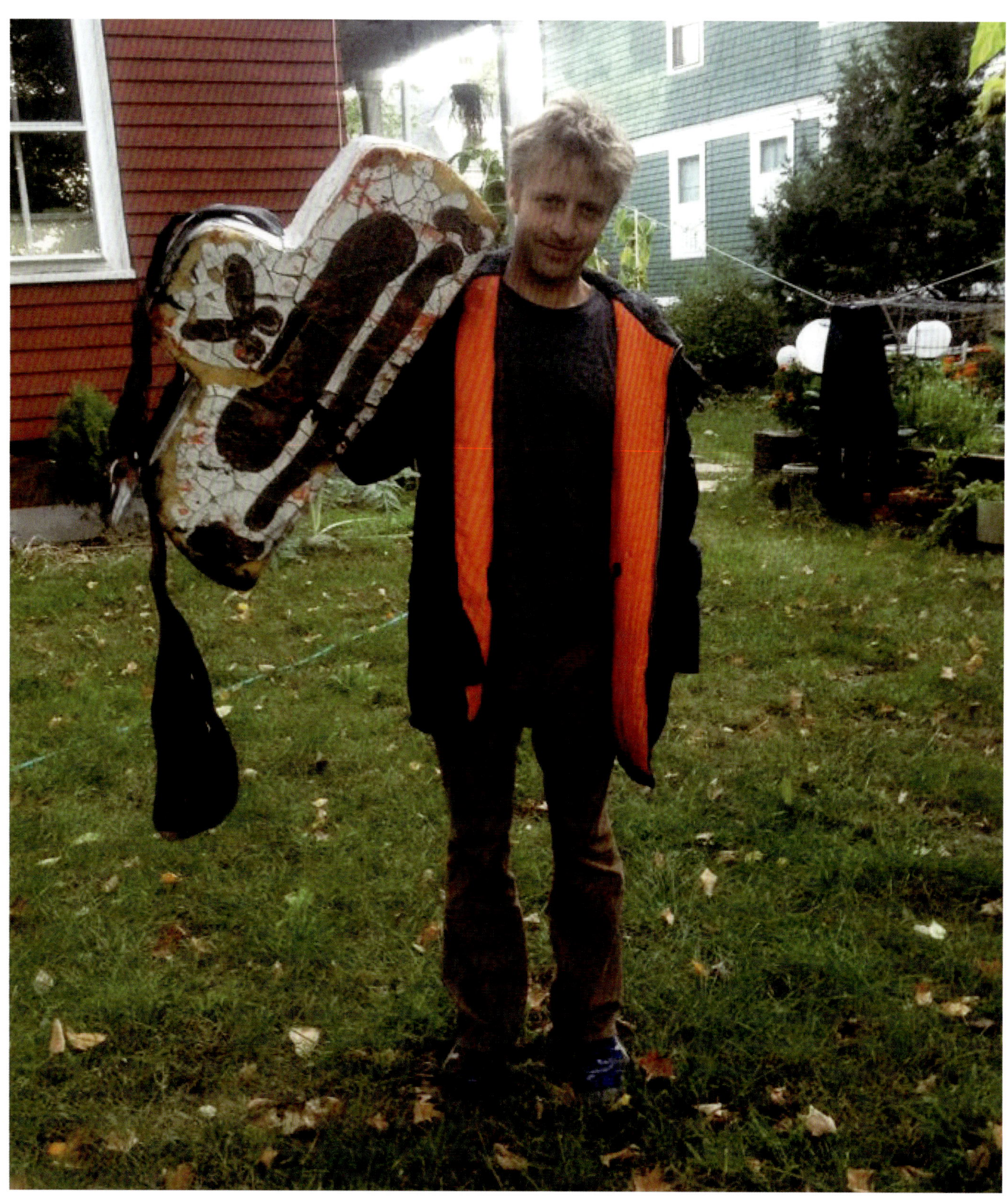

Interview & portrait By Asher Penn
Images courtesy Brian Gibson

Despite the fact that most of what he creates is loud and exciting, Brian Gibson works pretty quietly. Based in Providence, Rhode Island since the mid-90s, Gibson is best known as the bass player for the noise-rock duo Lightning Bolt with virtuoso drummer Brian Chippendale. Gibson is lesser known for his work with groups like Black Dice, Wizardzz, as well as his hilarious animated series / shit-destroying live band Barkley's Barnyard Critters. His most recent project is Thumper, a terrifyingly addictive "rhythm violence" video game. Now three years in the making, Thumper is a reflection of Gibson's ongoing commitment to creating new experiences that transcend expectations.

Where are you from?
Burlington, Vermont.
Were you an arty high school kid?
No. I was weird but I wasn't arty. I didn't fit in. There were some Goth kids, jocks, some academic superstars, art kids, and all these other groups. I wasn't a part of any of them. There were a couple of other kids that were like me and we wore vague button-down collared shirts and were really nondescript. No style. I thought I was going to go into biology.
Were you into music?
My grandfather bought me a bass guitar when I was a sophomore in high school. I got really into that and started playing with my brother who played drums. By my senior year I was playing shows with my brother and going out to see some shows. There wasn't much going on in Burlington that was that great. I was really excited anytime I got a chance to see any live music. If I was walking down the street and there was some fusion jazz band playing at a bar or something, I'd be like, "That's crazy...live music...I can't believe it. It's so loud." I wasn't very discriminating in high school.

How did you decide to go to RISD?
I think it just dawned on me around my junior year in high school. I'm the youngest in my family, all of my older siblings went to Yale. They were academic people and I wasn't as strong academically as they were.
You weren't a good student?
I found it hard to pay attention in class. I was realizing that art was the one thing I really enjoyed doing. I saw that my brother's friend Dare went to RISD and thought he was a really cool guy. He had a cool name too. I actually work with him now.
Doing what?
Making video games.
What did you study when you came to RISD?
Painting, illustration. I wanted to do animation.
What kind of animation were you into?
I liked Ralph Bakshi movies a lot in high school. Do you know this movie Wizards? He did some crazy stuff with live action and animation combined.
He did Fritz The Cat, right?
Yeah, and the animated Lord of the Rings. It has all this rotoscope stuff where they film live action and then draw over it. It creates a really bizarre unnatural feeling. He made some terrible movies too.
How did you meet Brian Chippendale?
I met Brian Chippendale during my freshman year. I think I saw him playing at a party. He was playing drums in a room by himself.
Just by himself?
Maybe there were two people sitting on the floor in that room with their heads between their knees and hands covering their ears.
Was he a really good drummer back then?
Yeah, and I was interested in finding a good drummer to play with. At that point my opinion was that a really good drummer made a band. When I arrived at RISD I asked my brother's friend Dare about drummers. He said Brian Chippendale was the best drummer in Providence.

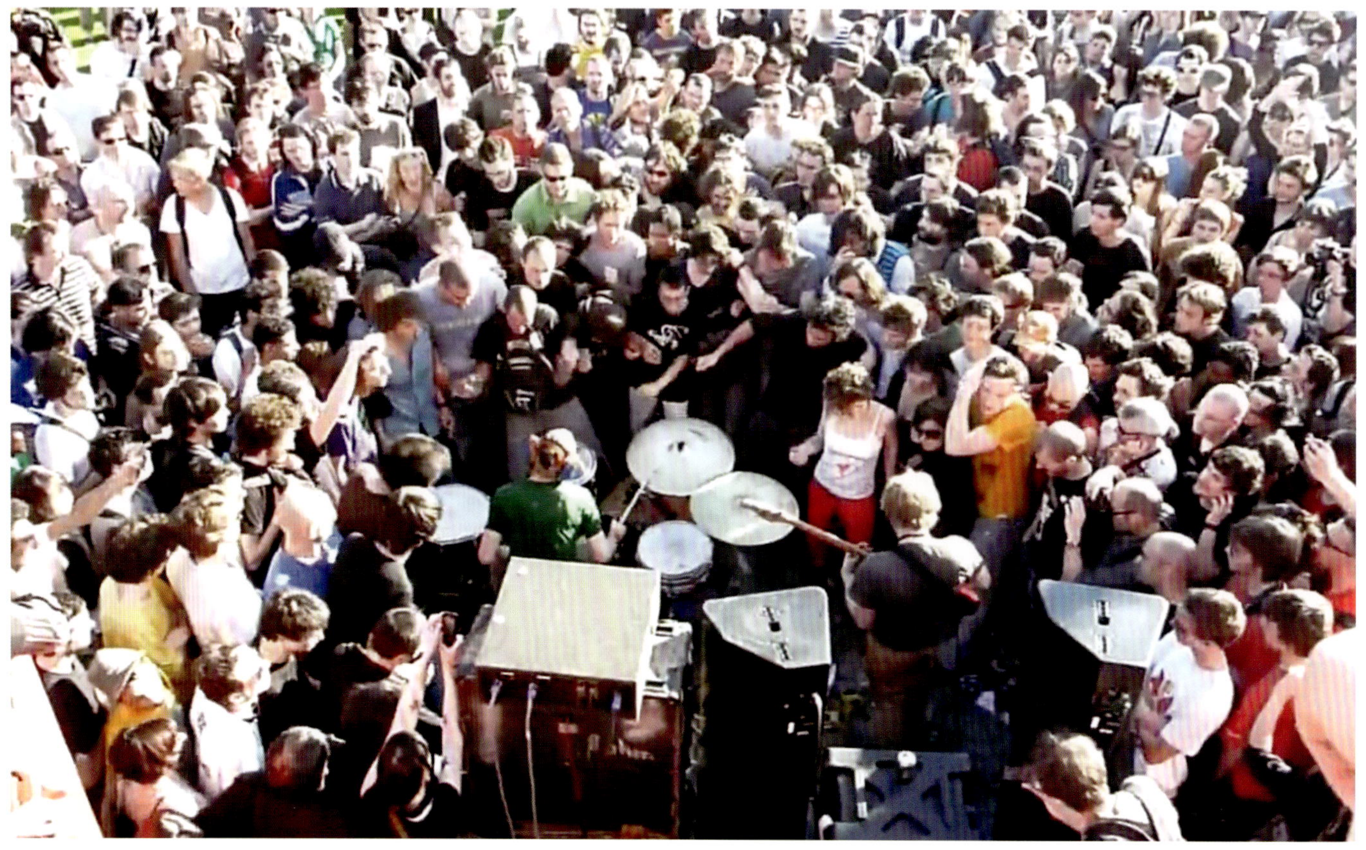

Lightning Bolt, Paris, 2009.

Were you seeing local acts when you moved there?
Yeah. Six Finger Satellite and Hydrogen Terrors were a huge thing when I came to Providence. I saw them a few times when I first moved here and it really made an impression. I think Providence also went through a big transformation after Boredoms came through in like 1994. They played Lupo's. It was a really good show. Yoshimi was screaming super high pitch as she was wailing on the high hat and this guy was playing funk guitar and the singer was jumping around. He had a clean white T-shirt on and short hair, conservative looking, but he was swinging around in the rafters and doing flips and stuff. The band at the time was so ridiculous, they were playing songs from the record Pop Tatari, and it felt like the Muppets band. It was just totally insane, really exciting. So many people in Providence cite that show as a personal turning point.

When you and Brian started playing together, was it immediately called Lightning Bolt?
We had a few conversations about what we should be called. The only other name I remember was Frog and Toad.

If I heard early Lightning Bolt would I recognize it?
Maybe not. It was slower, more nineties. Brian has always been the same level of drummer but he's gotten faster and faster. I wasn't using all the pedals I'm using now to make it super blown out and distorted so it had a cleaner feel to it. It was a bit rhythmically and sonically funkier.

Did you change your playing around Brian Chippendale's drumming?
After a while I started to get really into the way he was playing the kick drum. I started following it more directly, and tried to build a whole form around that. That — pounding kick matched with distorted bass — became a defining quality of Lightning Bolt to me.

What was your first show?
The first show we played as a two-piece was at Carr House, which is this coffee shop on RISD campus. We brought in a bunch of TVs with static and put red cellophane over them and turned out the lights so the room had this deep, dark-red glow to it.

Did Brian have the mask with microphone at the beginning?
I can't remember when Brian started using the mask. Maybe right after Hisham. We had Hisham Baroocha singing for us in the beginning for the first couple of years.

What did it sound like?
Kind of like Can? Japanese chanting sounding stuff. He had a delay pedal and he was singing a bunch of stuff and then swirling it around with his delay pedal. Just being pretty psychedelic and free-form.

Wasn't Hisham in Black Dice? What was Lightning Bolt's relationship to that band?
Well, I was playing drums with Black Dice in the beginning.

Oh, cool.
When I started playing with those guys it was the first time they had been in a band and they didn't really know what they wanted to do. There were some vague goals but we were really just screwing around.

Black Dice was kind of a hardcore band at the beginning right?
I actually think the whole hardcore thing was a kind of funny joke for Bjorn and those guys. None of us could decide if it was serious or not. It wasn't exactly in character, but the shows became really rowdy and fun so we embraced it. We wanted to do something crazy as friends and I think pulling off anything was really satisfying for us at that point.

Was Fort Thunder happening around this time?
Yeah. They must have all started around '95. I moved there in '97. I was only there for like a year. I actually got really bummed out when I was living there.

Why were you bummed?
Because I was broke and Brian and I were having a really rough band relationship at that point. I was going through my equipment, just blowing it up over and over again and having to buy speakers and cabinets. I just didn't have any money. I was working serving coffee to people on College Hill and felt totally stuck. I mean, Fort Thunder was a cool place but...

Probably a hard place to live. How did you participate there?
I did some comics in Paper Rodeo for Barkely's Barnyard Critters, but I wasn't really a big participant. I was kind of an outsider there. Barkley's Barnyard Critters came out of me wanting to do something with a bunch of friends that I had that were outside that Fort Thunder group. I wanted to do something that was just fun times with friends. The creative identity at Fort Thunder was very apocalyptic. I never really identified with any of that.

How did the band Barkley's Barnyard Critters start?
Me and a bunch of my friends were drunk at a party and I just started doing the Barkley voice. I was acting like McGruff, telling everyone not to do drugs. It was just some weird, dumb party scenario where the next day everyone was like, "Oh, it was really funny when you were being that dog." At some point later my friends Joe Bradley and Warren Bennett wanted to start a band called Barkley's Doghouse Blues Band. A band with animals — something really stupid that would be fun. Everybody in the band came up with their own animal personas. Warren instantly had this really perfect character for Brockton the vulture that he could do a voice for and everything. Joe was Charlotte the sheep. Everybody knew exactly what they were supposed to be. That band came together perfectly.

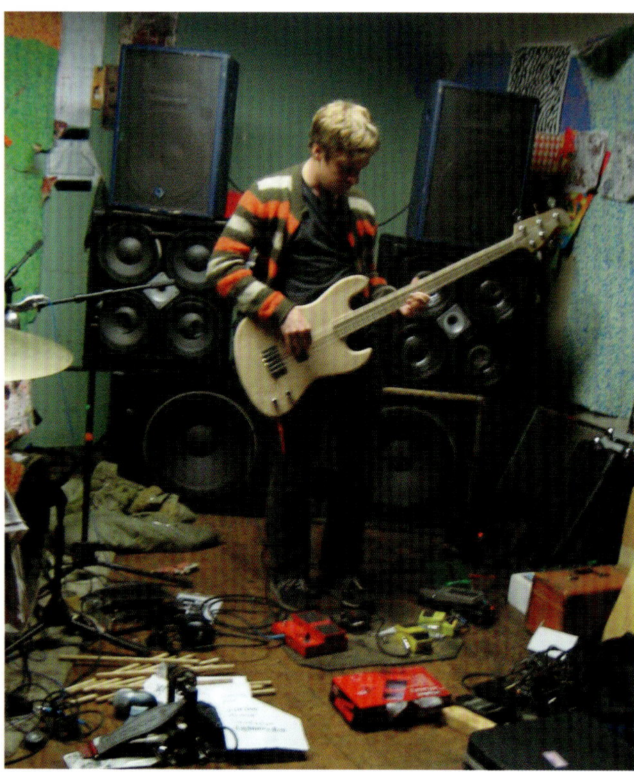

Practice Space, 2004.

Were you guys shit destroyers from the beginning when you played?
Not really. We always wanted to create this really theatrical thing, not the rowdy, screwing-things up, making-a-mess thing. But we never practiced enough. We never quite put together the crazy drama that we wanted for the show, so we just became animals having a good time. That's why shit always gets destroyed.

How did it become a cartoon?
I started drawing that stuff when I was in New York around 2000. I got to this point where I wanted to make an animation and put together stories with those characters. Like, "This is what Barkley would look like... This is what Brockton would look like..." The way I drew everything wasn't really endorsed by anyone else in the band. I just really wanted to do more with the characters.

Did you do all the voices yourself?
Initially I was getting everybody who played the characters to do their voices. For all the YouTube stuff I'm doing now I do all the voices because it's easier.

I have a few more questions about Lightning Bolt. When I looked you up on Wikipedia there were some very specific things about the stringing of your bass, how it's set up.
When I started playing with Brian, I was just playing a normal unmodified bass and it was really fun, but when we listened to the recordings it didn't have that much dynamic range — particularly with the pitch. It was all low, and hard to hear melodies. I added a banjo string to get the range of pitch that a full band typically gets with a guitar and a bass.

Why a banjo string?
Banjo strings are longer than guitar strings so they fit on the bass, which is longer. I wanted to add something that was accessible and had a really high range. Otherwise just bass to me is too limiting. I like being stripped down and limited as a band and not having a lot of options, but I didn't like how gray everything sounded without having that crisp, bright, high note in there. Later I got a whammy pedal too. Sometimes I'll use the whammy pedal and the banjo string together to get a super piercing high pitch.

I feel like with Lightning Bolt there is always a desire for sonic discovery.
Well it would be really hard to release an album if I felt like we were doing the same thing that we did before. I always feel like everything that I make artistically is always a bit improvisational and it's always iterative. I'm always trying to move towards something better, never feel like anything's arrived or complete. At the beginning of Lightning Bolt I was trying to find a kind of music that I could play that would complement Brian in the right way. But he's still changing, and I get bored quickly so it's a constantly moving target.

Your shows have a particular live energy. Lightning Bolt mosh pits were always different than other mosh pits.

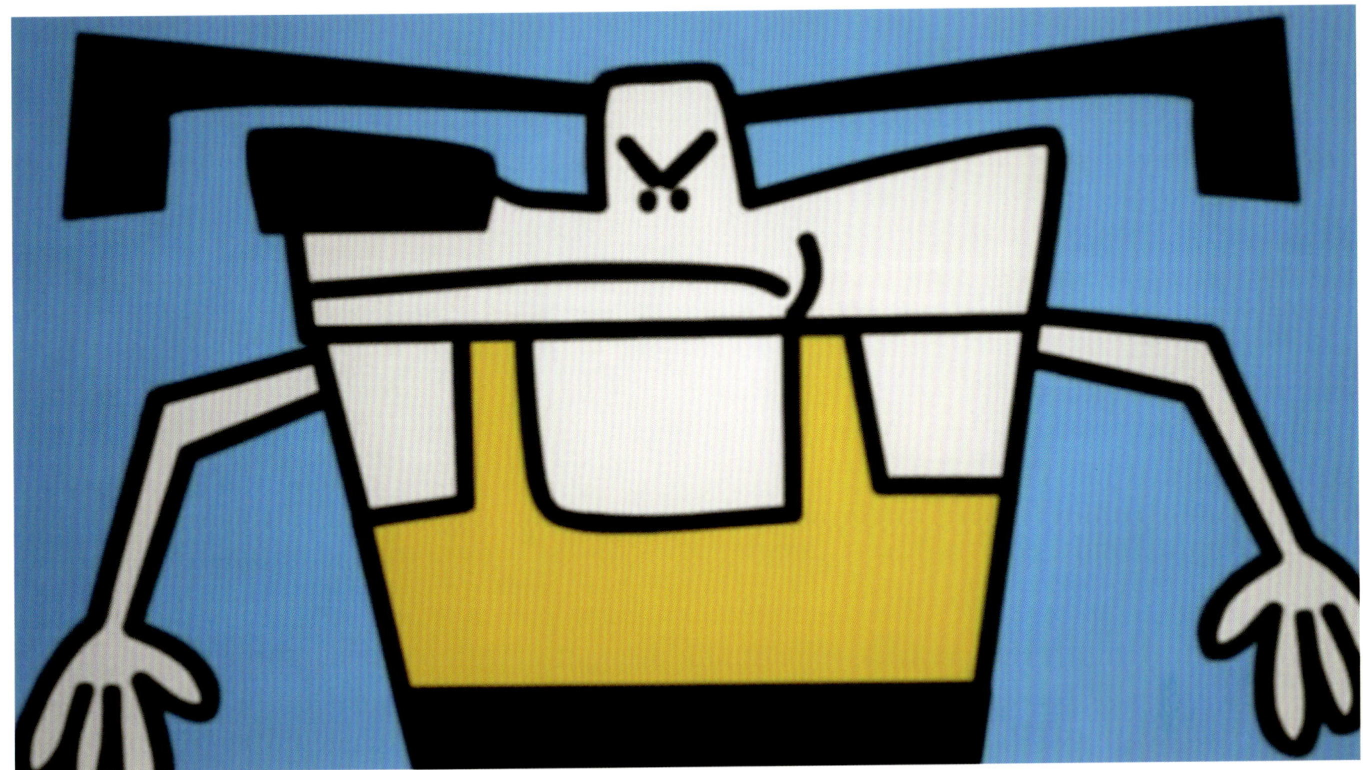

Barkley's Barnyard Critters, King Of The Ghetto, 2009.

I think if there is one thing that Brian and I share, it's that we both have this anxiety almost every second of the show about people getting bored. I think that always makes the shows more exciting because at any given time if something isn't working, we have to stop playing it right then and there and start playing something else. Or change it into something else to get it to work. I think both of us feel it physically when people aren't responding to what we're doing and it's a horrible feeling and we work really hard to change that when it happens.

That rules.

I see a lot of bands where they're not thinking about that at all. They're just playing their songs and they're not really paying attention to what the energy in the room is. For us a live show should have a certain level of interaction with the audience. If it's not there then it's a failure. I'm surprised that our attitude is as rare as it is.

How did you get involved in video games?

Ryan Lesser, a friend of mine, was and still is the art director at Harmonix. I saw him in a restaurant and I just straight up asked him if he had any work because I needed a job. I showed him some abstract paintings. He was familiar with other stuff I had done before and so he let me learn the tools that they were using there and try to contribute. They were making the game Amplitude at the time. I did a pretty good job so they hired me.

You worked on Guitar Hero, right?

Yeah, but I didn't have a huge contribution. I was doing effects and lighting, things like that.

How did Thumper start?

I had an idea for a mechanic that involved traveling through a moody world with sudden sharp right angle turns. I made a little movie of the gameplay. I suggested to Marc Flury that we start working on this game on the side, and treat the collaboration like a band. Something we do on the weekends for fun, not something that we're doing for financial gain or anything like that.

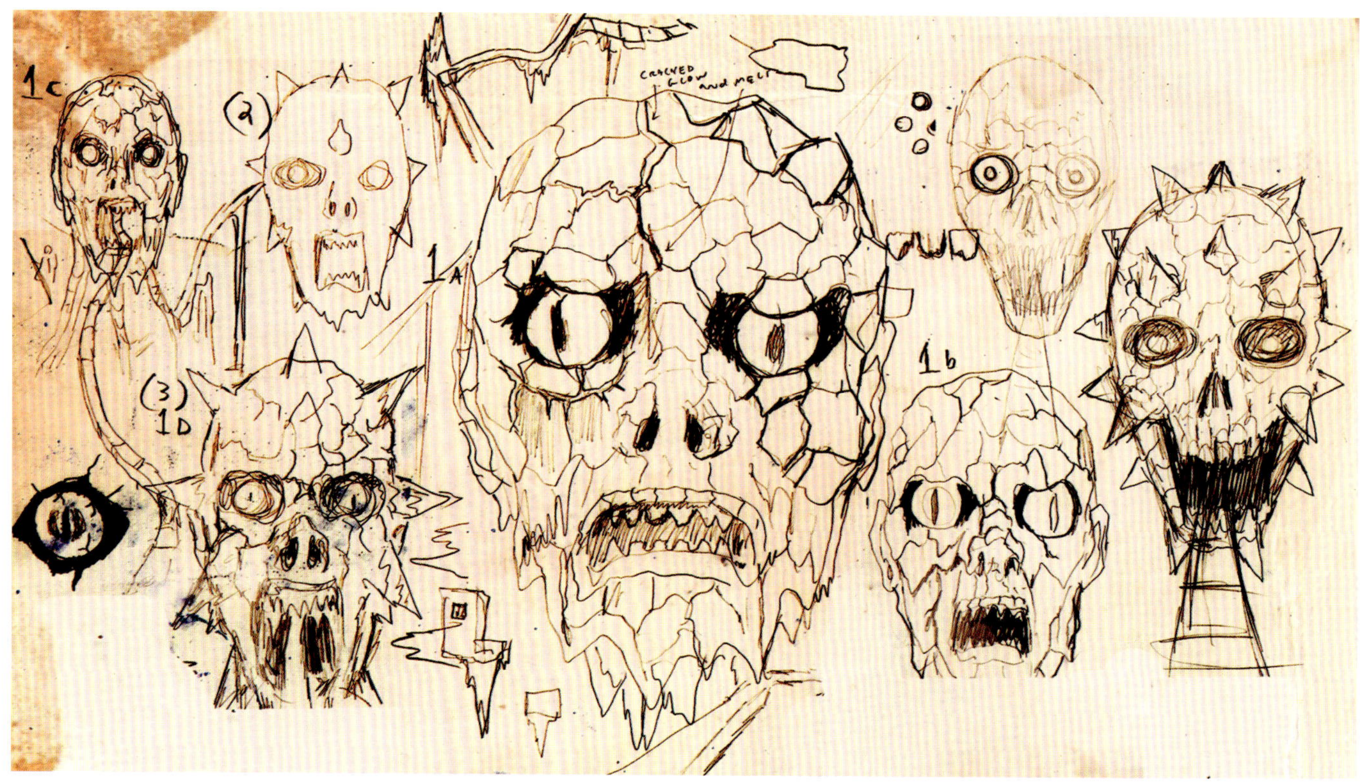

CrakHed Sketches, Mat Brinkman, 2012.

What's an engine for video games?
To build a game, you need to build
the tools that you're going to use
to build the game. Nowadays you can
actually just buy game engines where
people have already built the tools
that you're going to use to build your
game. A lot of those engines that are
out there are really powerful now, but
Mark and I were interested in building
a world from the ground up and having
the structure of the world embedded
in the game mechanics itself. We got
into the idea of having a game editor
that works the way Fruity Loops works
as a music editor. Have you ever used
Fruity Loops?

I've haven't but my friends have.
Fruity Loops is just a music
sequencer where you have a grid and
you can place samples along the grid.
We thought it would be cool to make
a world just like that grid where
you could define everything that's
happening along this path that you're
moving along — all the contours,
bends, gameplay, interactions,
everything. We had to build our own
engine to get that.

**Do you guys have a desired experience
in mind for the player?**
I've had this vague notion that
it should be really fast, simple,
physical. It should have a simple
interaction that makes the player
feel powerful. I also want it to be
very dark and trippy. I'd like to
invoke feelings of cosmic horror,
particularly of the Kubrick 2001
kind, where a very simple smooth
shape on the bare horizon can make
you feel terrified. I obviously want
it to feel like nothing else that's
out there.

There are characters too, right?
I think with a video game, if you're
going to motivate people to go on
this journey, you need to give them
compelling motivations. Heroes and
enemies can help do that for people.
When I started working on this I was
getting Mat Brinkman to help me.
He actually drew the first visual
concept for Thumper, the actual bug.
He came up with the name CrakHed.

What's a CrakHed?
CrakHed is the ultimate enemy boss, but
also is sort of a metaphor.

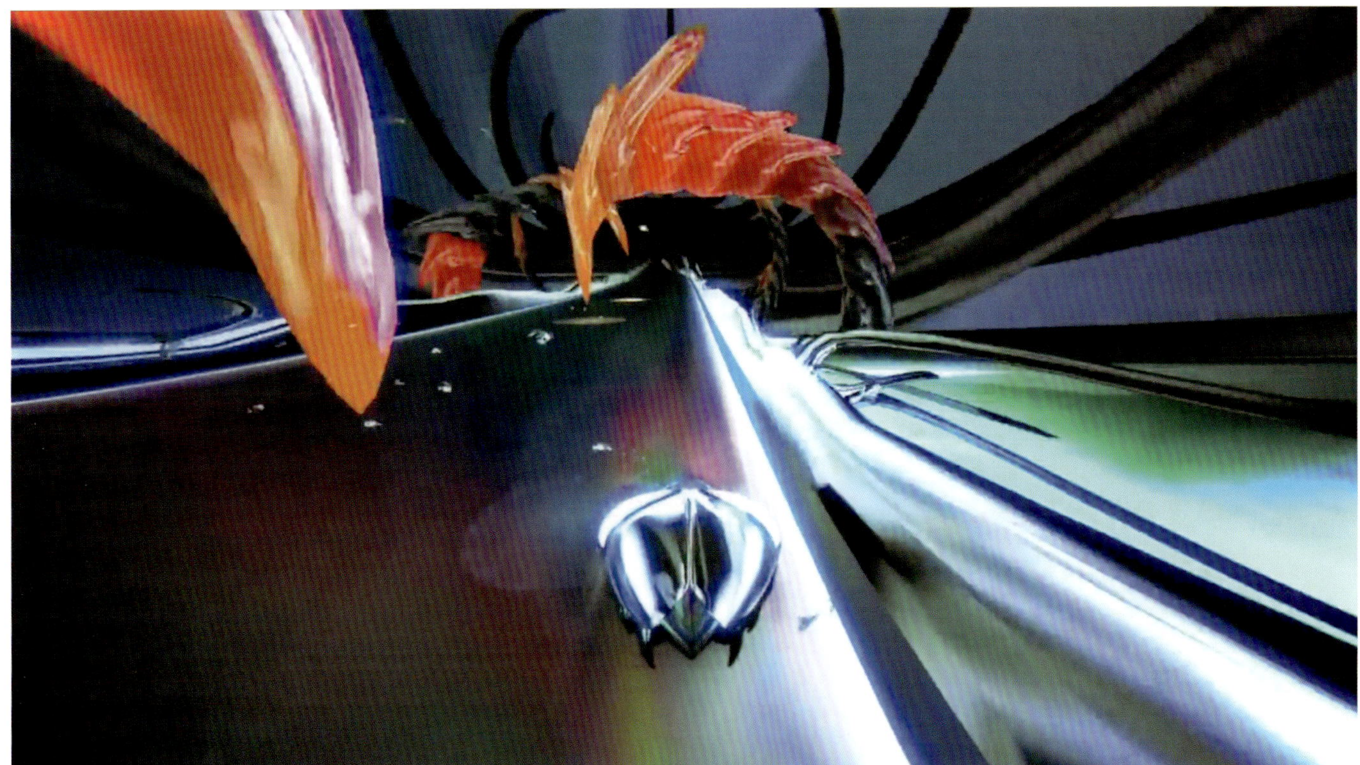

Thumper Gameplay, 2014.

We want the game to be super addictive. As you're in the game the CrakHed character gets more and more freaked and frazzled and fucked up. Hopefully that's what the players are experiencing as they're getting more and more addicted to the video game. It gets harder and harder and it progressively fucks you up. It turns you into this angry deteriorating disembodied head. Maybe by the end the player will realize that, in a way, they have become CrakHed.

Do any of your friends make games?
I have all these friends that are painters and comic book artists and sculptors and things like that. It's nice to work on something where you're not competing with anybody that you know. I don't know anybody person-ally who's working on independent video games. When you talk about it with people it's always interesting to them because it's rare. There's lot of really amazing video games out there but I do feel like video game culture is a little bit dry. It has a lot of room for new, interesting, and different things.

Indie game culture isn't the same as, say indie music?
Well it's such hard work to make a video game. People try to have these game jams where they get together and make a game over the weekend. Making a really good game usually takes many years. It's not like with a band where you can put something together and in two weeks put on a show. Or painting where you just make a painting in a day and show it. Sure, you can make a game quickly, but in general good games take so long that video game culture doesn't have the dynamic kind of life that music culture or fine art culture has.

It's not like art.
A good game isn't the same as good fine art. A game needs to plug into your programmed desires in this really specific way to motivate you to interact with it. Similar to the way a movie needs a good plot if you expect people to sit through it. Video games have artistic qualities as well, and that's what I'm interested in exploring — but it actually has to function well as a game. ☺

Peggy Noland
"Like Spring, Summer, Fall? No, that's not how I work."

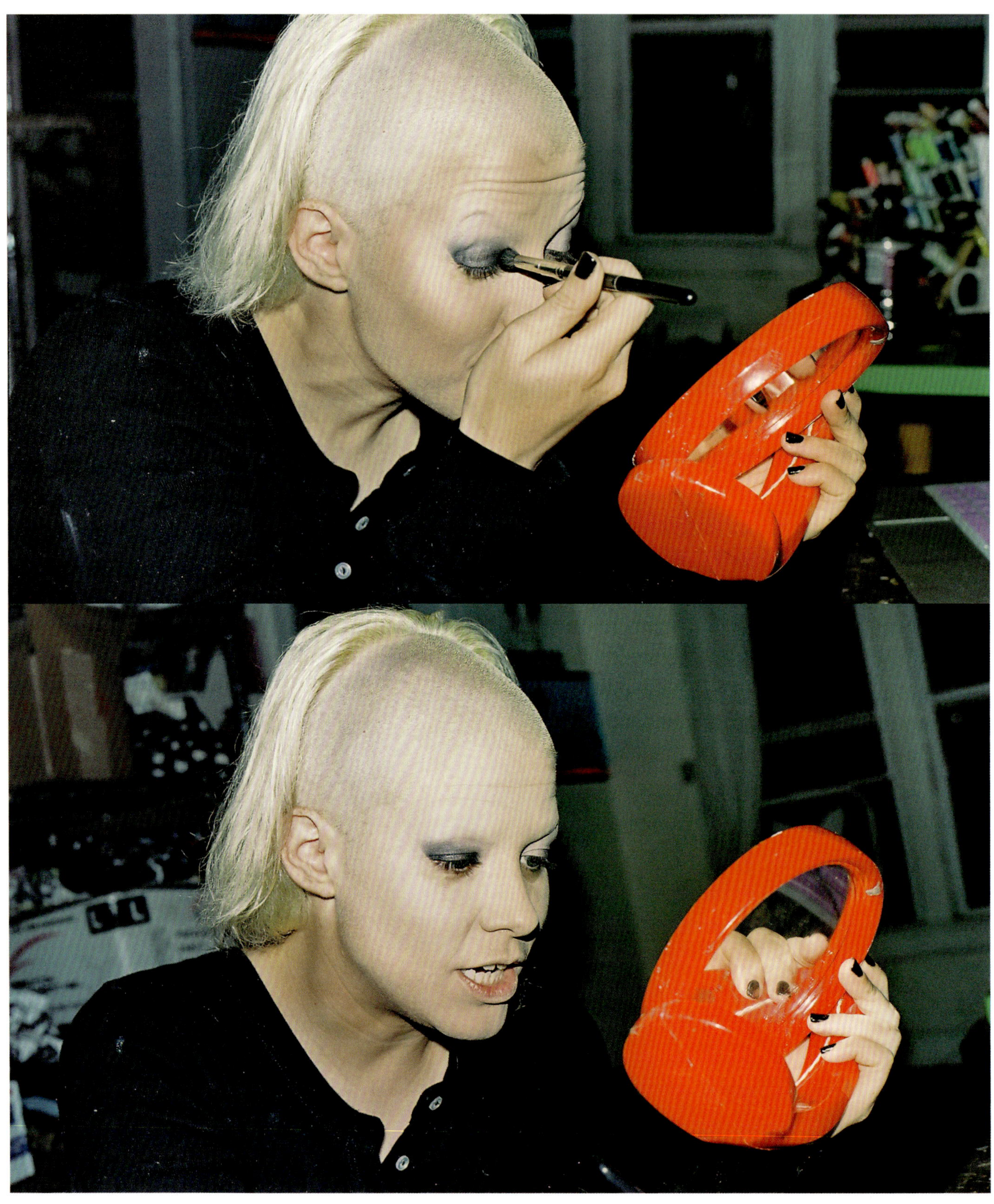

Interview & portrait by Cali Thornhill DeWitt
Images courtesy Peggy Noland

At the age of 23, Peggy Noland opened
a tiny storefront in her hometown:
Peggy Noland Kansas City. While
the ever-changing storefront has
remained the same in scale, Noland's
operations have expanded beyond
Missouri, with her bright, patterned,
personalized items embraced by
everyone from touring musicians,
fashion boutiques, and club kids
around the world. Now a resident of
Los Angeles, Noland's activities
continue to explore her signature
pop punk aesthetics all the while
maintaining a true dedication to the
fun DIY tactics they came from.

We're recording.
Oh my God! I'm nervous!
So, I'm Cali and I'm here with Peggy.
I'm Peggy, chillin' with Cali.
Hi Peggy.
What's up?
We should do this interview.
OK.
Peggy, where are you from?
I'm from Kansas City. Independence,
Missouri which is a suburb of Kansas
City. I feel comfortable saying
Kansas City though, because it's
close enough. It's like if you say
Independence, people aren't going to
know where you're talking about.
Kansas City is radical right now.
I guess it depends on who you ask.
**It seems like good things have been
coming out of Kansas City.**
Sometimes I wonder if it's wonderful
because I'm from there and I know
cool people, or if it actually is
wonderful. There's cool people
everywhere, in every city, right?
**There are but you need someone who's
like fucking really active. Because
most people are kind of lazy, right?**
I know what you mean. There's several
people that are really active that
I think contribute to making it
awesome. For sure.
You lived there for how long?
I lived there for 29 years. I mean,
I've traveled a lot, but that's where
I was paying rent. It's so cheap to
live there. My rent was like 200

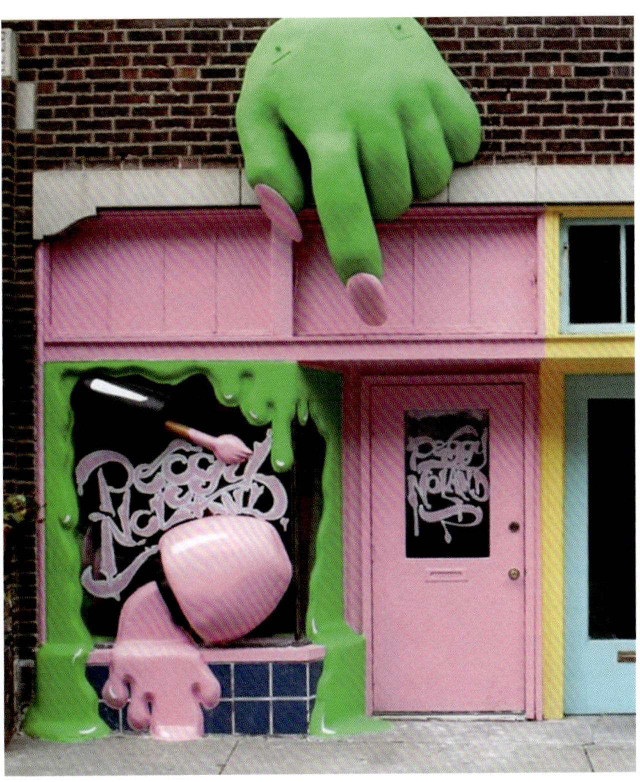

Peggy Noland Kansas City, 2009.

bucks a month for a giant place. That
leaves you a lot of extra money to
travel and do things. I think that's
why I was there for so long, because I
could leave and come back a lot.
**Were you a young starter? Like were
you young and leaving town and going
on adventures?**
Not like that. I was really naive
when it came to that stuff. I wasn't
like hopping trains as a teenager.
I didn't have a sheltered life by
any means, but I was scared for some
reason to do that stuff. I started my
own stuff young. I opened my store
when I was 22. I wasn't scared, but
I definitely didn't know anything.
I had no clue what I was doing. I
didn't expect it to last a year.
**Were you selling other people's stuff
at the beginning or your own?**
It started out as my own, but I
wasn't making it. I was having it
produced at a factory in New Delhi
that I used to work at.
New Delhi, India?
I was a production manager for a
clothing line in New Delhi. The
clothing company was in Kansas City.

Did you go to New Delhi?
Yeah, that's basically where I learned
about sewing and pattern making. I
didn't go to school for that. I didn't
speak Hindi, so if something was like
an inch or something too short and I
couldn't communicate that for whatever
reason, I would have to get on a
sewing machine and take it in at the
waist. It was easier to show than it
was to tell.

How old were you then?
I was 20 years old. That's when I
started sewing my own stuff.

Had you always wanted to make clothes?
No, never. Just out of high school
I thought I was going to pursue
religious studies. I took a couple of
classes at a college called Rockhurst
in Kansas City. I dropped out of the
program because I got offered that
New Delhi experience. I mean on one
side you have sitting in a classroom
and learning about world religions
and the other was like going to
India and living that day-to-day
experience.

**Were you still a spiritual person at
that point?**
Yeah. I grew up Catholic. My parents
are really different. My mom is
seventh-generation Catholic and my
dad is like extremely Agnostic, but
they're both so supportive of one
another.

**But you grew up Catholic. How was
that for you?**
Growing up Catholic was really
important to me, too. I personally
had a great experience in the Church.
I loved my church. I was spiritual in
that sense.

You were interested.
Definitely. And I was interested in
comparative religion, not theology. I
wanted to understand the world view,
not just my own. I didn't want to
make clothes.

Were you painting? Anything artistic?
No! Which is weird because my dad is a
full-time artist. I was like, "Oh I'm
not good at that." I was making stuff,
crafting as a kid. Making barrettes
and stuff from Hobby Lobby.

So how did you start your store?
When my job ended I was like, "I
can do this on my own." It was a
tiny, tiny store. It's like a tenth
of this space — what most people's
closets are like.

**The store is like a closet with
great big signs?**
Exactly. It's all storefront. You
walk in and that's pretty much all
you can see. The rent was reasonable
enough for me because it was so
small. I had a full-time job for
the first four or five years that I
had the store. Then it finally got
to a place where it could run itself
without me there. It doesn't make
me a ton of money at all, but it
doesn't cost me anymore.

**It takes care of itself. Who works
there?**
There's three girls that work there
that were students of mine at the
Art Institute.

But at first it was just you?
Oh my God. Yeah. It was just me.
Making clothes!

**What kind of clothes were you
making?**
They were wild, like what I would see
on blogs, or club kids in the early
2000s. That was really important
or popular then. I wanted kids in
Tokyo to like what I was making. I
was never making clothes for Kansas
City. That sounds bad, but you
know what I'm saying. I had a very
specific vision for my clothes — they
were for someone that wanted to look
outrageous on a daily basis.

But not like a costume.
I was making street wear. Most
people think they're costumes but
they're for wearing! Every day!
Like, on a Tuesday to go to the
grocery store.

How did it go over in Kansas?
I always felt so encouraged out
here, but as far as customers go,
I didn't have any. And that's an
important part of a business:
customers. It became clear to
me that I was just trying to do
something cool.

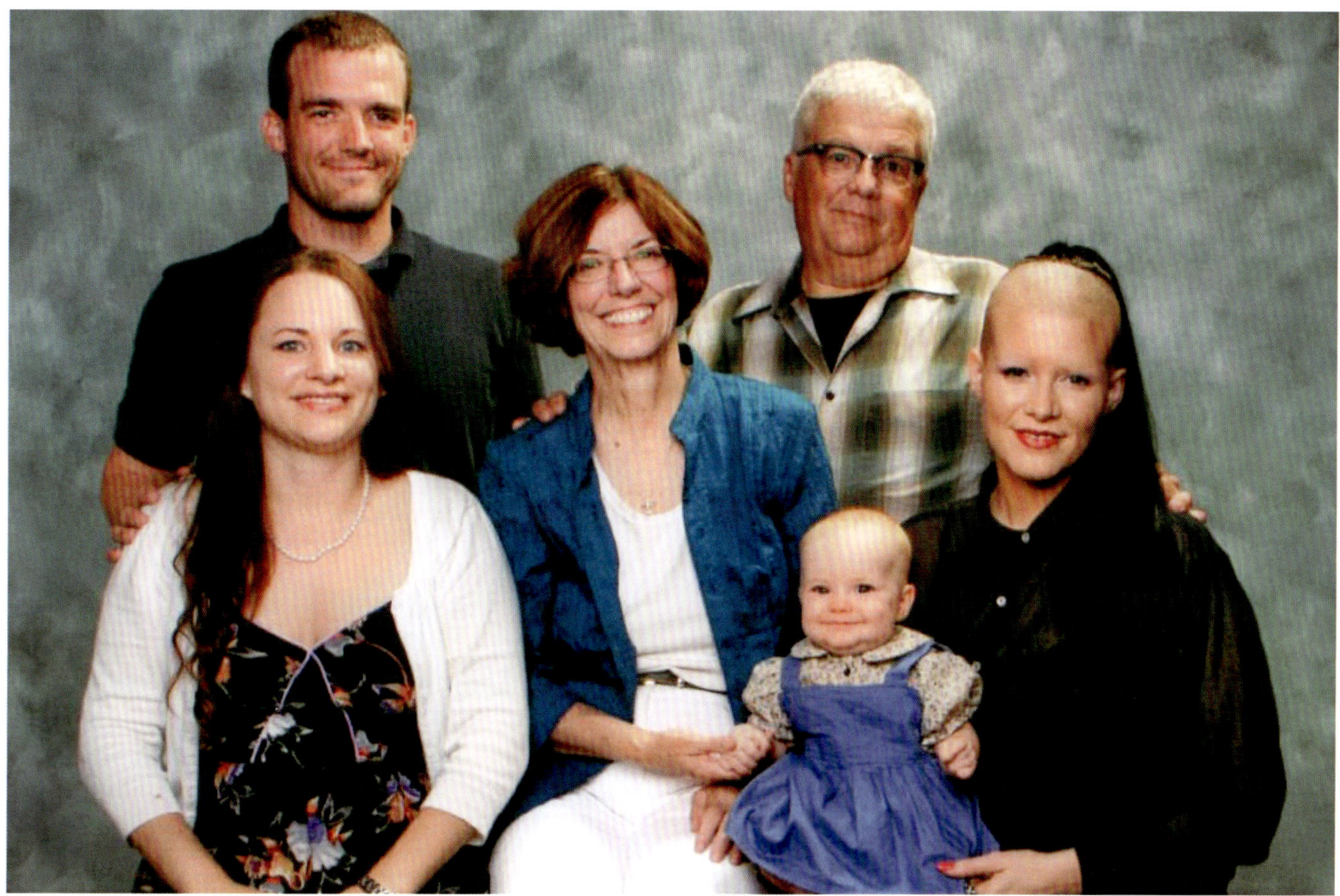

Noland Family Photo, 2011.

Not make money?
I thought that was what I was doing at first. There would be times when I had really boring stuff in the store that would just fly off the shelves. I was able to pay my rent that month but I was not inspired by it. I didn't think I was contributing anything. I didn't think it was cool. It was too average. It was too basic. I realized that by making stuff that felt cool to me, even if it didn't sell, I was way happier. I think most artists figure that out at some point.

Yeah. Please yourself first. That's really the main thing.
Exactly. I was willing to have another job in order to be able to make stuff that I like. Then I finally got my act together and got a website.

Was that around the same time you started making clothes for bands?
I made clothes for Lovefoxxx of CSS when they were first starting. That was huge for me.

How did she find you? Did you already know each other?
No. A friend brought a girl named Kianna into my store. She was in a band called Tilly in the Wall. They were touring with CSS at the time. I was already a huge fan of Tilly in the Wall and so I said, "Oh my God! Please let me make clothes for you, for your tour, for your show." I was so happy. She was so sweet about it, so I gave her a bunch of shit. They went on tour with CSS and Lovefoxxx's clothes didn't come from whoever was making clothes for her. Kianna wrote me an email and was like, "Do you care? She doesn't have anything to wear. I have too much. Can I give some to her?" For years after that I was making Lovefoxxx clothes. She was on the cover of Dazed and Confused in something I made. That was a big deal because I didn't know anybody. I was just this person with an overnight job in Kansas City, Missouri.

And a closet-sized store.
Yeah! It just happened so organically
and felt really exciting and rewarding
to have someone you admire, admire
what you do.
How did you end up moving to LA?
Well I was getting a lot of work
out here. Clients and musicians
and things. I also felt like I was
getting older. In Kansas City I had
this great store, an awesome job at
the Art Institute, a place I loved
living in. It felt so easy. It was
like, "Oh this could easily be the
rest of my life." That really scared
me. It was like a really nice problem
to have. Everything's perfect. I
gotta mess something up.
**What were you doing at the Art
Institute?**
I was teaching in the fibers
department. I taught sewing one
and two, pattern making, and
entrepreneurial textiles.
**Have your designs changed since
you've come to LA?**
Yeah, definitely. I'd never ever
puffy painted on anything.
**And now you puffy paint on
everything.**
On everything! I'm obsessed with
it. I always think like the 12 year
old girl in me would be like, so
happy or like so disappointed. Like
I like sewing, but it's so tedious
and boring at a certain point. It's
such a giveaway with the puffy paint
because it looks better if it's
messed up. It looks better when it's
a little bit fucked up.
I love that it's done by hand.
I think that's what people like
about it, because it gives them that
nostalgia.
**You also use logos a lot in your
clothes. Why do you love logos?**
I think that the logos felt responsive
to being so happily American. I love
commercialism and capitalism. I love
being advertised to. I love purchasing
things. I think that we're not
supposed to, in a way. Maybe a more
enlightened person is not supposed to
love being susceptible to that.

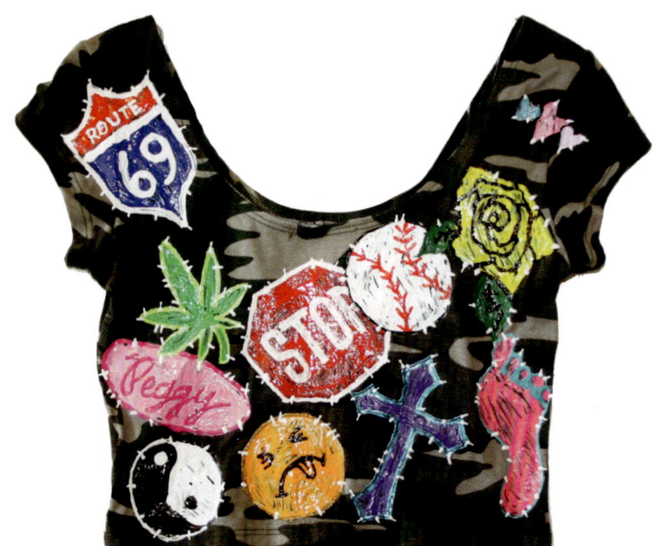

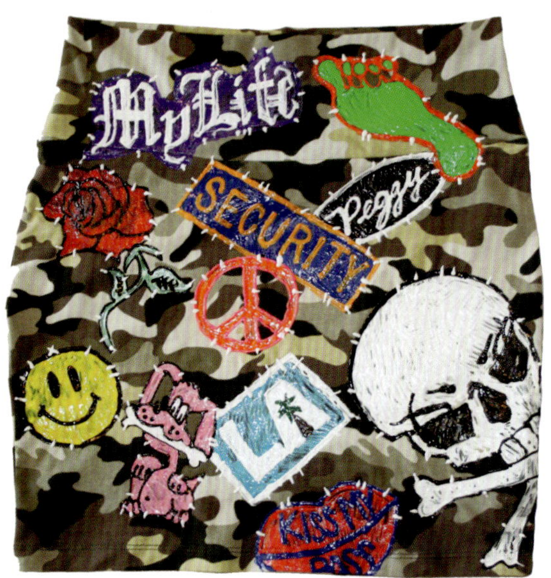

**Like underground people are supposed
to say, "Fuck the establishment..."**
Yeah, exactly. I get that and I feel
like my spirit is there, but I feel
like my wallet is definitely in the
store and I'm so happy about that! It
feels good to me so it's stupid to
pretend it doesn't feel good.
Yeah, fuck that.
I feel connected to enough other
things that aren't for sale — that
I cannot buy — so I also feel
comfortable buying and selling things.
I'm not a millionaire. I would love
to make money off of objects that I
care about and be able to make a nice
living off of that. That'd be awesome.

**How has it been going with Peggy
Noland, the clothing line?**
Way better since I've been here in LA.
Why do you think that is?
I don't know if it's because I'm making
different things or I'm making better
things but people are responding to
it. It's hard to know when it comes
to trend-based work: if it's hype or
if it's good. I don't ever feel like
I'm far enough away from it to have a
perspective of why something is.
**You and Seth are always working, but
it feels like a party.**
It is! I feel so lucky for that —
our aesthetics really compliment
one another. I think we both really
love what we do. We do different
and similar enough work that we can
challenge one another. We can also
ask each other technical questions.
So yeah, it's great here. Because
I definitely know the flip side of
that, hating your everyday. No more
of that, I think that's safe to say.
Do you have a plan for the future?
When I moved out here, I was
definitely like, "I want to open a
store." That was my plan. There's so
many great places to open a boutique
here. I would just drive around
and look at different neighborhoods
and visualize where I would like to
start my space. There were so many
different places that would be cute.
It would be cute in Echo Park. It
would be cute on Melrose. A lot of
different places could work. Then,
one day I was like, "Oh no. I know
exactly where I need it to be."
Where?
I don't want a store anywhere in Los
Angeles unless it's on Rodeo Drive.
I'm not even going to mess around.
How come?
I am kind of obsessed with this idea
of trending right now, and how we are
advertised to, and logos. That has
much to do with so many of the stores
on Rodeo Drive. It's about wanting
so desperately to have a piece of
the Prada lifestyle but all you can
really afford is the perfume. It
still makes you feel good.

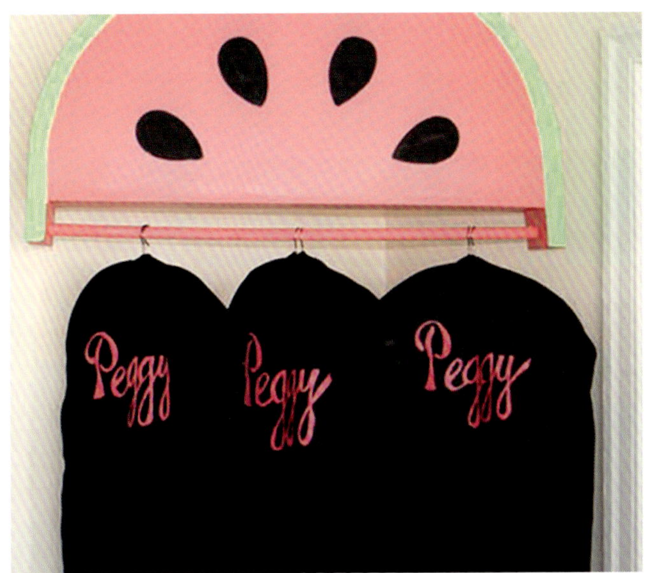

Rihanna Diamonds World Tour, 2012.

**So you have an idea of how your store
would fit in there?**
I have Google SketchUps of how I
imagine it looking and how I imagine
it to be — a thoughtful translation
of what happens on Rodeo Drive.
**You really approach retail as an
opportunity to be creative.**
I'm comfortable using retail spaces
as my art form. It's naturally what
I've done for seven years and I
didn't even know it at the time. I'm
not good at retail spaces, because
a good retail space means you turn
a profit. You make money. I don't
do that and I don't really have a
passion to make that my priority over
creating cool spaces, or making cool
clothes.
Kind of like an artist.
What I do is a really functional side
of art. People don't see clothing as
art, in general. I'm painting this
and it's on a dress. I'm not painting
it and hanging it on a wall, but if I
did, it would probably be called art
and not fashion.
Do you care?
I don't know if I care. I probably
went through a period where I did,
but it's just not my job to change
those definitions.
Last question: Do you make collections?
Like spring, summer, fall? No, that's
not how I work. ☺

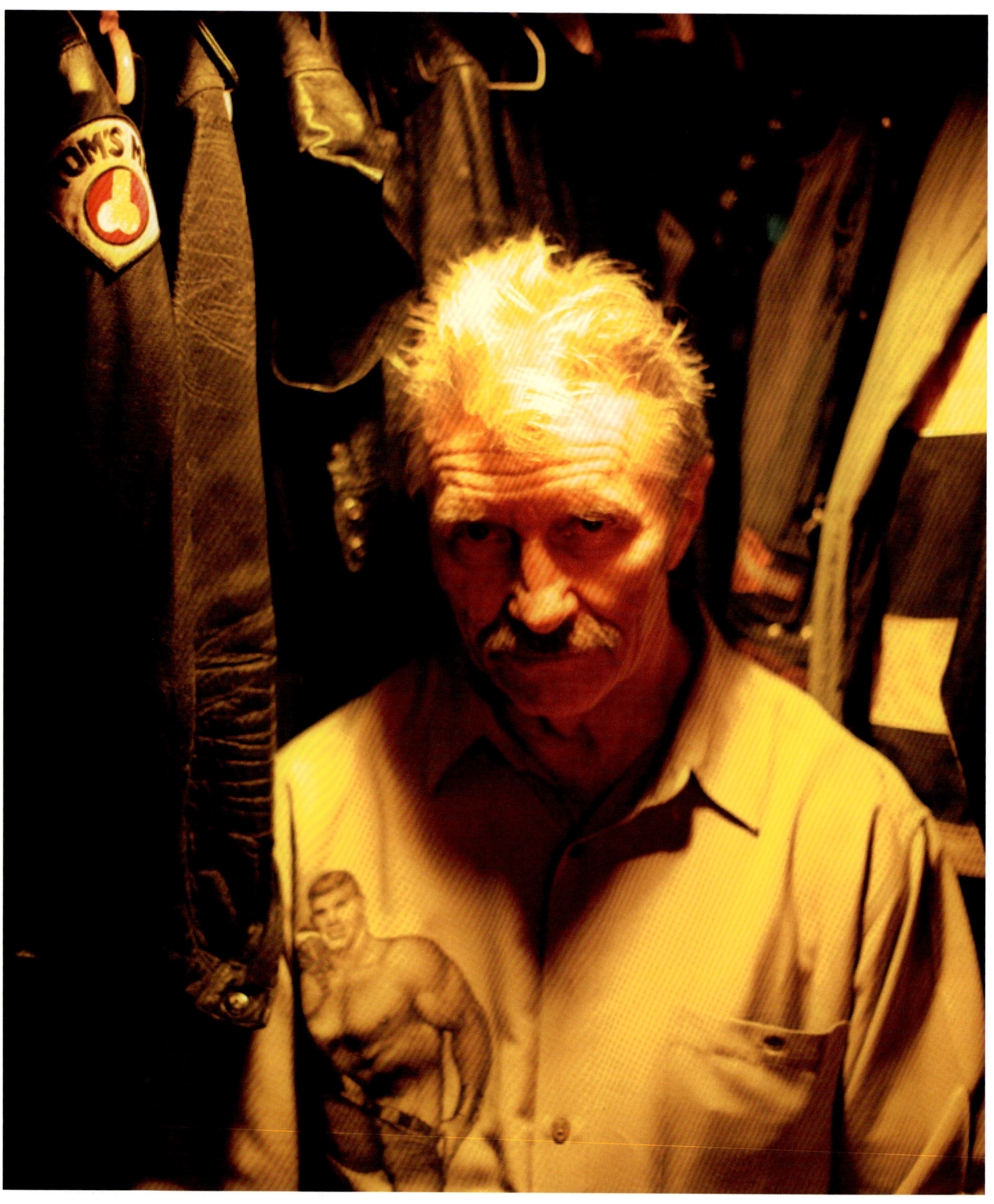

Interview by Michael Bullock
Photography by Cali Thornhill DeWitt

In 1980, Durk Dehner invited the trailblazing homoerotic artist Tom of Finland to live with him in Los Angeles. From then until his death in 1991 Tom split his time between the Echo Park residence and Finland, with Dehner wearing many hats: muse, model, lover, business partner, friend, and co-founder of the Tom of Finland Foundation, an organization dedicated to maintaining and building Tom's archive, and as it states on it's letterhead, "preserving, protecting and promoting erotic art." Last week the Tom of Finland Foundation celebrated it's 29th birthday, a particularly joyful occasion as it happened in tandem with a landmark retrospective at LA MOCA, a clear summation of the foundation's years of hard work and affirmation of Tom of Finland's proper place in history: as a master artist, visionary, and champion of sexual freedom whose body of work is important to society at large.

How did the Tom of Finland Foundation start?
My initial motivation for starting the foundation was as a friend. I took Tom on because he needed to have a business associate that could move things forward. I knew that he wasn't prepared to do that part of it and I just wanted to help him, especially in America. He wasn't from here and was often taken advantage of.

How did people take advantage of him?
People were always illegally reproducing his work. You could find it all over the place, poorly printed. Oftentimes it never stated who published it, but it was distributed across the country.

Who was actually printing it?
It was the mafia. There was a printer in the San Fernando Valley that was reprinting his work. It's funny, when we tried to get our first book published we ended up in their office. The printer shook Tom's hand and immediately said, "I wanna thank you. I've made so much money off your work that I was able to put my son through college." You could see Tom's face get bright red and he was shaking his head up and down, trying to be agreeable, but it was a complete slap in the face.

Did you still print with them?
We had to because at the time we couldn't find anyone that would print his work in Los Angeles. I mean here, in this metropolitan city they were so uptight about it. That continued for a long time. It was the same with galleries. They would rarely show explicit erotic work and if it was homosexual in nature, it was even more difficult. Museums certainly weren't buying or collecting it so we had to find our own way.

How did you do that?
We created our own galleries and our own art fairs that were designed to bring artists and potential collectors together. Through that, we developed our own collector base. I'm not saying the foundation did this by itself, I'm saying it was the culture, the community. It was underground for many years and then it gradually surfaced.

Why did the foundation care so much about helping other artists?
Tom felt that sexuality expressed in the visual arts is natural; it was one of the premises of his life and, when we don't allow it, we censor what we could do and inhibit ourselves. He was unwilling to compromise what was creatively coming through him and because of that he sacrificed a faster road to...

Financial success?
Not necessarily. As I said, we built a collector base. It was an interesting process because, through the fairs, our community gave value to its own artists and their work. By raising the prices on ourselves we allowed the artist to be more secure so they could create more work.

Do you still have the fairs?
We're organizing a fair in 2014 and we're also having an emerging artist contest.

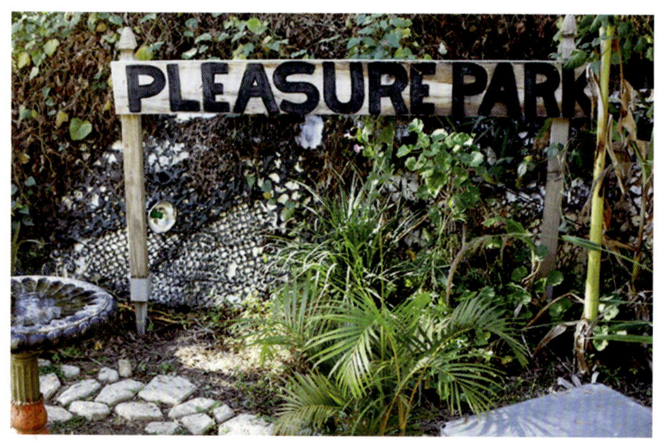

What are the guidelines for emerging artists at the fair?
The guidelines are very simple in that the only rule is that you can't have ever sold any of your work that is erotic in nature. We give support so that the artist will continue too nurture themselves. This is the 12th competition and the 18th fair we have done. We've had a high success rate in those competitions, with many artists such as Patrick Lee, Jay Jorgensen going on to have healthy careers.

Was Tom often asked to tone it down by publishers?
Yes. All the time, publications would say, "We'd love to print your work but we can't show raw sexuality." I mean we were just censored. We were invited by a respected gallery to be part of a museum exhibition in Lille, France. We picked the works and they came back to us two weeks later and said that the museum said no.

They uninvited you?
They said that because of the political climate there, gay marriage had just been approved and there was a lot of adverse reaction, so they were afraid that they might lose funding if they showed Tom's work. But the point is that it hasn't gone away. Artist censorship is very much alive.

That's why it's amazing to finally see Tom's retrospective show at MOCA. Can you explain how Tom and Bob Mizer figured their way around censorship as early as the late 50s?

Bob was the owner of the photo studio AMG (Athletic Model Guild), which put out a small periodical named Physique Pictorial that included photographs of male physiques and drawings by artists. At the time, it was one of the only ways that homosexual culture was getting fed and nurtured.

When did Tom draw his first cover for AMG?
In the spring of 1957. Then he became the house artist for that periodical all the way through 1970. The publication was extremely subversive. Bob's photo's always used costuming, like cowboys and Indians, gladiators, or Greek gods. It wasn't just because it was gay fantasy. In the 50s and 60s, they had to do it because in order to publish images of half naked men they had to be considered "historically valuable." That's why they were always depicting a previous time in history.

I never could have imagined those themes were invented to protect them. I just thought it was camp.
Even as late as the 80s it was still tricky. That's when Tom and I set up a mail order company together in order to sell catalogs of his drawings and merchandise. At that point, there were 13 states in America that had really aggressive postal authorities that were trying to file federal lawsuits against mail order companies, especially gay. Once, Tom wanted to include a drawing called Police Orgy that included a fisting scene but we had to cover that act because fisting was classified as obscene: fisting, piss, scat, bestiality, and pedophilia, those were the five that would land you in prison.

Piss would land you in prison?
Yup. So anyway, we have an award to honor people who have made an important contribution to our community and one of them was Larry Flint, and he was gracious enough to come speak at a dinner we had for about a hundred artists. He told them, "Stand your ground, stay strong, and never compromise." That brings us back to Tom. Those were his principles and the same principles this foundation was founded to support.

    Durk Dehnner & The Tom of Finland Foundation by Michael Bullock

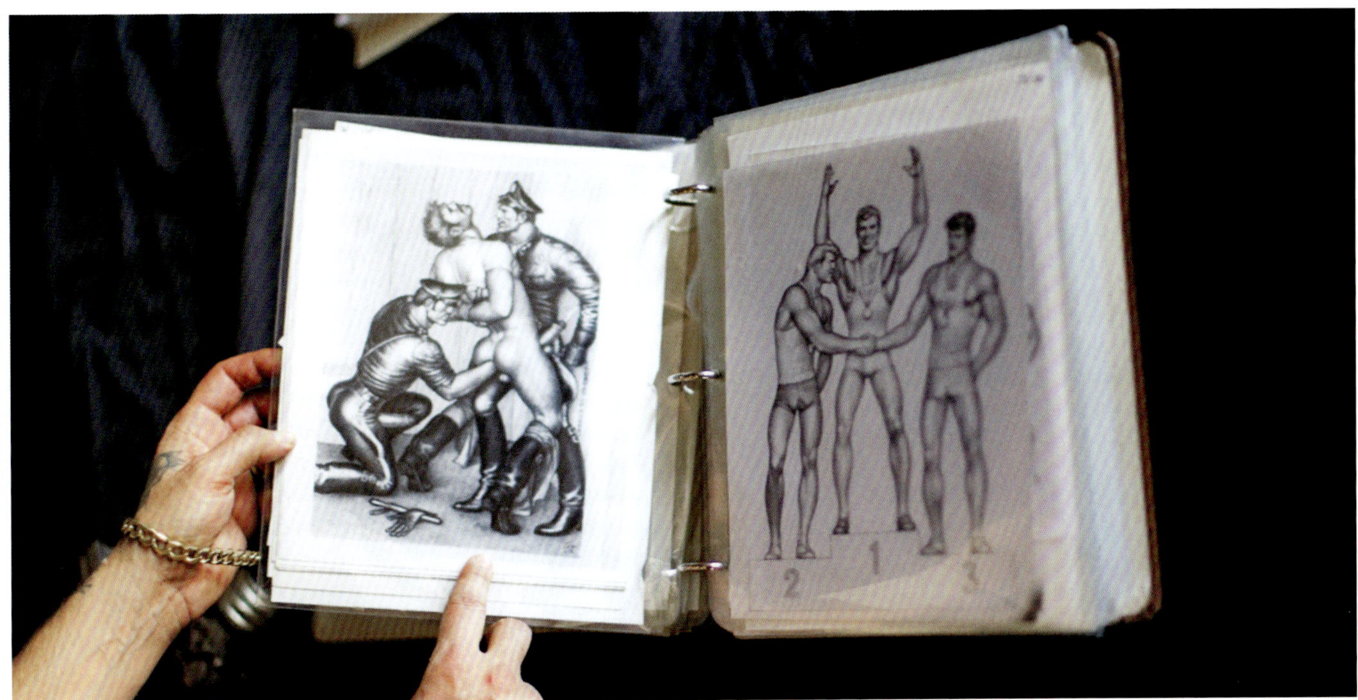

When did you first meet Tom?
I was 26 when I first discovered
Tom's work and I know what it did
for me. He laid into his drawings, a
message, an essence; he gave gay men
an identity that they could be proud
of. His drawings assured us that
we were whole and complete. At the
time, gay life was in the shadows,
behind closed doors. Tom literally
brought it into the light. A lot of
the time, he showed his men making
out in sunshine, out in the forest
because he wanted to communicate that
mother nature loved us, and that we
didn't have to buy into all of this
demeaning crap that society had been
dishing out.

Did he think of his work as activism?
He did, but you know he was Finnish.
The thing about Finns is that they
had been a suppressed people; they
were dominated by the Russians and
the Swedes and as a result they used
to be very modest. When he got older
he finally said it. There's a video
where he's speaking to some students
at Cal Arts and he finally says
it: that from the beginning he saw
the plight of the homosexual as so
pathetically horrible that he wanted
them to know that they were

perfect just the way they were.
He wanted straight people to back
off and let them have a chance. And
he wanted to tell them that they
deserved to be happy and to love in
the way that they wanted to love.
So he intended this, and this is
what happened.

**Was he able to see that he had
achieved that before he died?**
In the 80s he finally got it, that
he had succeeded and succeeded at
something pretty phenomenal. He
was able to communicate that gay
men weren't alone. I was part of
it and gay men all over were part
of it. We all nurtured each other
and it all was collective but Tom's
vision absolutely lead the way.
Harvey Shipley Miller, who was a
trustee from the Judith Rothschild
Foundation, called Tom of Finland one
of the five most influential artists
of the last century because his
vision transcended art and became the
culture. In the 80s, Tom of Finland
was everywhere, in bars of every
kind; it was in posters for events,
and in the music scene in England.
His imagery was with front men, like
Adam Ant, Judas Priest's Rob Halford,
and Queen's Freddie Mercury.

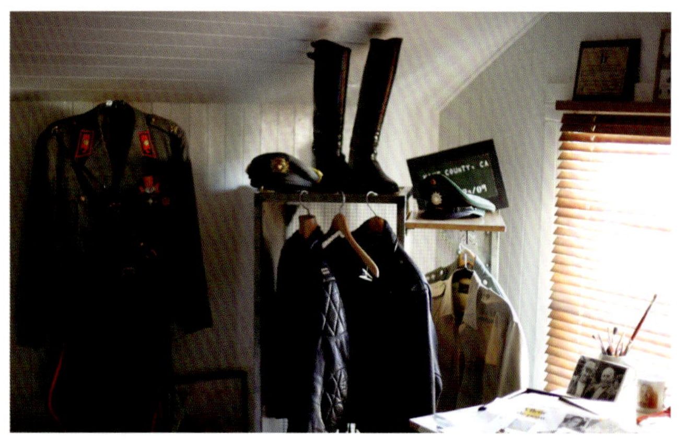

Not to mention his influence on gym culture.
Absolutely. If you go back to where this whole national-international gym culture came from, you follow it back to California in the 50s and early 60s. In Los Angeles, there were three gyms. There was Gold's, in Santa Monica; there was Vince's in North Hollywood; and Jack LaLanne's on Wilshire. Physique Pictorial inspired gay men to realize they didn't have to be that effeminate cliché of the time, that they could actually look masculine and muscular like the men Tom and Bob presented. By the 70s there weren't enough gyms in LA to keep up with the demand and it just kept going from there.

There was also that infamous Vivian Westwood T-shirt.
Yeah, it appealed to everybody. It became sort of like, "Who doesn't like Tom of Finland?" In his world, cops weren't trying to break up sex; they were encouraging it. The cops were sexual icons too. And everyone had a good time. There was humor. His hero's were always slightly embarrassed because they were caught in compromising situations. That's a very Finnish thing; their heroes are humanized so the audience can relate.

Does the foundation get criticized for being overly focused on sex?
The reason why the foundation was established, beyond managing Tom's archives, was to encourage and nurture work that is sexual in nature. Discrimination against sexual art is so dominant that it becomes a part of an artist's psyche. It's not that you have to always draw explicit sex but you should not have to even consider that you can't include it. We still watch movies where they're showing a woman front and back, but let me tell you — they're not showing a guy front and back. They'll show his butt, but they won't show his cock. What's that about? Let's just make it equal and get over this crap.

What does the foundation do to fight society's ingrained self-censorship?
We forget that we're a ritualistic people. As soon as we get socialized we want to hide it. That's why on the first of every spring, the foundation has it's biggest event, called the Rites of Spring. We have as many cocks around as we can. We have a cock altar, it's lots of fun. It's about celebrating; that's what Tom did. He celebrated the cock.

How far back does the archive go?
We only have a few things from the beginning, the 1950s, before Tom got published, and it's really a problem. That's something I want to hammer into artist's heads — capture everything that you do and keep an archive from the beginning. Do it as well as you can, because you have no idea how your art will be used 25 years from now.

One of the best things about the foundation is the supporting materials.
Yes. Recently, we realized that we needed to pay better attention to Tom's photographs. It was students from CalArts that slapped us across the face and made us realize they were also important. Tom photographed his models, developed his own film, and made his own prints. Then he would cut his prints up and put them into reference binders, which were a mixture of his photographs, other guys' photographs, and cutouts from magazines and everything. We realized that we needed to start showing them. Now we're producing exhibition prints of Tom's that are remarkable. He really stands as a photographer.

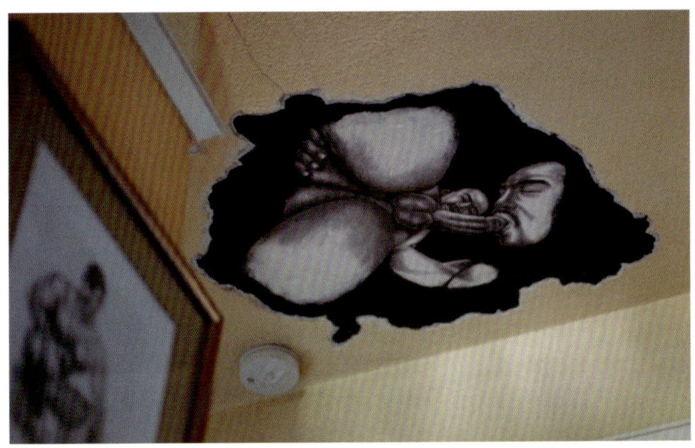

I loved the collages at the MOCA show. They were all of faces and it showed how focused he was on getting the right attitude through his men's expressions. There's the full range: joy, pleasure, mischief, bravado, and as you said, embarrassment.

Those collages that he used for reference are also being noted. He also did doodles, little silly drawings. He would take magazine cutouts, and would play with them — accentuate the right features to turn them into Tom of Finland men. All of this is now finally being looked at. He'll always be known for his pencil work, his graphics, but those materials are important.

When did you first realize his preliminary sketches were of value?

In 1984 Tom brought 1,500 rough sketches from Finland to store at the foundation. He never thought they were worthwhile outside of his archives. But I went, "Oh my god, these are amazing." So, immediately, I sent copies of them to our gallery in New York.

Which was Feature gallery.

Yes, Hudson is an amazing man, and did so much for Tom. Hudson exhibited Tom along with artists that he inspired like GB Jones. She's a female artist that recreated Tom of Finland's scenarios with lesbians. He also exhibited Martin of Holland, who made drawings of scat play. All of his men were covered in shit because shit is part of the gay tribal culture. It may not be manifested very much now but it was big then.

He exhibited all of them in his gallery in SoHo and never put up an explanation or a sign. This fucking sign shit... Trying to prevent someone from being offended. Like, fuck off, you know?

Did Tom ever get discouraged?

So much. I don't think there's any artist that has been ripped off as many times as him; it continued after he was dead. We still have to defend his copyrights. You have to fight for it and not let other people take what is yours. Tom got burned a lot. I saw him give up several times. It lasted about 48 hours. Then he had to start drawing again. When someone is passionate, they get pissed off and they never give up. Not every artist is like that, but he was.

Any closing thoughts?

Well... Tom is not owned by gays, he's owned by the world. I mean, his proprietary roots are with us, but we're absolutely willing to share him for everyone to benefit. In 2006 we had an exhibition in Paris at Gallery Richard of a hundred works. It was cold, December, and this elegant woman walked in wearing a red overcoat. She just stood in the middle of the gallery and panned the room, looking at the art with this radiant smile. I went up to her and asked her what she was thinking. She said, "I am standing at the bastion of freedom. Here lies the works of a man who never compromised what was in his heart. He represents freedom for all of us." And I think that's the way it is. ☺

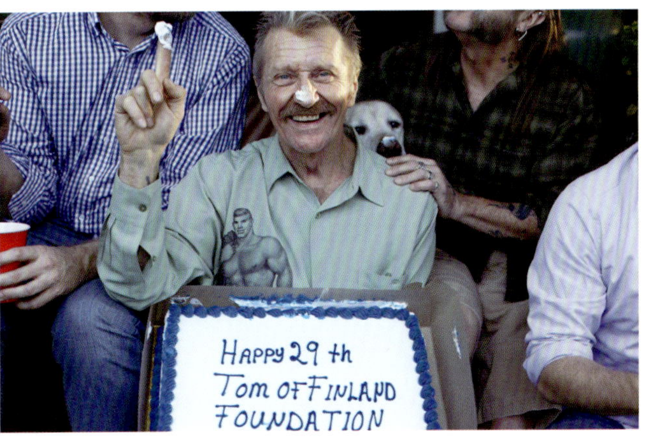

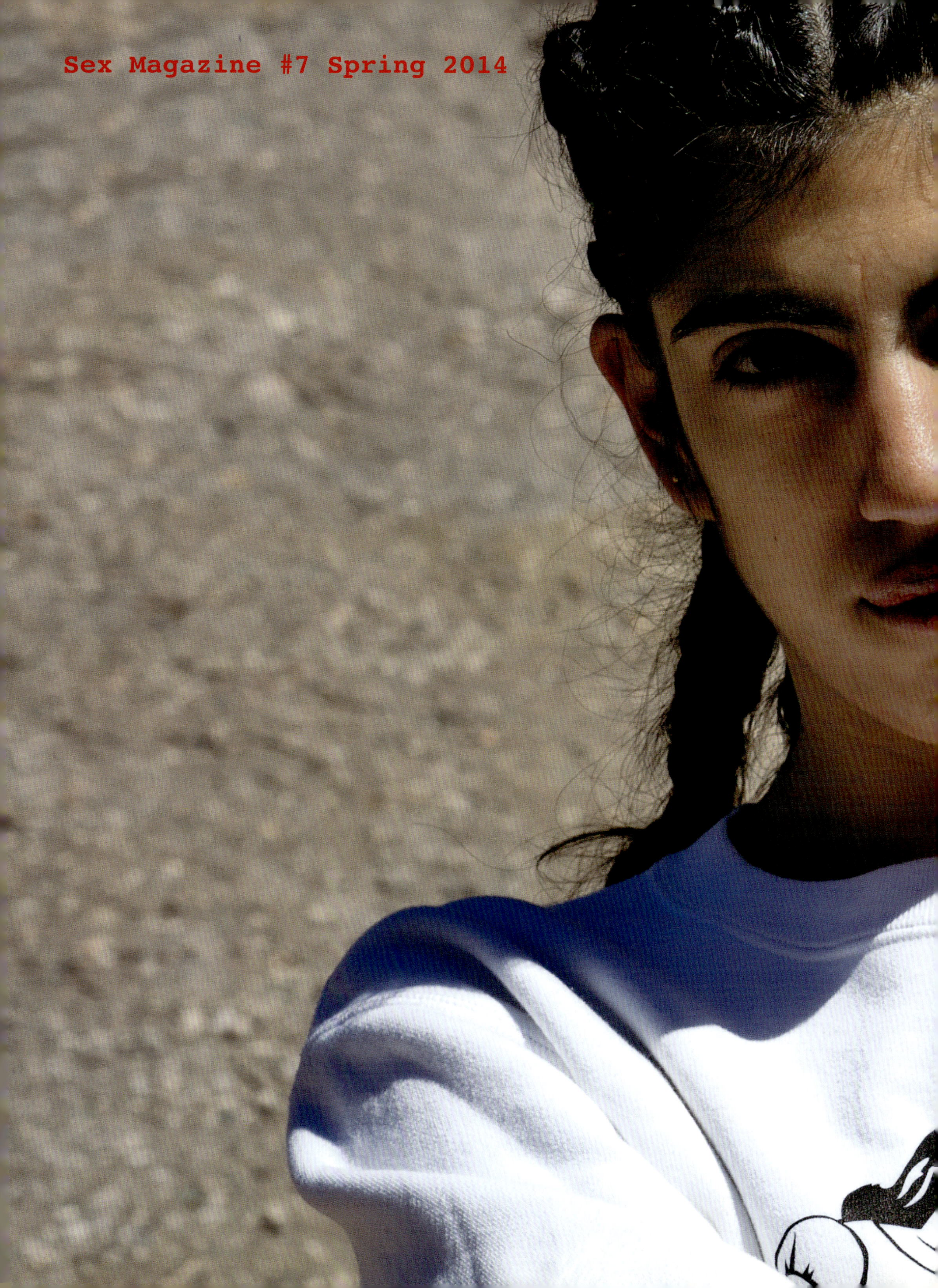
Sex Magazine #7 Spring 2014

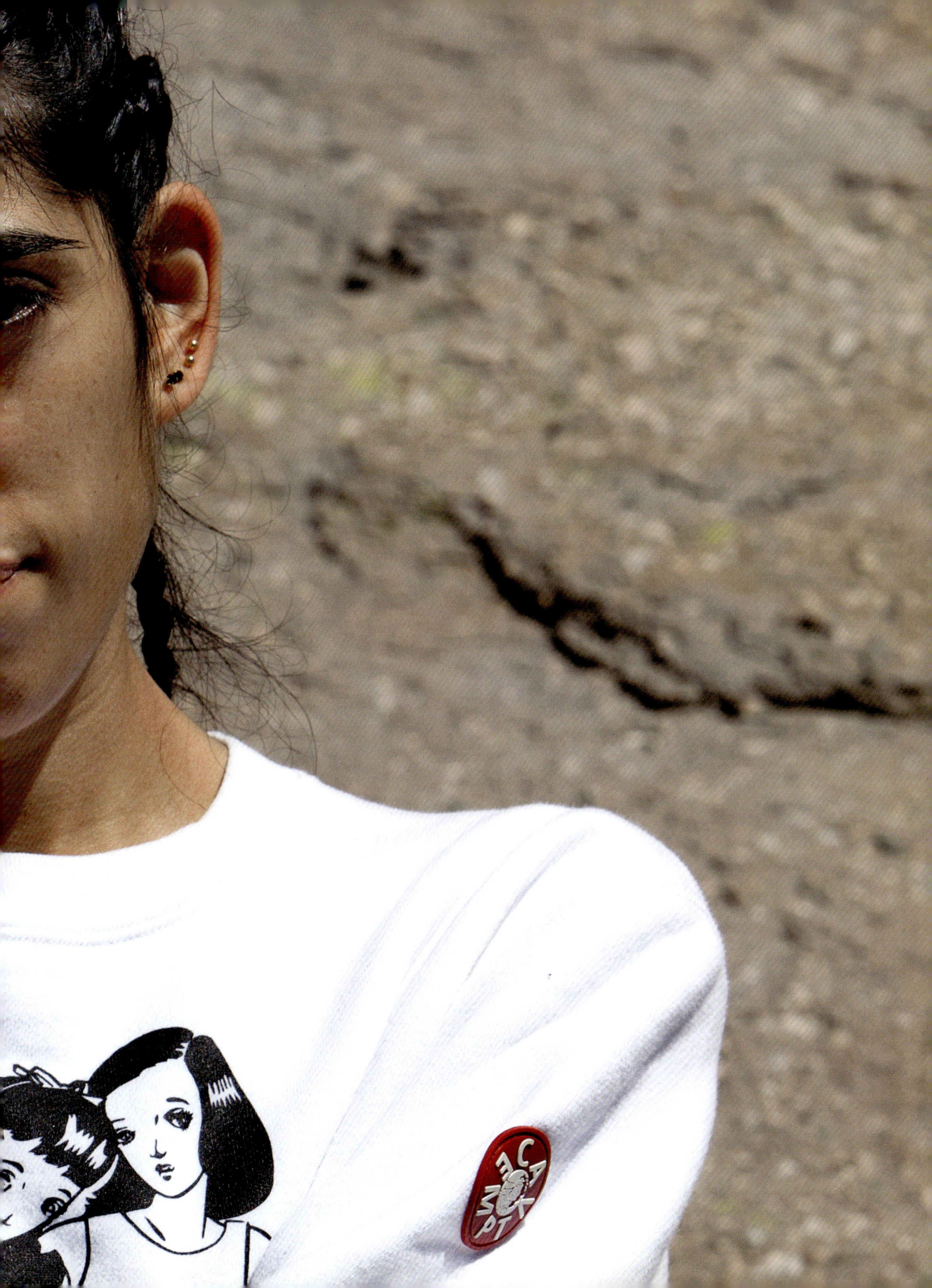

Korakrit Arunanondchai
"I don't have to define to myself what being an artist is yet."

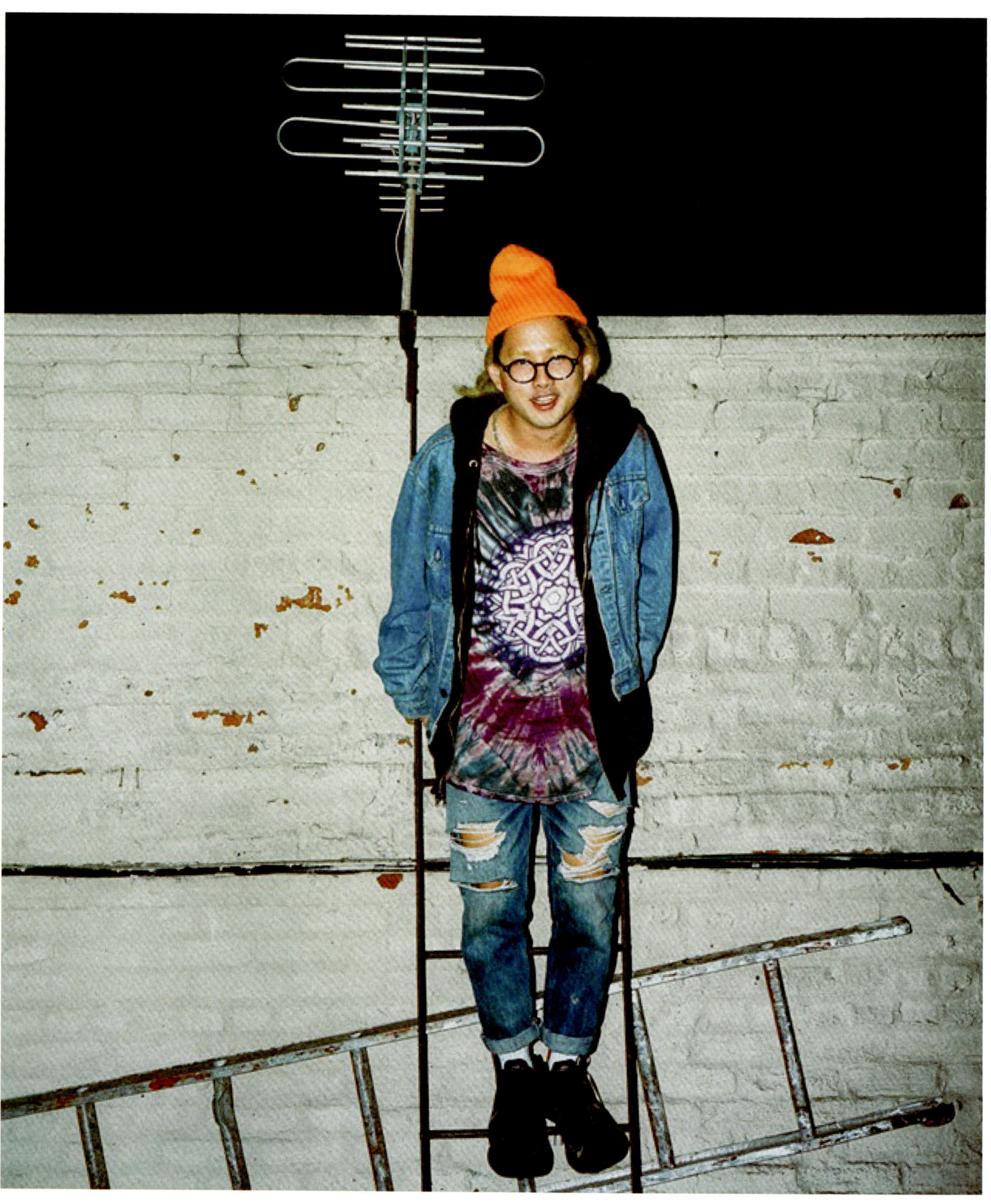

Interview by Asher Penn
Portrait by Chutchawarn Chut Janthachotibutr

Last week Thai artist Korakrit Arunanondchai performed the third installment in a series of "graduations," each separated by three years. The first one had occurred at Rhode Island School of Design in 2009, the second at Columbia University in 2011. Last week at MoMA PS1 Korakrit screened films while hosting a handful of musical and visual performers, (including himself), immersing an unexpected audience into an unusually personal, poetic, and sensational art experience. This contemporary Gesamtkunstwerk has always been Korakrit's goal, whose work in painting, sculpture, film, and collaborations with friends demonstrates how the act of making art can evolve into a transformation of self.

What's Bangkok like?
It's a big metropolitan city. Growing up there is different from visiting as a tourist. It's fairly religious. The majority of people are Buddhist. I went to a Catholic all-boys school for elementary and middle school.
You were raised Buddhist and went to Catholic school?
A lot of the good schools in Bangkok are Catholic. They're not super strict. The one I went to was called Bangkok Christian College. Once a week, we'd have a one-hour session where you have to go in and study your Bible and sing these translated and modernized Jesus songs together. Then we would have a bunch of rehearsals to put on a play and people would become a real team. It was this very crazy group experience, especially as it contained so much popular music and theatre.
How did you get into art?
Growing up in a Thai system, there wasn't a lot of exposure to art. I grew up reading lots of Japanese comics and watching Dragon Ball Z. I was really into things like Pokémon and drew comics all the time growing up.

What about the internet?
I mean, this was kind of pre-internet. When I graduated from high school, I still had dial-up and my brothers and I shared a computer. My relationship to pictures was cartoons, because they're the only pictures you consume, except for advertising and video games.
They didn't teach art at all?
Yes, but it was very rigid. Specific tasks, more like a craft class. One task was learning how to draw the Thai pattern. Everyone had to do it.

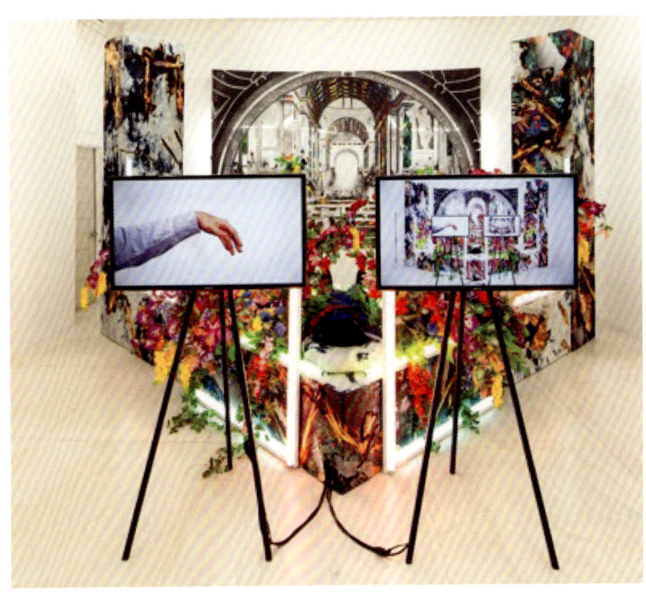

2012-2055, Columbia MFA Thesis Exhibition, 2012.

How did you get into Western art?
I moved to an international school for the last three years of high school. They actually offered real art classes where you could use nice art materials like Winsor & Newton oil paint. In Thailand they have to import it and it was so expensive. Here they actually gave you the oil paint, oil sticks, and stuff. It was baller.
Were you looking at art too?
I had this British art teacher that had gone to Slade and told me to look at the all the Young British Artists from the 90s. When we got to visit London, I just got dropped off at the Saatchi Gallery when they had that Sensation show up.

Images courtesy Korakrit Arunanondchai

That was the classic YBA Show.
Yeah. There were these Jake and Dinos
Chapman and Ron Mueck works. Then
at the Tate Modern there was Olafur
Eliasson's sun. It just blew my mind.
I saw this stuff and felt it was
totally what I was about at that time.
Because you related to it.
I related because all those artworks
are super sensational — in a way where
all people can relate through ideas of
scale and aesthetic. It's a good entry
point. It was good to see that people
could do this and that these artworks
could appeal to someone who didn't
understand art history.
How did you end up at RISD?
My older brother had applied to RISD
and said it was really good for
graphic design.

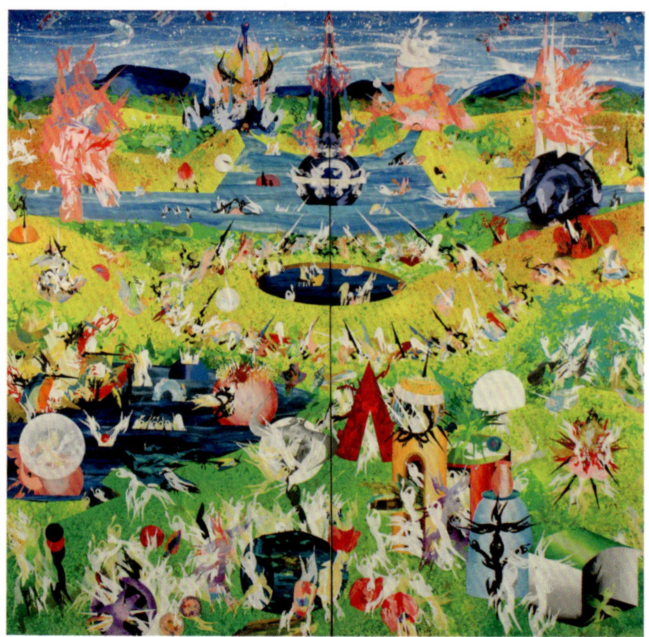

Garden, 2010.

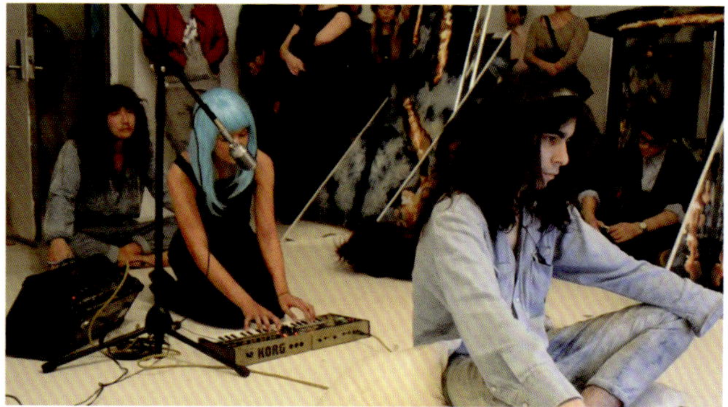

2011, Columbia, 2011.

You didn't want to study painting?
It wasn't practical. What am I going
to do after? There's no artist job
in Thailand. The plan was to study
architecture or graphic design. Be
practical, support myself, like most of
the other Asian people you see there.
So you ended up majoring in design?
I went to graphic design for two
weeks but felt really disconnected. I
switched to printmaking. That was the
cool thing to do at RISD at the time
— or at least how I remember it. They
let you do whatever you want. I was
making painting using silk screens,
hundreds of layers of it on top of
each other. By the time I graduated
I was taking painting classes that
made me realize I needed to know more
about the history of art.

Was that why you went to grad school?
Yeah, plus I needed a visa to stay
in the States, and I thought maybe
I could teach after. My mom's one
of the best English teachers in
Thailand, in my opinion, and I think
I wanted to continue that legacy of
teaching somehow.
What was Columbia like?
You would have so many people come by
your studio every day. I was trying
to take in as many different people,
their advice and criticism, and
combine it.
Was that when you started making films?
People were just saying, "You should
try video." At that time, I could
afford an SLR. Then Apichatpong
Weerasethakul gave a massive workshop
at Columbia that I sat in on. He
shoots everything in Thailand. When
my grandfather got sick with memory
loss I thought video was a great
medium for me to spend time with him.
How does making a movie change time?
It's like if me and you were talking,
and we're filming it, this whole
thing becomes an event. That summer
I was supposed to spend time with my
grandparents and my family. Doing
this video was a way I could always
be working.

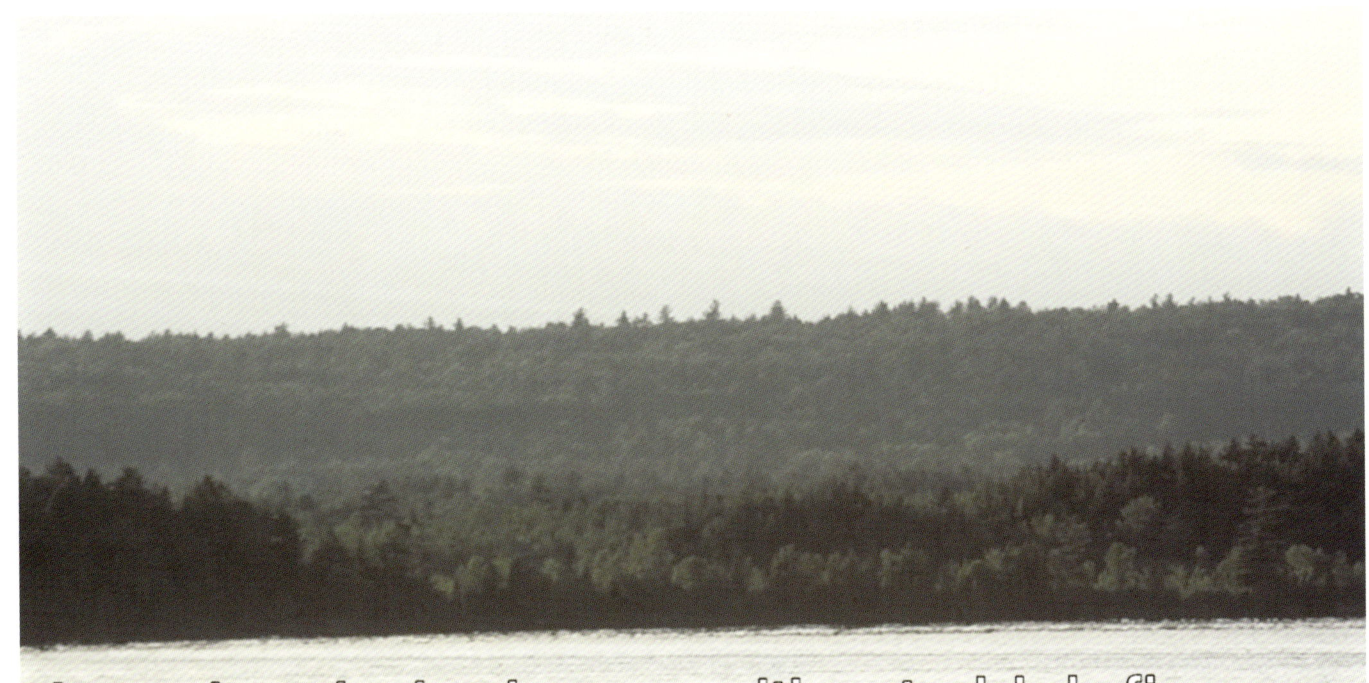

2556, 2013.

So you were making a documentary?
The way I make my video is by writing
a story with matching pictures. It's
kind of inspired by how Chris Marker
makes movies like Sans Soleil.

**I remember a video you made of a
performance you did at RISD. What
was that?**
When I was at RISD, I was making
everything from clothes to sculptures,
as well as paintings. The idea was
for everything to culminate with a
big musical installation, which ended
up happening around my thesis. It was
about death and rebirth — kind of
about me feeling sad about leaving
this art utopia.

**It sounds like you staged your own
graduation in a way.**
After I made it, I realized I
needed to make the same piece every
three years. It would never be
perfect, so every three years it
would be different. It's like my
version of a Gesamtkunstwerk. I'm just
not old or skilled enough to do it
completely yet.

**Wait, what's Gesamtkunstwerk? It's a
complete artwork, right?**

It's just a framework that I
operate in sometimes. For me, it's
about taking in the entire scope of
a situation and trying to be aware
of every single element. It's like
watching cinema but goes beyond
the frame. Your physical presence
is in there, too. It's like a
complete experience.

**Does this inspire the way you
collaborate with other artists?**
I think I collaborate in a way where
I try and plan a structure, and I'm
also a player in the structure.
And someone else can be a player.
So, with Alex Gvojic, who did the
lighting, I don't really say I want
this on, I want this off. I just
tell him what's going to be happening
and what the overall goal is and
let him figure it out. I'm not much
of a director.

**Do you consider these performances to
be ritualistic?**
Well, they're gatherings of people —
and that's what rituals are,
right? It's like the gathering
of people in a certain place to
do something together.

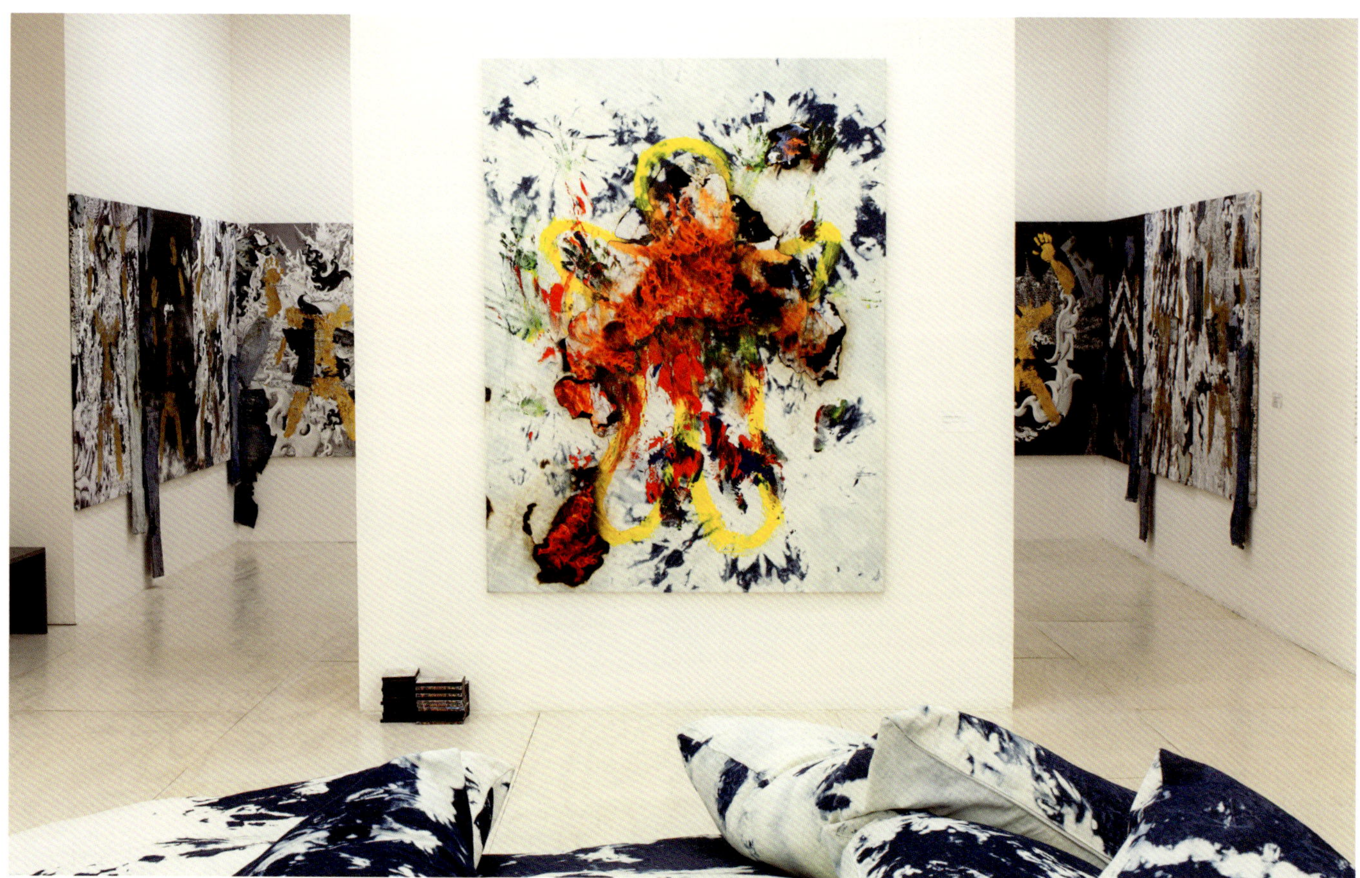

Installation at MoMA PS1, 2014. Photo: Matthew Septimus

Like an art opening.
With an art opening, there is something ritualistic about people coming together to try and look at objects and experience something.
How do you approach a film shoot?
It's all different. The kind I like to do best is when I just have a camera and tripod and walk around. My twin and I did this travel video where we would just go to different sites, kind of like a road trip movie. It wasn't planned, was more about being there and documenting it.
How does the film evolve after that?
The real ideas of the film come together with the editing and music. It's really music that glues it. I edit to music. With the trailers, I enjoy making them because they are filled with anticipation. This moment where a vague narrative appears with the feeling of anticipation is something I enjoy a lot. Most of the time I make the trailer before I even make the actual video.

Has making art allowed for experiences in your life that would have otherwise not happened?
Yes, totally. That's why I make art. This specific video trilogy project started with the impetus for me to go through something, to become the artist and person I want to be.
How do you identify yourself as an artist? How do you define that word?
I know what it means from different definitions in different contexts, but for me, I'd like to think it's still undefined. It keeps on getting defined, but I don't have to define to myself what being an artist is yet.
I've heard you describe your work as being about expanding a moment.
Well, everything's complicated, right? It's not about finding the truth of a moment, but the poetry within it.
Can you give an example of that?
That happened for me with this video where a Thai master painter critiqued a female body painter who was actually a go-go dancer on a TV show. It was

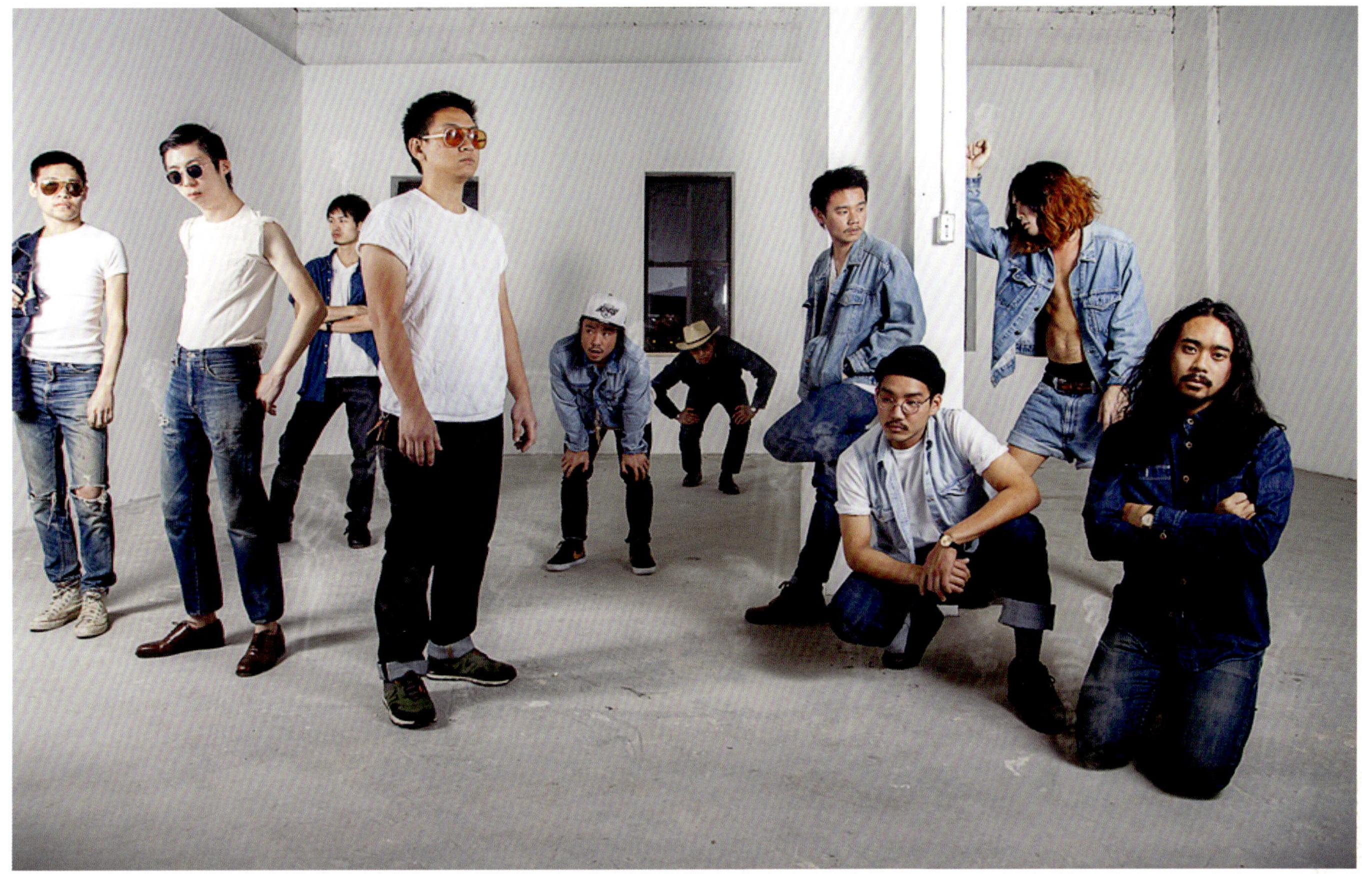

Painting with History in a Room Filled with Men with Funny Names, Clearing, 2013.

this moment where people were asking is this art or nudity put together through these two figures: one's male, one's female; one's in the sex industry, one is a national artist who built a temple. To freeze and expand that moment is a great way to talk about it.

Who are the Asian dudes wearing denim? Are they like a gang?
That was part of an idea of how to return to a collective. It started off with a show I did called Painting with History in a Room Filled with Men with Funny Names. Instead of making painting in the history of men making paintings, I wanted to draw a parallel to differentiate myself. Instead of belonging to a camp I could have my own camp, which was going to be with my fellow Thai men who had similar upbringings and went to the same all-boys type Christian school that I did. In reality it was just the Thai people I knew in New York but it became kind of a

community action, just coming together and doing things together. **Like smoking cigarettes in a room together. That's something a gang would do.**
That's how it started. Then, it kind of grew into this performance group and relationships. Now it's this thing I call Bangkok Boys. It's not just people from Bangkok. It's more of an open structure for collaboration — not just art. It's about coming together to create an image that later on maybe becomes reality.

They're also all wearing denim. Those fiery sweatsuits you made last year were so cool. What is it about clothes that interests you?
If you're talking about the image of coming-togetherness, clothing has a big role in that. The idea of loose uniform, belonging to something. With denim, the whole point was that it connected a lot of bodies and people together. There's just so much around everywhere. ☺

Andrew Feldmar
"Nobody suffers, nobody is crazy, if they weren't hurt."

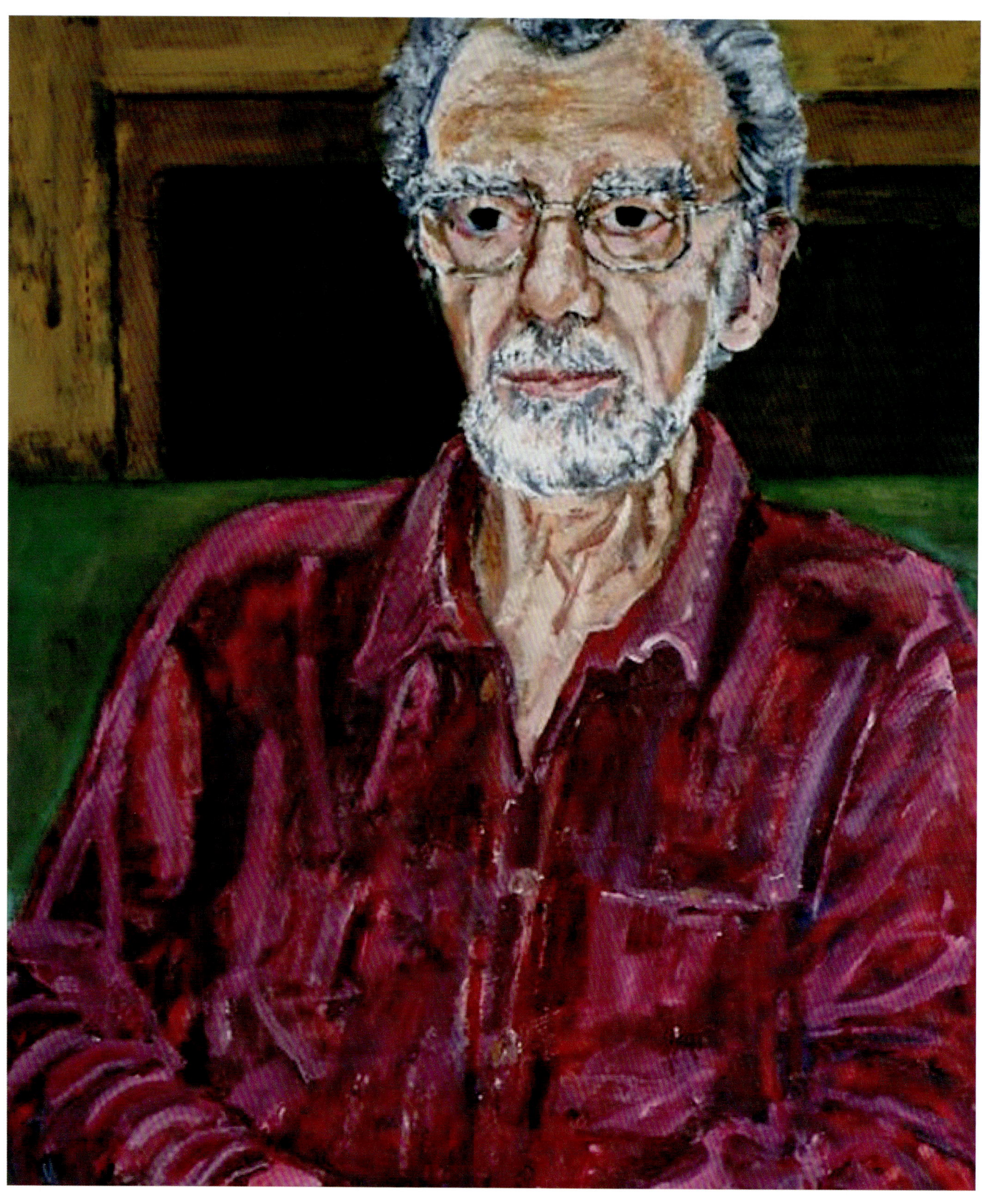

Interview by Asher Penn
Paintings by Meredith Feldmar

Full disclosure: Andrew Feldmar
is my therapist. I began seeing
him in 2006 and have continued to
sporadically seek his advice at the
most challenging moments. While I've
always wanted to interview him, some
very late googling yielded surprising
results: Feldmar was one of the first
to research the use of psychedelics
for therapeutic use in the 60s,
apprenticed and worked with
celebrated psychiatrist R. D. Laing,
and is currently an outspoken
advocate for the use of MDMA for
PTSD. Continuing Laing's "do no
harm" dogma Feldmar's wholly unique
approach takes therapy out of Freudian
analysis's past towards coming to
terms with the present moment.

Where were you born?
I was born in Budapest Hungary, 1940.
Not a good time or place for a Jew.
No. Family members had already
emigrated, feeling that things were
not going to be good. In 1943 Jews
were rounded up in Budapest. My
mother was taken to Auschwitz, my
father to a forced-labor camp, my
grandmother to the ghetto.
How did you survive?
Somehow my father arranged for a
young Catholic woman to take me. For
a year and a half I was living with
this woman and her kids. I had to lie
about my name.
How come?
Anybody who was hiding a Jewish kid
would be killed. I remember the father
of that household hitting my hand
because I was using a fork and knife
differently than how his children were
using it. I had to pretend I was just
like the other kids.
**How much of that period do you
actually remember?**
Very little. I try to remember that
part of my life but only fragments
come back — sitting on the arm of a
strange man, making the rounds. I
would look at the guy's face — if
there was no fear on his face I was
happy, but if I saw fear on his face
I got very frightened.

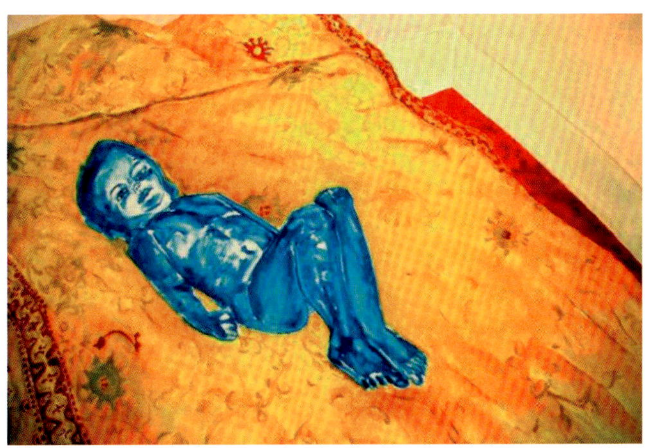

Concept (Blue Child on Yellow Spread), 1984.

**But you didn't really understand what
was going on?**
It was all just sound and fury and
color, but I was tuning into the
excitement, fear, emotions of the
adults around me.
What happened when the war ended?
In 1945 around my fifth birthday my
mother, father, and grandmother all
came back.
**You don't hear about that happening
often. What was Budapest like after
the war?**
Between 1945 and 1956, there was the
Russian Oppression with troops all
over Hungary. That's where I first
figured out what depression was about.
Depression is not a medical condition
— it's a political side effect of
oppression. Anybody who is oppressed,
whose expression is inhibited, will
end up depressed. So the whole country
was depressed. If anybody heard you
speak critically of the regime, the
secret police would knock on your door
at 3 AM and you'd end up in Siberia.
People were terrified.
How did you end up in Toronto?
When I was 16 my Father arranged
for a guy to sneak me through the
border to Austria. The Iron Curtain
was still down, the revolution was
defeated, so the borders weren't open
anymore. I escaped between Christmas
and New Years. I had to have a white
sheet around me so I wouldn't be
seen from the watch towers, there
were dogs barking... It was all very
exciting and dangerous.

Left: Portrait of Andrew Feldmar in Wine Hemp Shirt, 2007

What happened once you got to Vienna?
Vienna was so overrun by Hungarian refugees I couldn't even find a place to sleep. After three sleepless nights I negotiated with the policeman to take me to jail so I could have a good night's sleep. Then I found the British were recruiting for coal miners so I went England where they started to teach us English. Before I could get down to the mines, International Red Cross took me to Toronto where I had family.

What was it like being in Toronto?
It was good. I always felt like an alien in Budapest. I didn't feel I belonged, felt out of place — a strange feeling to have in the same apartment you've lived all your life. When I arrived in Toronto I was finally actually out of place, so I felt much saner.

How did you learn to speak English?
In order to learn English I started to read all sorts of things. I read everything by D. H. Lawrence, Lawrence Durrell, Henry Miller... I learned a lot from literature. I used to walk around with a dictionary. English grammar is fairly simple, but there is an enormous vocabulary. I had to learn about ten words a day, otherwise people thought I was stupid. If you don't speak the language people think you're dumb or deaf. People would talk slow and loud to me when that wasn't the problem at all.

How did you do at school?
The education system in Hungary was a lot better than in Toronto. I couldn't speak English but I got perfect marks in math, algebra, geometry, and trigonometry. I was also pretty good in physics and chemistry. They started to think I was some kind of mathematical genius. After completing grade 10 I told them I wanted to skip grade 11 and 12 and go straight to grade 13. I told them I'd learn English over the summer and that I'd rather fail grade 13 several times than go through the other grades. And to the credit of the principal he let me try it and I passed.

And you decided to pursue mathematics in university?
Mathematics was good while I was afraid of everything and was confused. It's so systematic, so clear. Whether you're right or wrong, there are no shady areas, it's all black and white. That was reassuring to me. Plus I didn't need any equipment or anything, all I needed was paper and pencil and I could amuse myself. It was as much an escape from interpersonal emotional reality as television could be. But by the time I felt a little more safe in the world and could speak better English, I wasn't interested in mathematics anymore, I was interested in what was going on with people, what was going on between us.

How exactly did you become introduced to psychology?
After my second marriage failed, I went into therapy for the first time.

You were married twice?
Yes. My first marriage broke apart after three and a half years, and my second marriage after three and a half years as well. I was totally oblivious as to why, and I thought it was the women who were impossible. I was also very upset, so I went into therapy. Early on, the psychoanalyst pointed out that the pattern was because at the age of three and a half all my connections were broken and the pain was such a surprise that I repeated it. He said I was somehow proud of being able to make people leave...the drive for mastery and the compulsion to repeat. When I realized he was right, I dropped mathematics. I thought: this is much more interesting.

How did you end up pursuing psychology formally?
I saw an ad that the University of Western Ontario was seeking a computer programmer in the Psychology department — a joint appointment to do programming for which they would help you get your Masters in Psychology faster than anyone. I got my Masters in two years without ever taking any undergraduate courses.

What was the computer program you had to write?
I had to write a program that would analyze the transcripts of initial psychiatric interviews and come up with a diagnosis that matched a psychiatrist's diagnosis, just from what the patients said.
That sounds kinda ridiculous.
It turned out to be, yes, but with one exception: I could predict with 100 percent accuracy who would be diagnosed an alcoholic. The algorithm was very simple — I just counted up how many times alcohol was mentioned and if it was mentioned more than twice the guy was an alcoholic.
Not much science there.
Right. I came from hard sciences. Here was psychology pretending to be a science whose aim is to predict and control human behavior. I thought: good luck!
Because you knew what science actually was.
Yeah. Psychology in the universities is based very much on statistics. When I was writing my thesis, you couldn't write a thesis without the use of statistics. You had to show that some result was statistically significant. I almost got my PhD for Mathematics in statistics, so I knew that they were misapplying that information. You can't use statistics for human beings — human beings are unpredictable.
Did you start working with psychedelics at the University of Western Ontario?
Well, my supervisor came from Regina, which in 1966 was the world center for psychedelic research. Duncan Blewett, the head of the Regina University Department of Psychology was a bright eyed, sparking acid-head. They wrote wonderful research, great literature, very inventive studies. They did group therapy where they would lock themselves in for 24 hours and everybody would take LSD. All the avant-garde experimentation in psychedelics started in Regina.

Was it legal?
It was all perfectly legal at that time. At a certain point my boss said, "I'm not gonna do this stuff anymore, are you interested?" I didn't know what I was saying yes to, but I definitely said yes. I usually say yes to things that I don't know anything about.
Had you tried any other drugs before?
No, never. I had my first LSD session right there. There was no interaction. He was sitting there reading a newspaper and I was tripping.
How does a psychedelic help psychology?
Duncan Blewett wrote a book called The Frontiers of Being where he says that what the microscope is to biology, the telescope is to astronomy, LSD is to psychology.
He was saying that LSD was a technology that allowed for the science to progress?
That's what was in the air. In Vancouver around that time there was a hospital called Hollywood Hospital that specialized in LSD therapy. It was probably one of the few hospitals in the world like that. You could fly in, they would give you a huge dose of LSD, 1,200 micrograms, and you would be cured you of your alcoholism.

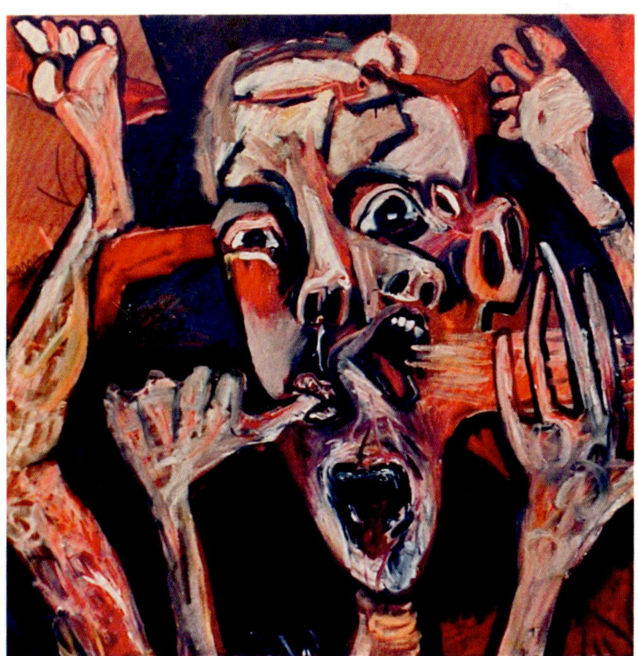

Excesses, 1986.

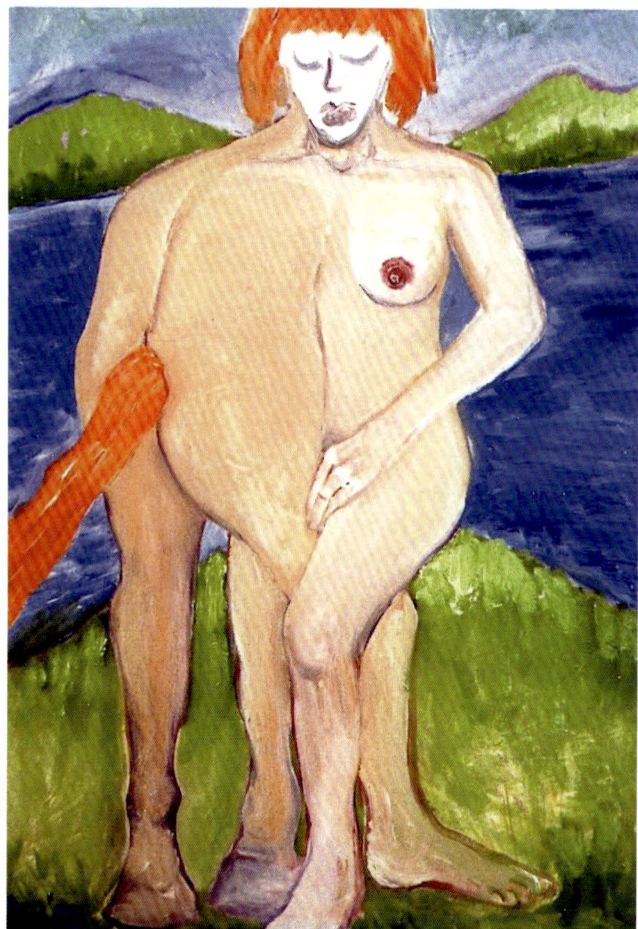

Iris Prays, 1986.

Hollywood Hospital was for alcoholics?
It was used with other drug
addictions, as well. Apparently the
CIA and other organizations from
the United States came there for
creativity training.
**It sounds like a very innocent
period.**
I was very lucky to have been there.
Then because of the excesses of
Timothy Leary, suddenly it was over
and dangerous.
**What can one learn from taking LSD
multiple times?**
LSD is one of those drugs where,
depending on the dose, when you
come back to an ordinary state of
consciousness you may not remember
much that happened. You may have a
vague memory that fantastic things
happened, but it's hard to bring back
those discoveries into an ordinary
state. In literature it's referred to
as state specific memory. Sometimes

with alcohol it happens — you get so
drunk that the next day you don't
know what you did until you get drunk
again.
**Or even just the feeling that pre-
occupied you.**
Right. The drug I'm working with now,
MDMA, is not like that. With MDMA,
whatever you discover while it's
lasting stays with you. You don't
forget it, it's not state specific.
The information transfers to your
normal state of consciousness.
**So MDMA is a lot more effective than
LSD?**
For therapeutic purposes, absolutely.
There are more and more instances in
the established medical community
where it is discovered that the use
of psychedelics speeds up therapy.
How do they make therapy shorter?
The essence of therapy is really
that everybody's PTSD: all the
varieties of diagnosis and labels
are essentially varieties of post-
traumatic stress disorder. Nobody
suffers, nobody is crazy if they
weren't hurt. So if you have been
hurt, sooner or later you have to
mourn and grieve of how you have been
hurt. But in order to get there, you
have to be out of survival mode.
The way that happens is with your
therapist: you establish some measure
of safety, security, and trust. For
some people that can take years.
Because if you were ripped off, if
you were hurt, if you were raped, if
you were abused, if you don't trust
people, why would you trust your
therapist, behind whose face there is
your abuser?
**And psychedelics speed up this
process of creating trust?**
What I found with LSD is that
suddenly all defensive habits would
disappear. I could trust somebody who
is trustworthy. I didn't have to be
paranoid anymore, my heart opened up,
I could suddenly feel safe enough to
mourn and grieve what happened to me.
What about bad trips?
If you look at any of the literature
that's worth reading, there's three

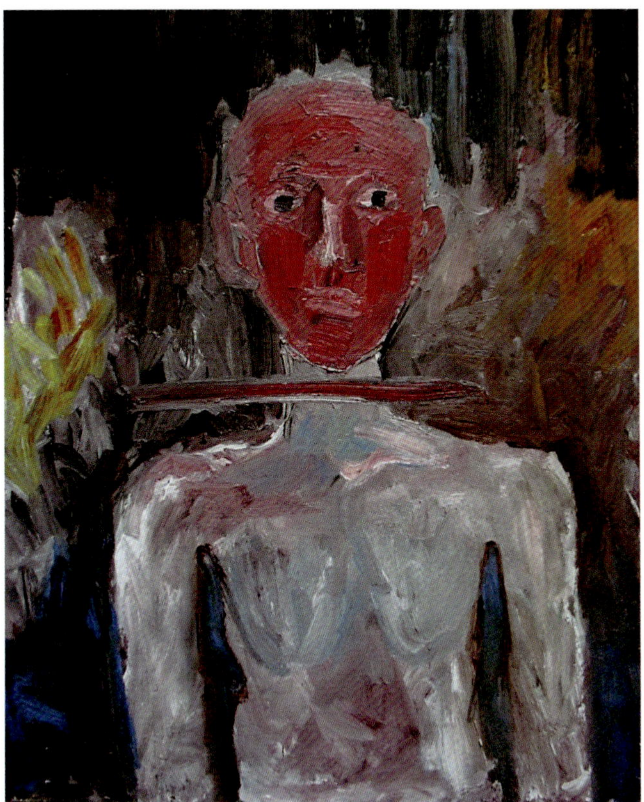

Hothead, 2003.

elements to a trip: the drug, the mindset, and the setting itself. Bad trips happen because of the setting or the mindset — it's never the drug. Bad trips are interactions between the person who's tripping and an unprepared, insufficient setting that can't support the person.

What happened after you got your Masters degree?

I got a two-month fellowship at UBC in psycholinguistics. When I came out I fell in love with Vancouver. I heard on the radio that they were looking for volunteers at the brand-new crisis center. I was one of the first ones to be trained to be on the phones with people who were suicidal and wanted to talk to somebody.

Did you enjoy that work?

I really enjoyed talking to people. The only frustrating thing was we weren't supposed to meet them face-to-face. I always wanted to meet them. That opened my mind up to the possibility that maybe I could be a therapist.

How did you pursue that?

I ended up getting a job as a Clinical Psychologist at the Health Center without any training in clinical psychology. You couldn't do that now. The head of the team said he was actually glad I had no training, because he didn't have retrain me — I could just learn from experience.

What kind of work were you doing?

Working with children. My supervisor believed that starting with children would teach you everything because they were guileless. So the father would see the psychiatrist, the mother would see the social worker, the children would see me. Then we would have case conferences.

What was it like working with kids in contrast to adults?

Fantastic. They were so honest. If you give them a sand tray with lot of little toys they'll play out the family dynamics. They basically tell you everything without even being aware that they are telling you their world. They play out their anxieties, fears, difficult situations. Taking them seriously and listening to them was very instructive.

Were there ever instances where you were concerned?

There was a kid who was labeled autistic. When I made a home visit, I found that the parents were crazy, not the kid. The father put the bed up near the attic, and at night he nailed a wooden plank on the crib so the kid couldn't crawl out while they slept in the basement. And the kid was labeled sick.

Did you eventually begin working with adults?

Once I began working with couples and families I realized that I was projecting my own family onto them.

How would you project?

I always made an alliance with the mother and fought with the father, which was my background. Despite my best intentions I kept on getting sucked in. At that point I realized I needed more training so I quit.

Is that how you ended up apprenticing with R. D. Laing?
Yes. There were two people who I thought I wanted to apprentice with — one was Erich Fromm, a Marxist psychologist, and the other was R. D. Laing. Both of them appealed to me because neither made the mistake of saying your suffering is something wrong within you. Both of them said if you're suffering it's because somebody's treating you badly.

How were you able to meet them?
It happened that in 1974, early in the year, both of them appeared on a circuit here in Vancouver. I got to hear and be with both of them. In 15 minutes I knew I couldn't work with Erich Fromm. Even today I really appreciate his writings, but as to personal interaction, I couldn't handle it. On the other hand I hit it off with Laing. By September my family was in London so I could start working with him.

Can you speak a little more about how Laing differentiated himself from the general psychiatric community?
Some people mistakenly call him an anti-psychiatrist. Whenever he was confronted with it he said he was a true psychiatrist and the others he fought against were anti-psychiatrists. He took his Hippocratic oath as a doctor very seriously, the essence of which was to do no harm. His major accusation towards the rest of psychiatry was that his colleagues were doing harm and didn't want to hear about it.

He seemed like a pretty reckless personality though.
When he was a therapist he was very careful about not doing harm. When he wasn't a therapist he wasn't so careful. The patient pays the therapist to be mindful. It's work to make sure that I'm not going to unleash on you the worst in me. If you don't pay me then you're taking your chances. Having a meeting with Laing outside of the therapy room was a totally different experience than inside.

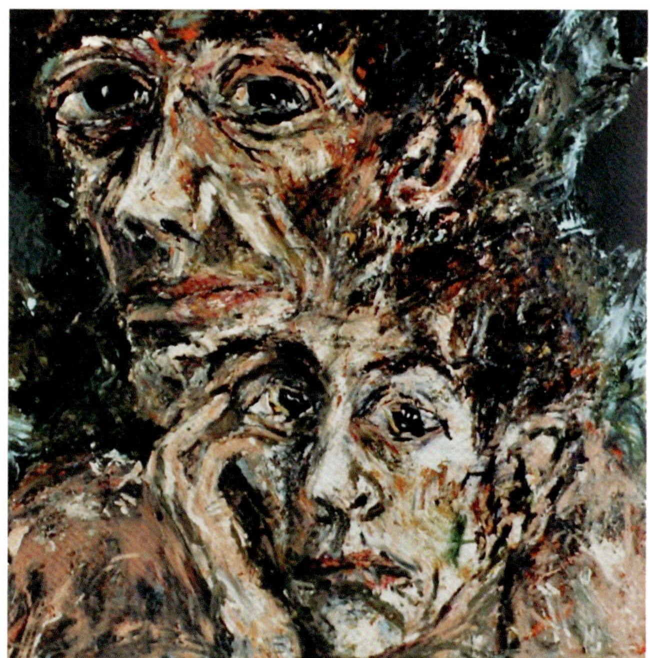

The Fall (Artist & Husband), 1987.

How much time did you guys spend together?
It was basically a year of intense togetherness — eight hours a week in various forms. Part of my training was that he would just call me up at any time day or night, saying here's a crisis, go out and deal with it.

How would he find these for you?
He was well known, so he would get crisis calls, and would just farm them out to me. I would just take a taxi to a given address and be precipitated into a situation.

What did you come out with from the year you spent with Laing?
Mainly self-confidence. I wouldn't have been able to say it at the time, but in hindsight I realized that you can't have self-confidence without somebody who you respect having confidence in you. It just so happened that Laing invested in me absolute confidence. At first I felt that he was mistaking me for someone else. It's almost like he was focusing as if I were 6'2" while I was 4'2". By the end of the year I grew to where he was looking. He treated me as if I would find my way and I did.

What happened when you came back to Vancouver?

I started from scratch. I didn't want to work for anyone else. No nonprofit organizations or anything, just a private practice. I decided if in six months I could make as much money as we needed as a family, then it would be clear that the community needed me. If not I would go to New York, London, bigger cities that would maybe sustain me. If that didn't work I would just drive a taxi, because that's the next best thing. You get paid for sure, the meter is running, and there's opportunity for conversation. I didn't know whether I could make it or not but I was willing to risk the worst.

And you didn't have to leave Vancouver. What is your practice like today?

I just reduced the number of days I work with patients to two. On Friday's I make house calls, family therapy, couples therapy. Mondays and Tuesdays are dedicated to MAPS: Multidisciplinary Associations for Psychedelic Studies. Then at least two times for a couple weeks a year I go to Hungary where I'm running The Soteria Asylum — a safe place, especially for young people, to be rescued from being labeled and degraded and taking up being a mental patient as a career. We try to have five or six people living together who otherwise would be hospitalized. We wait out and support them until they move out of their crisis. None of us freak out, they can take psychiatric medications, or not, as they want to.

You also do a lot of public speaking when you're in Hungary.

I give talks, lectures to infect people with this way of thinking — that there is no mental illness. I speak about how to raise children without shaming and humiliating them, trying to introduce a different way of educating.

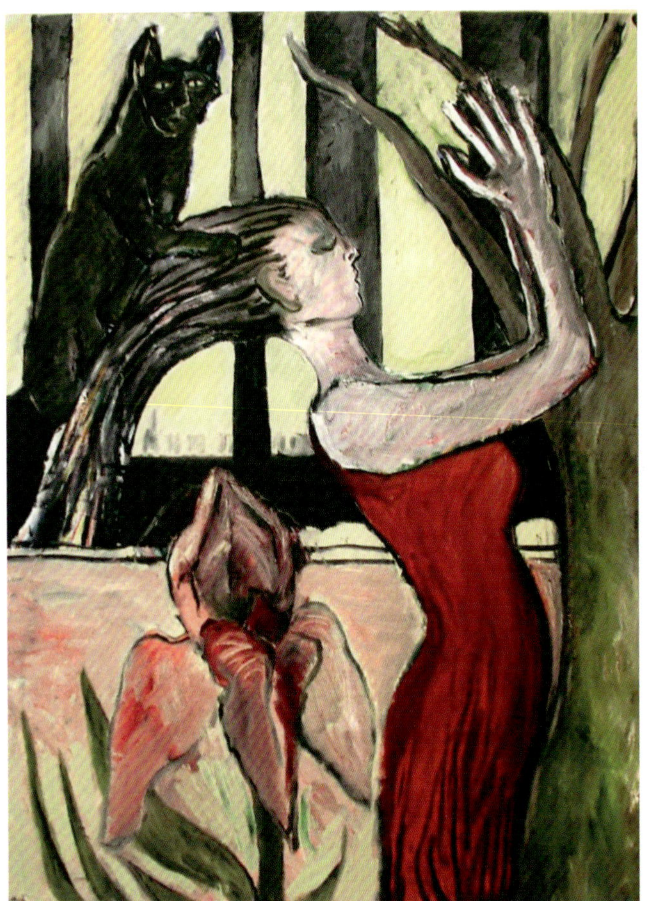

Iris Prays, 1986.

Last question: Your wife is a painter. What's your attitude towards art?

Well, if you look at it from an outsider perspective: my first wife was a cellist and a pianist. My second wife was a painter and a graphic artist. My third wife is a painter. So, obviously, throughout my life I have been moved to support and be around art. Where I live is filled with my wife's paintings — I feel like I'm living in the midst of luxury and visual stimulation.

Does it go beyond that?

There's really no explanation — I don't have any utilitarian attitude to it. It's just a form of expression. All art, from poetry to painting, points to that which is beyond language. I appreciate all forms of expression and I'm absolutely fascinated by the constant surprises revealed by creative people who are candid and spontaneous. ☺

Toby Feltwell

"What I think is interesting about street wear
is that it is basically negatively defined."

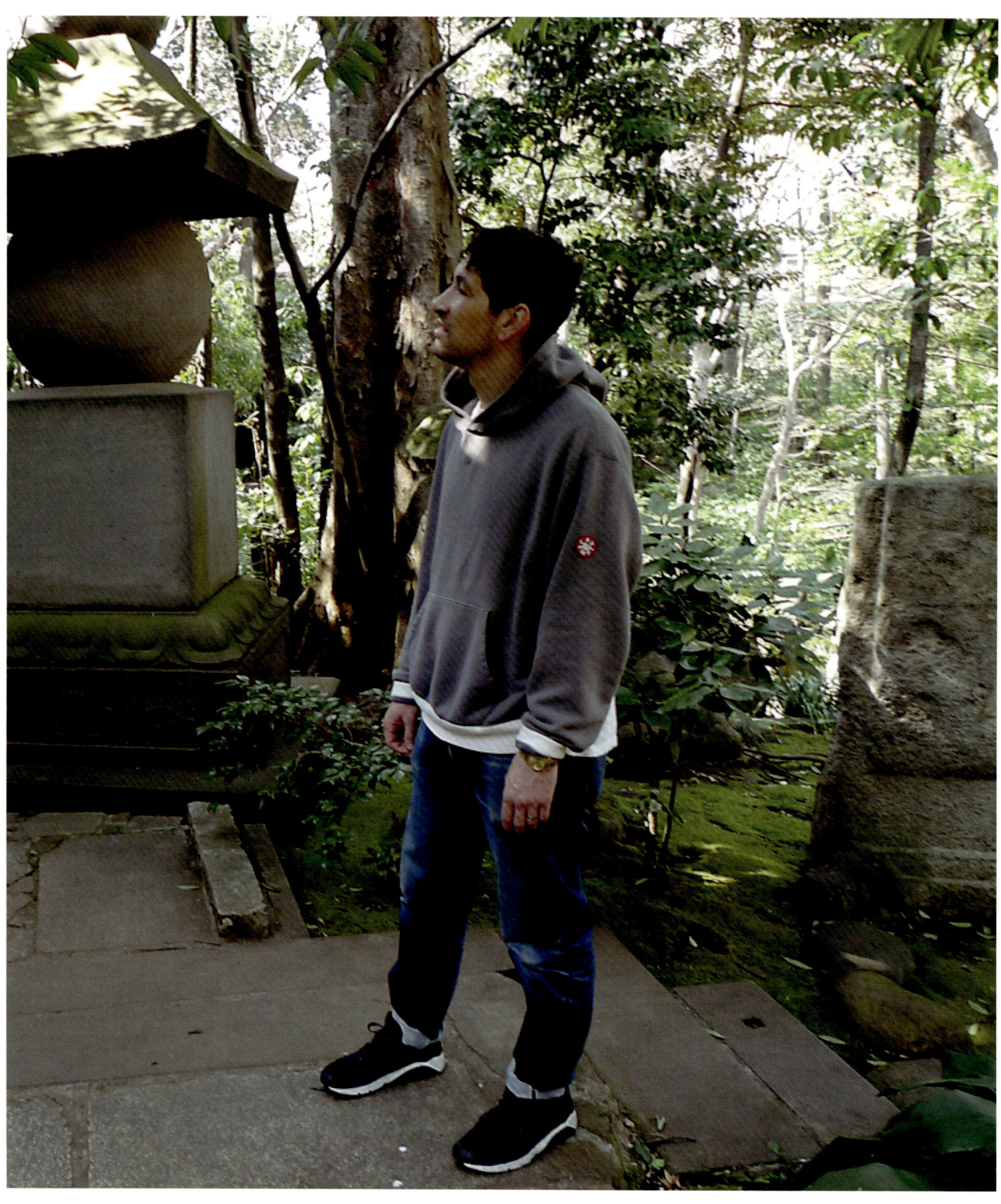

Interview by Asher Penn
Portrait by Will Bankhead

Toby Feltwell's career in music and street wear has existed largely behind the scenes. As an A&R for UK labels Mo' Wax & XL, his interest in Japanese culture found him brokering connections between East and West, leading to a longtime collaboration with Bathing Ape founder Nigo and the creation, alongside Pharrell, of Billionaire Boys Club. Today, Feltwell is the creative director of Cav Empt, the anomalous label started alongside veteran designer Sk8thg. With it's co-opting of standard markings found on almost all manufactured goods, C.E is a reminder of how the vernacular of street wear and branding can speak to the zeitgeist in a way that no other creative medium can.

Where were you born?
I was born in 1974 in Northamptonshire, England.
What was it like there?
Looking back it was quite dark and depressing. For most of my childhood Thatcher was in power so it was politically tense. Not a great time in Western civilization in general.
Were you in the suburbs?
Yeah, definitely. My parents were pretty young when they had me. They got married when my mum was a teenager. We lived in this small suburb with a lot of other young families. It was a first house kind of thing.
Did you skateboard?
I started skating when I was about 13. That was pretty important for everything else I got into. Back then, especially in England, skateboarding was kind of a package deal. You wanted to be as authentic as possible, so that meant listening to American punk bands that skaters listened to in California.
So you were getting American gear?
Yes, exclusively. Eventually I was only really interested in World Industries or something connected to that. We didn't really wear non-skate company products other than maybe some thrift clothes.

Were you going to concerts?
My friends were in a hardcore band so I was involved in that scene. I kind of grew up going to hardcore gigs. For years I was going to shows three or four nights a week. It was kind of a perverse thing to be into at the time because what was really happening in England right then was rave. The hardcore and punk scene was small and not particularly vibrant, but that's what my friends and I did.

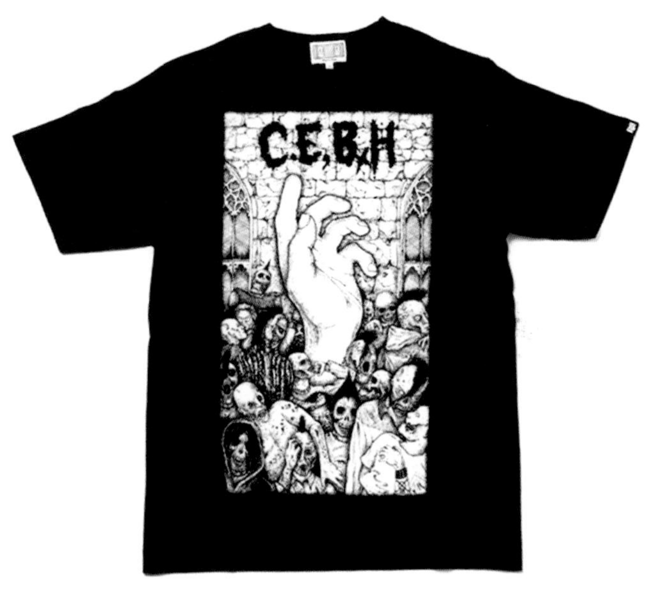

C.E x BOUNTY HUNTER "C.E.B.H" T-shirt, 2012.

Were you a creative kid?
I was good at drawing for my age and used to win prizes and stuff. Eventually we moved house to the countryside and I got a scholarship to do art. Part of the deal was that I was supposed to study painting at university but I didn't.
Why not art?
I went to interviews at a few universities for art, but they just weren't that interesting to me. I figured that if they weren't going to actively teach me something, and if I was going to carry it on, I could just do it myself. I ended up studying English Literature. I'm a sucker for praise and the guy that was in charge of the department thought I was good at it.

Images courtesy Toby Feltwell

Were you a good student?
I didn't really spend much time in college. It was a bit dull, to be honest. The kids there seemed like they wanted to flock together and make a new circle of university friends, which I wasn't really into.

Where did you hang out?
I spent most of the time hanging at Slam City Skates. My friend Andy Hartwell was the manager and it was a good vantage point to just see what was going on and who was around. You could just sit down and hang out for hours, you didn't have to buy anything. I met a lot of people through Slam.

Did Slam City Skates sell Japanese street wear?
Yeah, they did. They were probably the only store in London that stocked Good Enough and Bathing Ape when they started.

Were you into it?
Difficult to say, really... It didn't seem 100% authentic and I was kind of prejudiced against fashion that wasn't somehow connected to skateboarding. But it was interesting. You did somehow get that feeling of a global network of cool dudes.

Were you aware of Harajuku?
You'd see pictures of Hiroshi in i-D magazine. We all kind of knew what was going on. I went to Japan the first time when I was 20, so by that stage it all became quite apparent.

How did you learn to speak Japanese?
I got a friend to teach me some basics. It's easy enough to pick up. I was 20 years old and didn't have much to do. When I came back from Japan for the first time, having had the experience of going there, I could actually have more meaningful conversations and interactions with my Japanese friends in London, so I just kept it up.

How did you first hear about Mo' Wax?
There was a strong connection between Slam City Skates and Mo' Wax. I wasn't a huge fan, but I was friends with Will Bankhead, who was doing graphics for them.

How did you end up working there?
I left college and had no idea what to do. I was just going for really depressing job interviews. I wasn't interested and they weren't interested in having me. Will Bankhead told me to talk to Andy Holmes who had been at Slam and was the label manager at Mo' Wax at the time. The label had been signed to A&M Records, and they needed somebody to come in for a junior position.

What was your actual job?
I was basically sending out promos and doing dogsbody work. It was fun, though. You got records which you could trade or sell if you were stuck for money. I wasn't totally behind everything they were putting out, but they did put out some good jungle remixes. I was really into jungle — which made the work kind of legitimate to me. It was a pretty relevant place to be, given what I was into.

How did your position change over the years while you were there?
Eventually James Lavelle started trusting me to do more creative stuff like commissioning remixes and working with artists. Also because I could speak Japanese, I was helpful on that side of things. James was

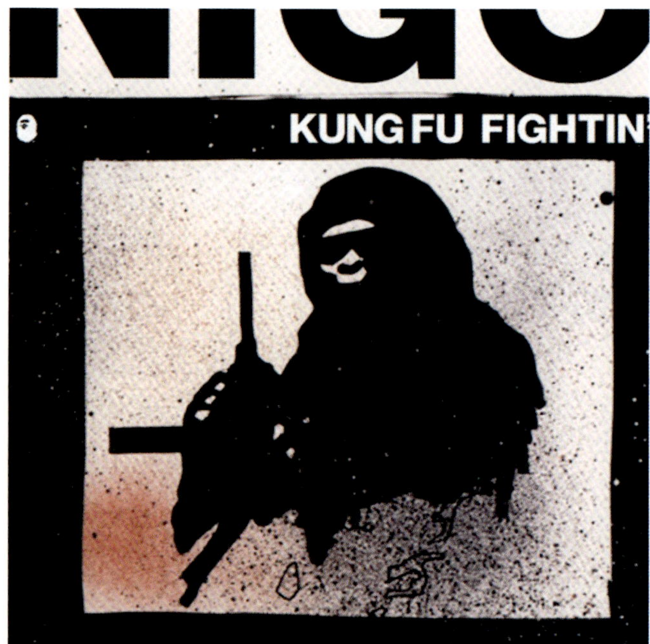

Kung Fu Fightin', Nigo, Mo' Wax, 2000.

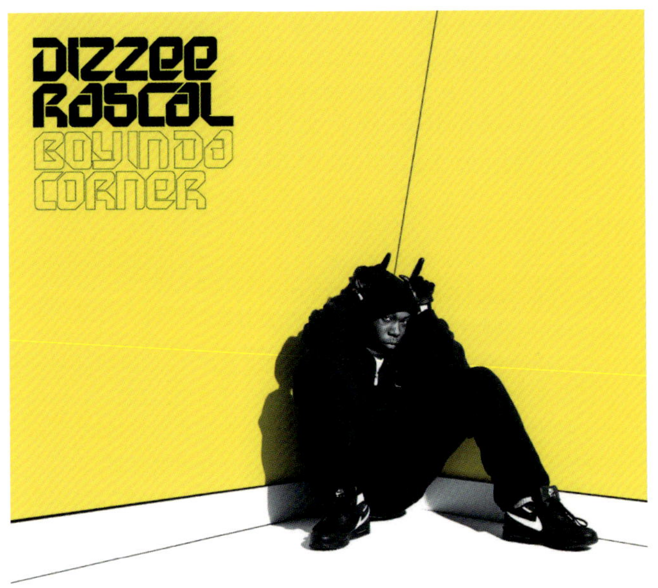

Dizzee Rascal, I Luv U, XL Records, 2002.

always interested in strengthening the connection and liked going there. I was making quite a lot of trips to Japan, looking after his connections. Eventually I took on more of an A&R role which eventually became label manager.

You ended up working at XL too, right?
Yeah. Basically Mo' Wax had never really had financial success. I mean, the DJ Shadow album sold well, but other than that it was just a red number on the balance sheet. This was during a period of a lot of consolidations and James was looking at alternatives to getting dropped. There was no way he could go back to being independent, so it needed some kind of support. XL seemed to be the best option.

How did you end up signing Dizzee Rascal?
When we started talking to Dizzee Rascal it was pretty clear that James wasn't going to be into it: although I played it to him, it wasn't what he was listening to. We were kind of concerned about being saddled with the Mo' Wax baggage cause we could see the relationship with XL getting dysfunctional. I asked Richard Russell if it would be cool for us to just do some stuff ourselves and put it out under XL without the Mo' Wax logo. We just kind of defected. That was really the end of Mo' Wax story an active record label.

That Dizzee Rascal record was a huge success.
There's always been moments in the UK underground scene when everything aligned and everybody saw into the same thing. It was pretty underground, but the underground was big. A lot of people knew who Roll Deep were and we probably found out about it relatively late.

By this point you were studying law, right? How did that start?
I got kind of bored of what I was doing day to day at Mo' Wax. It was fun but very low pressure. I didn't get paid much, but it was survivable. I needed to do something new.

What interested you about law?
I kind of looked up to the lawyers that we worked with in the label. They had a skill that other people didn't have. The basic knowledge that you need to operate a record label could be learned in half a day. With law you actually had to go and study for it and as a result were useful and sort of respected. They also acted pretty cocky because they knew that they were around a bunch of people that didn't know what they fuck they were doing. That was quite attractive to me.

Did you do night school?
Yeah, and the college of law was three minutes from my house which made it easy. I went from 7 till 10, two days a week for four years. It actually was quite a pain in the arse but I'm really glad I did it. I felt that I wasn't really using that many brain cells, working in the music business, so law school helped on that side of things.

What happened once you graduated?
I was supposed to leave XL and do two years of supervised work in a firm. In England that is the only way you can become a practicing lawyer. The legal director of XL's parent company was a really famous music lawyer and he gave me some good references. I got a training contract with a really good firm focusing on music law and copyright.

How did you end up working with Nigo?
Nigo had been asking me to go and work in Japan for a while — probably because he figured that Mo' Wax was on its last legs. I wasn't ever sure about living in Japan so I was reluctant to do it. Once I finished law school, knowing that I had to leave XL and go into this law thing eventually, I figured I would just do Japan for six months. I knew that Nigo would look after me and it was bound to be fun if nothing else.

Why did he want you to come to Japan?
He had just hit a plateau in his career. He'd accomplished more than anyone expected and he'd sort of run out of ambitions. He'd built an amazing house, the business was running fine, but he was in a bit of a funk. He's a very ambitious person and without having a direct, immediate goal, he lost the enthusiasm for a lot of things. I think my coming was kind of a good distraction for him.

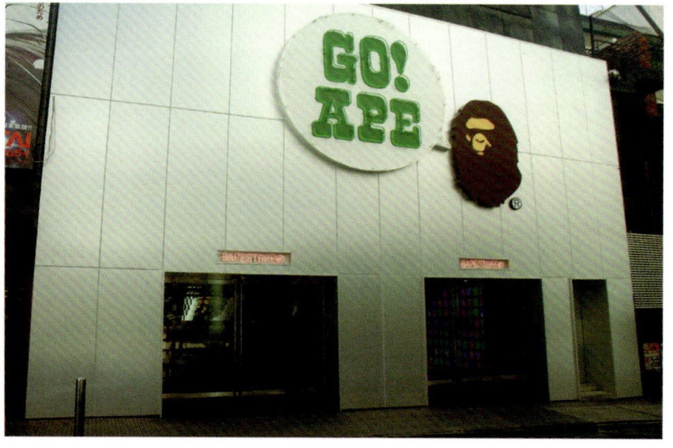

BAPE Store, Shibuya.

What would you guys do?
We spent a lot of time together not really doing work — just buying lots of records and talking shit all day. Buying records was super important, though. We would go record shopping twice a week which meant every record shop, checking out everything that was new. That was the key process while I lived in Japan; record shopping, driving around, talking about stuff, trying to work out what to do next.

Did he have any vague goals?
He had an ambition to open a store in New York, but was being discouraged by a lot of people in the company. There was a general feeling that they had come so far that they didn't want to try something that they might not be able to pull off and fuck up. Since opening a tiny shop and deciding to print some T-shirts BAPE had become a success, step-by-step, bigger and bigger. When you get to a certain level it gets more conservative and people are more worried about taking risks.

What kind of store did he want to make?
A lot of Japanese brands open a store in New York, Paris, or London just as a lifetime ambition. It doesn't really have any interaction or effect on the local population, it's just some kind of weird shop that everybody ignores and doesn't make money. Nigo didn't want to do it in New York if people didn't care about it. So when we were visiting New York we were forming these connections with Jay Z. We felt that maybe there was some possibility of building a store that we could actually open and people would know what it was. Then we met Pharrell and that accelerated everything.

Why Pharrell?
He was the first person that we met from that scene who really understood what Nigo was doing. Both of them needed to meet each other — they were on the same wavelength from the beginning. Within a few days of meeting, Pharrell asked Nigo if he would help with Billionaire Boys Club. Nigo volunteered to design it, which kind of took me by surprise. That became our whole new direction quite quickly.

Why did they have such a good rapport?
It wouldn't have worked if Nigo hadn't been so obsessed and immersed in what was happening in hip hop at the time, particularly with the language barrier. But if the references are the same you can have a real, deep understanding just based around that.

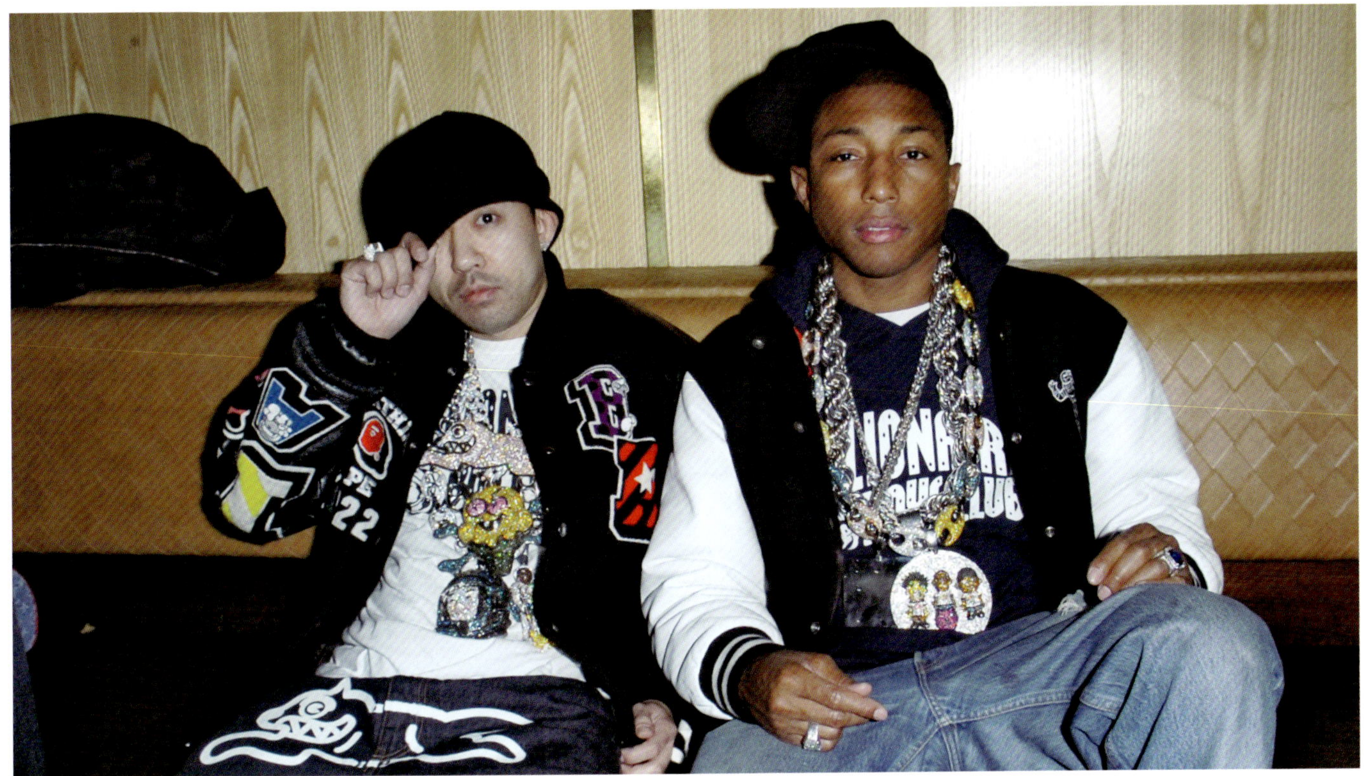

Nigo & Pharrell Present A Bathing Ape NYC 1st Anniversary Celebration, 2006. Photo: Djamilla Rosa Cochran, Getty Images

So you were translating, right?
I mean, obviously, I was traveling with Nigo helping him communicate, but I was also in on the plan. Pharrell had a very specific idea of what he wanted as a logo so I spoke to Sk8thg about it. Sk8thing drew it and Pharrell liked it which was kind of the acid test. We could interpret what he wanted and do it properly, it didn't just sound good, it really could work. And that's how it continued. I would get Pharrell's ideas and feed them back and get them made.

What about your legal work?
By the time a draft contract arrived from Pharrell's lawyers in New York I was about to start working at the law firm in London. It was handy timing cause I could just take over the contract negotiations for Nigo, which went on forever. The legal team in New York had never heard of this dude so they assumed that they didn't really need to take him that seriously. I was also locked into doing the law training for two years. When I eventually finished that, Nigo presumed I was just going to come back and start working with him, which I did.

What was your job in Japan?
When I came back to I began managing Bathing Ape's international business and the whole BBC operation. I was kind of responsible for all of it, everything from taking Pharrell's ideas and feeding them to everyone from designers to accounting. It was a staff of ten people, and Nigo was busy looking after BAPE generally. For most of the day-to-day stuff, it was down to me.

How did you stop working for BAPE and Billionaire Boys Club?
Nigo eventually sold BAPE to our Chinese distributor. I helped him with that sale, which was not really a fun process. It wasn't the original plan to sell when he did. As a part of that process, Nigo decided to get out of BBC too. He just wanted to have a more simple kind of life and just be friends with Pharrell and not business partners. It was quite complicated running the business between the U.S. and Japan.

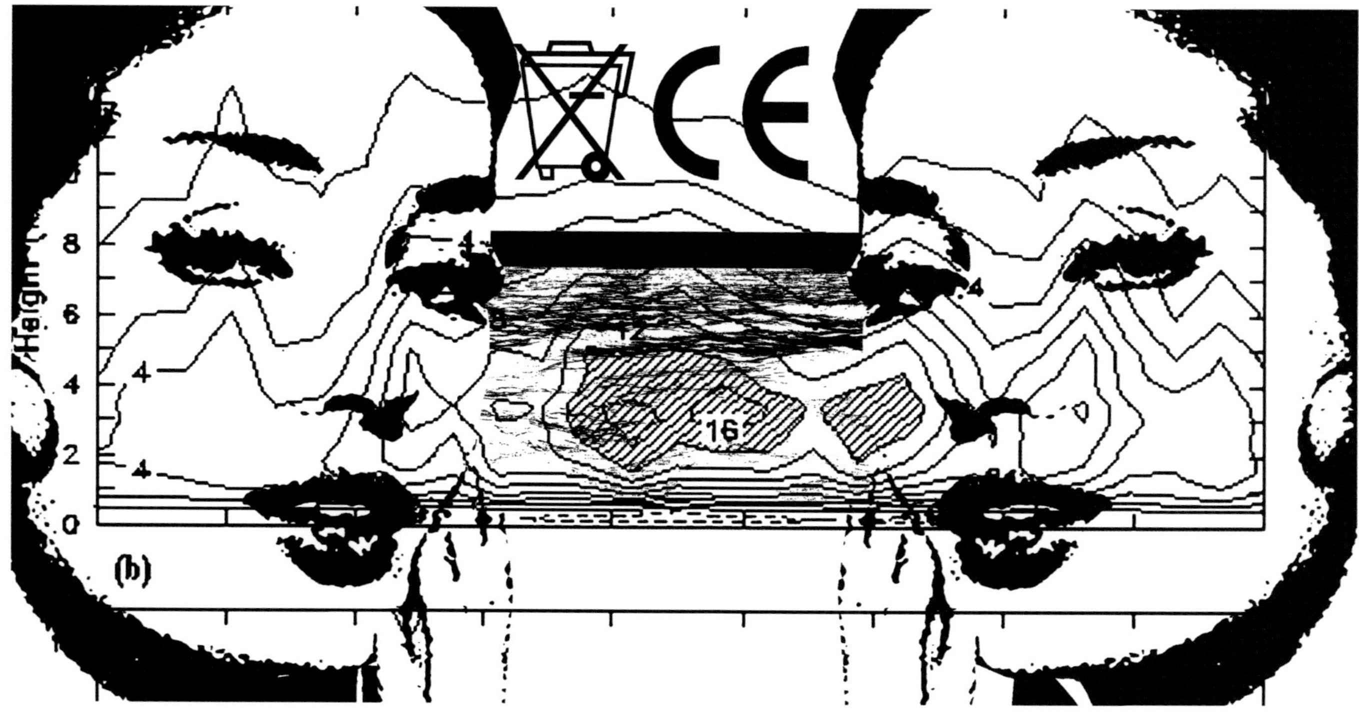

C.E Graphic, 2016.

Was this around the time that you started C.E?
I knew early on that the writing was on the wall for BBC & BAPE but Sk8thing and I were really kind of enjoying the process of how we worked together. I didn't want that to stop so starting C.E was the only way to ensure that.

What is it you like about working with Sk8thing?
He's a very interesting character. I find him easy to talk to. Of all the people in Japan that I met around that time, he was the one that would get my references.

What about the graphics?
The graphics themselves? I don't know. I guess they have that kind of authenticity. They look right in a way that is hard to explain. You can see why it's the output of a conversation but it also makes sense as a graphic.

And C.E was your first company on your own?
Yeah. Having the responsibility to stand behind something you created and say, "This is what I want to do," is something that none of us had had to face up to for a long time.

Where did you guys come up with the name C.E?
For some reason I had started reading Philip K. Dick books again. I had bought a Kindle and was looking for something light and easy to get me back into the reading habit. I think it was kind of back in people's minds — as the modern world seems to get closer to what he was talking about, it was strangely prophetic. Shin read it and he picked up on a character that has a Caveat Emptor tattoo, which he though was a cool concept. He took the name from there.

Caveat Emptor means "buyer beware".
Yeah. When I told some lawyer friends I was starting a brand called CE for Caveat Emptor, they thought it was brilliant, because it's a legal concept really. The basic position of commerce before consumer laws impose more obligations on the seller, meaning if you're buying something, then it's up to you to make sure you're getting what you're buying. It's a basic position of common law that's been modified to protect consumers over the years and has a heap of meanings when you apply it to a brand.

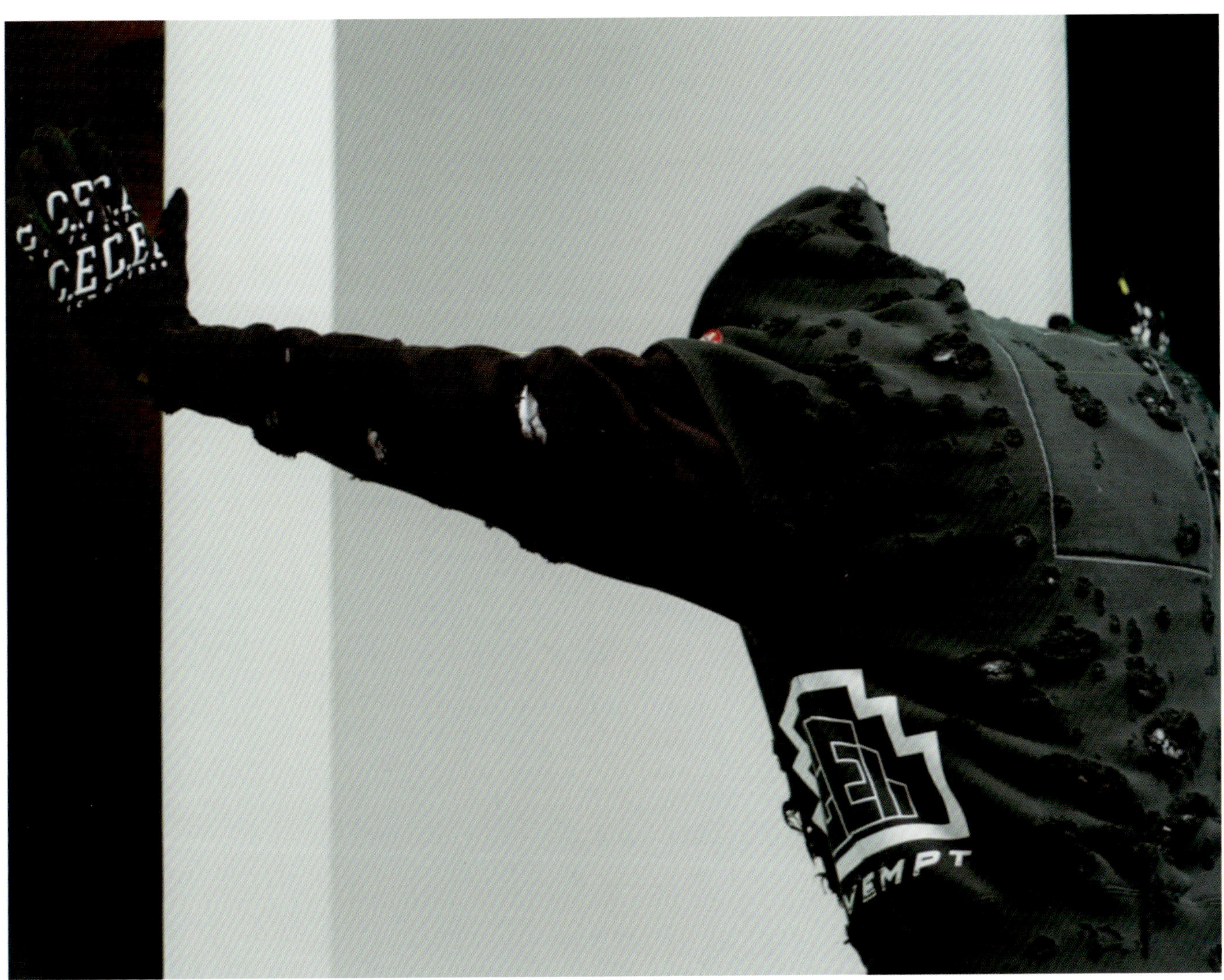

Actress, C.E SS14.

The marking CE is also ubiquitous. It's on the back of my phone.
That CE mark is a safety standard that allows goods to be imported into the European Community. Now that the world is a global marketplace, everybody wants to sell their products in Europe, but they have to comply to certain safety regulations and a CE mark shows that they're compliant. We like the idea of reverse adopting all these other products that are everywhere. You don't notice until somebody points it out and then you start seeing it everywhere.

It can make you kind of paranoid, which is pretty cool for street wear.
What I think is interesting about street wear is that it is basically negatively defined. It's about what you can't do. This changes with every generation but the idea is that you want to turn up to meet your mates and they gonna go, "That's cool." They're not gonna laugh at you for being totally irrelevant or outlandish. If you push it too far, then it's not street anymore. And it depends on what street you're on. The concept of it being a kind of peer pressure aesthetic is quite important to keeping it street wear, I think. People who are proper fashion designers who are influenced by street wear are often looking at street wear as an aesthetic phenomena rather than a social phenomena — and the social aspect is my experience of it. ☺

Doc Martens

"My walk home is sacred."

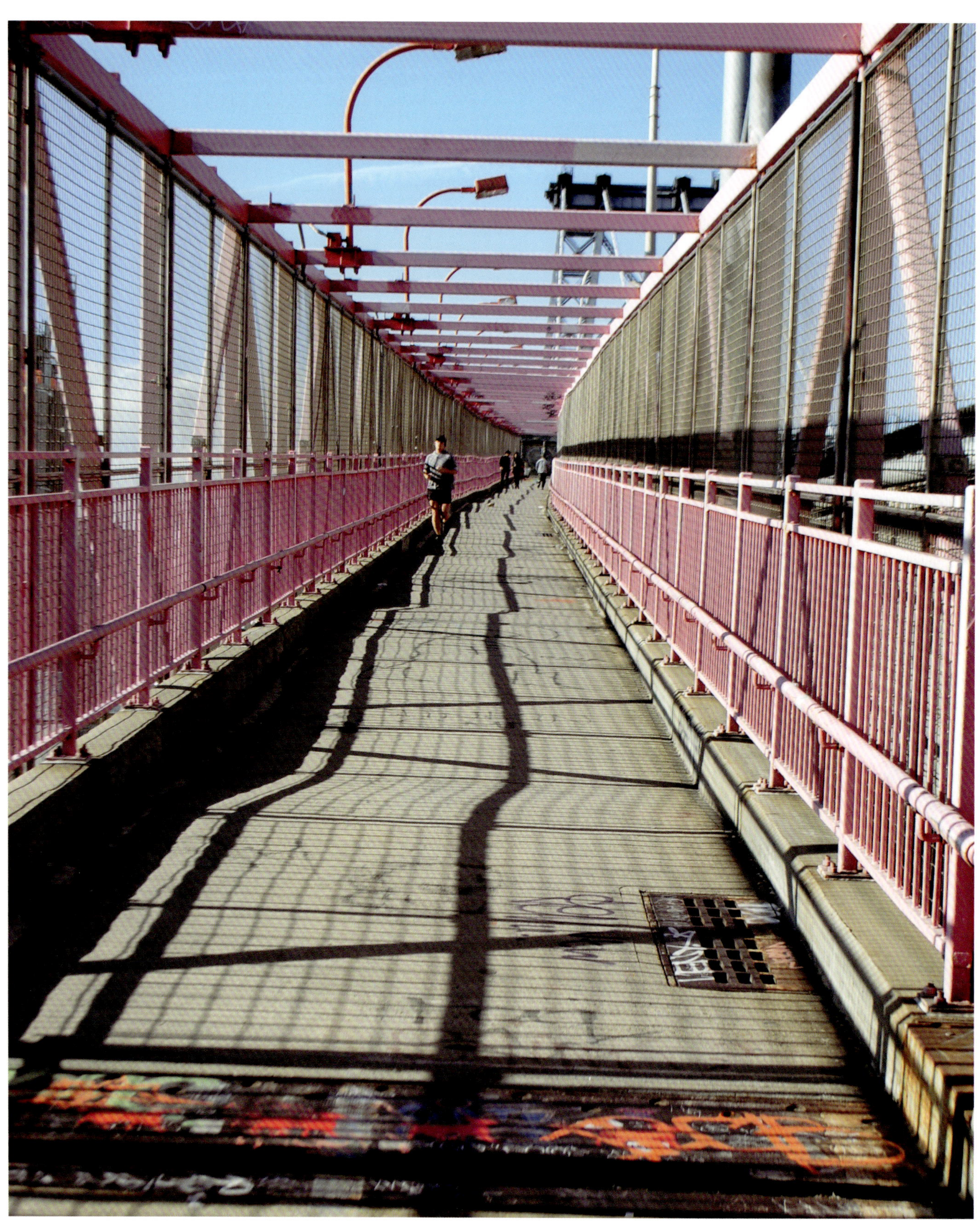

By Al Bedell

I tell people I like the month of February because it's my Birthday Month — "the pinkest, cutest, most Heart-Shaped month of the year."

My whole Thing is cardigans, hair bows, oysters in the afternoon, cats and puppies. I maintain a host of artificial signifiers in order to project a naive, celibate, and "Pure" persona, but I wish it could be real.

Telling passive-aggressive jokes, being quirky, going out without makeup — "This is my new Pinterest board about Tea Parties." Pleated mini skirts and loafers "in the club," hiding in the bathroom at a rave like a timid girl.

I am a timid girl. I'm not strong and I am afraid of everything. I'm even afraid of my best friends sometimes. If I could live in my Country Strong Pinterest board based on the Gwyneth Paltrow movie, I would. Illusions of pearl necklaces, fancy desserts and knitting patterns make me feel safe. I only want to feel safe.

Chastity is the thing I "value," or the thing I want people to believe I "value." I guess I don't really value anything.

I wish I were a child still. I wish I had a childhood abundant with cupcakes, dinner parties, lawn chairs. I wish I were a porcelain doll on a shelf, occasionally brushed by a maid with a feather duster.

February is the shortest month and I'm grateful for that. I like brevity. In such a brief month you can be whatever you want.

You can change your persona, your entire existence, if you feel like it. You can do whatever you want in 28 days.

I upgraded to Spotify Premium and fell back in love with music.

Lorde and Lana drenched my ears through my uncomfortable buds (I think my ears are abnormally shaped because all of my headphones hurt) during my Commuter Train to work and my Commuter Walk home.

5 days a week. 6 miles a day. Whatever.

My walk home is sacred. My tired feet deliver my hungover body through 14 neighborhoods, or six miles and two hours with Spotify Premium. I use my Walk to sync my playlists so I can listen to them on the train the next morning. The Walk is long but it allows me to cloud my relentless train commute with songs that I love.

A playlist titled Moody Girls is lengthened — Lorde, Lana, Fiona, Veruca, Cat P, Liz Phair. I have a significant Spotify Relationship with Liz Phair. Her songs about sex, men and Self Worth resonate with me.

"I wanna be Cool, Tall, Vulnerable and Luscious"

"Give me your Hot White Cum"

"It's nice to be Liked but it's better by far to get Paid."

Being a girl in New York isn't easy, and it's hardly fun, but you can make people believe it's glamorous — Gritty and Glamorous. It's totally okay to use men for money and it's equally fine to let men use you for sex. It's an exchange, a Buy and Sell situation. Strike while the iron is hot. Sex, Money, Glamour — New York City.

In NYC you have to be Hot, Cool, Determined, Well-Liked, and most of all, Resilient. Pinterest boards and fantasies of cotillions and spring picnics don't get you anywhere. It's nice to be respectful but it's better by far to be respected. And to gain respect, you need money. Shit Loads of Money.

I don't want these friendship brace-
lets or CZ studs in my ears. I don't
even want to love animals anymore. I
want to be hot and edgy, wear leather,
make money, outsmart men, take advantage of men. I'm sick of my butterfly clips, my Juicy Couture perfume,
my ballet flats and penny loafers. "I
only buy orthopedic shoes" I announce
to anyone who will listen. I want everyone to be aware of this Portrait of
Purity I'm trying to depict.

I bought orthopedic shoes on sale
once, another impulsive purchase to
make myself feel high for about 20
minutes. They didn't have my size so
I bought a pair a half size smaller.
They were marked down from $85 to $30.

Two hours later during my Walk home,
I had orthopedic blisters. I was
limping in $30 orthopedic flats that
were not even cute.

I may as well limp in shoes that make
me feel Strong and Resilient. I need
resilient shoes, shoes that demand
respect. Liz Phair wore Doc Martens
and I can wear Doc Martens too.
Bouncing Soles. Resilient. Made in
the UK. Made to Last. Country Strong.
I can limp for $200.

I just want a nice life for myself
and for all of my beloved friends.
We remind ourselves, everyday, that
this Struggle is worth it. You have
to struggle in New York. It's a thing
everyone talks about — it's trite but
true. Some of the truest things are
the most trite. Platitude feels Safe.
Strike while the Iron is Hot.

Whatsyourprice.com is a website for
Exchanges. Men reveal how much they
are worth and Young-Girls allude to
how much they should be worth based
on short bios with buzzwords like
'Ballerina, Yoga Addict, All Girls
School, Post-Grad, New to the City,
an Animal Lover, Great with Kids,
Whip-Smart, a Great Conversationalist, Wack Slut, Daddy Issues.'

In the 'Expectations for a First Date'
box I wrote 'Rest assured, someone's
gonna laugh.'

I tweet from my cubicle: 'Can I pull
off Doc Martens?' A resounding 'Yes, @_
YOUNGBABY_, yes.' $200 debt now.

Feeling Country Strong in my Doc
Martens, I go to work and write
about blouses for 8 hours (I'm a
catalog copywriter and I write about
clothing for 8 hours everyday.) Check
whatsyourprice.com and I receive some
offers: $41, $12, $99, $250. $250
eliminates the debt for my Doc's.

In just two hours, my shoes of
Resilience would be covered. I can keep
doing this, I can make rent, I can be a
Gritty Glamorous NYC Girl.

I make a new email account —
allymarie203@gmail.com; I'm Ally Marie
on this website and it doesn't matter
because men on whatsyourprice.com don't
care about your name.

They care about your photos and
"Conversational Skills" apparently.
"I'm Ally Marie, Young Baby, a Great
Conversationalist, I love animals and
architecture."

I sweat more than I usually do in my
cubicle as I prepare for my Reverse
Walk of Shame at 5:15 PM. I compose so
many future tweets in my head for my
first Paid Date. I want to make it seem
Gritty and Glamorous but I just feel
scared.

I'm not actually Pure, I'm wearing
Doc's, feeling resilient and about to
take a lonely man's money. I'm Whip
Smart and Country Strong. @_YOUNGBABY_
is a Struggling Edgy Bitch.

Of course it's raining. Even in
February, it's always raining in New
York. It adds to the allure of the
Glamorous Struggle. Sometimes I hope
it rains forever. Or just for the
next 28 days.

I want my Glamorous Struggle to be cloudy, veiled in snarky tweets and Spotify playlists and vodka and shit loads of rain. I don't want to remember it anyway. I promise myself that the struggle is worth it and it will be brief. My 30s will be truly glamorous (or just normal, content, comfortable, safe.)

From 34th to 52nd street I begin my Reverse Walk of Shame. I notice the backs of my ankles rubbing against my strong Doc's. "The rain will soften the leather," I think. I'm breaking my new resilient shoes in and it's just a brief struggle.

I'm early for the $Date (I'm always early) and my feet hurt — I haven't felt this kind of foot pain since I had to break in my first pointe shoes. "As an ex-ballerina, I love the Ballet, the Opera and Art!" I wrote in my whatsyourprice.com bio.

An Ex-Ballerina.

I was the youngest student to get pointe shoe privileges. I had 'Talent and Promise.' I wanted to be a ballerina — a porcelain doll — pink frills, butterflies, swans, tiaras, all of that. I was a dancer and dancers sacrifice their feet for beauty, perfection, validation. Those wooden shoes were going to make me stronger and more beautiful, delicate peach slippers ($95) made of satin and wood, designed to help me glide with elegance and control. It only takes a week to break pointe shoes in if you do it right, although some dancers take hammer and fire to their pointe shoes. Pointe shoes have to mold to your feet, to your movement. The shoes work for you once you train them. For one week, you're possessed by the agony of the shoe, but after that the shoes are yours. You are strong enough to bourrée across the floor on your tippy toes, supported by pointe shoes. You are in control and your shoes just support you.

"My Docs took three weeks to break in. It's painful but worth it in the end. And these boots will last for years. Best $200 I ever spent." I google 'how to break in doc martens' while I wait for my $Date to arrive.

@_YOUNGBABY_: of course im early and of course it's raining

I walk into the lounge and apologize to the beautiful hostess for my attire. Everyone is wearing high heels and black dresses. I'm wearing a mini skirt and fresh Doc Martens.

Only a few minutes pass and I see my $Date, a sad old man just relieved of his finance job in midtown. I was sure to mention in my whatsyourprice.com bio that I work in midtown. It's convenient.

"Hi, I'm Ally." I can't believe I'm Ally Marie right now. Lying about my name feels more uncomfortable than my constricted, blistering feet. We sit on low, cushioned cubes.

He asks me what I do, what I've done, and what I like to do. It actually feels nice to have a human being feign interest in me for a little while. I lie, or maybe I don't, I tell him that my only dream in life is to travel. "I want to see the whole world!" Once I was told by a seasoned escort to seem as naive as possible. I don't think I want to see the whole world. I barely want to see my own world. I'm grateful for the fog and the rain.

He talks about his children (they're my age) and his wife (he loves her but they only fuck twice a month), and what he is looking for on whatsyourprice.com. He would like to pay me a weekly $500 to be his "Girlfriend," go out to eat and get a hotel room where he can "touch me gently." He says he doesn't want to cheat on his wife and he'd never fuck me, just touch and kiss me.

I order another martini cocktail
thing called The Trouble Maker and we
laugh about me being a Trouble Maker.
The Trouble Maker cocktail was $18.
By the time our 2 hour session/$Date
is over, I finish four Trouble
Makers.

I excuse myself and do poppers in
the bathroom. I call my best friend,
"Oh my GOD this is the easiest money
I've ever made!" She says she's going
to make a WYP account ASAP. High on
poppers, I tell her, "YOU MUST."

"I like you because you're not
another Young Girl. You can hold a
conversation and you make me feel
special." Rest assured, I'm a great
conversationalist/liar.

He reaches for his drink and knocks
the glass over. Fumbling to catch
it, the glass lands on the marble
floor and cuts his hand. His hand
is bleeding and I ask a gorgeous
waitress for napkins. I wrap some
napkins around his ring finger and he
holds my hand for what begins to feel
like 28 days.

We leave the lounge and find out
that we both smoke cigarettes even
though we both wrote that we were
"Non-Smokers" in our bios. He is
still holding my hand. I wish poppers
lasted longer. He takes my face into
his napkin-bandaged hands and starts
to kiss me as I try not to wince. I
let him kiss me in the February rain
for a few minutes, trying to focus
on my damaged feet. "I love these
fucking shoes," I play on mental
loop.

"Which train are you taking?"

"The A," I lied, "it's right down the
street." He says he wants to make
this a weekly Thing and I tell him
"That sounds so, so good." I kiss him
on the lips again. I want to inhale
more poppers.

Two hours, basically 28 days later,
I'm free to walk from 54th St back
to my Bushwick abode. I walk past
Grand Central and think about taking
the Metro North to my dad's house in
Poughkeepsie.

@_YOUNGBABY_: I want to be in a twin
sized bed and feel safe and warm

I never want to be touched again and
I miss my dad. My dad would cry if he
knew what I just did. He'd probably
even give me rent money.

With an envelope of $250 in my Coach
bag and Resilient $200 boots on my
feet, I continue to walk. In an
attempt to distract myself from the
tears welling on my cheekbones, I
focus on the liquid pain in my shoes.
I'm definitely bleeding. Good.

It's still raining and I'm only
on 42nd Street. My "Moody Girls"
playlist is on. I relish the cloudy
feeling that is empowerment and
defeat like it's brand new. My feet
hurt so badly but it's worth it.

I get to Delancey Street and decide
to pay $2.50 for the train. I have
just walked over 50 blocks, my feet
feel foreign and I have money to
spend. I sit down in the train and
watch everyone look at me. I know
they know. They know the exact type
of bullshit a Young Porcelain Doll in
new leather boots just got herself
into.

I get back to my house, untie and peel
the Doc's from my feet. My socks are
wet with blood. I throw my money on
the floor and stare at it. Then I pick
it up and hug it like a teddy bear.

Next morning I wake up with the
lights still on and arrive to my
job in midtown at 8:46 AM. I like
February because it is heart-
shaped and the pinkest, but, most
importantly, I like February because
it is the shortest. ☺

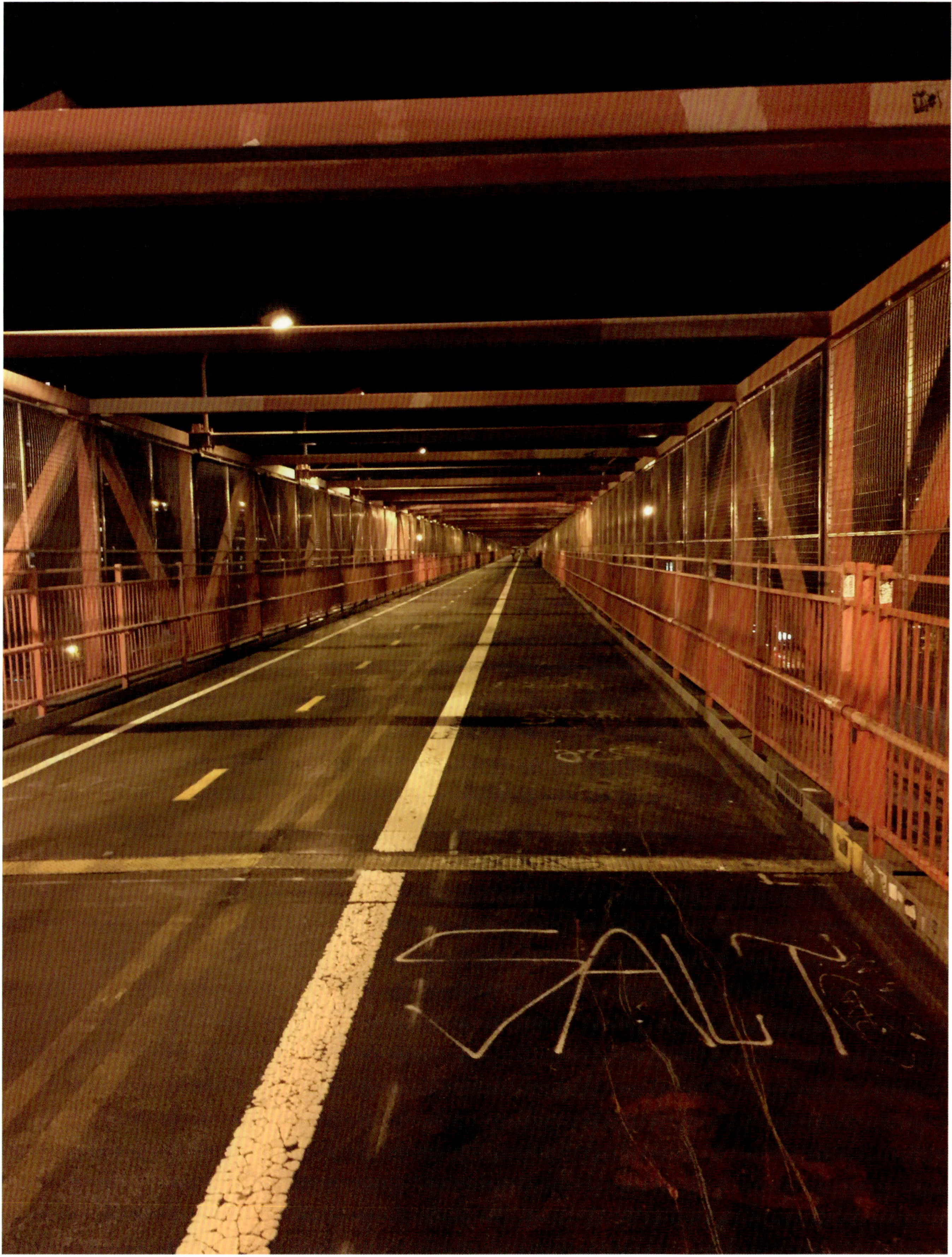

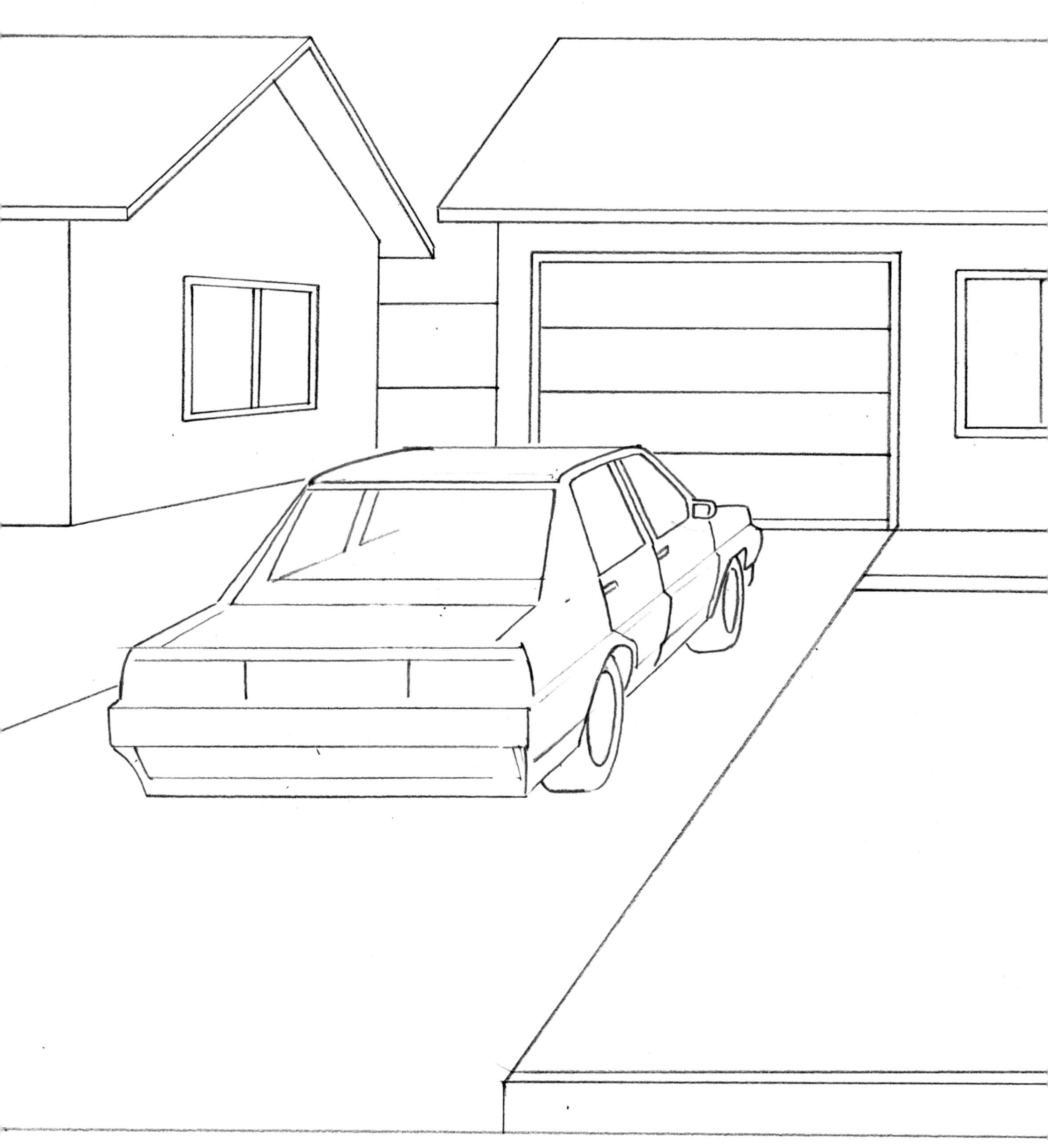

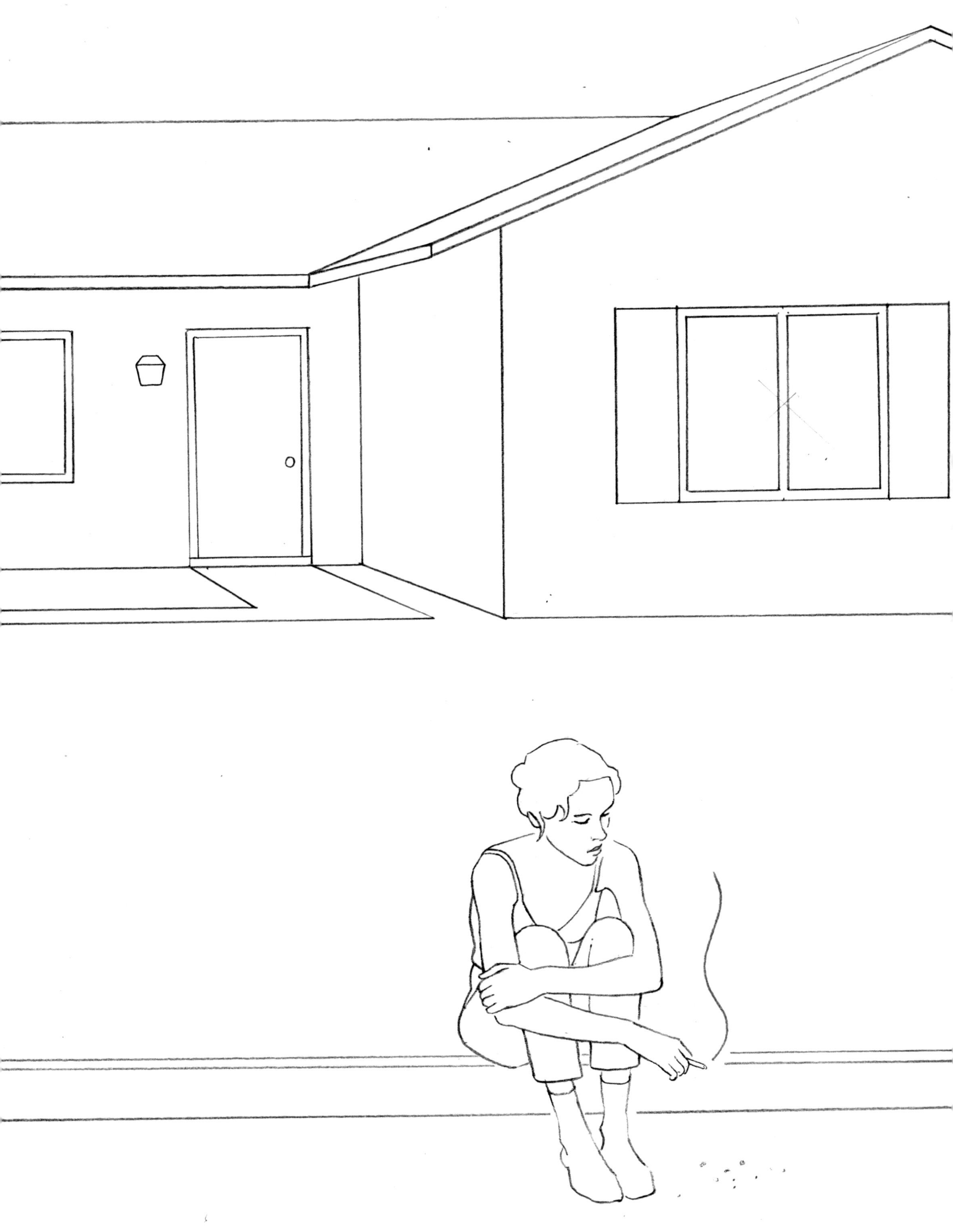

Olia Lialina

"Cyberspace is star backgrounds with blue
underlined links on them."

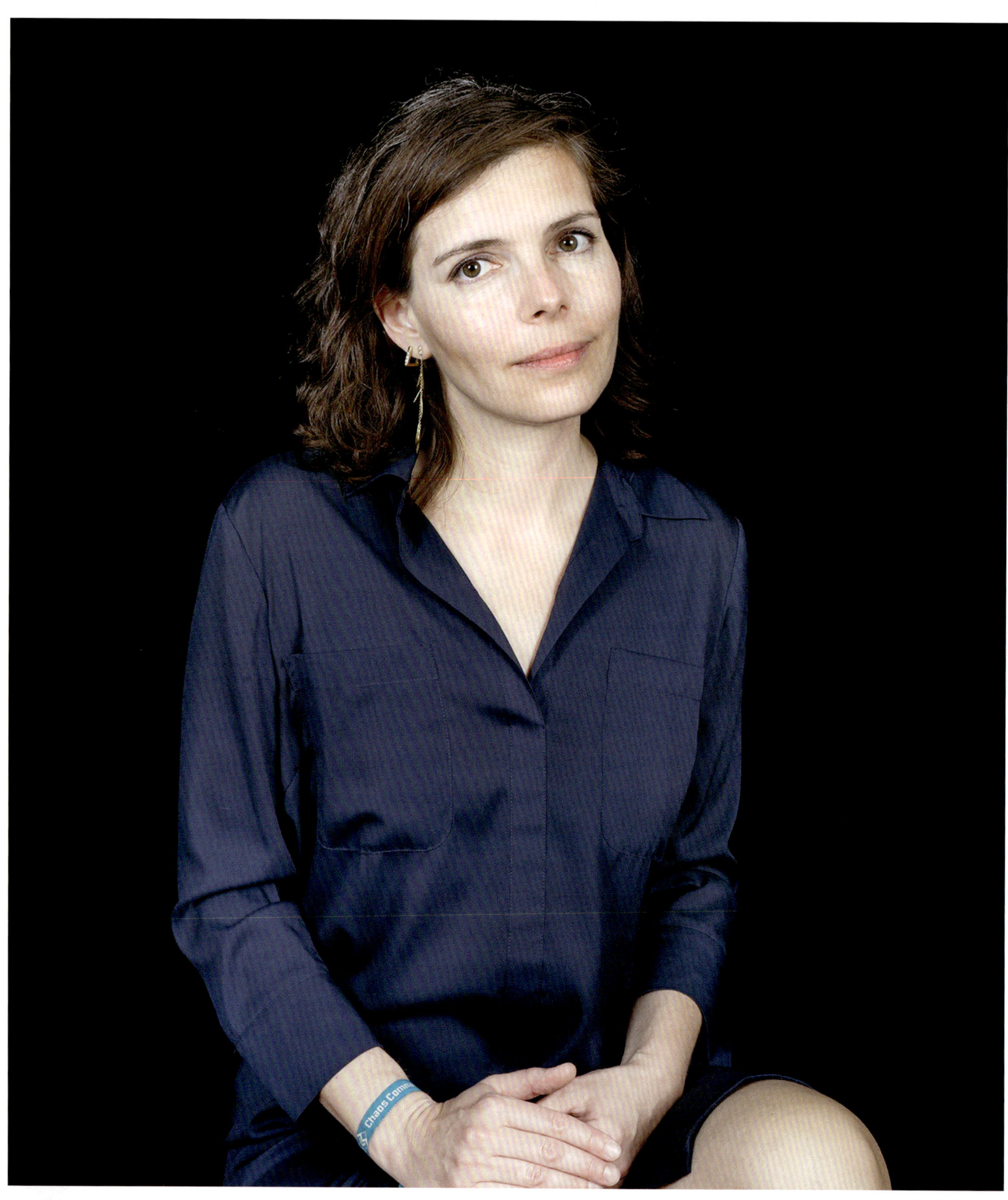

Interview by Jacky Connolly
Portrait by Natascha Goldenberg

Olia Lialina is a Russian-born net artist and professor of New Media at Merz Akademie Stuttgart. Her works are archived and available to view online at Art Teleportacia, Olia's web gallery. Her first seminal project, My Boyfriend Came Back From The War, is a cinematic, text and gif-based choose-your-own-adventure experience. She is also a prolific writer and theorist; her research focuses on the vernacular of the Internet and digital folklore. Recently, Olia's interrogation of this subject matter has been enriched by her and husband Dragan Espenschied's documentation of the GeoCities archive, One Terabyte of Kilobyte Age.

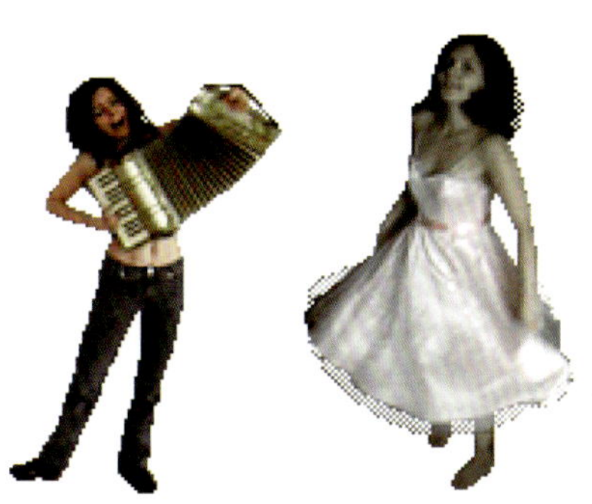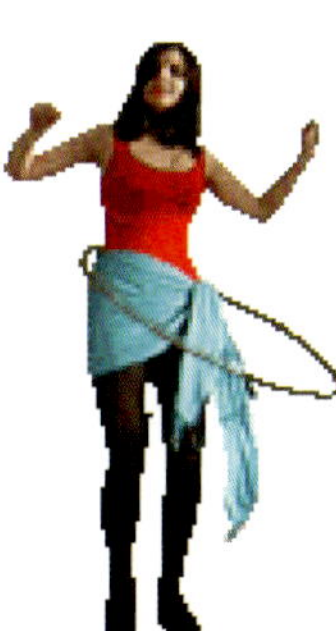

Animated gif Model, 2005.

What kinds of experiences did you have with computers before the Internet?
When I was a kid I was doing drawings on computer punch cards. My mother was a system programmer at a military institution, and she would bring home punch cards, not punched yet. Just pale blue, beige cards. It didn't have any meaning at that moment, it was just some paper.

Your mother was a programmer?
Yes, she wrote "apps" for automatization of control systems in Assembler and later PL.

Did you have a computer growing up?
No, I was really late with computer literacy in general. I was studying journalism and typography at Moscow State University and for their final thesis some of my fellow students had their work digitally printed. I was still working on a typewriter — I didn't have access at all.

How did you get your first computer?
In 1994, I was a film curator, and with my friends, we made an experimental film club. We asked Soros Foundation for money for the publication and general support — Soros at that time was funding a lot of artistic organizations in Eastern Europe. They were unusual though because money would be the last thing they would give. First they would give computers, which is what we got. Windows, 3.11 if I remember it right... I immediately started to make posters for our program in Microsoft Word.

What kinds of films did you show at the film club?
They were experimental films. The Cine Fantom Film Club was the child of Soviet conceptual film school, which was underground. When we started the club we were inviting people from abroad who were making experimental films. The club still exists in Moscow. Every Wednesday there are still screenings. It's been almost 20 years.

Did the computer you received have the Internet?
No. One of our filmmakers came back from New York and told us about the internet, that there is such a thing, and that he found in the internet the name of our club and our names. Then I started to try, and I made a page for the Cine Fantom Club.

Are you self-taught in HTML?
Yeah. I was learning through opening the source code of the pages, and modifying it. I didn't read any books on coding. It was still a nice way to learn how to program at the time. Today, the sources are so obscure you can't learn like this. Then I thought that I would try to make a film in the browser, and this is how it started; this led to My boyfriend came back from the war.

When I look at My boyfriend came back from the war, I see that it's sort of a textual storytelling experience, but especially with that flickering window, it's also a cinematic experience.

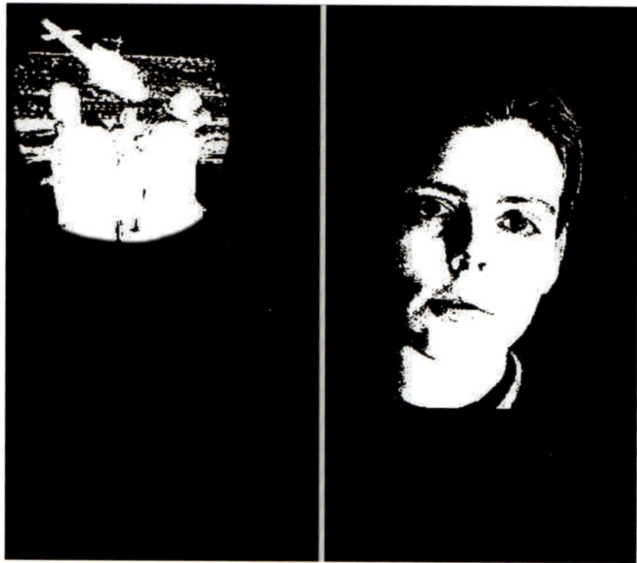

My Boyfriend Came Back From The War, 1996.

If it had been possible at that moment to make a video I would have, but it was not possible. I had to find a way to film it first and then to make a graphic out of it. One of the reasons it's in black and white was to save bandwidth so that people can in general see it. Otherwise it would be too slow. There are more than 100 files, and 20 graphics, and all of it's only 72 kilobytes, which is pretty unusual by todays standards. The trouble is that now it's too fast. You click on something, and it's immediately there. The narration is broken because of this speed.

I think back to gifs as a solution to show a film or video on the web before it was possible. Now, even as there are videos all over the internet, there's still something especially filmic about a gif. I was just looking at the Summer gif, on the swing, and I actually noticed for the first time that each frame is hosted on a different site.

This was a very dear project to me. This gif doesn't exist as one file – I didn't even try to make it. Sometimes I have trouble when the server is down for one of the hosting sites, and I have to communicate with the person who is hosting it. It can take some time.

It's dependent on a whole community. How many frames are there?
There are 18 frames, but there are 25 servers. So sometimes this path, it forks, as there are more servers than there are frames, so some people have the same frame. It's very nice... Maybe it can grow.

I was wondering about the universe gif that recurs in a number of projects throughout your website. Where is that from?
Star backgrounds are one of the most significant things on the web for me. When they started to disappear it was the first sign that the web was changing. I was just starting to teach, and we were making crazy things with the students, inside joke pages that you would send to each other made with an amateur style. Then by the end of 1999, you could hardly find such pages anymore. They would be redesigned or wouldn't exist. That was when I started to grab pages with star backgrounds.

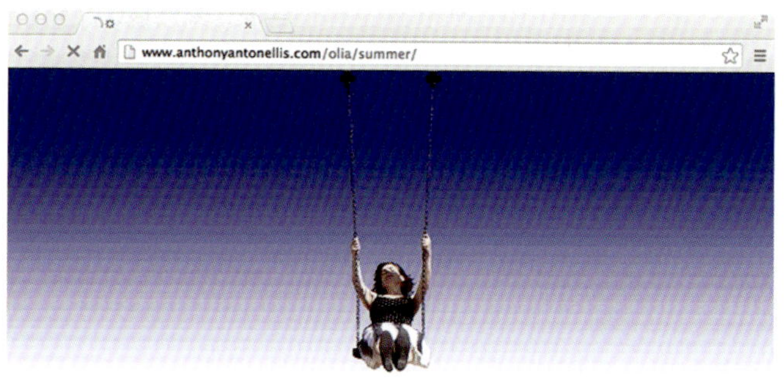

Summer, 2013.

Why were these backgrounds disappearing?
Well, it was clear for me as a designer why they vanished: They were bad to put text on, or looked immature. They are against any usability advice.

For all of the "professionals," they summarized the amateur culture at the time.
Yes. So I made Some Universe (2002) at that moment to show the beauty of those backgrounds.

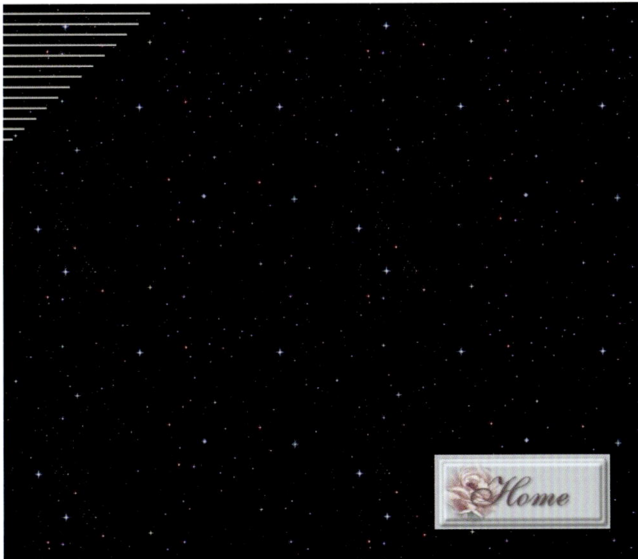

Homepage, 2013.

Why do you think the star patterns were so prevalent in those early sites?
Because the web was outer space. It was out there. Cyberspace is star backgrounds with blue underlined links on them. A lot of early website makers were science-fiction fans, so for them it was a very important motif. For a lot of gamers, the star background is a known theme for video games. For me, if you want to remember or respect or somehow relate yourself to the history of the web, you would put star a background in some way on your web page. My students know that to please me, there should be some star background in their project, especially when they show the first draft of something.

In your work, when the browser shoots diagonally across the stars or when the pages of an online newspaper peel back to reveal a starry "cyberspace," it feels as if you are peering through a browser window into the history of the internet. Beneath the glossy surface of the semantic web, we find the mysterious and tangled "black holes" that we used to fall into...these places have now been all but erased from view. On your website there are links to like your Pinterest and Facebook, but when you click they are mirrored 1997 versions of the sites that never existed.

It was all about imagining how these sites would have been like at that time. Not only technologically, but also conceptually. So in Facebook, you can only have 16 friends, because with the screen resolution in 1997 you could only divide the screen into 16 frames. We also try to translate the language, so you wouldn't "like" things — you would "vote up."

I love how on the YouTube there are movie theater curtains.
We didn't think about anything else. What we remember about that time, as soon as somebody was brave enough to implement the video on the page they would try to make it look like a cinema theater. There really weren't a lot of videos on pages at that time, and the videos we have are actually from 1997.

You have three children. How old are they?
My oldest daughter is almost 21. She studies film and theater theory in Berlin. Jurij is almost 11, and Zelda is almost 5.

choose a platform

suggested by **hugo** 2014-03-01
agree 3 | disagree 0 | **discuss 1**

Control over user data access

suggested by **hugo** 2014-03-01
agree 3 | disagree 0 | **discuss 1**

my data not being converted

suggested by 2013-12-23
agree 4 | disagree 1 | **discuss 1**

make screen shots.

suggested by **Aram Bartholl** 2013-12-22
agree 3 | disagree 0 | **discuss 1**

pull

suggested by **olia lialina** 2013-12-02
agree 3 | disagree 0 | **discuss 2**

User Rights, 2013

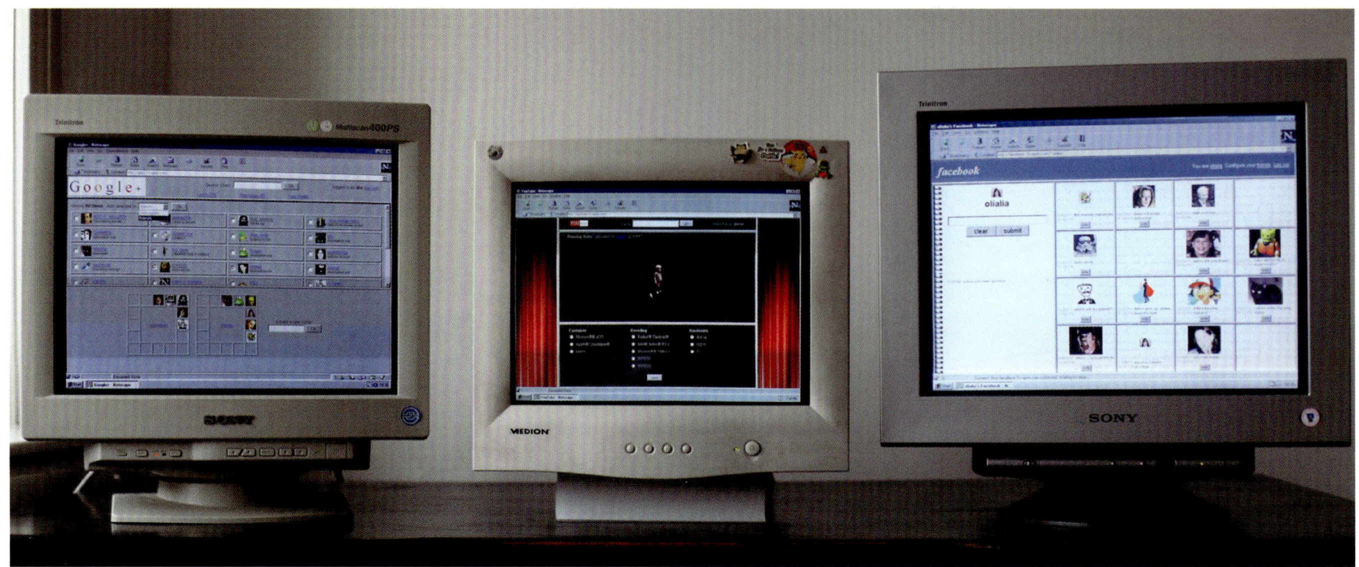

Once Upon, 2011—2012.

Do they play with computers?
They all do. Jurij plays Minecraft.
He also programs games already in
Scratch. With Zelda, everything
Jurij does, she is following him. It
was Jurij's idea to call her Zelda.
Sometimes people think that this is
some artificial conceptual name, but
she actually knows all the Zelda
games, knows the scene melodies. If
you suggest to her to dress as Zelda
for Halloween, she will want to dress
as Link... This is a funny twist in
the story.

What do you teach at Stuttgart?
I teach art and design, online
groups, and a colloquium on digital
culture and digital folklore — user
culture. In that class we look at
what's really unprofessional and
amateurish, what they did with
computers and online, and what they
still do now. The low digital culture
is still happening.

**This reminds me of your screenshots
of the GeoCities websites. How did
that project start?**
In the beginning of 2011, Dragan
and I finished the download of this
one terabyte torrent of GeoCities
websites. Dragan started to repair
them to make an archive readable and
usable and I started to look through
the pages and to make sense out of
it. Then we started a blog, One

Terabyte of Kilobyte Age. Dragan
developed a system that would
generate screenshots of every
homepage, so we could start to fill
the internet with its past. Tumblr
has a restriction that there can only
be three posts per hour so now there
are 72 new screenshots every day and
it's in chronological order. We are
currently in the end of January 1999.

The GeoCities blog is very popular.
It has a lot of followers for that
kind of content. There are some
pages that have become very popular.
I would really like to make now a
publication about this archive. I
think the title would be Bear With Me
or Bare With Me. That's what a lot of
people say on their early pages.

**I saw one site that you quoted on
Twitter: "It's not the best website,
but it will do."**
I collect what people say about their
own pages, what people think about
the web in general. The users at
that time didn't only try to make
something special with their page —
they were also very narrative. They
tried to explain why they made the
site, how it works, where to click
exactly. Sometimes next to an "Under
Construction" sign they would explain
maybe when exactly things would come
and what they would be.

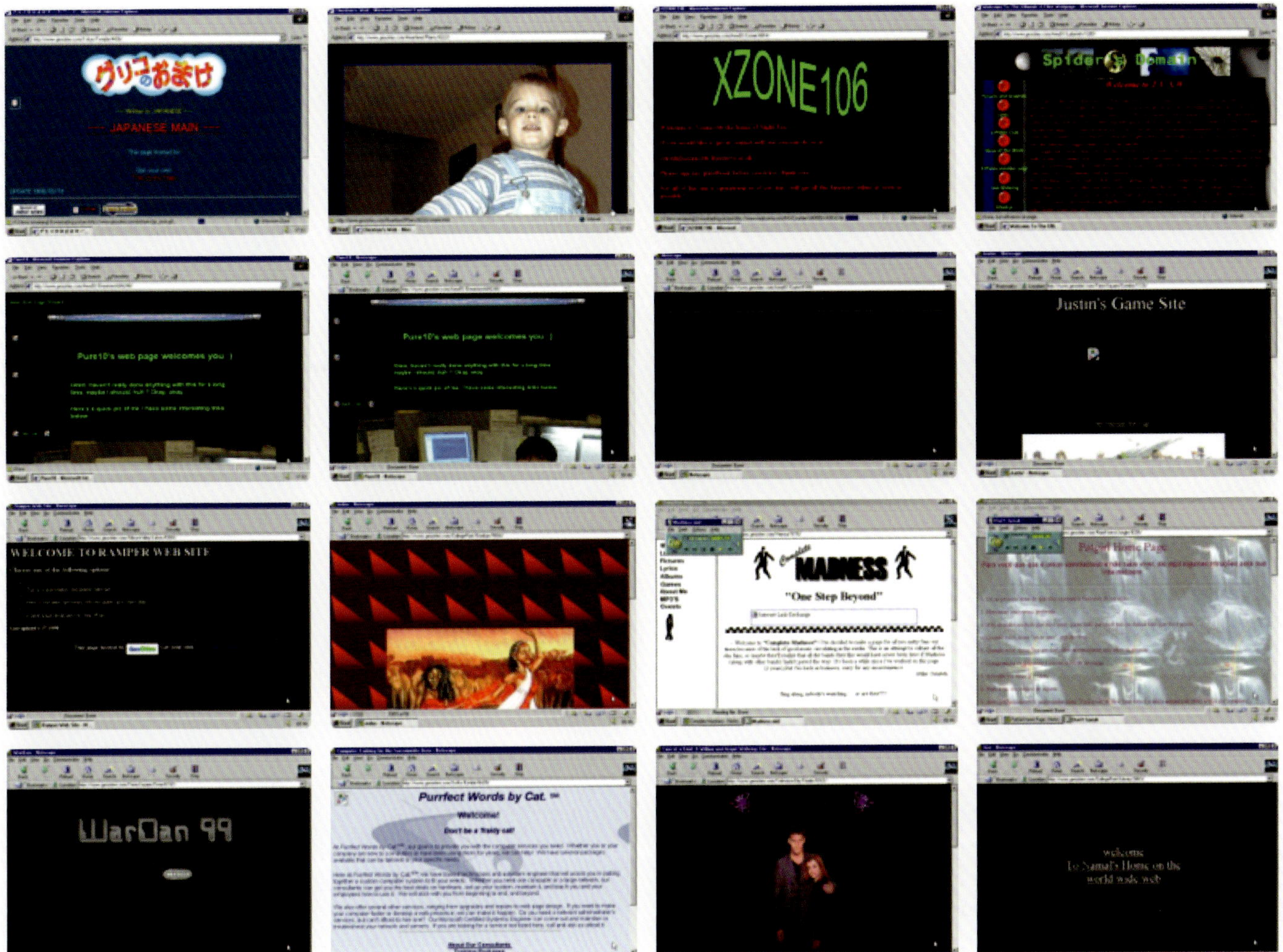

Once Upon, 2011—2012.

The narrative mode on these sites is very personal and revealing.
It's because all the time they had to make choices. This frame or no frames? Should it work in Netscape or in Explorer? What screen resolution? I am now posting Vines of these sites as well, to document the music on the GeoCities web pages. There is this book I ordered for my students called Designing for Emotion. The authors give advice to designers how to make pages that give the illusion that there is a real person behind it. This whole culture is ignored, even when they tried to achieve the effects that were fully present at that time. With the Tumblr, more people are getting acquainted and educated with the past of the web which is nice.
In A Vernacular Web, you were saying that these modes of web design will return. **You already see it on Tumblr, it's now stylish to use certain 90s web design elements when creating a new site. It is significant to have the original websites preserved in this way. So much cultural-historical information about internet culture is made accessible through these documents. How many more years will you be uploading?**
We have material for 12 more years. It's crazy just to think about it. Will people get tired of it, will Tumblr be closed? I don't know. Maybe our computer will die. We have some back-ups. Every day, I plan to stop to look at the new pages, and just again to go through from the beginning until this particular moment, because otherwise, I will never start to make something meaningful out of it. There's already too much information. ☺

Jacob Ciocci

"It's very confusing to figure out what it is that you do 'naturally' versus how you want to fit into the world."

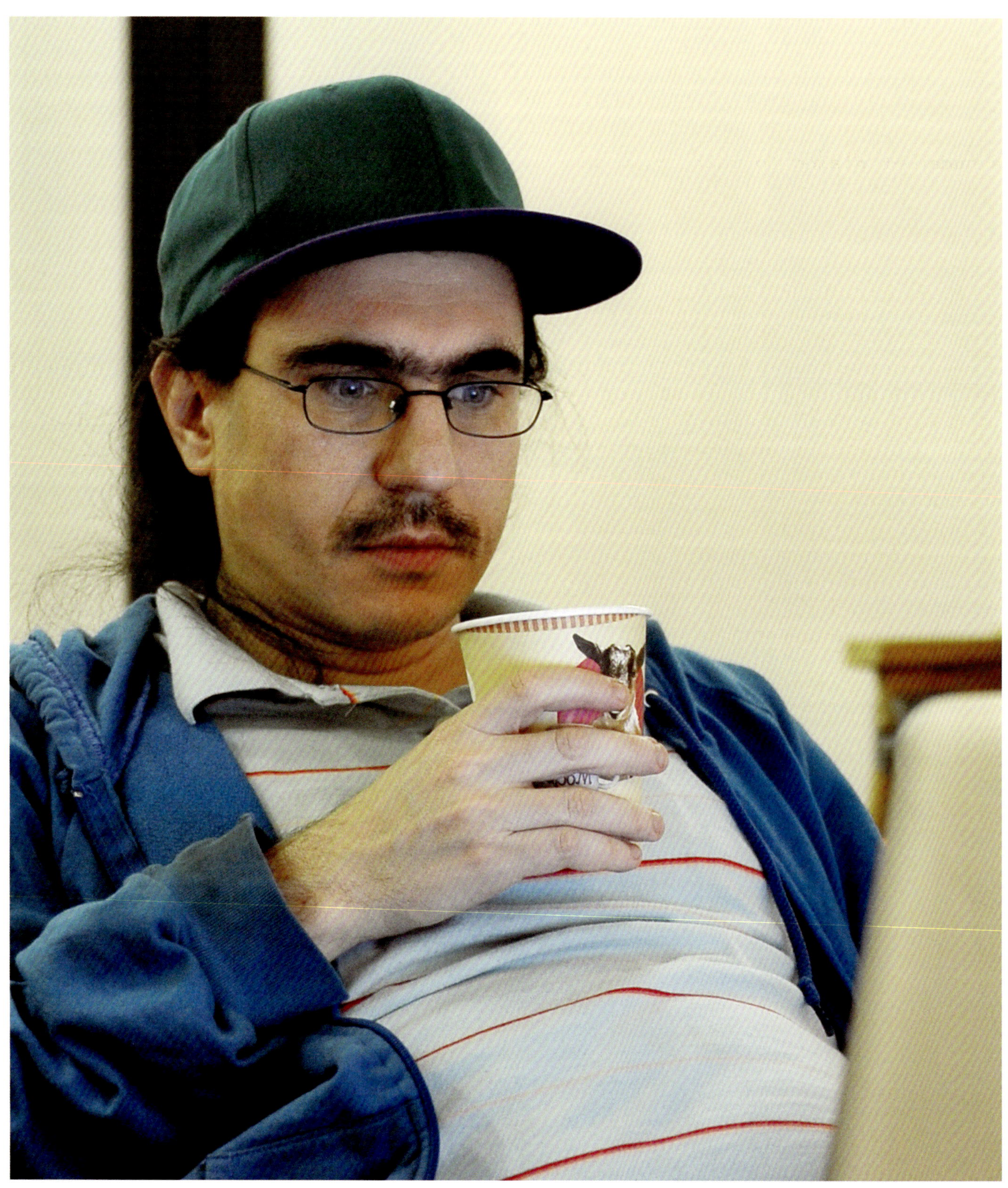

Interview by Asher Penn
Portrait by Jae Ruberto

Jacob Ciocci is best known as a founding member of Paper Rad, a collective of artists who in 2001 launched their gif-tastic website, bringing a previously localized aesthetic to the World Wide Web. An early student of all forms of computer art Jacob Ciocci's frequently collaborative work has taken the form of comics, paintings, video, music, and, of course, websites, bringing a humanist dialog to mainstream and underground culture alike.

Where are you from?
I was born in Lexington, Kentucky, then moved to Chapel Hill, North Carolina in the eighth grade. That's where I met David Wightman.
How did you meet?
We probably saw that we were both wearing a Nirvana shirt. I think we actually got to know each other the most through this a cappella group. We were also both into band stuff — he knew how to play classical music and I sang in a boy's choir.
What other stuff were you guys into?
David was the first person I knew personally that ever made a zine. It was called The Dandy Chicken. There was also a really great radio station at UNC called WXYC, which I would say was life changing for us. We would just listen to it all the time and find out who was who. That's how I found out about noise music and free jazz and all that stuff.
Were you into art in high school?
I drew all the time but it was mostly comics-based characters — I think I only ever really finished one complete comic of my own, mostly doodles of characters. I took an art history class in high school but it was really cursory.
What comics did you like?
I really liked Maxx. I also really liked Todd McFarlane and Rob Liefeld. Maybe we're moving out of a period where everybody hates them — I don't follow comics that much now — but certainly in the last 10—15 years everybody hated on them pretty hard.

They did the comics that some say destroyed the industry. The drawings have huge anatomically incorrect muscles, bad writing, were really colorful...I remember being obsessed with the detail mostly. I thought anything that had insane amounts of lines was better than something with less lines.
You went to Oberlin for college. What did you study?
I got a minor in Computer Science. It was for people who were not trying to be programmers, but wanted to get good at the basics and learn all the software. I minored in that and majored in fine art. Probably one of my favorite classes was Introduction to Contemporary American Religion. That blew my mind. I realized I was really interested in contemporary American culture and how it's related to the crazy history of our country.
Had you been interested in computers before then?
I took a programming class when I was 10 or 11. I guess one of my earliest collaborations with my sister Jessica was a text-based role-playing game we made on the PC. We made computer images too, but those and the game are probably lost forever.
What about the internet?
I didn't have any internet really in high school, but when I got to Oberlin my parents bought me a Mac and all of a sudden I had access to a T1 connection. It was a big deal — a "this is what I'm going to do for the rest of my life" kind of a situation. It was clear that computers were now going to be the dominant creative platform for both input and output in my life. It wasn't going to be just magazines, or painting, or whatever. Everything was forever going to be filtered through these machines.
Were there other students that were also interested in computers?
Yeah. Paul Davis and Cory Arcangel were both in the Conservatory. It was really inspiring to meet the two of them because what they were doing was different than what other people in their department were doing.

What was different about their work?
It was engaging on multiple levels.
It wasn't overly academic but it also
wasn't thoughtless. It was in between.
They taught computer art at Oberlin?
Yeah. There was one class where we
learned about internet art, and how
to make websites and interactive CD-
ROMs using Macromedia Director.
What was the first website you made?
I was interviewing this blind painter
for one of my independent studies,
so I made an experimental website to
document it. It was mostly images and
videos. It had very little text. It was
more like an abstract space in pastel
colors with interview snippets and
audio samples. I was trying to make it
look and feel spiritual, New Age.
**What was your attitude towards art
when you were in college?**
I was inspired by art that had some
sort of relationship to people outside of the gallery/museum/academic/
fine-art world. I remember outsider
art was something that I — and a lot
of other people — was inspired by.
**That reminds me of Fort Thunder.
Was it inspiring to you?**
I thought it sounded interesting and
had started to hear about music like
Black Dice, Lightning Bolt. Then for
Christmas, Jessica went to Million
Year Picnic in Boston and bought me
all these comics. They were really
mind-blowing, Ben Jones' early stuff,
Ron Regé Jr., Chris Forgues. I don't
think we could even get our hands on
any of the Fort Thunder stuff. When I
graduated, Jessica was already living
in Boston, so I was like, "This is a
no-brainer, I'll just move in with
her and we'll try and be friends with
these people."
So you met Ben Jones in Boston?
The first time we met Ben was at one
of his screenings. He went to MassArt
and started Paper Radio with Chris
Forgues there.
**So there was Paper Radio, Paper Rodeo,
and Paper Rad... I get them mixed up.**
Paper Radio was a Boston thing. I know
they had a period where they would do
it every week and it was free.

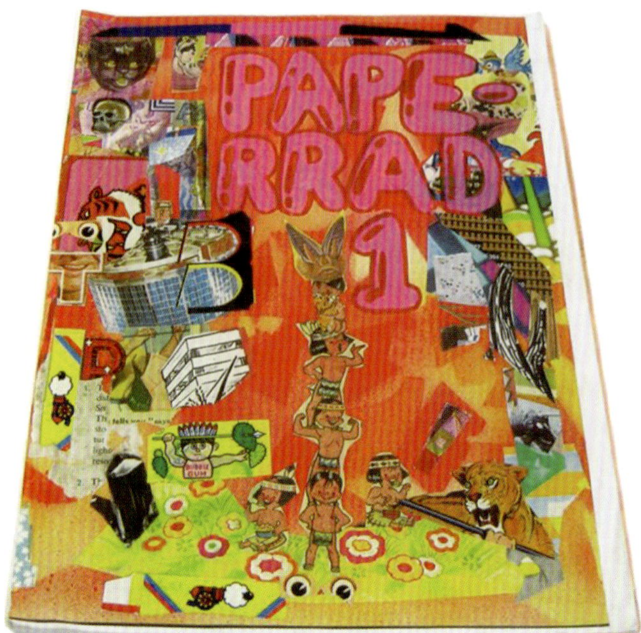

Paper Rad #1, 2002.

They were stealing the copies from
Kinko's and would just hand it out at
shows, events — leave it places.
I heard that Paper Rodeo was named
after Paper Radio. I think it was an
interesting situation where Ben and
Chris and their crew were inspired by
the Providence/Fort Thunder crew and
the Fort Thunder crew were in turn inspired by the Boston/Paper Radio crew.
And there was also Dearraindrop.
Joe Grillo was working under the name
Dearraindrop with at least a few other
people. I think it was initially the
name of the clothing line he did with
Laura Grant. Joe was making really
engaging, amazing stuff at the Museum
School and we'd go over to his house
to play music. His house just blew me
away. Joe had a really keen, advanced
set of interests in the stuff that he
collected from thrift stores.
How did Paper Rad start?
Paper Rad started as a website. Ben
wanted to make a website for all the
new stuff that me and Jessica and
Joe were making. After meeting Billy
Grant and Laura Grant, Paper Rad
became basically the six of us plus
collaborators. It was always very
vague to me who was in and who wasn't
considered a "part of it," which was
something I liked.

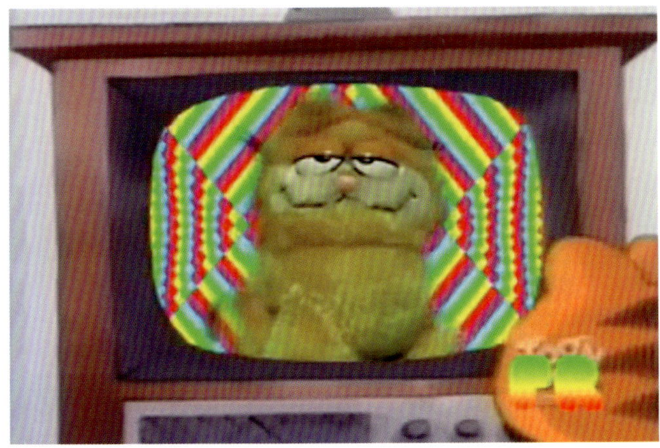

Paper Rad, Trash Talkin' DVD, Load Records, 2006.

You were making videos too, right?
When Jessica and I moved to our apartment in Boston we had free cable. We would watch it at night and just tape the funny parts, or the parts that we wanted to give to Ben, who would watch TV and send us clips too. I became aware that there were people trading videos, which seemed like an interesting proposition — just circulating these bizarre moments that seem to otherwise be lost. I think the first tape I saw like this was when I was still at Oberlin.

Kind of like Heavy Metal Drummer?
Yeah. It was a pre-internet, viral-style video. Remember: no internet meant no easily accessible, centralized archive of odd moments. If you saw something at three in the morning on cable or unearthed a bizarre tape from a thrift store, it felt almost imperative to try and document it and share it. Because no one else was...

How did things change when YouTube came along?
For me it was a big change. All of a sudden it was, "OK, now weirdness is no longer hard to find." Once YouTube happened, not only did sampling become easier, but the sharing of nuggets of gold became completely commonplace. Even though YouTube started in 2006 or something, I think we are still as a culture trying to figure out what this shift in access to weirdness means.

Your video work is a combination of found footage and animation.
Ben had already started making his own animations. He kind of pushed me and Jessica to make Flash animations, and Billy was making his own animations while still in high school in Virginia Beach. We all started making animations and it seemed intuitive to combine the animation onto VHS, mixtape format, with the found footage. That was sort of the beginning of the Paper Rad mix tapes.

What was the first Paper Rad mix?
I think the first one was PJ Vidz. PJ Vidz stood for (among other things): Peaceful Jackass Videos. Something with the spirit of Jackass in a way, but peaceful as opposed to snarky.

Paper Rad definitely had a New Age type of vibe.
That was one of the things that Ben, Jessica, and I all had in common. Our parents were into New Age mysticism. We grew up with this shared language of post-hippie spirituality transposed onto a suburban-American consumer-youth experience. BMX bikes + New Age = Paper Rad.

Were you doing video work outside of Paper Rad?
Paul Davis and I made a video that was a mash-up of Rihanna's Umbrella and that Cranberries' song Zombie. But instead of it being like a traditional audio mash up, or even a video mash up, we were instead directly inspired by people who were already manipulating ones and zeroes in digital video compression in order to create the effect which is now often called "datamoshing."

Datamoshing?
I'd written on the YouTube description for that video that the data on this video got all "moshed up," instead of "mashed up." We were always joking about how mash-ups should be called "mosh-ups" instead. Then one day I remember someone emailing me asking me if I could explain to him how to do "datamoshing." I LOLed and felt weird.

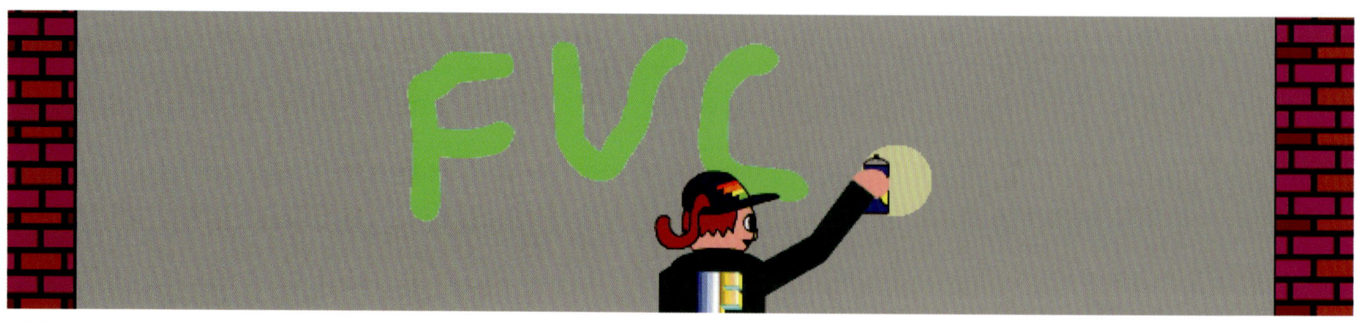

WYLD FiLE Banner. 2008.

Describe your comics from around then.
I was really inspired by how productive the Fort Thunder people were, how much they made, how focused and productive they were. My approach was to draw every night on ticker tape, which to me was a good example of a never-ending story. They were about a young boy named Little Dude, who is a lost soul just trying to find his way. Then there is this older guy named Box Eyes who's sort of his mentor or God, saint, spirit, whatever. Box Eyes is the guy that helps Little Dude get through.

I remember really enjoying that comic.
I think what a lot of people liked about them was that they were kind of more emo than the other comics being made in that scene. They were also about technology and computers. For two or three years that was what I did — tried to figure out what computers and digital culture meant for humanity, through these little drawings on paper that were distributed in zines first, and then on our website. The ideas and metaphors I started in those comics have carried me through all of the stuff that I do, even now.

You guys started doing art shows too.
Well there was a lot of cultural power in the name Paper Rad, but it wasn't because of the discrete fine art objects we were making. It was because of the ephemeral qualities of our work — the websites, the zines — and what we represented to a generation of young people. It was unclear to us, and even the galleries we worked with, how that would translate to a commercial gallery context.

At the time it felt a little awkward.
It was awkward at times, at other times I feel like it worked really well. We delved in headfirst and tried our best, but looking back on it I think certain things could have been handled with a little more nuance. Anyway, eventually more and more people started asking us to do things in other contexts too, like advertising.

Is that how WYLD FiLE started?
Yeah, we made music videos for clients. E*Rock from Portland started that and basically invited us to be involved. WYLD FiLE was clearly about making music videos for other people — mostly paid situations. Paper Rad was often more vague and expansive.

You guys were using Flash, right?
WYLD FiLE videos are probably almost all Flash. We all started using Flash because that was the one software that we could get our hands on for free. Some would say that comes from punk, but it comes from so many different attitudes. It's just a principal of using whatever tools you have available to make something great — not being held back by lack of access to fancy equipment.

The first time I saw Extreme Animals play live it felt like a combination of Lightning Bolt and positive, uplifting trance.
Yes, exactly. I'm pretty sure I introduced David Wightman to noise rock stuff like Quintron or Black Dice, Wolf Eyes, but he was listening to trance. He had a keyboard, and was like, "Here are these compositions I've been making, lets do them with noise drums and you playing noise and screaming on top."

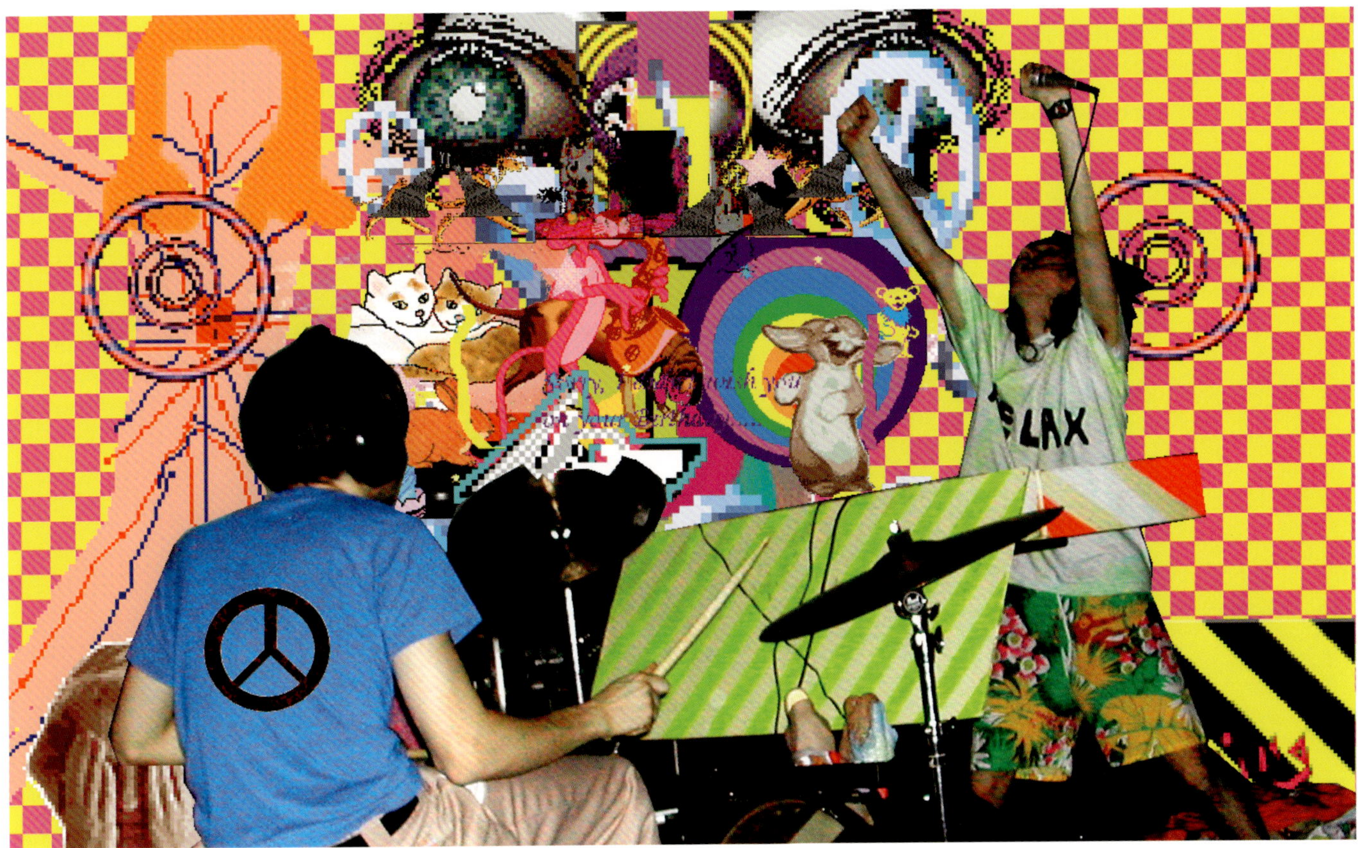

Extreme Animals, Summer of HTML Tour, 2003.

I had been listening to the Hackers soundtrack a lot when I first saw you. It felt on point.
Right. Then of course what happened was that all of American pop music (and arguably underground music too) shifted from a rock paradigm to an electronic music paradigm, and even more specifically: trance! So the meaning of what we were making completely shifted underneath our feet.

Is that why you added a guitar?
Yeah. I remember we were at this party recently and someone was saying, "Guitars are my cue to leave." I was like, "OK, definitely we've got to do more guitar." If something is so entrenched as a belief that it seems obsolete or irrelevant, then it's probably ripe for creative exploration. So Extreme Animals is pro-guitar, and in particular pro-nü-metal guitar. Plus David loves metal — he even taught a class on it at UCSD!

What kind of musical literacy is required to make Extreme Animals?
That is a great question, especially because David has a PhD in music composition, and has taught musicology. He is somebody who is really savvy and sophisticated at a pastiche mentality: combining different musical genres, tropes, or pop and sub-cultural references.

So it's all fairly self-conscious.
Some of it is strategic. We will definitely sit down and talk about what our band is doing and how it relates to what other people are doing...how it fits in or doesn't fit in within today's world. But, as much as we do that, we also just play around and do what comes naturally.

Right.
It's very confusing to figure out what it is that you do "naturally" versus how you want to fit into the world. That's the job of the artist — to get good at that. Figuring out how to filter out the world at a certain time, and let the world in at another, in a sophisticated, yet simultaneously intuitive, way. ☺

Nina Freeman

"I realized you could make games about anything —
kind of like with poetry."

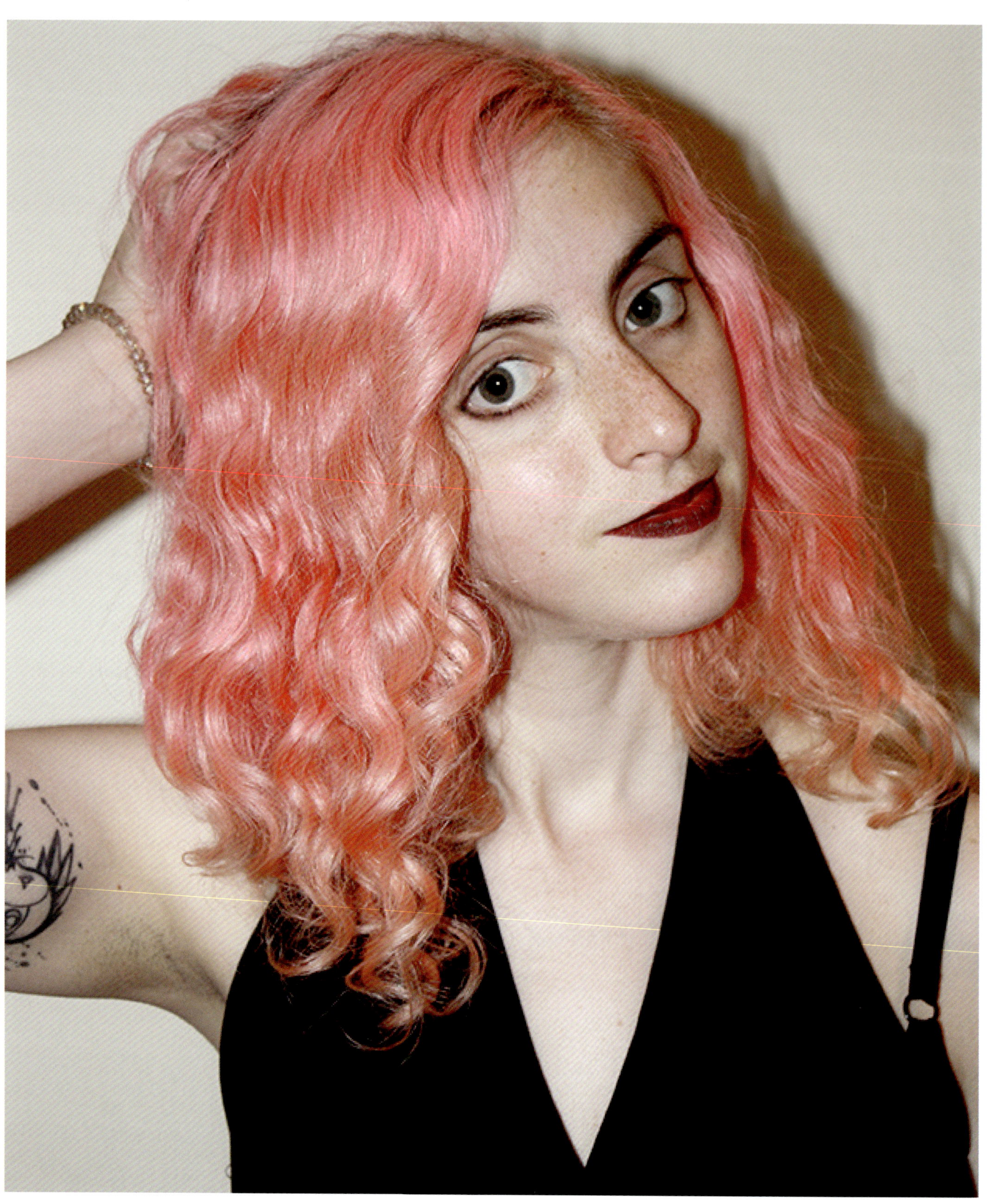

Interview by Asher Penn
Portrait by Emmett Butler

Despite her young age, Nina Freeman is already an exemplary voice in independent video games, both as an advocate for female programmers and experimentation within the field. With a background in poetry, Freeman's tiny, personal games range from the text based Mangia to the memory inspired My House My Rules, bringing the player to experience the intensity of the everyday. With a desire to educate and inspire, Freeman is also a co-founder of the Code Liberation Foundation, an educational outreach organization to help anyone who identifies as a women to learn programming from other women — an experiment that has already yielded exciting results.

How did you get into poetry?
I came to New York to study theater for my undergrad but wasn't totally jazzed on the crowd. Then I came into the company of a poet in residence at Pace University named Charles North, who's a second generation New York school poet. I ended up taking a bunch of poetry classes with him as well as getting involved with the St. Marks Poetry Project.
That place is the spot.
Yeah, there was a big history there which really interested me.
What kind of poetry were you into?
I love tiny poems about little things. Like writing about ordinary stuff like a trip to the grocery store or socks or something. Vignettes, really, which is funnily enough what I'm interested in doing in games.
Were you into video games when you were a kid?
I played tons of games. I was super addicted to this online game, Final Fantasy, for five years. I ended up playing that through high school and then into college. It's funny because when I first moved to New York most of my friends were people I met in the game. Even before I got into Final Fantasy online, I was into tons of games. Lots of JRPGs and old Sega games.

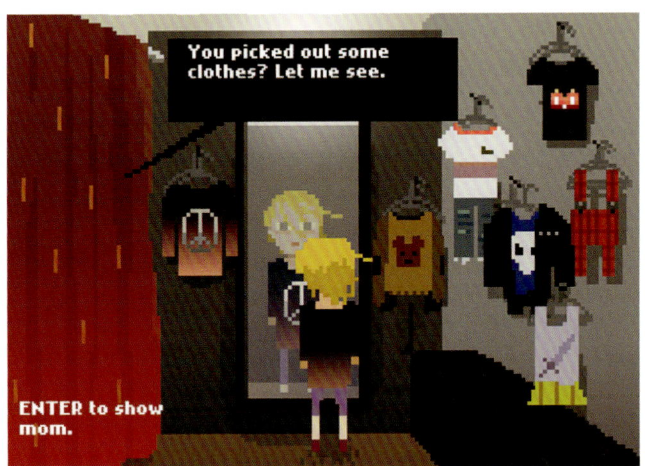

Ladylike, 2014.

Why didn't you study programming?
I had considered going to school for computer science. I had been making my own websites since I was really little. I'd also considered game design, because two of my best friends went to school for game design. My mom was a model though, and she really encouraged me to go in the performance direction, because I'd really done a lot of theater in high school, but web design was really my first hobby. I made my first website when I was like 13 on Homestead.
What was your first site?
It was a fan site for a series of books by Brian Jacques called Redwall. I was obsessed with the books when I was a kid, so I made little fan sites for stuff like that, and Pokémon, and all these different anime shows. I was always doing tech stuff when I was growing up on my own, in my room, not really telling anyone.
Kinda the opposite of theater.
Yeah. While I was at college I was also working in the computer science department, sort of filling the void of studying programming. It was just a student job, but once I'd been there for a couple years, they were sending me to Finland to do projects and participating in design challenges. I ended up actually participating in a lot of computer science when I was working there.

Did the poetry begin to crossover with the computer stuff?
My whole thesis was about sci-fi poetry, I was really interested in how technology wasn't looked at as much in the literature and poetry I was studying in school. I also started to write papers about video games. At the same time, I found myself becoming really involved with the chiptune scene in Brooklyn — people making music using old video game consoles like the Super Nintendo. There were these game developers that would go to these shows, Emmett Butler and Diego Garcia, and I became friends with them and they showed me all these indie games that I had never heard of.

What kind of games?
There's this game called Dys4ia, which is a small game that only takes a couple minutes to play by Anna Anthropy. She's a trans woman, and it's about her hormone therapy that she had. So, it's this seriously intense personal game. When I played it, I was totally blown away at how emotionally invested I became in this small game.

It sounds fairly adult and personal.
I'd never really realized that games could be like that. It was all pixel art, very simple, down to earth. I was used to sort of like the mainstream games like Minecraft. When I realized that people were making games like Dys4ia I realized you could make games about anything — kind of like with poetry. So I taught myself how to program.

What was your first game?
I think my first game was a Python text adventure that you would play in the terminal of your computer. It was sort of like this game called Zork, which is a really old text adventure game where you explore this world and story in text. I started doing lots of game jams, and became more and more involved with the indies in New York.

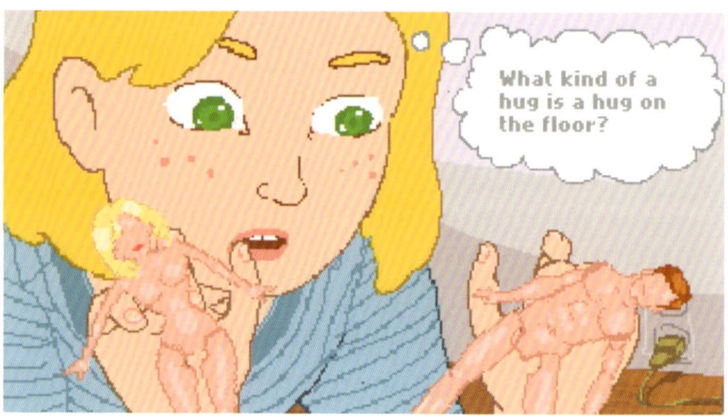

How Do You Do It, 2014.

How far back does independent game culture go?
That's actually something we talk a lot about right now in the games community. Right now indie is the big thing everyone is talking about, but games like Doom and Myst were indie games. Doom was just five guys working in their basement — they were really young. They actually distributed it as shareware, so those first players didn't even need to go to the store to buy it. They just downloaded it online using FTP or other file-sharing methods. There's a pretty rich history of people making games on tiny teams without budgets or big publishers, and a lot of those people become the ones making the games that are AAA now.

What were some of the other early games you made?
One of the first games that I made was called Hokuto no Huchen (Fist of the North Karp). It was a game about me as a little girl on a fishing trip I took with my dad. He caught the fish and was like, "Nina, here, take it off the line." Then he swung it to me, and it hit me in the face. That was always like a really hilarious memory to me. I was little and horrified because the fish felt gross. So I made a game about that. You play a little girl and she's trying to get as many fish off the line before she gets fish slapped. This was one of my first times experimenting with a game that was just about one of my childhood memories.

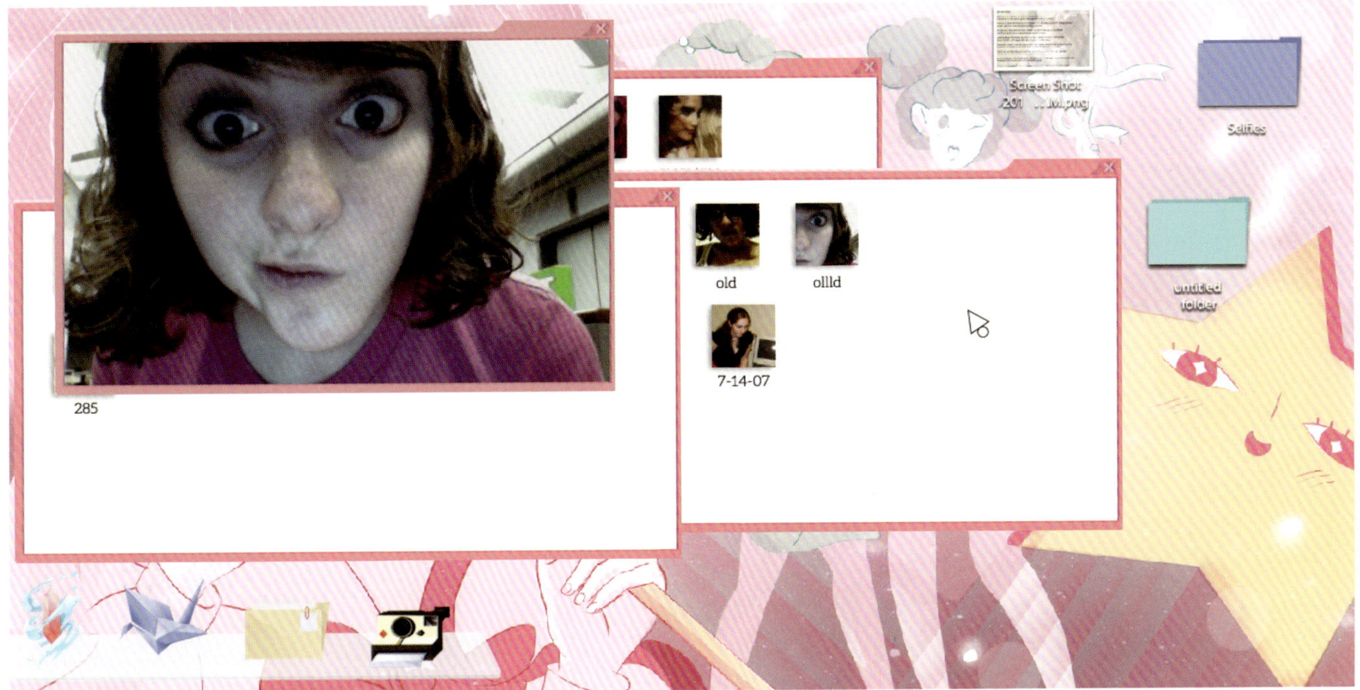

Cibele, 2015.

Your game Mangia is also autobiographical.
Yeah. I was diagnosed with this condition last year called gastroparesis, which basically means your stomach functions slower than normal. It was this awful year of doctors trying to figure out what was wrong with me, which was a pretty terrible experience. The game is about my misdiagnosis before I actually got the correct one. I wanted to sort of explore that experience of not knowing what was happening inside my own body and how I was trying and failing to deal with that mentally.

Why did you decide to do that game in text?
I wanted to express very specific things that would take a much larger game to do if it was with illustrated characters. I wanted it to be more personal and minimal. I am a writer at heart, so I knew I could get across a lot of these complex emotions in text. My hope was by giving someone this game that they could play through it to understand what it's like to go through something like that.

Could you talk a little bit about the Code Liberation Foundation?
I met this woman Phoenix Perry at the Game Developers Conference last year. She started in advertising, but made her way into games — she's a really good programmer. We were talking about how at the AI Summit talks there were only one or two women speakers and barely any women in attendance. A couple weeks later, she emailed me to get together with her and a couple ladies for pizza to talk about a project. I went over there and it was all programmers who had made games. Phoenix was like, "So, you're a bunch of women who are doing games, programming successfully. But there's so few of us, we should start taking our skills and offering them to those women who are interested in learning programming to make indie games."

And just for women.
Yeah, our classes are free and offered exclusively to anyone who identifies as a woman. We were lucky because NYU gave us some space for free to use that summer. Eighty people attended the class over the course of the summer.

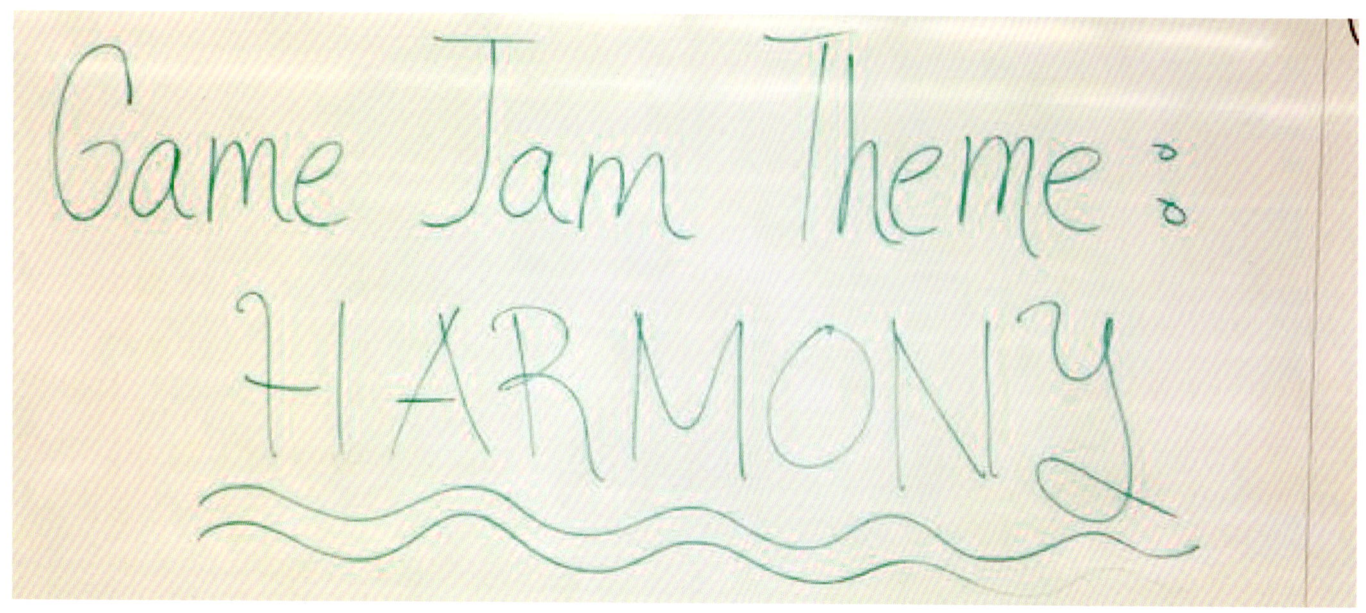

Code Liberation Foundation, 2014.

What did you teach?
It was an Introduction to C++ and Object-Oriented Programming. We were just trying to teach the fundamentals so that the students could go off and learn more about these games libraries with some kind of context. We went over stuff like what are variables, what are functions, what are classes — very basic things that you need to know for most popular programming languages.

What advantages does a female-exclusive environment allow?
There are obviously women out there who are comfortable going to take programming classes, but we're specifically interested in helping women who maybe feel or who have experienced stereotyping or abuse, in technical environments or just in the games world in general. Those women aren't gonna just go and take a regular programming class because of fear or intimidation. We're trying to help women who are really more comfortable learning in an environment where they feel safe.

Computer games aren't exactly marketed towards women either, right?
Yeah, it's totally focused on male gendered objects and images. There is a really long history of games and technology advertising being targeted at men, which creates an atmosphere where women don't feel like they belong there. We have this interesting PowerPoint full of advertising images from the 90s when a lot of the women who are taking these classes grew up. There are a lot of really weird Game Boy ads of girls that are weirdly hypersexualized. Like, there's this one where a girl is tied down to a bed. It's a weird joke about needing some time with your Game Boy, so you've got to get away from your girlfriend.

Well, Game Boy is pretty gender specific in it's name.
Ultimately, I can't say what the exact problem is that's causing the lack of women in games and programming. However, it's clear that the problem runs deep, so we should do everything we can to fix that. I think I got sick of just talking about how few women there are in games. I really wanted to go out there myself to find those women who were interested, but maybe felt scared, or didn't realize they had the potential. It's going well so far, and I'm meeting lots of great women. I know they're going to make really important games, and I can't wait to see what they do. ☺

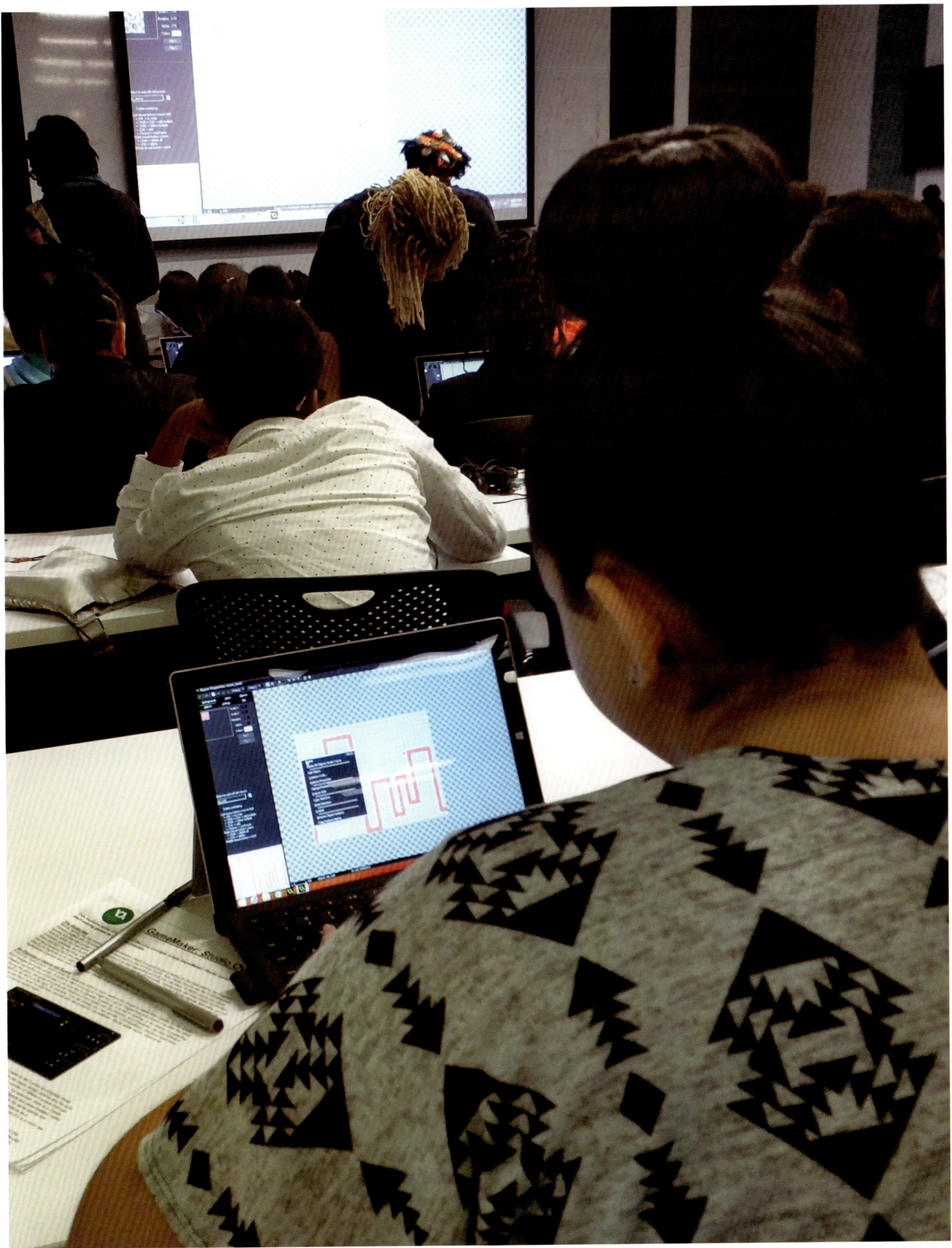

Code Liberation Foundation, 2014.

Juiceboxxx
"I have big fucked up dreams."

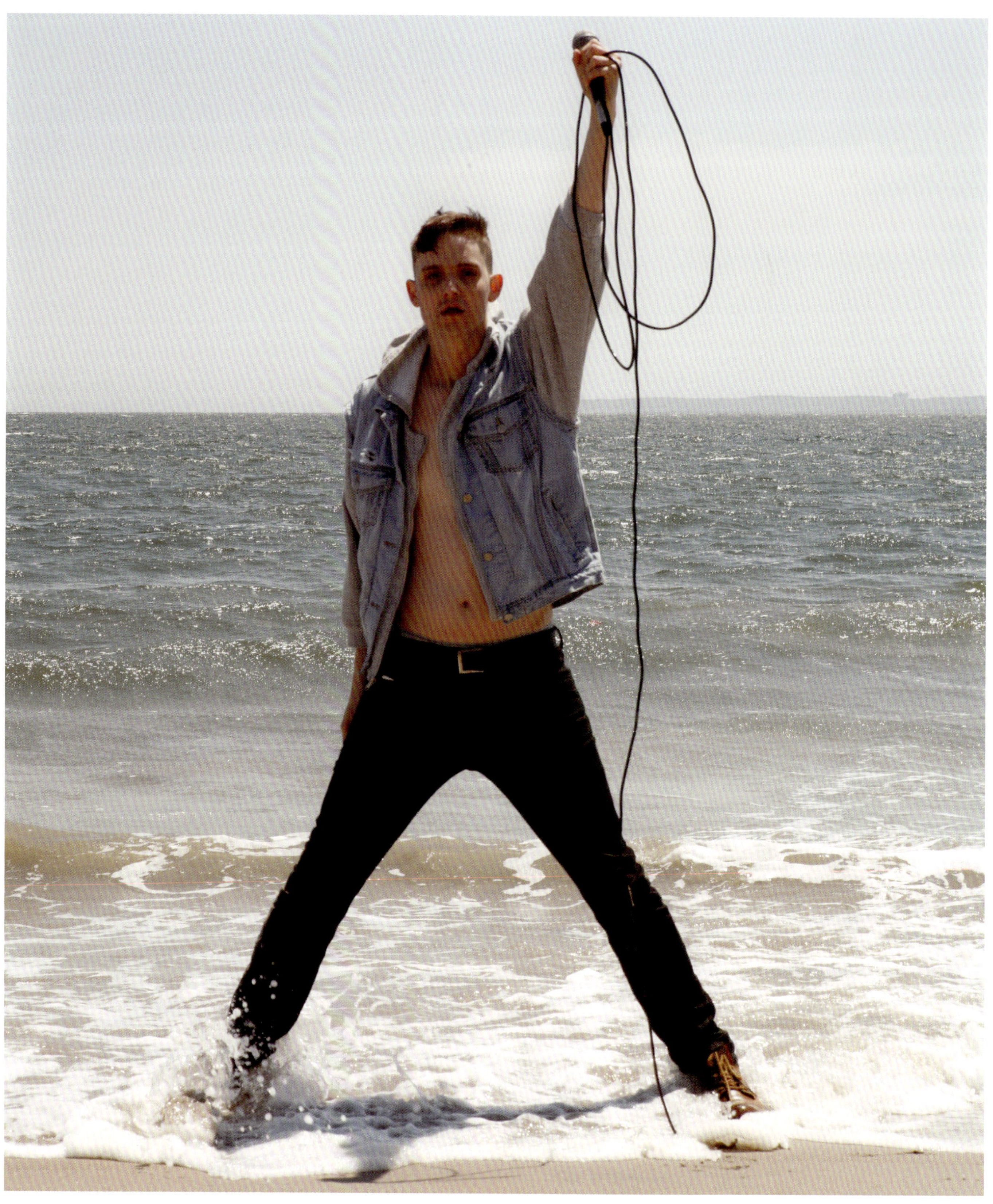

Interview & portrait by Asher Penn
Images courtesy Juiceboxxx

Spawned from the underground, and influenced as much by Bruce Springsteen as contemporary rap and noise music, Juiceboxxx is the most pop-friendly, life-affirming act since Andrew W.K. A self-taught artist and producer from the Heartland, Juiceboxxx's output is an expression of positivity through darkness. Since the age of 15, Juiceboxxx has taken his "never-say-die" live act to 18 countries, playing in basements and stadiums alike, with acts ranging from Japanther to Public Enemy. In the face of limited industry support, Juiceboxxx started his own label, Thunder Zone, releasing his own mix-tapes and albums, as well as unlikely merch such as an Extreme Animals VHS, Lil Ugly Mayne T-Shirts, and their signature energy drink. Today, at the age of 27, Juiceboxxx is still going harder than ever, upgrading from iPod to backing band and refusing to "surrender forever."

Juiceboxxx interview, Take 1. Well, there's only one take. So, you're from Milwaukee, right?
Yeah, outside of Milwaukee.
What's it like there?
You've never been to the Midwest before?
I went to St. Louis.
St. Louis is a little more southern. Milwaukee is the most German city in America. Part of that culture can be deeply felt in its love of beer. All my family is from the Midwest.
What do your parents do?
My dad was a high school photo-graphy teacher and my mom was a sign language interpreter at the local university. A good portion of all my family is involved in the educational system in some way. I have two aunts and two uncles that are school teachers.
How did you get into music?
Pretty young, pretty early. I dived in deep when I was like 11 with college radio. That was heavy for me.

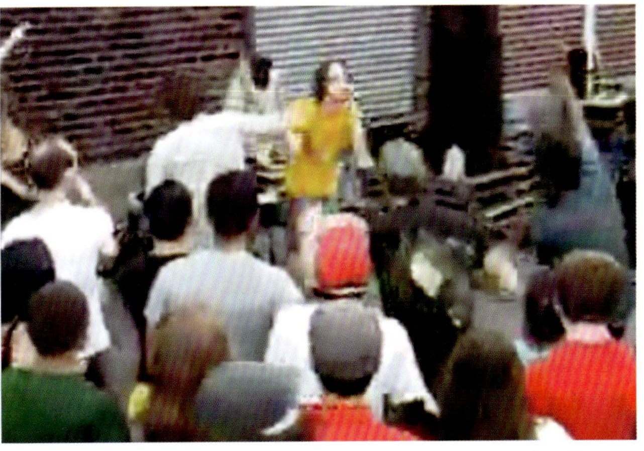

Juiceboxxx with Spank Rock, Todd P Festival, Brooklyn, 2006. Photo: Dan Clark

What was the station?
WMSE. It's still around. I was listening to that station for four years straight, hardcore. It was that classic college radio thing where if you listened to it all the time you get everything. There was the rave show, the punk show, the emo show. The underground rap show was happening and that was exciting. The Midwest was really happening for hip-hop music in the late 90s and early 2000s. You had Scribble Jam happening in Cincinnati. Eminem was coming up next to a group like Atmosphere, or a rapper like Dose 1. All that stuff was kind of happening on this college radio show — that kind of late-90s underground rap.
Like Eminem on Rawkus Records?
Yeah... So, you've got an interview with a white rapper and Eminem has already come up. I fuckin' brought it up in the first half a minute. Awesome. That's great.
How did you start rapping?
It was just intuitive for me. I started when I was 15. Before that I played in punk bands.
What did you play?
I played drums. But I wasn't just going to punk shows, I was going to rap shows, going to see people like Atmosphere, Del the Funky Homosapien, just whatever was happening in that sort of touring underground rap scene. These are things that seem pretty dated now, but at the time people took it very seriously.

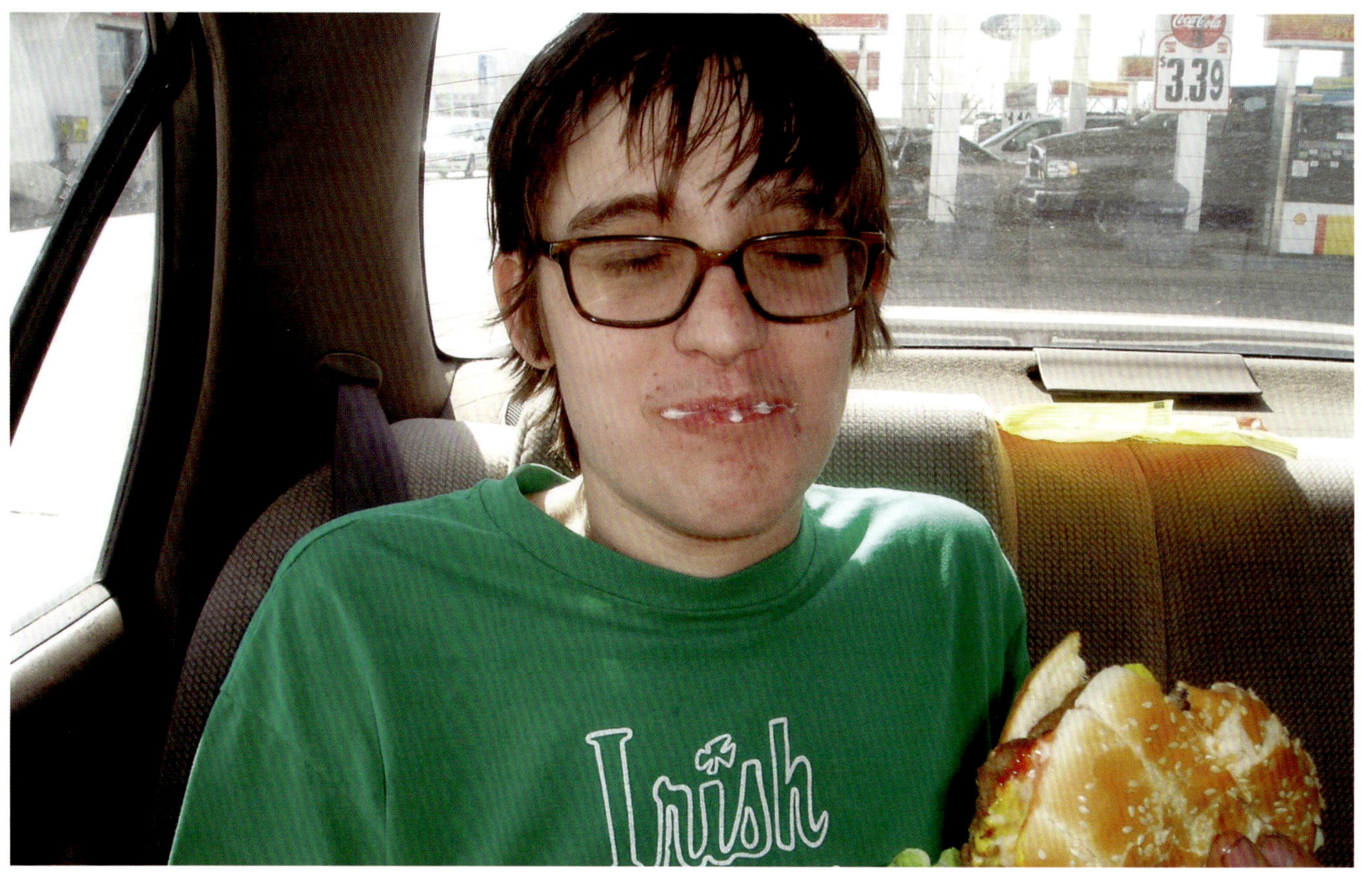

Spring Tour, 2004.

How did you learn how to make music?
Just on a computer. Truthfully,
I booked a show before I started
making the music. The first show I
played was at a community center
in the suburb I grew up in, with
this screamo band, Seven Days of
Samsara, who we all worshiped. There
were eight bands. I booked the show
actually and I think that's why I put
myself in.

How long had you been booking shows?
I started playing in bands and
booking shows when I was like 13,
14. There was a club that would do
all-ages punk shows from 5:00 PM to
8:00 PM, before it turned into a bar.
It was just perfect when I was 14
because my parents could drop me off
and pick me up and it would be done
by like 8:30.

**So you felt ready to be a frontman at
the age of 15?**
I wanted to have an outlet to play
shows. Maybe my ego was already too
big to just play drums or something.

Where did the name Juiceboxxx come from?
I didn't even come up with the name.
That's what's so fucked up about all
this. My buddy came up with it and I
don't even think he was in the band.
The first couple of gigs were as a
three-piece, but by our third or fourth
show the guys had lost enthusiasm.
I didn't want to cancel the show so
I showed up and I was like, "I'm
Juiceboxxx now." I couldn't come up
with a better name that day and it
just stuck. It's funny when your entire
creative life is based on these stupid
things you did when you were 15.

It's like a drunk tattoo.
Yeah, I mean, I don't have any
tattoos. I just have Juiceboxxx.

Did you play with an iPod?
This was pre-iPod. I mean, iPods
existed, but for a long time I just
had a CD player and it would skip
sometimes. Those early shows were
such an important outlet for me in
high school. We would go on weekend
tours to Chicago with friends.

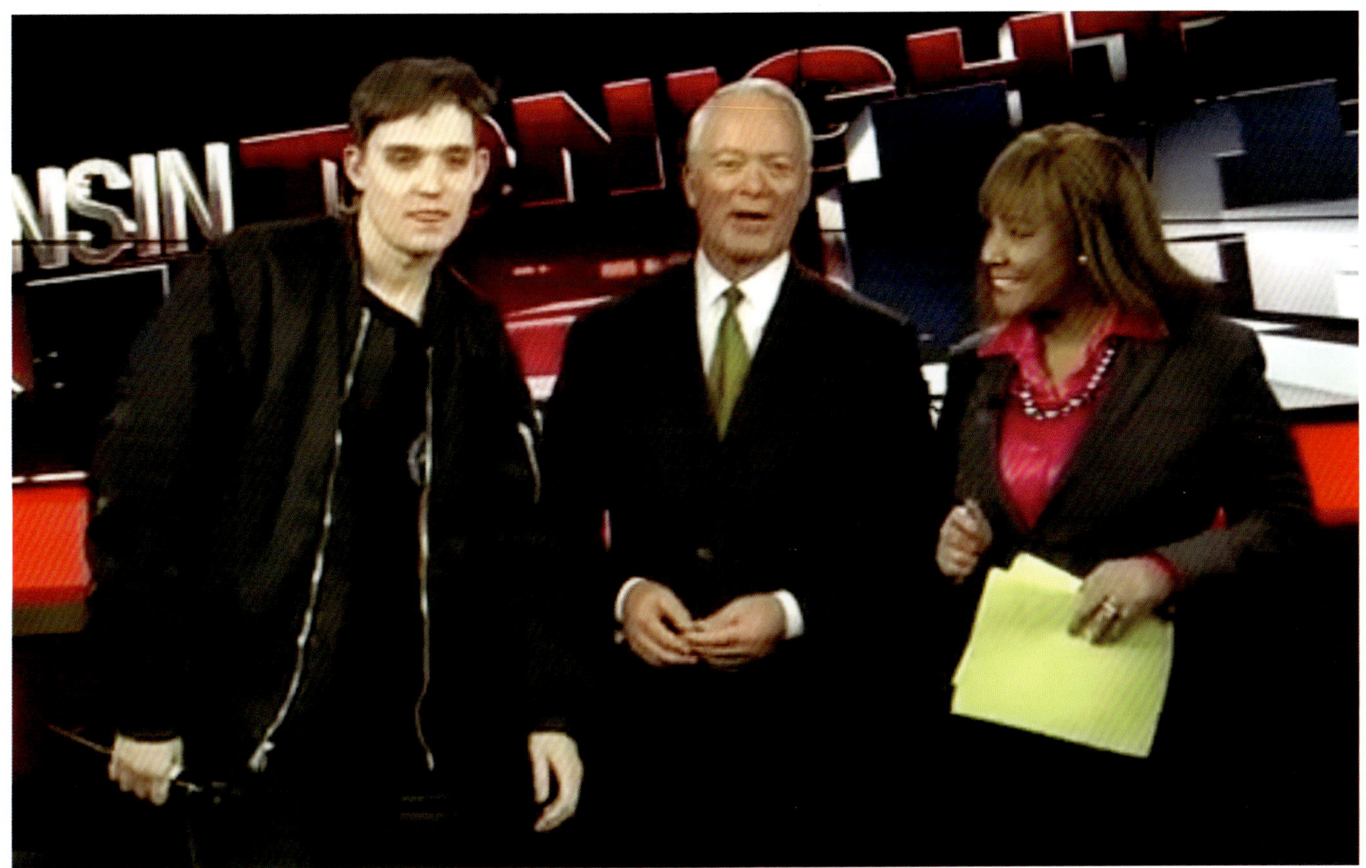

Wisconsin Tonight, 2014.

How were you making your tracks?
Just pretty basic things, you know. Nothing secret. The opposite of secret... Just think of the most generic thing you use and it's probably that.

Were there producers you were into?
I was listening to a lot of southern rap. I was listening to The Neptunes, Timbaland. I was listening to pop music.

Did you go to college?
For a year. I don't know why. It was at the local school that my mom worked at. It was a wasted year, totally useless. Then some weird shit happened where this dude got murdered on my front porch. This was the fall of 2006. I dropped out of school pretty much instantly after that. I just didn't want to waste any more time, so I started touring.

You've toured a lot since then.
It's just one of those things where if you're really unstable, the insanity of the road is like the most stability you ever get. That's how I felt. I haven't had my own, real apartment in like two and a half years — I just sublet places. I honestly wish I was on tour more. It's so fucked. I was sitting in some shitty fuckin' rock club on Friday night and I was like, "Man, I wish I was on tour right now." Most people would be like get me the fuck out of this place. It's covered in bad stickers and it smells like shit, but it trigged some Pavlovian impulse in me.

I bet you get better the more you play, too.
I mean, of course it makes you better. I wouldn't be foolish enough to keep doing this if I didn't see myself getting better. I wish I could tour more, but now I have a band and it's harder. Back when I just had an iPod, I could get on a Greyhound bus, or jump in a van with a band that was doing well and just open for them every night.

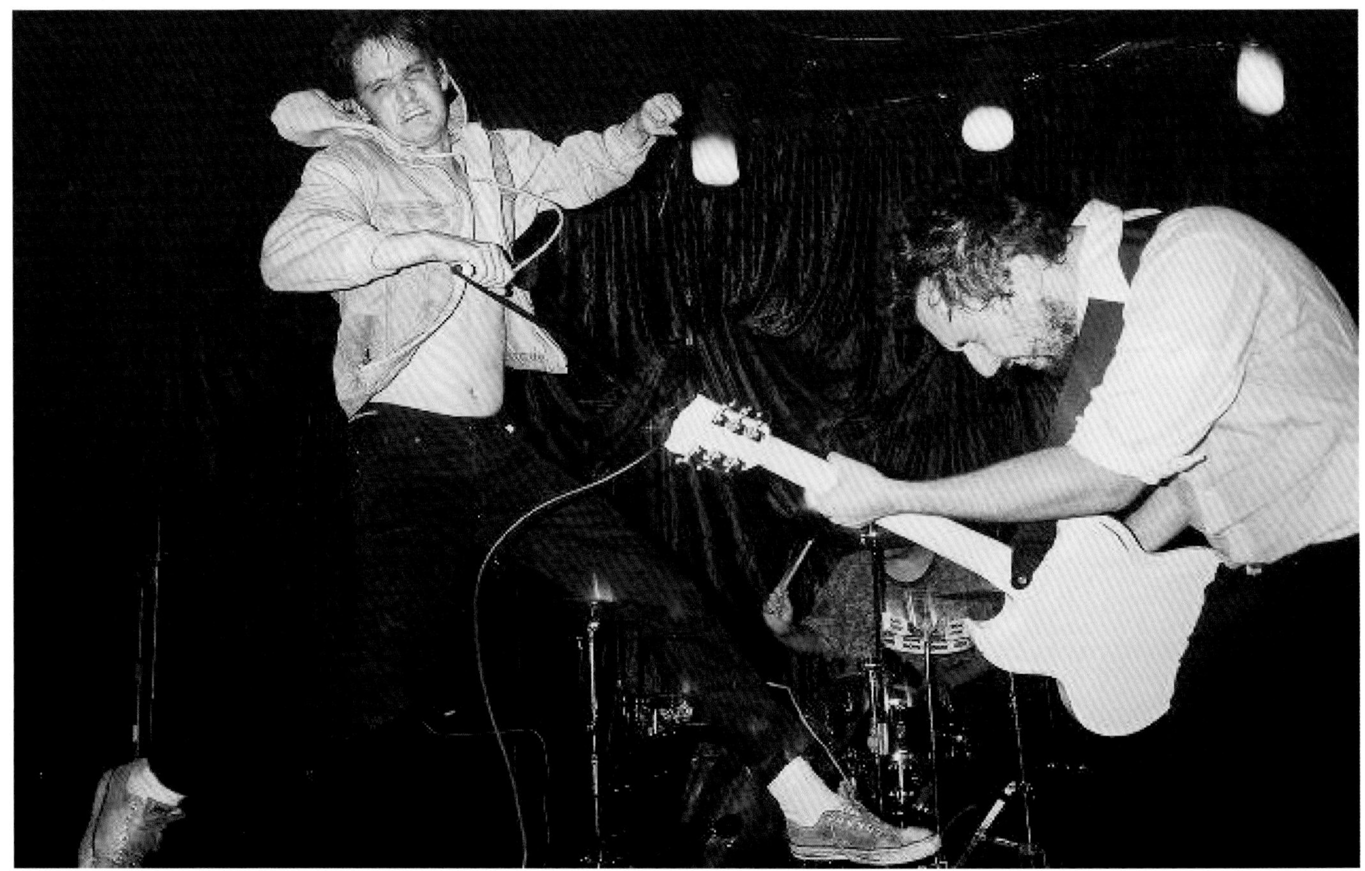

Juiceboxxx & The Heartland Band, The End, Nashville, 2012. Photo: Ben Todd

I've seen your shows. They're pretty intense.
Yeah, the shows have always been pretty aggressive. That's always kind of been a part of it. In high school I would stop songs in the middle — there would just be like weird freak-outs. It was definitely influenced by a certain noise-punk performance style. There were very few live rap shows I can say I've seen that inspired me as a performer. Later on getting into like Springsteen and Prince, or touring with Public Enemy, I really saw how high the bar can be raised.

How did you end up with Public Enemy?
I put out a free mixtape and Public Enemy's booking agent heard it and thought it would be funny for me to tour with them in Canada. That was really eye-opening. Before that, I didn't think you could do bands with rap music. It just never works. When I went on that tour I saw Public Enemy and they played for like two-and-a-half hours.

They were like the rap version of Bruce Springsteen and the E Street Band. It all kind of clicked, that if I wanted to express myself in a certain way I needed a band.

How did you get into Bruce Springsteen?
I think my gateway into Springsteen as an older teenager was Andrew W.K. I don't know if anybody else has made that connection, but I think both use language in a way that's so definitive. They have these things they keep coming back to and they kind of build their own world. A lot of rappers were doing that around the same time, like Young Jeezy, where they would have this imagery that kind of existed within their realm, catch phrases, slogans.

This reminds me of your label, Thunder Zone. How did that start?
It's kind of an extension of the aesthetics and the world I've built as Juiceboxxx. I have so many influences and I'm such a fan. It's beyond mercy.

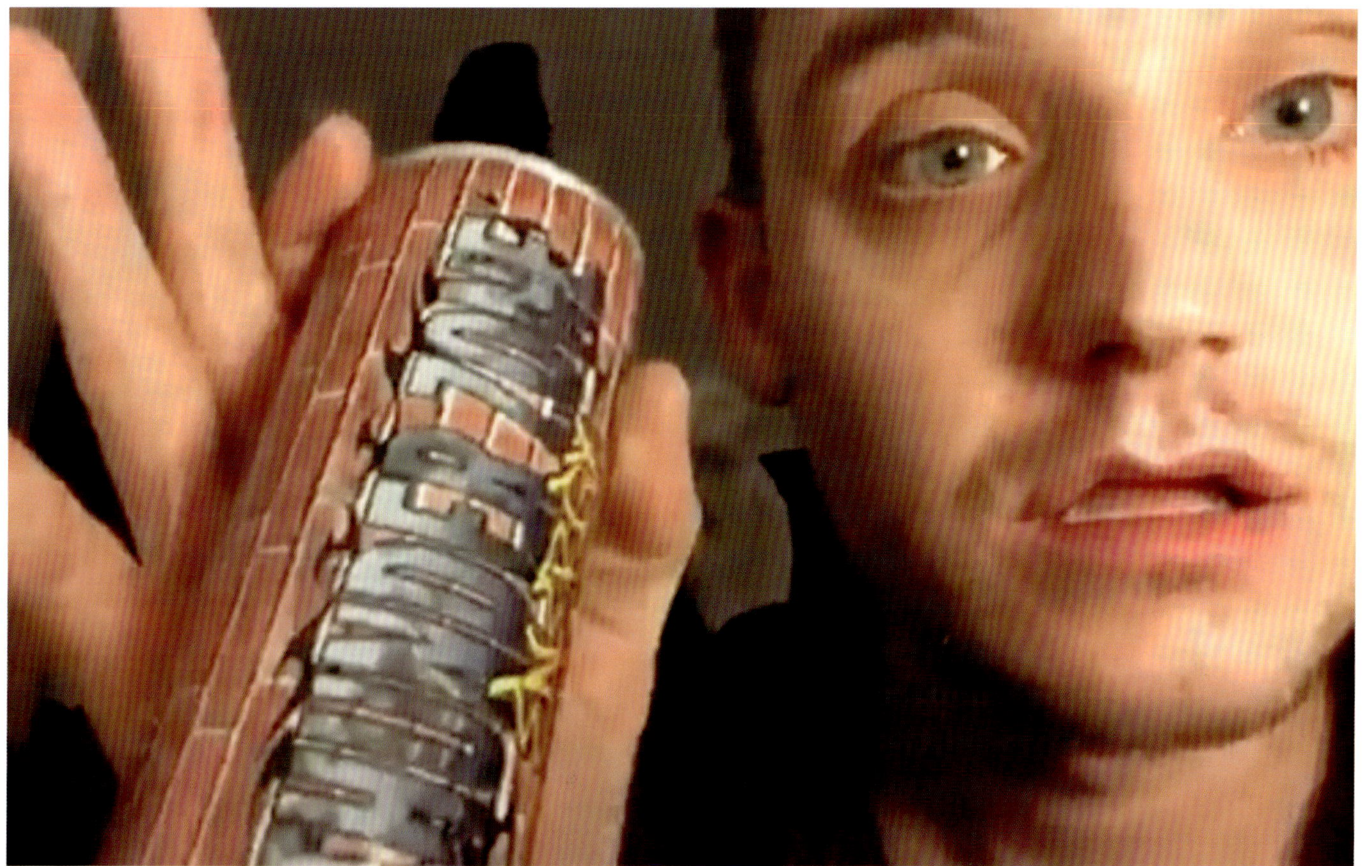

Thunder Zone Energy Drink Giveaway, 2015.

Was having an energy drink a part of that?
That was kind of what started it.
At the beginning I wanted to do a
record label that was also an energy
drink. Just something that would have
excited me as a fan. To go to the
website and this label is putting
out rap records and energy drinks
and the Extreme Animals tape and
these T-shirts. Just a collection of
things that could only come from one
person's vision.

How did State of the Thunder Zone start?
I got an iPhone for the first time — I
had a flip phone up until then. I felt
like I just needed to do a project
with the iPhone because I had it. 2013
was really like a dark year for me. I
was not in a very good place. I just
felt the need to document that energy
— this shitty weekly project that was
kind of terrifying to watch — extreme
in a casual way.

**You've got an album called I Don't
Want to Go into the Darkness. What is
the darkness?**

I don't know. Maybe it was sort of
a reaction to some communities I've
been involved with. I'm trying to stay
positive, even though I'm not always a
positive person. I think it's easy to
give up on your dreams, especially as
you get older. It's easier to kind of
settle into a certain zone. You have
to dream big and just be psyched about
the failure. Be psyched to look like
an idiot.

Do you think Juiceboxxx is underground?
I don't think so...I hope not, you
know what I mean? I have serious pop
ambition. I think there's a form of
Catholic guilt — the DIY punk rock
version — from being involved in
counterculture and underground music
since I was like 12 or 13. I have
some weird hang-ups that I have to
deal with. Like, I know I wouldn't be
doing music if I wasn't involved in
that world. I owe my entire creative
life to it... At the same time I have
to be honest. I have big fucked up
dreams. ☺

Odwalla88

"What happens when we're saying those things together is an exciting part about doing this together, rather than just one person."

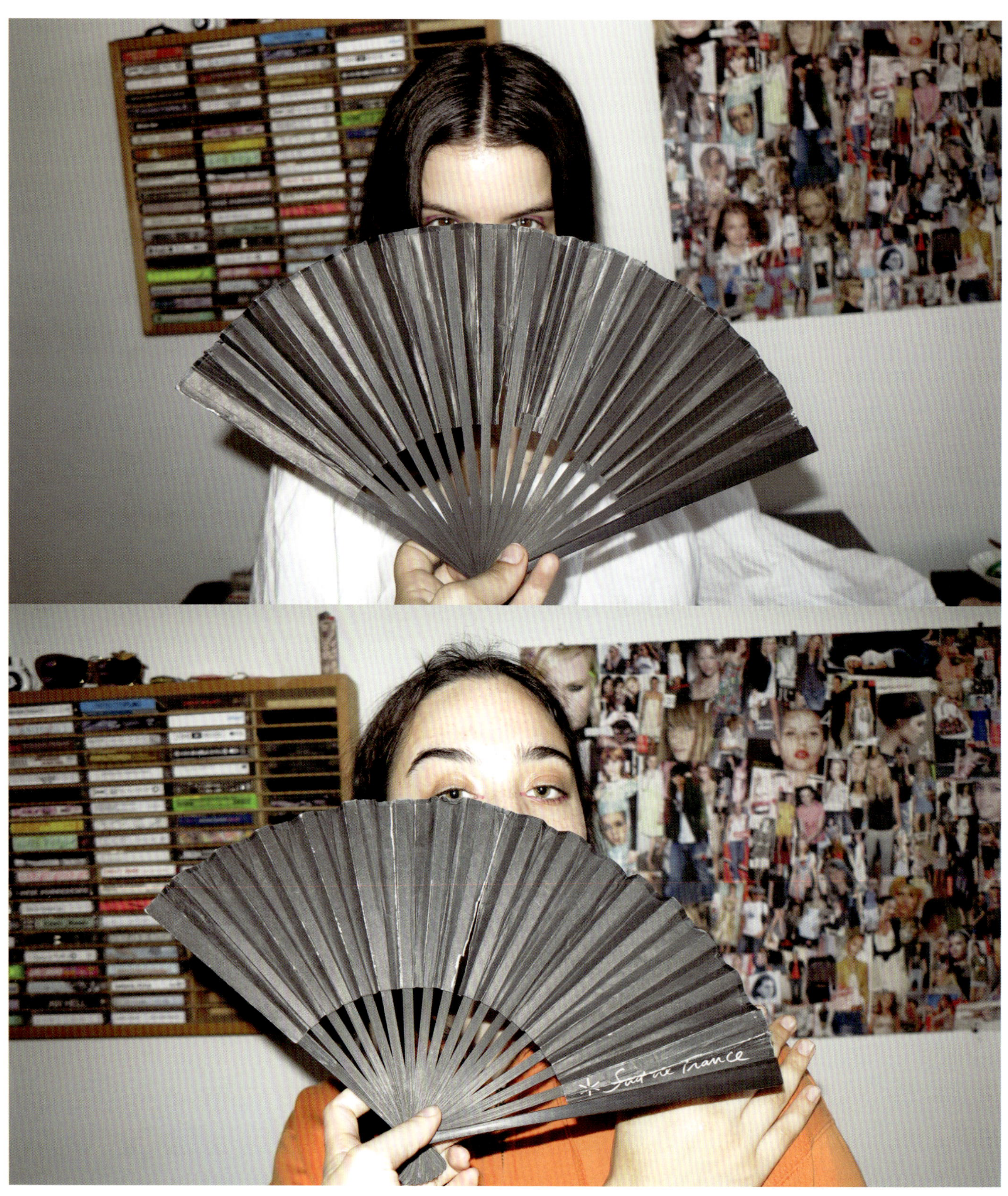

Interview by Brendan Fowler
Images courtesy Odwalla88

Whether or not you have seen or heard Chloé Maratta and Flannery Silva perform, I don't think Odwalla88 needs an introduction or explanation. It is so realized as a set and treatment of statements, built into Odwalla88 is it's own introduction that I believe functions best on its own. I will say this, though: they were sort of loosely explained to me and I was incredibly excited to see them play, but I was still unprepared for how intense they are live. Following the show I thought a lot about what I saw and worried that they could not be recorded in a way that could function anywhere near the level of the live performance. But as you will hear them say, they love bootlegs and it seems as well that the format of a coarse live recording really loves them back. Circa 2014 we are living in a time of so much retro-reference and I am constantly surprised by how little people seem to care about doing things — especially in music — that have already been done. Odwalla88 is that very, very rare new thing that would be new in any time. It's something that I didn't see coming and I am still surprised and challenged and riled by with every recorded listening and live witnessing.

I have to say as a preamble, I was excited when the magazine asked me to interview you because I really like talking to you two, and really like talking about your project, but I was reticent on some level because I feel like Odwalla88, as it presents itself in the world, is its own well-articulated statement, which is one of the things that I love so much about it. Spoiler alert: we are going to do an interview, but what do you think about the idea of talking about art like this?
Chloé: Fun.

Flannery: Well, I think in this situation I'm excited about it because we're talking to you, and I feel like every time we've met up we haven't really been able to hash it out, but we're psyched on each other, you know? So it feels like a very comfortable situation. But I think Chloé and I are always trying to describe to each other what this is and to other people, and that's definitely been a challenge. And there's a little bit of, not controversy, but there's some sensitive subjects that come up. And that's a challenge to talk about.
Chloé: To me it's just like when we were in school and we'd be in a crit and everyone wanted to crack the code wide open about stuff, like, "What does this mean and how do we all know the truest meaning of it?" and all of the things that maybe are supposed to stay hidden about it. But I love being in conversation with friends and people who make things, too, so it's a yin and yang.
Flannery: Making music, it's new, it's new for me, I guess for both of us, because it is less visual, it's more words, we're talking at you. **Yeah!**
Chloé: Yeah, in Odwalla we are screaming at you, rather. But music doesn't do the same thing, I don't think, where it's like you have to know a conceptual reasoning. **Odwalla88 certainly functions as a fairly direct address, but the parts that are less direct, or the parts that are more kind of gestural or something, I feel like are that way in a really considered way. So I guess that's the thing, my interest is not in cracking the code, as it were, my interest is very much in preserving and celebrating the code that is Odwalla88.**
Chloé: I don't think this is going to be the type of interview where you'll be like, "What does it mean to surf the wave?" you know?

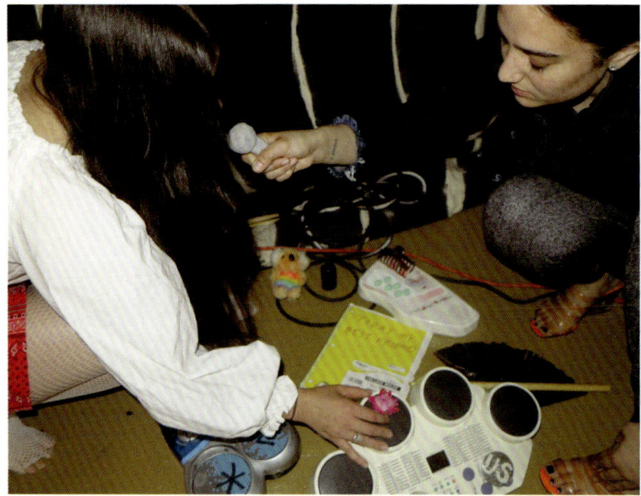
Odwalla88, Floristree, Baltimore 2013.

Well, that was actually my next question, so... But really, when did it start?
Flannery: I got a package in the mail, but I didn't order anything, and it was the First Act Electronic Drum Pad...
Chloé: ...We don't use it anymore. We bought it and we only used it at our first and second show, but it doesn't have an output. It's shaped like a foot, it's for a little kid, and it has little toes.
Really?
Flannery: We just want you to visualize it.
OK.
Chloé: But it didn't have an output, so I asked someone who I thought was really good at electronics to solder an output into it, but it feeds back really bad, the whole time there's this noise when it's plugged into the PA. But I bought that for Flan so she would be in a band with me because I had been doing my solo thing, Sissa, for about year, and I was like, this is not that hard, we should be in a band together. Because I was just doing vocal stuff, just a microphone, and I was like, we should make some noise, some sounds, together. That was about a year ago. Our first show was at Floristree with this band, Needle Gun, and —
Flannery: We sat on the stage, we didn't stand.

Chloé: Yeah, we sat down, which was weird.
Flannery: We were comfortable but weird.
Chloé: Yeah, very weird. I stood up for one song.
Wait, Flannery, how long did it take you to figure out that Chloé had sent you the drum pad?
Flannery: It was towards the last weeks of school, and I opened it and we were in the same room and I opened it. So it was like, it was cute, it was a very cute moment.
Chloé: She was so confused about what it was.
Flannery: Yeah, yeah.
Were you like, "It is a foot"?
Flannery: Yeah. "What does this mean?"
So the first instrumentation idea was percussion?
Chloé: Yeah, our first show we used that drum pad and then we put some loops together in GarageBand, which was in a similar way to maybe how we use our sampler now. So yeah, I guess the first thought was percussion. It was like, I want to bang on a drum pad. But we didn't even play it with sticks, we just played it by hand.
Flannery: And it was all the sounds that were within the foot, so it was kind of silly.
Chloé: Yeah, but I liked the cop car sound.
Flannery: Yeah, I liked that one. A couple of them were harsh. Or harsh enough.
Chloé: Only it sounded even harsher because it was amplified through the PA.
So this question feels a little bit code-orientated, but do you see it as a band or as a performance? I have my own feelings about that kind of stuff from my own trip, but how do you see Odwalla88?
Chloé: I think we see ourselves in the grand tradition of being in a band but not knowing how to play your instrument. Or not having great musical craft. But we would never play perfectly tuned bass through a pedal, you know?

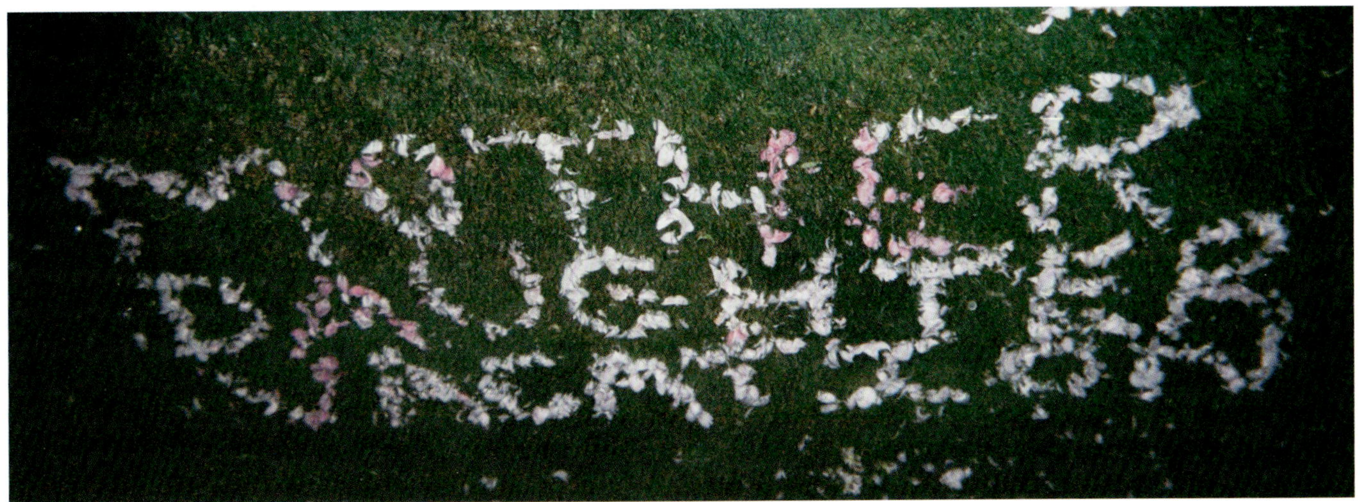

Flower Arrangement for Cell Phone Blog MDV, 2011.

Flannery: Yeah. But I think we've grown more into feeling like a band, because of having a list of songs that we play together, but, mmmm...
I guess what I really am asking is: you two both being artists and having your own art practices, what led you to wanting to do a project in the genre of "band"?
Chloé: Yeah, so you mean like playing alongside bands?
Exactly. Entering into that context as opposed to, or in addition to, any other context?
Flannery: I think for both of us what comes first is the words, for sure. I have always been writing poems or lyrics, so I think for me it felt like more of an accessible way to present that.
Chloé: Which is why we get called a poetry band.
Flannery: Yeah, which is — but yeah, I mean, we always talk about just wanting to make the music we want to hear, so I think that's the root of it.
Chloé: I feel like, also, I was going to a lot of shows that were all boy shows, bands would be all guys, and I would always be, like, I could never be in a band, but then after Sissa, the thing by myself — it sounds so, uhm, corny to call it my "solo project," but by doing that I was, like, we could definitely be in a band. It was almost like by performing by myself with just a microphone — I don't want

to keep using this metaphor of cracking the code — but it was like I cracked the code and it was all of a sudden apparent to me that we could just do it because people on stage weren't doing anything super magic, or super hard.
Flannery: Yeah. It doesn't have rules.
It doesn't have rules, it's true. Though I actually think that aside from you two, and of course some other people, that right now is a really extra-conservative time in music, and especially in underground music in a lot of ways, but that's a whole other thing. You two both just graduated from art school since the band has been happening?
Chloé: We played our first show two weeks before we graduated.
And Baltimore has a wonderful community that I think has a lot to do with the Maryland Institute of Art and people coming in from all over the place to go there and because it's inexpensive to live there and make work and make it work.
Chloé: The Baltimore community, there's so many rad and amazing people who live here that are really inspiring to me — I want to say a shout out to everyone who lives at Floristree — and I think in terms of support it's been very positive. After the kind of weird first show that was just us feeling out what it was like to write songs, or how do we put sounds behind the words —

Flannery: I think the reaction was like, "What was that?" And then there were a couple of people that were starting to describe it in a really sincere way. Max Eilbacher was one of those people, and then our next show was at his house, at The Bank in Baltimore. But yeah, overall, both for Odwalla and visual art, it's a very nurturing place to be. Very open. So yeah, in terms of Odwalla's home it's been really rad.

Chloé: And there's space to be a band or a project that performs. People will ask you to play at their house, even if you played a really weird show. And there's space to work on songs, like, "We've got to work on this stuff for the next show, let's write all new songs." There's space to be nurtured and space to grow.

And as a literal physical space. You two do a store with your other friend Max Guy, too?

Chloé: Yeah, Rock 512 Devil is a project space/bookstore/gallery/club-house. There's a book club that meets there. It's always changing and we're supposed to have hours and sometimes it's not open and then sometimes it's open every weekend for a few months. Flannery created this ASMR night of videos and performances, and she put together this reading of The Glass Menagerie. It is a small storefront, but both times it was totally packed.

Flannery: It was cozy. It's not that small, I was surprised how big it was.

Flannery: For The Glass Menagerie we used the windowsills as a stage, so it's very make-shift in a Baltimore way.

Chloé: But I don't know a lot of other cities where I could afford a store-front one block away from me and not have some crazy profitable business running out of it. It's special.

Flannery: Yeah, that's very telling of where Baltimore is at.

In another city it might have to be a really crazy teeny space if it were even possible at all. I wanted to pose this idea to you, though: I have been really thinking a lot about this idea of

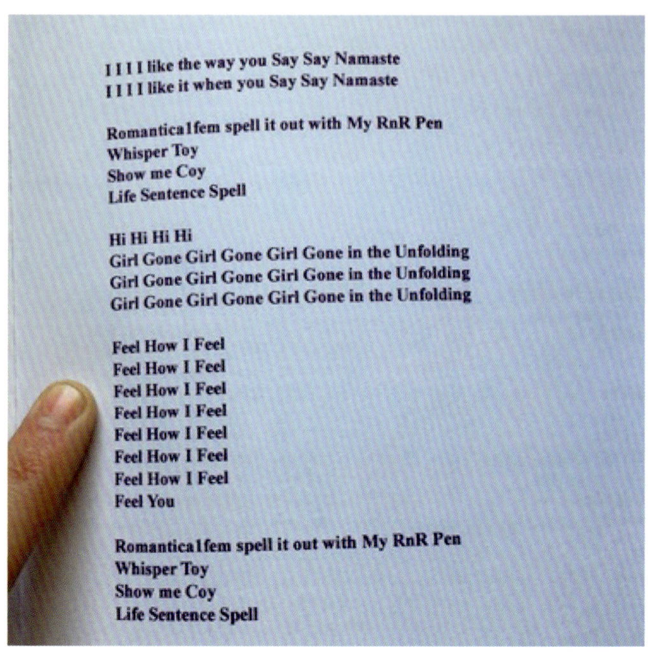

Odwalla88, Future Butterfly, The DA. Spunt Company, 2014. Photo: Marisa Takal

a sincerity spectrum, which I have not heard of classified as such, so the way I want to lay it out is on the one end if you picture totally sincere, literal, transparent, heart-on-sleeve, "honesty," and then on the other end, picture deception, maybe which even has sort of a malicious, nefarious connotation. I feel like often people tend to polarize, you know, segregate things into either totally sincere or totally insincere and dishonest. But in the middle somewhere I feel like exists this space of inter-sincerity or intra-sincerity, a spectrum between the two polarities that many things actually fall in. This is kind of a funny example, because we are in the middle of an interview, but an example could be when a sentiment is "real" — sincere — but the context in which it is presented may not be totally "real." Like, imagine an interview or something where the answers are really real and sincere but maybe the questions weren't actually ever asked or the whole thing was written by one person, so the final product serves to convey sincere feelings, "truths," but the

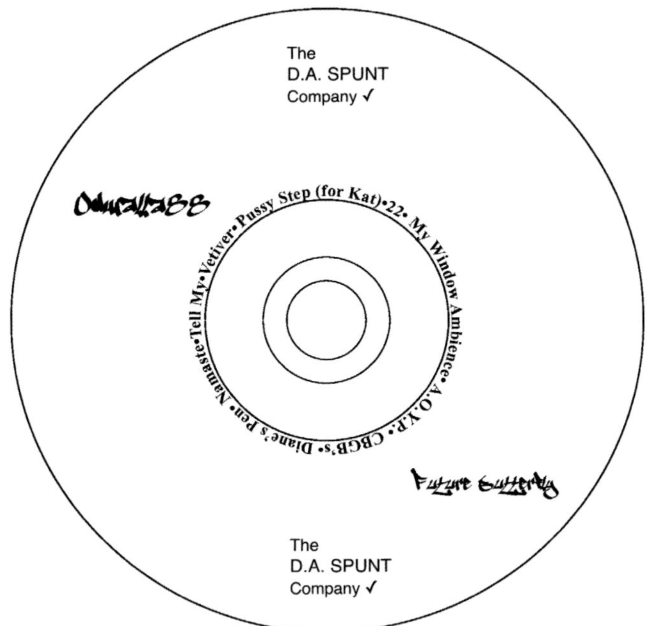

Odwalla88, Future Butterfly, The DA. Spunt Company, 2014.

presentation is a fictionalization of an event that never actually happened. You know what I mean?
Flannery: You mean like also the delivery of that?
Yeah, and I use that example just to set up the idea of this spectrum because I feel like it is kind of clear, but sometimes I think that things which may exist within this spectrum point less overtly to their place on the spectrum. I wanted to set that up because I think it's really interesting the way I perceive you to play around in it. I've had this conversation about Odwalla88 regarding the instances where you'll quote or you'll reference things and it's kind of unclear, it could maybe be sarcastic? I don't think you're using sarcasm in a mean-spirited way or a super cynical way at all, which are ends to which sarcasm is often used, but sometimes you will say things that kind of have sort of an attached cultural baggage already, but in a way that recontextualizes them.
Flannery: Yeah, totally. Max, our 512 partner, the last time he saw us he was like, "You guys are so sarcastic." I was like, "Hey! OK, I'll let that soak in."

Chloé: It's the delivery.
Flannery: Yeah, I think delivery is definitely where what is a sincere sentiment comes off as insincere. Or sarcastic.
Chloé: Because sometimes we say things in a bratty tone, not that it's a bratty thing we're saying.
Flannery: Yeah, I think that when I'm feeling more aggressive, the more aggressive moments, are when that side of it comes out. There's also a lot of repetition and a lot of mantra, so I think that the sayings can come off as more insincere.
Chloé: More insincere because they're said over and over again.
Flannery: Yeah, I think the repetition reinforces that.
Or maybe it complicates it. If you had a little spectrometer, like an intra-sincerity spectrometer, maybe if you said something one time it would register on one end, and then over the course of saying it five or ten times it starts to —
Flannery: Yeah, like saying "I care" a million times and how we just keep saying it and it gets exhausted.
Chloé: But I do care.
Flannery: But I do care, completely... We're totally not interested in cynicism and being sarcastic — we're just constantly trying to be aware of how to be positive and think of the happy things, but also talk about what makes us mad.
Still be critical.
Flannery: Yeah. That spectrum is definitely on the mind.
I was listening to this interview recently with a comedian who was saying that he likes to get into this certain un-comfort space, to take the joke someplace where people are uncomfortable and he likes to hang out in that space for as long as possible, push the limits of that space. I was thinking about you two and how I feel like the sincerity question space, you like to push that, you like to push those zones.

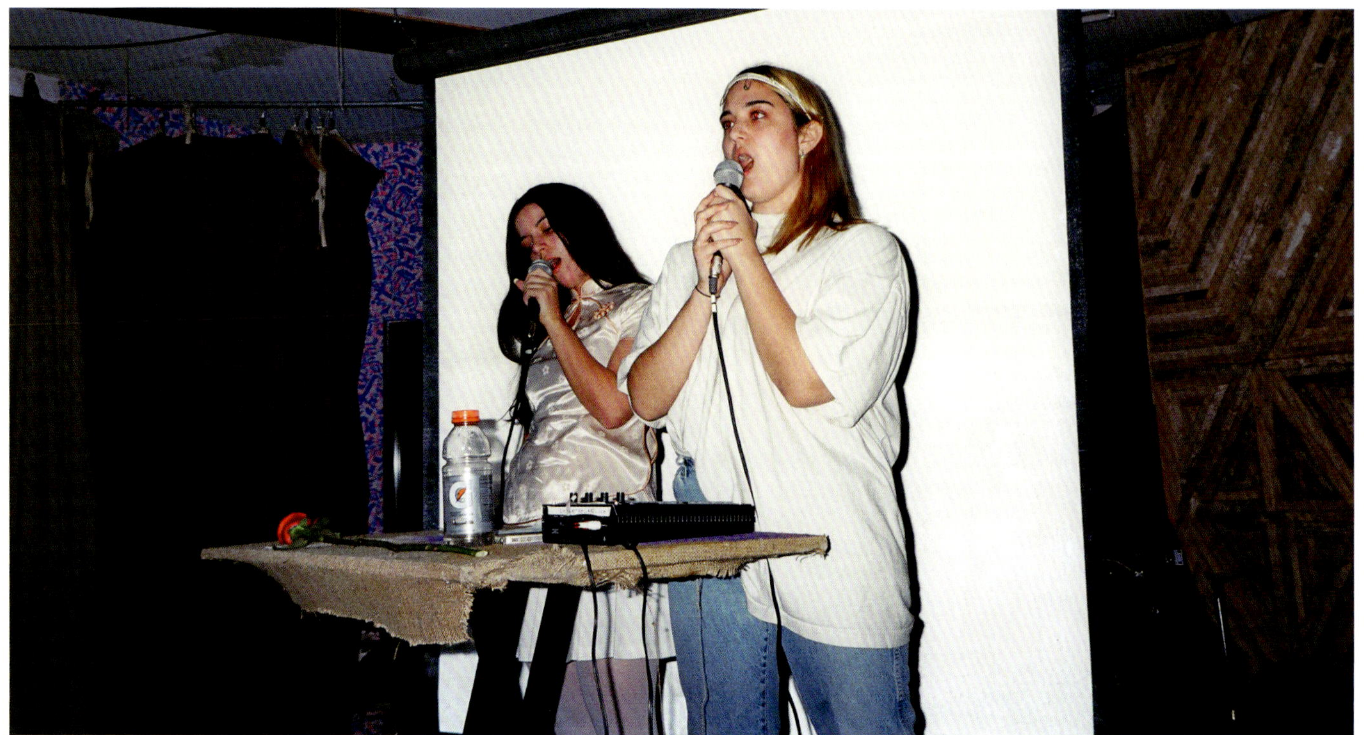

Odwalla88, Silent Barn, Brooklyn, 2014. Photo: Vinnie Smith

Chloé: I feel like that's something I've noticed when I listen to the bootlegs from our shows, the audio recordings, but this also has to do with how our song structure is maybe a little...I'm not trying to say we have this wild, avant-garde sound structure but —
Chloé: You know how sometimes people are like, "Oh, is that song done?" Or, like, "What's the song?" Sometimes the point at which the audience claps, or the pauses after a song, that's because of the content, or just the weird way it ended.
Flannery: I wonder if its the fact that we're not singing, we're just saying it. It just always comes back to the delivery for me, and the kind of monotone intensity of it.
It's a pretty strict style, your two voices and then at most two other sounds happening at a time, right? At most the drums and the sampler, or some combination of, and any single part has a lot of space to do what it needs to do, to explore. If you're repeating something as many times as you often are, it's like you get to really sink into it.

Flannery: What happens when we're saying those things together is an exciting part about doing this together, rather than just one person.
Chloé: I could never play an Odwalla song by myself because it needs two voices.
Flannery: Yeah, but when we were on tour and I lost my voice, Chloé did most of my parts. It was beautiful and really emotional to watch, but it maybe didn't have the sting.
Chloé: Because a lot of songs it'll be like Flan has her solo moment, and then I have my solo moment, and then it's this thing in the middle that we say together. Not to reduce it to that, but that's often how it jams out. Me saying all of the parts and then trying to use Flannery's delivery, how she said it, was so bizarre. I mean it was cool for one night, but it kind of freaked me out. Because it's about two voices, one voice by itself, one voice by itself, and then two together. I tried to sing those songs by myself when I jumped on a few of my friend's dates on a West Coast tour last summer and it was weird.

It was probably like you were doing some kind of a half cover kind of thing, right?

Chloé: Yeah, I would be like, "This is a song by my hardcore band, Odwalla88," and there'd be a long pause, and I would go into it...

Andrea [Longacre-White] made this observation the other day listening to your side of the split tape with You Nori about how rad it is that the difference between your own voices and those samples of your voices kind of flattens out on the recording. It gets hard to tell what is your voice "live" and what is your voice being played on the sampler. Is that something you thought about?

Chloé: I've never thought about that, but I like the idea of that because to me it's like if someone listened to it they would think it was a five person band and one person's job was to just go, "Tell my.../tell my.../tell my..." the whole time — like that's the girl who just does that. The first thing I wanted to figure out how to do, was to sample our voices. I'm not really into gear, but we were having a hard time figuring out what to buy, because people are weird about that stuff. For me it wasn't very accessible about what should I buy to start this band.

Flannery: It was like we didn't have a cool older sister to ask.

Chloé: When we got the [Roland SP] 404 that was the first thing I was so hyped to do, just be able to put our voices saying something in, and then make it say that many times, being able to yell into it and then loop the yell. I was so excited about that, because I don't know how to make beats.

Flannery: It was just like a powerful sound, to have that and then to be saying the same thing over, and then to kind of fade in and out of it.

Chloé: We either sample our voices or hardcore band's bootlegs — like at the beginning of a hardcore show and everyone's screaming. Those are our two favorite things to sample.

But I only like to sample the very beginning of songs, I realize.

Flannery: Live is preferable.

Chloé: Yeah, we like the sound of live bootleg stuff, which is why our tape is all bootlegs. People weren't happy with that.

You love the bootleg as a format.

Chloé: I like it just as much as regular recordings. I'm really excited about the things that we're working on right now with Max Eilbacher, how we're taking a long time to consider the vocals, consider how the samples sound and adjust the levels.

Flannery: He understands sounds differently than us, so it has this cool digi feel. It is a cool version.

Chloé: I like listening to live stuff, and I guess I don't have a good ear for tune or any of that stuff, which is why we don't sing. I'm not a skilled craftsman in that way.

Flannery: You're a musician.

Chloé: I'm a musician. I guess what I'm trying to say is I'm not hitting notes. And so for me, I don't have that ear, and so a bootleg sounds pretty great to me. Listening to it, that's what the show sounded like that we played, and we messed up a little bit when we played Pussy Step but that's what it was like to be at an Odwalla88 show in March of 2014.

Flannery: Yeah, I think it translates well.

Flannery: Mmmm, I don't know.

Chloé: I don't think so.

Flannery: I think they're both exciting. I'm excited about sharing both.

Yeah, I think so, too. Do you have a hierarchy of the relationship between a live performance and a document of the performance?

Flannery: It's interesting hearing or having the video recording of the thing, and then having just the audio recording of the live thing, because without seeing it, it almost felt more intense, more abrasive. Chloé has been recording the live sets on her tape recorder.

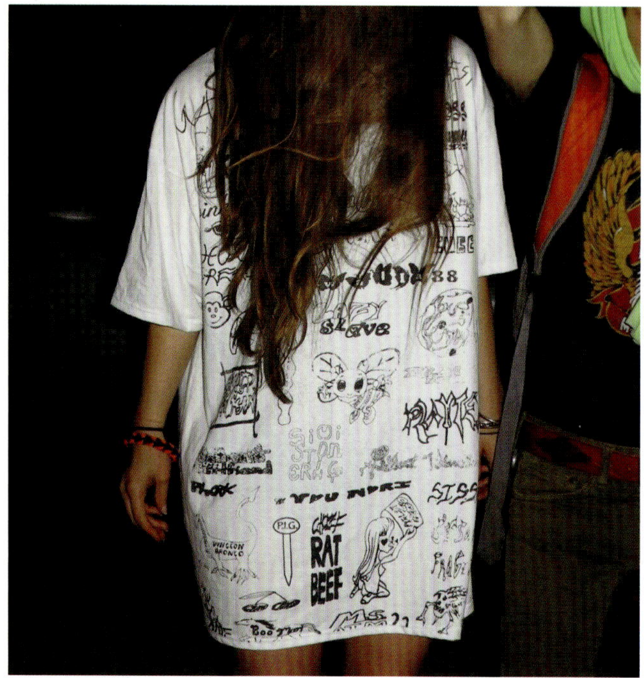

Fan in Fan Tee by Odwalla88 & Keke Hunt, Richmond, VA, 2014.

Chloé: But it sounds really bad.
Flannery: Bad in a way that we love.
Chloé: I didn't realize how bad it was until everyone said, "Oh, that tape you gave me..."

Is that your half of the split tape with You Nori?

Chloé: No, I'm pretty happy with that one, actually. That one is audio from a video which was recorded with a digital camera. I made this other bootleg tape where it was five minutes on each side and Noel Freibert held the tape player at one of our concerts from 20 feet away. That one is really not that cool...

Brendan: Too harsh.

Chloé: Yeah, it's too harsh. It's like a flat buzz punctuated by me dropping the microphone or something.

Brendan: I'm curious if there's anything to say about the way you two present live in the way it's so still? I feel like your movement is similar to how there's the sound economy, there's not that many elements, so each element becomes very significant. Similarly, physically you two are sort of staying in one place the whole time, and it's so intense.

Chloé: That's something, to quote Flannery, "To me it comes naturally." We both go to a lot of shows and when the performer maybe senses that this crowd isn't going wild with them 100% they will throw themselves into the audience, and be pushy and crazy and wild. For me, I'm always like, "Dude, that doesn't make your set look crazier or more intense if you're physically flailing all over the place." But that's cool, that's just their style, it's not bad or stupid, it's just — I think the way I stand in Odwalla is similar to how I did it when I played by myself, which is this bob back and forth, sway.
Flannery: It's swaying into the sound. But also, I can't stand up without swaying or else I'll faint. The Chloé sway started in a different way, so hers was more like feeling the words and feeling the sound.

Wait, is that true about fainting, Flannery? That's not true.

Flannery: No, it's true.
Chloé: No, it's so true, it's not even cool.
Flannery: I faint like once a year.

Brendan: Really?

Flannery: The sway and kind of the rock, it definitely felt like something that we're doing together and feeling together. So that, mixed with staring someone down or staring at something in the audience. I like to just keep one focus and just say it all into that.
Chloé: When we were on tour — I never said this because I think it would be kind of hokey — but I joked at one point with Flannery that we would say "Hi, we're Odwalla88 and we're really happy to be here even if we don't seem like it."
Chloé: We have an intense presence together, and I think about that a lot, whether or not that's too negative.
Flannery: It's a serious presence.
Chloé: One day I'll be in a funny band.
Flannery: Yeah, right.
Chloé: Yeah, right. 🙂

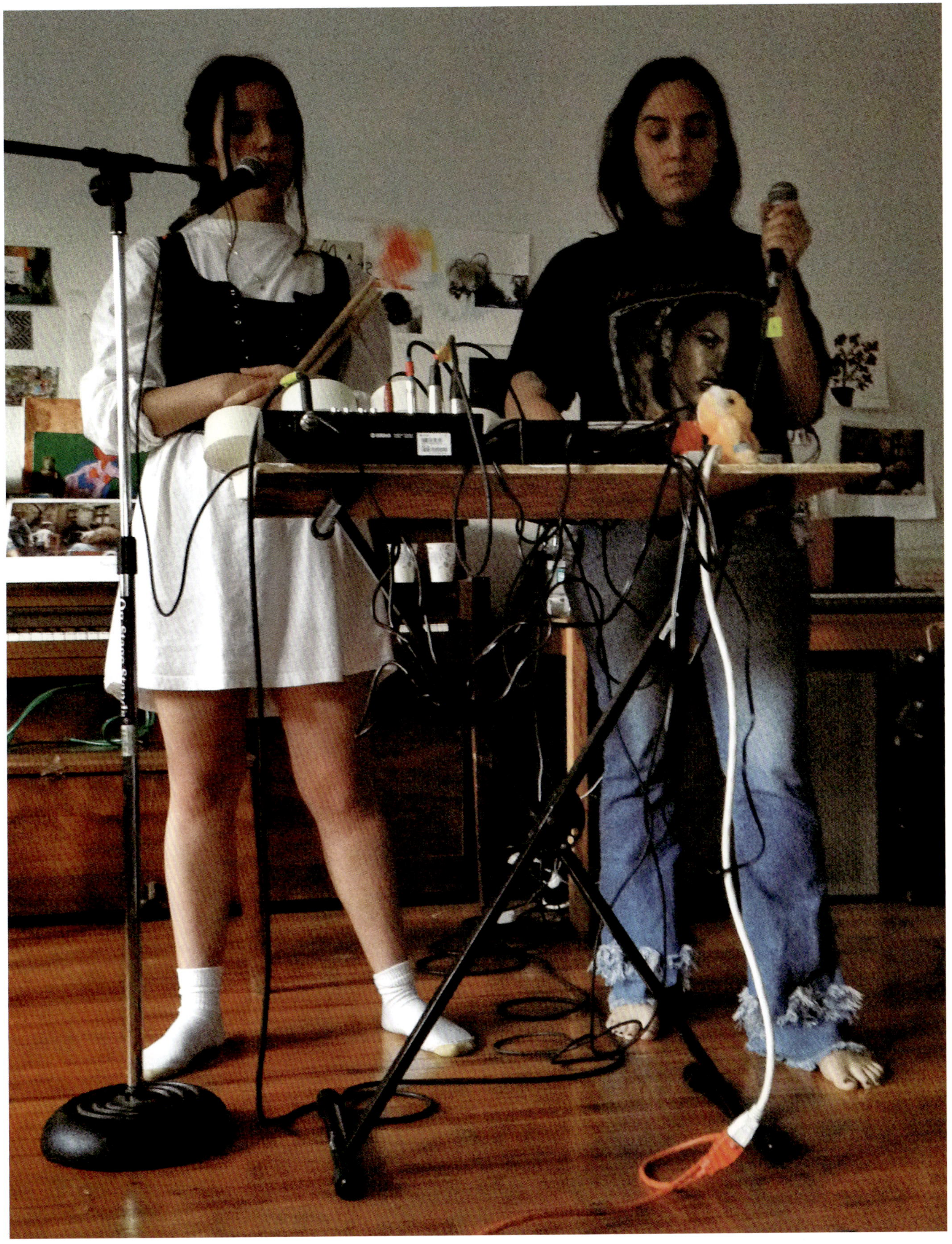

Odwalla88, Mommy Afterparty, to.be Office, New York, 2014. Photo: Asher Penn

On Bacon Index

"Determining whether something is a threat or challenge to your identity on the internet can be a frustrating game."

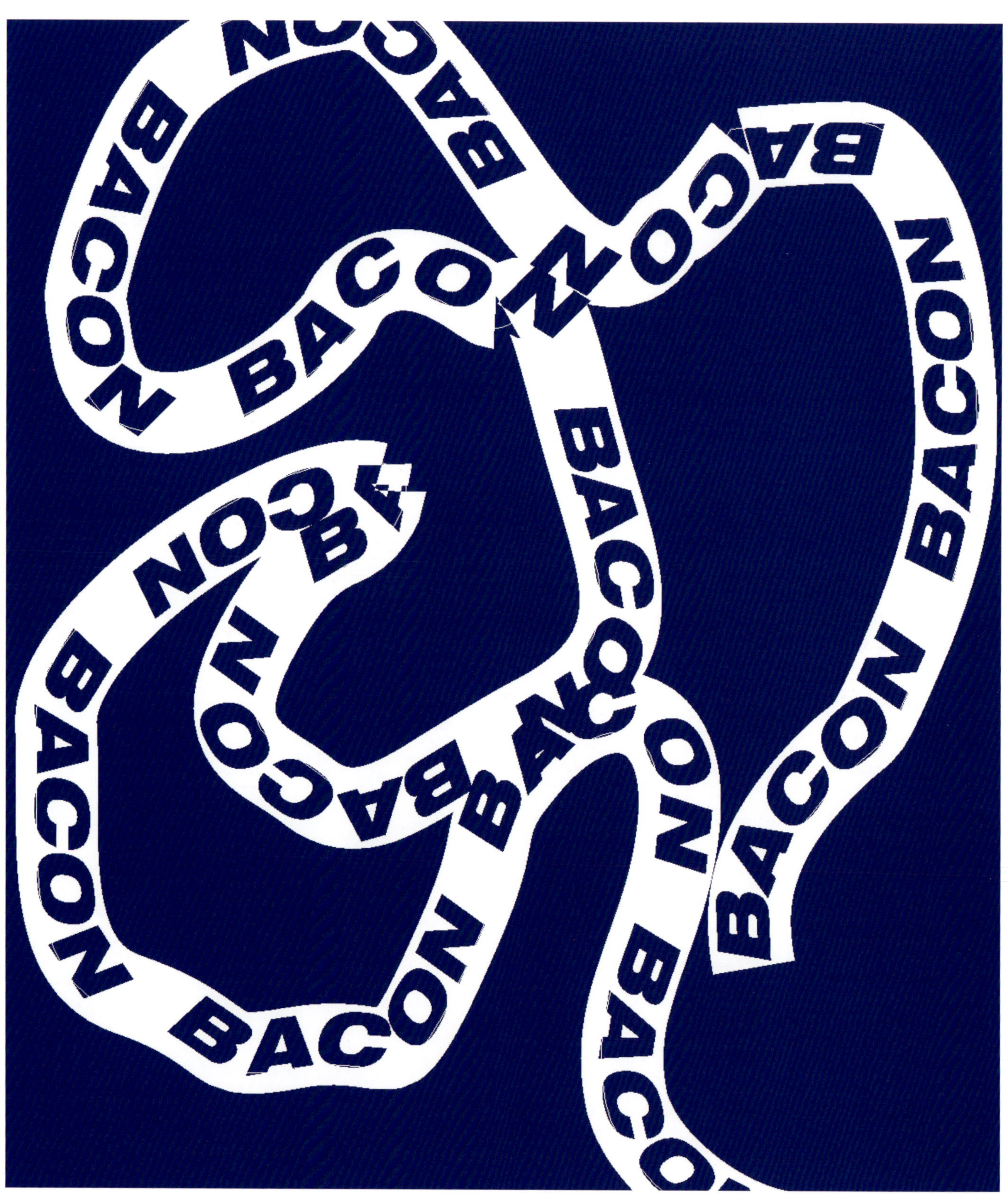

By Rosemary Kirton
Images courtesy Bacon Index

Introduction

Bacon Index is an independent Japanese brand which makes and sells street wear, amongst other things. The locus of the Bacon Index is its blog, through which a group of DJs, designers, and artist disseminate mixes, adverts, and shoots of their products. All of this is complemented by another practice, a dedicated feed of imagery relating to Kevin Bacon, which echoes through the design of their products.

This Japanese brand seems fundamentally informed by its unlikely mascot. Kevin Bacon is a significant figure outside of his acting. In the 1990s, he made an off-hand comment on a TV talk show professing he'd worked with everyone in Hollywood. A group of comedians picked up on this arrogance and plausibility, creating a version of the association game Six Degrees of Separation but geared towards the actor's statement.

Over the years Kevin Bacon's prowess has diminished but what came to be known as the Six Degrees of Kevin Bacon has developed beyond the actor's remit, to the point where Google has an add-on that indicates any given actor's "Bacon Number." It's clear Kevin Bacon acknowledges and adopts the phenomenon for his own ends, often appearing in adverts related to connectivity and relationality.

Bacon Index makes their user/consumer aware of Kevin Bacon through an archive of imagery they post through their Tumblr alongside candid shots of their minimal yet bold designs. The performance of this archive comes across as absurd and excessive, something a driven fan might do. Bacon Index is a sophisticated fan-form, where the hysterical adulation of fandom is then siphoned into the beautiful objects and mixes they produce in tribute.

Left: Bacon graphic, August 14th, 2013.

Street wear, Fandom, and Data

It's possible to identify many levels of the fashion industry ironically appropriating branded and cultural iconography in a manner which celebrates the knock-off or the counterfeit. Creating and distributing a forgery is a criminal act in and of itself, but it also functions to erode, or test, soft power — the influence a nation has on others through its ideals/culture as opposed to hard power being its infrastructure, military, resources. While it may seem close, Bacon Index keeps an intelligible step away from creating products that might unlawfully use the actor's image or name. Their professed love for movies and actors of Kevin Bacon's heyday also make it hard to write-off Bacon Index as a wholly ironic enterprise.

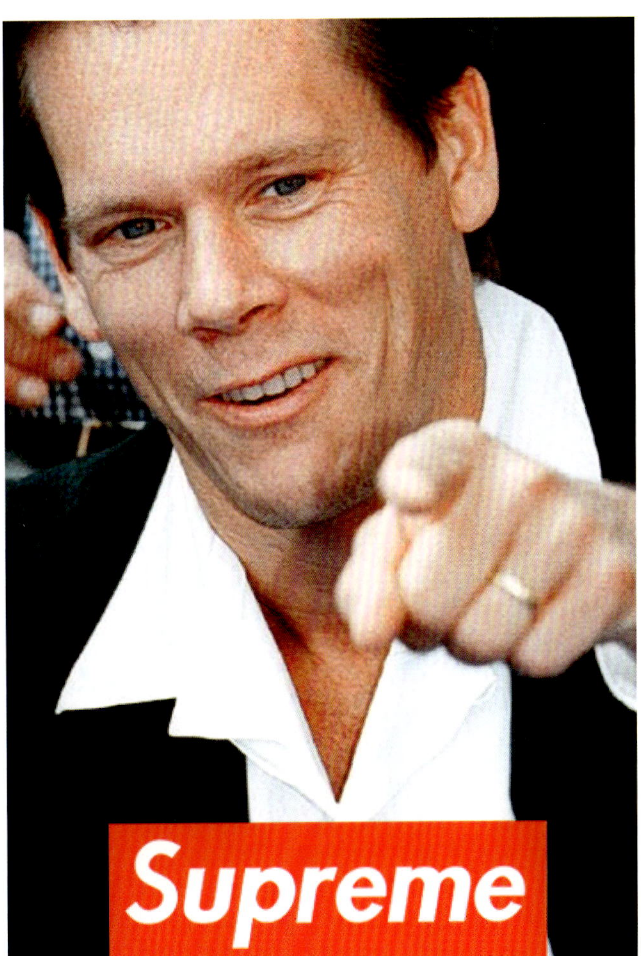

Bacon Index, 2011.

Similar in some way to Bacon Index, street wear brand C.E takes a wry stance on the economic trade standards of Europe by using the symbol designated to authenticate products, as their name/logo. Street wear brands are an emergent, DIY, localized form of fashion, that exist at a relative distance from high fashion and commerce. However these concepts/industries are increasingly diluted and cross-pollinated.

Street wear has been greatly elevated by e-commerce and proliferation of identity expression online, but the internet is also an arena in which authenticity can get quickly muddied, where security of identity and autonomy is subject to relentless abstract threat.

Determining whether something is a threat or challenge to your identity on the internet can be a frustrating game. There isn't much hope for the casual user, whose data, unlike the crops of their old FarmVille account, is being harvested by the services they occupy, and this is no doubt within the terms of their user agreement. To what extent and cause that data is exported and implemented is often unclear to the user too.

Bacon Index's seemingly indiscriminate archiving of Kevin Bacon imagery, would, if it weren't for the actor's fame, seem like a form of open surveillance, or just plain creepy, but in this context, it's playful fandom. The tireless work of fandoms, their fanart and fiction, are a legal gray area and at the same time, innovative, empathetic pools of creativity, a potential resource for the production forces behind the subject of the fandom.

Bacon Index's fan-archiving extends to the entire Kevin Bacon entity/celebrity — almost any image, whether poor quality or tenuous can be seen in the archive.

It's doubtful, but not impossible, that the actor is aware of these machinations and it's viable he'd be chill with it, like the whole Six Degrees of Kevin Bacon deal.

A Hysterical Index

The most likely place to encounter Bacon Index is online as a Facebook, Tumblr, or Instagram user. Although your timeline may feel banal, a consumer/user is constantly caught in traumatic or ecstatic negotiation of possible and existing contexts, just beyond immediate cognition, shifting all the time in minimal degrees, according to other users and the systems they populate.

While their identity may seem firmly fixed, Bacon Index's actual creative process seems to treat the actor as a lens through which they read and respond to the world, and that lens has an adjustable focus. To the point where you can buy designs featuring artistic renderings of Kevin Bacon, like the cap produced with artist Pon-Chan, or a less overt item like the BCN Junior hooded sweater or Bacon socks.

Their Tumblr evokes a "hysterical index," where indexing is exuberantly performed but doesn't provide a stringent indexical function. It even satirizes the kind of usefulness and functionality that users have come to expect from digital services. A hysterical index isn't necessarily technophobic, but a different way to encounter, collect, and distribute data than ones optimized for quantitative efficiency. As a user you expect efficiency from the services you engage with, and services expect you to surrender access to personal data in exchange. Your ongoing actions and updates provide information to that service too, which may ultimately improve its efficiency.

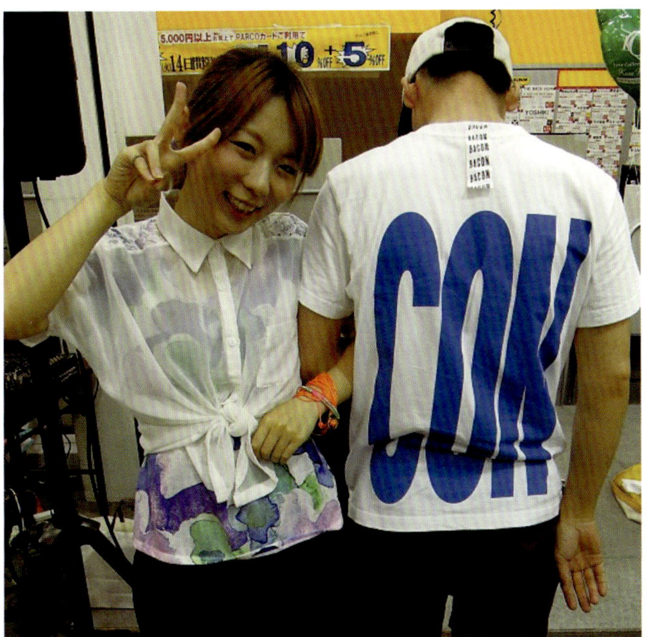

Bacon Index, 2013.

Brands rely on users to share and advertise their products for them through social media, and users, particularly younger ones who've known nothing else, feel comfortable with this. The way brands want to interpret their relationship with other users is decided and monitored by numerous people, and even though you may have the same interaction skill- set, they wield more knowledge, power and influence in these contexts, aside, of course, from exceptional users. And those users themselves are often singled out to be vehicles of authenticity through which brands can associate themselves and ultimately capitalize from.

The idea of a hysterical index is hard to realize when a user has to maintain and surrender an increasing volume of personal data, for purposes beyond their comprehension, in order to express themselves. Users who don't fancy themselves hackers or feel confident with encrypting their activity online, but can't bare to log off, find themselves in a predicament that pithy Tumblr HorribleGif sums up nicely:

"Like the metaphorical clone being tortured somewhere else, we cannot feel any direct sting related to data harvesting."

User Style

The German word "kummerspeck," literally translating to "grief bacon," means excess weight gained from emotional overeating. Happening upon the indulgence of Bacon Index's fanaticism might cause that metaphorical clone to gain a bit of weight — but is Bacon Index really any different from any other devoted fandom? Can it really be considered indulgent to enthuse about Kevin Bacon on the internet?

While you could argue it's just a zany, very millennial brand — and on initial inspection, Bacon Index might fit the description of "weird internet" (like the pejorative Weird Twitter, Weird YouTube, etc.) — this just writes off unfamiliar content, behavior, and users as "other." Japanese culture has often been interpreted in an exoticizied manner by Western media. Particularly emphasized, and even ridiculed, is Japan's fervor for American culture. As a fanatic project based around Kevin Bacon by a group of Japanese people, Bacon Index could easily be dismissed as that stereotype, or as playing with it, but to insist they're doing either of these things alone, would still be an insufficient summary. It's likely Bacon Index is regarded in a myriad of overlapping and fractional ways, specific to which of their multifaceted output an individual happens upon.

Despite algorithms helpfully tailoring timelines and feeds for relevancy, users have room, albeit not much, to happen upon unfamiliar content. Bacon Index might not post content for a long time and then spam five or ten posts, mostly images of Kevin Bacon, of course.

While as a brand this would represent bad practice, to a casual Tumblr user nothing about this behaviour could be considered exceptional or unusual. The trend-forecasting agency K-Hole's lifestyle concepts "acting basic" and "normcore" gained traction last year, if not mostly for being repeatedly misinterpreted. While acting basic might be seen as buying and wearing functional middle-class brands, normcore refers to being able to fluidly adapt to each environment a person finds themselves in, both through style and attitude.

This concept relies on the ability to sincerely blend into events/contexts/environments, not stand out. A fair amount of affluence and confidence is required from any individuals engaging in these concepts, in order to achieve or maintain them. Kevin Bacon, who was not lost for affluence or confidence, adapted to a life where he came to stand for a system of relation. Admittedly he didn't lose all autonomy, but what has he done lately, other than adverts for broadband?

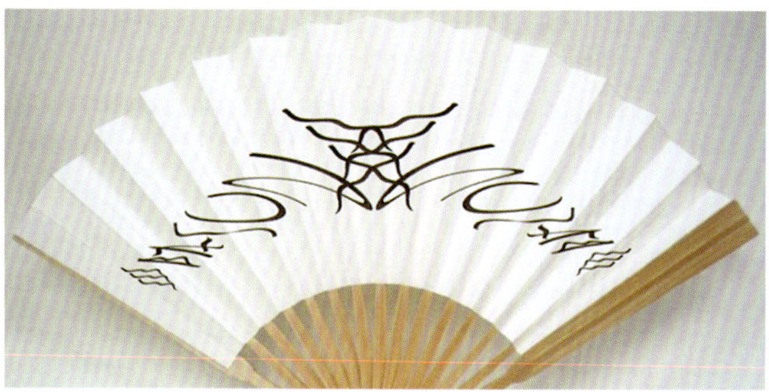

Bacon Fan, 2014.

Concluding: Bacon Index's Eulogy

First and foremost it's an absurdity that Kevin Bacon exists in such omnipotence. Bacon Index's kummerspeck, the weighty grief from the emotional over-consumption of Kevin Bacon, gets sublimated into their artworks and products. Bacon Index's popularity and actions have no doubt impacted upon the figure of Kevin Bacon — his integrity as a cultural figure has shifted.

In the past, Bacon Index claimed not to want to produce value, but definitely have and will go on to provide it for both the services they occupy as users, and Kevin Bacon. Like the metaphorical clone being admired somewhere, can Kevin feel the warmth of Bacon Index's adulation?

The continual update and reformulation of identity and data that the most average user performs is melancholic because it always exists as a poor facsimile of data surveillance. The normalcy of data surveilling emerges from the accessibility that public have to the daily life of celebrities like Kevin Bacon, made available to them through media and paparazzi. The trade-off for users is far more dirty than for celebrities — it's the same for a user liking a brand or posting a haul video online. Conventional brand-celebrity endorsements are often the subject of speculation because of the large amounts of money that changes hands, amongst other things. Bacon Index, as a brand/collective behaving like a fandom creating fan art, are sort of circumventing this bargain.

Almost every time a service changes its interface, or updates a user agreement, there's a sense of discomfort in the transition amongst users. It may not always be about adapting to the immediate change, but comes from an acknowledgment of the violence necessary for that change hidden in that bargain.

It's the necessary sacrifice of the user who surrenders more and more of their autonomy in order to streamline their experience. For a user to become exceptional relies on them harmonizing their operation of the mechanisms put forward by multiple platforms, with their ability to provide mutable meaning for communities that manifest, degrade, and intersect with immanence — that's a tall ask.

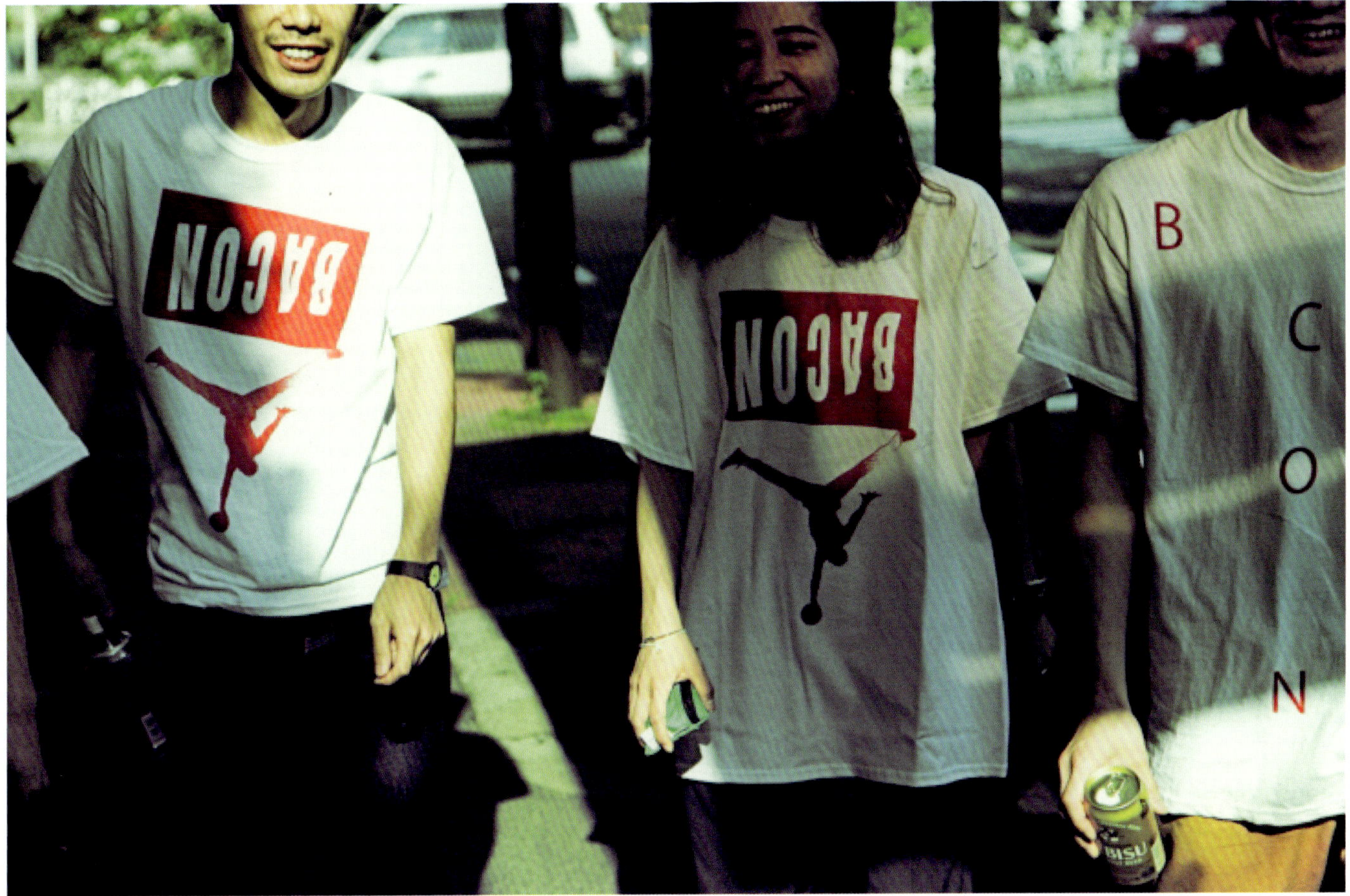

Bacon T-shirt Part 1, 2013. Photo: Ryosuke Kikuchi

It's absurd to imagine all users should become cyberpunk hackers or exceptional within their communities in order to evade unfair treatment of their data. In the absence of modernist infrastructure, the currency of identity can be exchanged for means of survival on a more fundamental level — we can't all afford or access camouflage technologies, from face changing software to vague stylistic turns like normcore or acting basic, to distort or destabilize identity.

Like clickbait articles concerning the shifting nature of identity online, contexts manifest and degrade with immanence from the tectonic movements of timelines and feeds. Even a casual user makes it their business to keep up with these different contexts. The compounding pressure of refreshing and interacting through these systems doesn't leave room for the user to mourn, and inspires a melancholic condition. Psychoanalyst case studies on failed mourning see individuals trying to become the locus of their trauma and then killing that self, in order to redress the balance of trauma and loss.

Bacon Index are decentralized users but united as one. That could just be a definition of a brand but many of their functions represent bad practice for brands, in a way that is perhaps expected from the tradition of street wear. In turn they also resist some of the formalisms associated with street wear in how they relinquish a lot of authenticity and formal fluidity in their commitment to Kevin Bacon.

I feel as though Bacon Index would stick with Kevin through thick and thin and that what they have is real. ☺

Alexa Karolinski

"I have a tendency to sound very negative because I'm German.
I feel like here in the States, you're trained to be super
optimistic and positive about everything."

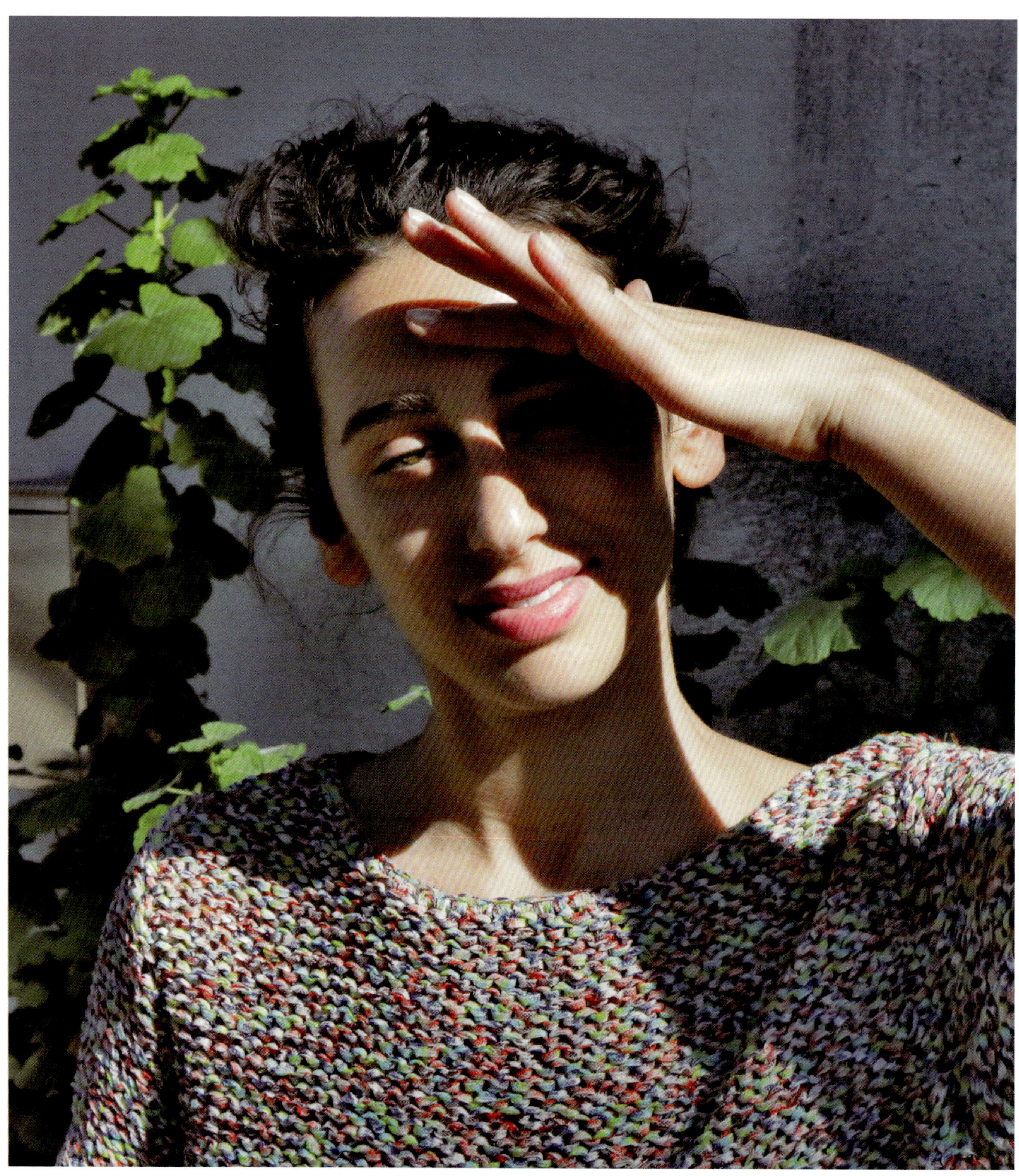

Interview by Fiona Duncan
Portrait by Eva Michon

Alexa Karolinski makes movies that
are so consistent in their vision, I
feel like I know her when I don't. Her
videos so far are mostly short: she's
made four fashion films with Mike and
Zoe Latta of the label Eckhaus Latta
and one for the brand 69, as well as
a sweet ad for the Berlin cosmetics
brand Uslu Airlines and a scrumptious
short starring Karley Sciortino. Her
latest is like a moving fashion editorial, a spin on Star Trek featuring
model-artist Britta Thie and clothes
by Nhu Duong, Anna-Sophie Berger, and
Arielle de Pinto. Alexa, a German-
Canadian, lives in Los Angeles with
her American husband Basil Katz. This
interview was conducted via Skype
video, with Alexa in her home — in
her garden, then her bed — in LA.

Where in Los Angeles do you live?
I live in Hollywood by the Hollywood
Bowl. It's really nice. I love LA.
When did you move?
I moved a year and a half ago. LA is
everything that people say, both good
and bad. It took a while but I can't
imagine living anywhere else right
now. I got a dog.
What kind of dog?
A Korean jindo dog. Basil's cousin
found her on the street. So, I guess,
she's — what do they say? She's a
rescue. In LA, you have to have a
rescue dog. If you have a new dog,
you're not going to get a lot of
respect at the dog park.
Do you have a favorite place in LA?
Underneath the Hollywood sign, like
literally the closest point that
you can get to the Hollywood sign,
there's this park. Grassy, not that
big, and technically for humans, it's
a beautiful park. People use it as
a dog park, and that's my favorite
place in LA. If you had come here for
the interview, I would have taken you
to this park. I go almost every day
at sunset. The echo, the soundscape,
is so weird. You can hear everybody's
conversation; the industry talk is
the funniest. Yesterday, when I went,
there was a bulldog event.

A what?
An English bulldog event. There were
about 30 English bulldogs, running
around and snorting, and their owners.
Did you take pictures?
I took a little Instagram video.
**So one theme that I've picked up on
a lot of your work that I wanted to
talk about is long-distance intimacy
and intimacy through technology.**
Really? That's cool that you see that.
**And that we're Skyping this interview
seems emblematic of that. Do you have
many long distance intimacies?**
Yeah, I mean, that's my life. My
whole family lives in Berlin. And now
my second family, my best friends,
live in New York and Berlin. I wake
up at 7 AM, so I can still get people
through Skype or on the phone who
are ending their workday in Berlin.
That's just a reality that I've had
to come to terms with. It's a nine-
hour time difference to Berlin.
That's the new normal.

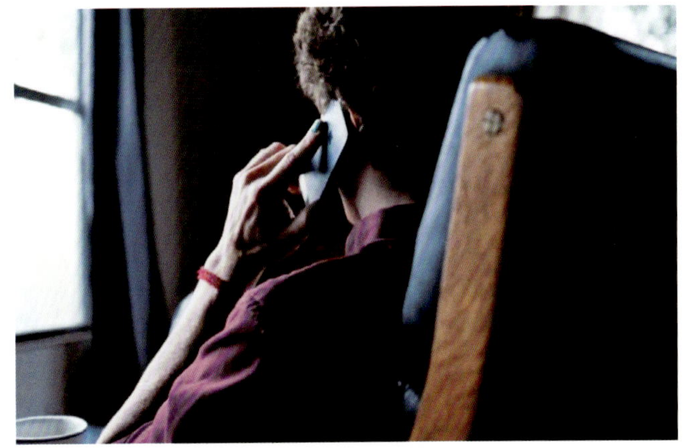

Uslu Airlines, LAX-TXL, 2014.

**I find my relationships become stron-
ger with some distance. We're forced
to create new ways of being together.**
Well, the problems become different
the older you get. I feel like when
I go back to Berlin and I have my
three-hour long drink with a friend
who I haven't seen in a long time, our
catch-up is different than it used to
be. You get to the deep stuff and to
the problems real fast, like it needs
to be deeper because there's less day-
to-day conversation and less time.

Images courtesy Alexa Karolinski

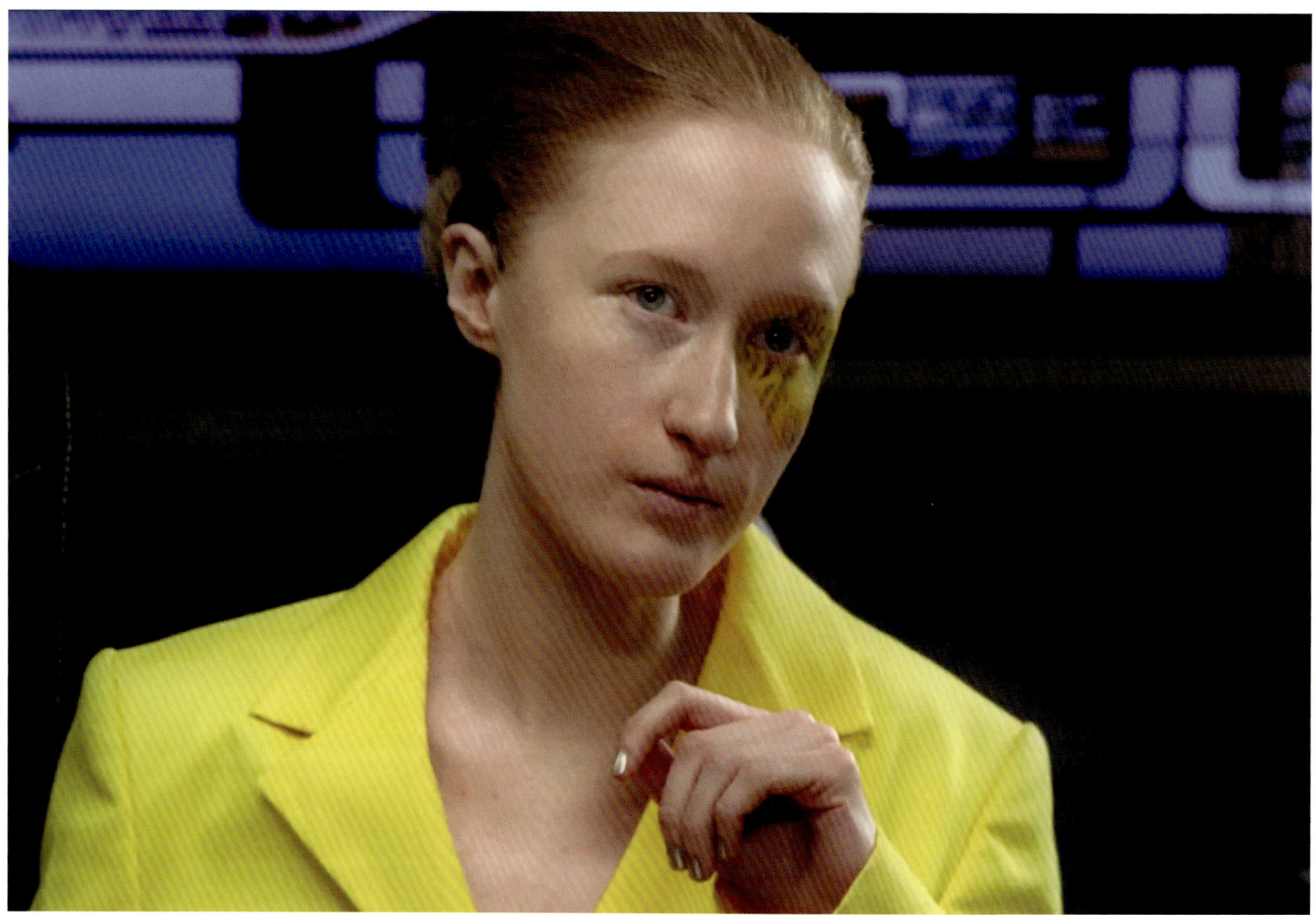

Anomaly, 2014.

Your videos are like a salve to the schizophrenia and alienation found online. I feel like I'm sharing in an intimacy, especially with those you've made with repeat collaborators, like Eckhaus Latta. How did you meet Mike and Zoe?
I met Mike and Zoe about two years ago in New York. I was just finishing SVA, and I really wanted to make movies, but I needed to find a way I could be hired as a commercial director. Since I didn't have musician friends who needed videos, the easiest thing for me to start with was fashion video, as I somehow mostly knew people connected to that world. I was doing videos for an online magazine for a while, I Like My Style. The people who ran that, Eva Munz and Adriano Sack, are friends from Germany. I Like My Style was among the first to feature Eckhaus Latta.

Then I asked my friend Emily Segal to introduce me to Mike and Zoe since she knew them from Providence. I met Mike and Zoe to talk about making videos for them. They hadn't really done any videos yet, and I remember we had this magical, epic, four-hour-long brainstorm. We still talk about it. Because it was beautiful. Back then, their studio was in Williamsburg; we sat there for four hours talking about what lacked in fashion video. By the end, we had 15 ideas for a video, although we never ended up executing any of those.
When did you know you wanted to be a filmmaker?
It was a gradual process. I went from studying art history, to working for Vice magazine in Germany, to working for culture television, writing reports about other people's art and work. With time, I just felt I wanted to make my own films.

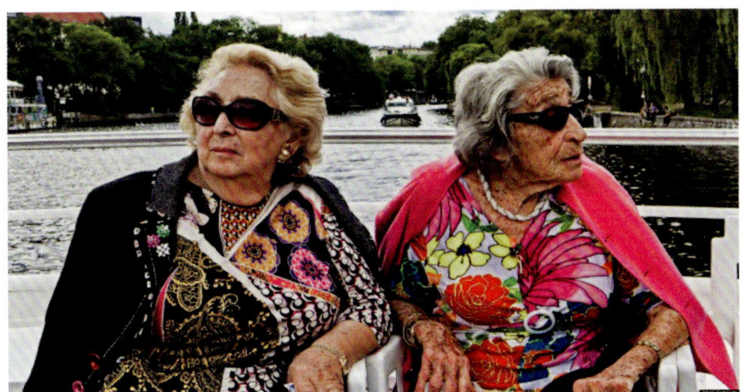

Oma & Bella, 2012.

Do you have favorite filmmakers?
They change all the time. The three
women who first come to mind are
Agnès Varda, Vera Chytilová, and
Chantal Akerman. Another filmmaker
I really respect, since I'm already
name dropping, is John Walter. John
Walter is New York-based, and was a
bit of my mentor while I was living
there. He's both a director, and an
editor extraordinaire. When he makes
films, he spends years on them, and
then they're perfectly told. You
should see this documentary, Theater
of War, that he made about Bertolt
Brecht's exile in California. When
a documentary is good, like really
good, no narrative film can compare.
**Your latest fashion video is
inspired by Star Trek. Did you watch
the show as a kid?**
It was on television, but I wasn't
a Trekkie. I've been watching so
much Star Trek with Basil in the
last couple of weeks to prepare for
this and it made me realize that
I'm married to an insane Trekkie!
I had no idea. Britta Thie, who's
the captain in the video, is also
the most intense Trekkie ever.
Britta will walk around Berlin
in a silver latex onesie. She's
seen every single Star Trek, every
series, every episode, like at least
four times. We did this video in
collaboration with the Star Trek Fan
Club Berlin. They meet there every
Saturday and do role-playing in this
youth center where they created
their own version of the bridge.
Members of the fan club play the
crew in the video.

Is Britta a member?
No. But when we went to this place
for the first time, Britta cried.
She was sitting in her future
captain chair in this place and
crying. She said that her whole life
is coming full circle right now. It
was beautiful.
**I love Star Trek for its inclusivity.
The ethics of show are really
inspiring. Did you talk to your collaborators on this video about that?**
Oh, yeah. We spoke about it a lot.
We did it with a German, Berlin-
based Star Trek fan club and
were thinking that if this was done
with a club in the States, these
people would probably visually
reflect the show's diversity more;
it would not just be white, blonde,
blue-eyed people, but that's the
reality of making anything in
Germany. In the video, we tried
to create different tribes around
the different fashion designers
featured, so for example, we have
Nhu Duong as part of the "Aggro
Minimal" tribe. We put the three
people on the bridge in Anna-Sophie
Berger. We also used Don't Shoot
the Messenger, an amazing Berlin
designer, and Arielle de Pinto for
the jewelry. Julia Burlingham did a
fashion editorial photo shoot while
we were making the video.
**Do you set limits between commercial
contacts and personal work? Even
your commercial contracts, like the
nails video for Uslu Airlines, are
so personal.**
Yeah, that's the struggle. I feel
like there will hopefully be
more and more of a difference, a
difference so extreme I don't need
to think about that compromise, or,
more ideally, they become one thing.
I know that in the commercial world
I need to do things a certain way,
there's very little creative wiggle
room. You just need to see the ads
that exist to understand that's just
how it is: you need to place your
own artistic vision within a brand's
or a client's vision for themselves.

That's a good way to approach it.
I think the most important thing
will be to always have other
projects that are all my own, like
the kinds of projects I've been
doing until now, where you just
work for yourself or with people
who also just believe in making
really cool things. But most people
don't like things like that I don't
think.

I don't believe that!
Commercially, I mean. Just look
at everything. I could rant for a
long time about what I think about
videos that exist online: "browser
friendly" commercial videos designed
to be played in a browser in the
background, catered to your being
able to do five things at once, to
skip forward or backward; they're
always made of unengaging,
beautiful images, like a cooking
or travel guide show aesthetic,
"pretty" being the only measure of
form. Like Instagram filters. Do I
sound too negative?

No.
I have a tendency to sound very
negative because I'm German. I feel
like here in the States, you're
trained to be super optimistic and
positive about everything.

**Yeah and that's why so much in our
culture sucks: because it's a "yes"
culture. It's anti-intellectual and
pro-industry. There's so much media
out there.**
Well, that's the real problem.
And that poses a real challenge
sometimes for my work, because
right now everybody's realizing
that video is an absolutely
necessary part of everything, of
online, but most people don't yet
know what that means or what they
want. Internet video is its own
thing. I often hear people talk
about "short attention spans." But
what do people mean when they talk
about other people's attention
spans? They want short videos
with many cuts. I think the whole
dialogue is wrong. I watch things
that I get extremely bored by, and
I don't believe this has to do with
my "attention span." I believe,
rather, that I'm not engaged with
it, and that's because it's not for
me. Something can be really well
shot and beautiful, all the elements
are there, and I don't know — I know
I don't like something if I feel
empty afterwards. A lot of internet
video leaves me feeling super empty
after. Like after watching a ton of
advertising.

**What do you mean by "internet
video"? How it is different than
other forms of film or video.**
I think the answer's in
distribution. You can make things
that go to television, to film
festivals, etc. Internet videos
are videos that are made for and
featured on the internet, and that
can be any kind of platform, whether
it be for a magazine or your Vimeo
page.

**Are you working on anything that's
not designed for the internet first?**
Yeah, I am writing a narrative
feature script and starting a new
documentary. Both ideally not for
the internet, or at least not at
first.

**Last thing — I wanted to talk about
food, because there's so much of it
in your work.**
Yeah. I'm very domesticated. That's
why I like living in LA. New York
often felt, I don't know...

**I eat salad from a box here, too
often. What's your go-to dish?**
Annie's macaroni and cheese. And
when I cook-cook, chicken soup. My
favorite thing is — I can't believe
I'm saying this out loud as it
sounds incredibly cliché — but I
love sitting and eating and drinking
with my friends. That's what I love
doing more than anything. I don't
really go out much, I don't party.
Even when I was living in New York,
I didn't really go to many of the
parties. I would much rather just
drink wine, smoke cigarettes, and
talk about stuff. ☺

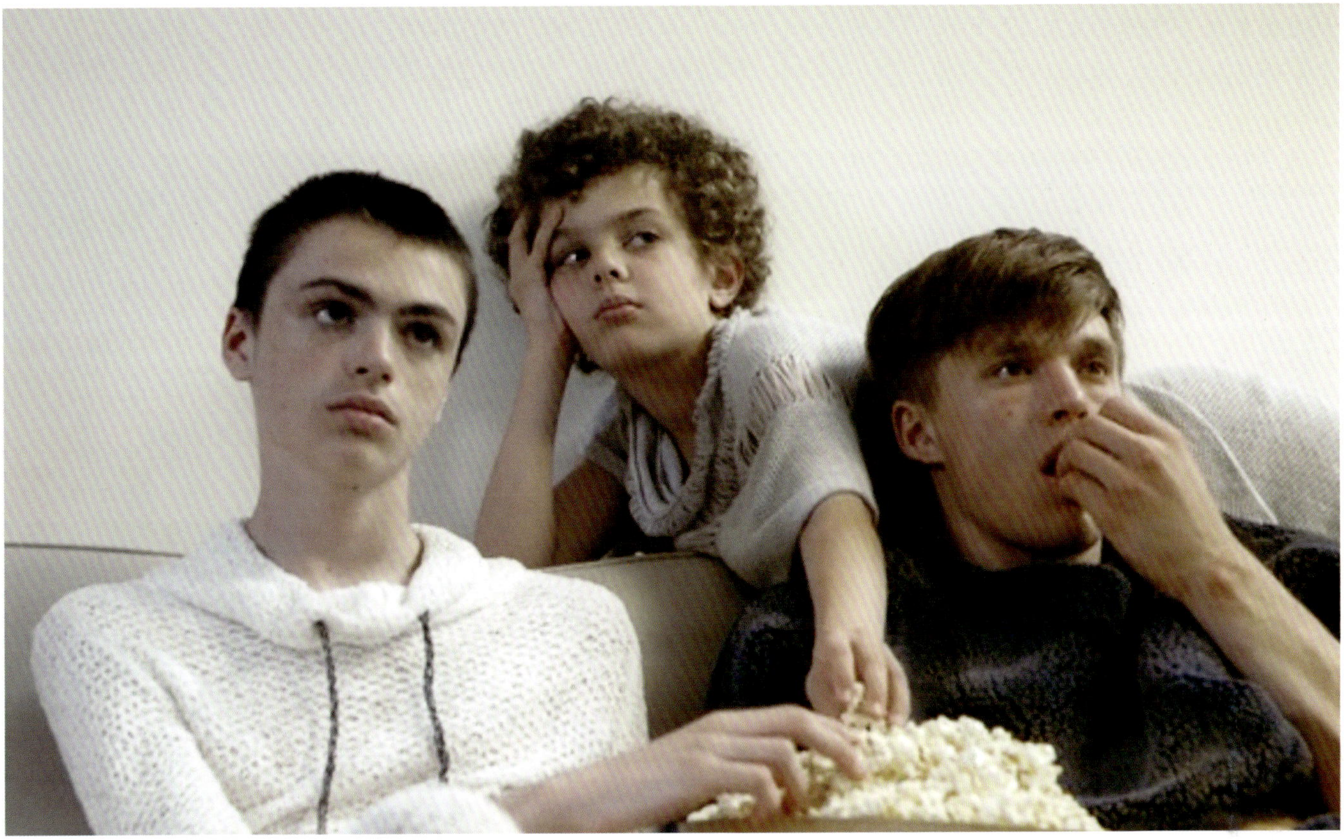

Eckhaus Latta, Family, 2013.

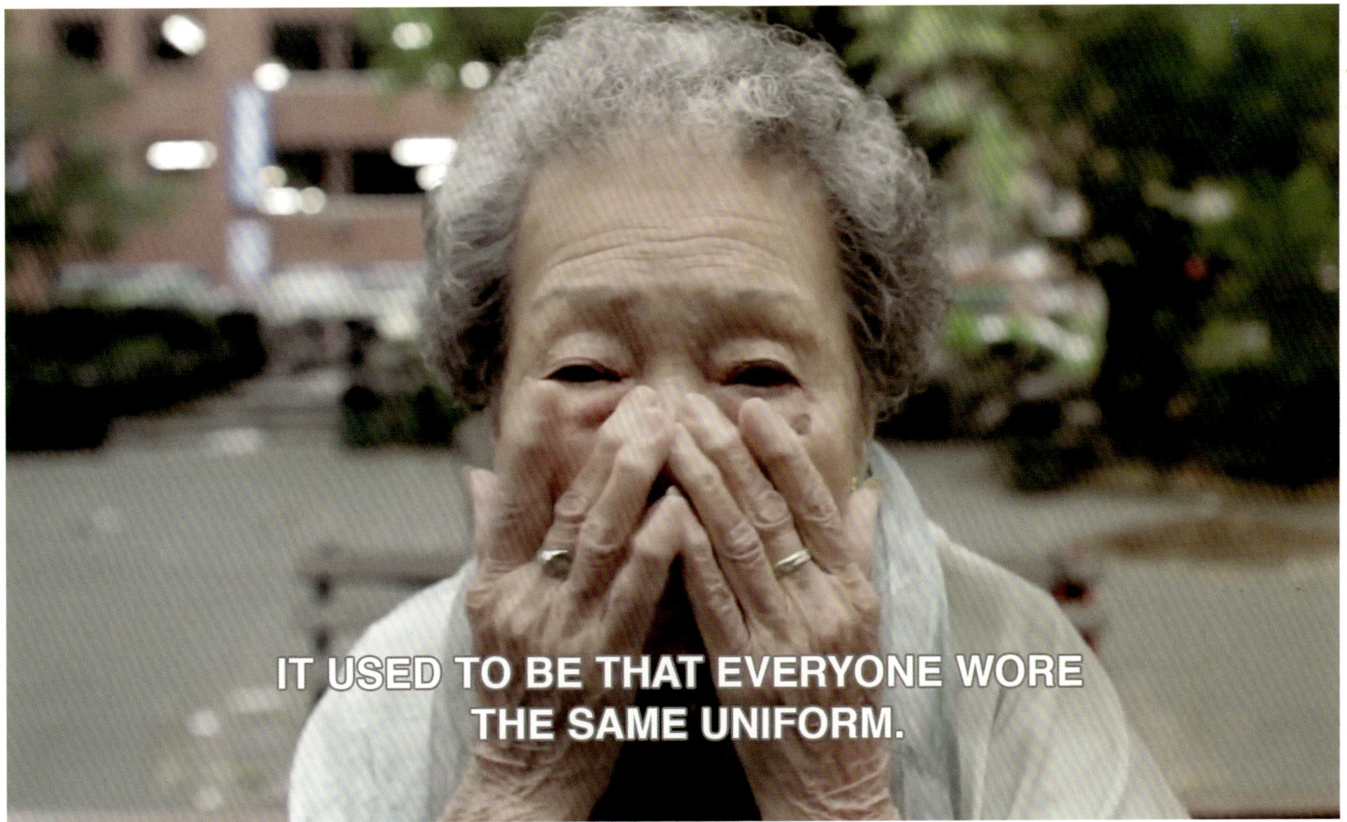

Eckhaus Latta, Uniform, 2012.

Frank Kozik
"I trained myself to do everything."

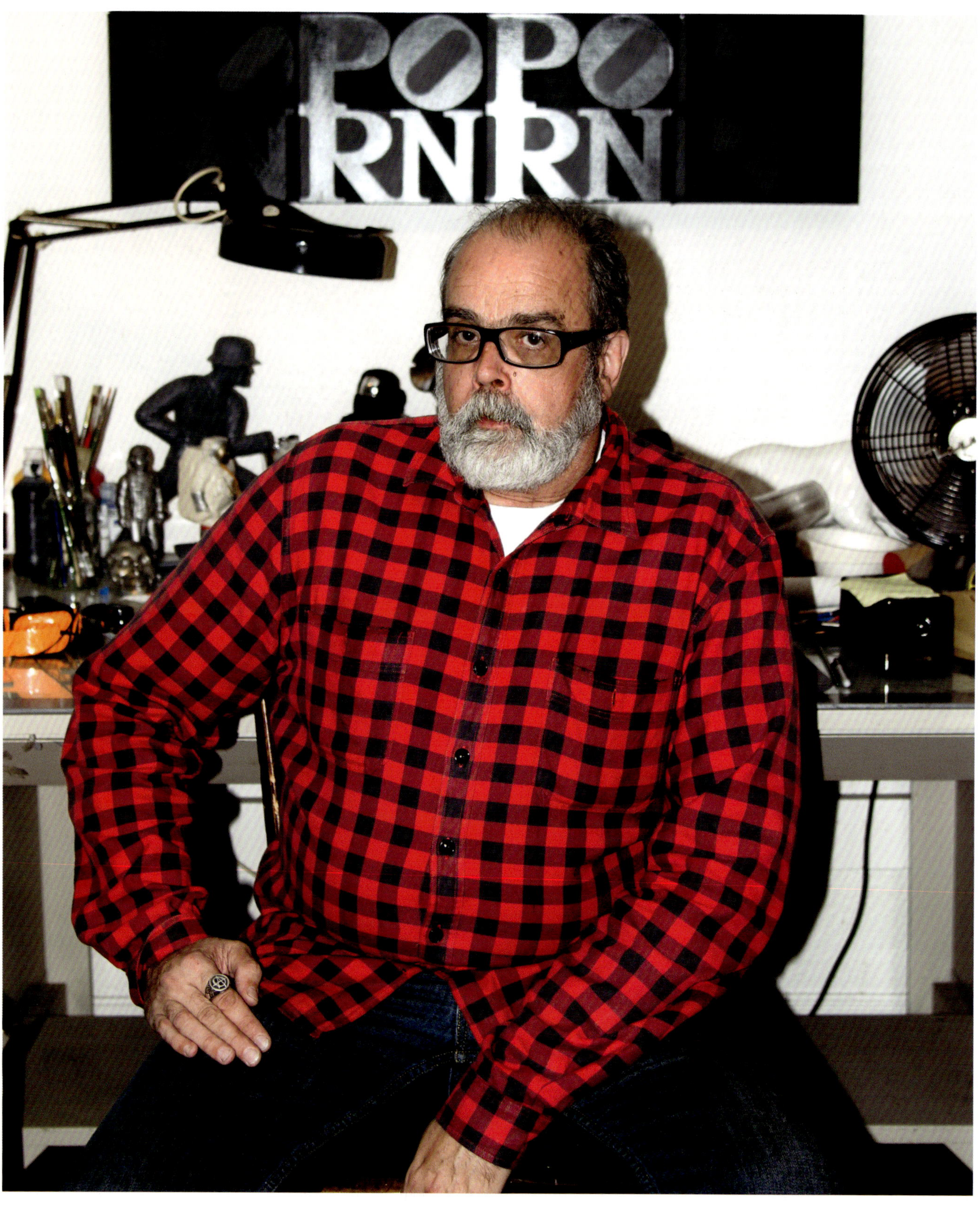

Interview by Asher Penn
Portrait by Andrew Eargle

Frank Kozik is an American designer
and illustrator based in San Fransisco.
Getting his start making flyers for
underground acts like Butthole Surfers
in weirdo 80s' Austin, Kozik is best
known for his iconic poster and album
art for groups like the Melvins
and Sonic Youth. With the rise in
popularity of grunge, Kozik's signature
combination of bold type and cartoon
lunacy became a paramount aesthetic of
the 90s, attracting high-paying clients which then allowed Kozik to start
his own label, Man's Ruin Records.
With a punk-rock ethos and pop-art
sensibility, Kozik has continued to
balance commercial work with his own
independent enterprises — making cool
shit for people to look at and buy.

**You grew up in Spain during the last
decade of the Franco regime. What was
your experience of that as a child?**
Well, my mother was well-to-do. If
you're a member of the ruling class,
growing up in a police state can fo-
ster quite a pleasant childhood. There
was no worry of crime or danger, and
we played in the streets without any
problem. We spent our summers on the
beach. I lived this idealized, almost
Victorian, childhood.
Were you exposed to a lot of art?
I lived in Toledo and Madrid, which is
basically living inside Classical Art.
Toledo is a preserved medieval city,
and every public building is filled
with art spanning from the Roman ages
to the 19th century. I would just go
to the Prado every day — it was free
for kids — I'd wander around and look
at paintings.
So how did you get into pop culture?
My mother married a succession of
wealthy men, and my father was an
alcoholic Air Force sergeant. I spent
most of my childhood with my mother,
an occasionally journeyed to England
and the United States with my dad.
When I got older, I started reading
books and getting exposure to ideas
from outside of Spain. When I was
about 14, I was given the opportunity
to move to the States with my dad.

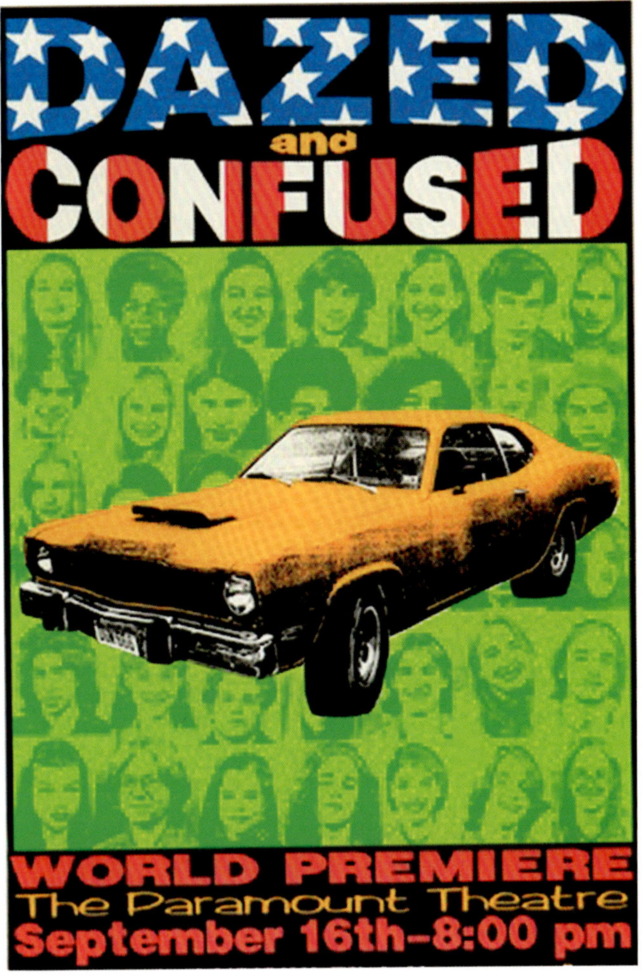

Dazed & Confused World Premiere Poster, 1993.

What was your dad like?
My dad was kind of like a good-
time Charlie — just chasing tail,
not an intellectual person at all.
He was the son of a city worker, was
drafted and fought in the Korean War.
He never had any higher education.
He was a bright guy, but he had
no outlet so he became a raging
alcoholic.
But you liked the States?
Yeah man! You have to understand
that I grew up in a place where it
really mattered who your grandparents
were. It was still a daily topic of
all conversation — the division of
families of the War and subsequent
ideologies. It permeated all of
society. Very classist, very
prejudiced, very judgmental, very
programmed. It was fucked. I happened
to have a liberal brain. I had a
creative brain.

Images courtesy Frank Kozik

What happened when you got here?
I went to school for a year before
I dropped out and got a job in a
hamburger stand. I bought a car, had
an apartment, smoked pot, got laid.
Life was good.

**How did you end up serving in the Air
Force?**
I got in some trouble, and it was my
way out. When I went in, I aced their
tests, so they just asked me what I
wanted to do. I told them I would
do whatever took the longest amount
of schooling. I went to technical
training schools for almost two
years. And the last two years, I was
in Austin, where there was nothing to
do except hang out.

**Do you feel like you got anything out of
the Air Force?**
The military was good for me because
when I went in, I didn't know how
to do anything. If you do get some
technical training, and you pay
attention to it, they will teach you
a methodology to achieve goals and
troubleshoot problems, to analyze
systems and stuff. I still apply a lot
of those methods today to what I do.

So, no college?
I didn't finish high school. I took
the equivalency thing but no college.
Any liberal arts education I have,
I've done for myself. I like to read
a lot and study, so that's never been
a problem.

How did you come to leave the Air Force?
By the time my enlistment was up, I
had made a lot of friends in Austin.
I was part of the local music scene,
had a girlfriend, a cool place to
live downtown. So I didn't re-enlist.
I just stayed in Austin.

What was the music scene like?
The music scene was amazing. It had a
good dozen or so ever-changing spots
to see all kinds of music, ranging
from cosmic cowboy-type music to punk
and new wave, to weird and whatever.
For two bucks you could see a show,
and everybody went. A lot of stuff
was going on and living was easy.
That's why so much stuff came out of
Austin in those years.

Who were some of your favorite Austin bands?
I was a big Butthole Surfers fan.
Scratch Acid was an amazing band. The
Dicks were really great. I would say
those three bands were my favorites.

Did a lot of touring bands come through?
Every band that toured would stop in
Austin to do a performance, because it
was like a little oasis stop between
the East Coast and the West Coast.
There was no place else those bands
could go in the middle of the country.
That's why I had a good career. I was
able to do all of the posters for the
bands doing one small show in Austin
on their way somewhere else.

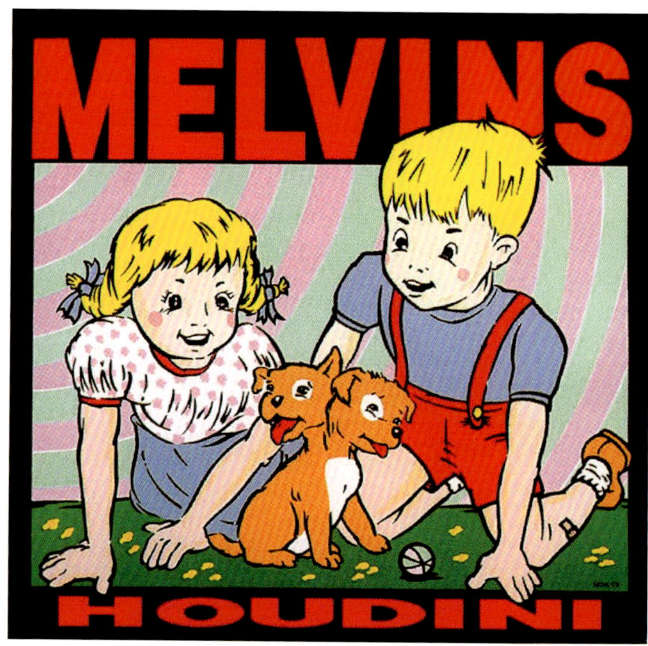

Melvins, Houdini, Atlantic Records, 1993.

How did you start doing flyers?
Before I did posters, I had been doing
some mail art. I had this marginal
correspondence going on with this
group in Portland called the Art
Maggots. A couple of the Art Maggots
moved down to Austin and rented a jam
house. I started hanging out with
them, drawing comics and nonsense
guerrilla street-art stuff. They would
xerox it and put it up around town.
At some point a local band or two
were like, "Hey, we really like these
posters that you guys are doing. Will
you do a poster for our band?"

So you started getting commissions?
I just started off doing little flyers for local bands which kind of turned into doing T-shirt designs for businesses, which turned into more posters for bigger clubs and bigger bands.

What were the early aesthetic influence for your first posters?
It was this weird mix of new wave shit I'd seen, some of the European Heavy Metal comic book artists; the industrial research publications were a big influence on me. Eventually my work became more colorful, wackier, and more fun.

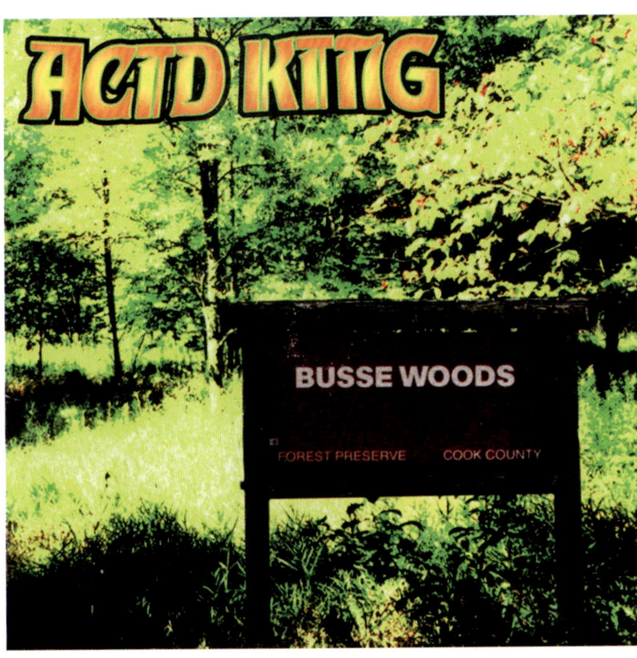

Acid King, Busse Woods, Mans Ruin Records, 1999.

Were you always drawing?
Not really. When I started corresponding with these punk rock people, they were drawing stuff and it got competitive. I trained myself to do everything.

How long was it until it was a viable business?
I didn't start making a living off of strictly my own, self-produced imagery until 1991. I quit my last job in 1987, and basically did commercial work: "We want you to draw an elephant on a surfboard with a margarita." That's what paid the bills. I still do it today.

1991 was the same year you moved to San Fransisco. What drove you there?
No reason. I was bored of Austin. I did end up doing well here, and I've been here ever since.

You did a lot of commercial work in the 90s, right?
I had tons of it. All the big companies, they wanted to sell to kids — grunge was the hot new thing in 1993, 1994. Subsequently, for the next three or four years, I got an ass-load of commercial jobs from Nike, beer companies, clothing companies, alcohol companies, tobacco companies, people who wanted to sell shit to kids. I happily took them all.

Can you speak a bit about your approach to commercial work?
I'm reasonable. They hire me to solve a problem. I'll ask them what they want, the physical parameters and the deadline. I ask them to reference any previous work of mine that they want me to sort of dive off of. I also ask "Is there anything you don't want to see?" Like, "Do you hate snakes?" You would be surprised, because a lot of times, they'll get pissed. It's like, "Don't you know the guy was in a plane wreck. You can't have planes."

Sounds pretty reasonable.
It's never adversarial. My job is not to cause the clients a problem, which is why I've gotten a lot of work over the years — word gets out. I'm doing it for money so I don't want to be problematic and agonize over the panel — I can do that on my own dime. They need something to help sell their product or their image. They trust me to solve their problem, and to do the best job possible. Since you can never really tell if advertising works what really matters is making the client happy.

It doesn't threaten your creative work?
You can still have a weird career and be an artist. Nobody cares that you did an ad campaign a month later. This commercial work allowed me to do things like start Man's Ruin Records. We put out 212 records that otherwise would not have been produced.

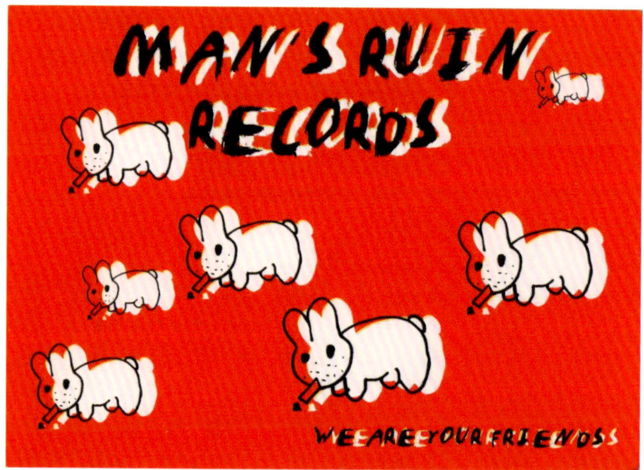

Man's Ruins Records, Promotional Postcard, 1997.

How did Man's Ruin start?

I was doing really well financially, and felt an obligation to pay my scene back. I also had a lot of friends in bands that were always complaining that, "No one will put out our record." Or, "They want to come in and produce all the songs and tell us what to do." Or, "No one will put out vinyl." And these were all bands that I liked. So I told my artists that we'll make a budget. You guys record whatever you want to do, and I won't tell you what to record. You don't tell me how to design the package, and we'll just put out something that's real. The profit will be a 50-50 split between future publishing. Completely cool, punk-rock square deal, and I can pay back all my friends' bands whom I loved, whose posters gave me a career. It went great until I started doing CDs. Bands wanted to make money so we did CDs, and that got really big. I had to hire a bunch of people, and had this big elaborate distribution system. Then, one day, Sony Distribution went bankrupt and left everybody holding the bag. When they went out of business, they owed me $1.5 million. I never saw a penny of that. The month we shut down the label was our biggest sales month ever, but no one was ever going to pay us for those sales. I pulled the plug on it and walked away.

Was Man's Ruin your first brand that you were running independently?

Pretty much. It was consistent logo work and concepts. There were several genres of music we were releasing. Each genre had its own conceptual/art approach to the packaging. We did a lot of promotional events, a lot of showcases. It was a hard sell at the time, but now I get people emailing me, offering $2,000 for a 7" that was seven bucks. The label was a critical success, but because of the distribution collapse and the advent of online, it was a commercial failure. I applied those lessons to the current brand I have with the toys.

How did you get involved with collectible toys?

I've been collecting toys forever, since the 80s. Then in the mid-90s, when I went to Japan, I would see this little Bounty Hunter toy around. It was a punk-rock version of the Captain Crunch character. I was like, "This is the coolest thing ever. What is this? Who makes this?"

So who was making them?

His name was Hikaru. We went over to his little store, and as it turned out, he collected my posters, so we hit it off. I had developed this Labbit character in the interim

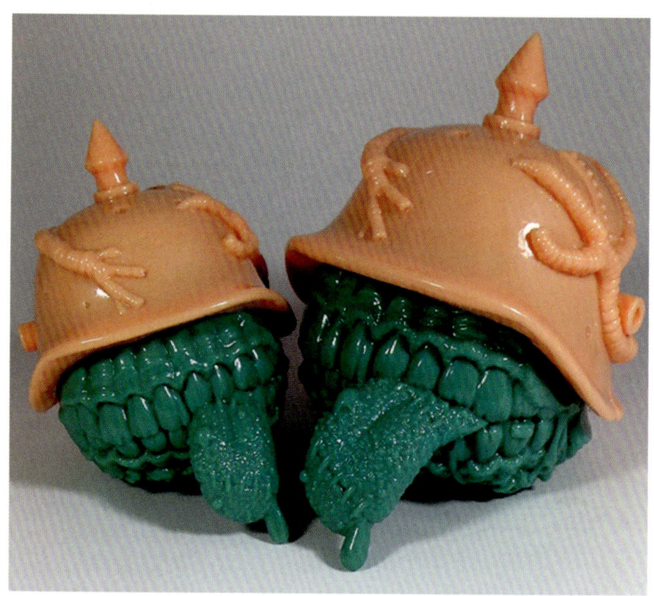

Freaky Fritz in Mint & Flesh, Hateball Set, 2014.

    Frank Kozik by Asher Penn

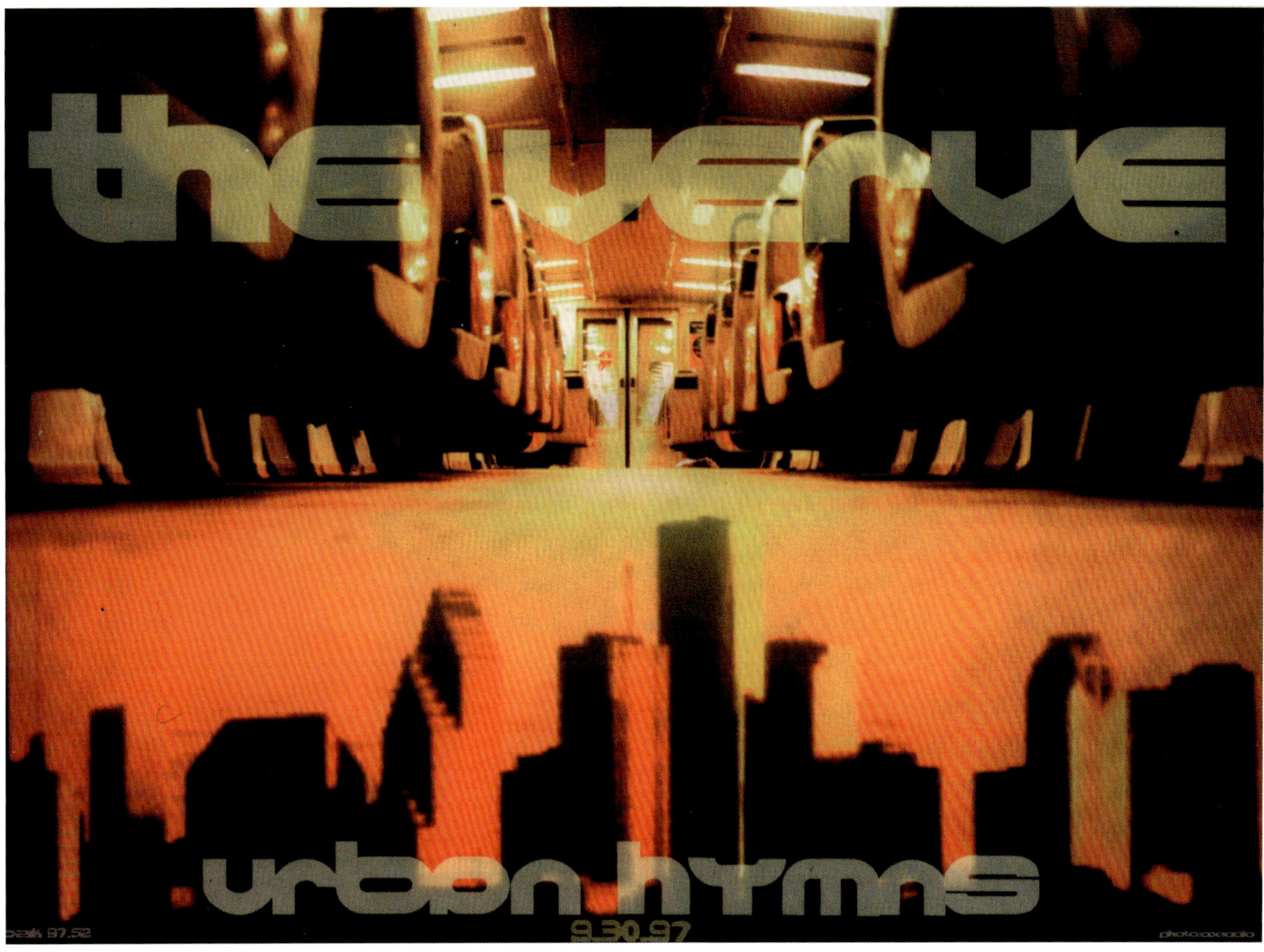

The Verve, Urban Hyms, Promotional Poster, 1997.

because I was obsessed with Hello Kitty, and he made my first toy in Japan. I ended up making toys in Japan for a few years, bringing stuff back to the states. Nobody cared, but I thought it was cool. Then in 2004, Kid Robot opened up over here and we started working together. It dramatically blew up for four or five years, peaking around 2008 or 2009. Now it's plateaued a lot online; a lot of my competition is gone, so I have a really stable market niche.

Do you feel like you've had any influences that have remained consistent over your career?
You know where it all comes from? I would see shit that I thought was cool, and would try to copy it. The shit I tried to copy changed over time. I don't think I ever developed anything innovative or new.

This reminds me of something you said in a previous interview about how important it is for artists to find a context.
If you want to be any sort of creative person, you have to find a world to fit into. Because if you're just out there on your own, no one's going to discover you. You have to meet like-minded people. You have to form both social and business relationships with a group of people who value your efforts, where your efforts contribute to the whole group experience. Then they will want to include you, and you'll be rewarded with recognition, or money, or whatever it is that you want. You can have fame, you can have notoriety, you can get a paycheck. But none of that happens in a vacuum. ☺

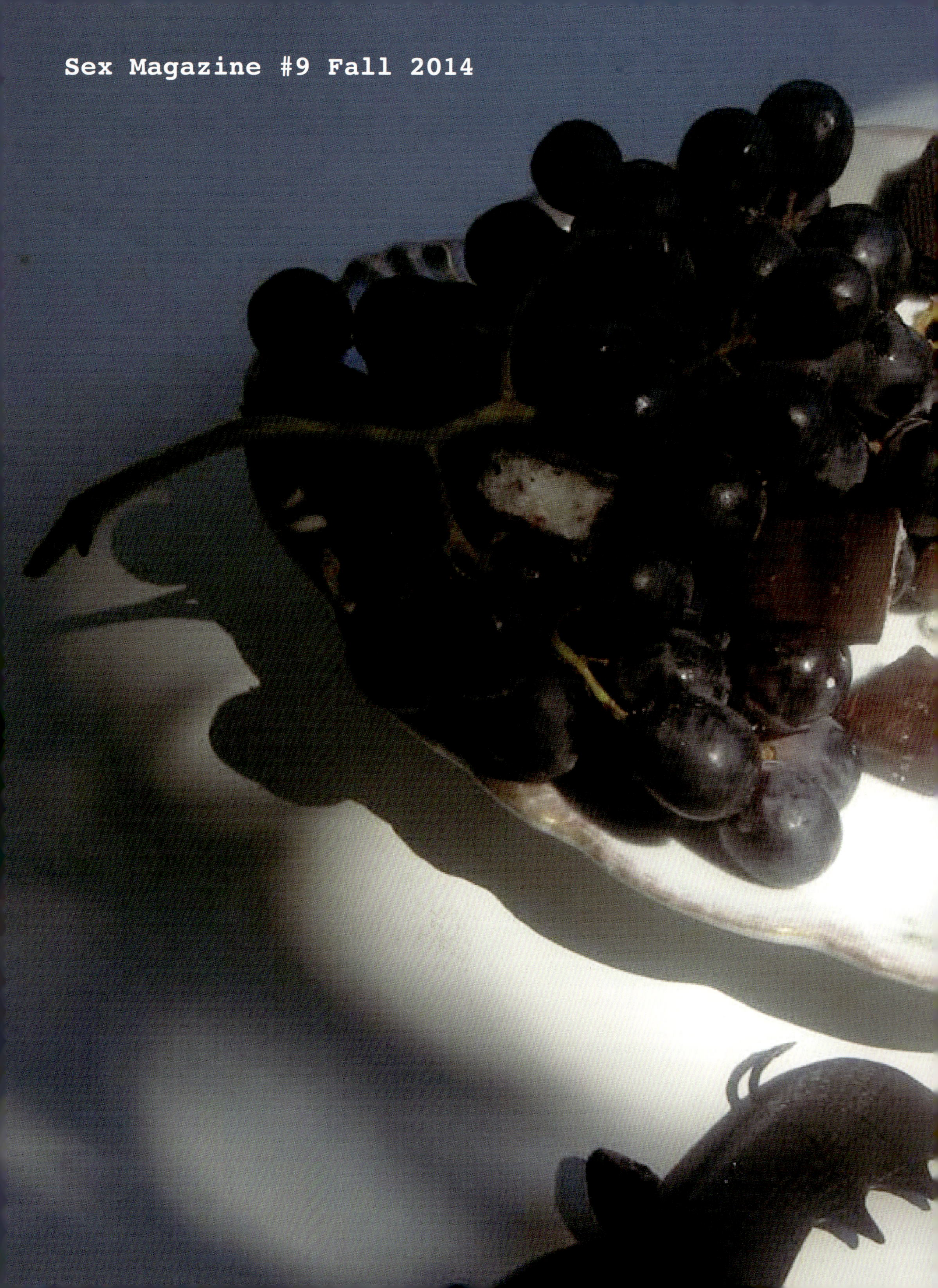
Sex Magazine #9 Fall 2014

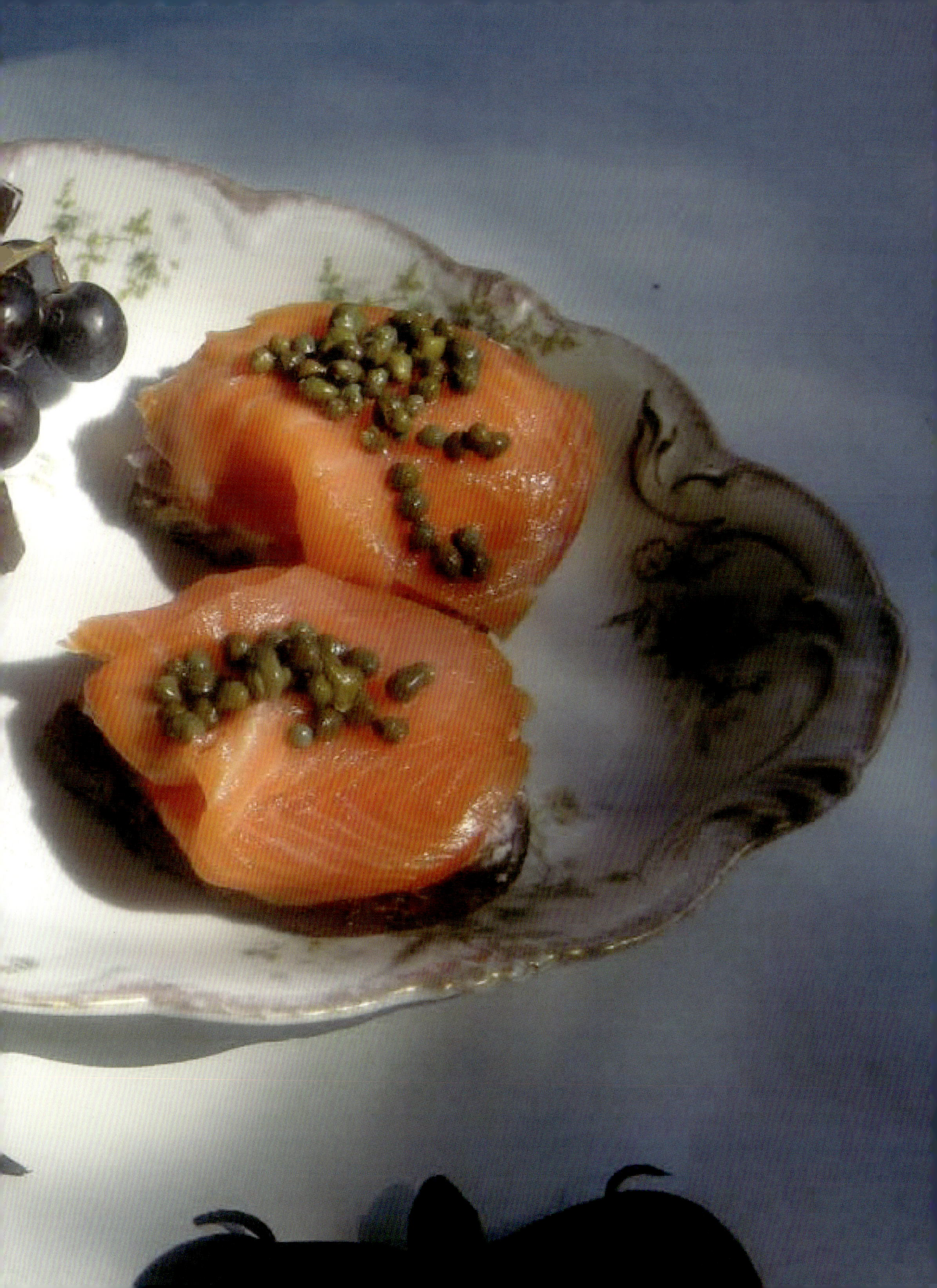

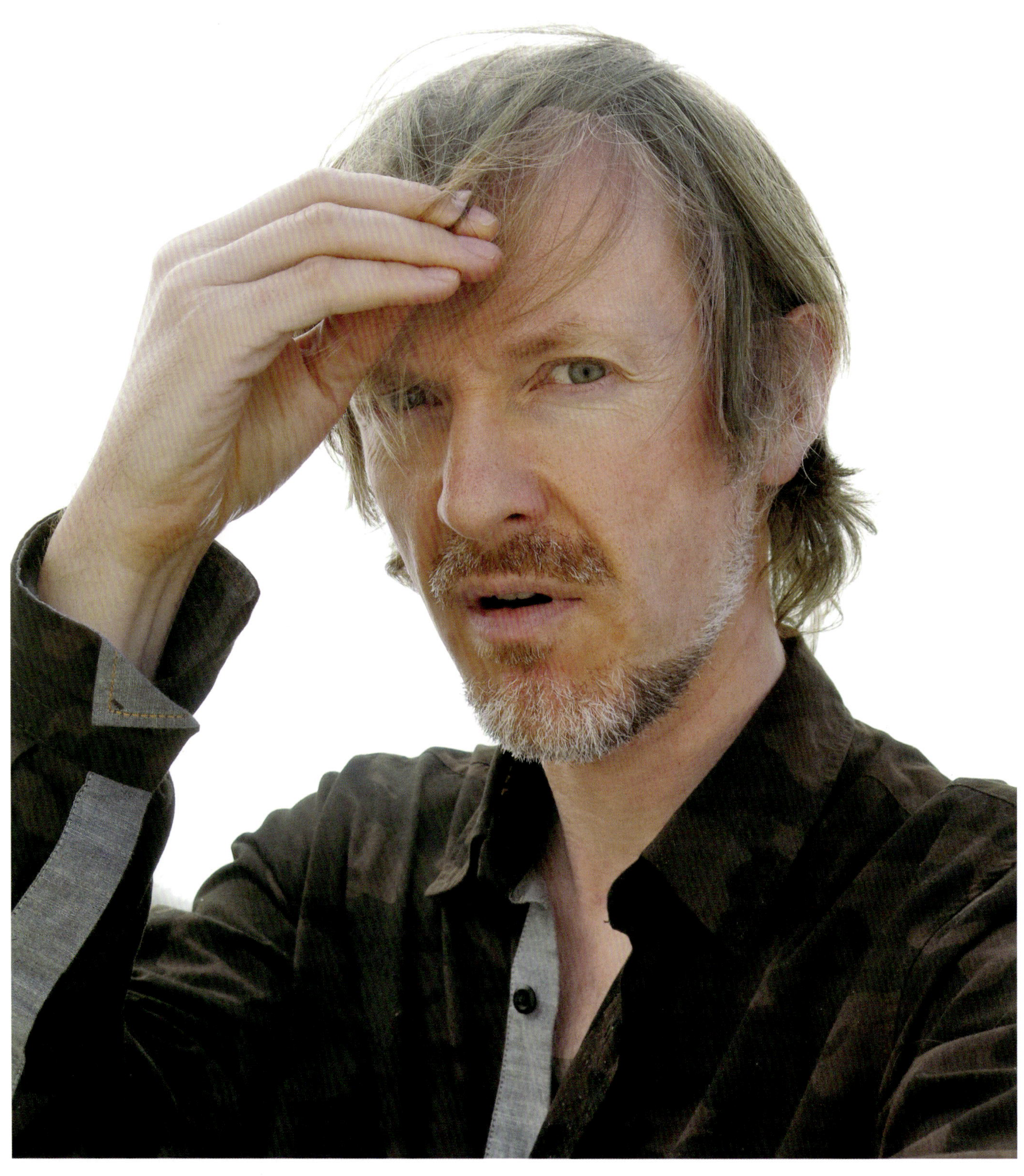

Torbjørn Rødland
"It was pretty clear that I wanted my photographs
to be of a different kind."

Interview by Asher Penn
Images courtesy Torbjørn Rødland

Torbjørn Rødland is a Norwegian photographer based in Los Angeles. Finding early inspiration from the Pictures generation, Torbjørn's images milk pleasure from motifs in commercial photography, exposing desire, power dynamics, and unsettling beauty. A photographer committed to his craft, Torbjørn has worked primarily in the art world, a context that has allowed to keep his highly problematized images pure.

So you're going to Norway this week?
It's actually next weekend. I have a show in my hometown, Stavanger.

What's Stavanger like?
It is the fourth biggest city in Norway and the most important for the oil industry, which is the basis for the new wealth in the region. Summers are cold and the winters are mild because you're on the water on the North Sea. The Gulf Stream heats up the water, so that keeps it from getting really cold.

What was your childhood like?
I was extremely introverted and isolated. I was asked whether I wanted to go to kindergarten and, of course, I opted out. I didn't have an interest in my peers — I didn't think I had any — so I stayed in my room with my drawings and scrapbooks of photographs I cut out of magazines.

What kind of drawings were you doing when you were a kid?
I made a caricature of a politician from TV at the age of five. From that early I was pretty set that I was going to do that for the rest of my life: be a caricaturist and work for newspapers. I was probably 16 when I started doing that for a local newspaper. Gradually I started to turn more towards the ambiguity and possibility in the art world.

How were you first introduced to photography?
My father was an amateur photographer and had a darkroom in the house. I started doing black-and-white darkroom work — probably at the age of 18 — a little bit at home.

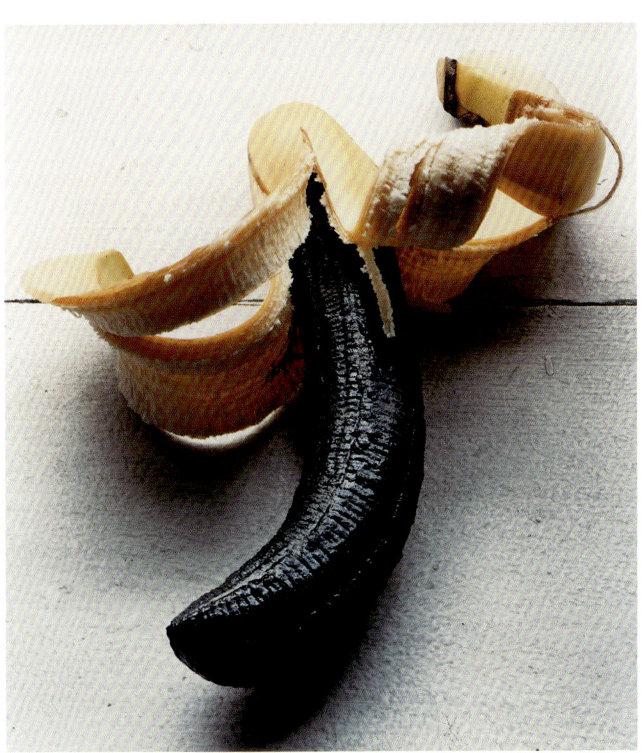
Banana Black, 2005.

How were you exposed to American culture?
Oh, like large parts of the world, Scandinavia is absolutely steeped in American movies, television, advertising, music, and literature. I was drawn to it from day one.

How did you find out about art?
Of course you're exposed to art through the school system and from your parents, but I didn't get a positive view of contemporary art from home. It seemed like something strange. At 19 I chose to study Cultural Studies at the local university and that's when it opened up for me. I got more excited about ideas, and realized that I didn't have to make the overly nostalgic or less interesting art that I had encountered.

Did you like the Pictures generation?
Definitely after I started making my own photographs. Postmodern American photography was the first art that really made a lot of sense to me, So it became the starting point. Cindy Sherman was important, Sherrie Levine's After Walker Evans project was important. Learning to look at photography in a different grain.

Were you seeing actual works or just images in books?
You know, seeing Untitled Film Stills in person, I was terribly disappointed. There was no more detail in the exhibited photographs than what I had seen in smaller reproductions of them in books. It was pretty clear that I wanted my photographs to be of a different kind — so that there would be more to discover when you were in front of the original print on the wall, which you hadn't seen in the smaller reproduction.

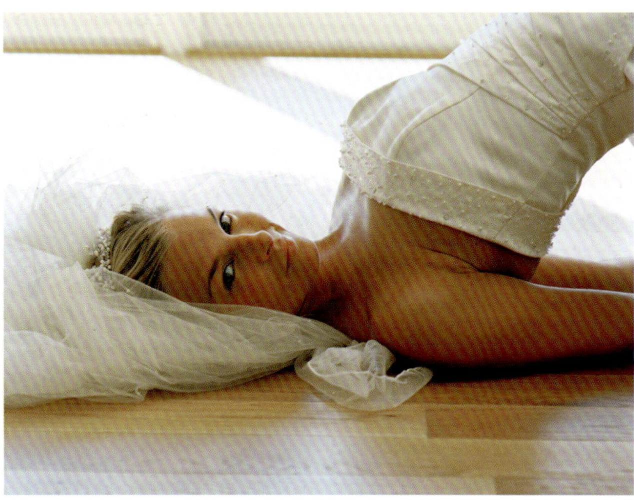
Arch Back Bride, 2007.

Your use of professional models was a nice nod to the Pictures generation.
I wanted to work with people whose job it was to become images — to be something general rather than a unique individual. I've always been drawn to universals. I didn't have much experience working with people and giving direction. Then, what I realized was that the seasoned fashion models were quite stuck on the faces and poses they were used to getting approval for. For the first project, Close Encounters, I halfway accepted and worked around that. But after seven Close Encounters I started working with a smaller camera for a while, a medium format, and I started finding my own models. I wanted to throw out even more photographic theatricality.

How did you get your own models?
I sort of embraced the most problematic male photographer role of approaching girls I found cute on the street and asking if I could photograph them. It was extremely difficult but it somehow made sense in the overarching project of breaking art rules. The more important it was for me to get a yes from a potential model, the more nervous I was. Very few said no, actually, probably because they felt sorry for this strange guy. I learned to choose people I could tell would give me what I needed, and not the fashion pout. After that I was better prepared to work with professional models, too.

Your interest in cuteness is another way you diverge from the Pictures generation.
I first embraced cuteness in the 90s and tried to push as far as I could in that direction. Later on I realized that there was some power play that followed cuteness into the pictures. Cuteness is linked to powerlessness. It's an appeal that cannot be fully controlled by the cute individual. It transcends theatre. In 1990s contemporary art it was a real taboo. That was one of the main attractions.

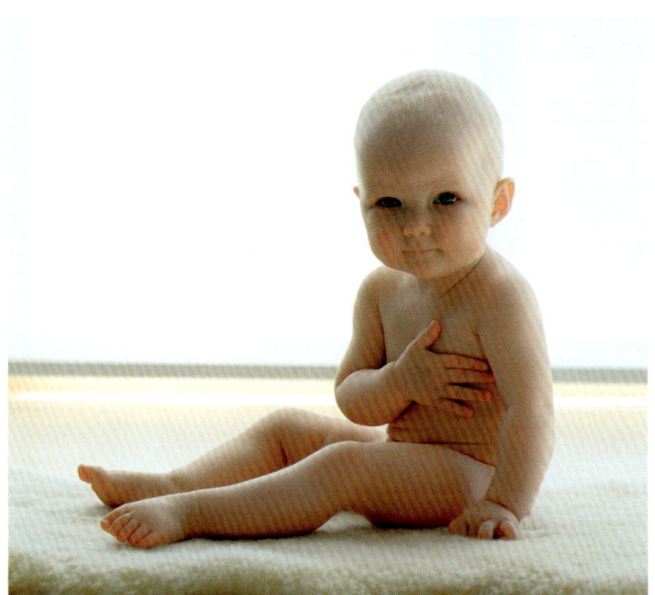
Baby, 2007.

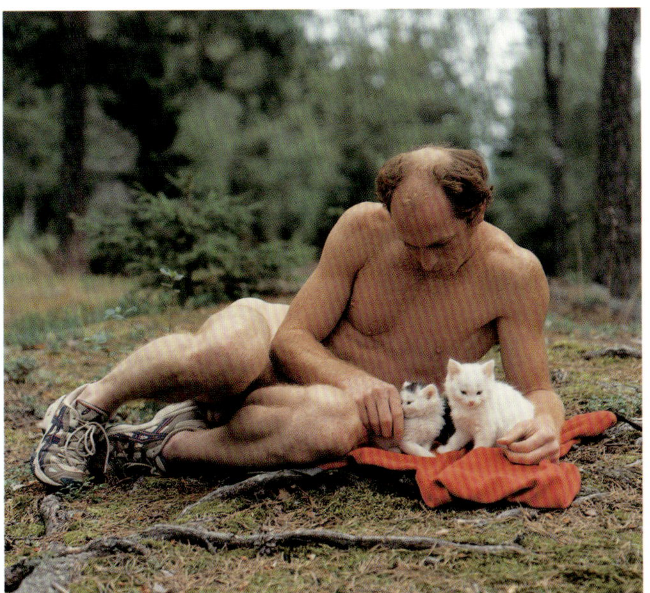

Nudist No. 6, 1999.

I've read that otaku culture inspired your work. How did you end up going to Japan?
I went in 2002 for a group show and ended up going back for a total of six months. The culture there accepts and cultivates cuteness in a very different way. It was just really in your face. Cute logos were dominating the corporate world. In Western culture cuteness was seen as a commercial lie, a quaint Hallmark card from the recent past. This all changed with YouTube and the internet in general. In the last ten years there has been a tsunami wave of insane cuteness in America. When I made my kitten photographs in the late 1990s it seemed like a very different situation.

The first piece I ever noticed of yours was Banana Black at PS1.
That must have been in the Greater New York 2005 show. I hadn't really turned to still lifes in a big way until that year, 2004—2005. Living in the East Village, I didn't know photographically what to do with the city. I was curious about basic visual symbols like whiteness and blackness, what happens to your impression of a banana if it changes color from white to black.

It seems like you've really avoided doing commercial work.
Early on I met quite a few photographers who set aside their young ideas and artistic ambitions to pursue the big money, and I saw that they were no longer excited about picking up a camera. Photography had become another dreary job. You could tell how they started despising it, despising themselves. It was very clear to me that whatever I had going, I could lose it if I didn't look after it.

You have to preserve it.
Exactly. Don't get me wrong: I love popular photography. I want to engage with daily lives, with internal worlds and feelings, and in an aesthetic that is partly derived from commercial photography. I'm focused on mythical aspects of popular imagery — aspects that are not linked to time and space, but rather underlying structures and stories.

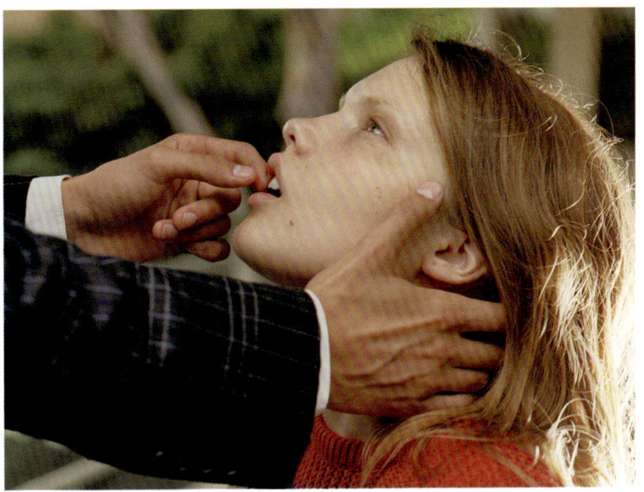

This Is My Body, 2013.

You're not selling anything, which changes a lot.
I think so too. But then there's this wide world of enthusiastic magazines that talk about art while they constantly want to trick you into promoting luxury items. I keep insisting that an art space with people who take seriously the complexity of the contemporary image actually exists for me. ☺

Princess Nokia
"I am moved by innocence, it always cheers me up."

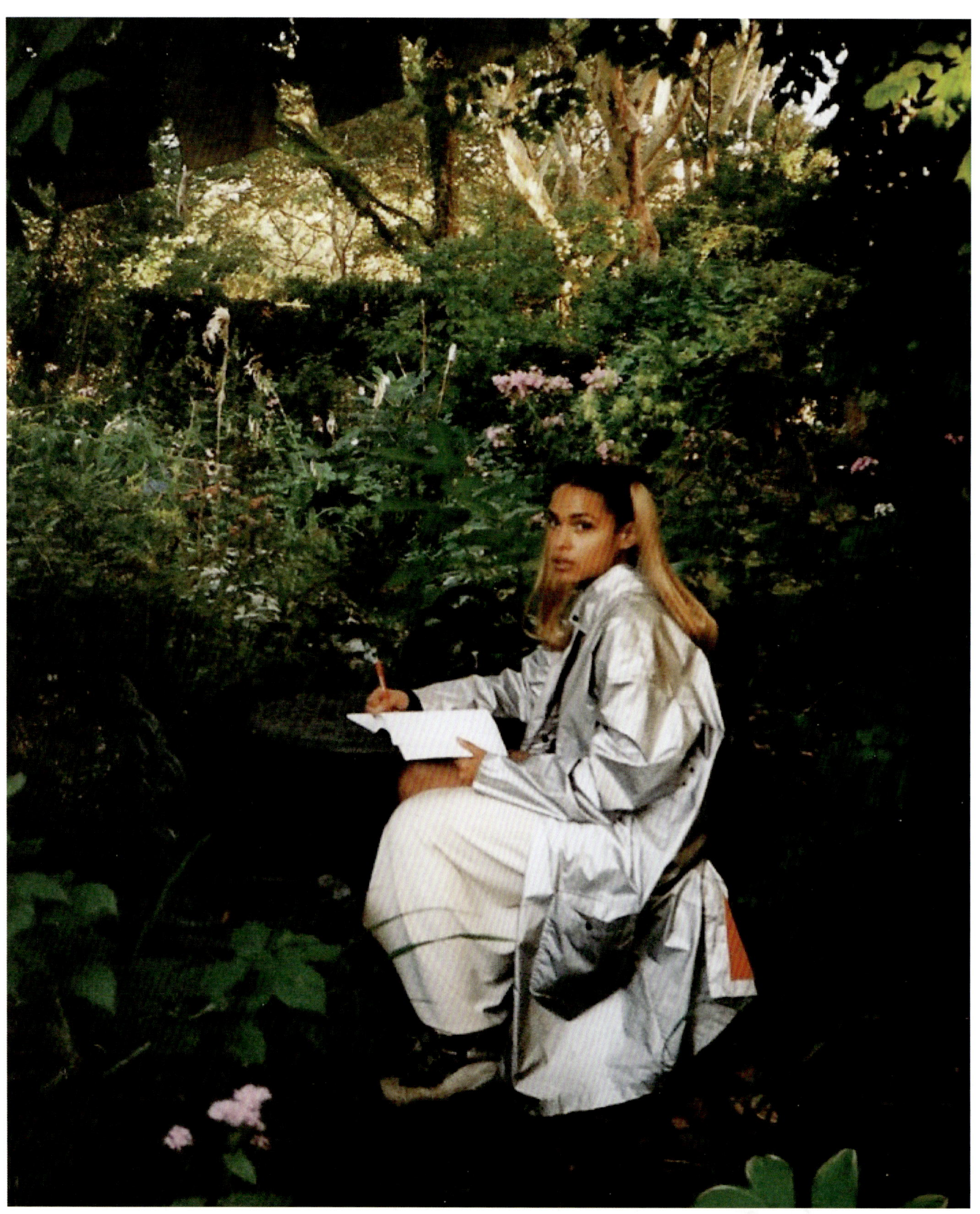

Goth witch, hacker angel, mother goddess, sensual tomboy...these are only a few of the unexpected combinations that describe Princess Nokia. Since the splash release of her video Bitch I'm Posh, the last two years have seen Princess Nokia's rapid growth as both a live and recording artist, culminating with the release of her debut EP, Metallic Butterfly, made in collaboration with the producer owwwls. The founder of the art and culture collective Smart Girl Club, and host of a weekly radio show on Know Wave, Princess Nokia wants to engage and empower women of all shapes, sizes, colors, and orientations. You can catch her at three in the morning, onstage, in front of screaming, sparkling club kids, or in Central Park on a Saturday afternoon feeding the ducks with her father. She truly is an anomaly.

Where did you grow up?
I grew up in East Harlem, on the Lower East Side, and in the Bronx. That's where I've currently been residing for the past four years: the South Bronx.
Your music is clearly inspired by strong women, particularly women of color.
Unfortunately, I've never had inspiring woman in my personal life to look up to. Perhaps that's why I admire and value so many female public figures. With that gap in my life, I looked to authors to fill that void and characters I could relate to. Young heroines such as Harriet the Spy, Matilda, and Mildred Hubble of The Worst Witch. As a child, I read Anne Frank and was moved. Then it was Sandra Cisneros (The House on Mango Street), Esmeralda Santiago (When I was Puerto Rican), Maya Angelou (I Know Why the Caged Bird Sings), and Julia Alvarez (En el Tiempo de la Mariposa) who taught me how to be a woman. I read and memorized their works feverishly. Their stories and perspectives as strong, nonconforming women of color taught me courage and resilience.

Can you tell me a specific moment when you felt strongly aligned with your sisters?
I am often deeply overwhelmed with this feeling of sisterhood. I feel it immensely when I do my radio show, Smart Girl Club, on Know-Wave, and I know there is a large group of women listening in and taking part in the discussion.
What exactly is Smart Girl Club? It goes beyond the radio show.
Smart Girl Club is a female-based production studio for Princess Nokia projects. I work with teams of exceptional women who collaborate and help me build my vision.

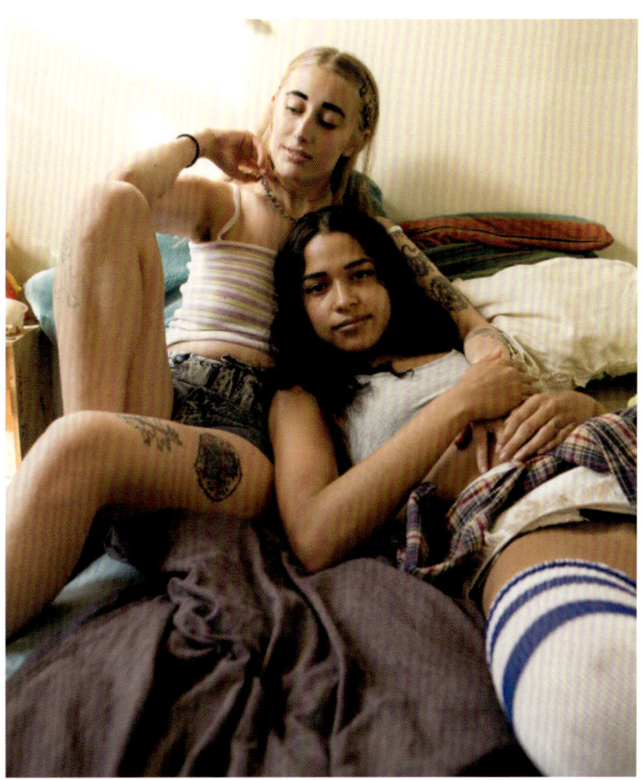

Milah Libin & Princess Nokia, 2014.
Photo: Jessica Lehrman

Where do you see it going?
Taking its roots from DIY, I see the collective reaching out to women on a large scale, making feminism and female camaraderie through the arts more accessible to all types of women, of all ages and groups. A summer camp, a holistic school, a recording studio...all safe spaces for women to work and cohabit amongst each other.

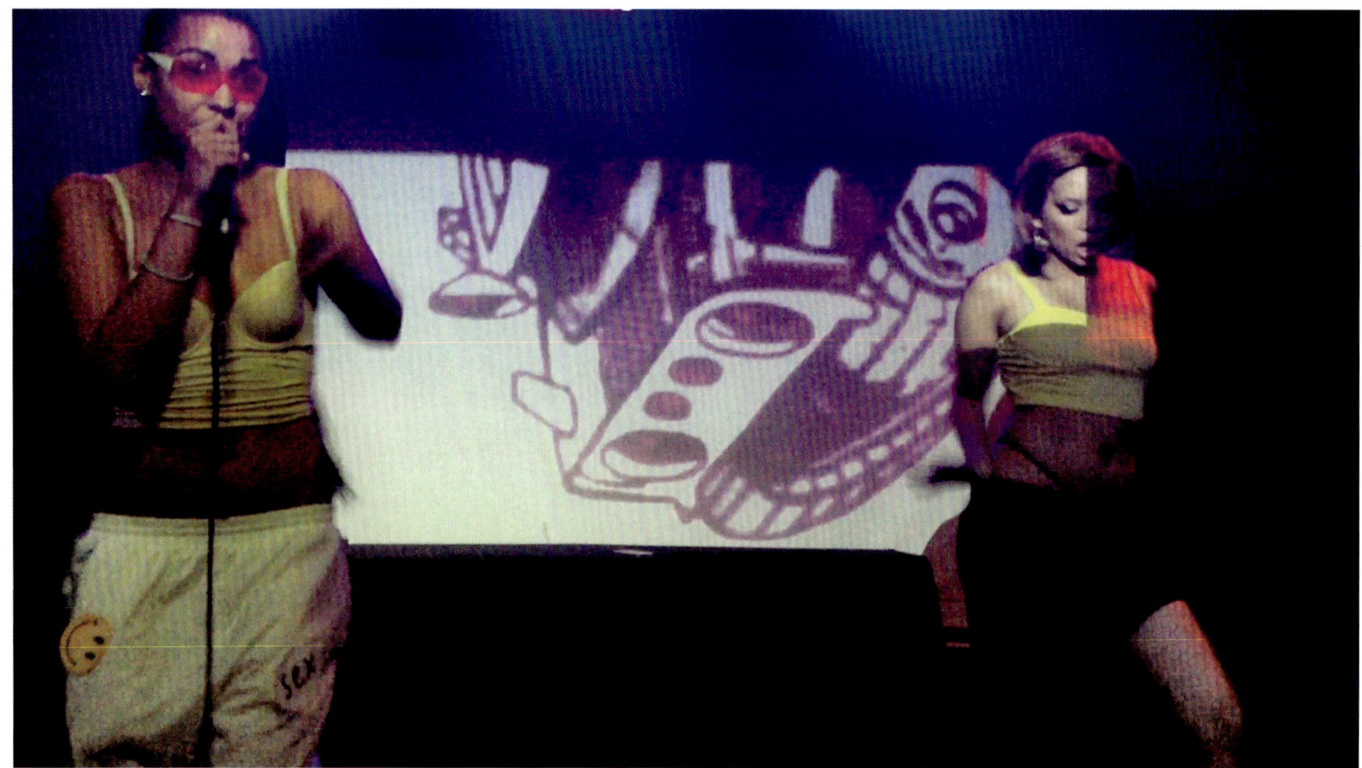

Princess Nokia, Santos, New York, 2013. Photo: Asher Penn

Like the Young Girls video that we just shot.
Yes! We had about 20 women and children, and it was one of the most beautiful experiences of sisterhood and female solidarity that I've ever had.

I feel like you also see a lot of female solidarity at your shows.
The other night, I performed a gig in London, and the pandemonium coming from this female audience was ridiculous. I never had so many young women in one space singing my music, crying, screaming. One girl gave me a hand-written letter and a gift.

How did you learn to make music?
With my brother and sister in elementary school. We all played instruments and practiced and goofed around a lot at the house. I really liked singing, so I joined the school choir in fifth grade.

What about performing live?
I did have a lot of experience performing live in plays, school concerts, and being a go-go dancer, so I really had no fear of going into performing and doing live shows.

How do you prepare for a show?
At this point, I try to remain calm and quiet before all of my shows, and not exert my energy...I take a disco nap.

How do you feel about playing with a live band?
I don't play with a live band. I tried it once and it was terrible. It wasn't their fault, it was mine. Owwwls puts so much artistry and energy into making the beats, and it wouldn't be honoring him correctly if I didn't incorporate the original instrumentals in the set. In the near future, I would love to start incorporating several live factors into the studio process.

What's it like working with Owwwls?
Making music with Chris Lare has been one of the most enjoyable experiences of my entire life. That guy is my best friend. We're always cracking jokes and talking about pop divas. We watch Mazzy Star and Portishead live sessions and he watches skate videos while I write lyrics. He has this body of music, and I throw ideas around until we find the right one.

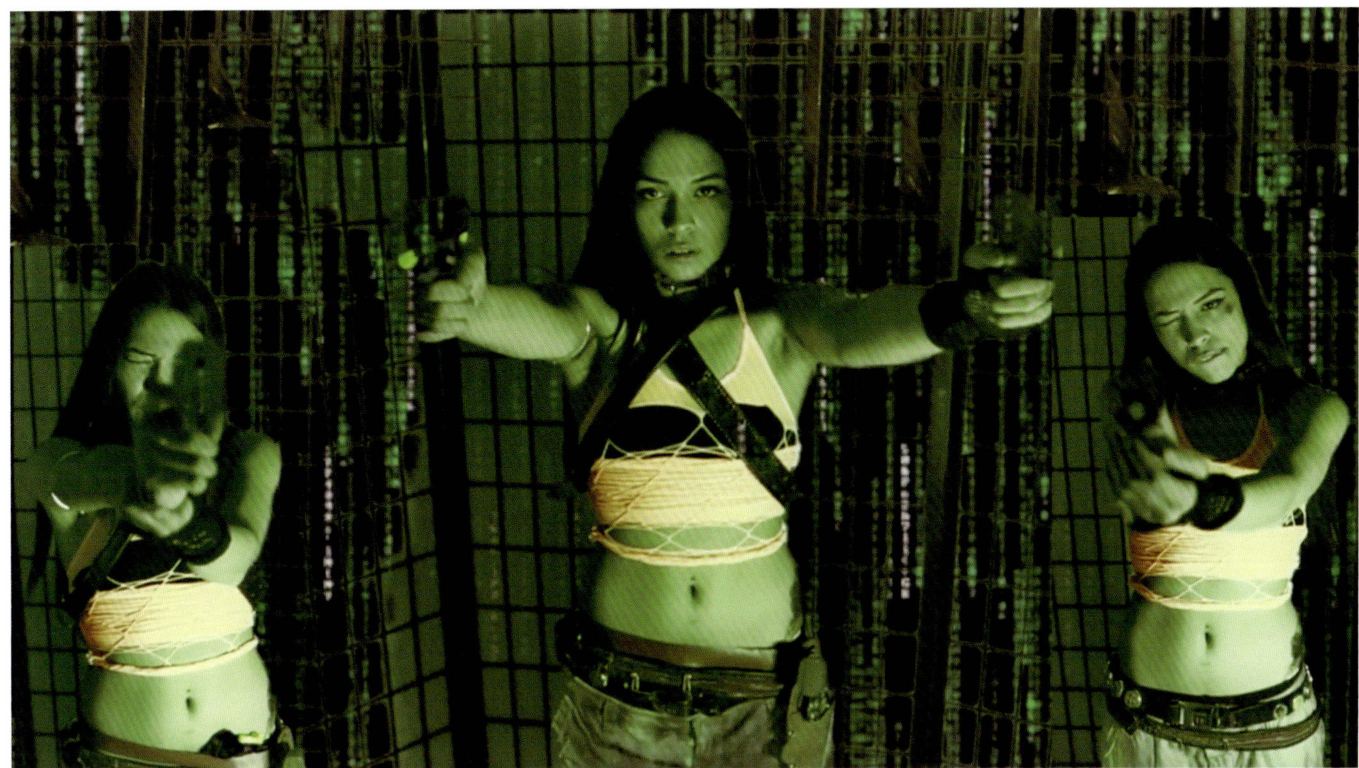

Princess Nokia, Cybiko, Directed by Milah Libin, 2014.

Then we record. I always hang around for a bit because I'm painfully meticulous about everything, but he doesn't mind. We take what we do very seriously.

I know you have a very strong and powerful relationship with your father — can you talk a little bit about that?

My father celebrated my uniqueness, and now so do I. This is why I am so adamant about control, expression, and my personal freedom. I don't feel like I have to change or impress anyone to move further vocationally. There isn't a gap missing. I don't put myself in compromising situations for approval from higher powers such as labels and mainstream expectations. Because of my father's unconditional and sweet love. I really think that I have been saved from the dark side of music.

What creative obstacles have you encountered?

I've had multiple people try to change my aesthetic or sound, censor me, or water my image down in the past. Obviously I wasn't having it, so I no longer have relationships with these people, and became more talented and more successful than they anticipated. My art and my career speaks for itself.

Where does your dream performance take place?

I would say a futuristic nightclub in Heaven, with my mom sitting front-row with God or Tupac as her date.

Would you start your own family in the future?

I believe that I am more keen on the role of a mother than a wife, truthfully. Having a beautiful family is a dream of mine. I love children, and I love the idea of raising them. So whatever God allows, I'll happily have.

Who do you want to cosplay as for the next Comic Con?

I was gonna be Princess Chi-Chi, but now I'm on the fence and I might change it...I'm painfully indecisive.

What is your go-to comfort movie?

Anything Miyazaki. I've probably watched Spirited Away and Ponyo a billion times. I am moved by the innocence, it always cheers me up. ☺

Susan Cianciolo
"Everything was handmade."

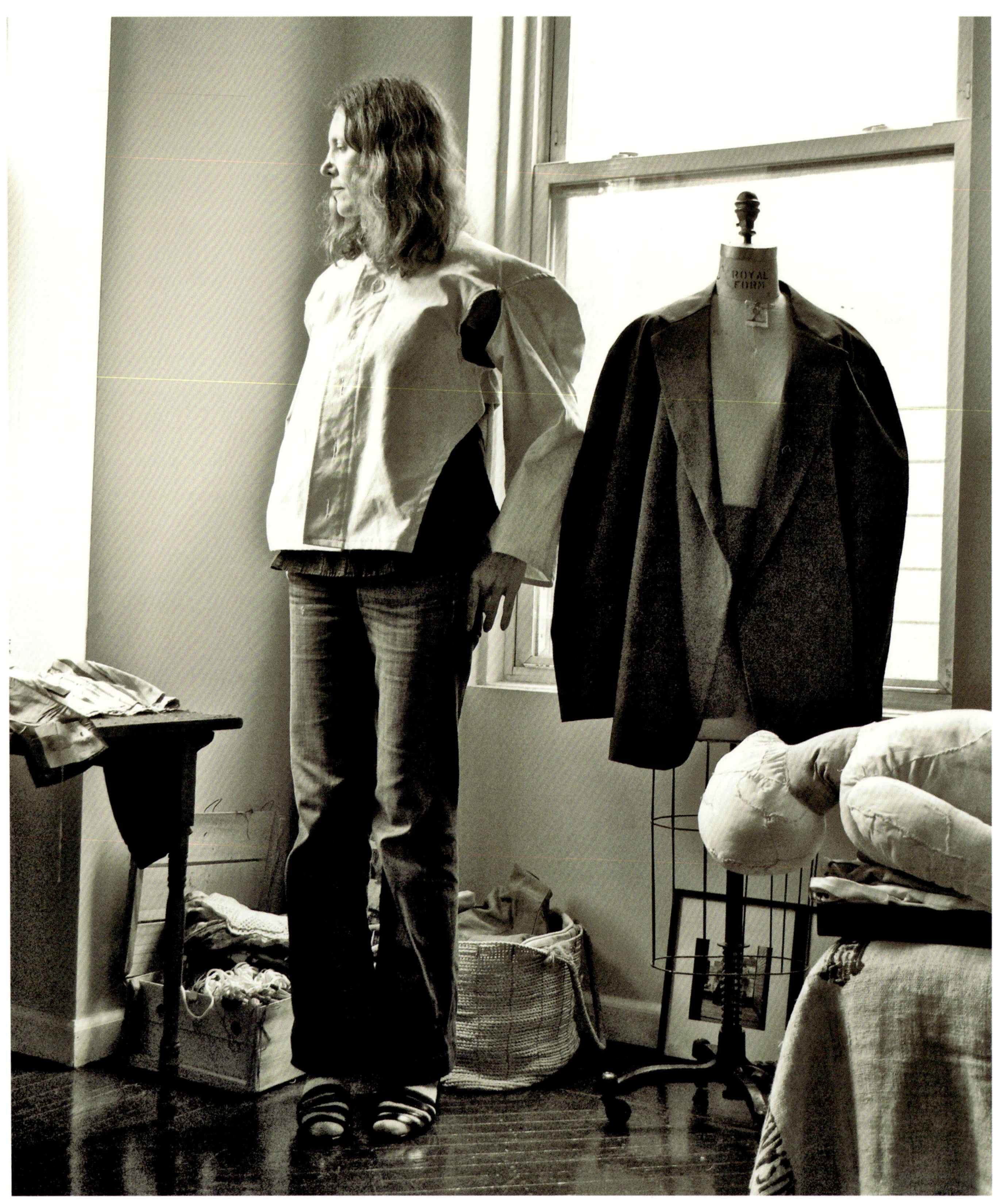

Interview by Asher Penn
Portrait by Wallace Lester

Susan Cianciolo is a pioneer of American independent fashion. Finding her start in the 90s alongside experimental art brands Bernadette Corporation, Imitation of Christ, and Mended Veil, Susan Cianciolo's signature frayed stitching and handmade alterations of thrift finds became an influential aesthetic for decades to come, as seen today on Etsy. Despite constantly shifting trends and economics, Susan has maintained a prolific and consistent career without compromise or expansion, allowing her to create and share truly unique clothing, artworks, and experiences.

Where are you from?
I'm from Rhode Island. I grew up in Maine with my dad part-time, but mostly I was in the inner city right outside of Providence. I grew up with my mom and grandparents there.

What did your parents do?
My dad has done real estate his whole life and had an antique business as well. My mom worked in a prison most of her life. She was a counselor for men's maximum high security. Later on, she became a parole coordinator planner. I remember taking trips to the women's prison on Christmas, working with a lot of different nuns, getting presents for the women that had kids. But she never allowed me to go into the men's prison.

I read in an interview that your mom also made dolls. What were they like?
It could be anything you could imagine. It was always different. I remember one year, we recycled all our walnut shells into a little bed for all these dolls. Then they became ornaments. She also made me a dollhouse with little curtains, little paintings. It was such a work of art, every little shingle.

Was a lot of stuff handmade growing up?
Every sweater I owned was hand-knit. Everyone wore hand-knit slippers. Growing up, my dresses were completely made by hand — whatever you can think of — the curtains, the blankets on the beds.

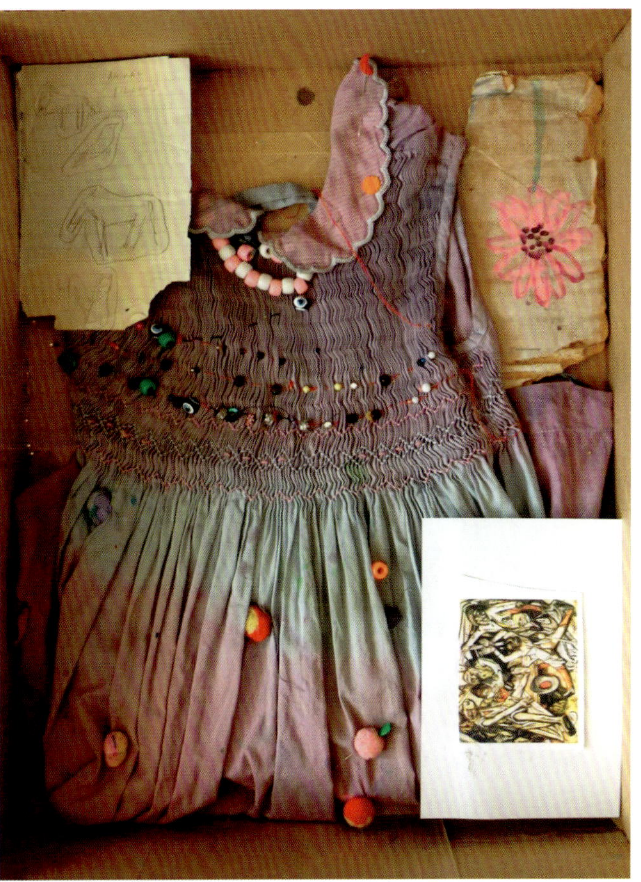

RUN Kit Collection, Children's Box, Maryam Nassir Zadeh, 2012.

How did you end up making your own clothes?
My mom bought me a subscription to Vogue. That's how I started. I asked her if I could go buy some Vogue patterns and start making things.

Did you want to dress cooler?
It was more that I was embarrassed to be brought up so poor. Here I was, in this house with grandparents and a great-grandmother, and everyone else had cars and lived in cool houses and had a regular mom-and-dad life. As a teenager it is so humiliating to not be like everyone else and be cool.

How did you learn to sew?
I learned from a woman who made wedding dresses. I went to Catholic school with her daughter, who was my best friend at the time. So, I asked my friend's mom if she would give me lessons. We'd meet in the evenings. I remember being in the basement and she was so good, I was so thankful she had the patience to teach me.

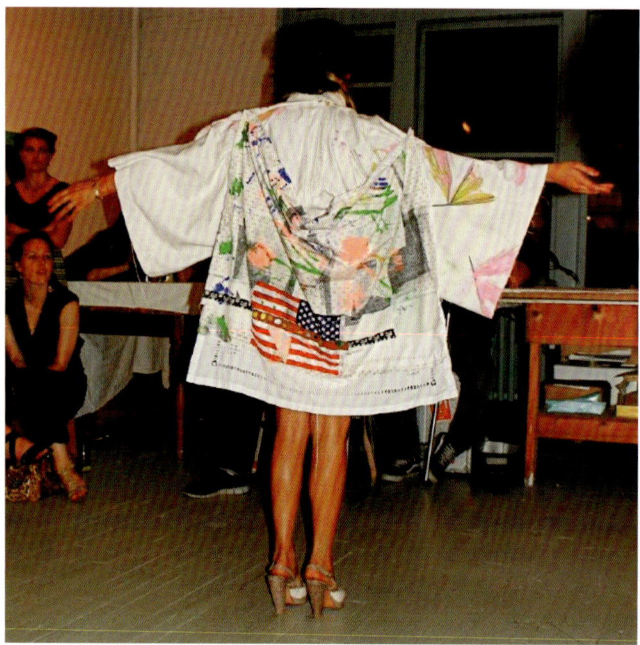

Hearts Open to Revelation Sky, Spring 2012
Collection. Photo: Rosalie Knox

You went to Catholic school?
Yeah, but it was very experimental.
The principal was a feminist nun
who ran all these programs in the
prison. She was super strong,
smart — a real renegade of a nun.
There weren't separate grades, so
the freshman and seniors were all
together. There were no classes
either: you had three-month blocks
where you did just one subject. I
decided I'd create an art studio
class for myself. I just sat and
drew forever and ever. We didn't
have any sports. There was a lot of
hanging out and smoking.
What was your religious upbringing?
Catholic, Protestant, Pentecostal,
and Episcopalian.
Wait, how does that happen?
At age four, I decided I was going
to become Pentecostal. I joined
with this family that had a church
down the street. I spent all my
time with them, went on tours with
them in their station wagon to meet
families, or just stay there all
day and read the Bible. My dad was
Sicilian Roman Catholic, so I would
do that when I was with him, and my
mom decided to become Episcopal, so
I would do that with her.

Were you spiritual from a young age?
Yes, my mom talks about that too.
She said it was really scary, very
shocking for a young person. I
remember giving her talks starting
around the age of four.
Talks?
Religious talks. Which is weird
because she's always seemed like such
a saint in the ways that she's helped
so many, and I always wanted to be
like that.
Doing good with what you do?
I was really tortured inside. How
could I choose fashion when my mom's
working at the prison? Couldn't I
pick a better way to help humanity?
But I couldn't get it out of my head
— fashion and art — and I didn't know
how that could possibly help anything.
**Was the first time you came to New
York to attend Parsons?**
Yeah, I was 17. We came for the
interview and I just said to myself,
"I love this place." It was so
exciting. I was honestly shocked by
all the other people. It was a big
deal. People on my block didn't ever
go away, let alone go to college. We
had loans and financial aid and all
of that stuff.
What did you focus on? Apparel?
My parents did not want me to do fine
art. I had to do a year of marketing,
merchandising, advertising, and then
go into fashion. They said I could do
art on the side. It's funny, a lot of
the professors kind of begged me to
go into fine arts. It was looked at
like fashion is evil. When I got into
the fashion program, every professor
said I should be in the fine arts.
**You started collaborating with
Bernadette Corporation when you were
a student. How did you meet them?**
Through Seth Shapiro. I don't know how
we met, but we'd sit around and talk
about God a lot and he asked me to
model for him. Then I helped him sew
pieces for his first collections. I
really wanted to help him. I loved what
he was doing. Then I met his cousin
Bernadette and joined in on Bernadette
Corporation for the performances.

I didn't know you modeled.
I like the fact that I got to know
what it was like to be the subject,
whether I was treated badly or if
it was exciting. I was glad I would
always know the rest of my life what
that person would feel like if I was
to be dressing them and directing
them and how hard it is, how much
your feet hurt, all the stuff you go
through. All the pain was so worth it
for that experience.

Were you working during school?
I was lucky. I worked at Bergdorf
Goodman and did the murals for all
the windows. They gave me so much
freedom it was unbelievable. I got to
do all the fashion illustrations for
all the boutiques, and giant murals
in the windows, and be up on ladders.
I learned how to paint really large-
scale and just do whatever I wanted
in there. I was also working as a
fashion illustrator and had graphic
design jobs.

You also worked for X-Girl...
And Badgley Mischka. They make
evening dresses for the Oscars.

**Wow. So you were good at executing
work that wasn't really your own?**
I feel like it's a good skill. It's
really hard. It feels like my soul
is dying inside. Around the time I
started working at Badgley Mischka, I
started really intensely doing my own
work. And I always did both, but I was
really pushing a lot by the end and
never sleeping and then when I left
them, I just knew I was immediately
ready to open my first collection.

What was your first collection?
I had a boyfriend that really wanted
me to clean my act up, get a job, and
be more professional. After I left
that job and I broke up with him, I
said to myself, "I am ready." I got
back in touch with Rita Ackermann
and showed her all my drawings for
my new collection and she said they
were great. Then I showed Bernadette
and she said, "OK, I'll style it,"
and Gabriel Asfour helped me. Then we
asked Andrea Rosen if I could do my
first show there.

That's really brave of you.
I know... You can't just go open
a collection. People really did
everything they could to convince me,
and I was scared to death.

What inspires a collection?
I get these insights or messages.
I don't know if you would call it a
vision — it's like this lightbulb
pops up and tells me, "This is what
you're going to do next," and I just
put on this tunnel vision and I do
it and I never deviate. I dedicate
my whole life to every show. I used
to push myself to death, like actual
hospitalization. I felt like I had
to sacrifice my whole self. It's
always been sacred to me. It's this
offering, and I'm willing to accept
if it's hated or if it's loved or if
no one comes or if 2,000 people come
— it doesn't matter.

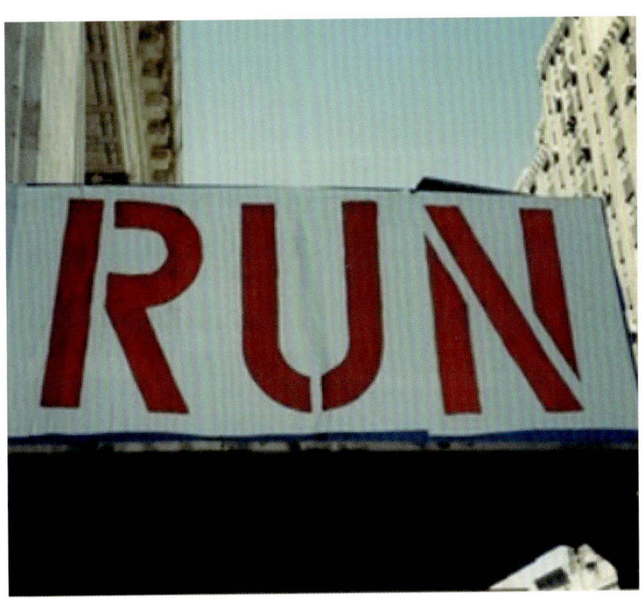

RUN Store, 2001. Photo: Brendan Fowler

Where does the name Run come from?
When I was 15, I was training as a
runner, racing for medals. Then I
met this high school girl down the
street that was much older than me
and she asked if I would train with
her every night, and we'd do hurdles.
My mom didn't believe me. She would
sneak down in the car and watch the
track. She thought I was out there
doing drugs.

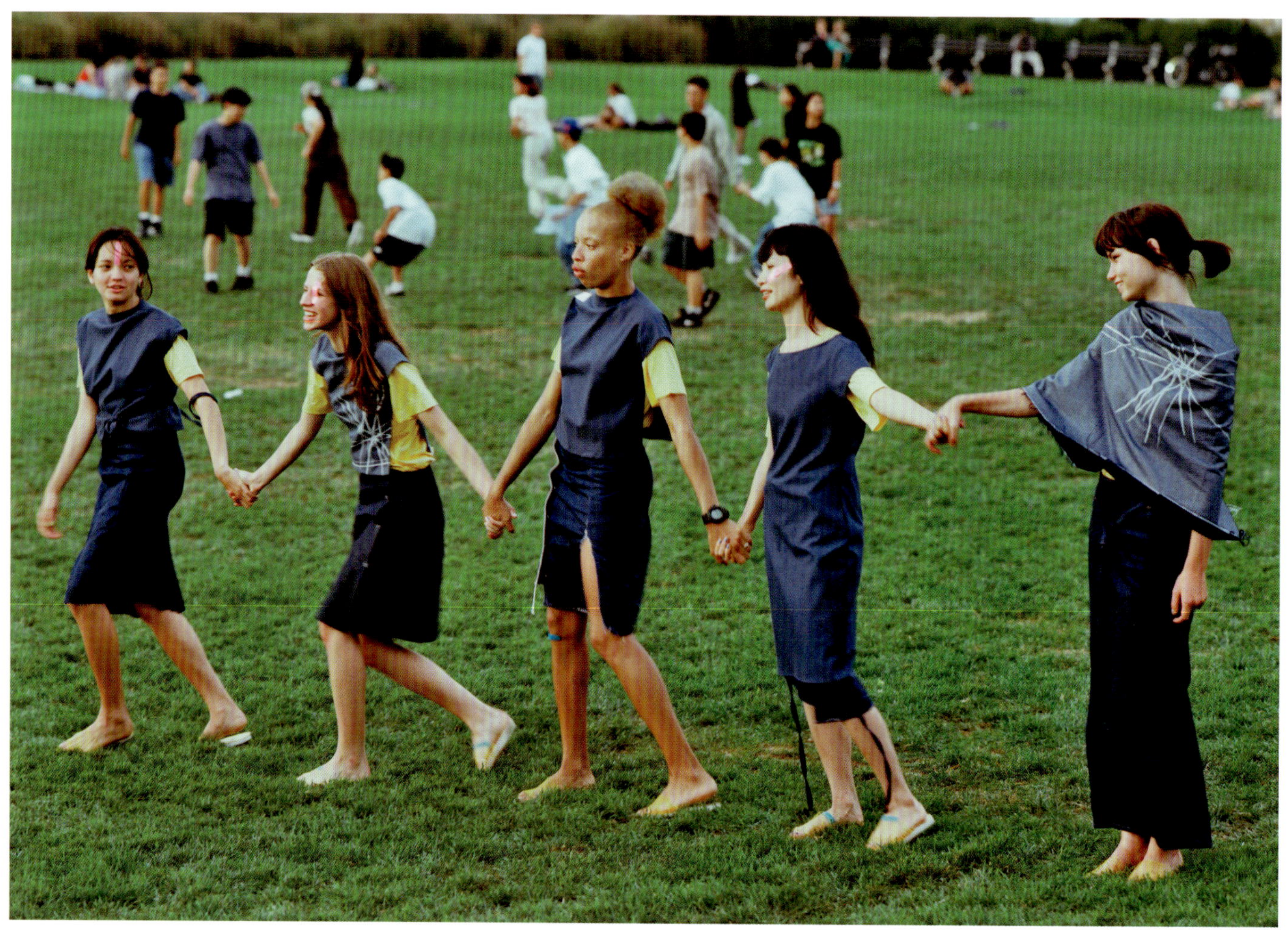

Pro-Abortion Anti Pink, Alleged Films, 1995. Photo: Cris Moor.

Ha ha.
I was really into running and now
I see its connection to the work.
I had to switch to something else
because I'm so messed up from it.
It's hard on the body. Running is
such a basic thing, and it came from
that deep love. During the Bernadette
Corporation times, I would sign
everything as Run and then when I
was going out — my very few moments
doing graffiti with Phil Frost — that
was my tag. I realized you can pick
really mundane, banal words and you
can transform them and then they have
other meanings. Like with Bernadette
Corporation, we were running from
responsibility or anything to do
with society. Then it became Run
Collection, because the studio became
so big at one point. It was this
giant collective of artists and Run
represented the studio.

**The first way I learned about your
work was from photos in fashion
magazines. The photo shoots were
always really different, not just
the clothes.**
When I began, I really hated
fashion shoots. They would make me
feel really claustrophobic and I
watched them turn into something
else in the industry, all this
glamour and fluff. I started to
remove myself from press and photo
shoots because I would get anxiety
attacks from the whole experience.
Then I met Marcello Krasilcic and
he started shooting my shows, and
photographing me, and doing photo
shoots with my clothes. I felt like
I had died and gone to heaven.
His aesthetic felt like it was my
brain. I felt that with Rosalie
Knox, too, and Mark Borthwick.
They're all very honest.

    Susan Cianciolo by Asher Penn

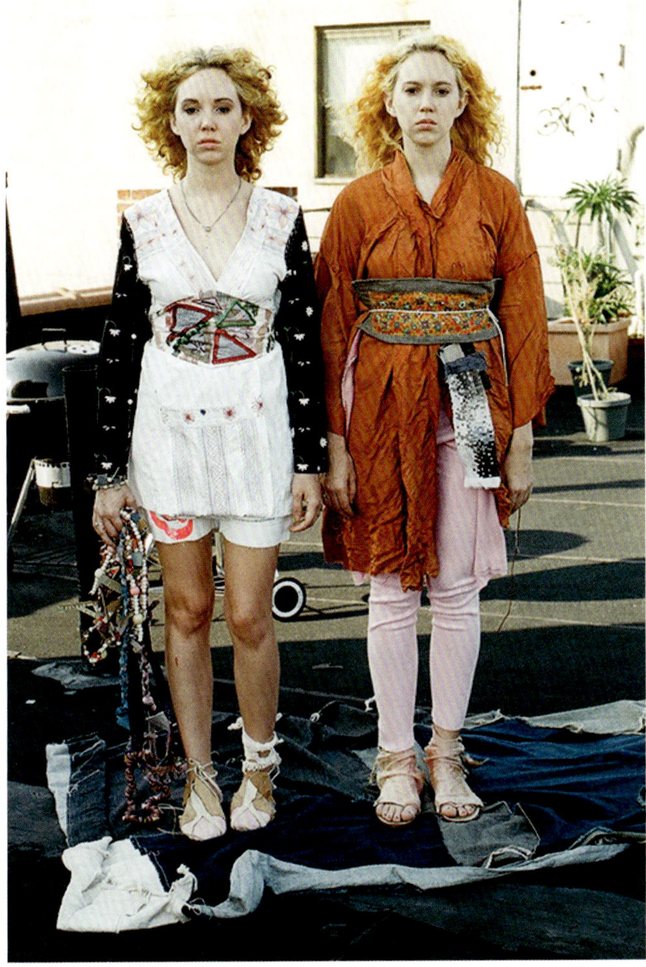

Lookbook, 2013. Photo: Brianna Capozzi

You seem to switch your self identification between fashion designer and artist.
Right now, I don't feel at all like a fashion designer. I love fashion with all my heart, but I don't feel a connection with it right now. I don't mean to be confusing, I feel myself to be an artist now, but that's been on and off. It's a curse because it's always so up and down.

I'm sure your patrons don't care. What is your relationship like with clients?
I end up being so in love with my patrons. It's a relationship of deep support and understanding. It's very real, as real as it gets. I would bend over backwards for them and I'll do any kind of special detail or work. It doesn't matter to me how much they're paying, and most of the time they convince me that they want to pay me more. They know the value. They're not messing around with me.

You wear your own clothes a lot, too.
I mostly used to wear it just so I would know how things felt, especially because we were doing such big production numbers for each collection. Recently I've been really enjoying feeling what it's like in other people's clothes and having that experience. I like all kinds of feelings of clothes. I'm not just into comfort.

How did you start making children's clothes?
I made a ton of dolls for friends who had kids, before I ever had kids. I'm sure I made kids' clothes too. Then I made my daughter Lilac a ton of things and when she got to a certain age, she said, "Sell it, sell it." Since I would always put Lilac in the show, I'd make some things for the show for her friends. Clients began seeing I had all these children's clothes and wanted to buy them.

Lilac likes being in the shows?
Oh yeah. When she walks on stage and sees all the people she brightens up. She wants to be in the show, she wants to help, she wants to be a part of it. Now she's become so much of a director that she wants to say how everything should be.

So she is also a collaborator?
I swear she always adds a better touch. It's so much more courageous. We disagree a lot, but it's great to have her collaborative aspect. There's just so much she's added to pieces that have made them 1,000 times better. And it's a way we can get along.

How do you think you have you remained independent so long?
Well, you have to roll with the punches. I know that when a recession hits, luxury items are the first things people drop, but I was never afraid to starve because I grew up so poor I never had anything to lose. I was fine if I was homeless. I went two weeks without food, knowing things would come around. Through all the ups and downs I found a perfect rhythm. Where I'm at now, after so much learning and risk taking, it was all worth it. ☺

Making Daisy Park
"Falling in love with your cellmate's girlfriend."

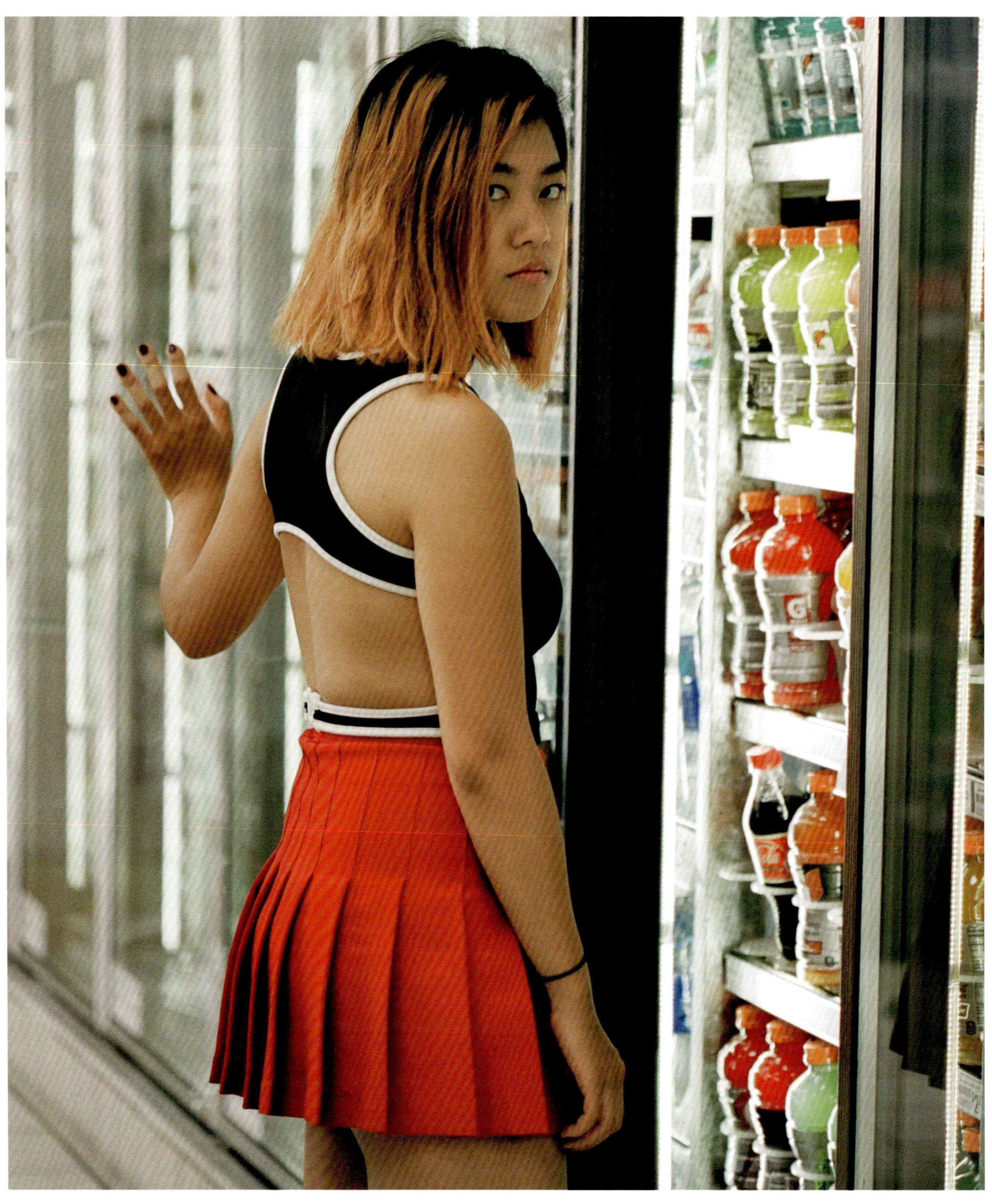

By Air Pop
Introduction by Asher Penn

Watching a movie grow from an idea into a reality is crazy. When Air Pop first told me about Daisy Park — a love triangle between two cellmates and a girl — I didn't get it. "Do they have to be in a minimum security prison?" It sounded like a lot of work. Actually everything sounded like a lot of work, from writing the script, locations, wardrobe, actors...making a movie is hard. Air Pop's approach to making Daisy Park is wholly unique because it utilizes all the skills and tools of the contemporary artist and applies it to the execution of a story. It also revels in elements of film that typically get glossed over: cool soundtrack, clothes, props. Lo-fi in all the right ways, Air Pop's Daisy Park reminds us how much fun independent movies can be, and the exciting, unexplored potential of true DIY filmmaking in 2014.

Here's how it happened.

The Idea. This is basically where it all started. I wrote this post; "Falling in love with your cellmate's girlfriend" almost three years ago on a personal Tumblr account, and that line haunted me for a while. I didn't even consider a film around the idea til much later. That simple situation of extreme isolation, the world still turning outside, and all of your prior control stripped. Having a girlfriend is quite common while being locked up, especially in minimum security prisons like in the film. What a bummer.

Beta Pictures. Asher and I first started discussing Beta Pictures in 2012. We couldn't believe how bad independent film had gotten and were trying to figure out why. Our main concept was a film studio that produced and distributed cool movies made by artists. Working outside of the studio system is both thrilling and necessary for our goals and really guided my decision-making.

Daisy. When Sophia Park was recommended for the role of Daisy, it was mostly because of the name... Just a total coincidence that she was perfect for the part. It was exciting to meet an individual who understands the idea of portraying someone and also totally down to transform themselves. She flew over from New York and stayed in Los Angeles for a few months. Our shooting schedule allowed for her to do her own thing a lot of the time and hang out with her friends. I was at first apprehensive about such a spread out schedule, but in the end it was pretty healthy actually. Many long drives out to Simi Valley, sharing music and hearing her crazy tales about the night before.

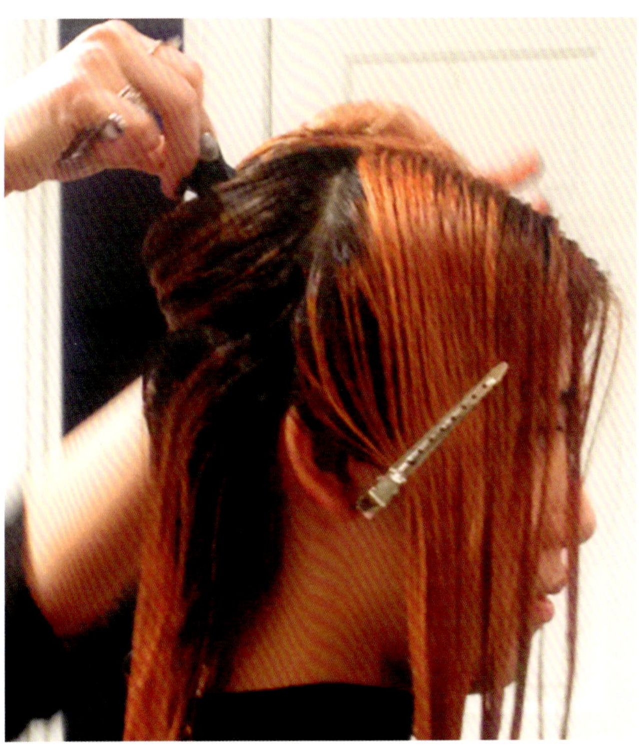

Sophia Getting Hair Dyed, Beverly Hills, 2014. Photo: Air Pop

Funding. Steve is the fucking best. I guess you could say he was the green-light or whatever. He helped fund the film very early on, really getting it off the ground, but he also killed it as the parole officer. Actually the day he signed the financial agreement, he asked if we could stop at the pet store. When we went in, he noticed the store employee struggling to grab his fish from the tank. He immediately grabbed the net from them and got them himself, all the while cracking jokes and making us laugh. That's Steve. I'm really glad his personality came through in the film and made it such a special scene.

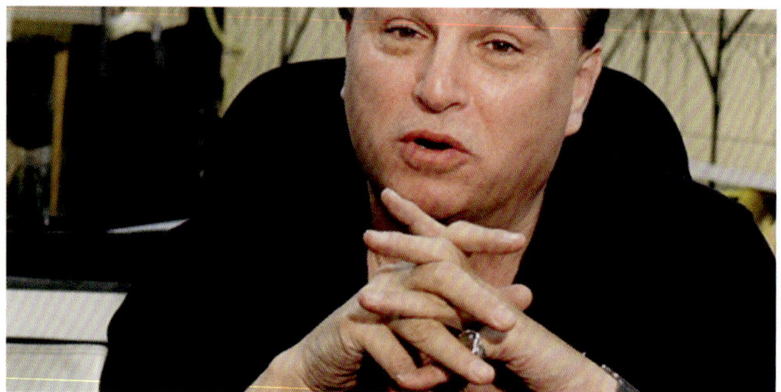

Steve, Daisy Park, Beta Pictures, 2014.

Gear. My camera setup was both shitty and amazing I guess. I built a wooden rig myself to house it all, and it turned out to be a pretty good design. I'm not really sure what people thought when they saw it, it's pretty bootleg. I'm not crazy about how everything looks with Digital SLR so I bought a pretty old Tokina lens off of eBay that gave the film a different feel. Mixing and matching older lenses with newer cameras is a really good starting point if you don't want that tacky digital look.

Cast. So no real actors, right? I guess I learned I'd rather work with some really cool people than really untalented cheap actors. I'm from Los Angeles, so obviously I could create the entire cast with low paying actors in an afternoon. That sounded really awful to me, so I decided to look around and meet some people. I think I got super lucky because it didn't take too long, but it was such a personal series of heavy decisions. Michael who played Raul looked straight up scary in a Facebook picture so I knew he'd be good. The guy that I wanted to play Jason just didn't work out and was pretty unreliable. I was only able

to communicate with him through Instagram Direct Messaging because he never paid his phone bill. I still love Jade though, he's great, maybe some other project one day.

Prison. A good portion of the film had to be set in a minimum security prison...where the fuck was I going to make that happen? I surfed Craigslist for months with no luck. It got pretty depressing at one point. Then, one day I searched for an art studio, first post result came up, looked good. I called them, ran over there, and handed them a check. It was that fast, unreal. That moment really saved the project and chilled me out a lot. My friend Miles that also plays Jason, decided to share the space and play music there. I still have the space and I plan on recording my next record there.

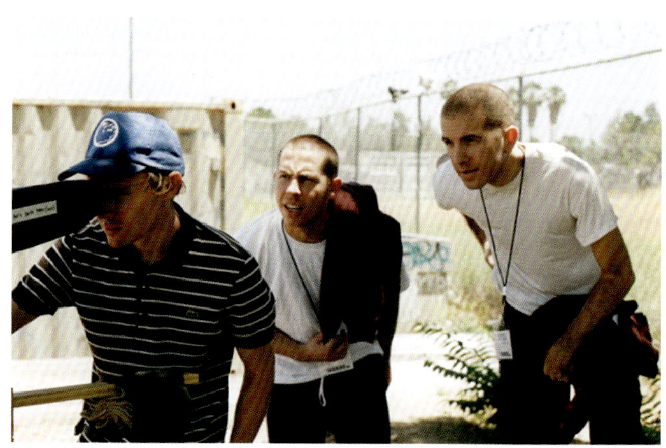

Air Pop, Brandon & Ian, The Yard, 2014. Photo: Michael Hernandez

The Yard. There's this really great open dirt field next to a skatepark I go to pretty frequently. I've gotten to hang with a lot of cool kids at that park. Miles first took me there a few years ago and it's pretty much become a weekly ritual for us. Anyway, it looks like a fucking prison yard and my buddy that works there hooked it up. I ended up naming the prison after my father (F.S. Morgan) which was just a joke. There's no metaphorical daddy-issue crap going on, he's the man.

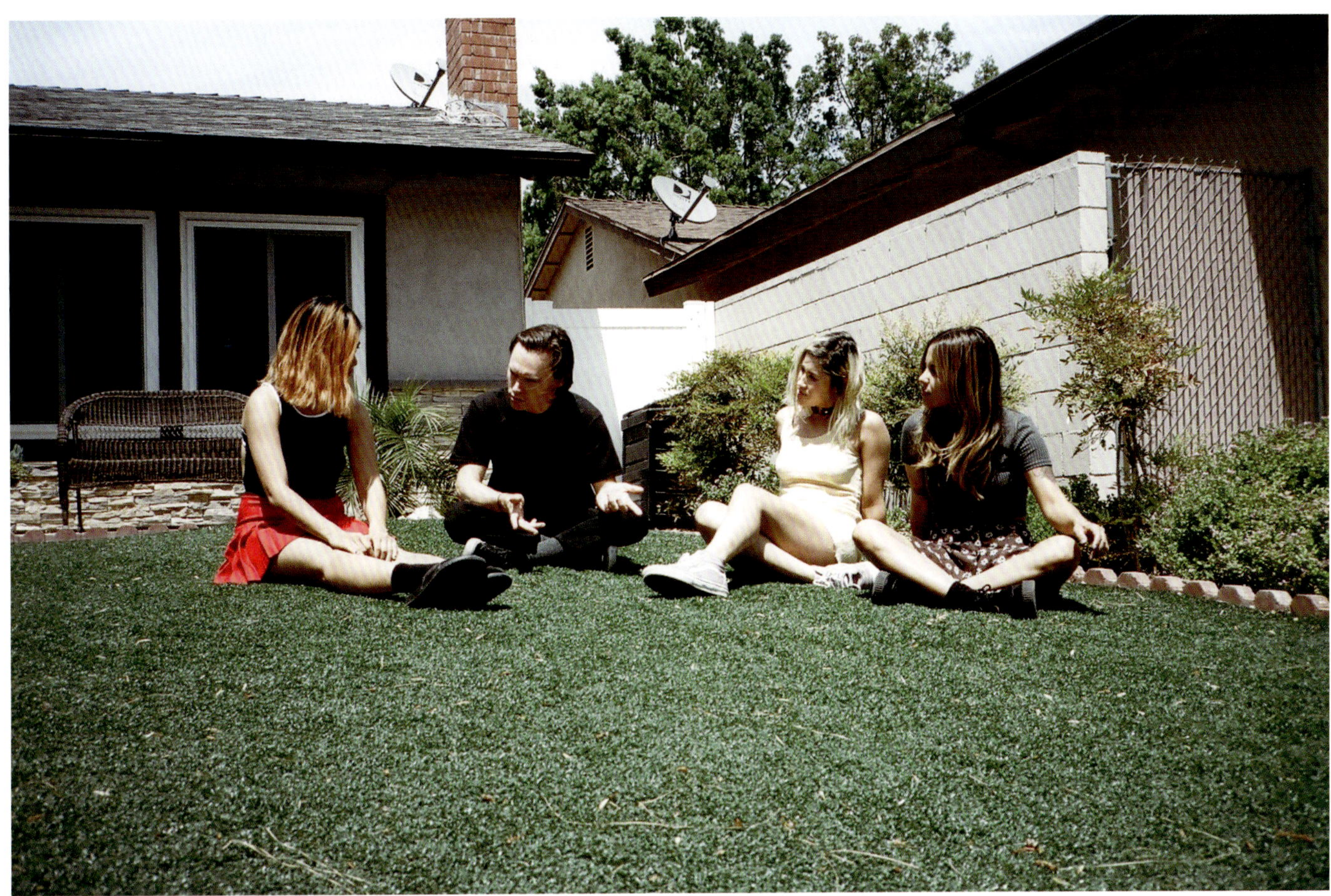

Sophia, Air Pop, Jenny & Brenda, The House, 2014. Photo: Nate Walton

The House. The grandmother's house is actually my brother and his wife's place. They were generous enough to let me film there, which worked out great. It was pretty far away from the city but totally worth it in every way. It's very suburban obviously and it was really funny filming the sex scene there. I had to shoot it from outside the window in the side-yard. Giving Ian and Sophia direction was rough because I had to yell weird sexual strategies so that they could hear me from inside. I already thought that their neighbors probably thought we were filming a porno.

Wardrobe. My girlfriend Allyson and I had long talks about the clothing for this project. What a girl wears everyday is an extremely valuable tool of expression that I really respect. We knew the overall direction for it and she did an incredible job of mixing online store purchases, thrift-store finds, and personal objects to execute a believable character. We also took some of the film budget, bought some extra clothes not for the film, and then doubled our money selling them on eBay...yeah, it's like that.

Directing. Being a director basically means you need to know exactly what the fuck to do everyday. Patience will save your ass, and you just need to chill out and focus. You know that really dumb thing directors say about how sometimes the actor surprises them and they deliver something truly special...well that shit is true and it's pretty fucking cool, and you don't need a professional actor to notice it.

Soundtrack. Before I started working on Daisy I had mostly been focused on music, and I knew it would be a major element of the film. It was a way for everyone to have a lingo and be able to talk to each other about something that they loved. Various genres and music tastes were able to mix in a more real life context as well. It was fun to write lines about the songs I created like, "This is some weak indie shit." A person's stance on a song or band can be pretty revealing. As far as making a lot of different sounding music, that was actually pretty easy and I've always felt very comfortable writing whatever style I want at any time.

Props. Creating a whole music world for the characters was crucial to the backbone of the story. I had the soundtrack figured out by making lots of fake bands, but wanted to take that idea even further. Music culture and the exchange of music may be our world's finest form of communication. It can build friendships and create a new vocabulary overnight. I designed a ton of fake band ephemera: T-shirts, flyers, posters, and cell phone cases...pretty fun.

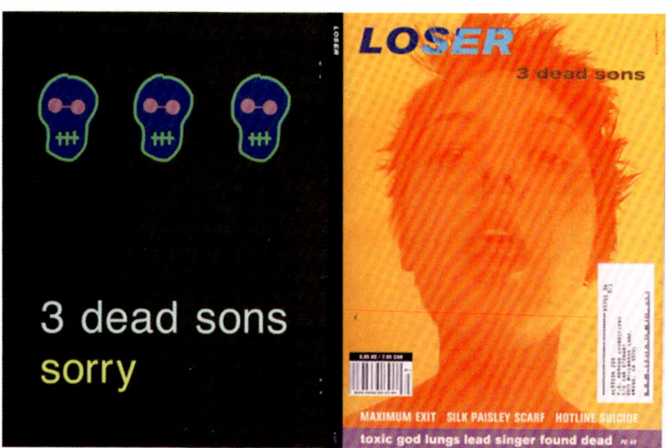

Loser Magazine Prop, Designed by Air Pop, 2014.

Drones. Fuck drones man. My friend Andrew is pretty good at flying them, but still. I appreciate the technology though and I think people will do a lot of cool shit with them. What worked though for the film, was this new view of their environment. You feel super sucked into the rooms and the close contact the whole film, but the ending takes you out of that.

I don't know that I'd intentionally use drones again, ha ha.

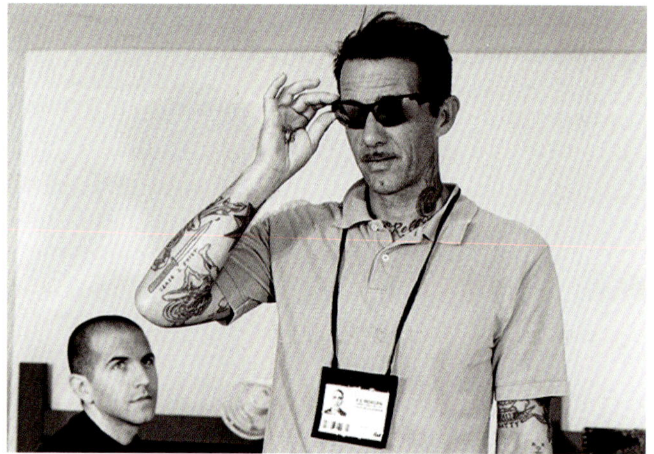

Ian & Cali, The Cell, 2014. Photo: Michael Hernandez

Cali. I've been a fan of Cali, both as an artist and a person, and have always thought that he would be amazing in front of the camera. Working with him was a total high point in the process. He totally understood the role and hopped right in. It was really hard not to laugh half the time — Ian and Michael kept laughing too. I found out that he and I grew up on the same street and went to the same high school, pretty wild.

Audio Dubbing. I knew that I wanted a more old school sound for the dialogue pretty early on. My favorite films are pretty much all overdubbed. I also needed a Korean mother to shout at Daisy through speakerphone. Randomly, I got in touch with my old friend Kyuhee who conveniently has been living in Seoul for the last five years or so (thanks internet). We didn't end up subtitling it, but trust me she's saying real shit.

Shit Talking. A huge part of life is shit talking, ha ha... Not just amongst women, but guys too. I wanted to write these experimental narration talking points just right. There's some truth going on in what they're saying, but in the end they still become an annoyance.

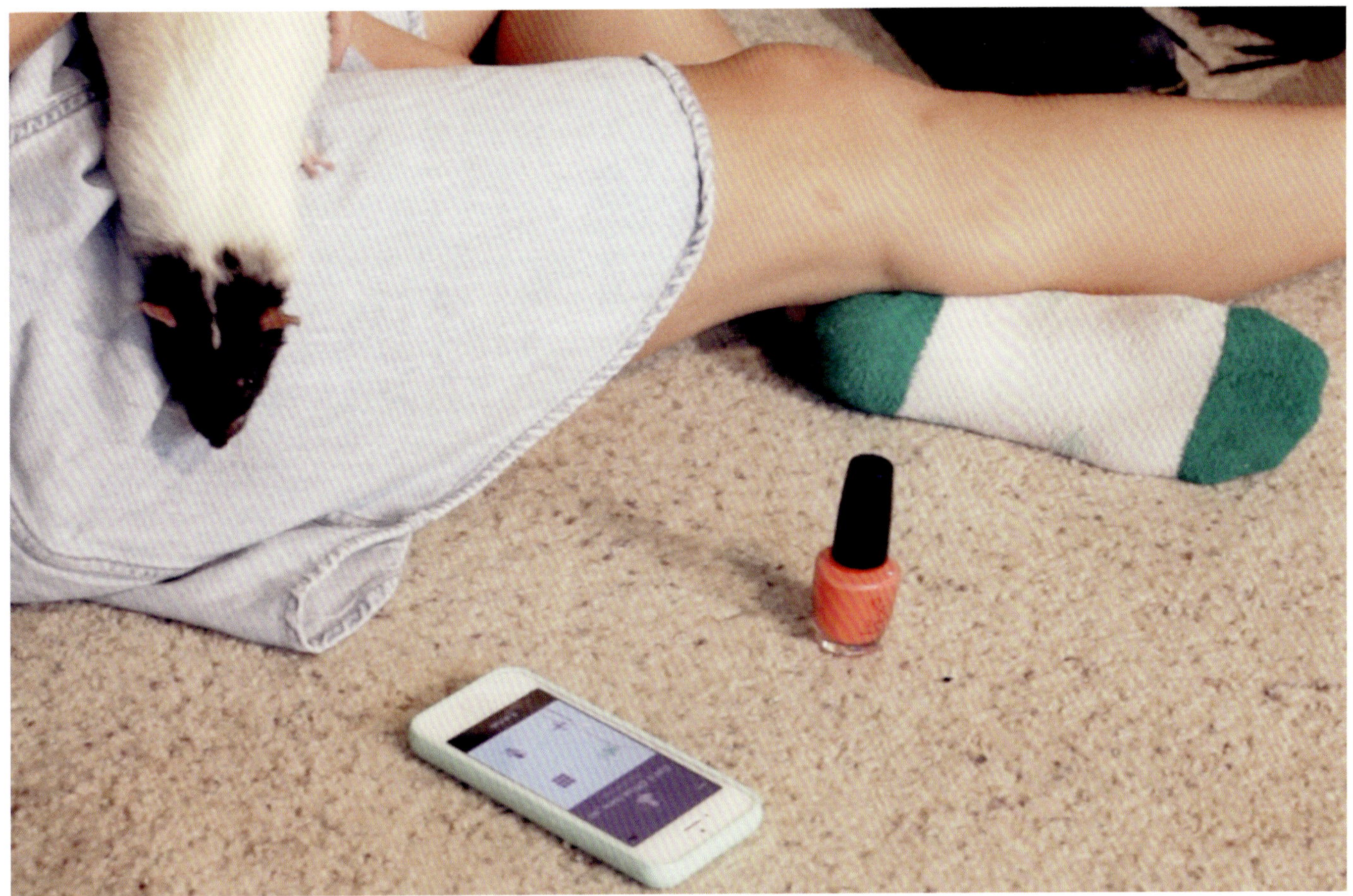

Sophia, Daisy Park, Beta Pictures, 2014.

They are meant to be anonymous and mysterious. I wasn't sure exactly how to visualize them, but in the end the noise worked out great. Those specs are actually generated from high-res photographs of my studio's dirty roof.

7-11. Anyone in California understands the importance of a 7-11, so getting to film there was a fucking blessing. Through some mutual friends I met a buddy whose family owns a couple of them. He hooked it up, and I was able to film there no problem. Even the dude working the counter at the time was cool about it. None of the customers bothered us, it was like too good to be true. Sophia and I only slept about 3 hours the night before too, got really lucky that morning. Sometimes shooting days that sound like logistical nightmares end up going smooth.

Editing. So yeah, you come home with all this shit that you filmed, and now you have to sit there staring for hours. There's no avoiding it. I definitely lost my mind a few times. At one point I was editing with a laptop on my studio roof sitting on a drum chair saying in a Drake voice out loud: "What am I doin'?" All bad.

The Premiere. I wrapped up the film in New York, my first time ever coming to the city. We premiered the film at Anthology Film Archives, a historic theater with great sound. The film looked awesome at such a large scale, damn. It's been a really crazy year. Watching other people see your film and totally get it is pretty fucking cool. I truly made this film DIY-style and I hope that artists will do the same and create a whole new wave of filmmaking. No one else is gonna do it. ☺

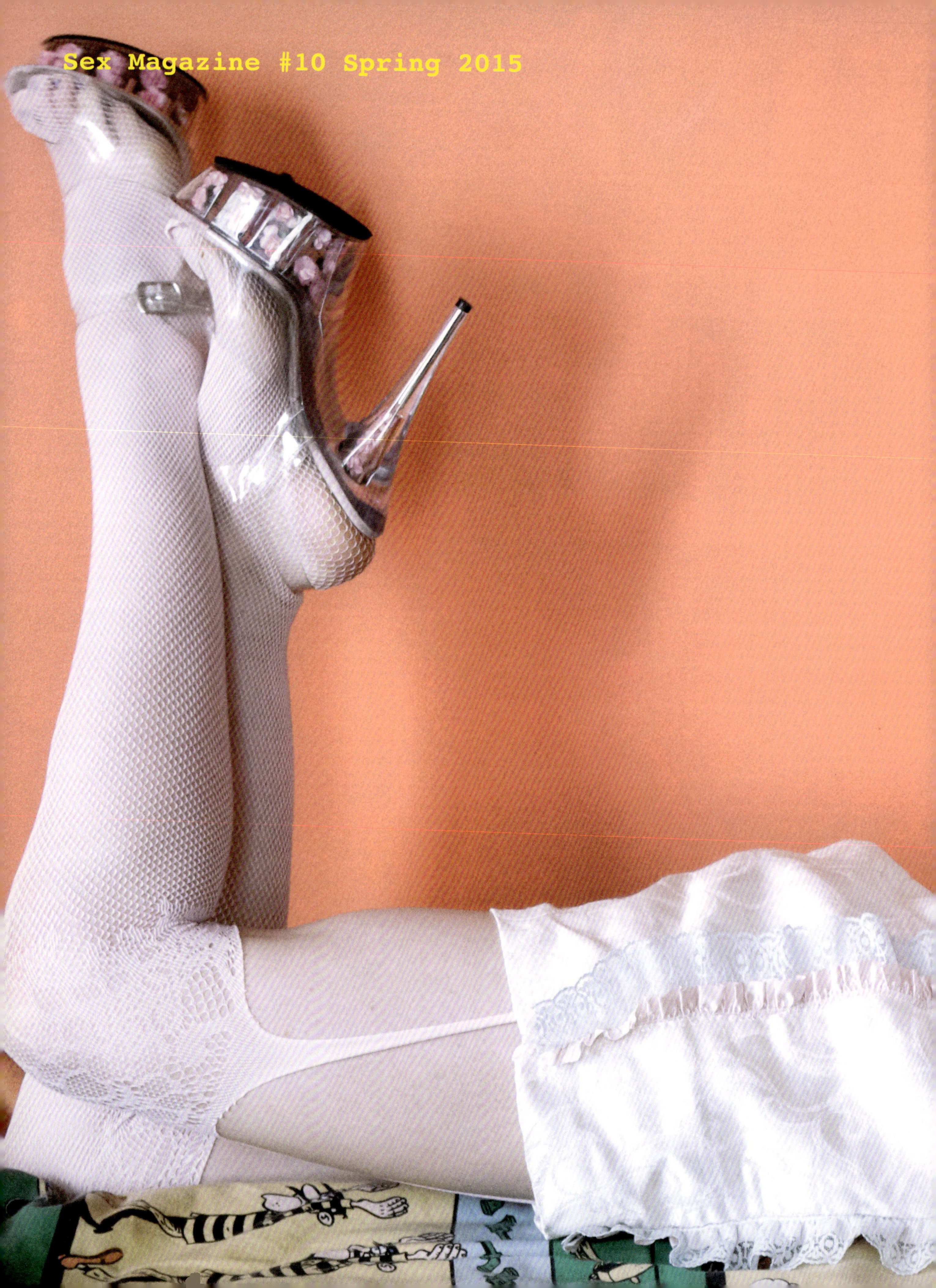
Sex Magazine #10 Spring 2015

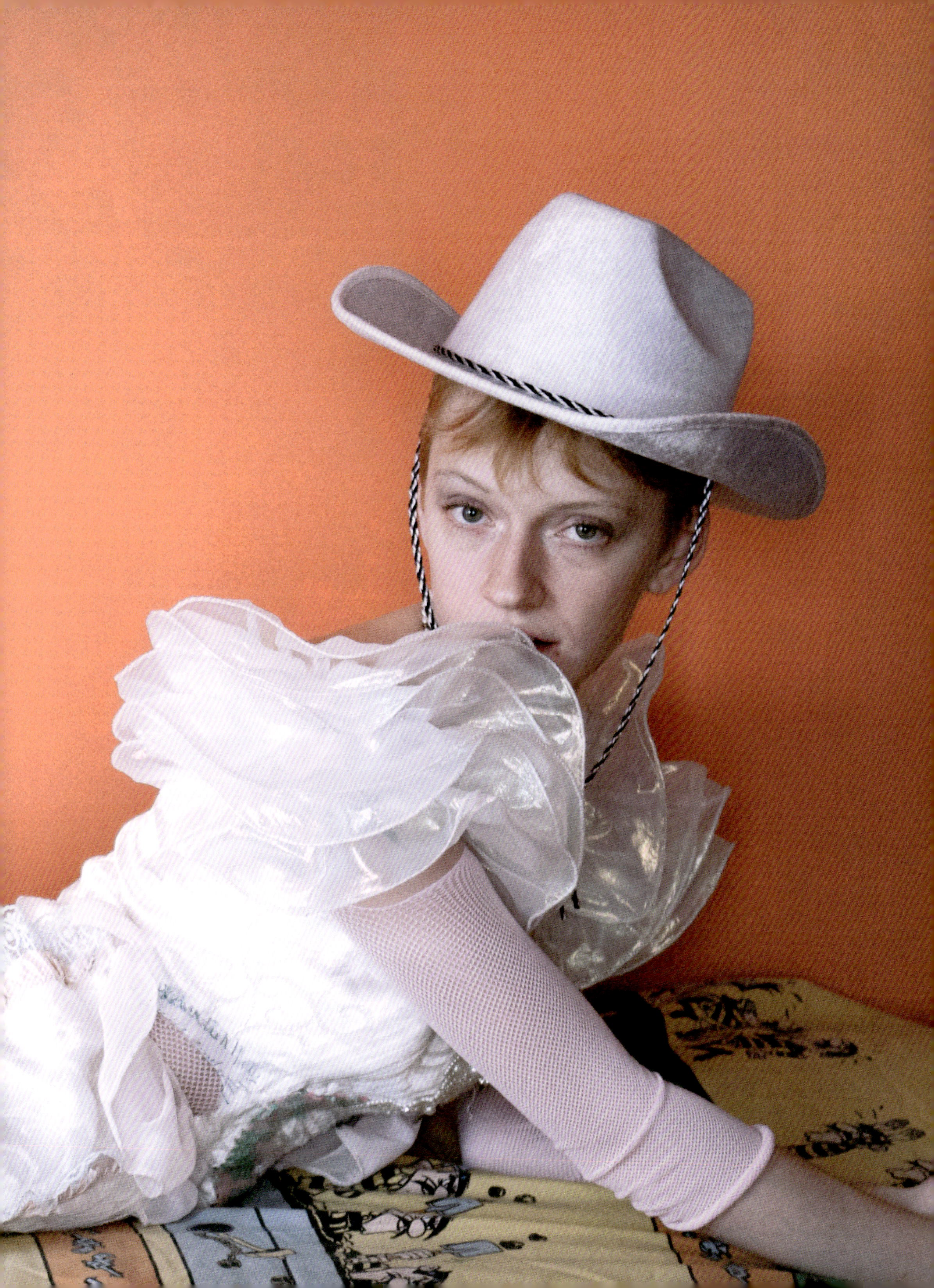

John Michael Boling
"A computer not connected to the internet is a very different thing."

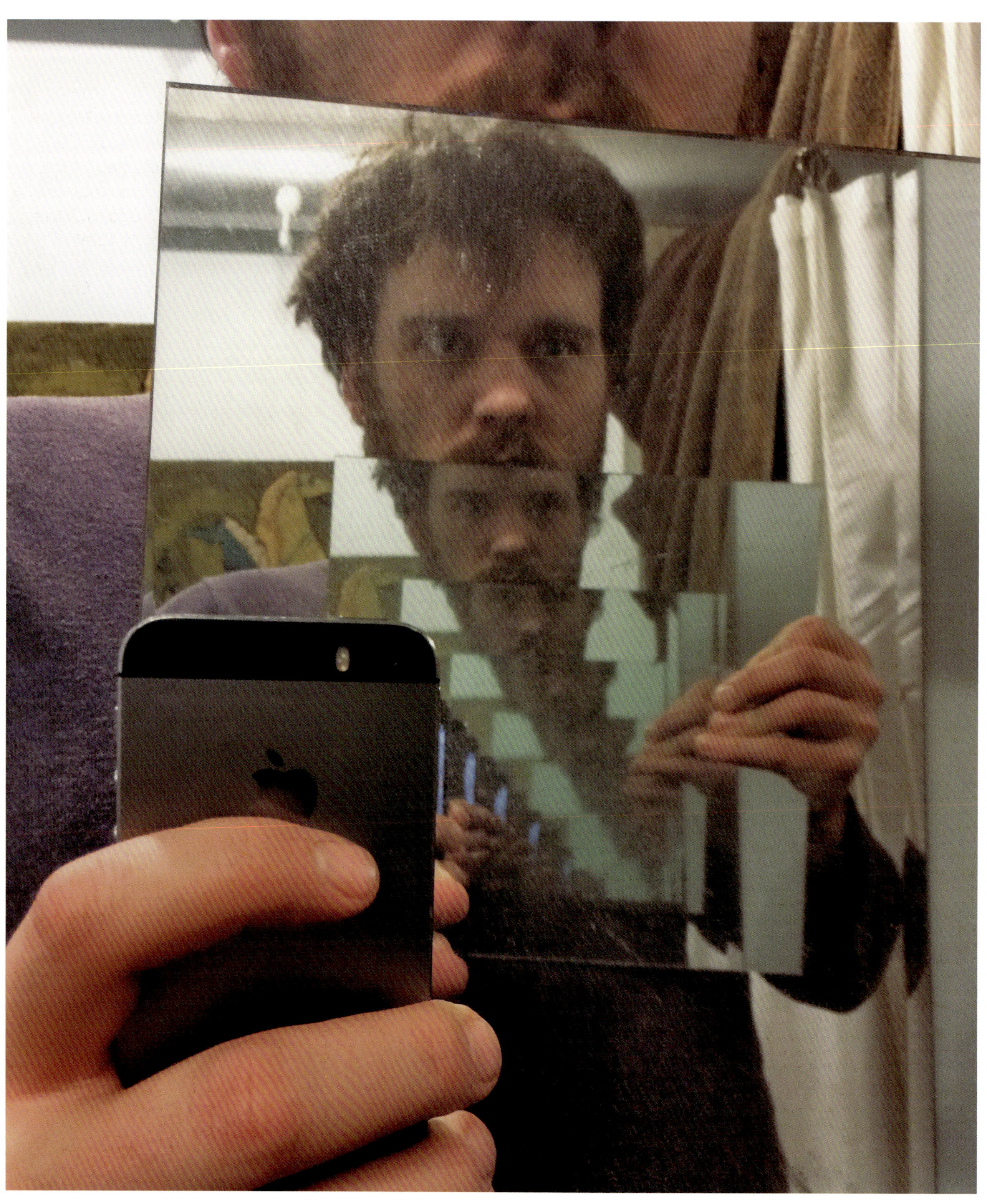

Interview by Asher Penn
Images courtesy John Michael Boling

John Michael Boling's contribution to the history of internet art is one of engagement. A prodigious user of personal computers and the WWW in their earliest incarnations, his work in digital montage, animation, and found video has consistently strived to push the limits of what is possible within the medium of internet art. Boling has also been a significant champion of post internet art in its formative years as a long-standing contributor to Rhizome, cofounder of the creative forum Nasty Nets, and cofounder of Are.na, a platform for personalized research. In the last year, Boling has distanced himself from the internet, returning to his roots to work on his first major work: a science-fiction anime television series made entirely on the open source software Blender.

So, you're originally from Georgia?
I was born in Rome, Georgia in 1983 and lived there for the first 18 years of my life.

Did you go to school there?
Yeah. In Georgia there's a really great program called the Hope Scholarship. If you go to college in-state and keep a 3.0 average they pay for your tuition and give you money for books and stuff. I went to film school at Georgia State University in Atlanta for a year, hated it, and transferred to the University of Georgia in Athens.

Why did you drop out of film school?
By the early 2000s, honoring my teenage dream of being a filmmaker didn't seem as fun anymore. That independent film culture from the late 80s and 90s had collapsed on itself and it was just too expensive to do anything. So my dad asked about art school.

Had you been into art before that?
Not really, but I was around it a lot. My dad went to art school, and my grandfather had an art gallery in Atlanta in the 70s. There was always art around the house.

What about doing stuff with the computer? When did that start?
My dad got us a 386 computer for Christmas in 1989. Pretty much every day since then I've been messing around with graphics on the computer.

What programs were you using?
When I was six I was using Deluxe Paint, which is this really cool bitmap graphics editor that was originally built for the Amiga. It was a really powerful program at the time. You could also make animations with it so I would spend my time making characters move around, mostly just playing around and having fun with it.

What about going online?
Shortly after we got that first computer, I dialed into a local BBS. I was like six or seven. I don't remember if it was a messaging interface or a forum, but I remember some guy, his name was Megalomaniac, sent a message saying something like "Hey, how's it going? What's up? I saw you're logged in."

That's gotta seem crazy.
I thought it was magic. I was really astounded by the possibilities knowing that you can connect with somebody like that. It wasn't until '94 that we got WWW access through Prodigy which was an early competitor of AOL. As soon as we got that, I saw there was a place I could put all these things I had been making. Prodigy was also the first of the dial-up services to offer free web hosting so I started to make websites.

What were they like?
They were just the goofy kind of nonsense websites an 11 year old would make. I remember one just had pictures of Dr. Teeth and the Electric Mayhem from the Muppets with an infinitely tiled background image of a Zagnut candy bar, and probably a few rotating skull animated gifs... The fact that you could just copy and paste a website's source code, make a few changes in a text editor and put out something new for people to see was amazing.

This was before Google too, right?
Yeah, the internet at that time was so different. You could kind of conceive of seeing it all in some way. When Yahoo first started, it was something like a user generated directory of websites. For instance, there would be a moderator who would take care of collecting and organizing all the skateboarding websites in California or something. You could just surf through the hierarchy on Yahoo and actually find stuff.

Were you aware of internet art from a young age?
Well, I didn't recognize it as that. There were probably weird things I came across that felt like art to me. It wasn't until I took a net art class in art school in 2005 taught by one of my mentors, Mark Callahan, that art online was sort of legitimized to me. It dawned on me that the stuff I found interesting and wanted to do could be looked at from an art perspective.

What was he showing you?
He showed us a lot of the new media and net art canon and introduced me to Rhizome which is where I came into contact with an early piece that Guthrie Lonergan had made. That Guthrie piece hit me hard. I felt like, "I've been doing stuff like this for fun on the side. Why don't I just do this stuff instead of all the other bullshit I've been doing?" Shortly after that Guthrie and I started emailing each other and became friends.

I understand that site del.icio.us was fairly central to the internet art community at the time. How did you get into it?
I had begun uploading stuff to http://www.gooooooooooooooooooooooooooooooooooooooooooooooooooogle.com/, my art site but nobody really knew about it. A friend had told me to check out del.icio.us. I went to it, typed in my domain and four or five total strangers had already saved it. I was immediately hooked.

Kind of like your first "like."
Del.icio.us was essentially the first Web 2.0 social network. If you saved a link, you could see a list of the other people who also saved that link. Through that process you could find cool people through the cool stuff they were saving. That doesn't sound very crazy now but at the time it was amazing. I can't really express how well it worked. I met so many friends there.

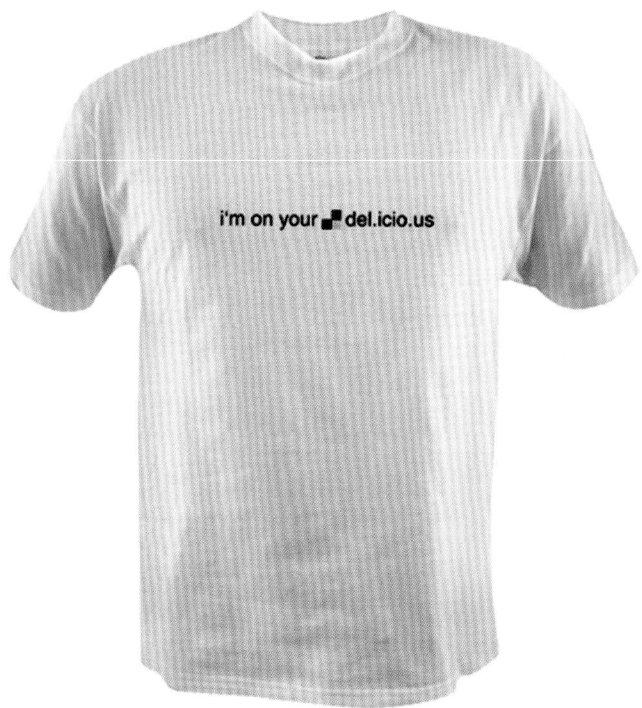

i'm on your del.icio.us, Nasty Nets post, 2006.

Were there any common things uniting the scene there?
The fact that we weren't using it exclusively as an archiving or collecting tool like most people used del.icio.us. We were also using it as a way to put out our own work, like an open studio or something. Most of us in the scene went to art school and had arts training. We were really the first generation who had grown up with the WWW and understood it in a real way. We were just starting to hit a point of maturity where the work was getting more intentional, but nobody outside of our circle really paid any attention to it.

It was a different era.
Yeah. Twitter was still in its infancy and still revolved around SMS, MySpace was more popular than Facebook, and Tumblr didn't exist. No iPhones. It was still casual and free. Then Yahoo bought del.icio.us and fucked it up and the web 2.0 social data agenda was embraced by all of the major tech players, and the iPhone came out and the internet really sort of changed into...well, what it is now.

Nasty Nets started before that, right?
Nasty Nets was an extension of the way a lot of us were using del.icio.us. Travis Hallenbeck who is something like the purest internet user I know served as the original point of departure for Nasty Nets.

He was kind of the inspiration?
Guthrie really internalized a lot of what Travis was doing and reached out to Joel Holmberg and I, wanting to band together. We reached out to Marisa Olson and started trying to figure out how to set up a place where we could do all the things we'd been doing on del.icio.us in a more customized way.

Kinda like a new place to hang out?
Yeah, it kind of felt that way immediately.

How did you guys figure out how to structure the site?
It was a Ouija board style website from a structural level. Four of us kind of figured out the initial layout and member set and it just mutated out of that. At the time I thought about it like a high school newspaper if the internet was your high school. It was like a club for professional internet surfers.

Professional internet surfers?
Yeah, just the idea of professionally surfing the internet as the foundation of a studio practice. Taking it seriously. Like, "This is my day job, I seek out and make things for the internet." When in reality nobody anywhere aside from a few oddities was really getting paid to blog. That wasn't a thing yet.

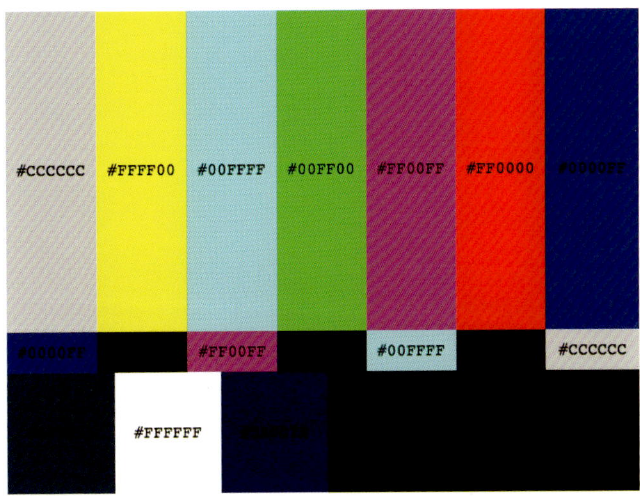

http://internetisnot.tv, 2008.

What were your goals for the work you were making at the time?
Often it was just, "What can I make tonight and put up tomorrow for everybody else to respond to?"

A lot of the work I've seen you do seems to come from extensive research.
Definitely. A lot of my stuff is about finding the right two things and placing them together in the right-wrong way. That is definitely the core motivation of my early work. I was trying to do whatever I could to reduce my involvement; that point of balance where the most minuscule alteration could create the most dramatic effect.

A lot of those early works remind me of Jack Goldstein or John Baldessari. Were you thinking about their work?
Honestly not until looking back. Most of the stuff I was looking at was on the internet and the only art I cared about was what was being made by my friends in the del.icio.us scene.

Like instead of art thats being made for the internet that might come from an art-historical context, it was art that takes its complete source of reference from the internet?
I think that's it right there, at least speaking personally. I was sort of doing it as a response to getting frustrated with art school, and getting that out of my system by using it as some filter for the internet.

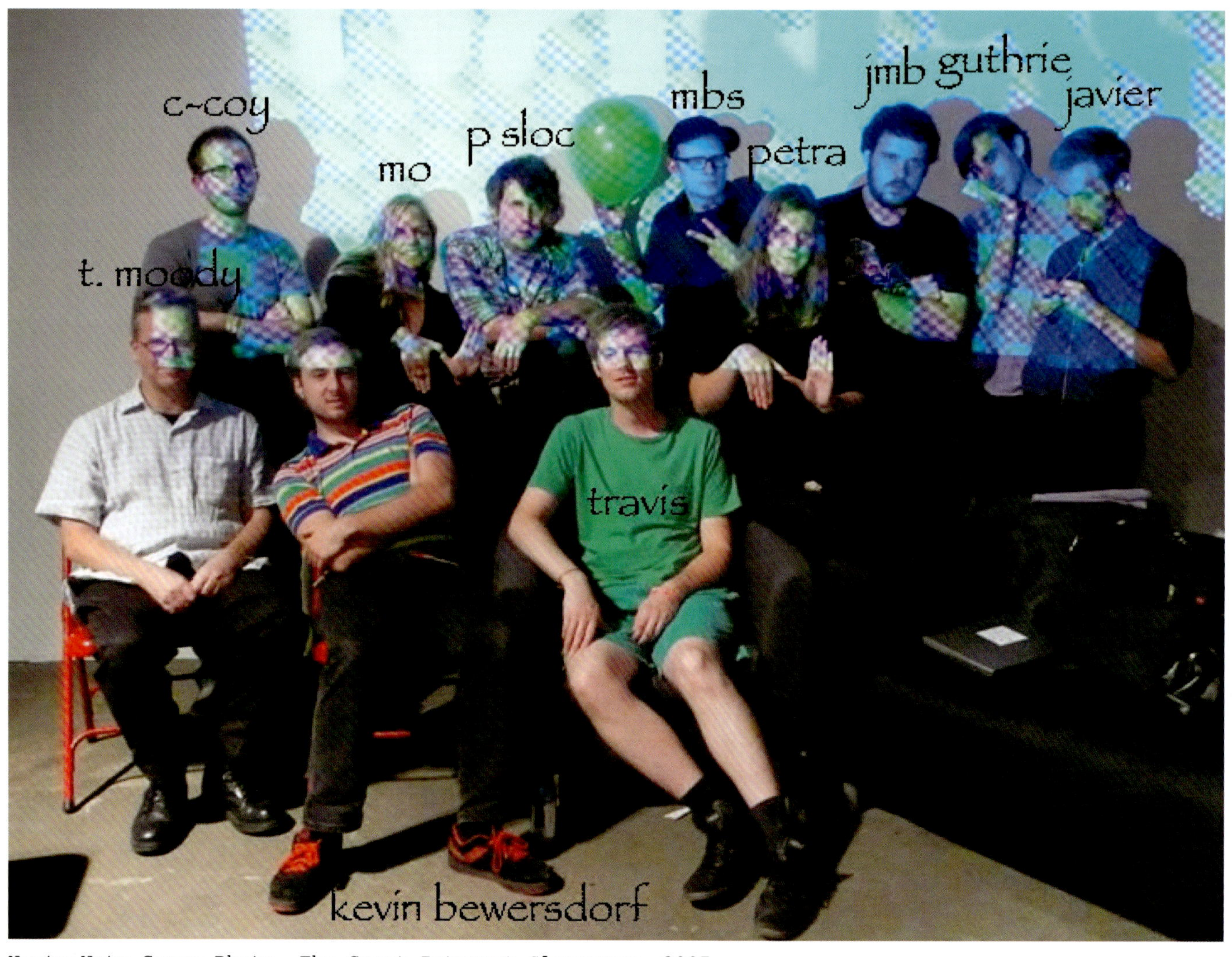

Nasty Nets Group Photo, The Great Internet Sleepover, 2007.

So you moved to New York right after you graduated?

Yeah. There was an artist who had visited our school and he had a loft space for artist assistants in Brooklyn so I worked for him a couple of days a week and got the apartment for free. I had to work a little bit extra to have enough money for macaroni and cheese, diet coke, and cigarettes. Most of my free time was spent on del.icio.us or just making something.

Were you able to start to hanging out with people you had met there?

I had known Marisa Olson through del.icio.us and Nasty Nets and was helping her out with a few of her projects. She started taking me out to openings where I got to meet Lauren Cornell and Cory Arcangel who have both been amazingly supportive ever since. Charles Broskoski was in town and we started hanging out a lot with Jamie Whipple. That combination of couches kind of crystalized New York as an outpost for the scene. Whenever someone came into town everyone would get together in real life and hang out. That was around the time that Nasty Nets and all that work really began to get more attention from the art world.

How did Nasty Nets end?

It was a weird end. I remember it got un-fun. There was some blog, maybe AFC or something, that contextualized it in a way that led to a flame war in the comment thread. It made it way too serious. People were getting catty about it. It got to the point where people were asking, like, "Where's the manifesto?"

It was never about that.
Not all the members of Nasty Nets
were even artists! It was a group
of people all coming from different
places all going in different
directions all interested in
different things. Nasty Nets was
just the part of the venn diagram
where everybody's interests met.
It definitely was not an art
collective. So we just ended it.
**Was that why you stopped making
work for a while?**
I stopped making work in part
because I was offered a job at
Rhizome. I had been blogging for
them, and when a full-time position
opened up Lauren offered it to
me. It sounded like a really good
opportunity for me to be part of
something I cared a lot about. So
I made an intentional decision to
spend my time and energy supporting
the scene and Rhizome's mission and
not letting my work as an artist
get in the way of that.
So you stopped making work?
I mean, I was also really way too
in my head and gummed up about my
own work and whatever I thought
other people expected. That was
also at a point where there was
a new generation of net artists
emerging.
**They were probably inspired by your
original crew.**
They weren't in our original crew
but had maybe known about it or
been influenced by it, or were just
on the same path as we were. I took
it upon myself, for better or for
worse, to investigate it and throw
it up on Rhizome.
How did you stop working there?
I think I realized that I didn't
want to pursue curating as a career.
My role became more administrative
than I had originally wanted. It
was a fantastic experience but I
got tired. I mean, working for a
nonprofit takes a lot of energy.
If you aren't 100% dedicated you
should leave and let someone else
who is pick up the torch.

**Was that around the time you began
working on Are.na?**
Yeah.
How did that start?
The original idea for Are.na came
out of what happened to del.icio.
us after it got bought and iterated
into god-knows-what. The scene that
had grown on del.icio.us had really
deflated. Before that, the site had
really worked. It delivered the
dream of the internet in terms of
finding strangers who are into the
same things you are and becoming
friends with them. There was so
much cool stuff done because of
it. When it evaporated I felt the
need to create a replacement for
it, something that was a force of
real connection in the same way.
Luckily I was able to join up with
a group of folks who had similar
motivations and we set out to
figure out what that tool/place
would be like.
**One of the first things I noticed
about Are.na was that it was a
social network that wasn't crack.**
You mean in terms of dopamine
responses?
Basically.
Yeah, I mean that's something Are.
na has avoided and not always
because we wanted to. It's
certainly how it ended up for the
better. The way we built it was so
it would not really have too much
of an opinion or even guidance on
how to use it. It was built to be
able to have new networks built on
top of it. I don't know of another
tool like it on the internet that
doesn't have an agenda.
**It's also an incredibly personal
research tool.**
We wanted to create a tool that
could augment and enhance human
knowledge and connection at the
individual and small group level.
For me, after working on it for
three years and using it daily,
it became my prosthetic memory. I
still think it's the coolest site
on the internet.

What are some of your favorite channels?
Dena Yago's got this channel called Language that's really important to me. Freak Hacks is the funniest thing of all time. I really like the Fictional Channels: Fictional Logos, Fictional Photography, Fictional Drugs etc. Pretty much any channel by Damon Zucconi is a must-see.

You started making work again when you made those two videos in 2013. How did that come about?
Yeah I was winding down my involvement with Are.na and hadn't been in the studio for five years. I just wanted to see if I could still do it. The Oneohtrix Point Never album R Plus Seven just came out, and a bunch of my friends had made videos for it so I was listening to it a lot. At some point the Boring Angel track came on and the idea flashed of emojis shuffling rapidly in sync with the arpeggio on the track. I spent a night testing it out and was super inspired by what I saw. It became an editing challenge to myself, and I spent the next two weeks making like 10,000 cuts on a 32x32 pixel video canvas. It was very self affirming to be able to realize I could still still make something that I found exciting and allowed me to elevate a lot of ideas I had been previously working on with montage.

And that led to the Kermit video?
I essentially started that the day after finishing Boring Angel. I just wanted to see how much of a story I could tell, how much I could max it out, exert emotional pressure on myself and the audience, while remaining true to the source material.

They're both pretty incredible accomplishments as works.
From a personal perspective, I knew I wanted to start making work again and wanted to shoot a couple shotgun blasts in the air, let people know I was alive. I also realized that I wanted to work on something bigger and more elaborate than music videos.

The TV show you're working on now?
Yeah. I began resurfacing old scripts and film projects I had been working on over the years. The one that I kept coming back to was called Best Friends Forever about a chat-bot that takes over the world by recruiting an army of teenagers. It was also the most impossible to do. I knew I'd never be able to get a budget to be able to do it myself in any way that I would be happy with.

Was that how it became an anime?
I had been watching a bunch of anime and was amazed by how economical it is. It's a really beautiful form of animation, what they get away with, what they achieve with so little. I started to wonder why nobody else was really doing this outside of the industry.

You've been working on it with Blender, right? Why did you chose that program?
I knew I wanted to work in 3D. I had a little experience with Rhino, had tried to learn Maya but wasn't really happy with what the rest of the landscape offered. I ended up on Blender's website and really connected with their mission from an interface perspective, and what they wanted to do with it long term. Coming from thinking about interface for three years while working on Are.na, they were just speaking my language, and it was clear that they had a plan. So I chose Blender.

And it's worked out?
I haven't felt bad about it a single day. It's gotten to the point where it's like playing an instrument. Once you have habituated the basic workflows and operations you really don't have to think anymore. You can just play the thing. It's hands down the most beautiful computer tool I have ever used.

It's open source right?
Yeah, so I don't have to worry about it getting bought and losing a feature. It also means that a bunch of dedi-cated weirdo hobbyists can make their own insane add-on tools and upload them for free for everyone to use.

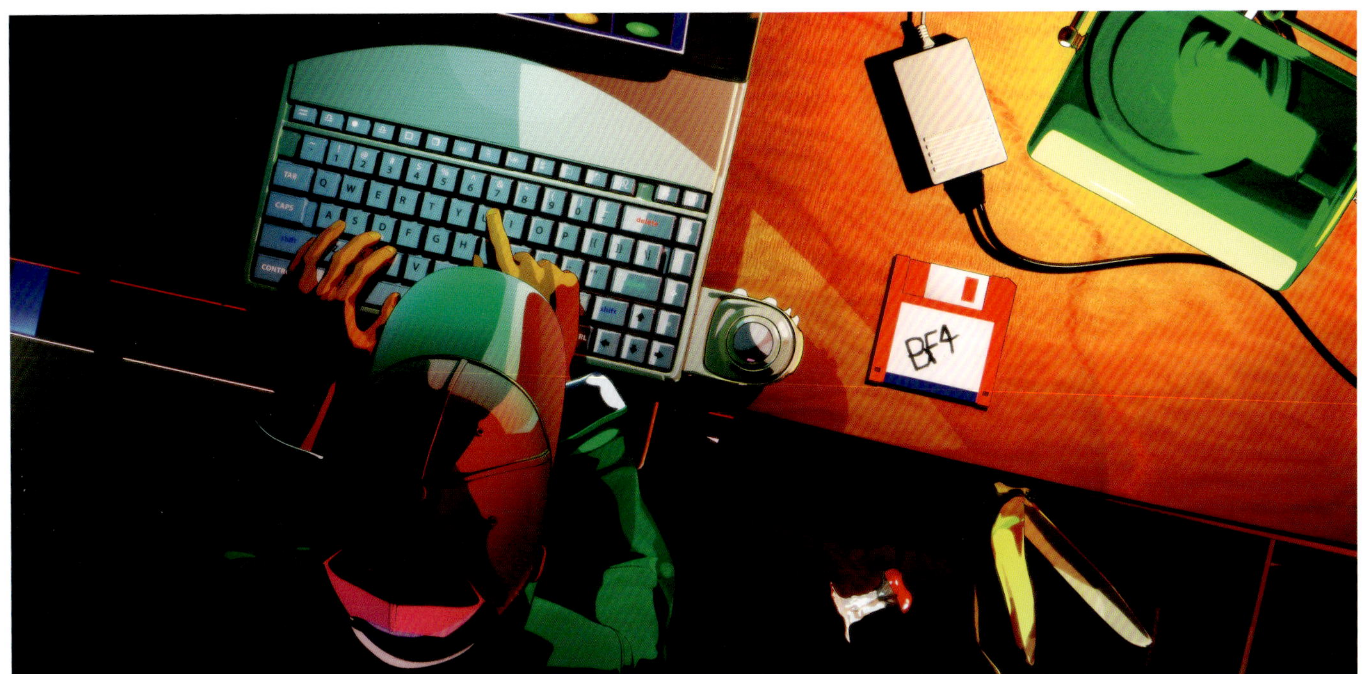

Kiran's Bedroom, Culture Sport, 2015.

You've been working on this in Georgia?
I knew I wasn't going to be able to do a project like this in New York so I moved down to Georgia and set up shop at my parents' farm for nine months. After a few months working there by myself I was joined by Jason Coombs and Joe Kubler, who went into intensive Blender training and now work with me on the show full-time. The space at the farm isn't insulated, so in January we had to move the operation an hour away to Athens, Georgia because it got too cold to work at the farm. That's where we are currently.

What's the space like that you were working in?
We were working in an old general store on the property. My sister had her letterpress there before I moved in. Before that it had been used by both a lawyer and a doctor as a personal study so there were dozens of bookshelves filled with encyclopedias and anthologies mostly from the first half of the 20th century. There was also my massive library of VHS tapes. And no internet.

How did that change your workflow?
Usually when I work I will start with a google image search for reference images and sort through them on Are.na. At the farm, if I wanted to figure out how to represent New York, I would pull out old VHS tapes of like Coming to America, Teenage Mutant Ninja Turtles, and Short Circuit 2 and pause on relevant images and take a photograph of that. I had to figure out everything with this analog reference library but I was never really stumped. Generally I would find something weirder or cooler anyways.

I remember Kevin Bewersdorf did something similar when he went offline.
Well, Kevin is the avant-garde. Everyone is always a few years behind him.

That must have been hard from a background of constant internet.
It was hard in a pretty interesting way. I mean I had been on the internet almost every day for 20 years, you know? The last six or seven years I had a job where I was sitting behind a computer on the internet. It becomes a phantom limb, an apparatus of the mind. It affected everything from the way my brain works to the way my body is used to moving. I would find myself opening a tab for no reason. A computer not connected to the internet is a very different thing. ☺

Lynn Hershman Leeson
"I've always been good at science."

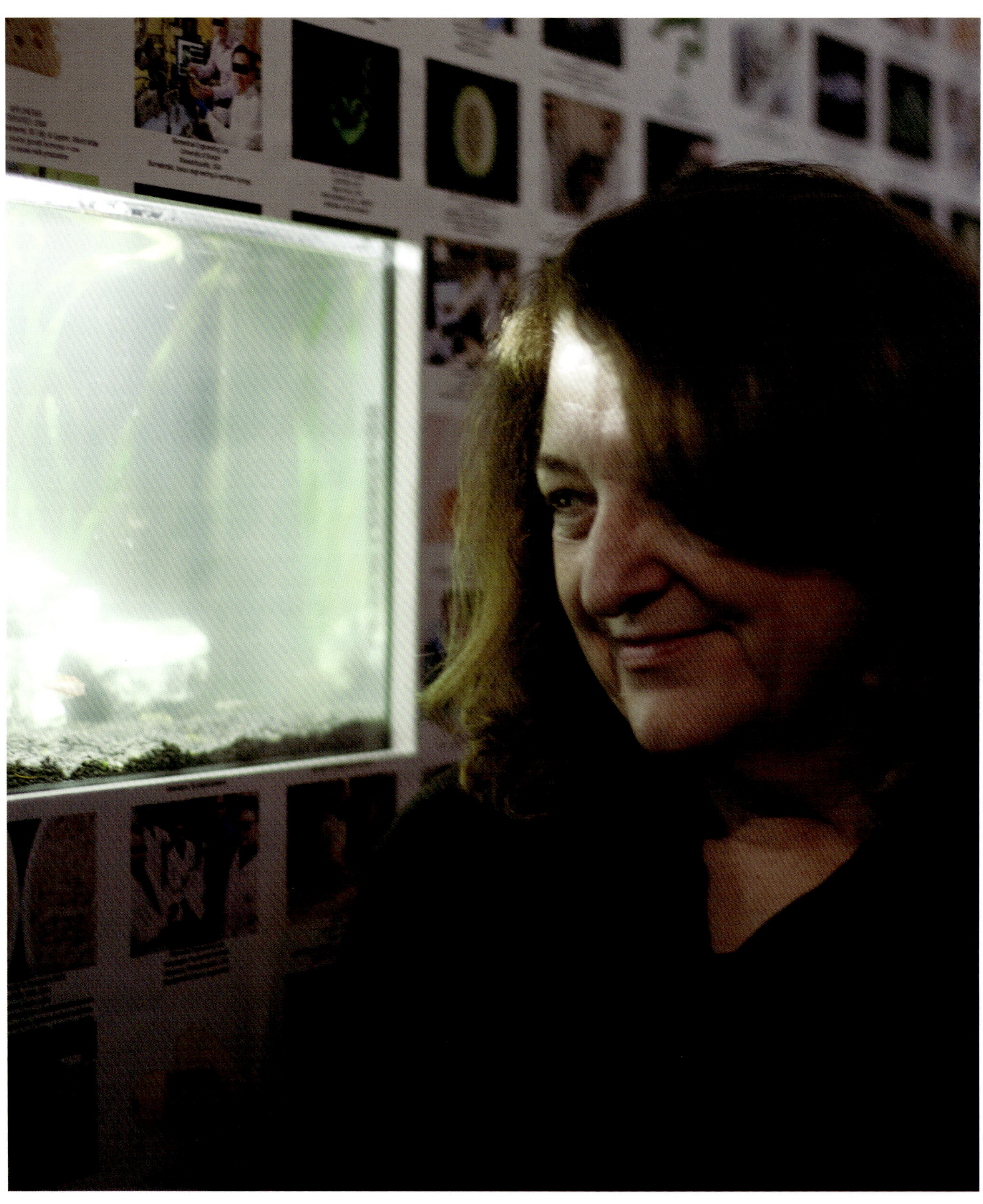

Interview by Jacky Connolly
Portrait by Fidelis Fuchs

Lynn Hershman Leeson is an artist, filmmaker, and media pioneer whose practice spans more than four decades. Her early work is almost prophetically relevant to our current condition; prevalent themes include the interfacing of humans and machines, our orientation towards technology, surveillance, genetic engineering, and virtual reality. Recently, Lynn's vast body of work has received a wave of overdue recognition with a retrospective of her work at ZKM Center for Media and Art in Germany and Origin of the Species, the inaugural exhibition at Bridget Donahue. Unwilling to accept the parameters set within the art, film, and science industries, Leeson's work continues today to push these boundaries — as can be seen in her recent installation, The Infinity Engine, and its soon-to-be released feature film counterpart.

I've been watching all of your feature films this past week, which has been great. !Women Art Revolution was really unbelievable. I just wanted to thank you for doing that, because it's really important. I've taken a course on women artists before and still it missed so many of the women you featured in the film.
So many people were overlooked, like Marcia Tucker for instance. No one recorded these important women. I thought somebody should shoot them and it turned out nobody else did.
It's just an amazing contribution. I was glad that you included yourself in it also. I was really blown away by that part in your documentary when you took all your work to the museum and they wouldn't take it.
I'm really glad in retrospect that they didn't take it, because now I can sell it. Because I had so few collectors my whole life my retrospective was far easier to accomplish.

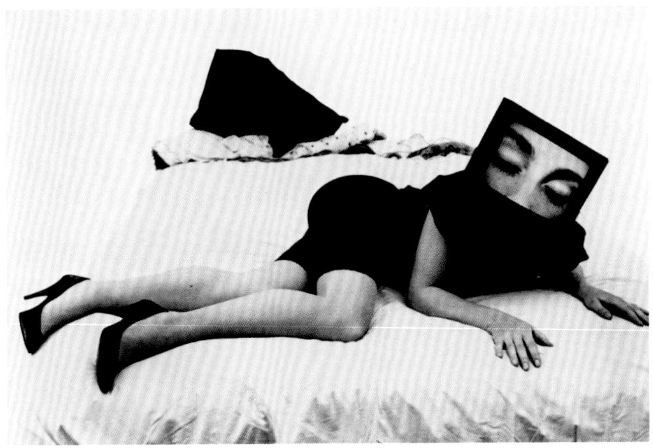

Phantom Limb #2, 1986.

How did you get interested in art? Was there an aha moment?
From my earliest memories, I was always making things. I never had a choice of whether I was going to be an artist — I can't do anything that functions, so it's what I do. The "aha" moment of whether I was an artist or not was probably after they closed my show at the University Art Museum in Berkeley and said media wasn't art. That was why I set up the hotel room, to show I didn't need anyone to define what was or was or was not art.
Was that the Dante Hotel?
Yeah. I consider that my first artwork. The idea of taking that risk and just doing it on my own was the first decisive moment.
I was wondering how you initially were compelled to create Roberta Breitmore.
When I did the hotel rooms I started to put things in the room from an imaginary person who might live there. Then I thought, "What if you liberated the imaginary person?" At first I wanted to do that with an actor but nobody would do it, so I had to. I never thought it was going to last as long as it did.
It was a four-year project, right?
Longer. Conceptually it started with outlines in 1972, and ended after the exorcism in 1979. I needed to have all that time to make her real, have her reflect that reality... What is the point that fiction starts and reality ends? What is believable and what's the blur?

Images courtesy Lynn Hershman Leeson

**When did you first become interested
in making work about technology?**
I think I was in high school and
I tried to Xerox something. I was
Xeroxing a drawing to get a record
of it and the paper crumpled up. I
really liked it and I kept trying to
reuse the Xerox machine to have it
make these weird images.
**How did you find out about
Interactive Laser Discs?**
I read about the National Gallery
doing something where you could
look at art in different ways with
this technology. I got in touch
with people from the company that
was doing the first laser disc. It
was called Video Disk Publishing
and they agreed to help me with
LORNA. At the time, nobody knew
about laser discs.
**It must have been a really early
technology.**
Yes. There were no icons or anything
to show how you move forward and how
you move back, so we had to invent
all that. We had to invent the terms
of how you played it.
**A lot of your work represents a
woman in the interior.**
Escaping.
**Sometimes they escape, like in
Teknolust the characters escape
their interior confinement.**
**It's funny, when I was watching
Teknolust, the character Ruby would
sometimes remind me of Roberta.**
Originally, when we were working on
Teknolust, she looked like Roberta,
but Tilda didn't want to wear any
makeup so we had to switch the look
to three different interpretations.
**How did you transition from art to
film?**
I was in a carpool with Eleanor
Coppola because our kids are the
same age and they used to have
screenings at their home all the
time. It just didn't look to me
like it was that hard to do, so I
literally just picked up the camera
and started. I took a Super 8 class
at the local community college. Then
I started just doing it on my own.

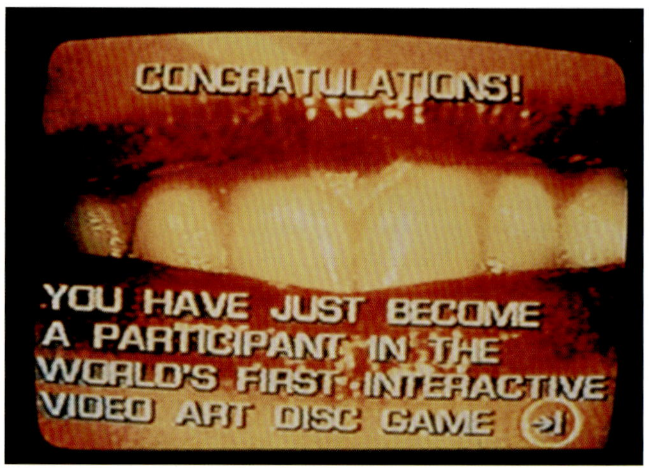

LORNA, 1983.

If I had gone to film school, I would
have felt a lot of restrictions
about what you're supposed to do.
When I was at Sundance with Strange
Culture, I was told that I broke the
fourth wall. I had to ask somebody
what that was.
**A movie is a really daunting and in-
volved process compared to video art.**
It was harder than it looked!
When you're a video artist you're
marginalized. I thought if I did a
feature film more people would see
it. That was kind of the impetus for
doing it.
How did you meet Tilda Swinton?
When I wrote Conceiving Ada, I
thought the only person to really do
it was Tilda Swinton, but I didn't
know her. When I called her agent
and told him my budget he said she
couldn't do it. Serendipitously I
was in Berlin showing The Electronic
Diaries and happened to accidentally
sit next to someone who said they
were Tilda's best friend in Berlin.
She said that Tilda was looking for
interesting projects, so she told
Tilda and Tilda called me. Her agent
said she could do it for five days
only, so that's what we did.
**I learned about Ada Lovelace in a
library science course at school. A
lot of people don't know her story.**
With the internet she became better
known. When I found out about her in
the early 90s, nobody knew about her
either.

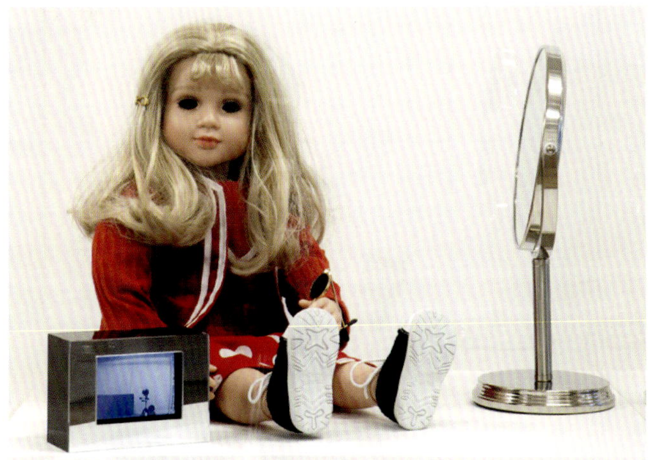

CyberRoberta, 1995.

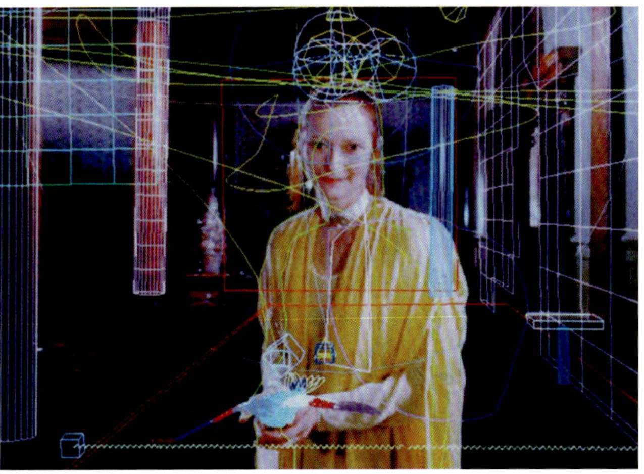

Conceiving Ada, 1997.

It's interesting that even in commercial uses, AI robots are often women.
That was one of the problems with Her. She was a secretary. Also I had problems with Her because I gave Spike Jonze my script for Teknolust when I asked him to be in it. We spoke a lot about my programmer who fell in love with Ruby. Then he worked this same idea into Her without crediting me whatsoever. Maybe he forgot where the idea came from, I don't know...

The way you depict women and technology is so radically different from other popular tropes. Teknolust has a totally different character to it.
These works are sort of inverted. At the time they were made everyone hated them. Teknolust was booed at Sundance. I had a contract with a distributor who wouldn't release it. Now, with time, people have begun to appreciate it and other things I've done...

I love when Tilda, as scientist Rosetta Stone, is surveilling her own clones through a screen in her microwave. Looking in on them trapped in this cyber-harem in the basement, watching a loop of Hollywood film clips of traditional Hollywood femininity for "inspiration."
She's playing a cat in the next film.

Is that The Infinity Engine?
I don't know if that's going to be the name of the film, but it's the name of the whole project. She plays a glowing green cat, named Tilda, that is used for AIDS research.

Is the cat animated?
No, it's going to be a real cat. I just added another cat, Quincy, and she falls in love with him.

Women that work with information technology or computers often work as librarians. They become human interfaces to do sort of simple tasks that AI isn't sophisticated enough for. This reminds me of the website you created for Agent Ruby. Did you come up with the idea for Agent Ruby before making the film, as sort of a vehicle for that artwork?
Exactly. I mean, you can imagine how hard it was to get Teknolust, this crazy movie about three clones, made, but at that time nobody was thinking about AI robots and the internet. There were 18 programmers from all over the world trying to figure out how to do it, because it was 1998. We found people from all over the world who would contribute parts of it because it was an interesting project.

Wow.
I mean, that's what all these projects are. A group of people who are interested in doing something that extends technology. Carnegie Mellon spent multimillions doing AI projects and none of them do as much as Ruby and DiNA, which we did out of nothing except goodwill. I'd be surprised if the whole thing cost more than $20,000. People just gave us software, and donated open source, so we could do it.

Yeah, you really can't say Siri is as good as Ruby.
Siri's not as good and she is 7 years younger. DiNA now has voice recognition and talks to you and remembers things and searches in a different way.
The documentation of The Infinity Engine installation is unlike any art exhibition I've ever seen. Could you talk a little about it?
The installation is a reproduction of a genetics lab. We had to register the ZKM Museum as a genetics lab, so we could get the GloFish in there. In the installation you travel through different rooms. There's a room with the GloFish that has the wallpaper of all the life-forms made through GMO since 2006. Then there's a room that has a lot of the court cases, patenting, who owns what, supreme court cases. Another room has 130 interviews with amazing scientists from around the world about the future of genetics and humanity. Then there's a face scanning room: it scans your face and then reverse engineers facial recognition to find out your origins; where you were from genetically.
How did you get that?
Dr. Josiah P. Zayner from NASA did it. Then the work creates a composite of users called Cyrus. Eventually you will be able to send in a selfie to add to the composites, and all the people's composites will be in the movie.
The face scanning thing is so heavy. I came in from an international flight and now to go through customs, they scan your face. It's scary.
Originally I wanted to do something that used people's actual DNA but it was too complicated and expensive with swabs or hair samples. Getting GloFish in Germany was already a problem... So we invented this way to do it through the facial recognition. I think it's going to be the future.

It's chilling that so much information about you could be found without your consent. How did you get interested in GMOs?
My whole family are scientists. My mother was a biologist, my father was a pharmacist. My brother and daughter are doctors. I was the only throwback. But I was always interested. I was always good at science.
So you're influenced through that connection?
I think so. I think science is like magic but I'm not afraid of it.
It's important for artists to pay attention to science right now.
That's why ZKM was the perfect place to show my work. There really is no museum in America, or even the world, that would consider this art or show this kind of work. ZKM is radical in that it deals with art and science and technology.
Did you have much formal education in science?
I studied biology at Case Western Reserve University. I took a lot of art classes at the Art Institute too.
You used to teach, right? Do you still?
I'm doing a class at the Art Institute in San Francisco. It puts me in touch with younger people. In the Bay area you just breathe new technology, so you know about things before they're public. People talk about it, like they talk about scripts in LA. It's an advantage.
What's your favorite thing to show, or screen, or talk about with students?
I usually show Metropolis or Beauty and the Beast.
How do you feel about the representation of the woman-machine relationship since Metropolis?
There is a tendency to use the evil robot woman. When you think about reproductive technology and female bodies, again the focus has been on control rather than actualization. I think the cyber forms that are going to come in the future are biological, not electronic. All these depictions of female robots is not the way it's going to happen.

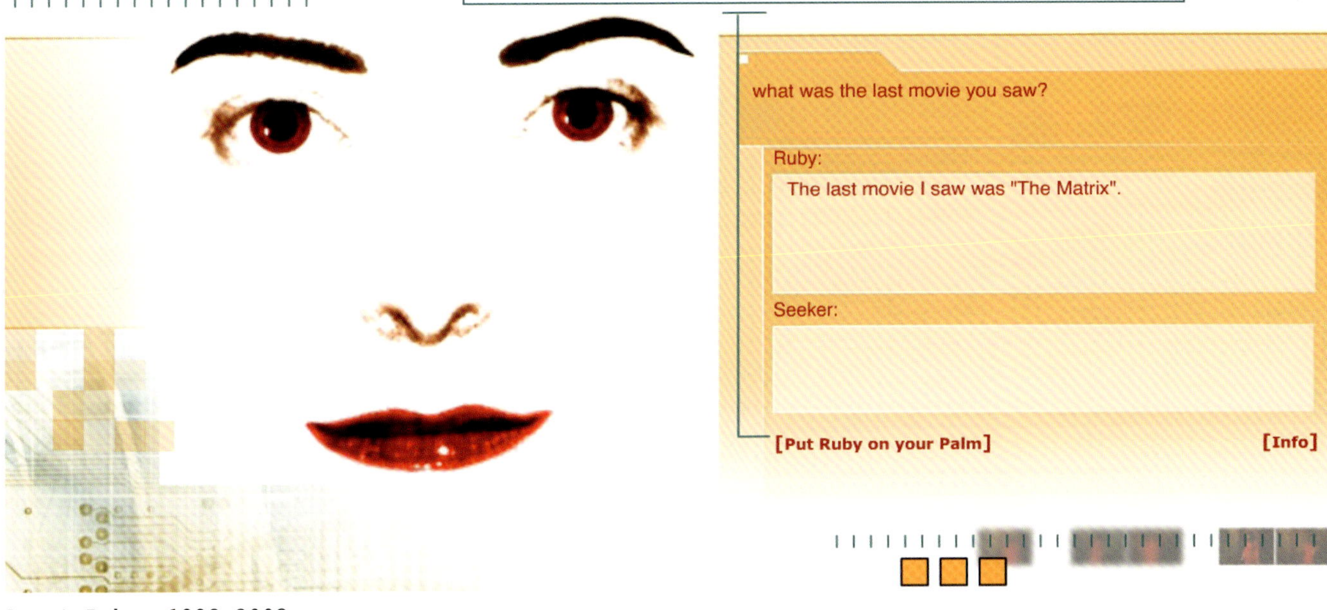

Agent Ruby, 1998–2002.

Yeah, people are already entering into cyborg territory.
Or having their DNA altered. In the United States, you can't use human genes because it's a violation of the 13th Amendment, which is slavery. But in the UK, they don't have those rules, so they took women who had trouble reproducing and they added and extra female chromosome. They gave birth to 50 babies that had two female and one male chromosome, and all their babies will have all three. It's biological change.

What's your general feeling about genetic engineering?
Our evolution is really shifting very rapidly, more than ever before, but we're destroying things. This is a way to survive the pollution, to create things that are alive; like you cross a spider and a goat and it has stronger milk. They're crossing things for reasons that they become more substantial and maybe they'll survive what we've destroyed. I want to talk to a professor at Stanford who thinks that we're entering the last phase of extinction.

Yeah, even if we haven't been engineered, the food we're eating has been.
Which is changing people, because we don't know what's going to happen.

Dolly, the sheep, was obese. Now they're finding that American children are heavy because of the GMOs.

How did you find the people you interviewed for your installation?
There are 130 clips, from about nine scientists. Some of them won the Nobel Prize after I interviewed them, but I knew that they would because of the things that they were doing that nobody else was doing. It's just research.

Did any of them know about your work?
Yes, the woman who won the Nobel Prize, Elizabeth Blackburn, agreed to be interviewed because she had seen Conceiving Ada. She said she felt like Ada. She found the aging gene and was seeing its relationship to cancer and how it works.

So when are you going to start working on the new film?
We're working on this script which needs one more push and then I want to make it this year. I've been trying to make it for a long time, but I think this is the year because The Infinity Engine will be done.

Who else is going to be in the new film?
I don't know yet. Marilyn Manson said he was interested.

That would be so cool.
Maybe he'll be the other cat. ☺

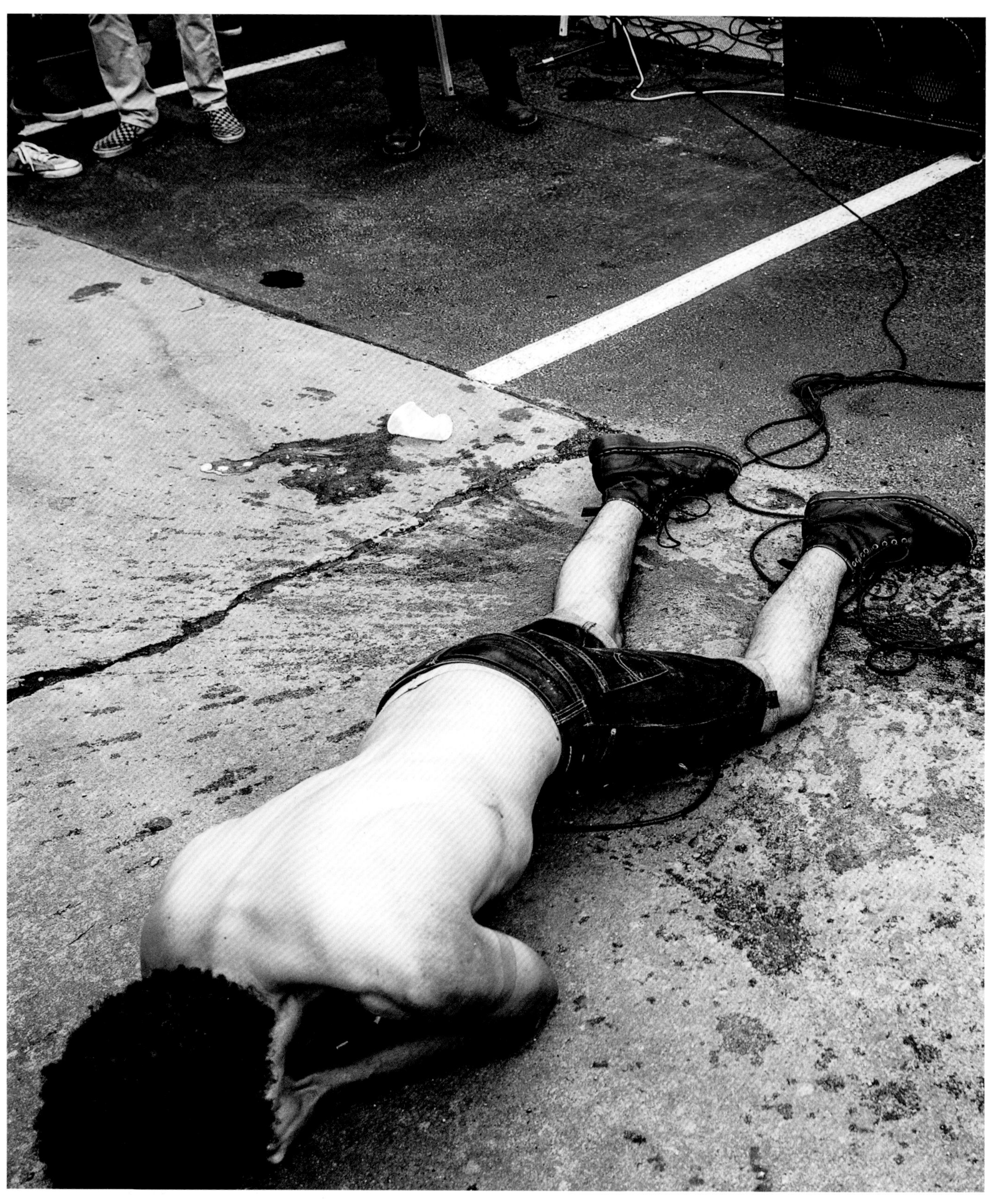

B L A C K I E
"I miss that feeling when you got the mic and they don't!"

Interview by Juiceboxxx
Portrait by Michael Craft

At 27, Houston musician B L A C K I E has already staked a legacy in the American underground rap, punk, and noise communities that he has moved through for over a decade. In a continuum of iconoclastic H-Town musicians that includes DJ Screw and Jandek, B L A C K I E's extreme and explorative music — synthesizing genres as disparate as rap, noise, hardcore, jazz, and grime — has influenced and inspired countless artists across the board. Known for his relentless live show and continual desire to push things forward, B L A C K I E's singular and perpetually moving style makes him a true force (and a bit of an unsung hero) in modern American music. Always intense, always surprising, and always exceptional: it was an honor to speak with B L A C K I E about life and music.

Alright, let's start at the beginning. What were you doing before you started B L A C K I E?
I played in some punk bands when I was a teenager. Those bands broke up, and we started doing math rock.
How old were you?
That started when I was 13 and I was doing that up until I was 17.
What was the main inspiration around starting B L A C K I E in the way beginning?
I had already been making really wild loops and beats for a long time but like, as soon as the bands I was in broke up I was just making it non-stop, full-time. I showed it to one of my friends from the next town over and he really liked it. And his girl liked it. They told me to keep rapping and make more of it.
Were you doing vocals on these beats or were they just instrumental?
I didn't do vocals on the beats until another kid from my town dissed me. That's when I started doing vocals. I was never really, from the beginning, "rapping." I was just pissed off. I had just been in punk bands and I had these beats. I was already screamin' on 'em.

And your response, that was a rap track.
Not really. It already had all the elements of what I would do for the next ten years or whatever, which is blown apart, kind of rhymin', mostly screaming. Not exactly like how I am right now, but real close, primordial.
So the foundation of B L A C K I E was kind of already there?
Yeah.
Do you still have those recordings?
I can't find that particular one, man. That's the one I want to find 'cause that was the one that predated everything. That one was from 2004. It was only 40 or 50 seconds long. It was already on the kind of power violence thing where it starts with a sample and it blows up and I'm screaming over the static and then it comes back to just whatever Winnie the Pooh sample, whatever weird kind of stuff I made.
So were you listening to power violence back then? What kind of power violence bands were you into?
I thought the hardcore bands had broken up in the 80s. I was into all the old school hardcore. But all of a sudden my friends showed me newer stuff, "Oh, there's this band, that band." "Mike, let's go to this show downtown."
Were you listening to rap around this time, too or were you mostly listening to...
I never stopped listening to rap, no matter how weird my stuff got or was, noise or screamo, whatever I was into, I was always listening to rap. Even now, I still listen to rap.
So, what were your first 50 shows? Were they all around Houston?
Yeah, Texas, yeah.
So, were you playing more punk shows?
Yeah, my first show, I probably played my first show when I was 13 or something. The very first show we ever played we got kicked off the stage.

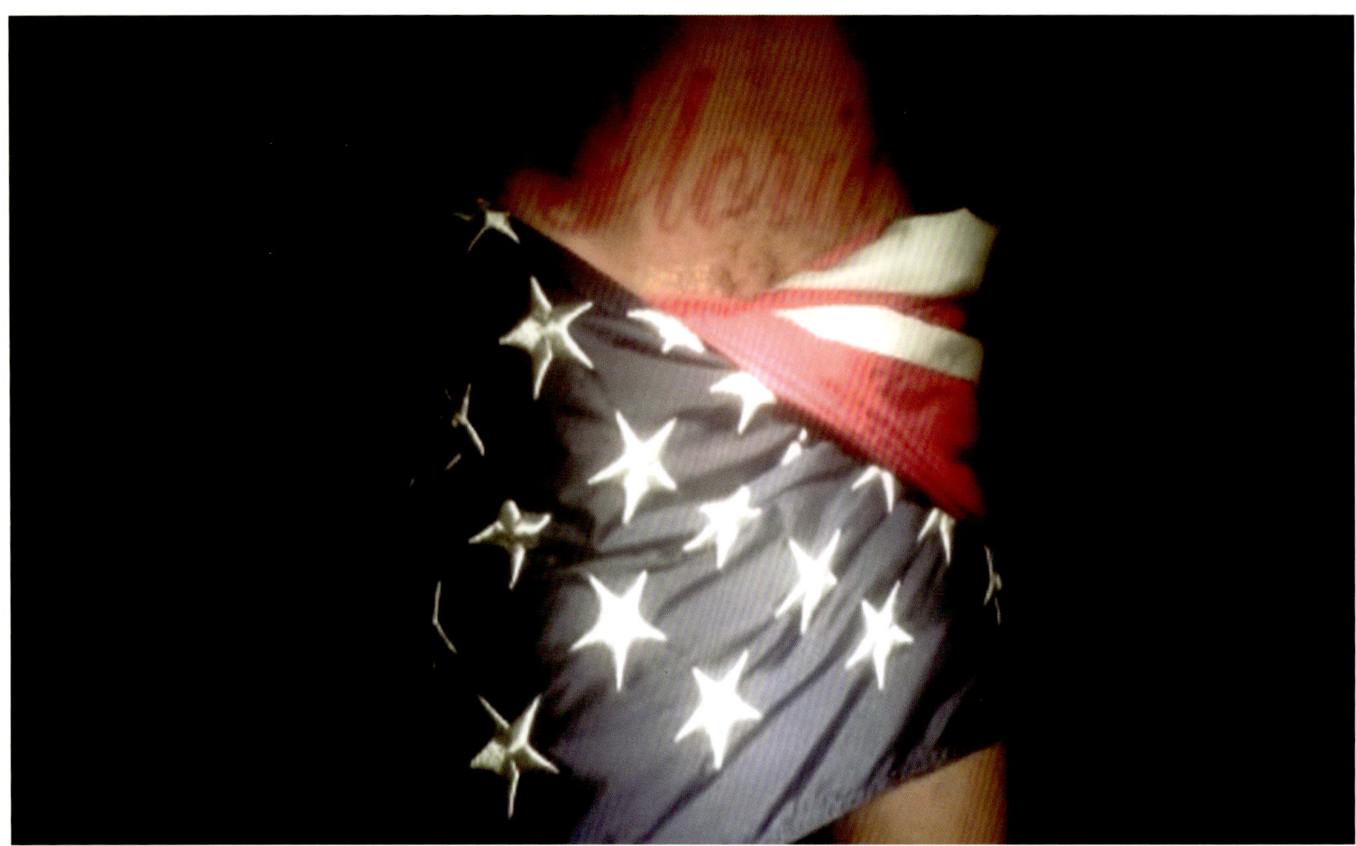

Warchild (Official Video), 2012.

What happened?
There was this thing here that they do every summer called the Strawberry Festival. Somehow our band got on it. We played last and we were way more aggressive than all the other bands, and our singer was jumping in the crowd and our drummer was breaking everything. So they kicked us off. They made us stop playing. Then the organizers turned off everything, it just antagonized everybody more...so our singer and our drummer just kept it up. But yeah, it's kind of a weird thing now but that's my whole existence. They still turn my microphone off. The last show I played in Houston, the mic broke, the house PA broke, and I had to keep screaming. That's the whole thing. We've always gotten kicked off. Everything always broke. They always unplug me. Since I was 13.
And how old are you now?
27.
What was the first time you went on tour?
The first time I went around Texas with my friend.

Was that as B L A C K I E?
Yeah, that was B L A C K I E.
And what year was that?
January 2009, with Brett Taylor.
And were you bringing speakers with you at this point? Did you have a version of your current speaker setup?
Back then I had more gear, if you can imagine that, but we could only cram two JBL speakers and a 5,000 watt amp in my friend's car.
Between 2005 and 2008 or so, when you were playing shows locally, were you playing a variety of things, or were you doing primarily punk shows or rap shows?
I would play as far as an hour away from my town, which is still in Houston. I played on anything I could get on. I would just bug anybody to play anything. Played at bowling alleys and churches. Got the cops called on the churches. I would rent a generator and put on my own mini-festivals at skateparks until the cops came.

At what point did you start to see a sort of progression in your fan base or progression in how you were perceived outside of your hometown?
People started getting with me in 2008. That's when I started playing within the actual city of Houston. I stopped playing in these weird bowling alleys and community centers. I was just focusing on playing clubs and bars downtown. That's when it got to the point where I could just jump out in the crowd and not get hurt 'cause people would catch me. That's when it started and it really clicked. It happened kind of quick 'cause just what I was doing and how loud it was, kids, they just had to kind of get with it.

From all the footage I've seen from that era, the crowd skews maybe towards punk kids, in a very general sense... Punk meaning anything from hardcore to noise or whatever.
There was one show in particular... I was opening for HEALTH, again. I opened for them a year before with my friends Cop Warmth. That was a real weak show. It was a year later and I jumped out in the crowd and they caught me and carried me out the club screaming. Before the show, HEALTH didn't remember who I was. They weren't really being friendly to me. Then after the show, they told me I needed to go on tour. They told me I needed to meet this guy, his name's Juiceboxxx, he's from Milwaukee. They told me about you after that show!

That's amazing 'cause B.J. from HEALTH played drums for me when I was hanging out in LA.
That's word, that's word.

So around 2008 maybe you're starting to play with, I don't want to say "the right kind of bands," but you're starting to play with some national acts that kind of get what you're doing and are really psyched about it. After that, when was your first real national tour?
The first tour was stupid.

Why was it stupid?
I only played five shows but the tour was almost three weeks long. I went to New York City and back but I didn't have any shows on the way back. Only had shows on the way up there. You know what I'm saying?

That's a rite of passage. Your first couple DIY tours have to be a total train wreck, but if you come out of that still loving it, then it usually gets a little bit better, which I'm sure it did.
Yeah, yeah. That definitely separates who does this for life and who's just gonna go home and go back to school or get a job and cry to their girlfriend.

So those tours were rough but you were still psyched coming out of it enough to keep going?
Man, to be honest, they weren't really that rough. I mean totally, they sucked, but this is by my standards, you know? Even though everything was fucked, I loved it.

Every record you put out is changing and it's always entering some weird new, unchartered territory. That's really where I think you separate yourself from a lot of your peers. I don't know, I guess this is a long-winded way of me asking you, you've undeniably had a good amount of influence on music over the past five years, but you're always moving into a new zone. Do you feel pressured to keep moving forward, or is it just something that's intuitive to you?
Man, that's a good question. I don't know why I do it. There ain't no answer. I just don't know. I just do it. Why do they cut my microphone off or unplug my gear? I keep doing it. Fuck them that's why.

Do you ever wish you were in a different position right now, or are you thinking more about your longevity and less about just the current moment?
It's B L A C K I E forever.

When did you first tour overseas?
2012.

**Was that a big moment for you to be
able to go to Europe and play?**
It was, but the crazy thing was that
my son was two or three months old.
So it was wild man. I just had a
baby. I went out there. I bought a
car and a house after I got back. My
life was going up.
**Those things mean the world. I feel
the same way, you know? So how are
you right now? We talked a lot about
how you came up. How are you now?
What are you working on now?**
I ain't really forcing nothing. If I
want to make something, I'll make it.
If I feel I want to play something,
I'll play it.
**That's not necessarily a bad place
to be if you're trying to make good
music.**
I feel I created what I wanted to
create with Imagine Yourself in a
Free and Natural World. I got the
peace, the inner-peace, of knowing
that I created exactly what I set out
to create. So I mean until I feel
energized again to make another kind
of art piece, I'm not gonna force
myself to do anything.
**Are you gonna be touring again any
time soon?**
I'm only playing ten shows a year
on the road from now on until I
feel different. I still feel like
rapping, like rapping for real and
also attacking the crowd. I miss that
feeling when you got the mic and they
don't!
**I haven't toured as much recently
either because I have this band
that I play with now and the expenses
are higher. Would you ever consider
bringing more people on the road with
you in the future?**
I want to, but it's finding the right
people. You know what I mean? A lot
of people want to work with me, want
to ride with me, but it's like look
man, what's the longest you've gone
without eating? Can you really do
this? You know, let's say you're
driving and I'm sleeping on the
passenger side. Are you gonna stay
awake? You gonna keep both of us

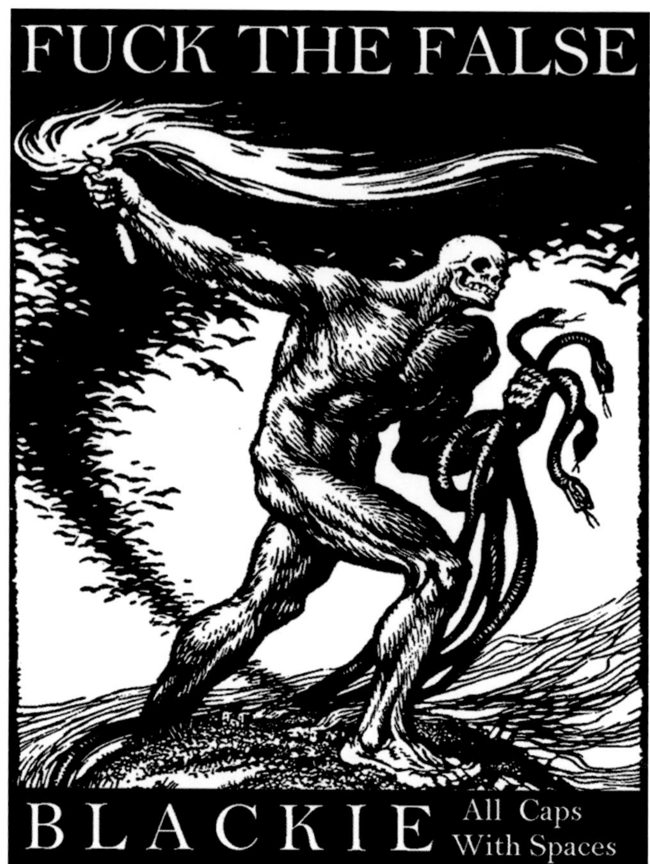

Fuck the False, 2013.

alive or are you gonna fall asleep
and kill both of us? It's just
sometimes I'm like man, let me just
do this stuff by myself. I know I'll
stay awake.
**Yeah, it's intense for you because
it's just you and a bunch of amps,
right?**
Yeah, man, sometimes. It's a real
journey out here. I got to ride the
fear. I called my friend when I was
on tour. I told him, "Hey, man, we
have to tour more. We gotta be like
Black Flag and those bands that used
to do this for real." He was like,
"Yeah dude but Black Flag wasn't a
lone black guy driving through the
southern United States."
How important is volume to you?
It's everything to me.
**When you were younger, what shows,
what bands kind of set the standard
for you in terms of volume?**
That guitar player in Melt-Banana.
His rig is so goddamn loud, still. It
just hurts your brain.

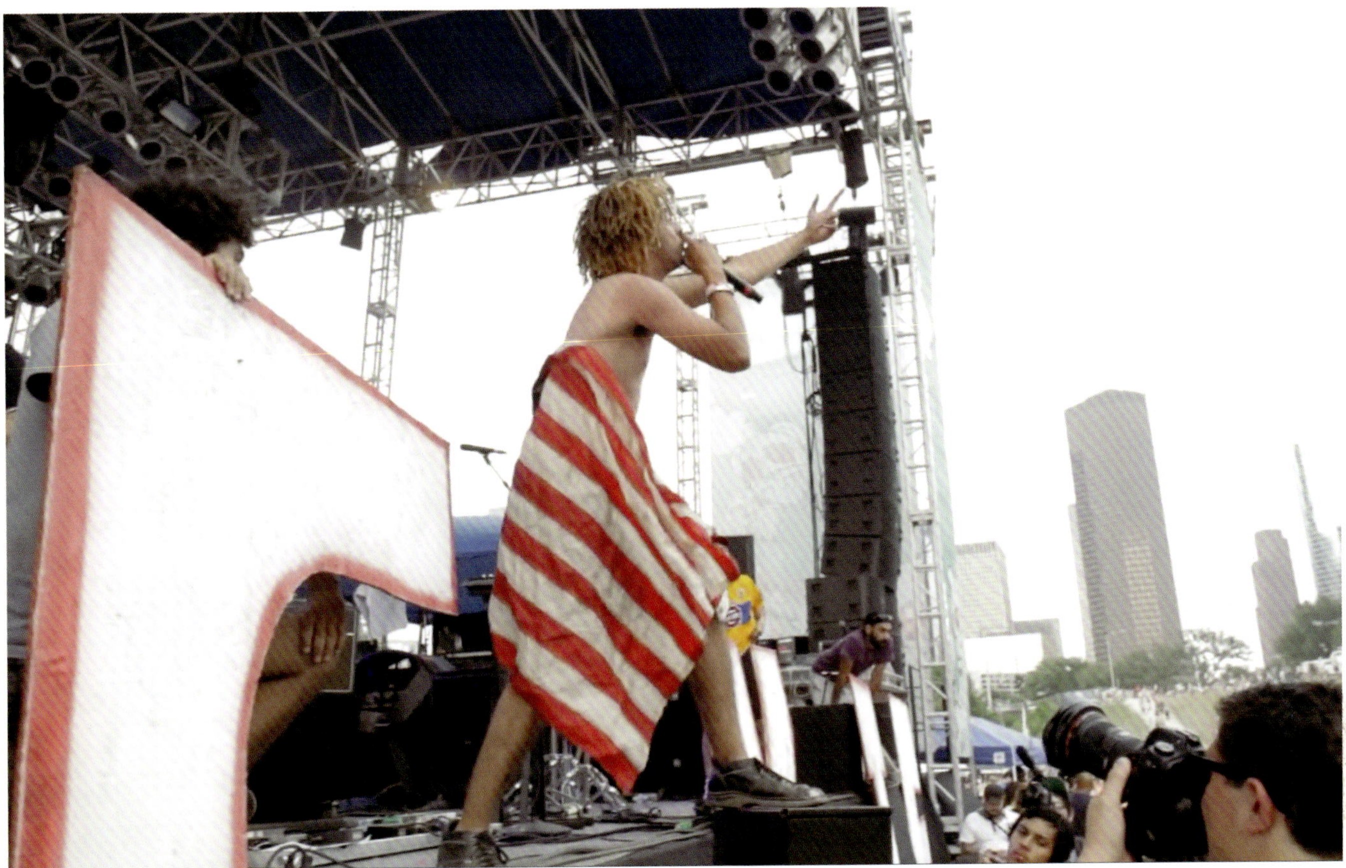

Free Press Summerfest, Houston, 2011.

I played three or four shows in Germany years ago with Melt-Banana and they blew my mind every night. How did you get into punk when you were young?
I got into punk because all these kids in junior high were talking about what they wanted for Christmas. And the kid in front of me in line said he was getting a bass guitar. I was next in line and they asked me, hey dude, what are you gonna get for Christmas? And I didn't know what to say. I still have problems talking to people. So since that guy said he was getting a bass guitar, I just said I was getting a bass guitar. And then I kind of, I never thought about it before. I thought hey, maybe I should get one. So then me and my dad were at a pawn shop and the first bass guitar the guy took off the rack had a Dead Kennedys sticker. And I didn't know what that meant or what it was, I just thought it looked cool. So I went on Napster and I typed in Dead Kennedys and I started downloading a bunch of weird songs, and I had never heard anything like that before in my life. I was like damn, that's kind of cool. This is weird as hell. They're spazzing man, and I'm kind of hyperactive. That's how I got into punk.
I mean the fact that you had that curiosity makes me think that you would have gotten into punk one way or another, but I don't know if that's true or not.
[Laughter] We're talking about my entire life and the rest of my life was just based off of a lie and just a random occurrence. If that guy had picked up a different bass, I would not be talking to you right now. None of this would have even possibly happened. It's all random.
Yeah man, you could be right. Well, you know, you should go back to that pawn shop and thank them sometime.
It's still there.
The pawn shop is still there?
Yeah. I go by it every other day. 🙂

Arcane Kids
"edutainment is NOT A CRIME"

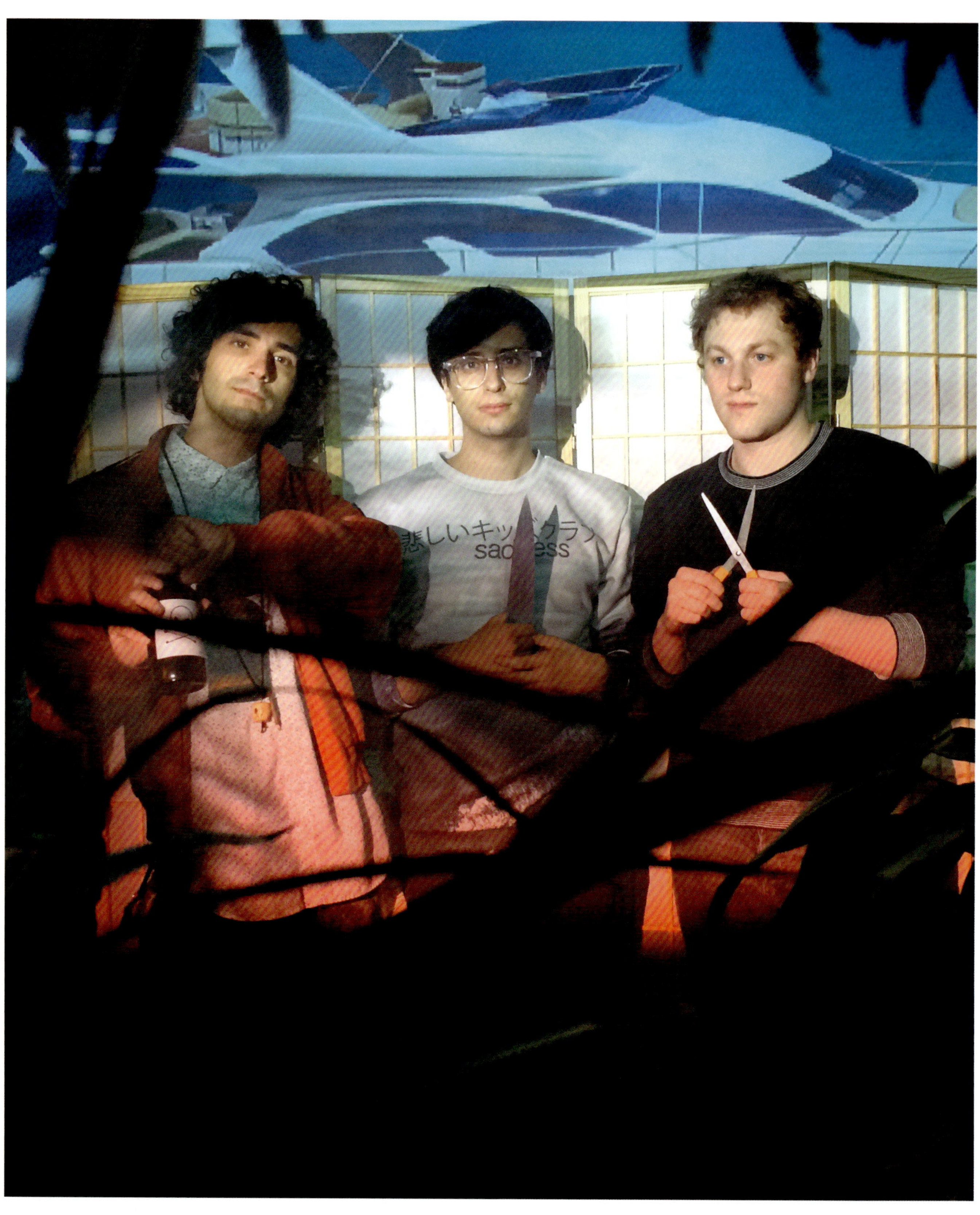

Interview by Asher Penn
Portrait by Yuliy

The word arcane means mystery, or a secret, which aptly describes my first impression of the Arcane Kids. When a friend told me to check out Bubsy 3D, an "edutainment" game that allowed you to explore a James Turrell exhibition at LACMA, all I wanted to know was who made this game. Was it a one-off? Googling the Arcane Kids I found myself watching the indescribably awesome trailer for Perfect Stride, a first person skateboarding game set in a dystopian future that asked the question, "What if in 1999 Tony Hawk didn't land the 990." Again, WOW. Reading their Manife$to (they had a manifesto!) it seemed that the games created by the Arcane Kids were far from random jokes, but rather were the highly principled output of one of the most defiant voices in independent video games today. When I asked to talk to them, they invited me to SK8 MUD, a virtual Denny's parking lot where you can type in commands to skateboard, drink a milkshake, listen to music, and talk.

ashermixtapehell: **HI**
lil_vertex: SUPPP
ashermixtapehell: **AM I CAPS?**
ashermixtapehell: **SORRY NOT TRYING TO YELL**
lordanime: this is a new feature
lil_vertex: YO U ARE HELLA CAPS
coolatv: hi
lil_vertex: HELLA SAME
ashermixtapehell: **STILL CAPS**
ashermixtapehell did a GNARLY OLLIE
lil_vertex: me flips magazine page
lil_vertex DIEZ
lil_vertex: if u use say then its caps
lil_vertex: but if u use forward slash, its not caps
coolatv99: DUH
yuliy: ;)
lil_vertex: SAY IS VERY FORMAL
lil_vertex: LIKE SHOUTING
ashermixtapehell: ok i think i got it
ashermixtapehell did a SICK OLLIE
lil_vertex OPENS UP CD PLAYER
lil_vertex LOADS OFFSPRING - CONSPIRACY OF ONE CD

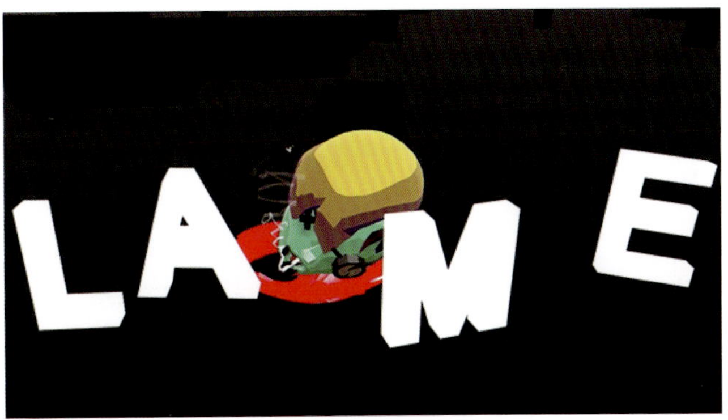

Game House, Beta Pictures, 2014.

lil_vertex did a TIGHT OLLIE into a SICK GRIND on that HOBBIT GRAND SLAM BREAKFAST
lil_vertex: i wonder,... if we will ever get to eat another hobbit GSB in our lifetimes
ashermixtapehell: so, i'm talking to coolatv, lil_vertex_, lordanime, and....
lordanime: our tech guru yuliy is hanging out
lil_vertex: namaste yuliy
ashermixtapehell: hi yuliy
yuliy: yooo
coolatv99: hey
ashermixtapehell: how many people are in the arcane kids? is it a loose collective?
lordanime: There are 5 of us, turbo loose
lil_vertex: ya its v project based, we usually form subgroups
ashermixtapehell: where does the name come from?
lordanime: We found a blank CD-R with the name written on it
lordanime: well we don't know what was on it
lordanime: it was fucked up
lil_vertex: ya it was in the dirt
ashermixtapehell: do you all have different skills?
lil_vertex: hmmm skills wise we have a ton of crossover
lil_vertex: everyone can do everything but we usually specialize based on what we like
lil_vertex: like i like sound / art / level design n shit
lordanime: we are all kinda just out of school, went through similar programs, so had the same basic skills

Images courtesy Arcane Kids

ashermixtapehell: did you all go to the same school?
lordanime: yeah, but we're not going to plug it
lil_vertex: ya i owe them A LOT OF MONEY still
lordanime PUKING
ashermixtapehell: wanna plug your majors?
lil_vertex STANDS ON A SOAPBOX
lordanime: i was a computer science major
lil_vertex: ELECTRONIC MEDIA ARTS AND COMMUNICATION
lil_vertex: so basically photoshop
coolatv99: computer science and game hell
yuliy: cs
yuliy: some dumb minors also
lil_vertex: ya we all did computer science in some capacity
lil_vertex: yuliy what did u minor in?
yuliy: electronic arts and math
lil_vertex: o dang
yuliy: i took the ultimately multiple choice based art history class to get that e arts minor
lil_vertex did a WICKED KICKFLIP
coolatv99: whoa
yuliy: 8)
lil_vertex: props
ashermixtapehell: what kind of jobs did you want out of college?
lil_vertex: i always wanted to make games but TBH i thought it was like... super unlikely that id be able to get a job doing it
lil_vertex: so i was learning relevant skillz but not actually game dev
lordanime: I wanted to be an architect, but also an art school drop out, So i did that and decided some creative programming thing would be better, so when I transferred i saw they had a game program
lil_vertex: i was thinking like maybe web design or something
coolatv99: im a product of the times
yuliy: same
lil_vertex: lol

ashermixtapehell: what kind of games were you into
ashermixtapehell: before you started making them?
lil_vertex: SHOOTERS!!!!!!!!!

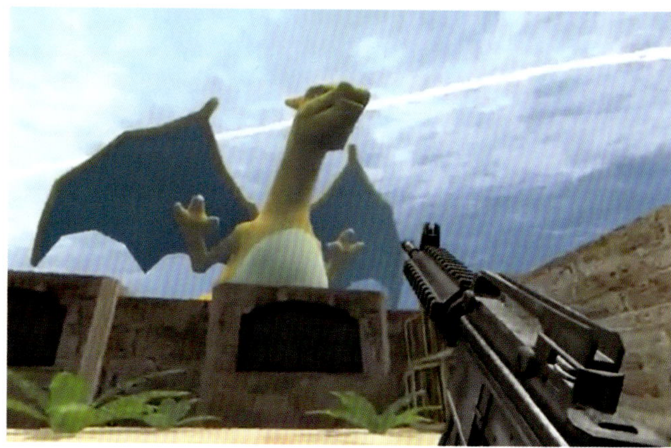

Pokémon Millennial Edition, 2014.

lil_vertex: i was really into quake and halflife
lil_vertex: i got my start by modding those gamez
lil_vertex: AND rollercoaster tycoon
lordanime: weird japanese stuff, tycoon games
lordanime: call of duty
lordanime: 2
coolatv99: gameboy and bad 10000 games in one office max bundles
lil_vertex: officemax-core
lordanime: i bought one of those and thought it was super good
lil_vertex: good value?
lordanime: i wonder what it would be like to slip your own games into those bargin bins
ashermixtapehell: did you all get into development through modding?
lil_vertex: were u guys doing any modding at all?
yuliy: i tried making wc3 mods caused i loved those RP maps
yuliy: but i never got really far with it
coolatv99: didnt have the ram back then
lordanime: i started off in flash, it made sense to me at the time that your game logic would be in an animated timeline
lil_vertex: bahaha

lil_vertex: ya i was using flash a
lot too
lil_vertex: i used to make a lot of
on rails shooters that were just
animations and buttons
lordanime: coolatv99 doesn't want to
admit his first games were in power
point
lil_vertex: i mean powerpoint has
GOTO... thats like 90% of what u need
lil_vertex: plus built in laser sound
FX
coolatv99: edutainment is NOT A CRIME
ashermixtapehell: hahaha
lil_vertex: did edutainment weekly
ever become a thing
yuliy: no but i get the reminder
every year
yuliy: when that blog ages
coolatv99: http://edutainmentweekly.
tumblr.com/

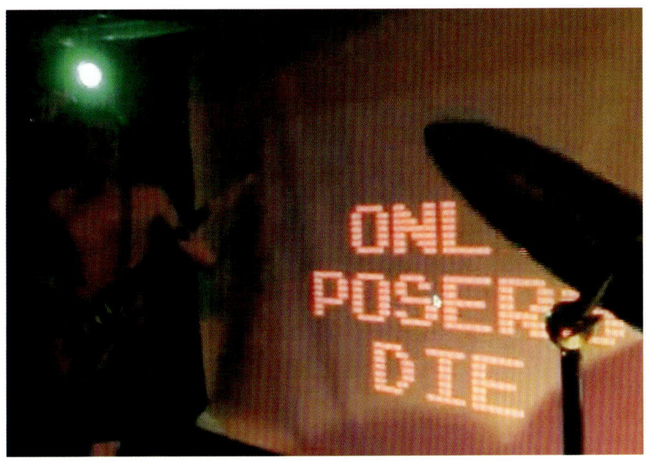

SK8PUNX, 2010.

**ashermixtapehell: so were you all
doing this stuff before arcane kids
started?**
yuliy: lil_vertext made me go my
first game jam
lil_vertex: B-) ruined your life
yuliy: yeah really fucked up my life
coolatv99: i made bad games in rpg
maker and game maker when i was a
teen
lil_vertex: haha
lordanime: we were all pretty green,
but once we started to make things
pretty consistently after "starting"
arcane kids is when i would say i
really started

lordanime: i used the word started
way too many times there
lil_vertex: hmm ya i like barely
finished anything before AXK
lil_vertex: couple of counter-strike
maps
yuliy: that one half life mod tho
with the brothers lil_vertex
lil_vertex: o frick ya
**ashermixtapehell: i read it started
in the basement of a music club?**
lil_vertex: ya most of us were
affiliated with this basement venue
lordanime: we thought we would ruin
the place with video games
lil_vertex: lol ya it was a very
wholesome DIY scene
lil_vertex: before the TERROR
**ashermixtapehell: were you guys
making music?**
lil_vertex: some of us were in bands
**ashermixtapehell: what kind of music
were you making?**
lil_vertex: we had a pretty good
shit-fi surf punk band..........
lil_vertex: NO BACKSIES
lordanime: 2nd place battle of the
bands
yuliy: ummm
yuliy: we won one
lil_vertex: yeah dude
yuliy: never forget fall battle
lil_vertex: AND we played an anime
convention......
lordanime: the anime convention was
my favorite
yuliy: yeah that was the best show i
think
lil_vertex: thats why we wrote "It'd
Be Cooler If You Were Into Steampunk"
lordanime: the cosplay ball
yuliy: was that the one with the fat
man stealth bat balloon?
coolatv99: i was there to see that...
very fateful
lil_vertex: i cant remember
lil_vertex: but ya asher all our
songs were like under 1 minute
ashermixtapehell: sick
yuliy: crystaline
lil_vertex: lemme link one our TRACKS
lil_vertex:https://nobacksies.
bandcamp.com/track/tom-arnold-
schwarzenegger

lil_vertex: that one is based on the trailer to True Lies
lil_vertex: ive never seen it
lil_vertex: but yuliy described it to me
lil_vertex: also this one is our most classic
lil_vertex:https://nobacksies.bandcamp.com/track/i-used-to-surf-but-now-i-work-for-the-government
lil_vertex: our maybe most popular song was called "I Bought A Sex Pistols V-Neck at JC Penny"
lil_vertex: u can find it on the bandcamp
ashermixtapehell: this is great
lil_vertex: a lot of the songs are garbage but there are some good ones in the trash heap
ashermixtapehell: so how did you end up ruining the really healthy diy scene?
lil_vertex: we decided to try and make games to go with some of the shows
lordanime: usually they were made in a day
ashermixtapehell: i figured you would have been more into electronic music cause of your games
lil_vertex: haha i was more into folk and punk originally
ashermixtapehell: can you describe a game you made in a day?
lordanime: our finest was mirage cat
lil_vertex: oh yeahhhhh MIRAGE CAT
ashermixtapehell: the one from zineth?
lordanime: its kind of a theme
lordanime: disappointment
lil_vertex: mirage cat was its own game originally that we made for the arcade
lordanime: you would trudge into the desert for just a little too long
ashermixtapehell: hahaha
lil_vertex: yeah you were trying to reach mirage cat
lil_vertex: but like... u knew the reality of it
lordanime: it was fun in the venue because people would hype each other up about mirage cat

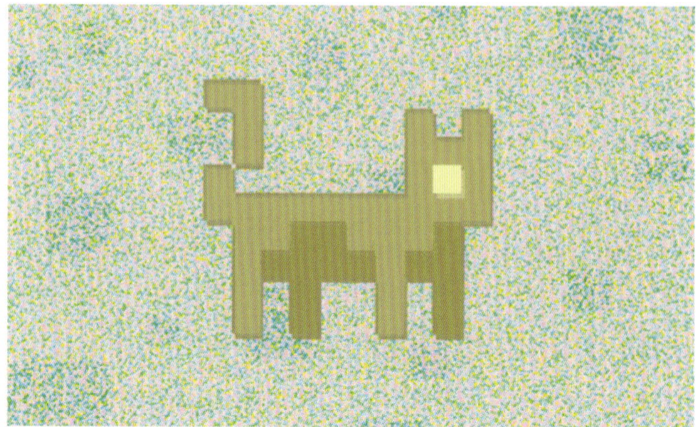

Mirage Cat, 2012.

ashermixtapehell: did you build arcade boxes?
lordanime: we would find computers in the campuses electronic waste
lordanime: then yeah, cardboard
lil_vertex: ya all our gear was from the dump
yuliy: lordanime found a lot of tvs on the road
lil_vertex: we had a pretty sweet stack of old TVs at one point
lordanime: there is a no backsies song about it
ashermixtapehell: did you ever make it to babycastles when it was at silent barn?
lordanime: nooooo :(
lordanime: but that was like our inspiration
lil_vertex: me and yuliy got to see the space at the silent barn but it wasnt running at the time
lil_vertex: at the ZOMBIE DOGS show
lil_vertex: but ya never actually been to a bbcastle show
ashermixtapehell: so are there a buncha early arcane kids games that are unreleased?
lil_vertex: yeah theres a lot of early trash thats unreleased
lil_vertex: NUDO was maybe the first branded arcane kids game?
lil_vertex: zineth was after that
lordanime: there was another in between that, lil_vertex does not want to talk about
ashermixtapehell: wait, whats nudo?
lil_vertex: nudo was a puzzle game, basically pre-arcane kids as we r now

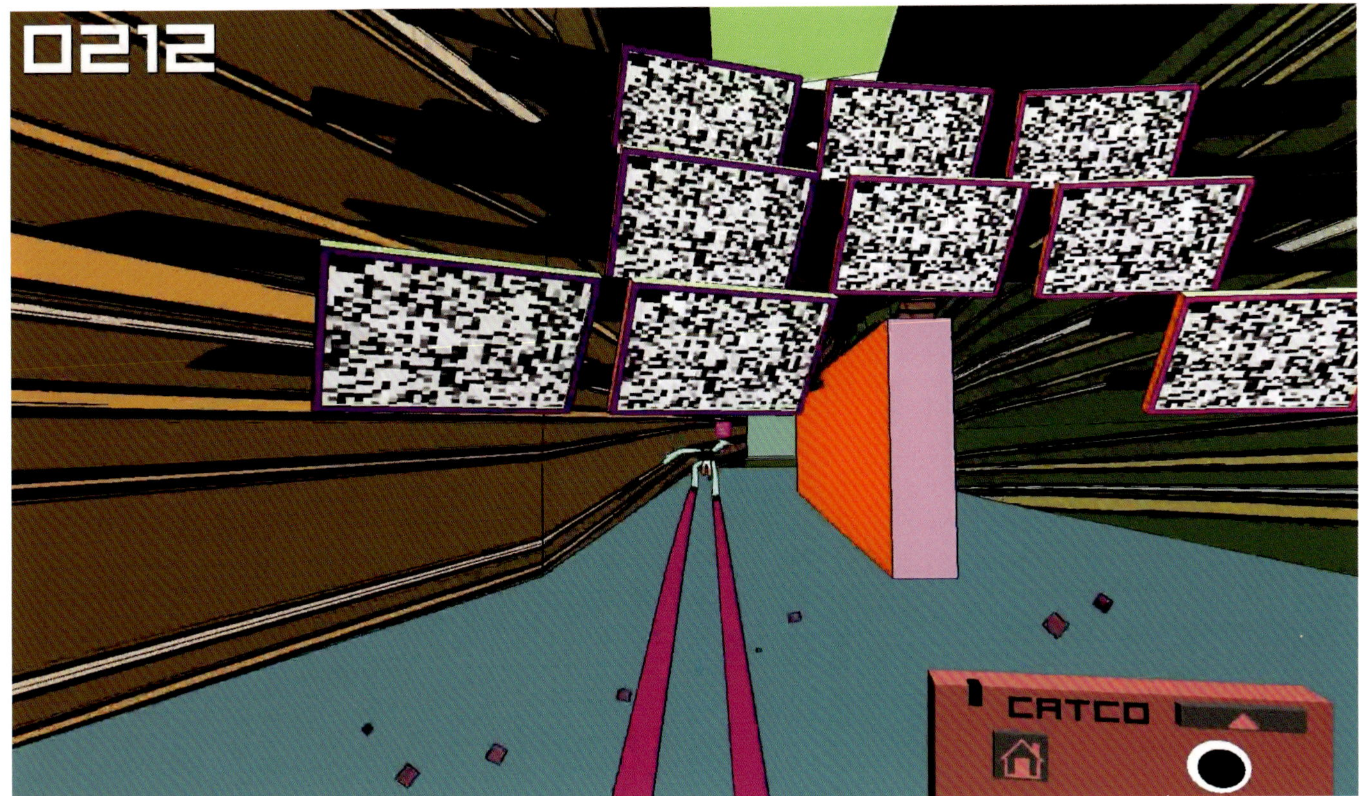

Zineth, 2012.

ashermixtapehell: how did zineth start?
lordanime: that was a project for class
ashermixtapehell: like senior thesis or something?
lordanime: yeah it was basically our final project
ashermixtapehell: there are 7 people credited with the game
lordanime: yeah other people in that class
lordanime: we were trying to do something big in a small amount of time
lordanime: so it was good to have other teammates
ashermixtapehell: yeah, i really didn't understand how a game like that could be created in a matter of months
lil_vertex: nosleep
lil_vertex: nosleep.borntoride
ashermixtapehell: what was the concept behind zenith?
lil_vertex: ZINEth
lil_vertex: spelling is crucial 2 the theme

lordanime: coolatv99 grew up on puns
lordanime: is it even a pun?
lil_vertex: portmanteau?
ashermixtapehell: like zine fair zine?
lordanime: the concept was, wouldn't it be cool to just skate a round in a big desert, while trying to play a cellphone game
ashermixtapehell: yeah that does sound cool
lordanime: we also wanted to just put random zine pages in the world
lil_vertex: the framing is that your job is to deliver zines
ashermixtapehell: yeah, it was weird, it reminded me of when i worked at printed matter
ashermixtapehell: i did that kinda stuff
ashermixtapehell: delivered zines
lil_vertex: haha nice
ashermixtapehell: except i couldn't fly and stuff
lil_vertex: and probably no virtual pets to keep u company...
ashermixtapehell: yeah it sucked
lil_vertex: lol

ashermixtapehell: i love zineth. ive never played a game like it.
ashermixtapehell: ZINEth
lil_vertex: theres some stuff thats kinda similar
lil_vertex: haha
lil_vertex: its like....... a game u can hang out in
lil_vertex: i like that vibe in games
lordanime: there is a multiplayer mode
ashermixtapehell: really?
lil_vertex: oh yeahhhhh
lordanime: one night we just played through a bunch of mario kart levels
lil_vertex: hahaha yeah there were custom levels
lil_vertex: rainbow road
lordanime: it was really fun
lil_vertex: those were like gamecube rips right?
coolatv99: game cube iso rips
lordanime: that is something we are trying to have at the core of perfect stride
lordanime: multiplayer that isn't impossible to find
lil_vertex: perfect stride is a LIFESTYLE game
lordanime: just hanging out
ashermixtapehell: it seems like zineth is inspired by the principles of skateboarding on a conceptual level
lil_vertex: appropriating capitalist architecture
ashermixtapehell: right
lil_vertex did a GNARLY KICKFLIP
ashermixtapehell did a WICKED OLLIE
lordanime: we never try to simulate the actual mechanics of things, just the emotions
lordanime: mostly because its easier
lil_vertex: ya u can get closer to it that way i think
lil_vertex: its VERY emotional
ashermixtapehell: so the concept of perfect stride is that tony hawk didn't land the 900?
lordanime: we just claimed that to increase blogability
ashermixtapehell: do you have a problem with skateboarding games?
lil_vertex: skate 3 is maybe one of the objectively best games

yuliy: real talk...
lil_vertex: did u know mark mothersbaugh composed some of the dynamic music in that game....
ashermixtapehell: so just corporate skateboarding games
lil_vertex: ya the 900 triggered an explosion of corporate skateboarding
lil_vertex: in the perfect stride universe its an apocalypse though
lil_vertex: the game takes place inside abandoned geocities dites
lil_vertex: so like all of the environments are the architectural versions of personal web pages
ashermixtapehell: wow
lil_vertex: the game is operating in that same space, its this dying web
ashermixtapehell: which is kind of like escape from LA
ashermixtapehell: how much more time do you guys have?
lordanime: we are all 18+ so plenty of time
lil_vertex PUTS ON JOHN CARPENTER SOUNDTRACK
lil_vertex: i can answer a few more

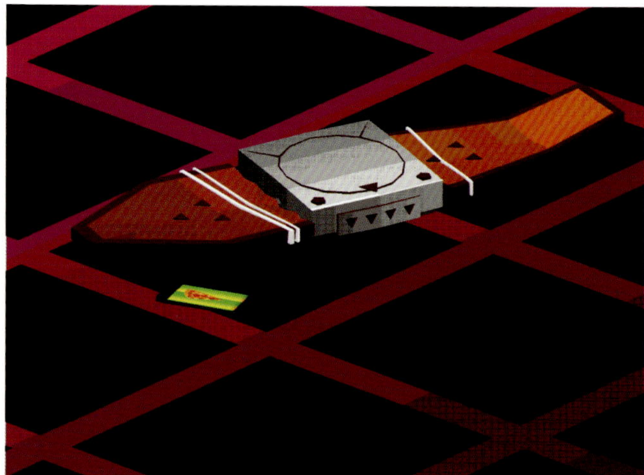

Perfect Stride, 2013.

ashermixtapehell: whats the story with the manifesto?
lordanime: search engine optimization
lil_vertex: its a collection of a bunch of ideas and themes that come up in our conversations
lil_vertex: idk a lot of ppl reach out to us because they want to do the kind of stuff we do

ashermixtapehell: yeah i saw your
guestbook. people are stoked
lil_vertex: we wanted to be like:
here are some of the things we're
thinking about in our work
lil_vertex: it was more to get other
people thinking critically about
their games tho
**ashermixtapehell: do you think that
people aren't critical enough?**
lordanime: we will be critical enough
for everyone
**ashermixtapehell: do you have plans
to enlist more arcane kids?**
lil_vertex: we have pretty huge plans
to expand...
coolatv99: !
lordanime: the tokyo branch
lil_vertex: Apps division
lil_vertex: Publishing & Acquisitions
coolatv99: money pit
ashermixtapehell: hahahah
**ashermixtapehell: are you guys into
art? the whole james turrell moca
thing doesn't seem random**
lil_vertex: yeah i feel like games
have so much to learn from art
lordanime: and the scene has a lot to
not learn from the art scene
lil_vertex: hahah
lil_vertex: bubsy is about
wonder..............
lil_vertex: like i actually really
wanted people to learn about james
turrells work
**ashermixtapehell: yeah it seemed to
come from a genuine place**
lil_vertex: the game sabotages itself
by ruthelessly using game techniques
like collectibles
lordanime: imagine experiencing
something as someone who is basically
a baby (bubsy)
lordanime: only knows his game world
**ashermixtapehell: kinda the best way
to experience art**
lordanime: i'd be tearing up
lil_vertex: the museum level ends
with that one piece
lil_vertex: i forget the name, its
the huge room with a pink void
lil_vertex: i spent a really long
time in there
lil_vertex: i cried

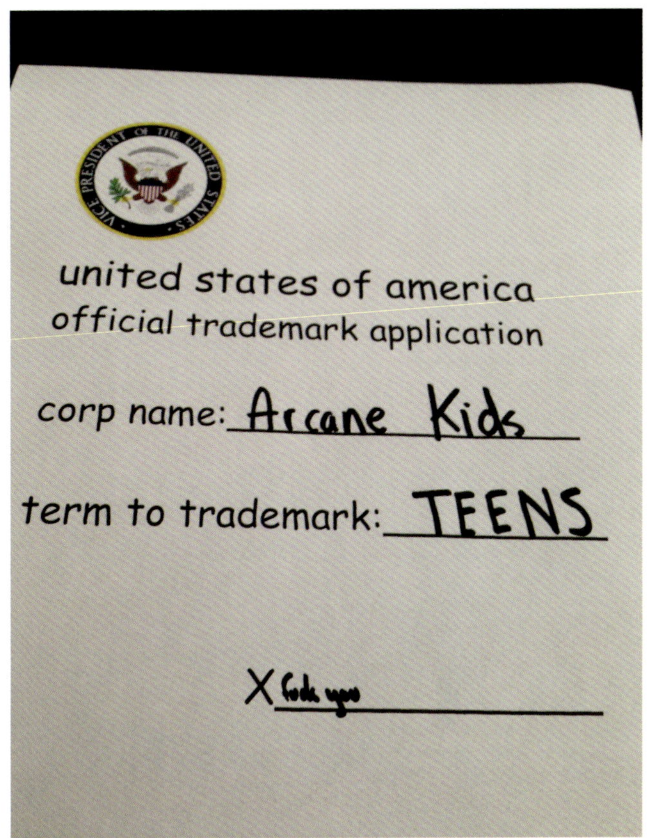

Arcane Kids Trademark Application, 2014.

lordanime: it does really mess with
parts of your brain you have no
control over
lil_vertex: his work w/ light and
space reminded me of the way video
games captivated me
coolatv99: i saw it after playing the
game and was not that impressed
lil_vertex: LOL
lil_vertex: it was also really
inspired by the one quote that was in
the game
coolatv99: (joke) (it was p good)
lil_vertex: if ur using light to
tell a story ur using the power of
stories, not the power of light
lil_vertex: (incredibly bad
paraphrasing)
ashermixtapehell: ok cool
**ashermixtapehell: i think that is a
good spot to end the interview**
lil_vertex: kool
ashermixtapehell: you guys rule
lil_vertex: nah u rule
**ashermixtapehell: thank you again
arcane kids**
ashermixtapehell did a GNARLY OLLIE 

Julien Ceccaldi

"I'll look at my reflection in the mirror,
and I'll tell it how ridiculous it is."

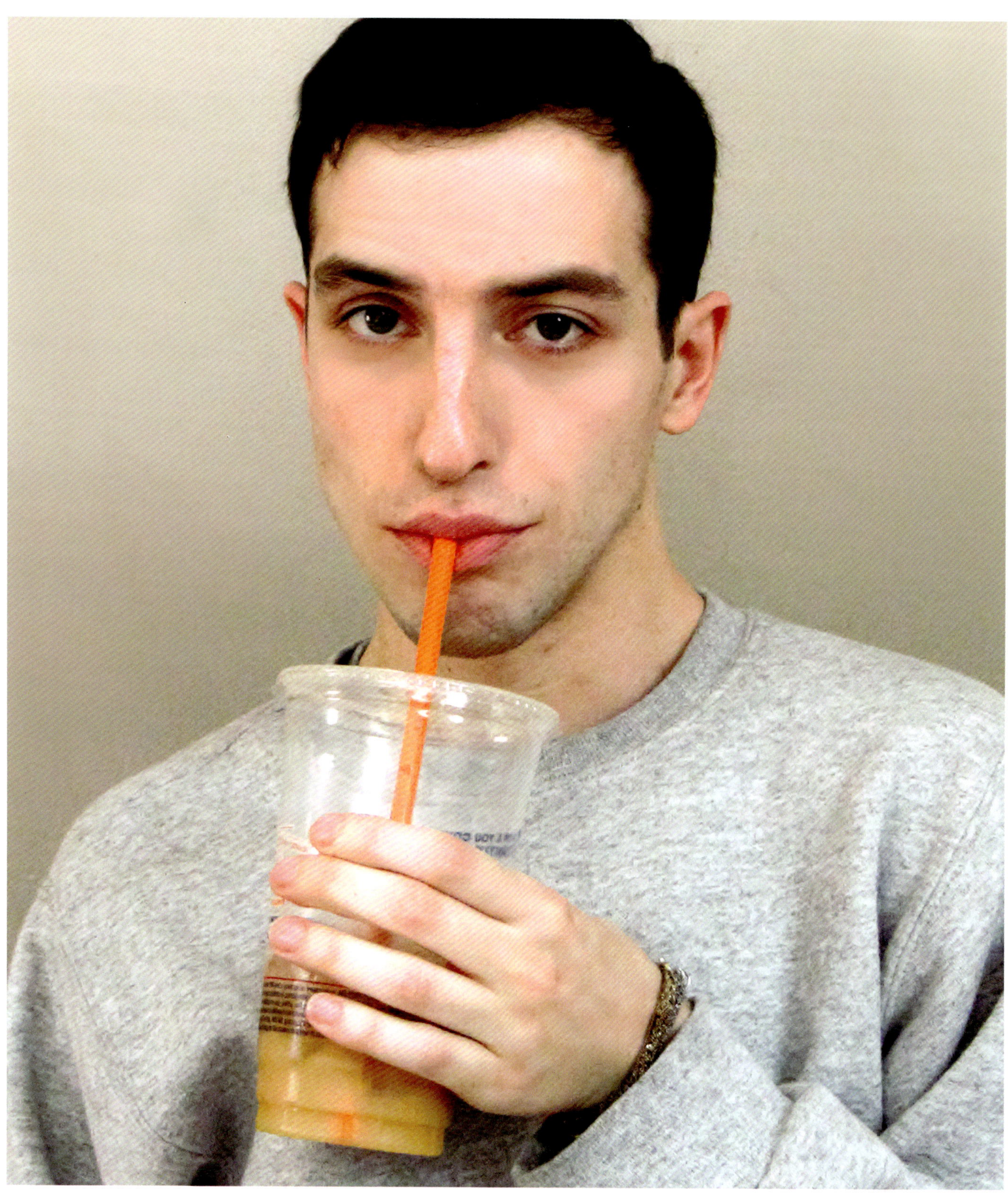

Interview by Fiona Duncan
Images courtesy Julien Ceccaldi

Eyes like bundles of grapes, checkmark noses, and ample, conical chins, broad built shoulders, narrow hips, and six packs, in style — a Julien Ceccaldi girl is unmistakable. She wants to be It, she yearns for it. She's fab, if only she could see herself from the outside. Inside, turmoil. She aches, in high fashions that bind like her deep insecurities. She doesn't fit in, or feel herself to, but like, who does? She fits in our hearts, heart on her sleeve. She heals. The Ceccaldi treatment: vulnerability and show, glitzy truths, see me? I see you. Where might you have seen Julien Ceccaldi's work? He's decorated canvas, clothing, comic books, vinyl sleeves, stained glass, and the cover of Artforum. He's made plays, and illustrated horoscopes for Kenzo. Sex has loved him long time. And here we have him in interview.

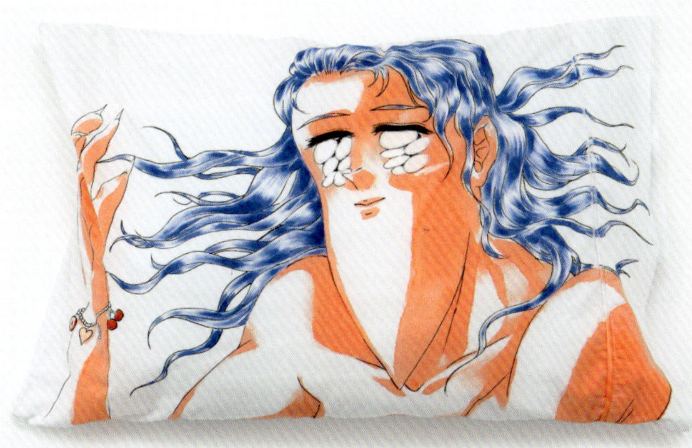

Blue Dreams Pillow, Paradise Garage 2013.

Where did you grow up?
In Montreal, Québec, and for a few years in France.
Were you a nerdy kid?
I tried not to be too much of a nerd, but I paid attention in class and then I'd go home and draw with my online friends, which is very nerdy.
I remember you telling me how you had online friends very early, like pre-millennium. Are you still friends with any of them?
No, I dramatically said goodbye to all of them on my 18th birthday via LiveJournal.

How come?
University had started, and there was this pressure put on me to stop drawing manga. I kept drawing in that style in secret, but exclusively on paper.
Where did you meet these friends? On forums?
On oekaki boards. They're bulletin boards that only let you post images you draw with the website's application. And then people comment on your work, usually with compliments. It's originally a Japanese program and the tools are tailored for manga artists. But the thing I liked even more were these websites that let users draw together on the same canvas, with a chat box at the bottom of the screen.
Who started these sites?
Artists would set up the application for a board or for a chat room on their personal website. The users would have this shared appreciation for the host's art. At one point I was on this one chatroom so often that the site's owner asked me to be an admin; it was an honor. She had a big fan base, so trolls would come deface the whiteboard often. I'd seen her work on the cover of a video game magazine, looked her up, and that's how I discovered her website.
Do you remember your first experience of a computer, of the internet?
We got the internet at home in 1996. I didn't see the appeal of chatrooms then. I preferred to go on the Capcom Japan website. I'd print off the pages that had character illustrations on them.
Cute. When did you start writing comics?
I won't count my attempts at drawing comics as a teenager — I kept giving up after two pages. In my early 20s, my best friend and I were partying a lot, to the point where we felt guilty for not making anything. So we sat down and wrote a list of things that made us laugh. It was mostly about the future as seen in early noughties RnB music videos: insane outfits, girls punishing a cheater

in a creative way, small spaceships entering in a big club-spaceship... We each did a little story about that, and about how fabulous people at the club must feel broken inside in secret — just like us. Then I derived dozens of 4-panel strips from this. The dialogues took a turn for the intimate, duplicating preoccupations I have about sharing too much about my personal life for example, and about what that means about my relationship to others.

Social dynamics.

Yeah, I wanted to talk about how everyone probably feels like they're on a different plane from everyone else, even within the group they are a part of. I wanted to talk about how a group doesn't actually exist, in the sense that it's not this solid, homogeneous block that you may perceive, because every single person in that group also personally feels excluded from it.

Totally.

Doesn't everyone feel like that?

Your comics are darkly relatable. The content could almost be mocking, like this is "young-girl" stuff, but you pull it off with empathy. How do you feel towards your characters?

The conversations and the monologues I write, it's how things sound in my head on a daily basis. I talk to myself all the time. I'll look at my reflection in the mirror, and I'll tell it how ridiculous it is. We're so sad, so lost, and so confused, it's almost funny.

When you publish a story that's about vulnerability or something associated with the neurosis of an individual, and then all these people identify with it, do you feel cleansed of that?

Wording out an issue through a character's mouth won't help me resolve it, but it will be a little weight off my chest. I try to never write about the very exact same problem twice. And yeah it's cool when people can relate. It's great.

I wanted to talk about some of your influences, like the French filmmaker Catherine Breillat. You're a big fan.

Yes, of everything she's done. Everything she's filmed, or written, or said in interviews, reveal things I've known all along without knowing. About the world and about myself. A Breillat heroine can lend her body to anyone and for free, even if, or maybe especially if, they're repulsive. But she can also be enraptured by plastic beauty. She might also give her entire self to one specific person. And it doesn't matter how deadly it feels to do that, because not being with that person will feel like an even worse death. All these possibilities of desire, and this mix of obscenity and romanticism, I take it like it's about me.

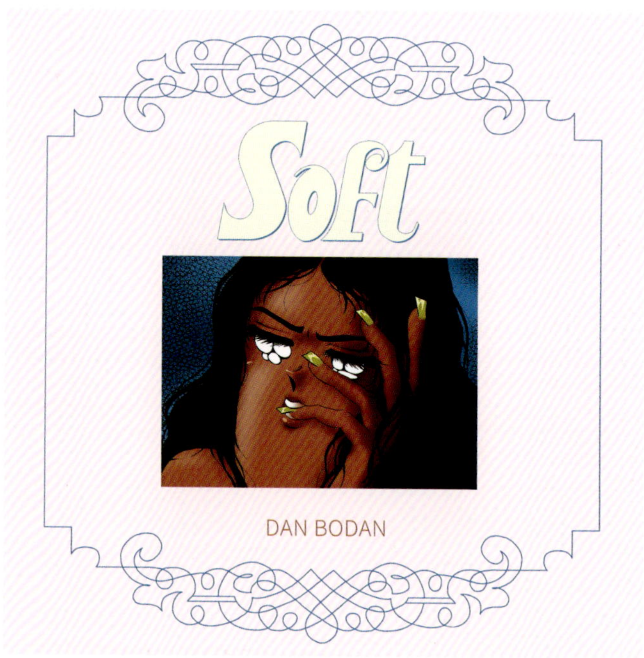

Dan Bodan, Soft, DFA Records, 2013.

I identify too, and I'm surprised, because she's so extreme. Someone once explained her radical statements on sex and gender to me as an inner dialogue externalized. They aren't spoken as essential truths, it's more like she's representing ideas about what men and women are.

It was me who told you that.

Ha. Of course. Stoner memory. Sorry.
Breillat talks about how men are this
and women are that, but she's really
talking about an all-encompassing
sexism that is so deep-seated it's
almost ancestral. She makes light of
it, and she definitely takes a stand
against it, without denying the part
of us that is attracted to violence
and death.

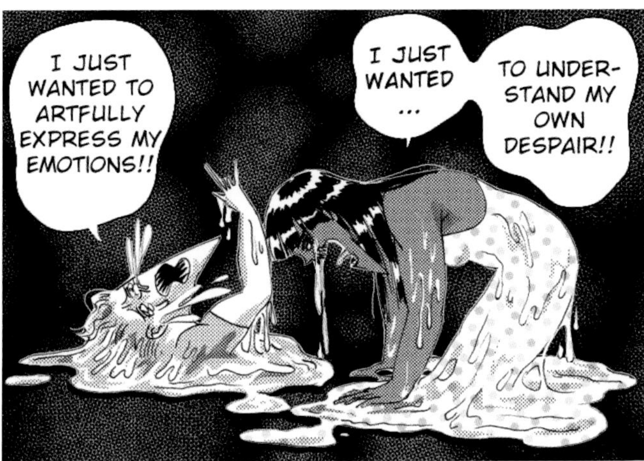

Inherited Struggle, 2014.

**Speaking of "men are this, women
that," are all men dogs? Or, why are
they in your comics?**
The first dogs I drew looked dopey
and horny, like the ones you've seen,
but they were chilled-out and cuddly
masculine gays. I was expressing my
conflicting feelings of attraction
and repulsion for masculinity. Then
that design came in handy when I
thought of a gag that involved some
random jerk. The women I draw are
never reprehensible, but the dogs
might be. Although lately I think
maybe we're all dogs: pitiful,
loving, begging dogs. Maybe that's
just me.
**"Now I wanna be your dog." More on
the influences. You have some strange
ones. You're really into YouTube
personalities, right?**
It's not so strange when you look at
the numbers though.
**Right, that's my oversight. It's
actually this huge phenomena that I
don't know anything about, except
through you.**

I think that's because the audience
is young. Like when you see these
YouTube conventions, where the YouTube
personalities do panels and meet-
and-greets, it's mainly preteens and
teenagers attending.
What kinds of videos do you watch?
I'll watch vlogs, junk food hauls,
questions and answers... Makeup
tutorials are very soothing to watch.
What's so soothing about them?
Listening to a guy or girl ramble
forever about makeup, it's like you're
killing time together, one on one, in
their bedroom. It's a window into a
very real world. The people I follow
are not professionals, they do very
everyday, makeup looks, but they
are earnestly trying to communicate
something with as much precision as
they can. They're on their own, and
the struggle to find the right words
is palpable. I feel like that all the
time, like my mouth isn't keeping up
with my thoughts. When you upload a
vlog on YouTube, you must be at peace
with yourself in that regard. You
have to accept that you've expressed
yourself as best as you could. Inexact-
itude happens, it's called life.
Who's a really well-known YouTuber?
Well, the biggest makeup guru is
Michelle Phan. She's a worldwide
celebrity. If she was on the street,
people would be taking photos of her.
I don't think I'm reaching. She's
built a literal empire from scratch.
But the YouTubers I really love right
now are Gigi Gorgeous and Trisha
Paytas.
**You also love Gilmore Girls. Did you
watch it when it was on-air?**
I did, in both French and English.
That would be a hard show to dub.
Yeah, rewatching it now, I catch the
jokes that got lost in translation, and
the ones that flew over my head. Fun fact,
I found out that Sookie was a bit of a
pothead when she was younger. It's not
even a subtle reference, you just have
to know what "baked" means. Also, it's
funny because she's a cook. Anyway, it's
surprising the program was so popular
with teens, considering there's only like
three teenage characters.

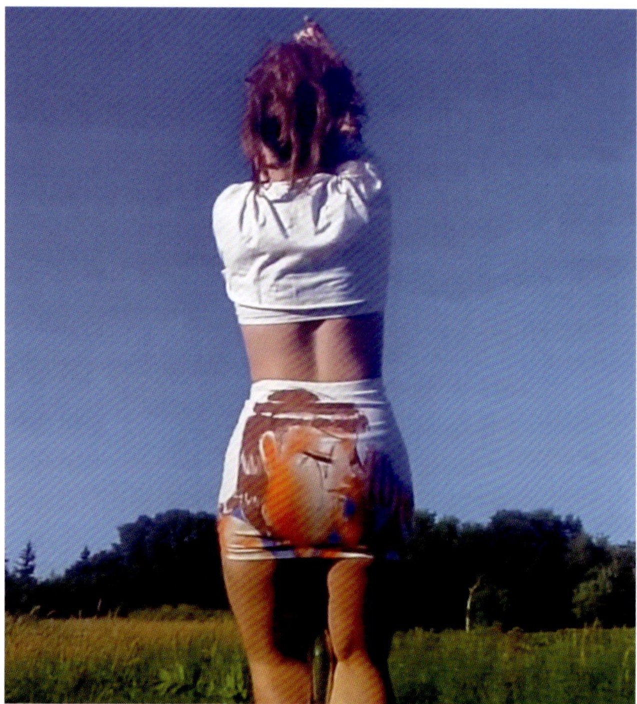

POLE Prairie, Directed with Mélissa Gagné, 2014.

There's all these oddball grown-ups.
Like Kirk, how old is Kirk? Who knows?
I loved Jess.
Rory and him are so hot together.
So hot. Real chemistry.
Actual chemistry 'cause they were dating most of the time he was on. There's nothing like Gilmore Girls. You can't know what the show's like until you sit down and watch an entire episode. It has a unique recipe and it's more self-aware than people initially assume.
Let's talk practice. When you're drawing do you find your hand follows your brain? Or does your hand do surprising things sometimes? Is it all deliberate?
Everything is very deliberate. In high school, our art teacher kept asking me to loosen up, but I've always been like, I don't want to say anal but...
You're tight.
And I'm getting tighter. In my first batch of comics, you can tell I was trying to draw with a loose hand. I didn't want my brain to consider anything other than the story and the words. I like to put effort in draftsmanship, it's obvious by now.

Yeah, your more recent work's got this gloss.
Up until I was 18, it was my goal to figure out how to replicate the glossiness of a professional, published illustration. I've picked up where I left off.
Are you still making clothes? How did that start?
My first shirts were spray-painted and done within 20 minutes; they looked gross and cheap. I sold them to my friends at craft fairs for next to nothing. The idea was that graphic tees are a joke within themselves. I was wearing them, even running a graphic tee business, so the joke was really on me. Clothes are a goofy support for a painting, so from the get-go, you know you won't be taken too seriously, and you can knock yourself out creatively speaking. I'm tired of selling clothes though. Fashion is fun, but retail can be so brutal.
Your characters aren't named, right?
Right, they're nameless. You can think of them as either interchangeable, or the same person throughout.
What about their gender?
My character designs are getting more unisex, with more slender silhouettes, which I'm compensating for with large sweaters and bald heads here and there. The comics reflect this uniformity. It's a world where on one hand, nobody comments on the way each other's body looks, yay! But on the other, there is no diversity, and the collective consciousness is dogmatic and binary. The one threat to this are visceral emotions; that's where the glimmer of hope is. I remember feeling less crazy when I first read all this Judith Butler stuff in school. I was basically being taught that everybody is in a constant state of performance, trying hard to maintain appearances at all times. I let out a sigh of relief: "Oh, it's not just me." 😊

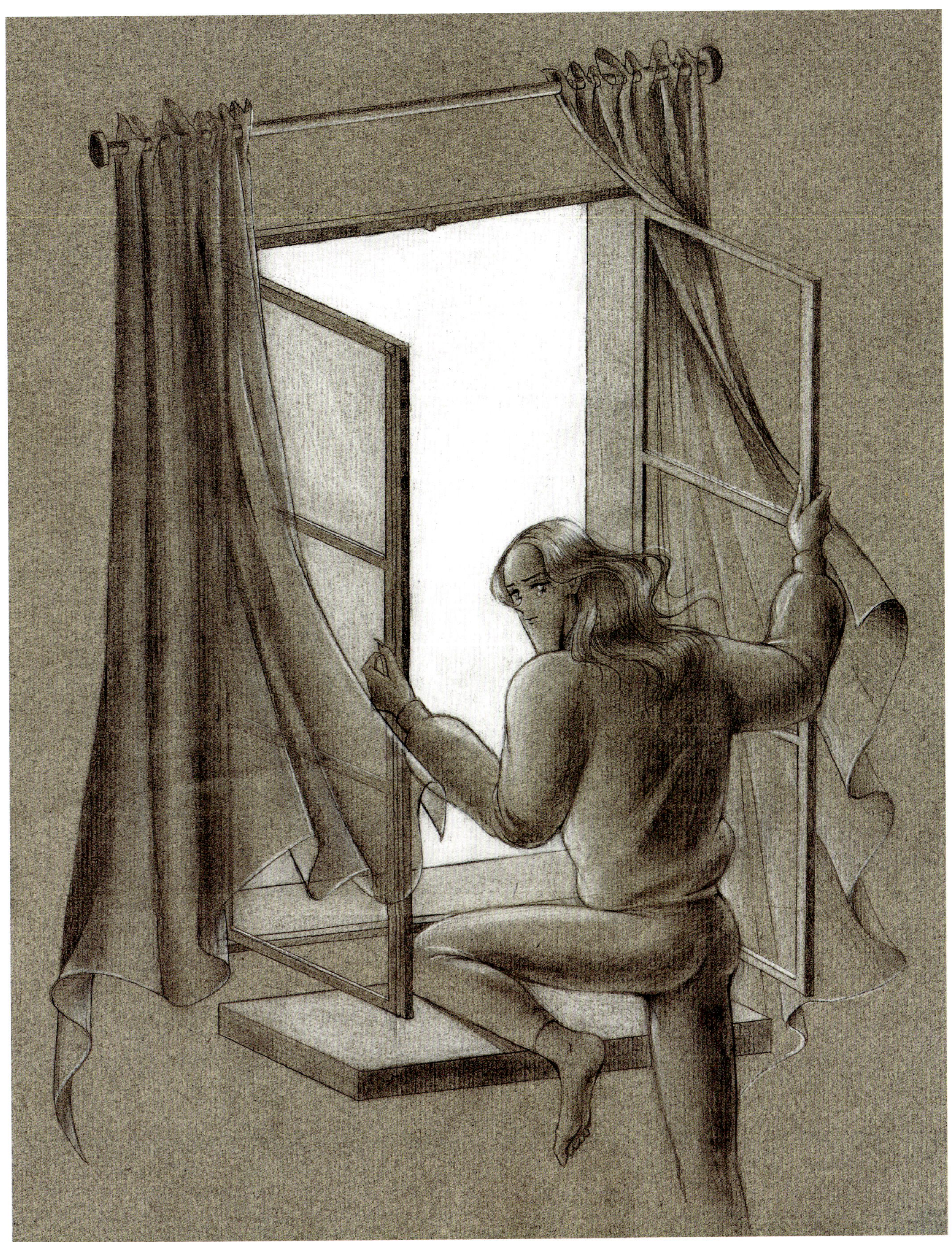

Defenestration, 2015.

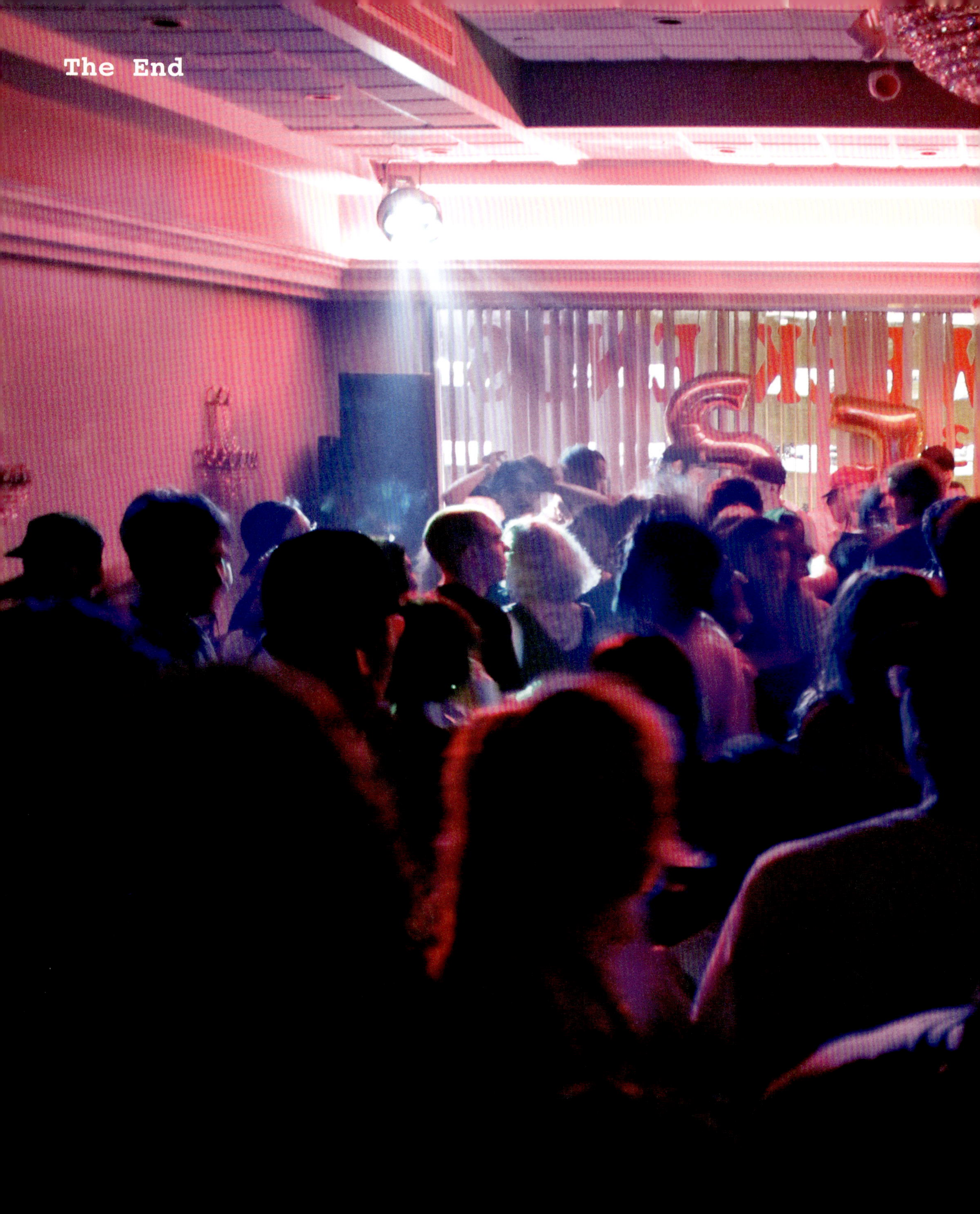
The End

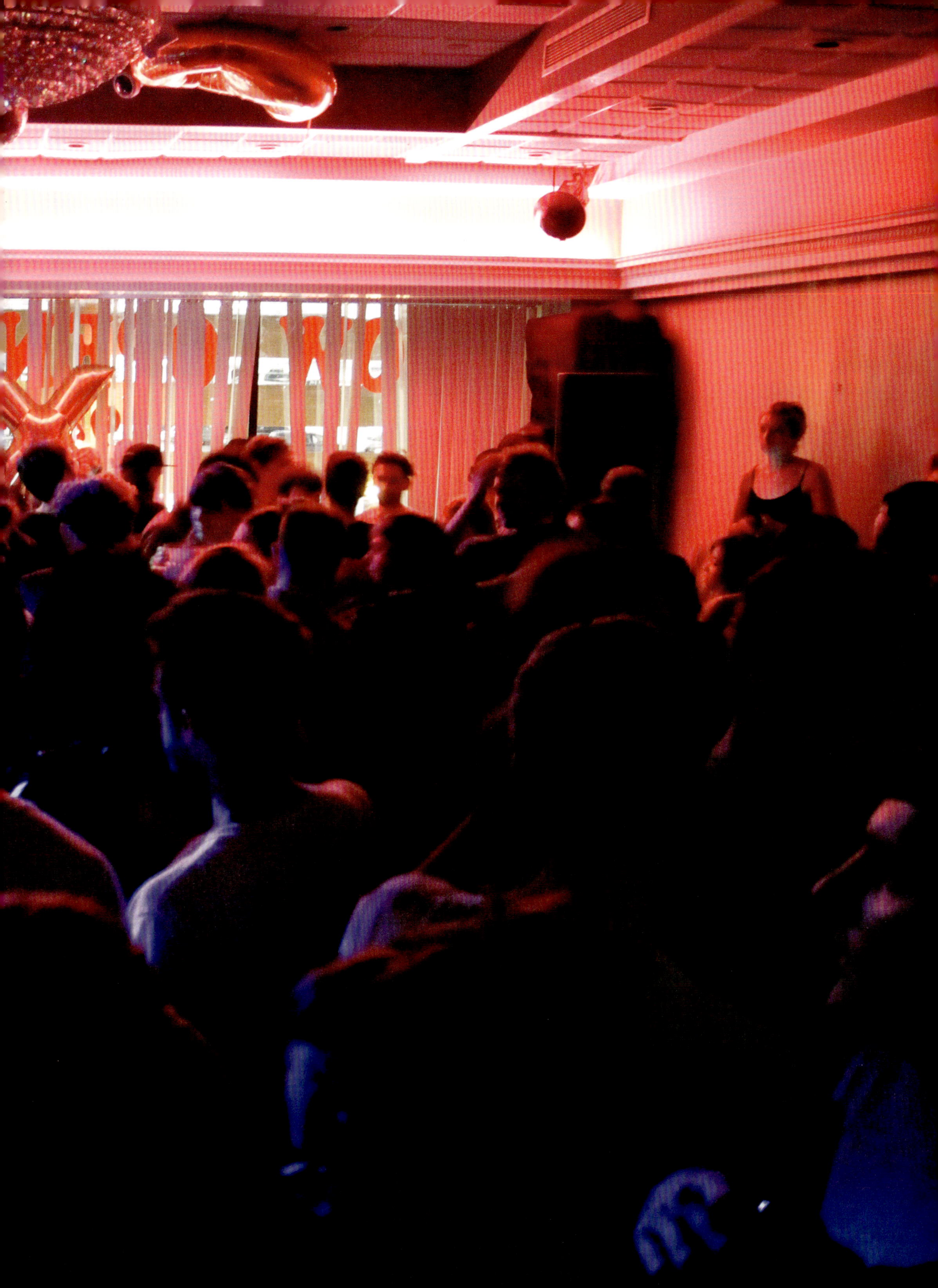

Contributors

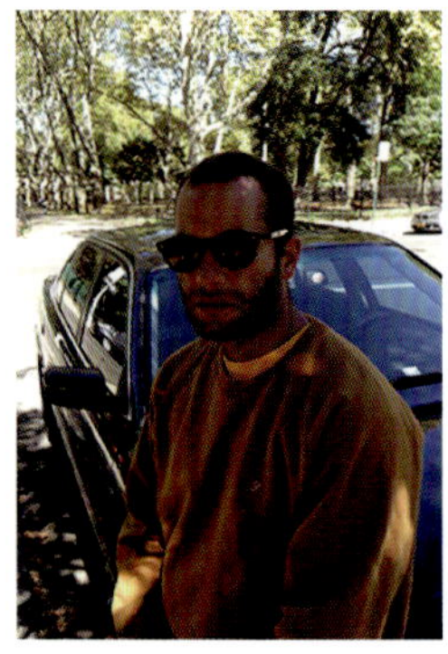

AARON BONDAROFF

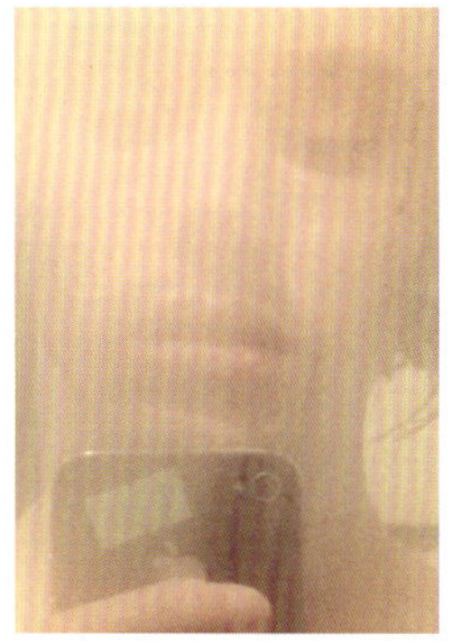

AIR POP

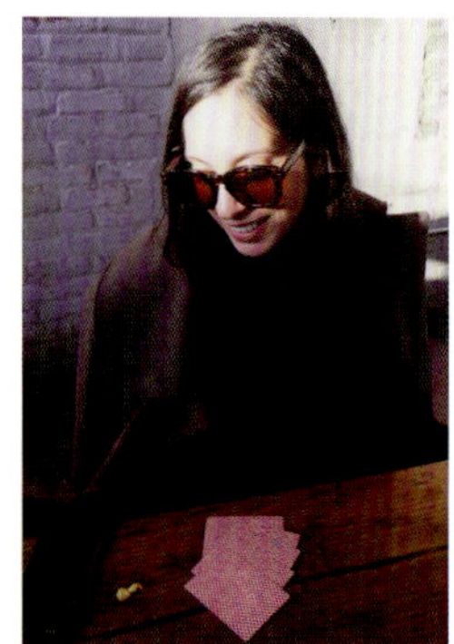

AL BEDELL

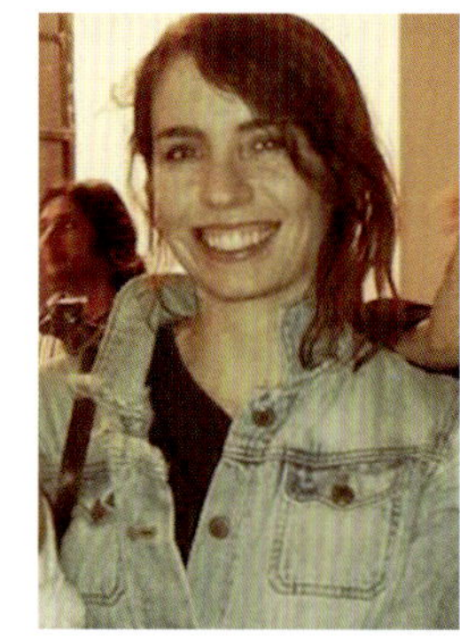

ALISSA MCKENDRICK

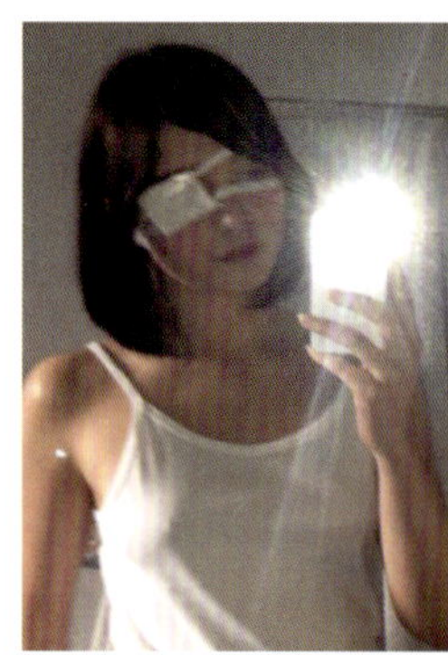

AMALIA ULMAN

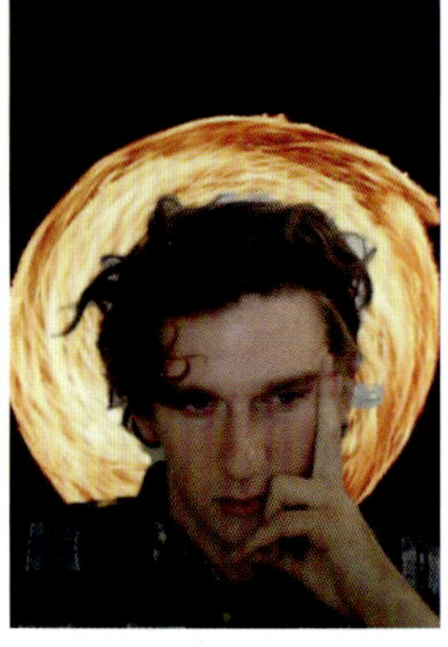

ANDREW EARGLE

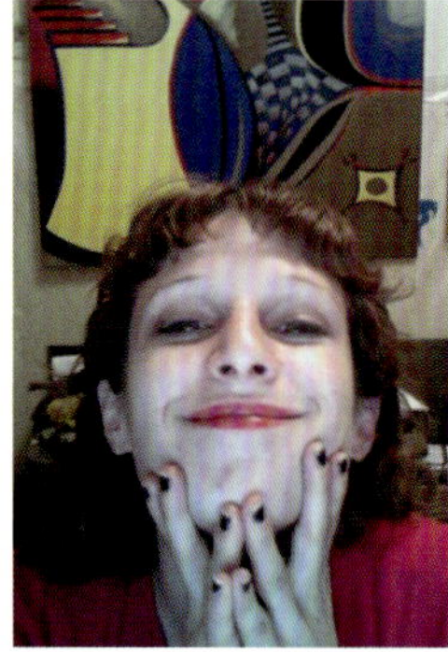

ANNIE PEARLMAN

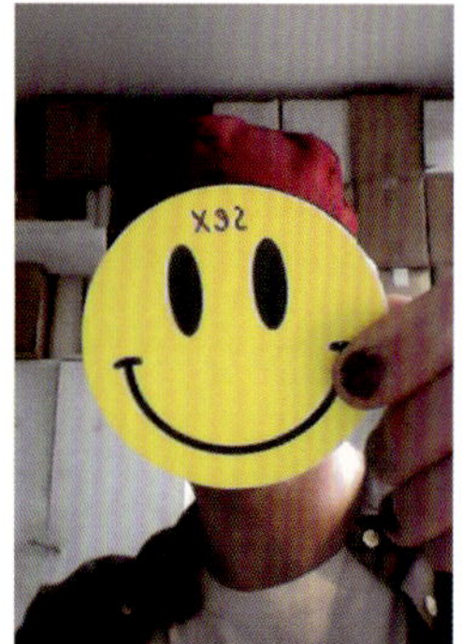

ASHER PENN

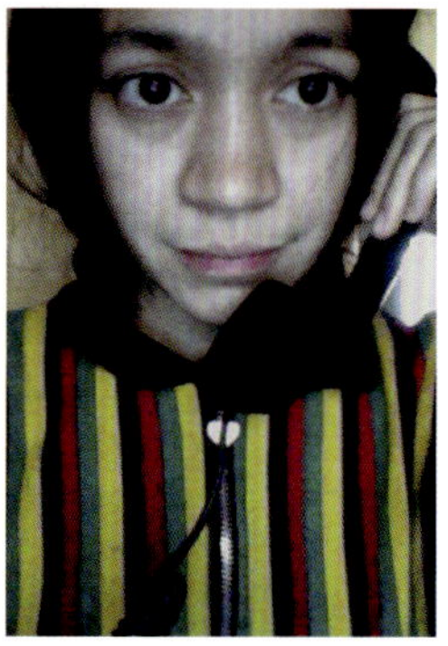

AVENA GALLAGHER

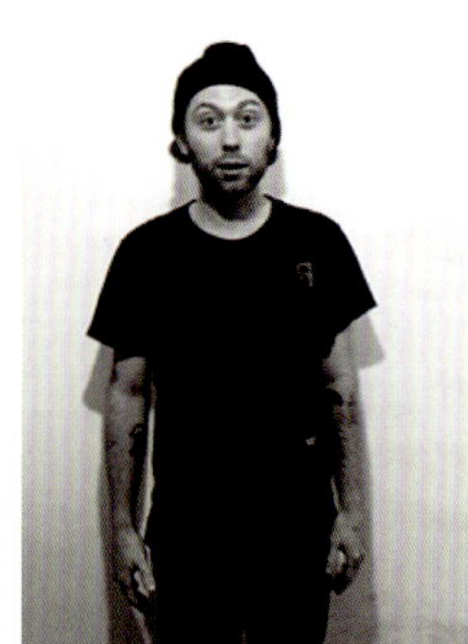

BRAYDEN OLSEN

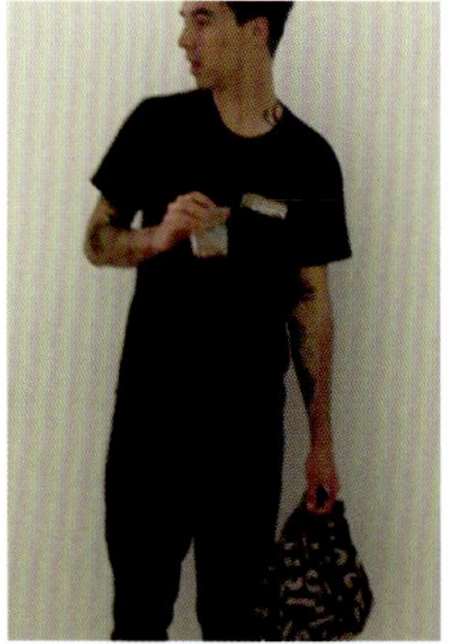

BRENDAN FOWLER

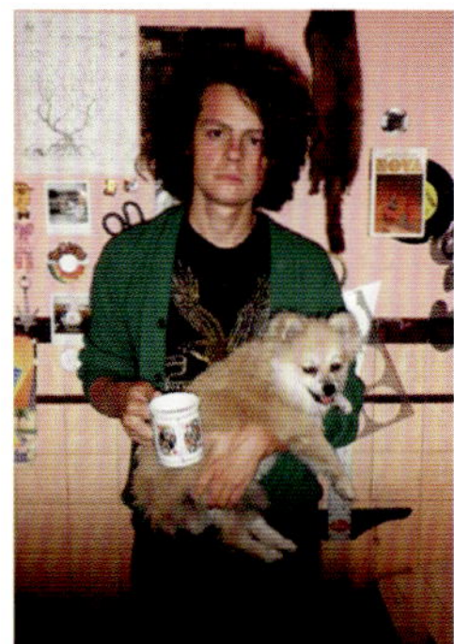

BRIAN BLOMERTH

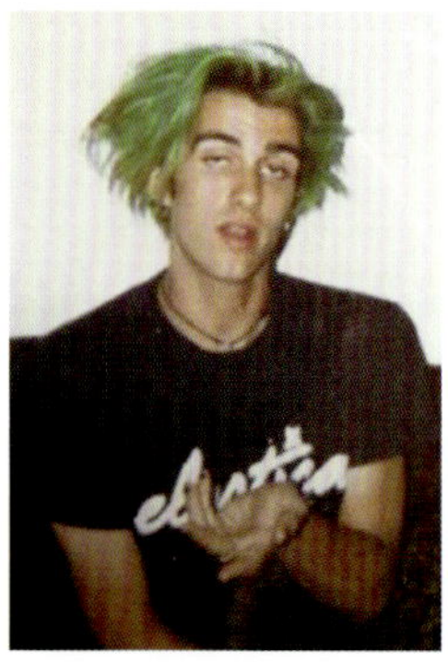

CALI THORNHILL DEWITT

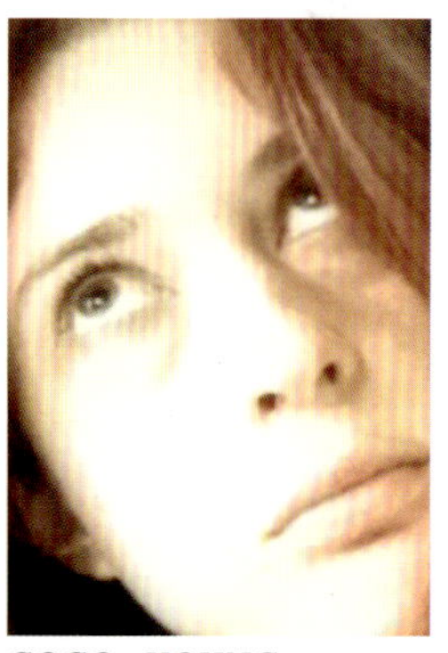

COCO YOUNG

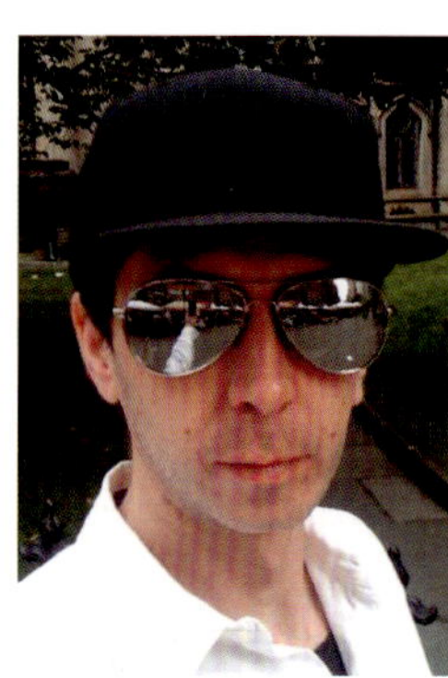

CRIS MOOR

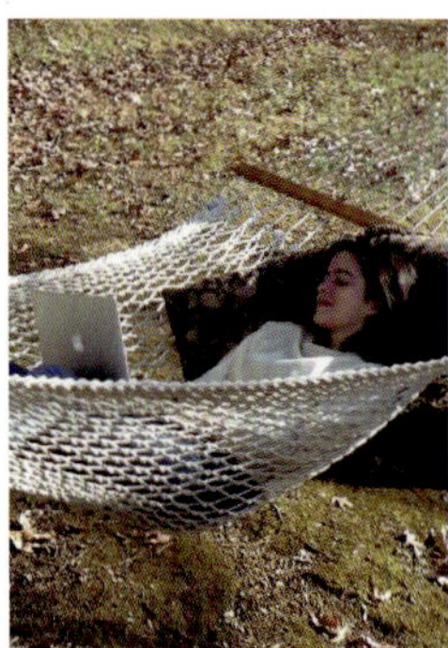

DENA YAGO

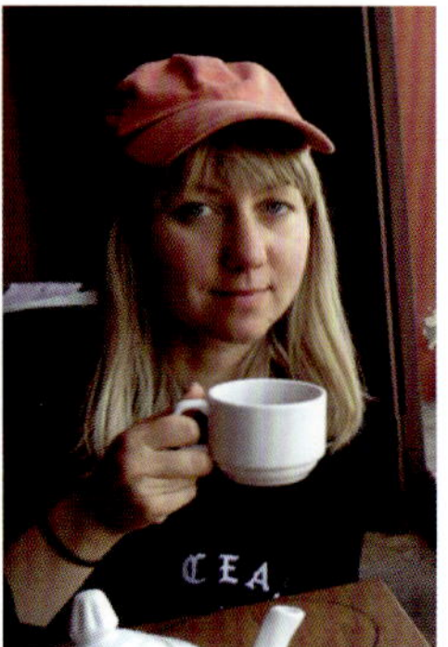

EVA MICHON

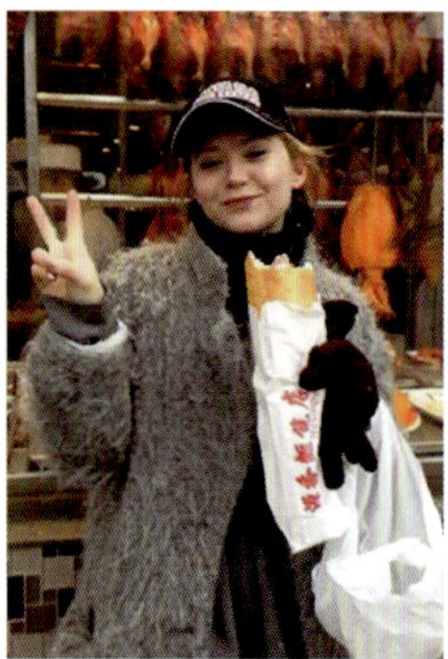

FIONA DUNCAN

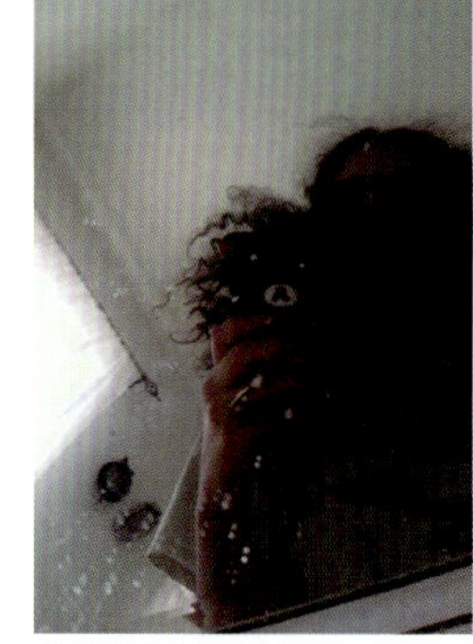

GABRIELLE TILLMAN

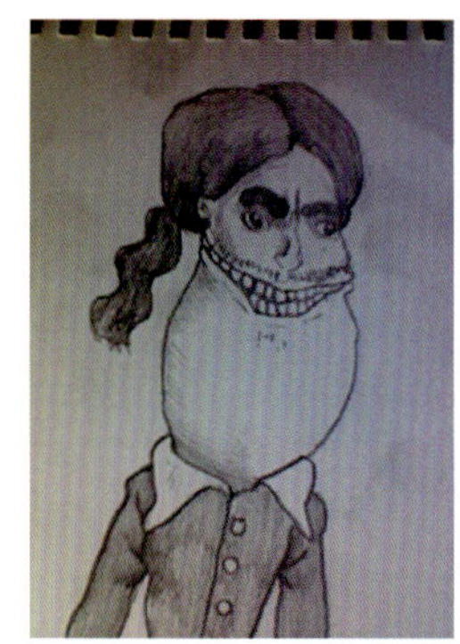

GOBBY

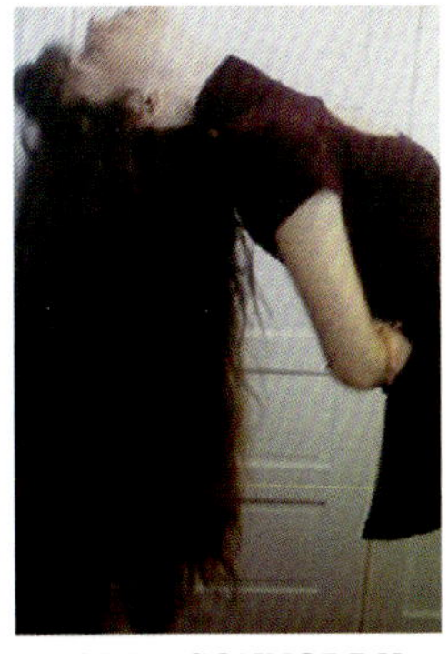

JACKY CONNOLLY

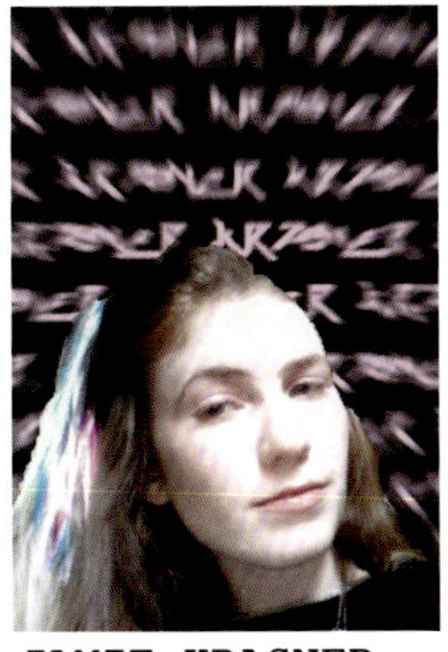

JAMIE KRASNER

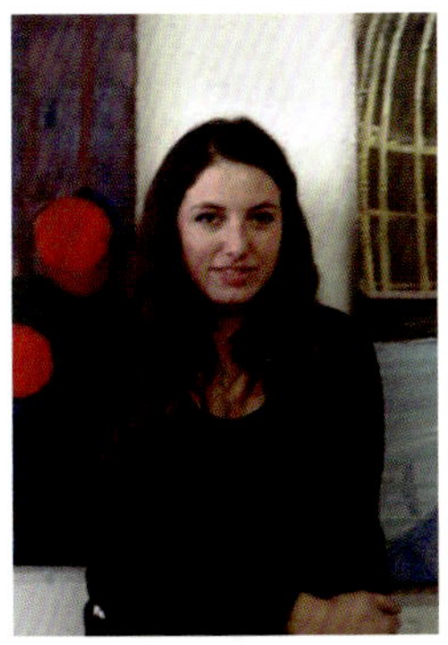

JESSICA WILLIAMS

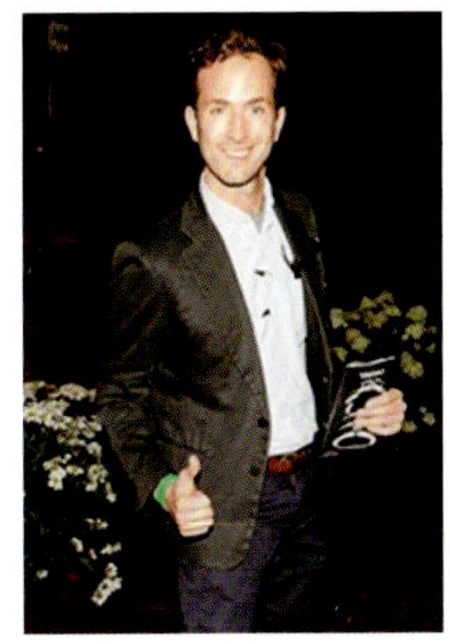

JOHNNY MISHEFF

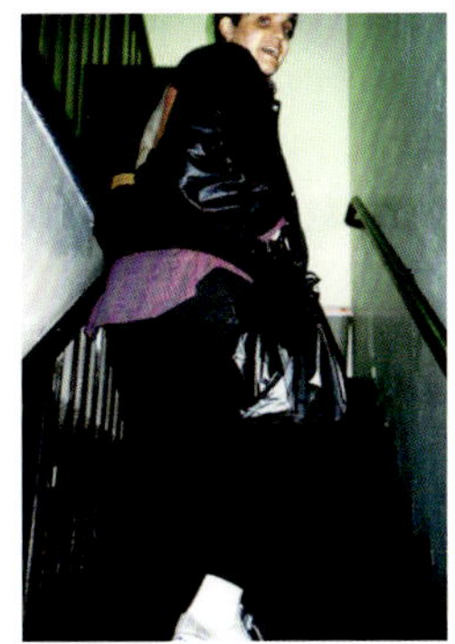

JUICEBOXXX

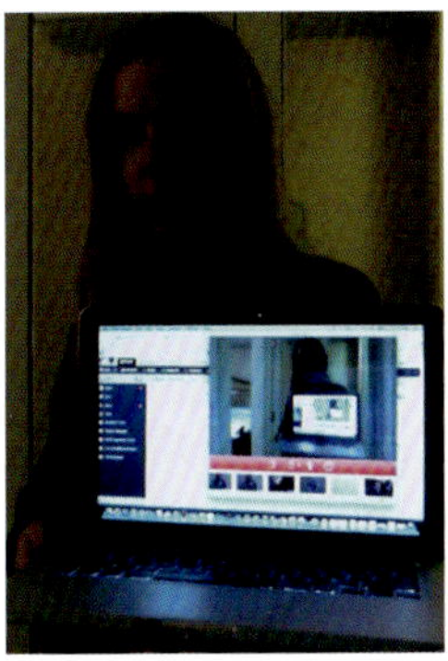

KAYLA GUTHRIE

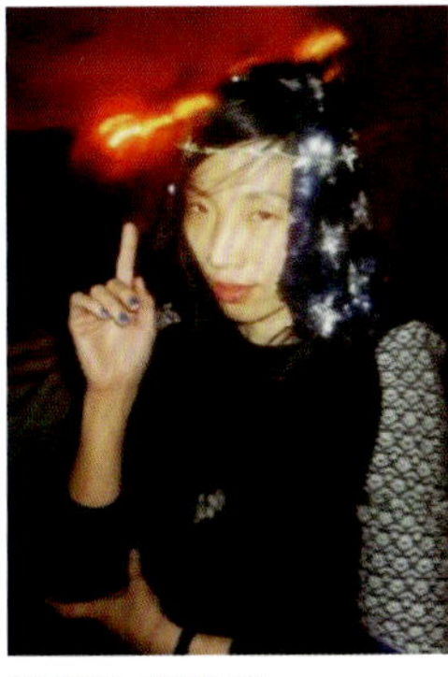

KIKI KUDO

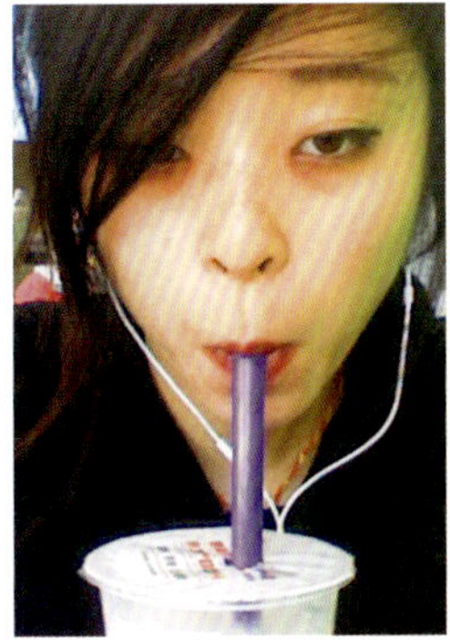

MAGGIE LEE

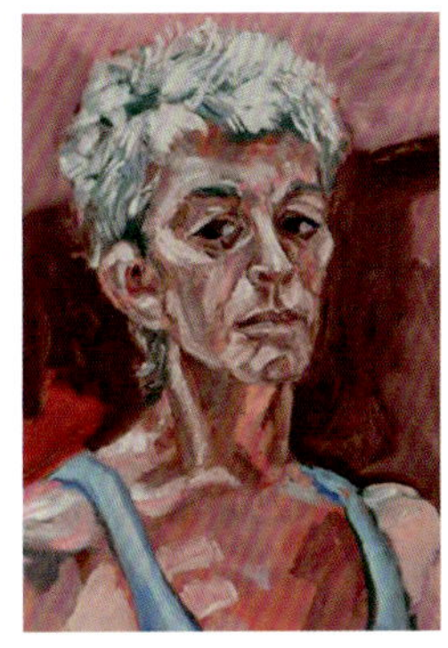

MEREDITH FELDMAR

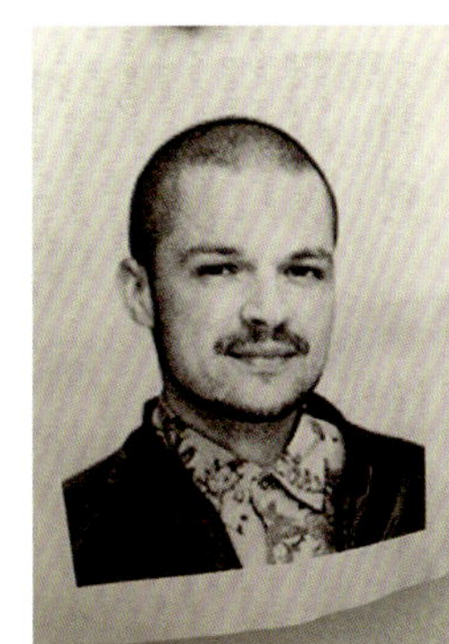

MICHAEL BULLOCK

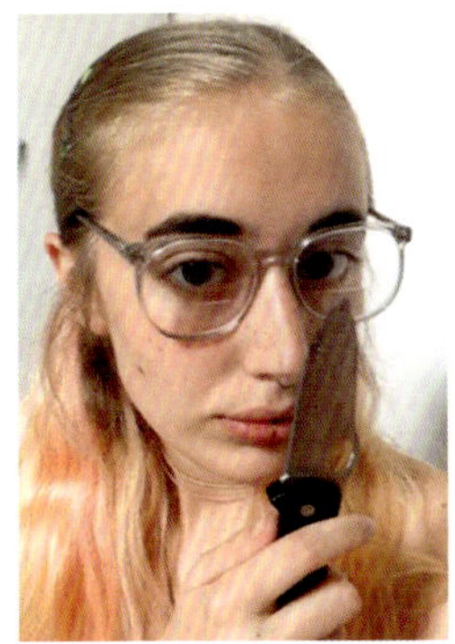

MILAH LIBIN

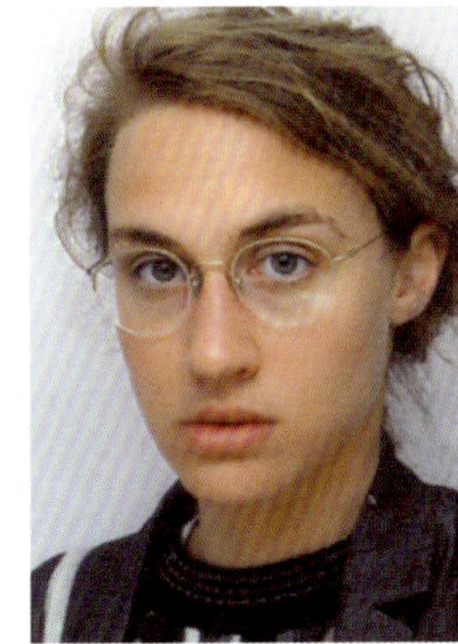

NATASCHA GOLDENBERG

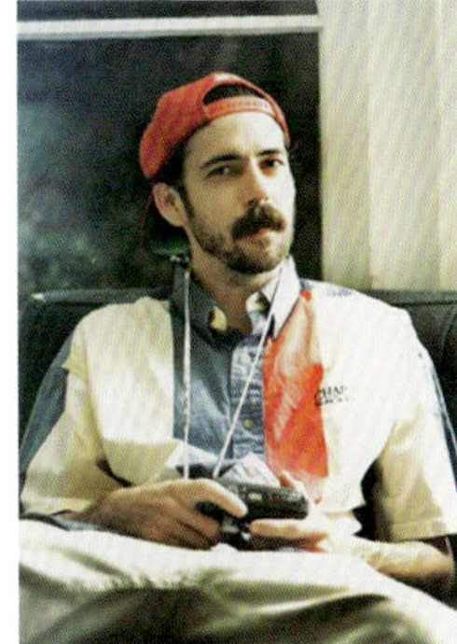

NATE WALTON

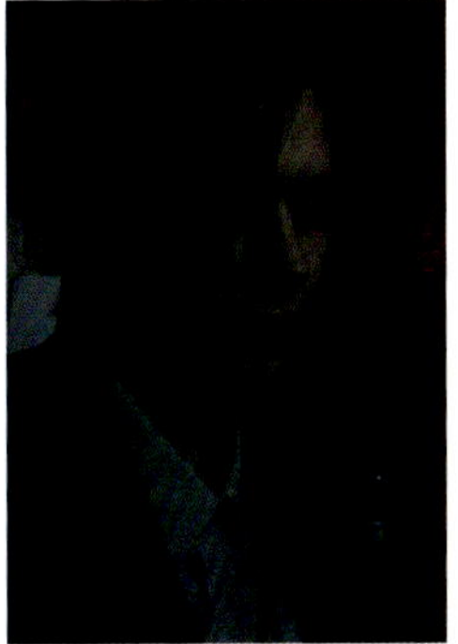

NATHAN ANTOLIK

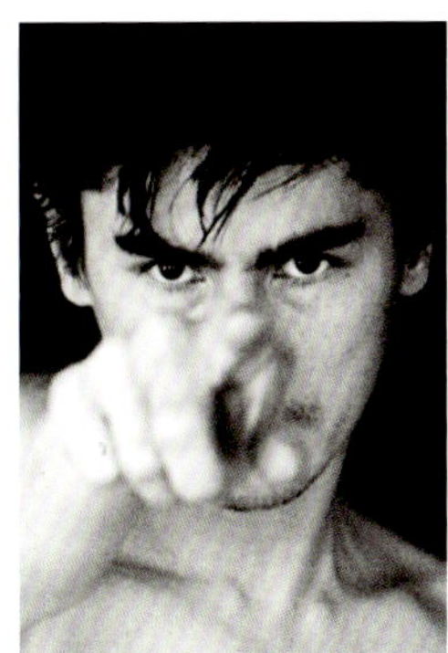

OTO GILLEN

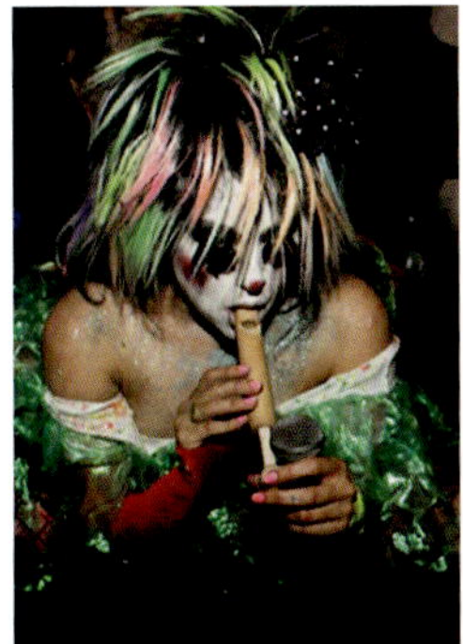

ROSALIE KNOX

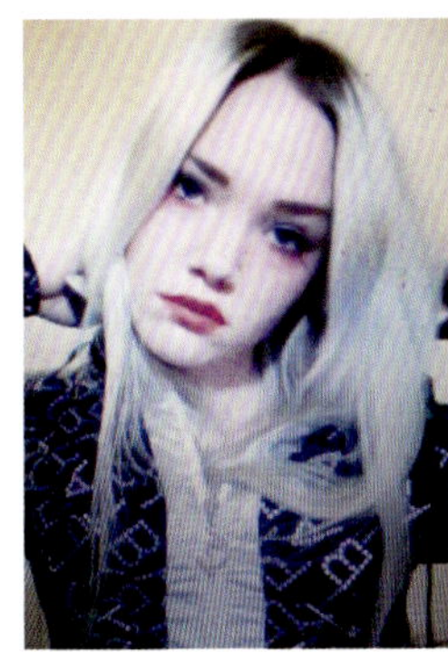

ROSEMARY KIRTON

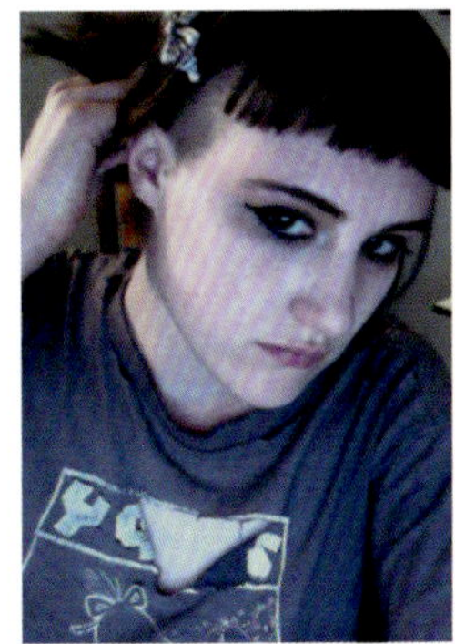

RAFFAELLA HANLEY

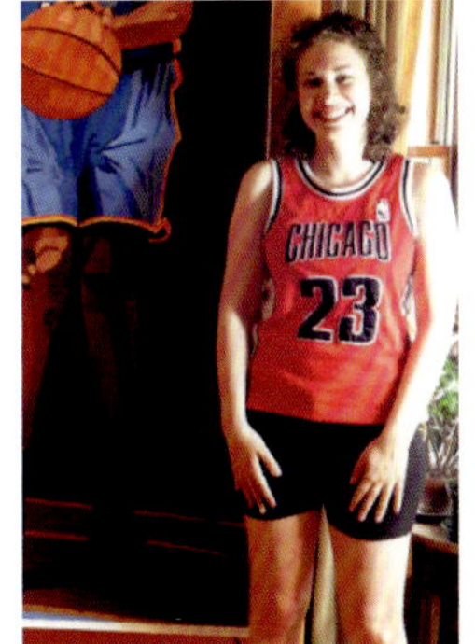

RACHEL BETH GLASER

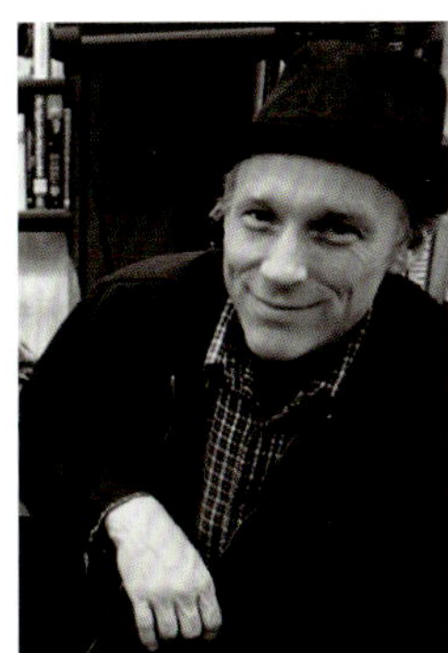

WALLACE LESTER

THANK YOU The Penn Family, Nathan Antolik, Maggie Lee, Air Pop, Jacky Connolly, Brendan Fowler, Will Luckman, Harsh Patel, Cali DeWitt, Kiki Kudo, Juiceboxxx, Avena Gallagher, Julien Ceccaldi, Amalia Ulman, Greem Jellyfish, Al Baio, Petra Cortright, Analisa Teachworth, Bunny Rogers, Fiona Duncan, Coco Young, Cris Moore, Nate Walton, Marlous Borm, Jackie Linton, Eve Essex, Bosko Blagojevic, Pierre Drescher, Arielle De Pinto, Andrew Feldmar, May Hong, Susan Cianciolo, Nick Dangerfield, John Michael Boling, Rosemary Kirton, Eva Michon, Jacer Racer, Gabrielle Tillman, John Birtle, Cammisa Buerhaus, Stefan Simchowitz, Keaton Ventura, Caitlin McMullen, Jenny Borland, Cab Bronski, Keith Connolly, Bridget Donahue, Brian Blomerth, Spencer Sweeney, Venus X, Nate Harrington, Raul De Nieves, Nina Freeman, Kayla Guthrie, Adam Tetzloff, Bill Strobeck, Amhara Burrowes, Prince Harvey, Sam Irwin, Nick DiLeonardi, Timothy Koehne, Amber Ventura, Cordelia Alquist, Kate Bell, Jessica Straker, Natalie Margolin, Ummi, Maya Fell, Nathan Whipple, Total Freedom, Letter Racer, Via App, James K, Gobby, Lee Bannon, Odwalla88, Dark World, 1080p, Lou Dallas, 2True, White Material, Blazer Sound System, Pepper Cotton, Bacon, C.E, Gerlan, Do It To Yourself, Big Boy Scene, Strictly Yours, Arcane Kids, The Zen Mafia, Real Fine Arts, Young Art, Bedstuy Love Affair, Bodega, White Flag Projects, KCHUNG Radio, Santos Party House, Trans Pecos, Times Bar, Bossa Nova Civic Club, S.W.A.T. Bar, China Chalet.

SEX Magazine: #1—10

Editing & compilation © 2016 Sex Magazine
Images and text © their respective owners.

Published in the United States by powerHouse Books,
a division of powerHouse Cultural Entertainment, Inc.
37 Main Street, Brooklyn, NY 11201-1021
telephone 212.604.9074, fax 212.366.5247
e-mail: info@powerHouseBooks.com
website: www.powerHouseBooks.com

Book design by Asher Penn

First edition, 2016

Library of Congress Control Number: 2016950510
ISBN 978-1-57687-782-1
Printed and bound in China through Asia Pacific Offset
10 9 8 7 6 5 4 3 2 1

http://sexmagazine.us